The Victims at the
Berlin Wall, 1961–1989

The Victims at the Berlin Wall, 1961–1989

A Biographical Handbook

Edited by
Hans-Hermann Hertle / Maria Nooke

for the
Centre for Contemporary History Potsdam
and the Berlin Wall Foundation

Co-authors:
Udo Baron and Christine Brecht
Martin Ahrends and Lydia Dollmann

Translation: Miriamne Fields, Berlin

Ch. Links Verlag, Berlin

This research project was funded and the printing of this book kindly supported by the Federal Government Commissioner for Culture and the Media (BKM).

The German National Library catalogs this publication
in the German National Bibliography;
detailed bibliographical information available online
at: http://dnb.d-nb.de.

Berlin, March 2011
© Christoph Links Verlag GmbH
Schönhauser Allee 36, 10435 Berlin, Tel.: +49-30-44 02 32-0
Internet: www.christoph-links-verlag.de; mail@christoph-links-verlag.de
Cover design: KahaneDesign, Berlin;
cover photograph by Wolfgang Grossmann, Berlin
Proofreading: Marie Frohling, Berlin
Typeset: Agentur Siegemund, Berlin
Printed and bound: Druckerei F. Pustet, Regensburg
ISBN 978-3-86153-632-1

Contents

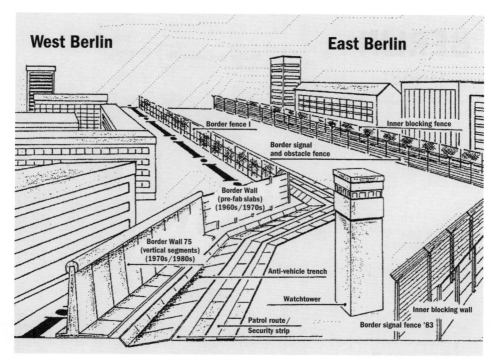

Sketch of border fortifications between East and West Berlin

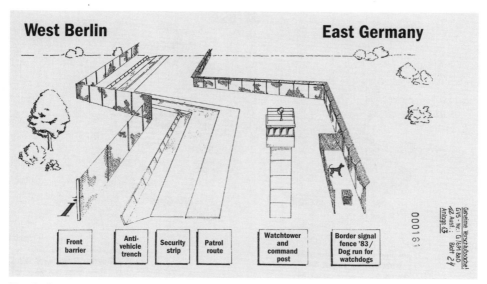

Sketch of border fortifications on the outer ring between East Germany and West Berlin

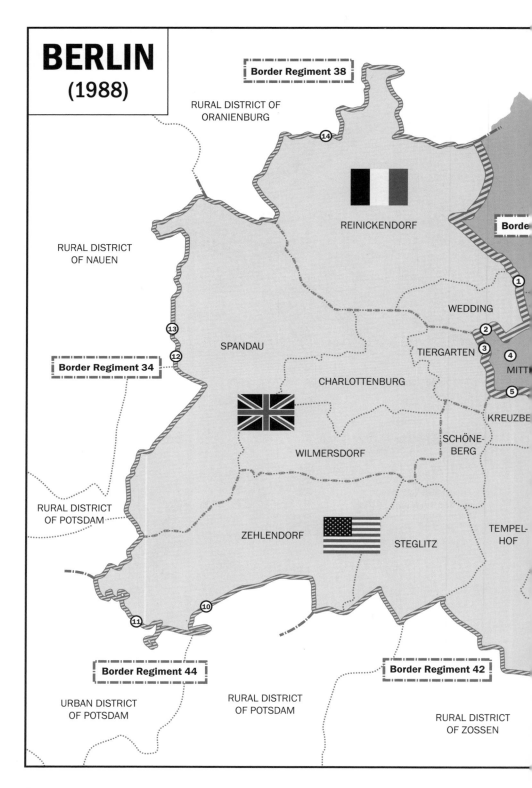

BERLIN
(1988)

Border Regiment 38

RURAL DISTRICT OF ORANIENBURG

RURAL DISTRICT OF NAUEN

REINICKENDORF

Borde

WEDDING

Border Regiment 34

SPANDAU

TIERGARTEN

MITT

CHARLOTTENBURG

KREUZBE

SCHÖNE-BERG

WILMERSDORF

RURAL DISTRICT OF POTSDAM

ZEHLENDORF

STEGLITZ

TEMPEL-HOF

Border Regiment 44

Border Regiment 42

URBAN DISTRICT OF POTSDAM

RURAL DISTRICT OF POTSDAM

RURAL DISTRICT OF ZOSSEN

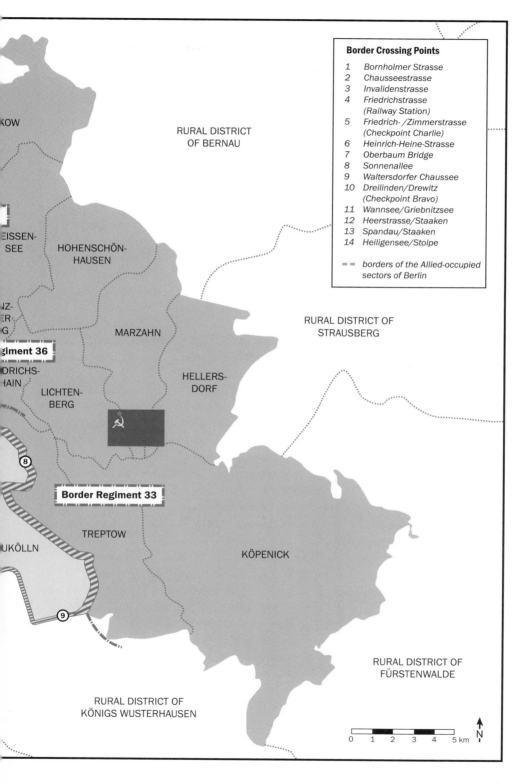

Border Crossing Points

1 Bornholmer Strasse
2 Chausseestrasse
3 Invalidenstrasse
4 Friedrichstrasse
  (Railway Station)
5 Friedrich- /Zimmerstrasse
  (Checkpoint Charlie)
6 Heinrich-Heine-Strasse
7 Oberbaum Bridge
8 Sonnenallee
9 Waltersdorfer Chaussee
10 Dreilinden/Drewitz
   (Checkpoint Bravo)
11 Wannsee/Griebnitzsee
12 Heerstrasse/Staaken
13 Spandau/Staaken
14 Heiligensee/Stolpe

— — borders of the Allied-occupied
    sectors of Berlin

RURAL DISTRICT
OF BERNAU

KOW

EISSEN-
SEE

HOHENSCHÖN-
HAUSEN

NZ-
ER
G

giment 36

DRICHS-
HAIN

LICHTEN-
BERG

MARZAHN

HELLERS-
DORF

RURAL DISTRICT OF
STRAUSBERG

⑧

Border Regiment 33

TREPTOW

UKÖLLN

KÖPENICK

⑨

RURAL DISTRICT OF
FÜRSTENWALDE

RURAL DISTRICT OF
KÖNIGS WUSTERHAUSEN

0 1 2 3 4 5 km

N

Preface

N othing conveyed a more lasting impression of the communist leadership in East Germany as a dictatorship than the Wall that divided Berlin from August 1961 to November 1989. It stood for almost 30 years as an icon of abomination: The world watched as desperate people used bed sheets to climb down from their apartment windows in search of freedom. We saw the photographs of border police officers, looking both agitated and defiant, as they retrieved the dead body of Peter Fechter, who helplessly bled to death at the Berlin Wall after his failed escape attempt in 1962. For the tens of thousands of East German citizens who wanted to escape the oppressive conditions in the communist state, the Wall was more than a mere figurative icon. It was a murderous reality and many people were arrested or killed as they attempted to surmount it.

However, as international political tensions began to ease in the 1970s, this concrete dividing wall in the city seemed to become an increasingly innocuous structure, as if its brutality could be concealed behind an unobtrusive coat of gray paint on the east side and by its colorful integration into the urban culture in the West. Following the political collapse of East Germany in November 1989, it looked as if the Berlin Wall might well become a forgotten phenomenon; so thorough was its demolition and disposal that today the remnants can only be detected with great effort. It took years after the two halves of the city were reunified before attention was drawn not only to the joy over its disappearance, but also to the memory of the widespread suffering that it had once caused.

Public discussions about the Wall and its victims became highly emotional during this time. Up to now there has been no reliable account of the number of fatal escape attempts or a definitive presentation of the biographies of these individuals. Instead, the public debate seemed to drive out with polemical shrillness what it lacked in verifiable knowledge. The attempt to draw attention back to the forgotten victims of the Wall triggered a macabre competition over the number of deaths, as if the historical judgment over the character of the communist dictatorship and its power instruments depended on how high that number was.

For this reason, in 2005 the Centre for Contemporary History Potsdam (ZZF) and the Berlin Wall Association (today's Berlin Wall Foundation) decided to conduct a joint research project with the aim of closing this knowledge gap about the people who had died at the Wall. This cooperative project, funded by the Federal Government Commissioner for Culture and the Media (BKM), was carried out over several years and, given the extremely diffuse and complex source material, used precisely defined criteria to ascertain the exact number of deaths. By researching their life stories, it defied the communist regime's efforts to cast the victims into oblivion. The biographical approach reveals insight into the motivations and life situations of the people who tried to flee, as well as of the people who died under other circumstances at the border. The study also provides an undistorted view of the "border system" that knowingly accepted the death of innocent people.

The publishers would like to thank the project directors and co-authors for their dedication to and sensibility in carrying out this unusually demanding project. It is our hope that the findings presented here will help to establish both a more conciliatory relationship between professional findings and moral empathy concerning research on the East German past and the division of Germany.

Potsdam and Berlin, January 2011

Martin Sabrow
Centre for Contemporary
History Potsdam, Director

Axel Klausmeier
Berlin Wall Foundation,
Director

Introduction[1]

B erlin, August 24, 1961: Eleven days after the sector border was sealed off with barbed wire and a few days after the first hollow concrete blocks of the Berlin Wall were erected, shots were fired in the border area near the Charité Hospital, not far from the Reichstag building. Transport police on a subway bridge saw a young man trying to flee across the Humboldt Harbor. They called out to him and fired warning shots, but the swimmer did not stop. One of the border guards aimed two shots at him, putting an end to the young man's escape attempt. He was hit in the head and sank beneath the surface of the Spree River. Günter Litfin was the first fugitive to be shot at the Wall. He was 24 years old.

Almost 28 years later, in the late evening of February 5, 1989, two young men approached the border fortifications at the Britzer Zweig Canal, which ran along the sector border between Berlin-Treptow and Berlin-Neukölln. The two men, trying to pass through the border fortifications, were under the impression that the order to shoot at the border had been revoked. They thought that the official visit of a high-level statesman to East Berlin created advantageous circumstances for an escape. When they reached the last border fence, however, they were seen by guards and came under fire from two sides. A final attempt to climb over the fence failed and the young men were forced to surrender. Standing with his back to the border fence, the 21-year-old Chris Gueffroy was hit by two individually fired shots aimed at him from a distance of 40 meters. One bullet went into his heart and he died within minutes.

Günter Litfin and Chris Gueffroy were the first and last fugitives to be killed by bullets fired by the border guards at the Berlin Wall. The first death, however, had already occurred on August 22, 1961, when 59-year-old Ida Siekmann tried to leap from the window of her apartment on Bernauer Strasse to the pavement below, which was part of West Berlin.

The 32-year-old engineer Winfried Freudenberg was the last person to die trying to escape to the West. He had made it over the Wall, having reached West Berlin in a homemade gas balloon on March 8, 1989. However, he lost control and the balloon rose too high. After flying in the freezing cold for five hours, Winfried Freudenberg's balloon crashed down into the West Berlin district of Zehlendorf.

Between 1945 and 1961, 3.5 million people fled to the Federal Republic of Germany from the Soviet zone of occupation and the later-established East German state.[2] East Germany was on the brink of collapse in the summer of 1961. On the night of August 12, Walter Ulbricht, the leader of the Communist Party, gave the order to have the sector borders in Berlin sealed off. Cobblestones were ripped out of the street, barricades were mounted and barbed wire was rolled out through the middle of the city. A few days later, on the night of August 17, construction troops began replacing the wire fencing with a wall made of hollow concrete blocks.

The border fortifications were expanded year after year and eventually concrete plates and watchtowers were mass produced. A virtually insurmountable border security system was created and, by the end of the 1970s, it was sealed off by an outer wall made of industrially produced concrete segments that were commonly used in agriculture as bearing walls for manure.

"Enemy-ward," which in East German jargon meant "from the east side to the west side," began the 15-to-150-meter-wide death strip with a two-to-three-meter-high "inner wall" or "inner blocking fence," and just beyond this stood a two-meter-high alarm fence. This "contact signal fence," which consisted of many rows of electrical wire, transmitted an acoustic and/or an optical signal when touched. The more advanced versions of this fence, such as the "Border Signal and Obstacle Fence II," were set 50 centimeters into the ground to prevent fugitives from crawling underneath the barriers. The modern fences enabled signals to be triggered "silently" so that the fugitive continued to believe he was safe long after the border command posts had their sights on him.

A dog run for watchdogs was installed parallel to the signal fence in the parts of the border that were difficult to oversee. The border soldiers' observation towers and bunkers stood in the next section of the border fortifications, which included a guard path for motorized patrols. The cable duct for the border communication system usually ran alongside the guard path, and next to it lay the security strip, carefully raked to allow every footprint to be seen. A line of high flood lights immersed the death strip in bright light so that visibility and shooting conditions were favorable even at night. The final obstacle in this system of barriers was the anti-vehicle trench that slanted downward from the East German side and rose vertically from the border side. It was sometimes reinforced with concrete plates.

This system of barriers ended with a 3.5-to-4-meter-high, ten-centimeter-thick concrete wall topped by a pipe that was designed to make it more difficult for fugitives to hold onto the barrier when they tried to climb over it. In some places a 2.9-meter-high close-meshed metal fence fulfilled this function.

"Friend-ward," which indicated the direction facing East Berlin, was a restricted border area that was only accessible with a special permit. It was controlled by the East German police, secret police and the voluntary "border troop helpers." A troop command of about 11,500 men was responsible for the security of the 156-kilometer-long wall that encircled West Berlin. The soldiers had the order to prevent "border breaches" using all means at their disposal, including their firearms.

The citizens in the East knew from hearsay or from western media that people had been shot and had died at the Wall. Günter Litfin and Chris Gueffroy, Ida Siekmann and Winfried Freudenberg – their deaths at the Wall were known to the public, causing shock and pain. But exactly how many people died at the Wall?

Who were these people and how did they die? How were their families and friends treated after the victim's death? What public and political reactions were triggered in the East and West when their deaths became known?

By now thorough research has been conducted on the history, structure and function of the East German border regime that secured the existence of the communist state for so long. The criminal prosecution of perpetrators who committed acts of violence at the Berlin Wall and East German border was nearly complete by November 2004.

This book strives to provide information about the number of fatalities that occurred at the Berlin Wall. It focuses on the lives of those 136 people and the circumstances under which they died. Their tragic fates are embedded in the larger historical context and positioned within the topography of the divided city. The study also addresses the difficulties in classifying who should be regarded as a victim at the Berlin Wall. It should be stressed, however, that the number of deaths *at* the Berlin Wall can in no way be equated with the much higher and undeterminable number of people who were victims *of* the Wall, the division of Germany and the communist regime in East Germany.

Previous Death Counts

A number of attempts have been made in recent years to calculate the number of people who were killed or died at the Berlin Wall.[3] Since the early 1990s, a series of publications have appeared, including numerical data and descriptions of a few typical death cases.[4] The death toll presented in these publications was usually based on lists that were compiled during the period when Germany and Berlin were still divided. These lists were created by different institutions, including the state security division of the West Berlin police, the Central Registry of State Judicial Administrations in Salzgitter, and the West Berlin association "Working Group 13th of August." These institutions collected all available information on deaths that had occurred at the Wall and the border since the 1960s. After 1990, numerical data also became available from the Investigating Agency for Governmental and Party Crimes, known as the ZERV, and from the Berlin public prosecutor's office.

Chief of Police in Berlin

Beginning on August 13, 1961, the state security division of the West Berlin police compiled a list of all the fatal injuries and incidents involving firearms at the Wall that were known to West Berlin. Information was reported by fellow fugitives, relatives and friends of the deceased, and by members of the East German police and border troops who had fled to the West. Part I of this list contained the known incidents involving a loss of life at the sector border or outer ring, regardless of whether another individual had been involved. Part II listed people who were injured; Part III registered "dubious cases" in which the circumstances of death could not be definitively clarified, and Part IV was reserved for "members of the NVA

(East German military) who were fatally injured," which meant border soldiers who had been shot and killed. When the list was completed in 1990, Part I contained 80 cases of death, although not all victims were identified by name. Part IV listed seven deaths. Part III listed unidentified individuals along with five people listed by name, who we now know were indeed shot and killed.[5]

The Central Registry of State Judicial Administrations in Salzgitter

The Central Registry of State Judicial Administrations in Salzgitter was established in November 1961. A list of death cases known to the institution over the years was published in 1991 in the "Salzgitter Report."[6] The report contains 78 cases of death for Berlin, but does not specify the exact criteria employed in compiling the list, as these had already been determined by law.[7] The purpose of the registry was to list incidents in which "suspicion of a criminal act was justified." Hence, its records included mostly cases of death and suspected cases of death that entailed an initial suspicion of third-party involvement and that it had been informed of by 1990. It received its information from the West Berlin police and through the interrogation of border soldiers who had fled to the West. Some information was attained more or less by chance.[8] Suspicion of a crime was, in fact, rather broadly defined, which resulted in the inclusion of a number of accidents.[9] The registry was a "preliminary investigation agency" of the public prosecutor's office. Since it operated in the West and the incidents occurred in the East, it often had to depend on unreliable information sources as well as conjecture, leading the journalists Werner Filmer and Heribert Schwan to conclude in 1991 that "the death list of the Central Registry Office in Salzgitter is understandably both incomplete and exaggerated."[10] The authors of the Salzgitter Report were quite aware of the tentative nature of their report since the registry had only limited means of gathering information and no access to the archives in East Germany.[11]

"Working Group 13th of August"

Founded by Rainer Hildebrandt as a registered association in West Berlin in 1963, the "Working Group 13th of August" continues to publish and annually update lists with the numbers, names and dates of death cases at the Wall and border. The working group's aim is to register "all victims who died in connection with flight and/or the border regime."[12] Its lists of victims include, for example, cases in which a fugitive died in an accident or by drowning, East and West German citizens who suffered a heart attack at a border crossing, unidentified corpses discovered in waterways, and most notably, a large number of border soldiers and East German policemen who committed suicide or who died in an accident while on duty, including incidents involving firearms. In 2008 the working group counted 222 deaths at the Berlin Wall. It also listed 13 additional deaths in Berlin under the headings "cases of death by other escape routes," "killed East German soldiers" and "killed Soviet deserters," increasing its total count to 235 deaths.[13] In many cases, however, the data is incomplete with the names, places and/or circumstances of death missing. Since the working group does not provide a list of its sources, its data require careful reexamination.

Investigating Agency for Governmental and Party Crimes (ZERV)

In the 1990s the Investigating Agency for Governmental and Party Crimes (ZERV) investigated the cases in which border soldiers or their commanders were involved in the death of a fugitive. The agency used the lists provided by the West Berlin police, the Central Registry Office in Salzgitter, and ZERV's own research in the Communist Party archive, most specifically, the Archive of the East German Border Troops and the Ministry of State Security, as the basis for its inquiry. These investigations succeeded in clarifying the events in a number of cases and having charges brought against the perpetrators. The ZERV, after it completed its investigations, published its statistical data on the death cases without identifying the names of victims. It named 122 fatalities for Berlin.[14] This figure contains the entire number of registered or known suspected cases in which East German armed forces were involved in the killing of a fugitive.

Berlin Public Prosecutor's Office

The Berlin and Neuruppin public prosecutor offices addressed the legal consequences of these deaths based on the investigations conducted by the ZERV. They focused on legally relevant acts of violence and the criminal prosecution of the perpetrators. In 1999, 86 border deaths were made known, a figure that included only those cases of death at the Wall that involved proven acts of violence by East German border security forces (primarily killing by firearms). Like the ZERV, neither public prosecutor's office published the names of the victims.[15]

Up to now no reliable, verifiable source-based count of the killings and deaths at the Berlin Wall that could stand up to a critical inquiry has been published. Depending on the sources, purpose and date of the survey, the figures vary between 78 (Central Registry of Salzgitter), 86 (Berlin public prosecutor's office), 92 (Berlin Chief of Police), 122 (Investigating Agency for Governmental and Party Crimes, "ZERV") and 235 (Working Group 13th of August).

The data in the Salzgitter Report are out of date because the registry did not have sufficient sources at its disposal at the time and its officially authorized mission limited its activities and perspective. The numbers provided by the ZERV are inadequate for two reasons: They do not take into consideration deaths that occurred by accident during an escape attempt and they include suspected cases that did not withstand the scrutiny of the public prosecutor's investigation process. Moreover, the ZERV reports do not explain the grounds for its suspicion of death or to which case group the death toll applied. The information from the public prosecutor's office, on the other hand, is based on proven cases that were examined on an individual basis through preliminary legal proceedings. But here only cases of death that involved legally relevant and proven third-party guilt were taken into account. Deaths that occurred under other circumstances were not included. Hence, the public prosecutor's figure represents the minimum number of fatalities that occurred at the Berlin Wall. The number of deaths presented by the "Working Group 13th of August" presents the opposite scenario: In its recently published lists, information is provided in varying degrees about the fatalities. In fact, this is the only institution to take into account those victims who died outside of the legal realm, for example, in an accident that occurred during an escape attempt. But many factors make this catalog of deaths problematic. The data, at least in part grounded in speculation, lack sources and proof, making them unverifiable from a scholarly perspective. The list is also flawed because it mistakenly counts survivors as fatal victims.[16] The criteria used for adding a person to the list are not provided or are inadequate. Consequently, real escape victims are mentioned in the same breath as people who died in incidental accidents, a fact that impairs the working group's self-proclaimed aim to preserve the honorable memory of the victims of the East German border regime.

A valid and verifiable standard for adequate documentation of the fatalities at the Berlin Wall must follow two central guidelines: It must be proven without a doubt that each person identified as a victim actually died. This means that ambiguous cases, as well as cases in which it is highly likely but ultimately not proven that a person died, must be treated as suspected cases of death. Secondly, a list of fatalities at the Wall must include only cases in which it has been proven that the person died as a direct consequence of the existence of the East German border regime. The victim lists provided by the "Working Group 13th of August" lack this scholarly verifiable standard. Consequently, its death count can only be regarded as an extensive list of suspected cases. Each individual incident needs to be verified or disproven by a precise scholarly examination based on clear criteria.

Definitions and Case Groups

A definition of the term "victim at the Berlin Wall" based on comprehensible criteria is a necessary prerequisite to achieving at least a roughly reliable estimate of the number of people who died at the Berlin Wall. The definition applied in this study established two conditions: There must have been an escape attempt involved in the death or a temporal and spatial link between the death and the border regime. Five case groups were established on the basis of these criteria:

- Fugitives who were shot and killed by members of the East German armed forces, or who were wounded and later died from their injuries, while they were trying to escape over the Berlin Wall.
- Fugitives who died while trying to escape over the Berlin Wall, or who committed suicide when they realized their escape attempt had failed, or who died from injuries suffered during the escape attempt.
- People from the East and West who were shot and killed by members of the East German armed forces or who were wounded and later died from the injuries suffered.
- People from the East and West who died at the Berlin Wall as a consequence of the East German armed forces' actions or failure to act, or who later died from their injuries
- Members of the East German border troops who were killed or wounded while on duty and who later died from their injuries.

What is decisive in each case is that a verifiable causal and spatial connection exists between the death and an attempted escape, or that a direct or indirect relationship exists between the "border organs'" actions or their failure to act at the site of the incident in the border territory. Our study's definition thus includes deaths not covered by the criminal prosecution of the perpetrators who committed acts of violence at the border, as this concentrated solely on cases in which another individual was directly involved.

Each case was individually examined for this handbook on the basis of these established definitions and case groups. All the data from the lists mentioned above, and from publications that have meanwhile been published, were compiled and examined by our project team. At the start of the project the databank registering cases of death at the Berlin Wall between 1961 and 1989 contained a total of 245 deaths and suspected cases of death that required checking (August 2005). On the basis of our own archival research and the new information provided by the lists from the "Working Group 13th of August,"[17] the number of suspected cases requiring examination rose to 575 (March 2009).

Sources and Archival Research

Broad archival and related material research was conducted to check the suspected cases and compile the biographies. For the first time, this project was able to evaluate the case files of the Berlin and Neuruppin public prosecutor's offices, prepared in the course of investigations on acts of violence at the Wall, and resulting in a total of more than 150 investigation files and over 70 pre-investigation files. These files contained the indictments and sentences, as well as the older investigative files of the West Berlin police, the Central Registry Office in Salzgitter, and the ZERV investigation findings – a wealth of source information and file data from both the West and East. The investigations were conducted on a large number of suspected cases that had never been brought to court because third-party involvement either did not exist or could not be determined. Hence, for an historical analysis, these documents, including preliminary investigation files, investigation files and court proceedings, are an important basis from both a quantitative and a qualitative point of view.

In response to an application to the archive of the Federal Commissioner for the Records of the Ministry of State Security in the former German Democratic Republic (BStU) – the "Stasi archive" containing the files of the East German secret police – we were provided with records on more than 100 deaths and suspected cases.

Clauses in the Stasi File Law (StUG), however, only allowed excerpts of these files to be released for view and not the originals in their entirety. The archive authority decided what sections to make available. Shortly before the research phase of our project was completed, the law was amended, allowing, under certain conditions, a non-anonymous view of files for the purpose of research. The project benefited from this change, but it is possible that, in certain cases, files exist that family members viewed, but which our researchers could not review in their entirety because of data protection and personal rights. Furthermore, when using Stasi files, it must be taken into account that individual files may have been destroyed in East Germany or may have not yet been made accessible.[18]

In the Federal Archives – Military Archive, the project team was able to research some 300 cases in the files of the East German National Defense Ministry, the East German border troops and the military public prosecutor's office.

Wide-ranging research, material viewing and evaluation also took place in the Federal Archives in Berlin and Koblenz, the State Archive of Berlin, the Brandenburg Central State Archive, the Police History Collection of the Berlin Police President, the Political Archive of the Foreign Office, the Archive of the Central Registry Office in Salzgitter and various press, radio and photo archives.

Research based exclusively on East German documents, however, is not free of bias with regard to past events and fates and biographies of the deceased, as these documents and files present information based on the values, interests and practical constraints of the authority that created the file. They are ultimately an expression of the power that the authority had over the individual in question.[19] Consequently, the secret police investigation files do not reflect the lives and thoughts of the people being spied on. They do, however, reflect the friend-enemy mentality of the people in power and the ruling authorities. Hence, they provide much information about the perpetrators, whose thought processes, biases and aims are conveyed through their choice of language and ideological considerations. In the files, for example, victims of the Wall are usually referred to as "fugitives of the republic" or "border violators." They were regarded and treated as "criminals." Terms such as "flight" and "fugitive" were avoided at all costs.[20] Furthermore, the investigation reports of the Stasi, in addressing the lives and motives of fugitives and other victims, often included half-truths, clichés and rumors based on false or unreliable information from spies or neighbors who were questioned. Finally, the Stasi agents' biases toward "republic fugitives" did not allow for any legitimate or personal reasons for wanting to leave East Germany. These views found expression in their claims that the death victim had a "negative attitude," was "influenced by the West," "criminal" or "socially deviant." Teenagers and young men were generally suspected of being unadjusted "rowdies" or "loafers" who had allowed themselves to be inspired by the "media of the class enemy" and the "decadent western lifestyle."

At the same time, it cannot be generally claimed that the military and Stasi files are without informative value. In fact, they are indispensable for documenting the events that took place in the border area and for reconstructing the circumstances of death. As the deaths at the Wall underwent criminal investigation, it became clear that although the presentation and evaluation of events was always subject to the logic and view of the perpetrators, they were indeed accurate in regard to recorded data on time and place, names and other particulars of the victims and perpetrators. In their reports, for example, the commanders of the border troops generally described the conduct of the border guards and officers as if it were in compliance with the rule book. It was not uncommon for clear misconduct, impossible even for the regime to overlook, to be glossed over or concealed. In spite of this, the courts came to the conclusion that the evidentiary value of the military and Stasi files in regard to the reconstruction of the events could not be ignored and that each case required examination and consideration.[21]

To gain insight into an individual's reasons for fleeing and the circumstances of his or her life independently of the official records from East and West Germany, the project team sought to contact friends and family and was successful in more than 70 cases, making it possible to integrate personal recollections and family contexts into many of the biographies. Contemporary witness reports, photographs and personal documents provided an individual view into the life of the deceased. Conversations with family members also showed that information that was not mentioned in the files had been passed on within the family. This included the individual experiences that led to disappointment with life in East Germany and to a break with the state or with the family. It should also be noted, however, that parents, siblings and friends were usually not informed in advance of a person's plans to flee, either out of the victim's desire to spare them the consequences of being an accomplice, or out of fear that they would not be sympathetic to the decision to flee. Many family members, even after viewing the Stasi files and witnessing the border guard trials, continued to have unanswered questions.

Findings

To evaluate the number of deaths at the Berlin Wall, the research, in accordance with the project's definition, focused on escapes with fatal consequences and other killings and deaths at the Wall, in the death strip and in the border area. The number of victims evaluated does not claim to account for all the victims *of* the Wall, which would have to include every fatality caused by the Berlin Wall and the 28 years that Berlin and Germany were divided.[22] Many people were victims of the Berlin Wall because they felt themselves to be defenseless against the communist regime, or because the distress caused by the separation from loved ones undermined their will to live. Some people took their own lives following a failed escape or after a request to leave the country was rejected.[23] Just how many lives were destroyed by the Wall in this way cannot be determined. The following data focuses on the number of Berlin Wall victims as defined by the project and should be understood as the lowest number possible. A total of 575 death and suspected death cases were researched and analyzed. In many suspected cases it was not always clear in the beginning what name and fate was concealed behind scanty information consisting of dates and locations. An examination of each individual case led to the following results:

- At least 136 people were verifiably shot dead, suffered fatal accidents or committed suicide after a failed escape at the Berlin Wall.
- At least 251 mainly elderly travelers died before, during or after passing through a checkpoint at a Berlin border crossing, usually as a result of heart attacks.

A total of 164 suspected cases were ruled out as victims at the Berlin Wall because there was neither an indication of an escape attempt nor a spatial link with the border regime, or because no death had occurred. These cases include, for example, fugitives who survived shootings with severe injuries, or individuals alleged by West Berlin sources to have been involved in escape attempts, which, however, was later proven not to have been the case. Dual counts due to imprecise information were excluded from the figures, as were suicides in Berlin waterways that could be proven to have no relation to escape attempts. These cases are addressed at the end of this book.

In another 16 cases it could not be determined on the basis of the available archival documents whether or not the person was a victim at the Wall or not. These include unidentified bodies found in the waterways for which no clear evidence of an escape or of a connection to the border regime could be found. These cases remain inconclusive and, along with another eight cases for which no archive material was found, are not classified in this study.[24]

Among the 136 deaths at the Berlin Wall, of which 97 were shot dead, there were:
- 97 East German fugitives and one Polish citizen who were either shot dead, suffered fatal accidents or committed suicide during an attempt to cross the border;
- 30 individuals from the East and West who were shot dead or suffered a fatal accident with no intention of fleeing;
- 8 East German border soldiers who were killed while on duty by military deserters, fellow soldiers, a fugitive, an escape helper or a West Berlin police officer.

Sixty-seven of the 98 fugitives were shot and killed. With one exception, the fugitives were East German citizens, including ten military deserters. A Polish citizen, Franciszek Piesik, was the only foreigner. He was one of the 28 people who suffered a fatal accident while trying to escape at the Wall. This number also includes fugitives who fell to their death on Bernauer Strasse or who drowned in the waterways at the Berlin border. Three fugitives took their own lives after their escape attempts failed.

In the second group containing people who died without the intention of fleeing, 22 of the 30 deaths involved residents of and visitors to West Berlin. Fifteen of them were shot and seven died in accidents. They include four escape helpers and Dieter Beilig, a young man who was known for his protests against the Berlin Wall in West Berlin. He jumped from the west side of the city into the border grounds at the Brandenburg Gate on April 2, 1971. The 30-year-old man was brought to the command post of the border troops that was located in the former Academy of Arts building not far from the Brandenburg Gate. A short time later he was shot at close range by an officer. To create a "legend" about his death, the Stasi manipulated evidence and falsified documents. Of the seven West Berliners who died in accidents, five were children from the West Berlin district of Kreuzberg who fell into the border waters while playing on the Gröbenufer riverbank and could not be rescued.

This group also includes eight East German citizens who were shot in the border area although they were not intending to flee. The 13-year-old Wolfgang Glöde, for example, was fatally injured while playing in the "Sorgenfrei" garden settlement when a shot was accidentally fired from a border soldier's gun while he was showing it to the interested boy. The 31-year-old Herbert Kliem was shot when he lost his way and mistakenly entered the border area while driving to pick up his wife and children. When he turned his motorcycle around to leave the restricted area, he was fatally shot. These kinds of deaths evoked strong resentment and protest among the residents living at the border and caused East Germany massive problems of legitimization.

A third group consists of the eight border soldiers who were killed while on duty. As guards, they were part of the system to secure the border and prevent escapes – and at the same time were exposed to the dangers associated with it. In three cases, the guards were killed by armed deserters. One guard leader on patrol duty was fatally shot when a fellow soldier mistook him for a fugitive. One of the border soldiers was knocked out by fugitives and died from his injuries; the remaining three border soldiers were killed in connection with an escape, either by an escape helper, a fellow soldier or a ricochet bullet that was fired from the gun of a West Berlin policeman.

The victims include men, women, children and youths:
- Nine children younger than 16;
- 34 youths between the ages of 16 and 20, including two young women;
- 67 young adults between the ages of 21 and 30, including two young women;
- 13 adults between the ages of 31 and 40, including one woman;
- 12 adults between the ages of 41 and 80, including three women;
- One young man whose identity and age could not be determined.

Most of the victims were young men between the ages of 16 and 30. They made up 78 percent of all the fugitives and attest to the readiness of young men in this phase of life to take on life-threatening risks. In contrast, married men made up only 20 percent and women only eight percent. Four women risked fleeing with their husbands or boyfriends.

More than half of the 136 victims died in the first five years after the Wall had been erected. Thirty-four people had already died at the Wall by the end of 1962:
- 1961–1969: 90 fatalities;
- 1970–1979: 30 fatalities;
- 1980–1989: 16 fatalities.

This distribution over time corresponds with the general escape movement over the entire period of division. The expansion of the border security system, the changes in East-West relations and the efforts on behalf of East Germany to gain international recognition, in particular through the CSCE (Conference on Security and Cooperation in Europe) process, strongly influenced these developments. Nevertheless, people continued to attempt escapes and were killed at the border up until the East German state came to an end.

Treatment of the Deceased and their Families

The deaths and murders at the Berlin Wall and the inner-German border, the Baltic Sea and Eastern Bloc borders, represented the pinnacle of violence stemming from the East German border security system.

The Communist Party leadership knowingly accepted the killings. Yet it was also aware from the very outset that acts of violence were registered by the West Berlin police and dealt with by West Berlin's public prosecutor's office, and that the Central Registry of State Judicial Administrations in Salzgitter documented and investigated all cases it became aware of for the purpose of criminal prosecution. Shots fired at the Wall also brought East Germany into greater disrepute in both halves of the country. They created an echo beyond the country through the protests of the U.S., British and French city commanders in Berlin, and damaged the international reputation of East Germany and the Soviet Union, which supported it.

These circumstances are referred to in a Stasi report in conjunction with the killing of the fugitive Michael Bittner at the Berlin Wall in November 1986 as follows: "The political sensitivity of the state border to Berlin (West) made it necessary to conceal the incident. Rumors about the incident had to be prevented from circulating, with information passing to West Berlin or [the] FRG."[25] In order to keep shots and, of course, killings at the Wall as secret as possible, the "processing of corpse cases, should they involve incidents on the state border to West Berlin,"[26] was placed in the hands of the Ministry of State Security (MfS), where the deaths were regulated by "ordinances," "instructions" and "observations." The border troops were to transfer injured fugitives from the death strip to certain hospitals – preferably the People's Police Hospital in Berlin-Mitte and the Drewitz Army Hospital near Potsdam. Dead fugitives were taken to the Forensic Medical Institute at the Humboldt University (Charité) or to the Bad Saarow Central Army Hospital for autopsies. Even the severely injured were not generally transported by ambulance, but on the loading bed of army trucks or military Trabants, with no medical care whatsoever. Upon arrival at a hospital or the coroner's office, the Stasi took command. The investigation departments ("Line IX") of the two regional Stasi administrations in Berlin and Potsdam were responsible for these fugitives, as was, in particularly important cases, Central Department IX at Stasi headquarters. Injured fugitives were isolated in separate rooms at the People's Police Hospital, kept under guard and transferred as soon as possible to the Stasi prison hospital or the Stasi remand prisons in Berlin or Potsdam. The Stasi had sole power of disposal over the dead: It took over their possessions, effects and exhibits; in the case of Christian Buttkus it even confiscated and archived the fatal bullet removed during the autopsy. And it was the Stasi alone that determined what happened to the body: starting with the autopsy and followed by the issuing of the death certificate, the application to set up a "corpse case" with Department I A (political crimes) of the East Berlin state prosecutor's office, running the public prosecution file, receiving the autopsy report, issuing the death certificate at the Berlin-Mitte registry office, receiving the funeral certificate, to the transfer and cremation of the body, which generally took place at the Baumschulenweg Crematorium. In dealing with all these institutions – and after that with the family members – the responsible Stasi agent had to assume a false identity "as a police officer acting on behalf of the Berlin general state prosecutor."[27]

The border troops wrote reports on every attempted escape incident. In the case of deaths, these usually went to Erich Honecker, the Politburo member responsible for security matters and later secretary general of the Communist Party. Their further investigations concentrated on analysis and, where appropriate, removal of weak points in the border security system that had possibly facilitated the escape attempt.

The actual investigation of the crime scene, collection of evidence and questioning and interrogation of witnesses, including the border guards involved, was again mainly the task of Stasi Departments IX in Berlin and Potsdam, in particular their "special commissions," which cooperated closely with a further Stasi line, Central Department I.[28] But concealing the incident and the crime scene always took priority over crime scene investigation for these "investigation organs," if this could prevent events from being observed and registered on the West Berlin side. Members of Department IX in Berlin and Potsdam carried out regular clandestine investigations into the victims and their families, as well as possible motives and third parties aware of the escape attempts. At the same time, they had the task of informing the victims' next of kin and, when they considered it appropriate, placed family, relatives, friends, colleagues and neighbors under observation.

It was "not advisable to come straight out with the news," according to the Stasi's "ordinance for processing corpse cases." Beginning with a general conversation with the as yet uninformed widow, father or mother "may produce many valuable pieces of information on the border violator."[29] The extent of the information subsequently revealed on the death also called for "great tact." The following formulations were stated to have proven useful:

"a) ... lost his life through a border provocation of his own causing,

b) ... had a fatal accident of his own causing,

c) ... drowned in a border waterway."[30]

As version b), "had a fatal accident of his own causing," apparently prompted many additional questions on where the incident took place, agents were instructed to make use of version a), "as it is thus easier to explain why no information can be provided on the precise location of the incident."[31]

The agents were to refuse to "show the corpse" to the next of kin and had to attain their agreement to a cremation and request their signature for a declaration for this purpose. The Stasi paid the costs of the funeral up to the presentation of the urn, in a number of cases using money taken from the pockets of the victims themselves.

According to "instructions" from the Potsdam Stasi administration, the relatives were to be informed that "a memorial ceremony will not take place on principle."[32] Only when the urn was buried did officials allow "a memorial ceremony [to] take place in the smallest circle, for which a priest may also be selected." By attending almost all burials, Stasi agents even robbed the family of its privacy in bidding farewell to the victims; they monitored the sermons and shadowed the mourners. In conversation with the family, agents were to assure that "no information on the incident becomes public, whereby suitable elements from the investigation results may be used tactically to achieve this objective (morally degenerate person, criminal tendencies, etc.)." The precise details given to the family members about the cause of death depended on the results of the investigation – and above all on what had already become known to the public about the "incident" via "western organs and propaganda, injured and arrested parties, other East German citizens."

In many cases, the public and the family found out about deaths for various reasons – and the Stasi was unable to conceal the details. When this occurred, East German propaganda often villainized the dead as "criminals." But usually the Stasi proceeded, as the biographical texts show, according to the directives. The family members were informed about the death – usually with no information on the exact circumstances – but were obliged to remain silent or lie on the matter to third parties, or they were simply told lies about the cause of death. False circumstances of death were even constructed as evidence. In some cases the death was neither confirmed nor denied even in response to inquiries, and the names of victims were kept secret – although the Stasi was aware of them.

Employees of the forensic medical institutes, hospitals, state prosecution offices, the East German police, registry offices, funeral institutes, the Baumschulenweg Crematorium and the graveyard administrations cooperated with the Stasi or served as its instruments and took part in the manipulation of evidence and falsification of official documents, such as death certificates, at the Stasi's request or instruction.

After 1990, a number of the doctors, state prosecutors, police officers, registrars and crematorium and graveyard staff formed a kind of cartel of silence along with the Stasi agents. This is the reason why the disappearance of the bodies of Roland Hoff, Siegfried Noffke, Dieter Beilig, Dr. Johannes Muschol, Silvio Proksch and Michael Bittner could not be explained.

Many families did not find out the truth about how their loved ones died until the 1990s, when the East German archives were opened and the perpetrators of the crimes on the border were prosecuted.

The Criminal Prosecution of Perpetrators Responsible for Fatal Shootings at the Berlin Wall

In the years after 1990, the Berlin public prosecutor's office brought 112 charges against 246 people in connection with the acts of violence at the Berlin Wall: charges against soldiers who shot and killed fugitives, and against their military and political superiors. All trials have been concluded.[33] About half of the accused were acquitted. In many cases, the name of the person who fired the fatal shot(s) could no longer be established; in others, no intent to kill could be proven. Shots fired at armed deserters were even legitimated by a decision of the highest judicial authority. The Federal High Court ruled that desertion was a crime according to the East German military penal law of 1962. The killing of deserters, it said, is excused because, in this "special case," the unlawfulness of the deed could not be apparent to those who carried out the shootings.[34]

Altogether 132 of the accused had final sentences passed on them for various manslaughter offences – as direct or indirect offenders, as accessories, instigators or for aiding and abetting, including:

- 10 members of the Communist Party leadership,
- 42 members of the military leadership, and
- 80 border soldiers.[35]

In addition to the cases in Berlin, the Neuruppin public prosecutor's office brought 21 charges against 39 border soldiers who fired fatal shots and ten charges against 12 commanding officers; in these 31 cases, the shots were fired on the outer ring around West Berlin.[36] Nineteen of the accused border soldiers were given suspended sentences for manslaughter, and one border soldier was sentenced to ten years' imprisonment for the murder of Walter Kittel. Seventeen of the accused were found not guilty; the cases against two soldiers could not be opened for health reasons. All twelve commanding officers were given suspended sentences.

When establishing the guilt of a person and handing down punishments, the courts took into account subjective extenuating factors in favor of the accused, such as:

- their integration into the hierarchy of a totalitarian system;
- the repression of justified doubts regarding state-given orders;
- the constant political indoctrination with the resultant corruption of the sense of what was right;
- the time that had passed since the crime;
- the young age of the accused at the time of the crime; and
- the advanced age of the accused at the time of sentencing, with the resultant increase in sensitivity to punishment.

The prison sentences were graded according to the position of the accused in the military and political hierarchy, and, on the whole, were surprisingly short:

Border guards (usually suspended)	6–24 months
Regiment commanders	20–30 months
Commanders-in-chief (and their deputies) of a Border Brigade or Border Command	6–39 months

Commander-in-chief of the border troops (and his deputies) and members of the NVA leadership	12–78 months
Members of the Communist Party leadership	36–78 months
Members of the National Defense Council	60–90 months.

Following the preliminary examination and after it had been established that the killing of a person was also a punishable offence in East Germany, the German federal courts applied West German law when passing verdicts and fixing sentences. This law was – with a few exceptions – more favorable to the accused than East German law, because it was more lenient. The courts' verdicts followed the jurisdiction of the Federal High Court, according to which the deliberate killing of unarmed fugitives cannot be justified, as it is "an obvious, unbearable offence against fundamental dictates of justice and against human rights that are protected under international law."[37] Orders, regulations and laws that allowed the use of firearms to prevent escapes and thus, ultimately, to kill fugitives were therefore not recognized as sufficient justification.

In view of the immurement of the entire population, killing, violation, criminalization of and discrimination against a large number of people, many found the number of acquittals too high and the punishments that were given too lenient. The suffering of many families and the injustice done to several generations in East Germany remain largely unatoned for. But we owe it to the criminal justice system that, because of the investigations and trials, the human rights violations in East Germany and the crimes committed by the Communist Party have been comprehensively documented.

Remembering and Commemorating the Victims at the Berlin Wall

The fatal shots fired and fatal accidents suffered at the border incited horror, helplessness and anger. In the East any expression of resentment or criticism could have led to an arrest. The West Berliners, on the other hand, had to accept what was happening before their own eyes, helpless to do anything about it. The fatal escape attempts in particular caused angry protests and inspired spontaneous initiatives to preserve the memory of the dead and criticize the border regime. As early as September 1961, memorial signs were erected on Bernauer Strasse for the first victims who lost their lives while trying to flee out of their windows. The names of the dead were hung on monuments wrapped in barbed wire on Bernauer Strasse. On October 5, 1961, the day Udo Düllick died, an angry crowd of West Berlin citizens gathered on the riverbank at Gröbenufer in Kreuzberg. A wooden cross was spontaneously erected to the unknown fugitive. The death of Peter Fechter on August 17, 1962 led to especially fierce protests. Shot by border guards while trying to flee, the 18-year-old construction worker bled to death right behind the

Wall in the death strip for the world to see. His death came to symbolize the deadly threat posed by the Berlin Wall. A memorial cross was set up to Peter Fechter the very day he died, initiated by the young West Berliner, Dieter Beilig, who had participated in many protest actions against the border regime after the Wall was built. Dieter Beilig himself fell victim to fatal shots in October 1971, after he jumped down from the top of the Berlin Wall into the death strip at the Brandenburg Gate and was arrested. The East German leaders were able to conceal his death and keep it a secret. Only recently, with the opening of the newly-erected Academy of Arts building on Pariser Platz, has his death been acknowledged at the site of the border troop command post where he was shot.

In light of these depressing events, over the years numerous monuments and memorial sites were created by friends of escape victims and West Berlin citizens to the people who died at the sector borders. In 1989 there were more than 50 memorial sites.

In addition to spontaneous activities, a number of organized initiatives were instigated by associations and state institutions to commemorate the victims.[38] On October 18, 1961, a commemorative event was organized by the Kreuzberg district office for Udo Düllick on the Gröbenufer riverbank where a cross stood in his memory. The memorial site was later expanded to include a memorial stone for other border victims. In the months after the Wall was erected, the Wedding district had memorial stones set into the sidewalk on Bernauer Strasse to the people who died there. Many are still there, commemorating the victims today. In November of 1961, the "Curatorship for an Undivided Germany" set up a monument made of stones similar to those used to build the Berlin Wall. The monument to the victims of the border regime stood on the center strip of the avenue "Strasse des 17. Juni," across from the Brandenburg Gate. Today it is located farther west, not far from the Victory Column. In an act initiated by the SPD faction of the Berlin Parliament on August 24, 1962, a memorial stone was dedicated on the west side of the Humboldt Harbor to Günter Litfin, who, one year earlier, became the first fugitive to be shot at the Wall. It was in this manner that a number of memorial sites emerged along the sector border in memory of the victims.

Residents of and visitors to West Berlin were not the only people to seek out these sites. Prominent politicians from Germany and abroad also commemorated the victims there during their visits to the divided city. At official memorial ceremonies wreaths were laid in memory of the dead.

While people in the West were commemorating the fugitives as victims of the border regime, East Germany was stigmatizing them as criminals. In contrast, the border soldiers who were killed while on duty were given funerals with all the military honors, and their memories were kept alive as reminders of what had happened. Commemorative plaques and so-called "rooms of tradition"[39] were created to celebrate their "heroic deaths on behalf of the protection of Socialism," contributing to the ideological propaganda against the West. Many institutions, including schools, work brigades, border troop units, youth clubs and even special events, bore the names of these men. Memorial rooms and commemorative events were established at many sites. The state-ordained commemoration of the dead border soldiers in East Germany was pitted against the active civic participation in remembering the victims of the border regime in the West. On the tenth anniversary of the day the Berlin Wall was erected, the West Berlin Senate, for example, supported the "Berlin Citizens Association" in its effort to set up white wooden crosses along the line of the border in honor of the known victims. Later these crosses were assembled at the Reichstag building and on Bernauer Strasse. When the Wall was torn down in 1990, many of these memorial signs in the East and West disappeared. The monuments to the killed border soldiers were removed for political reasons, but on the west side they disappeared amidst the euphoria of quickly dismantling the border grounds. But a few of the memorial signs did survive, or were created again, or moved to a new site. The "white crosses," for example, were moved temporarily to the Tiergarten Park between the Brandenburg Gate and the Reichstag. When the plaza in front of the Reichstag was redesigned, a new memorial site was created with white crosses near the original location on the bank of the Spree. It is situated very close to the "Parliament of Trees" memorial site that was designed by the Berlin artist Ben Wagin a year after the Wall fell. This installation on the border strip along the Spree River was created out of original pieces of the Wall. Today the monument is partially integrated into the newly erected Bundestag library. In combination with the white crosses on the other side of the Spree River, this memorial ensemble reminds tourists and other visitors to the parliament quarter of this area's historical importance.

In 1989 the Association of the Victims of Stalinism (VOS), founded in 1950, asked the mayor of Berlin for his support in organizing their annual memorial ceremony for the victims of the Wall. In response, the Senate decided that the ceremony, which had until then been conducted by the VOS at the monument to the victims of Stalinism on the Steinplatz plaza in Berlin-Charlottenburg, would henceforth be organized by the Senate staff. The official memorial ceremony took place on August 13, 1990 at the cross dedicated to Peter Fechter on Zimmerstrasse, not far from Checkpoint Charlie, and was attended by the city leaders from East and West Berlin, as well as by representatives of the federal government. Today the cross has been replaced by a memorial pillar in memory of the death of the young construction worker. It is here, at this site, that the state of Berlin commemorates all the victims of the Wall each year on August 13.

As the Wall was being torn down, efforts began to preserve at least a part of the border fortifications in memory of the division of the city and in commemoration of the victims of communist tyranny. Out of this initiative, which was strongly supported by members of the West Berlin Reconciliation Parish, by resolutions of the Round Table in Berlin Mitte and, finally, by the federal government – represented by the German Historical Museum – the Berlin Wall Memorial was erected on Bernauer Strasse as a site of national commemoration, dedicated on August 13, 1998. The memorial's design initially led to polarization and critical reactions. Victim associations in particular complained that the grounds were unable to convey the horror of the border regime. When, in 2004, an installation initiated by the "Workgroup 13th of August" was erected at Checkpoint Charlie out of 1,065 tall wooden crosses in memory of the victims of the Wall and border, the public expressed a strong desire for a permanent memorial site that would allow for both individual and public commemoration of the fatal victims. The Berlin Senate adopted the discussion of an appropriate form of memory and commemoration into its "General Concept for Remembrance of the Berlin Wall," passed in 2006.[40] With funding from the Berlin Senate and the federal government, the memorial site at Bernauer Strasse is currently being expanded and developed into a national site of remembrance. In addition to the memorial ceremonies conducted each year, prayer services have been held since August 13, 2006 in the Chapel of Reconciliation for the victims who died at the Berlin Wall. Independently of this, the victims continue to be remembered at many sites along the former line of the border through private initiatives and local district activities.[41] In 2009, in commemoration of the 20th anniversary of the fall of the Wall, plans were made to add more memorial signs to the 100 memorial crosses and commemorative plaques that already exist – for example in Tempelhof and Pankow – and to rename streets. The memory of the crimes committed in connection with the East German border regime functions as an affirmation of the shared German-German history. The state honored the victims and their families through the Criminal Law of Rehabilitation[42] and through the Grave Preservation Law,[43] which allow relatives to claim financial support and guarantee that victims' gravesites be preserved for an unlimited period. Because many relatives did not know of this law and, in most cases, the graves had already been destroyed, very few gravesites of victims of the Wall actually exist today. This is one more reason why the memorial sites for the victims of the Berlin Wall and the commemoration of their lives and deaths continue to be so important.

1   Text: Christine Brecht, Hans-Hermann Hertle and Maria Nooke; editing: Hans-Hermann Hertle and Maria Nooke.

2   See Hans-Hermann Hertle, *Die Berliner Mauer – Monument des Kalten Krieges*, 4th revised edition, Bonn, 2009.

3   See Hans-Hermann Hertle / Gerhard Sälter, "Die Todesopfer an Mauer und Grenze. Probleme einer Bilanz des DDR-Grenzregimes," in: *Deutschland Archiv* 4/2006, pp. 667–676.

4   See Werner Filmer / Heribert Schwan, *Opfer der Mauer. Die geheimen Protokolle des Todes*, Munich, 1991; Volker Koop, *"Den Gegner vernichten." Die Grenzsicherung der DDR*, Bonn, 1996; Wolfgang Rathje, *"Mauer-Marketing" unter Erich Honecker. Schwierigkeiten der DDR bei der technischen Modernisierung, der volkswirtschaftlichen Kalkulation und der politischen Akzeptanz der Berliner "Staatsgrenze" von 1971 bis 1990*, Dissertation, 2 Bd., Kiel, 2001; Hannelore Strehlow, *Der gefährliche Weg in die Freiheit. Fluchtversuche aus dem ehemaligen Bezirk Potsdam*, Potsdam, 2004; Roman Grafe, *Deutsche Gerechtigkeit. Prozesse gegen DDR-Grenzschützen und ihre Befehlsgeber*, Munich, 2004; Uwe Gerig, *Morde an der Mauer*, Böblingen, 1989.

5   "Opfer der Mauer." Polizeiliche Liste des Polizeipräsidenten in Berlin / Abt. I, o. O. (Berlin), o. J. (1990).

6   Heiner Sauer / Hans-Otto Plumeyer, *Der Salzgitter-Report. Die Zentrale Erfassungsstelle berichtet über Verbrechen im SED-Staat*, Munich, 1991.

7   See Hans-Jürgen Grasemann, "Fluchtgeschichten aus der Zentralen Erfassungsstelle Salzgitter," in: Bernd Weisbrod (ed.), *Grenzland. Beiträge zur Geschichte der deutsch-deutschen Grenze*, Hanover, 1993, pp. 28–50.

8   On the criteria of the Central Registry, see Sauer / Plumeyer, *Salzgitter-Report*, pp. 23–31, quote p. 27.

9   See Sauer / Plumeyer, *Salzgitter-Report*, pp. 279, 281.

10 Filmer / Schwan, *Opfer der Mauer*, p. 153.

11 "Die Erfassungsstelle hat das in der DDR begangene Unrecht nicht vollständig dokumentieren können. […] Es

ist ein Report, der erst dann wissenschaftlich vertieft werden kann, wenn die im vereinten Deutschland zugänglichen Erkenntnisquellen ausgewertet sein werden," (Sauer/Plumeyer, *Salzgitter-Report*, p. 21).

12 Alexandra Hildebrandt, *Neue Zahl der Todesopfer des DDR-Grenzregimes – Keine Endbilanz*, Berlin, 2004 (137th press conference of the "Working Group 13th of August" on 12.8.2004), p. 3.

13 Alexandra Hildebrandt, 1303 *Todesopfer – keine Endbilanz. Neue Zahl der ermittelten Todesopfer des Grenzregimes der SBZ/DDR/SED*, Berlin, 2008 (153th press conference of the "Working Group 13th of August" on 12.8.2008).

14 See Zentrale Ermittlungsstelle Regierungs- und Vereinigungskriminalität, *Jahresbericht 2000*, Berlin, 2001.

15 For our research project it was possible to view an unpublished list of names from the public prosecutor's office in Berlin ("Liste aller Toten an der innerdeutschen Grenze," Date: 21.9.1999).

16 See the chapter "Alleged Cases of Death" in this book.

17 Under the heading "Deaths at the Berlin Wall" the "Working Group 13th of August" list in 2006 included a total of 239 cases. The following year the figure was reduced to 231. The difference was based on 14 deletions and six new entries. In 2008 the figure changed to 222 cases. The nine fewer deaths was the result of 13 deletions and four new entries. In addition to cases "believed dead" of which it was proven that the individuals in question had actually survived, and a few double counts in its list, the working group included 39 water corpses, eight border guard suicides and ten soldiers who were killed while on duty in accidents with firearms or in other incidents.

18 See Roland Lucht, "'Ablagen liquidieren – ›spezifische‹ Vorgänge tragfähig gestalten'. Schriftgutvernichtung des MfS während der »Wende« und der Auflösung der Staatssicherheit," in: Dagmar Unverhau, *Hatte »Janus« eine Chance? Das Ende der DDR und die Sicherung einer Zukunft in der Vergangenheit*, Berlin u.a. 2003, pp. 81–97.

19 See Alf Lüdtke/Peter Becker (eds.), *Akten. Eingaben. Schaufenster. Die DDR und ihre Texte*, Berlin, 1997, and Klaus-Dietmar Henke/Roger Engelmann (eds.), *Aktenlage. Die Bedeutung der Unterlagen des Staatssicherheitsdienstes für die Zeitgeschichtsforschung*, Berlin, 1995.

20 On the ambiguity of the perpetrator language, see also: Thomas Auerbach, "Liquidierung = Mord? Zur vieldeutigen Semantik des Begriffs in den MfS-Unterlagen," in: *Horch und Guck* 17 (2008), Vol. 59, pp. 5–7.

21 In some cases the courts expressed their opinions on this explicitly in their verdicts, for example. in their sentencing of the men who shot Horst Kullack and Willi Block. See here "Urteil des Landgerichts Potsdam vom 1.11.1995," in: StA Berlin, Az. 2 Js 39/95, Bd. 2, Bl. 1–28 (duplicated file); "Urteil des Landgerichts Berlin vom 13.1.1995," in: StA Berlin, Az. 2 Js 71/91, Bd. 5, Bl. 8a–8e.

22 For the moving depiction of a difficult German-German family history in the context of the Cold War, see also Peter Wyden, *Die Mauer war unser Schicksal*, Berlin, 1995.

23 See Udo Grashoff, "*In einem Anfall von Depression ... .*" *Selbsttötungen in der DDR*, Berlin, 2006, in particular the section on "Selbsttötungen als Folge der 'Einmauerung' der DDR," pp. 128–157; Dieter Müller-Hegemann, *Die Berliner Mauer-Krankheit. Zur Soziogenese psychischer Störungen*, Herford, 1973. As director of the Wilhelm-Griesinger Hospital in East Berlin between 1964 and 1971, the author treated many patients suffering from mental disorders that were caused by the Berlin Wall. See also the detailed chapter "Other Cases of Death" in this book.

24 See also the descriptions of 24 people in the chapter "Inconclusive Cases" in this book.

25 "Abschlußbericht des MfS/KD Pankow zur OPK 'Morgentau', 25.7.1988," in: BStU, Ast. Berlin, AOPK Nr. 5895/88, Bl. 118.

26 See here on the following "Ordnung [des MfS] für die Bearbeitung von Leichenvorgängen, o.O., o.J.," in: BStU, MfS, HA IX Nr. 5134, Bl. 10–16. There were similar directives for the inner-German border.

27 Ibid.

28 The "MfS-Hauptabteilung I" was active in the NVA and border troops under the heading "Verwaltung 2000" or "Bereich 2000" and responsible for "military counter-intelligence." This included, above all, the prevention of military desertions through the acquisition of informers, comprehensive spying on members of the army, as well as discovering and investigating attempts to desert. See Stephan Wolf, *Hauptabteilung I: NVA und Grenztruppen, MfS-Handbuch, Teil III/13*, published by Bundesbeauftragter für die Unterlagen des Staatssicherheitsdienstes der ehemaligen DDR, 2nd edition, Berlin, 2005.

29 See "Ordnung [des MfS] für die Bearbeitung von Leichenvorgängen, o.O., o.J.," in: BStU, MfS, HA IX Nr. 5134, Bl. 13.

30 Ibid.

31 Ibid., Bl.14.

32 "Weisung des Leiters der BVfS Potsdam zur Regelung der Zuständigkeit und des Zusammenwirkens von Dienst-einheiten der Bezirksverwaltung bei der Bearbeitung von verletzten oder getöteten Grenzverletzern und durch Folgeerscheinungen verletzten oder getöteten Personen an der Staatsgrenze der DDR zu Westberlin im Bezirk Potsdam, Potsdam, 20. 5. 1970," in: BStU, Ast. Potsdam, BdL Dok. Nr. 400576, Bl. 3–11, quote Bl. 10. Here also the following quote.

33 On criminal prosecution of deaths at the Wall, see Henning Rosenau, *Tödliche Schüsse im staatlichen Auftrag: Die strafrechtliche Verantwortung von Grenzsoldaten für den Schusswaffengebrauch an der deutsch-deut-schen Grenze,* 2. edition, Baden-Baden, 1998; Klaus Marxen / Gerhard Werle, *Die strafrechtliche Aufarbeitung von DDR-Unrecht. Eine Bilanz,* Berlin, 1999; dies. (eds.), *Strafjustiz und DDR-Unrecht. Dokumentation, Bd. 2: Gewalttaten an der deutsch-deutschen Grenze,* 2 Teilbde., Berlin, 2002; Toralf Rummler, *Die Gewalttaten an der deutsch-deutschen Grenze vor Gericht,* Berlin / Baden-Baden, 2000; Karl Wilhelm Fricke, "'Grenzverletzer sind festzunehmen oder zu vernichten'. Zur Ahndung von Tötungsdelikten an Mauer und Stacheldraht," in: *Die politische Meinung,* No. 381 / August 2001, pp. 11–17; Erardo C. Rautenberg, "Die strafrechtliche Aufarbeitung des DDR-Systemunrechts im Land Brandenburg aus staatsanwaltschaftlicher Sicht," in: Klaus-Christoph Clavée / Wolf Kahl / Ramona Pisal (ed.), *10 Jahre Brandenburgisches Oberlandesgericht,* Baden-Baden, 2003, pp. 97–130; Roman Grafe, *Deutsche Gerechtigkeit. Prozesse gegen DDR-Grenzschützen und ihre Befehls-geber,* Munich, 2004; Hansgeorg Bräutigam, "Die Toten an der Mauer und an der innerdeutschen Grenze und die bundesdeutsche Justiz," in: *Deutschland Archiv 37 (2004),* pp. 969–976.

34 See "Urteil des Bundesgerichtshofes in der Strafsache gegen Rolf S. und Ernst R. im Fall Michael Kollender, Az. 5 StR 137 / 96, vom 17. 12. 1996," dok. in: Klaus Marxen / Gerhard Werle (eds.), *Strafjustiz und DDR-Unrecht. Dokumentation, Bd. 2: Gewalttaten an der deutsch-deutschen Grenze, 1. Teilband,* Berlin, 2002, pp. 277–281.

35 Bernhard Jahntz, *Die Bilanz der Strafverfolgung des SED-Unrechts,* Vortragsmanuskript, Wustrau, 2007.

36 See *Schwerpunktabteilung der Staatsanwaltschaft Neuruppin für Bezirkskriminalität und DDR-Justizunrecht, Bilanz 2006* (Ms.).

37 See "Urteil des Bundesgerichtshofes in der Strafsache gegen Karl-Heinz W. im Fall Manfred Weylandt, Az. 5 StR 167 / 94, 26. 7. 1994," dok. in: Klaus Marxen / Gerhard Werle (eds.), *Strafjustiz und DDR-Unrecht. Doku-mentation, Bd. 2: Gewalttaten an der deutsch-deutschen Grenze, 1. Teilband,* Berlin, 2002, pp. 179–187, quote p. 182.

38 See Rainer Klemke, "Zwischen Verschwinden und Gedenken – die Erinnerung an die Berliner Mauer heute," in: Anna Kaminsky (ed.), *Die Berliner Mauer in der Welt,* Berlin, 2009, pp. 214–227.

39 "Rooms of tradition," ("Traditionszimmer" and "Traditionskabinette") were rooms set up in schools, factories, barracks and other East German institutions to preserve the so-called "anti-fascist traditions of the working class" and to honor communist resistance fighters and socialist role models according to the guidelines of Marxist-Leninist ideology.

40 See http://www.berlin.de/sen/kultur/kulturpolitik/mauer/gesamtkonzept.html.

41 See *Gesamtkonzept zur Erinnerung an die Berliner Mauer,* 2006, ibid. See also Anne Kaminsky (ed.), *Orte des Erinnerns. Gedenkzeichen, Gedenkstätten und Museen zur Diktatur in SBZ und DDR,* Berlin, 2007.

42 Law on the rehabilitation and restitution of victims of illegal prosecution measures in acceding territory from Oct. 29, 1992, revised by publication on Dec. 17, 1999 (BGBl. I, p. 2664), last amended by Art. 1 of the law of Dec. 22, 2003 (BGBl. I, p. 2834), § 18.

43 Law on the preservation of graves for the victims of war and tyranny in the publicized version of January 29, 1993 (BGBl. I, p. 178), last amended by the Law of December 21, 2004 (BGBl. I, p. 3641).

136 Victims at the Berlin Wall, 1961–1989

Fugitives who were either shot, suffered a fatal accident or took their own lives at the Berlin Wall between 1961 and 1989; individuals from the East and the West who did not intend to flee but were killed or suffered a fatal accident in the border territory

Ida Siekmann

born on August 23, 1902

fatally injured on August 22, 1961
after jumping out of her apartment window
at Bernauer Strasse 48
at the sector border between
Berlin-Mitte and Berlin-Wedding

Ida Siekmann was born on August 23, 1902 in Gorken, a small village that at that time belonged to the West Prussian district of Marienwerder and today is part of Poland. It is not known when she left the East Elbian province and went to Berlin.

In 1961, the year the Wall was built, she lived at Bernauer Strasse 48 in Berlin-Mitte. Like all the buildings and properties on the south side of the street, her apartment building was located in the administrative district of Mitte, part of East Berlin. But the street, including the sidewalk in front of the building entrance, belonged to the administrative district of Wedding, part of West Berlin. Since 1945 this border dividing two city districts had also served as the boundary line between the Soviet and French sectors of Berlin. While the sector border was still open, close family contacts and neighborly relations existed between the densely populated residential areas.

Ida Siekmann crossed the border regularly since the border situation required her to enter her building from West Berlin. Moreover, she was likely to have paid regular visits to her sister, who lived just a few blocks away in the western section of the city. When the Communist Party leadership sealed off the entire sector border on August 13, 1961, the situation for Ida Siekmann, who lived alone, changed dramatically. Like hundreds of thousands of Berliners, she was cut off overnight from relatives and acquaintances living in the other part of the city. But because the 58-year-old lived in a building located directly on the East Berlin border, she was more strongly affected by the new barrier and control measures that were introduced.

During the first days and weeks after the Wall was built, many of the residents of Bernauer Strasse attempted to flee from the border houses: They did not want to be separated from relatives and were under constant harassment by the East German authorities. Shortly after the border was shut off it was still possible to leave through the front door of the buildings. By August 18, however, all the front doors that exited onto the West Berlin sidewalk had been nailed or walled shut and new entrances had been created through back courtyards. Members of the workers' militia and police units were posted in the building corridors and staircases and checked the documents of everyone who wanted to enter a building or apartment.

These measures instilled fear in the residents and, in desperation, many of them jumped from their windows or climbed down a rope to escape to the West. The West Berlin fire department stood on the sidewalk and tried to catch them in their rescue nets to prevent them from getting injured. On August 21, Ida Siekmann watched as the entrance to her building was barricaded shut. Early the next morning she threw her bedding and other belongings out the window of her third floor apartment. Then she jumped. Perhaps she was scared of being discovered. The West Berlin firemen had no chance to catch her in their rescue net. She was badly injured when she hit the sidewalk and died on the way to the nearby Lazarus Hospital – one day before her 59th birthday.[1]

The circumstances of her death were diligently recorded in East Berlin. The East German police noted in one of their routine reports: "On August 22, 1961, at 6:50 a.m., Ida Siekmann […], single, jumped out the window of her third floor apartment in the front building and onto the street […]. S. was carried away by the West Berlin fire department. The blood stain was covered up with sand."[2]

On the west side, her death at the Berlin Wall set off a wave of indignation. Decades later, a West Berlin police officer who personally witnessed Ida Siekmann's fall recalled how shocked residents and passersby had been.[3]

The press reported in detail on the "fatal jump to freedom" and made it perfectly clear that the East German leadership bore responsibility for the tragic occurrence: The "Berliner Morgenpost" wrote that "Ulbricht's brutal measures against our fellow-countrymen in the eastern sector of Berlin have taken a human life yesterday." The "Bild-Zeitung" called the death of an East Berliner "an indictment of the communist regime."[4] Newspaper articles also noted the widespread frustration over the fact that the western Allies and German federal government had shown such reserve in reaction to the blockade measures. After the Wall was built, Federal Chancellor Konrad Adenauer did not rush to West Berlin. He arrived on the day Ida Siekmann died and was strongly criticized for waiting this long.[5]

An official funeral service was held for Ida Siekmann on August 29, at the Municipal Cemetery on Seestrasse in Wedding. A large number of West Berlin residents attended the service. Red roses and white carnations in the colors of West Berlin decorated the coffin. Official representatives of the district, Senate and federal government expressed their condolences to the sister of the deceased. After the burial, Ernst Lemmer, federal minister of all-German affairs, and Helmut Mattis, the district mayor of Wedding, placed a wreath in front of the building at Bernauer Strasse 48 which bore the inscription: "deprived of freedom." Many residents and passersby paid homage to the deceased at the site where she died. One writer noted at the time that the sidewalk was always covered with wreaths and flowers.[6]

The district office of Wedding erected a monument for Ida Siekmann at her death site. It consisted of three wooden logs enveloped in barbed wire.[7] Regular memorial services took place there over the following decades. German and foreign state guests also paid their respects to the site as a form of public commemoration on the west side of the Wall. Robert Kennedy, the American attorney general, and Federal Chancellor Konrad Adenauer also made a stop at the monument dedicated to Ida Siekmann. Like so many other politicians, they too laid a wreath and honored the deceased with a moment of silence – a gesture that was also an expression of their rejection of the border regime established in East Germany.

Christine Brecht

1 See "Sprung in den Tod um frei zu sein," in: *Berliner Morgenpost,* 23.8.1961, and "Flucht-Sprung in den Tod," in: *Bild-Zeitung*, 23.8.1961.
2 "PdVP-Rapport Nr. 234, 23.8.1961," in: PHS, Bestand PdVP-Rapporte, Archive-No. 8037, Bl. 8.
3 See Doris Liebermann, "Die Gewalt der anderen Seite hat mich sehr getroffen." A conversation with Hans-Joachim Lazai †, in: *Deutschland Archiv 39* (2006), pp. 596–607.
4 See *Berliner Morgenpost*, 23.8.1961; *Bild-Zeitung*, 23.8.1961.
5 See "Kanzler sagt schwere Zeiten voraus," in: *Frankfurter Rundschau*, 23.8.1961.
6 See Eckart Kroneberg, "Beschreibung einer Mauer," in: Hans Werner Richter (ed.), *Die Mauer oder der 13. August*, Reinbek, 1961, pp. 90–101, here p. 100.
7 See *Berliner Morgenpost*, 16.9.1961.

Günter Litfin

born on January 19, 1937

shot dead on August 24, 1961
in the Humboldt Harbor near Charité Hospital
at the sector border between
Berlin-Mitte and Berlin-Tiergarten

Günter Litfin was born in Berlin on January 19, 1937 and lived in the city district of Weissensee. He grew up during the Second World War and later experienced the country's reconstruction and the gradual division of the city. His father Albert worked as a butcher and in 1945 helped found the local CDU district chapter, which his wife Margarete also joined. The four sons were baptized Catholic and attended the St. Joseph School in Berlin-Weissensee. The family was clearly rooted in a milieu that was not supportive of the East German government and its mission to "establish socialism."[1] The sons continued to maintain this attitude as adults: In 1957 Günter Litfin and his younger brother, Jürgen, joined the West Berlin CDU, which unlike the CDU block party in East Germany, existed illegally in the eastern part of the city.[2]

After completing an apprenticeship as a tailor, Günter Litfin got a job in a West Berlin tailor workshop. He was fashion conscious, dressed elegantly and dreamed of becoming a costume maker for the theater. At first the young man commuted daily from his parents' apartment in Weissensee to his job near the Bahnhof Zoo. But "border-crossers," as people who worked in the West and lived in the East were called, were under increasing pressure in East Germany. To avoid conflict Günter Litfin found an apartment in the West Berlin district of Charlottenburg, but he did not register his new address with the police because that would have made him a "republic fugitive" – someone who has deserted East Germany – and would have meant that he could no longer visit his relatives in East Berlin. Günter Litfin's brother later described him "as the calming force in the family and the one everyone could confide in."[3] After his father died in May 1961, Günter strongly felt it was his responsibility to be there for his mother.

Consequently, he postponed his permanent move to West Berlin – until it was too late. The construction of the Berlin Wall suddenly put an end to his plans for the future. Günter Litfin spent August 12, 1961, a Saturday, with his mother and brother visiting relatives on the west side of the city. When they took the S-Bahn back to Weissensee late that evening, they had no idea that measures were being prepared to close the border. The shock was great the next morning when they heard on the radio that the sector border had been completely sealed off during the night. Günter Litfin, unable to accept the existence of the Wall, began looking into possible escape routes.

A large number of successful escapes were undertaken during the first few days after the Wall was built. Many East Berliners found holes or used an unobserved moment to cross the sector border, which was not yet completely guarded.[4] No one could imagine at this point that the border guards would actually aim their weapons at someone fleeing. But on August 24, 1961 the fatal consequences of the newly established border regime were displayed for the first time. It was just after 4 p.m. when Günter Litfin began his attempt to reach West Berlin by fleeing between the Friedrichstrasse and Lehrter train stations. According to reports from the East Berlin police, he crossed Charité Hospital grounds and climbed over a wall bordering the bank of the Spree River[5] when members of the transport police discovered him. From the railroad bridge where they were standing, they ordered the fugitive to freeze and fired a few warning shots. They opened fire when Günter Litfin jumped into the Humboldt Harbor. He was fatally wounded by a bullet in the back of his head just before he reached the West Berlin bank on the other side. East Berlin firemen pulled his body out of the water three hours later.

Meanwhile hundreds of West Berliners had gathered on the west side of the harbor and watched as the dead body was carried away. The press reports over the next few days reflected the outrage that Günter Litfin's death had triggered in the West. "Ulbricht's human hunters have become murderers," ran a headline of the "BZ" newspaper. The "Frankfurter Allgemeine Zeitung" also condemned the border guards for their "brutal cold-bloodedness."[6] West Berlin residents expressed their strong resentment through spontaneous protest demonstrations. On the morning of August 27, a banner was hung on the west side of the Humboldt Harbor with an inscription in German: "No matter how berserk Ulbricht becomes, Berlin remains free. And will never go red."[7] A year later a memorial stone to Gunter Litfin was placed at this site.

The reaction in East Berlin was quite different. Under the headline "Shots Disregarded," the East Berlin press presented the fugitive as someone "who was pursued because of his criminal behavior."[8] "Neues Deutschland," the Communist Party's "central organ," and its head propagandist, Karl Eduard von Schnitzler, showed no compunction in disparaging the deceased by name. Staff members of the Ministry of State Security harassed and intimidated Günter Litfin's relatives. His brother was unaware of what had happened when he was arrested on August 25 and interrogated the entire night. The same day his mother's apartment was searched without explanation. Both were left in the dark as to what had happened to Günter Litfin. They first found out that he had been shot and killed at the Wall through an announcement on the West Berlin news program, "Abendschau," that reported the fatality on August 26.[9]

Although the circumstances of his death were generally known from western news reports, the East Berlin authorities demanded that the relatives of the deceased remain silent about the incident. This explains the ambiguous language of the obituary that stated that Günter Litfin had died suddenly and unexpectedly "from a tragic accident." At the funeral, which took place on August 31 at the St. Hedwig Cemetery in Weissensee in the presence of Stasi personnel, the truth could not be revealed. According to Jürgen Litfin, because the majority of the guests knew that his brother's death was not an "accident," the funeral became a farce.[10]

After the East German state collapsed, legal proceedings were introduced against the two men responsible for shooting him. They had to appear before the Berlin district court in 1997 and take responsibility for their actions. According to the verdict, they were found guilty of joint manslaughter. As with most of the border guard trials against guards who had shot fugitives at the Wall, the sentences handed down were mild: The men were sentenced to one year and one year and six months respectively, and then released on probation. In its closing statement the court commented on "how little all these sentences do justice to the illegal nature of the acts in question and how strongly symbolic they are."[11]

Christine Brecht

1 See Jürgen Litfin, *Tod durch fremde Hand. Das erste Maueropfer in Berlin und die Geschichte einer Familie,* Husum, 2006.
2 See Günter Buchstab (ed.), *Verfolgt und entrechtet. Die Ausschaltung christlicher Demokraten unter sowjetischer Besatzung und SED-Herrschaft 1945–1961,* Düsseldorf, 1998.
3 Conversation conducted by Christine Brecht with Jürgen Litfin, 2.6.2006.
4 See Bernd Eisenfeld/Roger Engelmann, 13.8.1961. *Mauerbau, Fluchtbewegung und Machtsicherung,* Berlin, 2001.
5 See "Rapport Nr. 236 des PdVP Berlin/OS für die Zeit vom 24.8./25.8.1961, 25.8.1961," in: PHS, Bestand PdVP-Rapporte, Bl. 188; "Rapport Nr. 236/61 der Trapo/Abschnitt Berlin/Operativstab für die Zeit vom 24.8.1961, 00.00 Uhr, bis 24.8.1961, 24.00 Uhr, 25.8.1961," in: PHS, Bestand Trapo-Rapporte, Bl. 17; "Bericht der [SED-]Bezirkseinsatzleitung Berlin über den 24. August 1961 an Walter Ulbricht, 25.8.1961," in: BArch, VA-07/39575, Bl. 22–26; "Rapport Nr. 234 der Hauptverwaltung der Deutschen Volkspolizei, 25.8. 1961," in: BArch, DO 1/11.0/1351, Bl. 170.
6 *BZ,* 25.8.1961; *Frankfurter Allgemeine Zeitung,* 26.8.1961.
7 "Journal der Handlungen des Stabs des PdVP, 27.8.1961," in: LAB, C Rep. 303-26-01, Nr. 239, Bl. 116.
8 *Berliner Zeitung,* 25.8.1961.
9 See interview by Maria Nooke with Jürgen Litfin, 8.1.2001.
10 See ibid.
11 "Urteil des Landgerichts Berlin vom 17.1.1997," in: StA Berlin, Az. 27/2 Js 141/90, Bd. 3, Bl. 15–29, here Bl. 28.

Roland Hoff

born on March 19, 1934

shot dead on August 29, 1961
in the Teltow Canal
on the outer ring between
Teltow (Teltow district) and Berlin-Steglitz

"The inhuman division of our city," reported the "Berliner Morgenpost" on August 30, 1961, "claimed a third life yesterday. At the zone border in Lichterfelde, an unknown fugitive was murdered by the Vopo [East German Police] while trying to swim to freedom through the Teltow Canal."[1] The East German authorities had long known the identity of the deceased by then,[2] but they did not reveal his name for decades. Even the victim's relatives were not notified. Not until the East German archives were made accessible was it discovered that the man whose escape attempt ended fatally on this late summer day was the 27-year-old Roland Hoff.

Roland Hoff was born on March 19, 1934 in Hanover, where he grew up with his three sisters. One of his sisters recalled that the only son was their mother's favorite and continued to live at home even after he had completed an apprenticeship as a pipe-layer.[3] He did not move out until he went to East Germany at the age of 27 in June 1961. Like so many West Germans who resettled in the East, he was not motivated by political convictions.[4] His mother believes that he drove to the inner-German border and requested residency in East Germany because he feared being penalized for having driven his moped while under the influence of alcohol. After completing the admissions procedure at the Barby Reception Camp near Magdeburg, Roland Hoff was assigned an apartment and job in Lusatia in Saxony. But only a short time later he wrote to his mother that he was already thinking about coming back to the West.[5] The Berlin Wall put an abrupt end to these plans. Apparently Roland Hoff spoke out openly against the closure of the border at his workplace ten days later. This resulted in his discharge "due to absenteeism and inciting slander against the state in violation of the measures of 13.8.61."[6] He failed to respond to the summons to appear before an arbitration court "for the purpose of clarifying his employment situation." Instead he packed his belongings, sent them by mail from Forst to his mother in Hanover and headed off in the direction of Berlin on August 29.

That day in Teltow, a suburb in the southwest of Berlin, construction was being carried out to facilitate surveillance of the East German side of the Teltow Canal.

The border to the West Berlin district of Lichterfelde on the other side ran through the middle of the canal here. A group of forty construction workers were busy clearing an embankment under the surveillance of border police and militia work units. According to a Potsdam police report, Roland Hoff must have managed to disguise himself as a worker and reach the bank undetected. At 2 p.m. he jumped into the border waters with a briefcase under his arm and swam to the West Berlin side. "Don't shoot! Please don't shoot" he called out after the first shots were fired. But four border guards continued to fire at him until he was fatally wounded in the head and sank beneath the water's surface.[7]

The workers on the east side of the Teltow Canal who had witnessed this violent act were horrified and spontaneously stopped their work. One worker expressed his displeasure loudly, calling the border soldiers "concentration camp guards" and "murderers," and was consequently detained temporarily and interrogated.[8]

The authorities also took strong action against the workers of a nearby industrial plant, the "Teltower Geräte und Reglerwerk," who expressed their sympathy with the victim. A flier from the factory leadership accused an employee of making light of and defending the escape attempt because she had described the guards as murderers.[9] The flier is a good example of how East German propaganda villainized a victim in order to legitimize the brutal action taken against fugitives: "A henchman of the Cold War was not able to complete his assignment. A louse on the body of our worker and peasant state has been squashed before it could bite."[10] This kind of propaganda, which equated the victim with the enemy, was a clear and intentional public demonstration of the harshness of the authorities. Similar examples can be found in the East German press reports that employed the same clichés and prejudices. "Neues Deutschland," for example, characterized Roland Hoff and Günter Litfin, who was shot and killed a few days earlier, as "sinister elements," "criminal characters" and "riffraff." The East German "Märkische Volksstimme" responded to the West Berlin Senate's protests with the statement: "You speak of freedom and lament that East German border control officials shot criminals who disregarded all the warning calls and shots and violated our border in an attempt to escape the punishment they deserved."[11]

Within a very short time police and firemen, as well as journalists and photographers, arrived at the site where the shooting had taken place and aimed their cameras at the men in uniform on the other side of the canal. In the western media and in commentaries the shots were unanimously condemned and the brutality of the act was criticized.[12] In response to this most recent fatality the West Berlin authorities conducted an investigation of the alleged criminals and would continue to do so in every case that followed. A reward of 10,000 German marks was offered for tips that would lead to the identification of the perpetrators in this unprecedented search operation. A wanted poster showing one of the marksmen was hung at many places along the Wall as a deterrent.[13] In the following years, defectors to the West provided West Berlin authorities with the names of the border guards involved in the shooting, but they could not take action against them yet. After the Wall fell, however, the three former border guards were brought to trial, but the courts were unable to determine which one was responsible for the fatal shot.[14] The East German authorities never divulged Roland Hoff's name. His mother, after hearing western media reports, was convinced that it was her son who had been found dead in the Teltow Canal and she notified the West German authorities. But her lifelong efforts to receive information from the East German authorities remained unsuccessful.

A memorial stone to the unknown fugitive was unveiled on the West Berlin bank on the first anniversary of his death and is still there today.

Christine Brecht

1 "Das dritte Todesopfer der KZ-Schergen," in: *Berliner Morgenpost*, 30.8.1961.

2 See, for example, "Bericht des Kommandeurs der 5. Grenzbrigade der DGP an das MdI, 29.8.1961," in: BArch, Pt 10591, n. pag.

3 Conversation conducted by Christine Brecht with Margarete W., Roland Hoff's sister, 3.11.2006.

4 See Andrea Schmelz, *Migration und Politik im geteilten Deutschland während des Kalten Krieges. Die West-Ost-Migration in die DDR in den 1950er und 1960er Jahren,* Opladen, 2002.

5 See "Vermerk der Polizei Hannover, 21.11.1961," in: StA Neuruppin, Az. 61 Js 23/95, Bd. 1, Bl. 100–101.

6 See "Funkspruch der DGP, 29.8.1961," in: BArch, Pt 10591, n. pag.

7 See "Zwischenbericht des VPK Potsdam, 29.8.1961," in: BLHA, Rep. 471/15.1, Nr. 223, Bl. 38–40, and "Tatortbefundsbericht des VPK Potsdam, 29.8.1961," in: Ibid., Nr. 568, Bl. 137–138. See also the eye-witness statement from Thilo S., 14.9.1993, in: StA Neuruppin, Az. 61 Js 23/95, Bd. 4 , Bl. 56–69.

8 Ibid, here Bl. 63. The exact quote: "You concentration camp guards, you are worse than the Nazis. You murderers!" See also information of the MfS-ZAIG from 31.8.1961, in: BStU, MfS, ZAIG Nr. 510, Bl. 1–6, here Bl. 6, and "Bericht des Kommandeurs der 5. Grenzbrigade der DGP, 29.8.1961," in: BArch, Pt 10591, n. pag.

9 Statements by former employees after their flight to West Berlin in September 1961, in: StA Neuruppin, Az. 61 Js 23/95, Bd. 1, Bl. 59–65.

10 "Der Impuls," flyer, 4.9.1961, in: StA Neuruppin, Az. 61 Js 23/95, Bd. 5, Bl. 42–44.

11 "Mordhetze in der Frontstadt," in: *Neues Deutschland*, 2.9.1961; "Unsere Staatsgrenze ist unantastbar," in: *Märkische Volksstimme*, 6.9.1961.

12 See *Berliner Morgenpost*, 30.8.1961; *Der Kurier*, 30.8.1961; *Telegraf,* 30.8.1961; *Spandauer Volksblatt*, 30.8.1961; *Der Tagesspiegel*, 30.8.1961, and reports on RIAS from 30.8.1961.

13 See, for example, the MfS report on supposed western war mongering, 1.11.1961, in: BStU, MfS, ZAIG Nr. 525, Bl. 3–39.

14 See "Urteil des Landgerichts Potsdam vom 22.4.1996," in: StA Berlin, 27 Js 99/95, Bd. 6, Bl. 175–228, and "Urteil des Landgerichts Potsdam vom 15.4.1996," in: Ibid., Bl. 229–232.

Rudolf Urban

born on June 6, 1914

crashed to the ground on August 19, 1961
while fleeing from his apartment
on Bernauer Strasse
at the sector border between
Berlin-Mitte and Berlin-Wedding
died from consequences of his escape
on September 17, 1961

The driver Rudolf Urban was 47 years old when the Berlin Wall was built. He lived with his wife at Bernauer Strasse 1 in East Berlin at the time. He was born in the four-story apartment building near the Reconciliation Church. Like all the buildings on the southern side of the street that belonged to the administrative district of Mitte, they could only be entered from the sidewalk situated in West Berlin. This unusual situation at the sector border had affected the lives of the residents for years, but it became extremely acute when the East German leadership began sealing off the inner city sector border on August 13, 1961.

In response to the barriers blocking all roads and crossings between the two sides of the city, a number of people tried to flee to West Berlin from the border houses on Bernauer Strasse.[1] The East German authorities took drastic measures in response to these actions. They sealed all the entrances and windows of the border buildings and placed armed guards in the hallways and stairs of the buildings. Bernauer Strasse became notorious during this time because the western media publicized these events with pictures and reports. A West Berlin author described the oppressive situation: "Only the residents on the upper levels can still speak to their acquaintances in West Berlin from their windows. The building doors are nailed shut, the ground floor windows are walled up. Ulbricht's 'Socialism' is creeping along the corridors in mason's stockings."[2]

Like so many other residents, this form of harassment led Rudolf Urban and his wife to attempt to flee. In an interview in 1980, Mrs. Urban said that it was not an easy decision for her husband to make. She had pushed to leave from the very first day, but he was reluctant at first. He did not want to abandon what he had been working towards for so many years and insisted that he had done nothing wrong. On the evening of August 18 the couple heard loud hammering and realized that the building entrance that opened onto the West Berlin sidewalk was being nailed shut. This is what tipped the scales for her husband. "When they nailed the front door shut, he turned around and said, 'Now we are going.'"[3]

The next day was a Saturday. It was August 19 and the American vice president Lyndon B. Johnson had just arrived in West Berlin. His visit was supposed to

45

restore the West Berliners' faith in the United States after the protecting powers had shown such reserve in response to the sector border's being sealed off, a reaction that was incomprehensible to West Berliners.[4] On the east side of the city the Urbans began preparing their escape. They planned to slide down a rope from a window of their first floor apartment. Frau Urban recalled later that they had refrained from taking the safer route from the window of a ground floor apartment out of consideration for their neighbors. The ground floor apartments were not yet evacuated, but watch guards were posted in the staircase and checked the papers of everyone who went in and out of the building. It would have been impossible to climb out their neighbors' window without making them an accomplice to the Urban's escape. So the couple attached a rope to their window frame instead and slid down one after the other to Bernauer Strasse. But both Rudolf Urban and his wife slipped, injuring their hands and feet, and had to be taken to the nearby Lazarus Hospital.[5]

Many years later, two former nurses recalled how, when the Urbans arrived, they were both in a severe state of shock. Rudolf Urban was evidently wearing a number of suits, one over the other, because he didn't want to leave them behind in his East Berlin apartment.[6] The nurses didn't want to bother the patient with questions about the circumstances of his accident.[7] He had crushed his heel bone and was treated as an in-patient. Rudolph Urban caught pneumonia while in the hospital and died in the West Berlin Lazarus Hospital on September 17, 1961. He was 47 years old. He was buried in the Dorotheen Cemetery on Liesenstrasse in Wedding.

At the time the West Berlin public was not aware of Rudolf Urban's escape or his week-long stay in the hospital. Authorities and media first publicized the East Berliner's fate after he had passed away. A police report from November 1961 stated that "he died from injuries received during an escape."[8]

The Wedding district later placed a memorial of wood and barbed wire at Bernauer Strasse 1 at the site of the accident to commemorate Rudolf Urban. According to newspaper reports, East Berlin policemen railed and threw stones at the workers while they were setting up the monument.[9] Each year on the anniversary of the day the Wall was built, memorial services were held for him and other victims of the Berlin Wall. In October 1965, when East Berlin demolition crews began tearing the border houses on Bernauer Strasse down to the ground floor façade, a temporary covering was placed over the monument so that it would not be damaged.[10] When the new concrete wall was erected in 1980, the building from which Rudolf Urban had fled ultimately gave way to the expansion of the East German border regime.

Christine Brecht

1   See "Statistik der Grenzdurchbrüche vom 13.8.–31.8.1961 des PdVP/Stab PdVP/Abt. Information," in: LAB, C Rep. 303-26-01, Nr. 239, Bl. 158–164.

2   Wolfdietrich Schnurre, *Die Mauer des 13. August,* Berlin, 1962, p. 65.

3   The interview with Frau Urban was conducted for a documentary film by Hans-Dieter Grabe. See "Lebenserfahrungen. Bernauer Strasse 1–50 oder Als uns die Haustür zugenagelt wurde," ZDF 1981.

4 See Kurt L. Shell, *Bedrohung und Bewährung. Führung und Bevölkerung in der Berlin-Krise,* Cologne/Opladen 1965, pp. 44–45, and Andreas Daum, *Kennedy in Berlin. Politik, Kultur und Emotionen im Kalten Krieg,* Paderborn 2003, pp. 48–53.

5 See interview with Frau Urban, l.c.

6 Interview by Maria Nooke with Margarete Umland and Sophie Hermann, nurses in the Lazarus Hospital, 17.1.2001.

7 Interview by Maria Nooke with Ursula and Günter Malchow, residents and staff in the Lazarus Hospital, 7.4.2002.

8 See "Bericht der West-Berliner Polizeiinspektion Wedding über die seit dem 13.8.61 geflüchteten Vopo und andere Personen, 14.11.1961," in: PHS, Bestand Grenzvorkommnisse, n. pag.

9 See "Vopo-Flüche gegen Mahnmal," in: *Spandauer Volksblatt,* 18.11.1961.

10 See. "Schutt soll auf Mahnmale prasseln. SED-Abrissaktion in der Bernauer Strasse wird zur Provokation," in: *Die Welt,* 4.10.1965.

Olga Segler

born on July 31, 1881

injured on September 25, 1961

while fleeing from her apartment at Bernauer Strasse 34

at the sector border between

Berlin-Mitte and Berlin-Wedding

died from consequences of her fall on September 26, 1961

Olga Segler was born to parents of German descent in 1881 in a town called Prischt that later belonged to Ukraine. No other official documents providing information about her life exist. She was eighty years old in 1961 and lived at Bernauer Strasse 34, near Brunnenstrasse, in the East Berlin district of Mitte. Her building, like the other ones on that side of the street, formed the border to the western part of the city. Consequently, the elderly woman found herself in an unusually precarious situation when the border was sealed on August 13. For one, she was separated from her daughter, who lived just a short distance away on the West Berlin side of the sector border. Moreover, she experienced the East German authorities' increasingly ruthless treatment of Bernauer Strasse residents. For almost six weeks Olga Segler endured life in a barricaded building with watch guards posted in the corridors and staircases to prevent people from escaping to the West. They monitored the movement and behavior of the residents 24 hours a day.

The East German authorities regarded the border houses on Bernauer Strasse as a "focal point of border breaches."[1] According to an East Berlin situation report, in September 1961 the most common method of escape included "jumping from apartment buildings located directly on the state border into rescue nets held by the fire department, or roping down the fronts of buildings."[2] Within the first three months after the Wall was built, more than 150 people reached the neighboring West Berlin district of Wedding through escapes of this kind. Many were injured during the dangerous undertaking and had to be treated by a doctor.[3] The first fatality occurred on August 22 when Ida Siekmann, a 58-year-old woman, was fatally injured while jumping from her apartment.

The situation on Bernauer Strasse escalated further in September. The East German authorities began a major evacuation operation on the morning of September 24. Two thousand people were to be moved out of their apartments, most of them against their will. The West Berlin police and fire department expected that many residents "would in the last minute try to flee to freedom before their apartments are evacuated."[4] Dramatic events took place as a consequence of the evacuation. A 77-year-old woman who was ready to jump hung in the air for minutes outside her window because members of an evacuation crew tried pulling her back into her apartment while West Berliners from below pulled her downward. She finally fell into the rescue net of the fire department.[5]

Olga Segler decided to jump from the window of her second story apartment on September 24. Her daughter waited down below on the sidewalk, encouraging her to jump. The firemen caught the eighty-year-old woman in their rescue net but she injured her back on impact and had to be taken by ambulance to the nearby Lazarus Hospital. Olga Segler died the next day.[6] Her heart had given out as a consequence of the overexcitement she experienced during the escape.[7]

The East German authorities registered Olga Segler's escape attempt as a "border breach," and the official report referred to her successful "flight from the republic."[8] Believing that the fatally injured old woman had survived, they opened an investigation against her.[9]

Meanwhile, on the other side of the Wall, Olga Segler was being publicly mourned. Her funeral was held at the municipal cemetery in Berlin-Reinickendorf. A memorial was dedicated at the site of her fall in November 1961. It resembled the monuments of wood and barbed wire that had been dedicated to Ida Siekmann and Rudolf Urban, both of whom had lived on Bernauer Strasse and lost their lives trying to escape. For years to come, new wreaths and flowers were placed at the monument on memorial days.

The building where Olga Segler had lived was torn down in 1966 except for the ground level façade. This haunting relic of a building, with walled up windows, functioned as the border wall until 1980. Later, the last remains of the original building were replaced by a concrete wall.

Christine Brecht

1   "[MfS]Bericht, 1.11.1961," in: BStU, MfS, ZAIG Nr. 525, Bl. 9–39, quote Bl. 32.

2   "Information Nr. 21 zum Rapport Nr. 283/61 der HV DVP/Operativstab über Einschätzung der Lage in den Grenzkreisen der Staatsgrenze West, der Staatsgrenze im Bezirk Potsdam und im demokratischen Berlin, 13.10.1961," in: BArch, DO 1/11.0/1354, Bl. 196–199, here Bl. 199.

3   See "Bericht der West-Berliner Polizeiinspektion Wedding über die seit dem 13.8.61 geflüchteten Vopo und andere Personen, 14.11.1961," in: PHS, Bestand Grenzvorkommnisse, n. pag.

4   "Bericht der West-Berliner Polizeiinspektion Wedding über die Zwangsräumungsaktion der Vopo in den Häusern im Zuge der Bernauer Straße (SBS) am 24.9.61, 26.9.1961," in: Ibid.

5   See Berliner Morgenpost, 26.9.1961; Der Tagesspiegel, 26.9.1961.

6   See Telegraf, 26, and 27.9.1961; Der Tagesspiegel, 26.9. and 1.10.1961; "Ereignismeldungen der West-Berliner Schutzpolizei, 26.9.1961," in: PHS, Bestand E-Meldungen, n. pag.

7   See "Bericht der West-Berliner Polizeiinspektion Wedding über die seit dem 13.8.61 geflüchteten Vopo und andere Personen, 14.11.1961," in: PHS, Bestand Grenzvorkommnisse, n. pag.

8   See "Spitzenmeldung des MdI/Bepo/1. GB/II. Abt. über einen Grenzdurchbruch in der Bernauer Str. 34, 25.9.1961," in: BArch, VA-07/16927, Bl. 257; see also "Rapport No. 266 der HV DVP/Operativstab, 26.9.1961," in: BArch, DO1/11.0/1353, Bl. 176.

9   See "[MfS]Strafkarte für Olga Segler, 15.9.1961," in: BStU, MfS, Strafnachricht, Speicher XII/01.

Bernd Lünser

born on March 11, 1939

fatally injured on October 4, 1961
while jumping from the roof of the building
at Bernauer Strasse 44
at the sector border between
Berlin-Mitte and Berlin-Wedding

When the Berlin Wall was built, hundreds of students from the eastern section and outskirts of the city were cut off from the universities where they studied in West Berlin. The 22-year-old Bernd Lünser was caught by surprise when the sector border was sealed off in the middle of the semester break.

He was born in Berlin on March 11, 1939 and, after his parents divorced, lived with his mother in the Friedrichshain district of Berlin. His father lived in West Berlin. After graduating from high school at the age of 18, he completed a brick-layer apprenticeship with an East Berlin company before beginning his studies at an advanced technical college in West Berlin in the winter semester of 1959/60. He had wanted to become a civil engineer and his instructors and fellow-students at the State Engineering School of Architecture in Berlin-Neukölln commented that he was exceptionally talented and popular.[1] The police and press reports do not shed light on what led him to study in West Berlin, but presumably, like many other people of his age group who commuted daily from their homes in the East to colleges and universities in the West, he was dissatisfied with the educational system in East Germany.

According to his father, Bernd Lünser had been determined to complete his studies in West Berlin even after the border was closed and began looking desperately for a way to reach the West before the new semester began in October.[2] His hopes for attaining a legal permit to cross the border were dashed and he was unable to find an adequate escape route. Consequently, Bernd Lünser died tragically on October 4 while trying to rope down from the roof of an East Berlin border house on Bernauer Strasse. The circumstances of his death attracted attention in both the East and the West because it was the first time since the Wall had been built that West Berlin police officers returned the fire of East Berlin border guards.[3]

The entire width of Bernauer Strasse belonged to the West Berlin district of Wedding, but the buildings on the south side of the street were situated on East Berlin territory. After the Wall was erected, this area continued to be a starting point for escape attempts, which is why the East German authorities evacuated many of the buildings, walled up the windows and doors and increased surveillance. Bernd Lünser planned to get around the barriers and border guards by climbing onto the roof of a house on Swinemünder Strasse in the evening. From there he planned to cross the rooftops until he reached the corner building at Bernauer Strasse, from where he intended to use a clothes line to scale down the front of the building. But he was discovered by border guards.

When the guards began to pursue him, Bernd Lünser called out loudly to West Berliners who happened to be passing by on the street below. "Help me. I want to jump!" he cried from high above. They notified the sector patrols of the West Berlin police. Meanwhile on the other side of the street the first shots were fired. A short time later, firemen were prepared to catch the young man in their rescue net,[4] but Bernd Lunser and one of his pursuers entered into a scuffle on the roof of the building at Bernauer Strasse 44. They both slid to the edge of the roof. Bernd Lünser was able to break free and jumped to the ground, but he missed the firemen's rescue net by a few meters and hit the concrete with full force. He died immediately.

During these dramatic events, bullets flew to the West Berlin side and the West Berlin police returned the fire. The East German policeman who had wrestled with Bernd Lünser on the rooftop was hit in the thigh. In East Berlin police and Stasi reports, the West Berlin police were accused of having opened fire without the East Berlin border police's firing any shots to the West.[5] Similarly, Karl Maron, the East German Minister of the Interior, took a firm stand in a letter of protest to the West Berlin commanders and Senate, in which he condemned the alleged attempted murder of an East German border guard as an "egregious provocation" that endangered peace. He referred to the fugitive as a "criminal" who was trying to elude his arrest after being caught red-handed.[6]

The West Berlin police claimed they had not opened fire until they, as well as the firemen and residents, were endangered by the shots being fired from the other side. Hence their use of firearms was justified.[7] The West Berlin Chief of Police, Erich Duensing, strongly commended his officers for striking back at the right moment.[8] A speaker of the U.S. State Department also argued that the West Berlin police had been forced to defend themselves and demanded that the Soviet Union prevent any more shootings at the sector border.[9]

Proceedings, opened in 1990 against the border guards involved in the shooting, were unable to determine who had fired the first shot. The defendants were consequently found not guilty. Later research proved false the belief that there had been another fugitive with Bernd Lünser on the roof who had also died.[10] This false theory had been based on West Berlin eye-witness accounts that were noted in police and press reports and cited for many decades.

The exchange of fire on Bernauer Strasse evoked strong outrage in both the East and the West, but only West Berlin was concerned with publicly commemorating the death of Bernd Lünser. Many West Berliners sought out the place of his death and placed flowers there. Later, students who had known Bernd Lünser from the university placed a wooden cross on the site that, like the memorials to other victims of the Wall, was wrapped in barbed wire.[11] Bernd Lünser was buried on

October 11, 1961 at the cemetery on Bergstrasse in Steglitz, a West Berlin district. The East Berlin authorities denied his mother permission to attend the funeral service. Instead she expressed her sadness in a telegram that was read out loud at the grave.[12]

Christine Brecht

1   See "Bericht der West-Berliner Polizei, 12.10.1961," in: StA Berlin, Az. 27/2 Js 140/90, Bd.1, Bl. 23.

2   See "Bernd Lünsers Vater: Er wollte hier sein Studium beenden," in: *Berliner Morgenpost*, 6.10.1961.

3   See Kurt L. Shell, *Bedrohung und Bewährung. Führung und Bevölkerung in der Berlin-Krise*, Cologne/Opladen, 1965, pp. 340–348.

4   "Bericht der West-Berliner Polizei, 5.10.1961," in: StA Berlin, Az. 27/2 Js 140/90, Bd. 1, Bl. 6–7.

5   See "Spitzenmeldung des MdI/Bepo/1.GB (B)/II. Abt. betr. Grenzdurchbruch einer männlichen Person in der Bernauer Strasse 44, 4.10.1961," in: BArch, VA-07/16926, Bl. 53–55; "Abschlussbericht des MdI/Bepo/1.GB (B)/Kommandeur betr. Grenzdurchbruch in der Bernauer Strasse durch Bernd Lünser, 6.10.1961," in: Ibid., Bl. 58–61, and [MfS]-Bericht, 1.11.1961, in: BStU, MfS, ZAIG Nr. 525, Bl. 9–39.

6   See "Mordanschlag auf Volkspolizisten," in: *Tribüne*, 6.10.1961, and *Neues Deutschland*, 6.10.1961, and *Berliner Zeitung*, 6.10.1961.

7   See "Bericht der West-Berliner Polizei, 5.10.1961," in: StA Berlin, Az. 27/2 Js 140/90, Bd. 1, Bl. 6–7.

8   See "Bei Gefahr wird zurückgeschossen," in: *Der Kurier*, 5.10.1961.

9   See "Washington warnt vor Schiesserei. Pankow spricht von Provokation," in: *Spandauer Volksblatt*, 6.10.1961.

10 See "Urteil des Landgerichts Berlin vom 16.10.1997," in: StA Berlin, Az. 27/2 Js 140/90, Bd. 4, Bl. 93 a–93 d.

11 See "Ein Kreuz mahnt in der Bernauer Strasse," in: *Die Welt*, 25.10.1961.

12 See *Berliner Morgenpost*, 12.10.1961.

Udo Düllick

born on August 3, 1936

drowned on October 5, 1961 while under fire
in the Spree River near the Oberbaum Bridge
at the sector border between
Berlin-Friedrichshain and Berlin-Kreuzberg

Octtober 7, 1961 was the first anniversary of the founding of the East German state after the Wall was built. State-run businesses and organizations throughout the country were having celebrations. Udo Düllick, who worked as an engineer for the Deutsche Reichsbahn, the East German railway company, in Berlin-Lichtenberg, attended the obligatory company party on the evening of October 5. The 25-year-old had long been fed up with the political pressure that permeated the communist state. His sister recalled that it was hard for him not to complain or to repress his critical thoughts.[1] Udo Düllick's anger escalated that evening when he got into an argument with his supervisor at the company party. During the fight he evidently tore the epaulets off the other man's Reichsbahn uniform. This conflict was probably what finally led Udo Düllick to flee. That very night he took a taxi to Warschauer Strasse in the Friedrichshain district and tried to swim from a spot not far from the Oberbaum Bridge across the Spree River to West Berlin.[2]

Udo Düllick was born on August 3, 1936 in Werder near Strausberg, east of Berlin, and spent his childhood there. He was a vivacious child, veracious and rebellious. His family was Catholic. He had a brother who was six years older. His mother died young and his father remarried and had another child, Udo Düllick's younger half-sister. Udo Düllick first trained to be a bricklayer, and later studied engineering in Dresden. When his older brother moved to the West in 1959, Udo Düllick stayed in East Germany and continued to live with his parents. He spent the weekend of August 12–13, 1961 with his girlfriend in West Berlin. When the two of them traveled back home on August 13, they most likely had no idea that the sector border that had been sealed off the night before was to be permanent. Later, in reference to the Berlin Wall, Udo Düllick told his stepmother that he could always find a way to the West if he had to.[3]

He was a good swimmer, which is probably why he risked escaping through the border waters on that October evening. It was almost midnight when he approached the bank of the Spree River. He removed his jacket, pants and shoes on the grounds of the Osthafenmühle and jumped into the water. Border guards posted on the nearby bridge noticed the fugitive immediately. After they set off flares and warning shots, they fired their guns at him. Then the water police began to pursue him by boat. Udo Düllick swam for his life. He repeatedly dove under the water to avoid the bullets. West Berliners on the other side of the river watched the dramatic events and wanted to help the young man, but they could not go beyond the embankment wall because the entire width of the Spree there belonged to East Berlin. Udo Düllick had almost reached safe ground on the other side when he suddenly sank beneath the water's surface. His dead body was retrieved from the West Berlin side an hour later.[4]

His pursuers were convinced they had hit him with their bullets. A situation report from the East Berlin commander stated: "The individual was fatally wounded by the shots fired and went under."[5]

But West Berliners soon established that the body of the fugitive did not have any bullet wounds. The biopsy determined that exhaustion from the chase had caused him to drown.[6] The mistaken cause of death was, however, also cited in West Berlin police and press reports. Eye-witness accounts claimed that two or three fugitives were involved. Consequently, for decades westerners continued to claim that two fugitives had died that night. Only after the East German archives were made public was it possible to determine without doubt that Udo Düllick had been alone when he attempted to escape.[7]

In West Berlin, the death of the fugitive, whose identity was not known at first, caused great sadness and led to a wave of protests.[8] No less than 2,500 people gathered on October 7, 1961 to attend a funeral service on the Gröbenufer in Kreuzberg. Young people set up a large wooden cross wrapped in barbed wire as a sign of their condemnation of the communist regime. Protest slogans such as "Hounded to death by concentration camp guards" were painted on banners and signs.

Over the next few days hundreds of West Berliners came to the Gröbenufer and placed flowers and wreaths at the site. On the "Sunday commemoration of the dead," a few weeks later, a memorial stone with the inscription "the unknown fugitive" was erected next to the cross.

Over the following years memorial services took place there regularly. The funeral on October 18, 1961 was also an official event. A memorial service conducted by the Kreuzberg district assembly was broadcast live by RIAS, the radio station in the American sector, after which the deceased was buried before a large crowd at the Jerusalem Cemetery in Kreuzberg. Since his religion was not known, the ceremony was led by both a Catholic and Protestant clergyman.[9]

Udo Düllick's parents heard on the news about the death of a man at the Oberbaum Bridge and worriedly contacted the West Berlin authorities. But communication between East and West was difficult after the Wall was built and it took a number of weeks before they knew for certain that the man who had died was actually their son. The West Berlin authorities did not reveal his name to the press out of respect for the relatives who feared repercussions by the East German state.[10] The Catholic church congregation in Rehfelde, the town next to his hometown, held a requiem for Udo Düllick in November 1961. The East German secret police demanded that the circumstances of his death not be mentioned.

Christine Brecht

1 Conversation conducted by Christine Brecht, Hans-Hermann Hertle and Maria Nooke with Irene Düllick, Udo Düllick's sister, 3.9.2005.
2 The contemporary investigation of the West Berlin police yields same findings. See StA Berlin, Az. 27 Js 143/90, Bd. 1, Bl. 1–89.
3 See conversation conducted by Christine Brecht, Hans-Hermann Hertle und Maria Nooke with Irene Düllick, Udo Düllick's sister, 3.9.2005.
4 For details about the course of events, see "Spitzenmeldung des MdI//Bepo/1.GB/B./VI. Abt./Kommandeur betr. Schusswaffengebrauch am 5.10.1961 gegen 24.00 Uhr im Gebiet des Osthafens, 6.10.1961," in: BArch, VA-07/16926, Bl. 83.
5 "Lagebericht der SKB/1.GB/Abt. Operativ, 6.10.1961," in: BArch, VA-07/4787, n. pag.
6 See "Vorläufiges Gutachten von West-Berliner Gerichtsärzten über die Sektion eines unbekannten jungen Mannes, 7.10.1961," in: StA, Az. 27 Js 143/90, Bd. 1, Bl. 29–30.
7 See "Verfügung [27/2 Js 143/90] der Staatsanwaltschaft II bei dem Landgericht Berlin, 4.10.1994," in: Ibid., Bd. 2, Bl. 281–284.
8 See "Ein schwarzes Kreuz an der Mordstelle," in: Der Kurier, 9.10.1961, and "Ereignismeldung der West-Berliner Schutzpolizei über die Lage an der Sektor- und Zonengrenze," 13.10.1961, in: PHS, Bestand Ereignismeldungen, n. pag.
9 See "Abschied von dem unbekannten Flüchtling," in: Der Tagesspiegel, 19.10.1961.
10 See "Niederschrift der Zeugenvernehmung des Bruders von Udo Düllick durch die West-Berliner Polizei, 17.11.1961," in: StA Berlin, Az. 27 Js 143/90, Bd. 1, Bl. 57, and "Bericht der West-Berliner Polizei, 17.11.1961," in: Ibid, Bl. 58–59.

Werner Probst

born on June 18, 1936

shot dead on October 14, 1961
in the Spree River near the Schilling Bridge
at the sector border between
Berlin-Friedrichshain and Berlin-Kreuzberg

Born and raised in Berlin, Werner Probst was 25 years old when he tried to flee to the western part of the city in October 1961. He lived with his parents in the Friedrichshain district and worked as a driver for a state-run company. Before the Wall was built he had worked for a West Berlin transport company. Werner Probst, however, was not a typical border-crosser. Beginning in February 1959, the Ministry of State Security maintained him as a so-called secret informant ("GI") under the code name "Harry."[1] Information about the background, lifestyle and political views of this Stasi informer was found in a file entry documenting his spying activities.[2]

When Werner Probst agreed to work with the Stasi, he had no job training and could barely write. Evidently, he quit school early and had been caught stealing as a youth.[3] As was common practice by the East German secret police, his criminal record was used as the "basis for his recruitment."[4] His case officer wrote that by working as an informant for the Stasi, Werner Probst could "make up for his past mistakes and have his punishment revoked."[5] Moreover, the Stasi was interested in the contact "to shady characters" that he supposedly had in the so-called demimonde and criminal world in both halves of the city: "Since the GI has a lot of acquaintances in the underground," the recruitment report stated, "he will be assigned to provide tips and shed light on these people."[6] After being hired as a secret informant, Werner Probst began hanging out with border-crossers, prying on racketeering and reporting regularly on the people he met in the West Berlin bars. It appears that his cooperation with the Stasi was motivated less by ideological convictions and more by an interest in gaining a personal advantage. He earned desirable western currency for his spying activities and enjoyed a degree of freedom of movement.

When the Berlin Wall put an end to this, Werner Probst could not or would not accept the new situation. He was temporarily arrested just three days after the barriers were erected when he was found trying to enter West Berlin at the Friedrichstrasse Station border crossing while inebriated. The Stasi responded to this incident with a threat: "The next time he's arrested the contact with us will be broken."[7]

His case officer suggested that Werner Probst be placed as an informant in the West and was able to keep him in line for a while.[8] But when this plan was dropped because he lacked the qualifications for an apprenticeship in encryption, Werner Probst apparently saw no further reason to stay in East Germany.[9] According to his Stasi file, the State Security believed he had difficulties accepting that he could no longer travel to West Berlin and his "border breach" was mainly motivated by his desire to get to his savings held in a West Berlin bank account.[10] Whether this accurately depicted his motivations is not known since he left behind no explanation of his actions.

On the evening of October 14, 1961, the 25-year-old East Berliner went to the Spree not far from his parents' apartment and entered the water beneath the Schilling Bridge with the intention of swimming to the West Berlin bank on the other side. Border police who were guarding the river from the bridge noticed him at around 10:30 p.m. One of the guards illuminated the water surface with a spotlight while the other two set off signal and warning shots before opening fire on the swimmer.[11] Werner Probst made it to the exit ladder on the West Berlin quay wall. Injured on his thigh and in his head, he pulled himself up the ladder steps before collapsing, fatally injured. His violent death was documented in a matter-of-fact military tone: "When the person reached the ladder, shots were fired. P. was hit and collapsed directly onto the bank of West Berlin territory. At this moment the water police who had been notified arrived, pulled the border violator from the embankment and brought him by boat to the Oberbaum Bridge. The individual was already dead on arrival."[12]

The nighttime shots on the Spree bank in Kreuzberg were also registered by the West Berlin police, but it was not immediately clear to them what had happened.[13] Within a few days enough evidence had been gathered to lead them to conclude that the shots had been directed at a fugitive fleeing the East. Werner Probst's half-sister, who lived in West Berlin, told the authorities what she had learned from his parents. They were informed on October 16, without place or time being specified, that their son had been shot and killed while attempting to flee. His parents' request to see him before his burial was refused.[14] Border guards who later deserted to the West made statements that finally provided conclusive information connecting Werner Probst's death to the shots fired at the Schilling Bridge. On the basis of this information, in October 1961, the West Berlin police placed charges of homicide against unknown members of the East German company of the 1st Border Brigade that was stationed in this area.[15]

Thirty years later the case was re-opened and three former border guards were identified as the alleged perpetrators. The public prosecutor's office initially regarded the crime as murder committed out of base motives since the victim had already reached the western bank at the time of his death, but in the end the men were charged with joint manslaughter.[16] The district court of Berlin found the three defendants guilty of this charge in May 1995. The question of which of them bore responsibility for firing the fatal shot that killed Werner Probst could not be clarified during the trial. As was the case in most of the border guard trials, the court sentenced the defendants mildly, since they had committed the act "on the basis of an – albeit obviously unlawful – order within a command hierarchy in which they stood at the very bottom."[17]

Christine Brecht

1   See hand-written statement of commitment from Werner Probst, 10.2.1959, in: BStU, MfS, AIM 7188/61, Personalakte, Bl. 49.

2   See Helmut Müller-Enbergs, "Zum Verhältnis von Norm und Praxis in der Arbeit mit Inoffiziellen Mitarbeitern des Ministeriums für Staatssicherheit," in: Klaus-Dietmar Henke/Roger Engelmann (eds.), *Aktenlage. Die Bedeutung der Unterlagen des Staatssicherheitsdienstes für die Zeitgeschichtsforschung*, Berlin, 1995, pp. 56–76.

3   See "Vorschlag zur Anwerbung eines GI [des MfS]/HA II/4-b, 26.1.1959," in: BStU, MfS, AIM 7188/61, Personalakte, Bl. 43–44.

4   See the entry "Inoffizieller Mitarbeiter-Kandidat; Werbungsgespräch," in: Siegfried Suckut (ed.), *Das Wörterbuch der Staatssicherheit,* 3. edn. Berlin, 2001, pp. 202–203.

5   "Auskunftsbericht [des MfS]/HA II/4 betr. GI 'Harry', 13.7.1959," in: BStU, MfS, AIM 7188/61, Personalakte, Bl. 50.

6   "Werbungsbericht [des MfS]/HA II/4-b betr. Werbung des Probst, Werner, 25.2.1959," in: Ibid., Bl. 48.

7   "Treffbericht [des MfS]/HA II/4 betr. GI 'Harry', 24.8.1961," in: BStU, MfS, AIM 7188/61, Arbeitsvorgang, Bl. 217–218, here Bl. 218.

8   See "Vorschlag [des MfS]/HA II/4 betr. Absetzung des GI 'Harry' nach Westberlin, 14.9.1961," in: BStU, MfS, AIM 7188/61, Personalakte, Bl. 120–123; "Schreiben [des MfS]/HA II/4 an die [MfS]-Abt. XI im Hause betr. Ausbildung eines IM mit Chiffre, 12.9.1961," in: Ibid., Bl. 124, see also "Treffbericht [MfS]/HA II/4/B betr. GI 'Harry', 26.8.1961," in: BStU, MfS, AIM 7188/61 Arbeitsvorgang, Bl. 219.

9   The hand-written memo stated: "The suggestion is untenable. 'Harry' writes too poorly, which makes encryption training impossible." See "Vorschlag [der MfS]/HA II/4 4 betr. Absetzung des GI 'Harry' nach Westberlin, 14.9.1961," in: BStU, MfS, AIM 7188/61, Personalakte, Bl. 123.

10 See "Bericht [des MfS]/HA II/4 betr. Probst, Werner, 16.10.1961," in: Ibid., Bl. 131–132, here Bl. 132.

11 See "Spitzenmeldung des MdI/Bepo/1.GB/IV. Abt. über die Verhinderung eines Grenzdurchbruchs am Posten 37a," in: BArch, VA-07/16926, Bl. 132–133, and "Bericht [des MfS]/HA I an Generaloberst Mielke über die Verhinderung eines Grenzdurchbruchs durch Anwendung der Schusswaffe mit tödlichem Ausgang, 16.10.1961," in: BStU, MfS, AIM 7188/61, Personalakte, Bl. 136–137.

12 "Bericht des MdI/Kommando Bepo/Operativer Diensthabender über verhinderten Grenzdurchbruch mit Schusswaffengebrauch, 15.10.1961," in: BArch, VA-07/4724, Bd. 1, Bl. 119.

13 See "Bericht der West-Berliner Polizei über den Schusswaffengebrauch im SBS an der Sektorengrenze, 16.10.1961," in: StA Berlin, Az. 2 Js 254/91, Bd. 1, Bl. 92.

14 See "Bericht der West-Berliner Polizei, 30.10.1961," in: Ibid., Bl. 97–98.

15 See "Strafanzeige der West-Berliner Polizei wegen Totschlags von Werner Probst gegen 'VP'-Angehörige, 26.10.1961," in: Ibid., Bl. 91.

16 See "Anklageschrift der Staatsanwaltschaft bei dem Kammergericht Berlin, [2 Js 254/91], 19.11.1992," in: Ibid., Bd. 3, Bl. 22–48.

17 "Urteil des Landgerichts Berlin vom 5.5.1995," in: Ibid., Bd. 3, Bl. 227–28.

Lothar Lehmann

born on January 28, 1942

drowned on November 26, 1961
in the Havel River on the outer ring
between Sacrow (Potsdam city district)
and Berlin-Zehlendorf

Lothar Lehmann was 19 years old when he lost his life trying to flee to West Berlin in November 1961. Only pieces of his life and the circumstances of his death are documented. According to official documents, he was born on January 28 or 29, 1942. Contradictory information also exists concerning his place of birth.[1] Thus, it remains unclear whether Lothar Lehmann came from East Prussia or was born in Falkensee, a community outside of Berlin that borders the West Berlin district of Spandau, where he grew up in the care of foster parents and where he attended school in the 1950s. After completing 8th grade he trained to become a metalworker at the state-owned agricultural machine-building company in Falkensee. He spent his free time breeding pigeons and cycling with a local company athletics group.[2]

In September 1961, a few weeks after the Wall was built, the 19-year-old began his military service. There was no general conscription at this time, hence his enrollment was – technically speaking – voluntary. In truth, however, a major propaganda campaign strongly pressured most young men to commit themselves to an "honor service" for the 'Socialist Fatherland.' This pressure increased considerably after the Wall was built. The FDJ, the Communist Party youth organization, began a national campaign in August 1961 under the motto: "The Fatherland is calling! Protect the Socialist Republic!"[3] Its aim was to recruit as many young people as possible into the military to provide the necessary reinforcements for police and army units assigned to "border security."

Lothar Lehmann was sent to the border. He was assigned to a Gross Glienicke police unit that was stationed outside of Berlin, not far from his home in Falkensee. His unit belonged to the "border police" that guarded the border between the East German district of Potsdam and West Berlin. Just what motivated the 19-year-old to flee is not known. It does not appear to have been a spontaneous decision. In early November he had let his mother know that he wanted to flee to the West. While on vacation he casually asked her for the address of relatives living in West Germany, remarking: "Won't they be surprised when I get there." When she worriedly pointed out to him that people were shot at the border, he acted sure of himself, saying things would be fine.[4]

A number of police officers, soldiers and army conscripts like Lothar Lehmann decided to desert during the first weeks and months after the Wall was built, despite the fact that drastic punishments awaited them if they were caught.[5] Guard duty on the border grounds offered advantageous opportunities to escape. Moreover, many of the border guards rejected the intensified barrier measures and feared that they might one day have to shoot at fugitives themselves. In this early period, East German border guards who had deserted were reporting to the West Berlin authorities daily.[6] Lothar Lehmann, however, was unlucky. He died trying to escape without anyone in West Berlin even noticing.

This happened at the bank of the Havel River in Sacrow near Potsdam, an area Lothar Lehmann knew well from his bike training trips.[7] The border to the West Berlin district of Zehlendorf ran through the middle of the river. On November 26, 1961, Lothar Lehmann, a member of his unit's boating group, was in charge of repairing boats on the Havel riverbank in Sacrow. As evening approached, and when no one was looking, he entered the water wearing a life jacket with the intention of swimming to the other side. Evidently the water was so cold that he suffered a physical shock and lost consciousness. Border guards saw him in this condition, pulled him out of the water and brought him to the Potsdam District Hospital. According to a report from the East Berlin commander, Lothar Lehmann died "around 9 p.m. despite attempts to revive him and without external influences during the arrest and transport."[8] The autopsy conducted later determined that "indirect drowning caused by cold shock and cardiovascular collapse" was the cause of death.[9] These facts were confirmed by an investigation that was conducted as part of the legal prosecution of injustices committed in East Germany in the 1990s.[10]

Lothar Lehmann's mother put down on record in 1992 that his parents had learned from members of the border police on November 26 that their son had drowned while trying to desert.[11] Over the following days they were questioned about his reasons for fleeing and his escape plans, during which time their son was presented to them as a criminal. The mother did not admit to having known about his plans out of fear that she would be accused of being an accomplice in his "flight from the republic." The East German authorities insisted that the parents not speak to anyone about the escape attempt. At the victim's funeral in the municipal cemetery in Falkensee, his death had to be referred to as an "accident."

Lothar Lehmann's friend, Wolfgang S., however, had a hard time believing the official version of the story, particularly since behind closed doors rumors were spreading in the town. According to his own statements, he tried to find out the truth by engaging in a conversation with two border police officers. He learned from them "that Lothar wanted to flee and that he went into the water wearing a life vest. He lost his life doing so, they told me. But they evaded answering my questions about the incident."[12] After that he started asking around in Sacrow and found out where the incident had occurred. Wolfang S. succeeded in fleeing to West Berlin in January 1962 and informed the authorities there of everything he knew about his friend. Lothar Lehmann has been officially registered in the West as a victim of the Wall ever since.[13]

Christine Brecht

1 See "Niederschrift der Zeugenvernehmung eines Freundes von Lothar Lehmann durch die West-Berliner Polizei," in: StA Berlin, Az. 2 Js 137/91, Bl. 15; "Strafanzeige der Berliner Polizei wegen Totschlags von Lothar Lehmann gegen Unbekannt von Amts wegen, 30.1.1992," in: Ibid., Bl. 123a; "Vermerk der Berliner Polizei zum Tod von Lothar Lehmann, 5.2.1992," in: Ibid., Bl. 139.

2 See conversations conducted by Maria Nooke with Manfred G., Lothar Lehmann's fellow sportsman, 26.6.2008 and 16.7.2008, and "Niederschrift der Zeugenvernehmung eines Freundes von Lothar Lehmann durch die West-Berliner Polizei, 23.5.1962," in: StA Berlin, Az. 2 Js 137/91, Bl. 15-20.

3 See "Aufruf der FDJ, 18.8.1961," in: BArch, DY 30/IV 2/12/55, Bl. 130.

4 Transcript of the Falkensee police witness hearing of Lothar Lehmann's mother, 21.1.1992, in: StA Berlin, Az. 2 Js 137/91, Bl. 125-128, here Bl. 126.

5 See Rüdiger Wenzke (ed.), Staatsfeinde in Uniform. Widerständiges Verhalten und politische Verfolgung in der NVA, Berlin, 2005.

6 See, for example, the event reports for the months August to December 1961, in: PHS, Bestand Ereignismeldungen der West-Berliner Schutzpolizei, n. pag.

7 See conversation conducted by Maria Nooke with Lothar Lehmann's fellow sportsman, Manfred G., 16.7.2008.

8 "Lagebericht der Stadtkommandantur Berlin für die Zeit vom 26.11.61, 00.00 Uhr-26.11.61, 24.00 Uhr, 27.11.1961," in: BArch, VA-07/4725, Bd. 2, Bl. 108.

9 "Sektionsprotokoll des Bezirkskrankenhauses Potsdam, 28.11.1961," in: StA Berlin, Az. 2 Js 137/91, Bl. 138.

10 See "Verfügung der Staatsanwaltschaft II bei dem Landgericht Berlin, 10.2.1992," in: Ibid., Bl. 142-144.

11 See transcript of the the Falkensee police witness hearing of Lothar Lehmann's mother, 21.1.1992, in: Ibid., Bl. 125-128.

12 See transcript of West Berlin police witness hearing of a friend of Lothar Lehmann, 23.5.1962, in: Ibid., Bl. 18.

13 See Bundesministerium für Gesamtdeutsche Fragen (ed.), Verletzungen der Menschenrechte. Unrechtshandlungen und Zwischenfälle an der Berliner Sektorengrenze seit Errichtung der Mauer, Bonn/Berlin, 1962, p. 20; Bundesministerium für Gesamtdeutsche Fragen (ed.), Ulbrichts Mauer. Zahlen, Fakten, Daten, Bonn/Berlin, 1962, p. 15.

Dieter Wohlfahrt

born on May 27, 1941

shot dead on December 9, 1961
at the corner of Bergstrasse / Hauptstrasse
on the outer ring between
Staaken (Nauen district) and Berlin-Spandau

Born in 1941 in Berlin-Schöneberg, Dieter Wohlfahrt had been crossing the border between the East and the West regularly ever since he was a young boy. He came from an educated middle-class Catholic family and grew up as the eldest of three children in Hohen Neuendorf, a northern suburb of Berlin. Like his deceased father and his siblings, he had Austrian citizenship and was therefore able to cross the border to West Berlin and West Germany without restrictions. When, at the age of 14, he was denied the right to attend secondary school in East Germany, he moved to the West Berlin district of Wilmersdorf to live with his aunt.[1] There he was able to attend the Bertha-von-Suttner School that had its own "east class," which gave students from East Berlin and the surrounding area of Brandenburg the opportunity to get a high school degree. As long as the sector border was open, a number of Dieter Wohlfahrt's fellow classmates commuted regularly, some of them twice a day, between the East and West. Many of them shared a common rejection of the communist regime as a result of personal experiences, and consequently they were a tight-knit group of friends. When the sector border was permanently closed off in August 1961, Dieter Wohlfahrt, who was then studying chemistry at the Technical University, did not hesitate to get involved in helping former classmates, their friends and relatives to escape to West Berlin.[2]

He joined a group of students which included Detlev Girrmann, Dieter Thieme and Bodo Köhler, who, with great skill and prudence, were continually coming up with new ways to get around the many barriers and controls.[3] In the first weeks after the Wall was built, they were able to get a number of fugitives out through the sewage system. Dieter Wohlfahrt played a major role in these escapes since he had an Austrian passport that still allowed him to maneuver back and forth between the two halves of the city. It was his job to travel to East Berlin as a so-called "cover man" and to inconspicuously open and close the manhole covers where the fugitives entered the canalization system. His former classmate Karin Albert and the man she later married were among the people who had been able to make it to the West in this way. They had known Dieter Wohlfahrt to be an unassuming and inconspicuous young man from whom they had not expected such courage and determination, but they recalled that he thrived in his work to help people escape.[4] Consequently, he did not hesitate to offer the 17-year-old Elke C. his assistance. She had just recently fled from Staaken to West Berlin and wanted to help get her mother across the border at the same spot. Karl-Heinz Albert and another friend also agreed to help. On December 9, 1961, they drove with Elke C. and her friend in a borrowed VW van to the outskirts of Spandau to the agreed upon site at the corner of Bergstrasse and Hauptstrasse.

The others stayed behind when, at around 7 p.m., Dieter Wohlfahrt and Karl-Heinz Albert climbed over the rope that marked the border to the West. Hidden by the darkness, they used bolt clippers and engineer pliers to cut through the three layers of barbed wire fence that blocked off the border there. Karl-Heinz Albert recalled later that all of a sudden Frau C. came running toward them from the other side, calling out for her daughter.[5] Moments later they heard someone yell "Stop! Border Police!" and he had barely enough time to throw himself on the ground before the first shots were fired. Albert was not hit and managed to crawl beneath the barrier back to West Berlin, but Dieter Wohlfahrt remained motionless on the territory of East Germany, just five or six meters from the border line. West Berlin police and members of the British military police soon arrived at the site and tried to approach him, but their attempt to help was thwarted by the East German border guards' threat to use their guns. The dying young man was not offered any help from the east side. He remained on the ground, lying between the tiers of barbed wire, for over an hour without showing any sign of life before he was carted off.[6]

The East German authorities made slanderous accusations against Dieter Wohlfahrt and his friends. The official statement claimed that an armed attack had taken place on the "state border" during which young escape helpers had opened fire. Firearms and dynamite that were supposedly found with the deceased were presented to the public as evidence of the "criminal tools of the agitator Wohlfahrt."[7] His friends in the West were able to offer credible assurances that none of them had been armed, and the western investigative authorities rejected these accusations as mere propaganda. A police spokesman was quoted as having said that "The Communists' claim that the young men had pistols and plastic bombs with them was clearly made up out of thin air. It is their old method of saying 'the deceased is guilty.'"[8]

Nonetheless this accusation from the Cold War era continued to have an effect even after the East Germany state collapsed. Confidential military and Stasi reports show that East German border police had attacked Dieter Wohlfahrt from behind that evening, but they presented the events as if he had been armed and had fired the first shot.[9] It is highly likely that these documents were at the time falsified or manipulated as propaganda, but this theory cannot be proven. The legal proceedings against the former border policeman who shot Dieter Wohlfahrt were dismissed in 1996 with the explanation that the accused criminal may have acted in self-defense.

For those who had known him, the violent death of the twenty-year-old Dieter Wohlfahrt was a tremendous shock. His mother and siblings in Hohen Neuendorf were questioned by the East German secret police and instructed not to leave their residence for the time being. The Stasi organized the funeral, which took place on December 14 in Nauen, but only Dieter Wohlfahrt's family was permitted to attend.[10] In West Berlin the people mourning the fate of Dieter Wohlfahrt went well beyond his group of friends. The Catholic student community organized a requiem for him in the St. Matthias Church in Schöneberg. Professors of the Technical University commemorated him during their lectures. The site of his death was marked by a wooden cross.

The West Berliners not only directed their anger at the people responsible in East Germany: An observer at the time pointed out that it was the first time that a death at the Berlin Wall had also triggered protests against the political leadership in the West.[11] Student representatives expressed their criticism in an open letter to the Allied commanders, the mayor of Berlin and the interior minister in which they wrote: "Given the inhumanity of the fact that the wounded man was lying there for two hours without any help, we cannot understand how both our police and the British protecting powers were not able to find a way to assist the injured man." They concluded from this that "The reserve demonstrated from our side will only encourage the eastern ruling powers to continue to show no consideration for human life."[12]

Christine Brecht

1   See "Niederschrift der Zeugenvernehmung der Tante von Dieter Wohlfahrt durch die West-Berliner Polizei, 9.12.1961," in: StA Berlin, Az. 27/2 Js 145/90, Bd. 1, Bl. 13. On the family background and history, see also "Bericht [des MfS]/Abt. VII/Potsdam betr. Dieter Wohlfahrt, 11.12.1961," in: BStU, Ast. Potsdam, AU 1753/62, Bl. 272, and "Abschrift der Tel.-Mitteilung des Leiters der MfS/KD Oranienburg betr. Vorkommnisse im Zusammenhang mit der Familie Wohlfahrt, 11.12.1961," in: Ibid, Bl. 273–274.

2   See interview conducted by Maria Nooke with Dr. Ruth Wellmer-Hesse, one of Dieter Wohlfahrt's former teachers, 15.4.1999.

3   See Marion Detjen, *Ein Loch in der Mauer. Die Geschichte der Fluchthilfe im geteilten Deutschland 1961–1989*, Munich, 2005, pp. 95–115.

4   See conversation conducted by Christine Brecht with Karin and Karl-Heinz Albert, Dieter Wohlfahrt's former schoolmate and partner, in assisting escapes, 30.4.2007.

5   See ibid. and "Niederschrift der Zeugenvernehmung eines ehemaligen Flüchtlings, Fluchthelfers und Freundes von Dieter Wohlfahrt durch die West-Berliner Polizei, 9.12.1961," in: StA Berlin, Az. 27/2 Js 145/90, Bd. 1, Bl. 7–10; see also "Niederschrift der Zeugenvernehmung eines ehemaligen Flüchtlings, Fluchthelfers und Freundes von Dieter Wohlfahrt durch die Berliner Polizei, 19.5.1993," in: Ibid, Bd. 2, Bl. 364–373.

6   See "Abschrift der West-Berliner Polizei aus dem Tgb. des RKB 146, lfd. Nr. 453/62, 9.12.1961," in: StA Berlin, Az. 27/2 Js 145/90, Bd. 1, Bl. 2, also preliminary report of the West Berlin police, 16.12.1961, in: Ibid., Bl. 22–23.

7   "Grenzsicherungskräfte der DDR beschossen," in: *Neues Deutschland*, 11.12.1961; see also "Hintergründe der Anschläge aufgedeckt," in: *Neues Deutschland*, 12.12.1961.

8   "Rote Mordschützen fanden neues Opfer," in: *Der Kurier*, 11.12.1961.

9   See "Bericht des MdI/Bepo/2.GB (B)/Der Kommandeur betr. Provokation am 9.12.1961, 10.12.1961," in: BArch, DY 30/IV 2/12/74, Bd. 1, Bl. 91–96, and "Einzel-Information des MfS/ZAIG über Grenzprovokation an der Staatsgrenze nach Westberlin am 9.12.1961, 10.12.1961," in: BStU, MfS, Z 525, Bl. 40–46.

10 "Protokoll des MfS/BV Potsdam/U-Abt. betr. Einsargung und Beerdigung des beim Grenzdurchbruch tödlich verletzten Dieter Wohlfahrt, 14.12.1961," in: BStU, Ast. Potsdam, AU 1753/62, Bl. 270, and "Mitteilung des [MfS]/Abt. XII betr. Grenzverletzung, 11.12.1961," in: Ibid., Bl. 275.

11 See Sebastian Haffner, "Der Mord an der Mauer. Ost und West sahen zu, wie Dieter Wohlfahrt starb," in: *Christ und Welt*, 15.12.1961.

12 "TU-Studenten fragen: Warum wurde Dieter Wohlfahrt nicht geholfen?," in: *Der Tagesspiegel*, 12.12.1961; see also "Studenten kritisieren die Polizei," in: *Die Welt*, 12.12.1961.

Ingo Krüger

born on January 31, 1940

drowned on December 11, 1961
in the Spree River near the Marschall Bridge
at the sector border between
Berlin-Mitte and Berlin-Tiergarten

Ingo Krüger was born in Berlin-Dahlem on January 31, 1940. His father died while serving as a soldier in the Second World War. After his mother re-married, the family moved to the eastern section of the city. Ingo Krüger grew up in Niederschöneweide in the eastern district of Treptow.[1] His stepfather worked for the East German television company and his mother was employed as a "people's judge" in East Germany.[2] After finishing school Ingo Krüger completed an apprenticeship as a cook and after that he worked for a state-run company that was responsible for the gastronomy of the East German government's guest houses. The family appeared loyal to party principles and accommodating to the system, but further examination revealed that it did not cut off its contact with relatives and friends in West Berlin. Ingo Krüger's fiancée, Ingrid K., also lived in the other part of the city. They had met in childhood while attending the same school in Berlin-Johannisthal. The couple began dating in 1958 even though Ingrid and her mother had moved to West Berlin. His continued contact with her is what first caused Ingo Krüger trouble with his company a year before the Wall was built. Colleagues who worked as informants for the Stasi scrupulously documented his contacts to the West, inflating them into "agent activity."[3] When Ingo Krüger was questioned, he claimed that his fiancée intended to move to East Berlin after the wedding. He also applied for his own apartment in the East.[4]

Ingo Krüger and his fiancée were separated from one another when West Berlin was sealed off on August 13, 1961. They continued to find ways to see each other and made dates at remote areas at the edge of the city where they could exchange letters and presents through the barbed wire. But over time these meetings became more difficult to organize and Ingo Krüger was even temporarily detained once on his way to one of their meetings and was warned that he should stay away from the border.[5] To continue seeing each other they developed a new strategy. Ingrid R. registered her permanent address with relatives in West Germany because – unlike West Berliners – West Germans were still allowed to travel to East Berlin.[6] After that she was able to visit her fiancé again. But when the couple realized that the closed border was becoming a permanent situation, Krüger began preparing his escape.

Since he was an experienced skin diver, it seemed a good idea to escape through one of the many border waters with the help of diving equipment. Apparently a lot of people had had a similar idea because the number of people joining diving clubs in East Berlin skyrocketed after August 13, 1961.[7] Ingo Krüger began preparing his escape in early November and observation reports show that Stasi agents were watching his every move.[8] His escape route was to begin in the city center and continue across the Spree River to the Reichstag building. A number of his friends helped him to prepare and his fiancée was also in on the plan. At around 11 p.m. on December 10, 1961, Ingo Krüger took a taxi with two friends to the Spree bank at Schiffbauerdamm. He was already wearing his diving suit under his coat. A friend who monitored boat traffic on the Spree was waiting for them. She advised him to enter the river beneath the Friedrichstrasse train station to avoid the East German customs boats that assisted in guarding the border.[9] This way the boat crew would not see him. Ingo Krüger put on his scuba and entered the water. His friends stayed on the embankment and tried to keep an eye on him in the water, but they soon noticed that something had gone wrong.

Meanwhile Ingrid R. was waiting in vain on the other side of the West Berlin bank. She watched in horror as East German customs officials began searching the water with hooks and spotlights. They eventually pulled a body out of the water and onto the boat.[10] Despite the poor visibility, Ingrid R. was certain that the body belonged to her fiancé and that his escape attempt had failed. She was still hoping that he had survived the ordeal, but according to Berlin border police reports, the 21-year-old fugitive was already dead when they retrieved him from the water near the Marschall Bridge.[11] According to the corpse entry book of Humboldt University's Institute of Forensic Medicine, Ingo Krüger died on December 11 at 12:10 a.m.[12] The autopsy book registered the cause of death as "presumably death by drowning."[13]

The East German authorities told Ingo Krüger's parents and fellow colleagues at his work that his friends and fiancée had helped him prepare his escape and that they were responsible for his death.[14] One of his friends was arrested for assisting "flight from the republic." Another friend was blackmailed into working with the Stasi.[15] At the time of the funeral on December 23 at the East Berlin cemetery on Baumschulenweg, Ingrid R. still did not know what had happened to her fiancé. Letters she sent to Ingo Krüger's mother were not answered for weeks. The terrible truth finally reached her in a roundabout way in January.[16]

The exact circumstances of Ingo Krüger's death remain unclear. Theories that he died violently could not be confirmed. The Stasi investigation came to the conclusion that "K[rüger]'s death was brought about by a failed (breathing) instrument."[17] But investigations carried out in the 1990s as part of the legal prosecution of violence at the Wall and border established that he died on that December night as the consequence of a cold shock.[18]

Christine Brecht

1   See "Niederschrift der Zeugenvernehmung der Mutter von Ingo Krüger durch die West-Berliner Polizei, 9.11. 1977," in: StA Berlin, Az. 2 Js 147/90, Bl. 42–45.

2   As part of de-Nazification and Stalinization, after 1945 in the Soviet zone/East Germany, laypersons, who were regarded as non-suspect and reliable, were given crash-course training to become so-called "Volksrichter," or people's judges. See Hermann Wentker, *Volksrichter in der SBZ-DDR 1945 bis 1952. Eine Dokumentation*, Munich, 1997.

3   See "Abschrift eines GI-Berichtes [des MfS]/HA PS/Abt. I, 21.1.1960," in: BStU, MfS, AOPK 20505/62, Bd. 1, Bl. 62; "Aktenvermerk der Kaderleiterin/VEB Gästehäuser der Regierung [für das MfS] betr. Ingo Krüger, 30.12. 1960," in: Ibid., Bl. 249.

4   See "Aktenvermerk der Kaderleiterin/VEB Gästehäuser der Regierung [für das MfS] betr. Ingo Krüger, 9.1. 1961," in: Ibid., Bl. 250.

5   See handwritten arrest report of the Bepo/4.Komp., 25.10.1961, in: Ibid., Bl. 310.

6   West Berliners were banned from traveling to East Berlin as of 24.8.1961. The ban remained in place until the first entry permit agreement was set for the Christmas holidays in December 1963.

7   See East Berlin police protocol, 7.4.1962, in: LAB, C Rep 303-26-01, Nr. 495, n. pag. According to the report, after diving clubs had become very popular after the Wall was built, all diving athletes were investigated by the police.

8   See "Abschrift eines GI-Berichtes [des MfS]/HA PS/ Abt. I betr. Ingo Krüger – Koch Thälmannplatz", in: BStU, MfS, AOPK 20505/62, Bd. 1, Bl. 337–338, also "Beobachtungsbericht des MfS/Verwaltung HA VIII/Abt. I/ Referat 3 zu Ingo Krüger, 29.11.1961," in: Ibid., Bl. 370–378.

9   See Manfred Suwalski, "Die Entwicklung der Zollverwaltung der DDR (1945–1990)," in: Torsten Diedrich/Hans Ehlert/Rüdiger Wenzke (eds.), *Im Dienste der Partei. Handbuch der bewaffneten Organe der DDR*, Berlin, 1998, pp. 577–592.

10 See also "Ereignismeldung der West-Berliner Polizei, 11.12.1961," in: PHS, Bestand Ereignismeldungen der West-Berliner Schutzpolizei, n. pag.

11 "Rapport Nr. 342 der HV DVP/Operativstab, 11.12.1961," in: BArch, DO1/11.0/1358, Bl. 192.

12 "Bericht der West-Berliner Polizei, 29.10.1991," in: StA Berlin, Az. 2 Js 147/90, Bl. 67.

13 Ibid.

14 See "Auswertung des MfS/HA PS von einem Vorgang im Gästehaus der Regierung am Thälmannplatz, 12.7. 1962," in: BStU, MfS, AOPK 20505/62, Bd. 2, Bl, 214–224, here Bl. 214, 223–224.

15 See "Abschrift eines Befragungsberichtes [des MfS]/HA PS/Abt. I, 23.3.1962," in: BStU, MfS, 3245/65, Bd. 1, Bl. 91, 113, 114, 117, 168–169.

16 See letter from Ingo Krüger's grandmother to his fiancée, 4.1.1962, in: StA Berlin, Az. 2 Js 147/90, Bl. 13–17.

17 "Auswertung [des MfS]/HA PS/Abt. I betr. Vorgang Ingo Krüger, 20.8.1962," in: BStU, MfS, AOPK 20505/62, Bd. 2, Bl. 216–225, here Bl. 224.

18 See "Verfügung der Staatsanwaltschaft II bei dem Kammergericht Berlin (27 AR 74/97), 4.3.1998," in: StA Berlin, Az. 2 Js 147/90, Bl. 170–171.

Georg Feldhahn

born on August 12, 1941

drowned on December 19, 1961
in the Teltow Canal, near the Massante Bridge
at the sector border between
Berlin-Treptow and Berlin-Neukölln

A West Berlin customs official made a ghastly discovery while doing his rounds on the Teltow Canal on Sunday, March 11, 1962: The body of a young man was floating in the water near the Späth Bridge in Britz in Neukölln. The other side of the canal formed the border to the Soviet sector. The corpse was wearing the uniform of an East German border policeman and had, it turned out, been in the water for weeks. The head and face were disfigured by injuries caused by ship propellers and beyond recognition, but West Berlin newspapers cited police information that the death was caused by drowning and that there was no evidence of violence.[1] The West Berlin authorities also publicized the identity of the dead man: His name was Georg Feldhahn. He was 20 years old when he died and had been serving in East Berlin's 1st Border Brigade.

Although it seemed logical that the young man had died while trying to escape, West Berlin authorities were unable to confirm this at the time.[2] Contact between East and West Berlin had been frozen ever since the Wall was built, hence it was not possible to make inquiries to the authorities on the east side of the city.[3] Officials even contacted West Berlin relatives in an attempt to get in touch with members of the deceased's family, but were unsuccessful. Consequently, the background and circumstances of his death remained unclarified until the East German state collapsed. It was later revealed that Georg Feldhahn did, in fact, die while trying to desert from the military.

The documents that he filled out before signing up to serve at the border show that Georg Feldhahn was born during the war in 1941 in Friesack in the Havelland and grew up in that rural region west of Berlin.[4] He never knew his biological parents. He wrote that his father died in the Buchenwald concentration camp in 1942. As far as is known, he was separated from his mother at the age of four months and placed with his older sister in an orphanage.[5] After the war the siblings were adopted by foster parents who brought them to their home in the small town of Buschow. After completing school Georg Feldhahn trained to operate a tractor at a state-run farm before he was recruited at the age of 18 to enlist with the East German border police. He committed to a three-year service during the recruitment interview at the East German police district office in Rathenow. The protocol notes that he expressed a readiness to be transferred and expressed the wish to serve his duty in Thuringia. According to his own statements, he did not have any relatives outside of East Germany.[6] His service was to begin in September 1959, but instead of being assigned to Thuringia, he became a member of the border units stationed at Gross-Glienicke in Seeburg, an area bordering the West Berlin outer district of Spandau. After the Berlin Wall was built, Georg Feldhahn was transferred from the outer border to the inner-city sector border where he joined the 6th Border Brigade that operated in the south of the city between the Treptow and Neukölln districts.[7]

Desertion was not uncommon during the first weeks and months after the Wall was built. Hundreds of border guards used their duty at the border grounds to turn their backs on East Germany. Stasi reports registered a total of 28 cases of desertion to West Berlin in just the first two weeks of October 1961.[8] West Berlin explicitly encouraged the border guards to take that "leap to freedom." Using loud-speakers and fliers, the "Studio at the Barbed Wire," a radio station of the West Berlin Senate, encouraged them to refuse to obey the communist regime. One of their appeals was, "Don't let yourselves be buffaloed. Trust your feelings for the freedom of each individual. Don't let yourselves be pressed into the mold of your system."[9]

The official documents do not shed light on what led Georg Feldhahn to undertake his escape attempt. It also remains unclear whether his flight was a spontaneous act, as the Stasi presumed, for lack of any other indications, or whether it was a decision planned long in advance. He had not drawn any attention to himself before the day of his escape. The Stasi informants in his unit had not been aware that he was planning an escape nor that he had contact with people living in the West. The files merely assert that before reporting to duty on the day in question, Georg Feldhahn had been drinking in the city with two comrades.[10] His shift at the border strip began at 9 p.m. near the Massante Bridge on the bank of the Teltow Canal. Around 10 p.m., on orders from his duty leader, he inspected the signaling device on the barbed wire fence, but never returned to his post. Instead he gradually approached the bridge that led to West Berlin. When he noticed that he was being observed and followed, he fired a number of shots from his machine pistol without hitting anyone. Then, before return shots could be fired, he disappeared.

Given the available evidence, the East Berlin investigators assumed that the fleeing man had successfully crossed the canal near the pipes running beneath the bridge.[11] The unit commander was quoted in the final report as having criticized the other guards for behaving too passively "instead of confronting the traitor and possibly employing firearms." The Stasi also focused extensively on the "question of the unit's guilt" and claimed that "F. could have been shot without difficulty before he crossed the canal."[12] Doubts about the success of Georg Feldhahn's escape did not arise until the next spring when West Berlin newspapers reported on the body retrieved from the water. It would appear, the Stasi wrote, that he fell into the canal while trying to escape and drowned in the freezing water.[13]

Nothing more was entered into the files held in the Stasi and border troop archives. The East German authorities did not disclose any other information about the case. Thus the fate of Georg Feldhahn remained unsolved for decades and was ultimately forgotten. Even his sister did not learn about his death until the nineties.[14] It is not known whether his foster parents, who have by now passed away, ever knew what had happened to their son.

Christine Brecht

1   See "Ertrunkener Vopo gefunden," in: *Bild-Zeitung*, 12.3.1962; "Toter Grenzpolizist war aus Seeburg," in: *Berliner Morgenpost*, 13.3.1962.

2   See "Vermerk der West-Berliner Polizei, 20.3.1962," in: StA Berlin, Az. 7 AR 90/93, Bd. 1, Bl. 25.

3   See Gerhard Kunze, *Grenzerfahrungen. Kontakte und Verhandlungen zwischen dem Land Berlin und der DDR 1949–1989*, Berlin, 1999.

4   See questionnaire of the MdI/HV DV. P, filled out by Georg Feldhahn, 6.7.1959, in: BStU, MfS, AP 9819/63, Bl. 5–10, handwritten resumé from Georg Feldhahn, 6.7.1959, in: Ibid, Bl. 11.

5   It was not possible to attain more information about Georg Feldhahn's parents.

6   See "Einstellungsprotokoll des Volkspolizei-Kreisamts Rathenow/Offizier für Kaderfragen, 6.7.1959," in: Ibid., Bl. 12, and the investigation report of the VPKA Rathenow/ABV, 6.7.1959, in: Ibid., Bl. 13.

7   See "Spitzenmeldung [des MfS]/HA VII/7/U.Abt.1.Grz.Brg. (B/106) betr. Fahnenflucht des Bp.-Angehörigen Georg Feldhahn, 20.12.1961," in: BStU, MfS, AP 9819/63, Bl. 27.

8   See "Wochenberichte [des MfS-ZAIG] über feindliche Manöver, Absichten und Massnahmen gegen die DDR, 1.10.–6.10.1961, 7.10.–14.10.1961," in: BStU, MfS, ZAIG Nr. 4395, Bl. 1–30, as well as the numerical data in: Stephan Wolf, *Hauptabteilung I: NVA und Grenztruppen, MfS-Handbuch, Teil III/13*, Berlin, 2004, p. 69, also Torsten Diedrich, "Die Grenzpolizei der SBZ/DDR (1946–1961)," in: Torsten Diedrich, et al (eds.), *Im Dienste der Partei. Handbuch der bewaffneten Organe der DDR*, Berlin, 1998, p. 219.

9   Quoted from an [MfS] report on supposed western war-mongering, in: BStU, MfS, ZAIG Nr. 525, Bl. 3–39, here Bl. 28.

10   See "Spitzenmeldung [der MfS]/HA VII/7/U.Abt.1.Grz.Brg. (B/106) betr. Fahnenflucht des Bp.-Angehörigen Georg Feldhahn, 20.12.1961," in: BStU, MfS, AP 9819/63, Bl. 27–30.

11   See ibid. Also "Abschlussbericht des MdI/Bepo/1.GB (B)/VI. Grenzabteilung/Kommandeur betr. Abschlussbericht zur Fahnenflucht des Gefr. Georg Feldhahn am 19.12.1961," in: Ibid , Bl. 19–22, here Bl. 21.

12   "[MfS] Spitzenmeldung HA VII/7/U.Abt.1.Grz.Brg. (B/106) betr. Fahnenflucht des Bp.-Angehörigen Georg Feldhahn, 20.12.1961," in: Ibid., Bl. 29.

13   See "Aktenvermerk [des MfS] betr. Georg Feldhahn, 25.1.1963," in: BStU, MfS AP 9819/63, Bl. 33.

14   See "Niederschrift der Zeugenvernehmung der Schwester von Georg Feldhahn durch die Rathenower Polizei, 9.6.1996," in: StA Berlin, Az. 27 AR 177/95, Bd. 2, Bl. 42–44.

Dorit Schmiel

born on April 25, 1941

shot dead on February 19, 1962
at Wilhelmsruher Damm
at the sector border between
Berlin-Pankow and Berlin-Reinickendorf

D orit Schmiel was born in Berlin during the war in 1941. Her father died serving as a soldier in the Second World War. She and her older brother were raised by her mother and stepfather in the East Berlin district of Pankow. Ever since she was a child, Dorit Schmiel had traveled regularly to the western part of the city to visit relatives, go shopping, watch movies or go dancing. She experienced the sealing off of the sector border and the loss of freedom to visit the West as a painful turning point in her life.[1]

Dorle, as she was called, was twenty years old at this time. She worked as a seamstress in a state-run manufacturing company and had recently moved in with her fiancé, Detlef T. She was also friends with the brothers Eberhard and Dietrich B. and the latter's girlfriend, Brigitte K. None of them was able to relate to the political situation and the ideological demands of the communist state. The situation became unbearable for them when the Wall went up. Eberhard B. recalled later that her friends were convinced that, regardless what the party and government promised, there was going to be less freedom and fewer economic improvements.[2] They decided to leave East Germany in early 1962 when it became apparent that the division of the city was going to remain permanent. News of successful escape attempts was heard about daily. One of Dorit Schmiel's cousins had managed to get through the barbed wire at the border in the north of the city. They wanted to try to escape at the same spot on the night of February 19, 1962.

It was already past midnight on a misty, cloudy night when the five friends approached the border to West Berlin's Reinickendorf district from the east side at Rosenthal in Pankow. They observed the movement of the border guards from a good distance before approaching the security area along the cemetery grounds. Using a wire cutter, they cut a hole in the first fence and, one after another, they crawled through the fence into the security strip on the other side. They then lay down flat on the snow and slush-covered ground and began gradually crawling forward. They had almost reached the last two rows of fences when three border guards noticed them and began to shoot at them.[3] Although the official East German reports claim otherwise, the guards opened fire without calling out first or firing warning shots to the defenseless fugitives who were lying on the ground.[4] A bullet hit Dorit Schmiel in her stomach and she cried out. Only then did the guards stop firing and approached the young people, ordering them to stand up. Detlef T., Dieter B. and Brigitte K. obeyed the order. The 16-year-old Eberhard B. was also able to get up by himself although a bullet had wounded his shoulder. But Dorit Schmiel remained on the ground, to the horror of her friends. She was bleeding profusely and crying in pain. Detlef T. recalled that the guards finally grabbed her by her arms and legs and carried her off like a piece of meat.[5]

She was brought to the next street, Wilhelmsruher Damm, and placed on the ground. It took at least 30 minutes for an ambulance to arrive. The two wounded people were taken to the People's Police Hospital in Berlin-Mitte. Eberhard B. reported that Dorit Schmiel kept asking "Do I have to die? Do I have to die?" all the way to the hospital, but once they arrived she did not utter a sound and was breathing weakly.[6] The hospital files show that she had suffered from a shot through the stomach and died from internal bleeding just a short time later.[7]

The other fugitives were interrogated for hours that very night. A month later they were put on trial. The indictment said that their joint escape attempt represented an act "that seriously endangered society" and which could have endangered the peace by inciting "provocations from the class enemy."[8] The Pankow district court sentenced them to prison terms ranging from ten months to two years.

Thirty years later Dorit Schmiel's friends saw the three border guards who had shot her held responsible for their actions. During the trial, at which the friends served as witnesses and joint plaintiff, it was not possible to determine which guard had fired the shots that killed Dorit Schmiel and wounded Eberhard B. The court was nonetheless convinced that all three defendants had willfully accepted the death of the fugitives. They were found guilty of joint manslaughter in coincidence with attempted manslaughter and were sentenced to 18 month in prison, a sentence that was commuted to probation.[9]

Everyone who had known Dorit Schmiel was deeply shocked by her death. As long as she lived, her mother held her cousin partially responsible for her daughter's death, falsely believing that he had enticed her daughter and friends to attempt the escape.[10] But both family and friends have no doubts about the circumstances under which the 20-year-old lost her life. News of the East Berliner's violent death also reached West Berlin through relatives. When the Wall still stood there were a number of memorials erected to preserve the memory of her fate.[11]

Christine Brecht

1   See conversation conducted by Christine Brecht with Marianne K., Dorit Schmiel's cousin, 15.11.2006.

2   See "Niederschrift der Zeugenvernehmung eines Mitflüchtlings von Dorit Schmiel durch die Berliner Polizei, 29.8.1991," in StA Berlin, Az. 27/2 Js 146/90, Bd. 1, Bl. 195–202, here Bl. 195.

3   See "Abschlussbericht des MdI/Bepo/1.GB (B)/1. Grenzabteilung betr. Versuchter Grenzdurchbruch, 19.2. 1962," in: BArch, VA-07/8461, Bl. 1–4.

4   Conversation conducted by Christine Brecht with Dietrich B., 1.12.2008; Conversation conducted by Maria Nooke with Eberhard B., 3.12.2008. See "Urteil des Landgerichts Berlin, 23.3.1994," in: StA Berlin, Az. 27/2 Js 146/90, Bd. 4, Bl. 46–99, here Bl. 65.

5   See "Niederschrift der Zeugenvernehmung eines Mitflüchtlings von Dorit Schmiel durch die Polizei in Esslingen, 16.8.1991," in: Ibid., Bd. 1, Bl. 180–182, here Bl. 181.

6   Conversation conducted by Maria Nooke with Eberhard B., 3.12.2008. See also "Niederschrift der Zeugenvernehmung eines Mitflüchtlings von Dorit Schmiel durch die Berliner Polizei, 29.8.1991," in: StA Berlin, Az. 27/2 Js 146/90, Bd. 1, Bl. 195–202, here Bl. 197.

7   Entry in hospital sheet, People's Police Hospital, department of surgery, 19.2.1962, in: Ibid., Bd. 1, Bl. 144–145.

8   "Anklageschrift der Staatsanwaltschaft Berlin-Pankow, (I Pa 195/62), 7.3.1962," in: Ibid., Bd. 1, Bl. 206–208, here Bl. 207.

9   "Urteil des Landgerichts Berlin vom 23.3.1994," in: Ibid., Bd. 4, Bl. 46–99.

10 Conversation conducted by Christine Brecht with Marianne K., Dorit Schmiel's cousin, 15.11.2006.

11 See "Junge Union für Gedenkstein für Maueropfer," in: *Berliner Morgenpost*, 20.2.1987.

Heinz Jercha

born on July 1, 1934

shot dead on March 27, 1962
at Heidelberger Strasse 75
at the sector border between
Berlin-Treptow and Berlin-Neukölln

Heinz Jercha, a native Berliner, was living with his wife and child in the western part of the city when the Wall was built. In the spring of 1962, the young father, a butcher who had fled East Germany a few years earlier, joined an escape assistance group initiated by a former colleague, Fritz Wagner, who helped people in East Germany escape to the West. They dug a tunnel beneath the barriers at Heidelberger Strasse in Berlin-Neukölln, a street that bordered directly on the East Berlin city district of Treptow. The underground passageway began in the basement of a building at Heidelberger Strasse 35 and came out at the building number 75 on the East Berlin side of the divided city. Since March 21, 1962, Heinz Jercha and the others in the group had helped dozens of East German citizens escape to the West. On March 27, they again risked going to the other side of the Wall to pick people up and bring them to West Berlin. However, Stasi documents reveal that this time Heinz Jercha was ambushed and shot at by Stasi agents.[1] Badly wounded, the 27-year-old crawled back through the tunnel to West Berlin, where he died a short time later. "Those swine shot me," were apparently his last words.[2]

Escape operations, criticized and prosecuted in East Germany as "human trafficking," experienced their "heyday of heroism" in West Berlin during the first years after the Wall was built. They were supported by the authorities and the population in many ways.[3] Heinz Jercha was the second person following Dieter Wohlfahrt to be shot at the Wall while trying to help others to escape and his death triggered strong expressions of solidarity and sympathy in the West. After his death, people everywhere demanded that Jercha's widow and five-year-old daughter be provided for by the Senate and the authorities responded to these demands by granting the family of escape agents who were killed the same status as relatives of someone who died in war: They were henceforth entitled to a small pension.[4] Politicians publicly expressed their recognition of the fact that Heinz Jercha had risked his own life to help others.[5] Representatives of the federal government, the Senate and West Berlin districts paid their last respects by attending his funeral on April 5 at the Wald Cemetery in Zehlendorf.[6]

The circumstances under which Heinz Jercha died remained unclear for a long time. The East German leadership denied any responsibility and kept the files that proved that the escape agent was shot by a member of the Stasi under lock and key.[7] West Berlin police investigations determined that Heinz Jercha was together with Harry Seidel on the evening of March 27. Seidel, along with Fritz Wagner, was one of the key players in the early escape operations. They had joined forces in early 1962 to build the tunnel in Heidelberger Strasse.[8] But unlike Fritz Wagner, who had offered his escape services to East Berliners for money, Seidel acted out of personal and idealistic reasons. Heinz Jercha stumbled onto the operation through Wagner's broad professional network and helped Seidel with the excavation work.[9] When they completed the tunnel, Jercha and Seidel took on the risky task of picking up the escape candidates at the East Berlin end of the tunnel each evening and leading them back to West Berlin. They acted cautiously, and Seidel later admitted to the West Berlin police that they were armed with pistols for their own protection.[10] Seidel also had contact with an escape operation run by students and, without Wagner's knowledge, he and Jercha were also using the tunnel to bring other young East Berliners to the West.[11] During one of these operations Heinz Jercha got into a conversation with two East Berlin students to whom he had given a ride in his VW Beetle after their successful escape. They asked him if he would help a friend of theirs who desperately wanted to leave East Germany, and they offered to pay him money. Jercha agreed.[12] The escape tunnel had meanwhile been betrayed by an East Berlin resident who had won Seidel's trust. Seidel had no idea that the man worked as a Stasi informant under the code name "IM Naumann," but this was how the Stasi found out about the escape operation on March 24. They developed an "operative plan to liquidate the tunnel," with the main aim of arresting Harry Seidel, who they believed was the "organizer of the trafficking operation."[13] On March 25, Stasi agents were on the lookout in the basement of the East Berlin building where the tunnel ended. On the evening of March 27, Seidel and Jercha successfully led an elderly couple through the tunnel unnoticed. Afterwards the Stasi arrest commando was given the order to take action as soon as Seidel appeared. The Stasi officer in charge later wrote "the comrades were to sharpen their knives for this one" and he added emphatically that what he meant was "they were to have their guns ready and if necessary use them."[14] Seidel and Jercha returned a short time later to carry out the escape operation that Jercha had organized on his own initiative in agreement with the two students. Seidel later put on record that when they reached the East Berlin side, he had waited on the basement stairs while Jercha went upstairs to meet the fugitives in the building corridor.[15] But instead the Stasi arrest commando was waiting for him. According to the Stasi files, one of the men ordered him to surrender, at which point he shone his flashlight into their eyes and without a struggle quickly ran away. The Stasi men opened fire immediately and chased him but they were unable to stop either Jercha or Seidel from escaping through the tunnel to West Berlin. One of their bullets, however, ultimately killed Heinz Jercha. The autopsy found that it was a ricochet shot that hit him in his chest, wounding him fatally.[16]

On the basis of the Stasi files opened after the East German archives were made accessible in the nineties, an investigation was opened against the four Stasi agents who were identified as having shot Heinz Jercha. In this case, however, narrow limits were placed on the legal prosecution because the court conceded that at the time their intention had been to arrest a West Berliner who had illegally entered the territory of East Germany. Given this fact, the use of firearms that led to Heinz Jercha's death could not be penalized as homicide. The proceedings were dropped without an arraignment.[17] A memorial plaque on Heidelberger Strasse today recalls the fate of Heinz Jercha.

Christine Brecht

1 "Bericht der VfS Gross-Berlin/Kreisdienststelle Treptow betr. Schleusung in der Heidelberger Strasse 75 am 27.3.1962, 27.3.1962," in: BStU, MfS, HA I Nr. 6086, Bl. 146–148.

2 Transcript of a West Berlin police witness hearing of the resident from whose basement the tunnel was dug, 30.3.1962, in: StA Berlin, Az. 29/2 Js 148/90, Bl. 60–61, here Bl. 60.

3 For context, see Marion Detjen, Ein *Loch in der Mauer. Die Geschichte der Fluchthilfe im geteilten Deutschland 1961-1989,* Munich, 2005.

4 See "Er starb für die Freiheit anderer," in: *BZ,* 29.3.1962, also "Schnelle Hilfe für die Witwe von Heinz Jercha," in: *BZ,* 30.3.1962.

5 See "Man liess ihm keine Chance", in: *Berliner Morgenpost,* 29.3.1962, also "Lemmer: Ermordeter Jercha ist Märtyrer der Mauer," in: *Der Kurier,* 29.3.1962.

6 See "Abschied von Heinz Jercha," in: *BZ,* 6.4.1962.

7 See "Schüsse in Westberlin. Infame Lüge der Frontstadtpresse," in: *Neues Deutschland,* 29.3.1962, also in contrast to this the contemporary West Berlin investigation files, in: StA Berlin, Az. 29/2 Js 148/90, Bl. 1–166.

8 See Marion Detjen, Harry Seidel, in: Karl Wilhelm Fricke/Peter Steinbach/Johannes Tuchel (eds.), *Opposition und Widerstand in der DDR. Politische Lebensbilder,* Munich, 2002, pp. 340–350.

9 On the history of this tunnel escape, see Dietmar Arnold/Sven Felix Kellerhoff, *Die Fluchttunnel von Berlin,* Berlin, 2008, pp. 72–77.

10 See "Niederschrift der Zeugenvernehmung von Harry Seidel durch die West-Berliner Polizei, 30.3.1962," in: StA Berlin, Az. 29/2 Js 148/90, Bl. 58–59, and the report of the West Berlin police station 215, 28.3.1962, in: PHS, Bestand Grenzvorkommnisse, n. pag. According to it, the pistols were confiscated on March 27 and Seidel was detained temporarily.

11 See on this "Niederschrift der Zeugenvernehmung eines Fluchthelfers durch die West-Berliner Polizei, 29.3.1962," in: StA Berlin, Az. 29/2 Js 148/90, Bl. 43–46.

12 See "Niederschrift der Zeugenvernehmung eines Tunnelflüchtlings durch die West-Berliner Polizei, 31.3.1962," in: Ibid, Bl. 63–65.

13 See "[MfS-]Operativplan zur Liquidierung des Stollens Heidelberger Strasse 75, 26.3.1962," in: BStU, MfS, HA I Nr. 6068, Bl. 142–144, and "Sachstandsbericht der VfS Gross-Berlin/Kreisdienststelle Treptow betr. Operativ-Vorgang 'Krampe,'" 30.3.1962, in: Ibid., Bl. 38–48.

14 "Bericht der VfS Gross-Berlin/Büro der Leitung betr. Falsches Herangehen bei der Liquidierung eines unterirdischen Ganges und Entweichung eines Verbrechers, 28.3.1962," in: Ibid., Bl. 138–141, here Bl. 140.

15 See "Niederschrift der Zeugenvernehmung von Harry Seidel durch die West-Berliner Polizei, 30.3.1962," in: StA Berlin, Az. 29/2 Js 148/90, Bl. 58–59.

16 See West Berlin autopsy report, 28.3.1962, in: Ibid. Bl. 10–13, and report of the West Berlin forensic investigative department, 30.3.1962, in: Ibid., Bl. 39–40.

17 See "Verfügung der Staatsanwaltschaft II bei dem Landgericht Berlin, 27.8.1997," in: Ibid., Bl. 278–285, also "Verfügung der Staatsanwaltschaft bei dem Kammergericht Berlin, 23.8.1993," in: Ibid., Bl. 269–275.

Philipp Held

born on May 2, 1942

drowned in the Spree River
in April 1962
probably at the sector border between
Berlin-Friedrichshain and Berlin-Kreuzberg

P hilipp Held was born on May 2, 1942 in Worms am Rhein in West Germany. He had a sheltered childhood there, but it was overshadowed by the early loss of his father who had died in a car accident in 1955. After finishing school, Philipp Held trained to become an electrician. After this he began studying engineering. His mother was proud of her only son. But his mother opposed his friendship with Bärbel W., whom he met when he was 19, and after this point the mother and son began to have disagreements. Philipp Held and his 16-year-old girlfriend felt misunderstood and patronized. They made an unusual decision that would have grave consequences. Without telling their parents, they drove to the inner-German border in September 1961 and got out in East Germany near Helmstedt. Bärbel W. had grown up there until she fled to the West with her mother in 1956.[1] At the border they both announced their desire to resettle in the East. They had to go through the admissions procedure at the Barby Reception Camp near Magdeburg. They were examined and registered as a "new arrival" and "repatriate," according to the official East German terminology.[2] Afterwards they were permitted to move to Eberswalde in the north of Berlin where Bärbel W.'s father and other relatives lived.

But Philipp Held and his girlfriend had a hard time adjusting to the living and working conditions in East Germany. Moreover, they were not exactly greeted with open arms in Eberswalde. They felt controlled and reprimanded by adults there, too. Not long after their arrival, they wrote letters to their parents in the West that suggest that they already regretted their move to the East.[3] It was not until then that the couple seemed to realize that with Germany now divided by the Wall, the way back was not open to them. During a visit to East Berlin they realized that the border was "dreadfully guarded and walled up."[4] In desperation, they began looking for a way out. Since Bärbel W. was still a minor she tried to obtain an exit permit from the East German authorities. For Philipp Held, who according to East German law was of full age and who already had vocational training, the application seemed hopeless. From the point of view of the East German state, both economic and ideological arguments spoke against allowing the young qualified male worker who had moved from the capitalist West to leave again. The situation escalated when, in January 1962, East Germany introduced general conscription and Philipp Held worried about being drafted into the National People's Army. He feared that as a soldier entrusted with confidential information, he would never be allowed out of the walled-up country. In the end he felt he had no other choice but to risk trying to flee, and his last letter to his mother contained a vague hint of this intention.[5] His girlfriend and landlord were also informed of his intention without knowing any details. When he disappeared on April 8, they assumed that his escape had been successful. It was only after they did not hear from him for a number of days that they began to worry.

Members of the East German border police noticed the body of Philipp Held in the Spree River on April 22, 1962. All evidence suggests that he drowned while trying to swim from the grounds of the Osthafen Harbor in Berlin-Friedrichshain to the West Berlin bank on the other side. The report written by the border police unit on duty that night stated that "the body floating towards the Oberbaum Bridge was retrieved from the water by the water police at the Schilling Bridge around 6 p.m. […]. The body belonged to Held, Philipp […] H. had his identity papers in a cellophane bag on him."[6] The fact that the deceased had identity papers wrapped in a waterproof bag with him was a clear indication to East German authorities that they were dealing with an "attempted border breach." Further investigations determined that at the time of retrieval, Philipp Held had been floating dead in the water for approximately ten days. His corpse had gotten caught in the wire of an underwater barrier. Since no bullet wounds were found on the body, the East Berlin investigation office assumed that the deceased had drowned.[7]

The actual circumstances of his death were never clarified. Neither the authorities in the East nor those in the West, nor friends or relatives, were able to find out exactly how, when and where Philipp Held had died.

The East Berlin prosecuting authorities waited a number of days before informing his mother that they had retrieved her son's body from the water. The official letter dated April 26, 1962 stated succinctly that her son had been killed in an accident. She tried, with the help of authorities in Worms, to have her son's body delivered to her. She then found out, to her great dismay, that her son's human remains had been cremated without her permission. She strongly mistrusted the official statements coming from the East German authorities and suspected that they were trying to conceal a violent crime. She turned to the West German press to have her view made public, which is how the rumor started that Philipp Held had been shot. The "Bild-Zeitung" ran the headline "Pankow tried to cover up the act." It reported that there was hardly any doubt of the fact that Philipp Held "was murdered by Ulbricht's border guards."[8] When the Berlin public prosecutor's office re-opened the investigation in 1990, it was unable to confirm this theory.[9] All the available documents support the view that Philipp Held had drowned while trying to escape in April 1962.

Christine Brecht

1 See "Bericht der Nachrichtenstelle Helmstedt (Dienstbereich Polizei-Abschnitt LK Helmstedt)/Niedersächs. Verwaltungsbezirk Braunschweig, 22.5.1962," in: StA Berlin, Az. 27 Js 151/90, Bd. 2, Bl. 4–7.

2 Between 1949 and 1989, close to 600,000 people moved from the West to the East, mostly for personal reasons, including many so-called "repatriates." See Cornelia Röhlke, "Entscheidung für den Osten. Die West-Ost-Migration," in: Bettina Effner/Helge Heidemeyer (eds.), *Flucht im geteilten Deutschland,* Berlin, 2005, p. 97–113.

3 See letters from Bärbel W. [copy of the Worms police], 13.9.1961–10.5.1962, in: StA Berlin, Az. 27 Js 151/90, Bd. 1, Bl. 50–64.

4 See letters from Bärbel W. [copy of the Worms police], 15.10.1961, in: Ibid., Bl. 51.

5 See letter from Philipp Held [copy of the Worms police], 5.4.1962, in: Ibid., Bl. 27–28.

6 "Grenzrapport Nr. 112/62 des MdI/Kommando Bepo/Op. Diensthabender, 23.4.1962," in: BArch, VA-07/4739, Bd. 2, Bl. 127.

7 See "Handschriftliche Aktennotiz [des MfS] /HA VII, 5.5.1962," in: BStU, MfS, ZAIG/1 9300/3, Bl. 58.

8 *Bild-Zeitung,* 5.5.1962.

9 See "Schlußvermerk der ZERV, 11.12.1991," in: StA Berlin, Az. 27 Js 151/90, Bd. 1, Bl. 132–136.

Klaus Brueske

born on September 14, 1938

**shot dead on April 18, 1962
at the Heinrich-Heine-Strasse border crossing
at the sector border between
Berlin-Mitte and Berlin-Kreuzberg**

On the night of April 17, 1962, three young East Berliners undertook a daredevil escape attempt: They tore through the obstacles at the Heinrich-Heine-Strasse border crossing with a truck. Amidst a hail of bullets from the East German border guards, they managed to break through to the West Berlin side. Two of the passengers got away with mere injuries, but the 23-year-old Klaus Brueske, who was driving the escape car, was fatally injured. The next day a West Berlin newspaper ran the headline "He died driving them to freedom."[1] The East German press presented the circumstances that led to Klaus Brueske's death in a very different light. "Neues Deutschland" reported that they were "shot while breaching the border" and added that "on April 18, 1962 a certain Klaus Brueske was shot and killed while violently breaking through the border. His act placed the lives of members of the border security organ in extreme danger."[2]

Klaus Brueske was born on September 14, 1938 in Berlin, the fifth of eight children. He had spent his entire life in the Friedrichshain district, which had been part of the Soviet sector since 1945. After quitting a masonry apprenticeship, he became a driver. Beginning in January 1961 he found employment at the AEG where his father also worked. The company was located on the west side of the city, and he commuted every day between East and West Berlin. When the border was sealed on August 13, 1961, his father chose to remain in West Berlin, but Klaus Brueske was reluctant to give up his familiar surroundings in the East. He found a new job in the East as a driver for the same company where his older brother worked.[3] Over the following weeks and months, however, his friends grew increasingly discontent with the situation in East Germany. They began to discuss possible ways of escaping and explored the border area. Over time a plan to break through the border crossing at Heinrich-Heine-Strasse with a truck began to take shape. No fewer than seven young men wanted to participate in the escape.[4]

Klaus Brueske borrowed a truck from the company on April 17, 1962, claiming that he had to move. He loaded the truck with sand and gravel in order to increase the vehicle's ability to break through the Wall. That evening he met his friends in a bar, and later Peter G. told western authorities how they had spent their last East

German money and gotten drunk "in an atmosphere of morbid humor."[5] When the seven youths left the bar they were startled when an East German policeman addressed them. Even though the policeman did not seem at all suspicious, they decided to separate for a while and meet at the truck again later that night. Only three of them showed up at the designated time. They waited a bit before leaving without the others. Klaus Brueske sat at the wheel, Lothar M. was in the passenger seat next to him and Peter G. lay down on the back of the fully-loaded truck platform.

It was past midnight when the young men raced through the border crossing at a speed of 70 km/h. As the truck broke through the first and second barriers, border guards aimed two bursts of fire at them, firing 14 shots altogether. The vehicle was hit many times but continued to speed across the border line, not stopping until it collided with a property wall on the West Berlin side.[6] The three fugitives were brought to the nearby Urban Hospital and treated for injuries and wounds. But for Klaus Brueske the help came too late. The autopsy report states that two shots through the back of his neck did not kill him immediately, but led him to lose control of the vehicle. Upon impact with the property wall he was buried in sand and suffocated painfully.[7] The border guard who fired the shots was held accountable for his actions forty years later. In April 1994 he was found guilty of manslaughter coinciding with attempted manslaughter and sentenced to one year and two months probation.[8]

The East German authorities saw the escape attempt by Klaus Brueske, Peter G. and Lothar M. as an "especially glaring example of border breaching" and conducted a long and extensive investigation that focused on two areas, one of which concentrated on the events that occurred at the Heinrich-Heine-Strasse border crossing. It found the shooting of the fugitives to be expressly justified and in line with orders, but the layout of the security obstacles was criticized for its deficiencies. Consequently a slalom path leading up to the border crossing was added to help prevent vehicles from breaking through in the future. Repair and reconstruction work was carried out immediately following the escape. Moreover, the investigators began to put their sights on Klaus Brueske's friends and relatives in East Berlin. The deceased's apartment was searched by Stasi agents and co-workers and siblings were interrogated. When it was discovered that Klaus Brueske's older brother knew about his plan to escape, he was suspected of complicity and held in detention for four months.

Neither Klaus Brueske's mother nor his siblings were permitted to attend the funeral that took place in West Berlin in the municipal cemetery in Lübars.

After a second person, Heinz Schöneberger, was killed at Heinrich-Heine-Strasse in December 1965, a West Berlin group called "Working Group 13th of August" erected a wooden cross there in March 1966. Photographs of Klaus Brueske and Heinz Schöneberger were placed next to the cross.[9] Memorial services take place at the memorial each year on the anniversary of the day the Wall was erected.[10]

Christine Brecht

1 *Der Abend,* 19.4.1962.

2 *Neues Deutschland,* 19.4.1962.

3 See "Niederschrift der Zeugenvernehmung des Vaters von Klaus Brueske durch die West-Berliner Polizei, 19.4.1962," in: StA Berlin, Az. 27 Js 160/90, Bd. 1, Bl. 32.

4 See "Niederschrift der Zeugenvernehmung eines Mitflüchtlings von Klaus Brueske durch die West-Berliner Polizei, 10.5.1962," in: Ibid., Bl. 38–39.

5 Ibid.

6 See "Chronik der IV. Grenzabteilung/1.GB vom 26. Juni 1961 bis 31. Dezember 1962," in: BArch, VA-07/16661, Bl. 17 and 19, also "Grenzrapport Nr. 108/62 des MdI/Kommando Bepo/Op. Diensthabender, 19.4.1962," in: BArch, VA-07/4739, Bd. 2, Bl. 184.

7 West Berlin autopsy report on Klaus Brueske, 19.4.1962, in: StA Berlin, Az. 27 Js 160/90, Bd. 1, Bl. 14–18.

8 See "Urteil des Landgerichts Berlin vom 24.4.1998," in: Ibid., Bd. 5, Bl. 1–2.

9 See "Nachricht der West-Berliner Polizeiinspektion Kreuzberg betr. Mahnmal (Holzkreuz) für Heinz Schöneberger, 7.3.1966," in: PHS, Bestand Grenzvorkommnisse, n. pag.

10 See "Fotodokumentation des MR der DDR/MfS/GÜSt Heinrich-Heine-Straße zur Kranzniederlegung im Vorfeld der Grenzübergangsstelle, 13.8.1988," in: BStU, MfS, HA VI Nr. 1573, Bl. 95–97.

Peter Böhme

born on August 17, 1942

shot dead on April 18, 1962
at Gleisdreieck Griebnitzsee
on the outer ring between
Potsdam-Babelsberg and Berlin-Zehlendorf

Peter Böhme began attending the National People's Army Flak and Artillery Officer's School in Geltow near Potsdam at the end of December 1961 but soon regretted this career decision. A few days later he wrote to the school director: "I have no interest in the career of an officer and don't feel I am able to learn what is necessary for the job. Moreover I don't see it offering any prospects for my future. This is why I am requesting a transfer back to my old unit."[1] When he was confronted by his brigade leader, the 19-year-old argued that he did not want to become a poor officer like some others he knew and would prefer to study to become an athletics teacher at the German Advanced School for Fitness Training in Leipzig. His supervisor, however, ended the "discussion" by requesting that he reconsider his view. Consequently, Peter Böhme came around and declared that he was willing – at least to pretend – to carry through with the planned training.[2]

The conflict marked a turning point in Peter Böhme's life. It was not the first time that the young man had gotten the short end of the stick in a conflict with parents, authorities and supervisors. But this time he decided he would not give in to the pressure and planned to flee to the West at the first possible opportunity.

Born and raised in Saxony's Chemnitz, called Karl-Marx-Stadt during communist rule, Peter Böhme often had problems with the Socialist establishment as a high school student. When he was 16, he was threatened with expulsion from school because he and a friend had bought a pair of studded jeans in West Berlin that were officially frowned upon in East Germany.[3] After graduating from secondary school he began an apprenticeship as a motor mechanic, but had to quit the training after he fled across the sector border to West Berlin – still open at the time – and had to be brought back by his father. The East German authorities evidently refrained from punishing the young man for his attempted "flight from the republic." Instead they demanded that Peter Böhme enlist with the National People's Army for several years. Obliged to join the East German army, he did only the bare minimum, but nonetheless managed to complete the usual stations of basic training, sergeant instruction and the application to officer's school.

At the officer's school Peter Böhme soon befriended Wolfgang G., who was the

83

same age and who had been transferred to Geltow from Cottbus at the same time. Wolfgang G. had also been forced to serve in the military as a consequence of minor offenses and openly admitted that he did not want to be an officer.[4] They were both tired of constantly being told what to do and soon agreed that desertion was the only way to get out of this situation.[5] In early April 1962 they began the necessary preparations. Wolfgang G. was later quoted as saying "We couldn't serve this hateful regime any longer."[6]

On the night of April 16, 1962 the two officer students removed two pistols and ammunition from the weapons cabinet of the Flak Artillery School. They had wanted to be able to defend themselves in an emergency, Wolfgang G. later explained to the West Berlin police.[7]

When, contrary to expectations, the missing weapons were noticed, they had to quickly disappear from the barracks. They walked to Potsdam where they hid the entire day while the search for them continued. That evening they took a taxi to Potsdam-Babelsberg and cautiously approached the border to the West Berlin town of Kohlhasenbrück. Arriving from the Griebnitzsee station, they walked along the S-Bahn tracks that once went to Berlin-Wannsee but were then no longer in use.

Two guards, Jörgen Schmidtchen and Klaus R., were on duty together that night. According to the military files, they were waiting in a former gatekeeper's house when around 2:30 a.m. they heard a noise and went outside to see what it was.[8] Thinking that the approaching men were on patrol duty, Schmidtchen, the guard leader, went up to the two men in uniform and asked them about their patrol, Wolfgang G. later testified. Then suddenly a fierce exchange of fire broke out during which Peter Böhme and Jörgen Schmidtchen were fatally injured. Wolfgang G. remained uninjured and was able to escape to West Berlin.

The fact that the desertion of two NVA soldiers cost two people their lives was politically explosive given the East-West conflict. The West Berlin press expressed solidarity with the fugitives. The "Bild-Zeitung" wrote: "A fugitive who is shot at by Ulbricht's henchmen is acting in self-defense … but shooting a fugitive intentionally, that is murder!"[9]

In East Germany Peter Böhme and Wolfgang G. were demonized as "common criminals," who, through their desertion, revealed themselves to be "enemies of the German Democratic Republic."[10] Despite the lack of evidence, the East German authorities charged Wolfgang G. with the death of Jörgen Schmidtchen and demanded that he be extradited, which the West German federal authorities refused to do. A voluminous file reveals that for many decades the Stasi continued to spy on Wolfgang G. in the West.

The memory of Peter Böhme's fate, meanwhile, was forgotten in both the East and the West. His death was the focus of preliminary proceedings in the nineties, but because the case never came to trial, the public was, for the most part, unaware of it. Research conducted as part of the legal prosecution of violent acts at the Wall established that it was actually Peter Böhme who had shot Jörgen Schmidtchen before he was fatally hit by the other guard, R. The proceedings against R. were dismissed in August 1992. The court conceded that he acted in self-defense when he fired shots at the deserting officer students. But the public prosecutor concluded that Peter Böhme was guilty of the murder of Jörgen Schmidtchen since he opened fire without being directly threatened.[11]

Christine Brecht

1. See "Abschrift des Schreibens von Peter Böhme an den Gen. Oberleutnant M. zur Weiterleitung, 5.1.1962," in: BArch, VA-01/13496, Bd. 1, Bl. 350.
2. See "Abschrift des Unterhaltungsblatts [Protokoll] für den Offiziersschüler Peter Böhme über ein Gespräch über die Zurückziehung einer Bewerbung zur Offiziersschule, o.D. [18.1.1962]," in: Ibid., Bl. 351.
3. See "Einschätzungsbericht [des MfS]/HA I/LSK-LV/U.-Abt. Stab/Potsdam über den Deserteur Peter Böhme, 22.4.1962," in: BStU, MfS, Rechtsstelle Nr. 118, Bl. 68–72; "Ermittlungsbericht [des MfS]/HA I/LSK-LV/U.-Abt. Stab/Potsdam über Peter Böhme, 22.4.1962," in: Ibid., Bl. 73–77.
4. See "Einschätzungsbericht [des MfS]/HA I/LSK-LV/U.-Abt. Stab/Potsdam über den Deserteur Wolfgang G., 22.4.1962," in: Ibid., Bl. 78–81.
5. On desertion from the military as a form of resistance and refusal see Rüdiger Wenzke (ed.), *Staatsfeinde in Uniform? Widerständiges Verhalten und politische Verfolgung in der NVA*, Berlin, 2005.
6. "Sterbender gibt Feuerschutz," in: *BZ*, 19.4.1962.
7. See "Niederschrift der Zeugenvernehmung des Mitflüchtlings von Peter Böhme durch die West-Berliner Polizei, 19.4.1962," in: StA Berlin, Az. 27 Js/56 Js 277/03, Bd. 1, Bl. 34–35.
8. See "Bericht der Bepo/2.GB/B/Der Kommandeur betr. Schwerer Grenzdurchbruch unter Anwendung der Schusswaffe und mit tödlichem Ausgang am 18.4.1962, 17.4.1962 [falsche Datierung]," in: BArch, VA-07/18345, Bl. 257–263.
9. "Berlins Kripo sucht Mörder des Flüchtlings," in: *Bild-Zeitung*, 21.4.1962.
10. "Bericht der NVA/Flak-Artillerie-Schule/Untersuchungskommission zum besonderen Vorkommnis an der Flak-artillerieschule, 18.4.1962," in: BArch, VA-01/13496, Bd. 1, Bl. 314–334, quote Bl. 320.
11. See "Verfügung der Staatsanwaltschaft bei dem Kammergericht [2 Js 150/90], 18.8.1992," in: StA Berlin, Az. 2 Js 150/90, Bd. 2, Bl. 202–207.

Horst Frank

born on May 7, 1942

shot dead on April 29, 1962
in the "Schönholz" garden settlement
at the sector border between
Berlin-Pankow and Berlin-Reinickendorf

After the Wall was built, the grounds around the Wilhelmsruh S-Bahn station in the East Berlin district of Pankow were a favored starting point for escape attempts. A number of people succeeded in reaching the West Berlin district of Reinickendorf by escaping through the border fortifications of this area.[1] But East German border guards used their guns to hinder an escape there on April 29, 1962. The 19-year-old Horst Frank tried to "break through" to West Berlin – as it was officially referred to in East Germany – at around half past midnight. According to a border police report, he had "already climbed over the second wire fence when our guards called out to him. Since F[rank] continued his flight, our guards fired seven shots at him. F[rank] was transported to the People's Police Hospital where he died at approx. 4 a.m."[2]

The East Berlin border report documents the violent death of the young man, but gives little impression of what actually transpired between two fugitives and three border guards. When Horst Frank was shot that night he was very close to reaching his goal. He and Detlev W. had been crawling through the border strip for four hours. They had both managed to reach the last barrier, a three-layered barbed wire fence, without being noticed. His friend was lucky. The two border guards did not see him and he was able to escape to West Berlin. But they did discover Horst Frank. From a distance of 20 meters, they opened fire on the fugitive lying on the ground. When a third border guard was alerted by the shots, he also began firing at the 19-year-old, who was hopelessly tangled in the barbed wire. Horst Frank was hit three times. A bullet penetrated his stomach and lung, causing him to die shortly thereafter.[3]

The court that tried the three guards many years later was unable to determine who had fired the fatal shot. Nevertheless, all three men were found guilty of joint manslaughter and handed down probation sentences ranging from one and a half years to one year and three months.[4]

Horst Frank came from Saxony. He was born on May 7, 1942 in Lommatzsch. After completing a gardening apprenticeship, he moved to East Berlin just a few months before the Wall was built. He worked for a state-owned horticultural company in the Weissensee district and shared an apartment with other workers in a company dormitory. While visiting his parents in Lommatzsch over the 1962 Easter holidays, he got into a conversation with Detlev W., who was two years younger. The young men had known each other since childhood and found that they shared something in common: They both wanted to leave East Germany.[5] Detlev W. later put down on the official record that his main reason for leaving was to meet his biological father who lived in the West. He did not disclose what his friend's reasons for leaving were. A general conscription had been introduced in East Germany in January 1962 and the fact that Horst Frank was soon to be recruited into the National People's Army is likely to have played a decisive role in his decision to flee. His military summons to attend his medical examination, dated March 23, 1962, was one of the few things that Horst Frank had on him when he was shot.[6]

The two friends agreed to flee together. They met a week later, on April 28, 1962, in East Berlin to carry out their plan. Horst Frank had already checked out a spot on the sector border in Berlin that he thought was suitable for an escape attempt: the Schönholz garden settlement that bordered the West Berlin district of Reinickendorf in the north of the city. Equipped with wire cutters, they waited until dark before approaching the border grounds. Detlev W. recalled that they cut through the interior wall and found themselves within the border strip, an open field that was approximately 80 meters wide. Horst Frank had evidently prepared the escape well. Instead of hectically running off, they remained on the ground and crept forward slowly and cautiously. They often stopped and ducked to avoid being seen by the border guards. They noticed a trip wire in time and were able to get past it without triggering an alarm. When Detlev W. reached the border fence, he suddenly heard shots, but did not realize that his friend was caught in the barbed wire and had been hit. The border guards' shots were also heard on the other side of the border fence. Residents, police officers and members of the French military police watched as the seriously wounded fugitive was transported away. Since Horst Frank had not shown any signs of life, the people in the West assumed that his wounds had been fatal. Residents erected a wooden cross at the site the next day.[7]

In fact, Horst Frank died shortly after he was pulled out of the barbed wire fence. But that did not hinder the East German authorities from charging him with an "attempted border breach." The files of the Ministry of State Security show that an arrest warrant for the severely wounded young man was immediately requested, leading to his transfer to the prison division of the People's Police Hospital and the preparation for his immediate interrogation.[8] Frank never regained consciousness and died that very night.

The Stasi waited four or five days before informing his relatives of his death and releasing the corpse to them.[9] The funeral took place in Lommatzsch on May 12, 1962.

Christine Brecht

1 See "[MfS]-Bericht, 1.11.1961," in: BStU, MfS, ZAIG Nr. 525, Bl. 3–39.

2 "Grenzrapport Nr. 119/62 des MdI/Kommando Bepo/Op. Diensthabender, 30.4.1962," in: BArch, VA-07/4739, Bd. 2, Bl. 26.

3 See "Anklageschrift der Staatsanwaltschaft bei dem Kammergericht Berlin [27/2 Js 149/90], 5.8.1994," in: StA Berlin, Az. 27/2 Js 149/90, Bd. 2, Bl. 16–18.

4 See "Urteil des Landgerichts Berlin vom 23.11.1995," in: Ibid., Bl. 106–123.

5 See "Niederschrift der Zeugenvernehmung des Mitflüchtlings von Horst Frank durch die West-Berliner Polizei, 21.5.1962," in: Ibid., Bd. 1, Bl. 12–13, also "Niederschrift der Zeugenvernehmung des Mitflüchtlings von Horst Frank durch die Berliner Polizei, 17.2.1993," in: Ibid., Bl. 190–195.

6 See "Abschlussbericht des MdI/Bepo/1.GB (B)/I. Grenzabteilung/Kommandeur zum versuchten Grenzdurchbruch am 29.4.62 gegen 0.30 Uhr, 29.4.1962," in: BArch, VA-07/8641, Bl. 15.

7 See "Bericht der West-Berliner Polizei (Polizeiinspektion Reinickendorf) betr. Festnahme eines Flüchtlings nach Schußwaffengebrauch, 30.4.1962," in: PHS, Bestand Grenzvorkommnisse, n. pag.; also "Wieder ein Vopo-Opfer," in: *Der Abend,* 30.4.1962.

8 See "Protokoll der VPI Pankow/Abt. K, 29.4.1962," in: BStU, MfS, Archivakte A 121586, Generalstaatsanwalt von Gross-Berlin, Bl. 3, sowie "Karteikarte des [MfS]/KD Pankow, 29.4.1962," in: BStU, MfS AS 754/70, Bd. 16, Bl. 16.

9 "Schlussvermerk des PdVP Berlin/Abt. K, 5.5.1962," in: BStU, MfS, Archivakte A 121586, Generalstaatsanwalt von Gross-Berlin, Bl. 18.

Lutz Haberlandt

born on April 29, 1938

shot dead on May 27, 1962
on the Alexander embankment near Charité Hospital
at the sector border between
Berlin-Mitte and Berlin-Tiergarten

The East Berliner Lutz Haberlandt chose to flee to the western part of the city on a Sunday. It was a sunny day and unusually warm for that time of year. On the same day, May 27, 1962, the mayor of Berlin, Willy Brandt, called on the West Berlin population to stay calm. There had been an exchange of fire between an East Berlin border policeman and West Berlin police officers four days earlier that had caused quite a stir. A young fugitive was shot and the East German border policeman Peter Göring was fatally wounded. Despite demands from politicians in the West for the shootings to stop, the violent attacks on people fleeing did not cease. Lutz Haberlandt was shot and killed when he tried to escape.

Born in Berlin in 1938, Lutz Haberlandt, the second of three children, grew up in the Prenzlauer Berg district. After eight years of schooling he completed a brick-laying apprenticeship after which he worked as a mason. His father is believed to have worked in West Berlin before the Wall was built and, according to the Stasi file on the family, they had a number of relatives in the West. The Stasi categorized Lutz Haberlandt as "indifferent to politics," which suggests that he was not a supporter of the communist regime.[1] At the age of 24 he was still living with his parents on a street that was then called Dimitroffstrasse, today's Danziger Strasse. That particular Sunday he left his home around noon and went to a local bar. He had a beer and got into a conversation with a friend whom he happened to have met there. Questioned by the Criminal Investigation Department later, the friend denied knowing anything about his friend's plans to escape and stated that he had left the bar drunk and gone home.[2] Lutz Haberlandt's parents also told the Stasi during an interrogation that they had no idea that their son was planning an escape, nor did they know what had motivated him.[3]

Lutz Haberlandt was probably not totally sober when he headed for the inner-city later that afternoon and entered the grounds of Charité Hospital, situated directly on the border. At about 4 p.m. two transport policemen who were guarding the area from a nearby railroad bridge noticed him there.[4] The two guards later recorded that they observed the young man as he climbed onto the roof of a shed, removed his jacket and shoes and lay down in the sun. After a while he suddenly jumped down from the roof and climbed over the property wall into the cordoned-off border strip. Other border guards posted about a 100 meters away on a tower of the courthouse on Invalidenstrasse also noticed the young man do this. After firing a warning shot, the border guard K. aimed two shots directly at Lutz Haberlandt from the tower. One of the bullets hit him in the head, penetrating his skull and causing him to collapse. Doctors, nurses and patients at the nearby Charité psychiatric clinic who had witnessed the scene said that he was left lying in the shrubbery for about forty minutes.[5] He was probably dead when the guards carried him away.

Other border guards had also fired shots to prevent him from escaping. A few bullets entered into West Berlin territory. Policemen on the west side returned the fire and a bullet grazed an East Berlin border guard's helmet. East German propaganda claimed that the West Berliners' use of firearms was a "severe provocation" and reacted as they had in the past with accusations and finger pointing.

A few days after Lutz Haberlandt's violent death, the West Berlin police received anonymous tips that helped to establish the identity of the victim.[6] The information was provided by relatives of Lutz Haberlandt who lived in East Berlin. It was reported that the day after his death, East Berlin policemen and a state prosecutor appeared at his parent's home at four o'clock in the morning to inform them of his death. The mother asked if her son had been shot, which they confirmed. Then they searched the apartment and pressured the parents into agreeing to have the corpse cremated. The funeral took place on July 8 at the Weissensee Cemetery.

Preliminary proceedings against the former border guards involved in the shooting of Lutz Haberlandt were opened in the nineties. It was determined without a doubt that the deadly bullet had been shot by Private K. He was sentenced as a young offender in March 1996 to a year and a half on probation.[7]

Christine Brecht

1 See "Einzel-Information Nr. 335/62 [des MfS-]ZAIG über den beim versuchten Grenzdurchbruch am 27.5.1962 in der Nähe des KPP Invalidenstrasse tödlich verletzten Lutz Haberlandt, o.D.," in: BStU, MfS, ZAIG Nr. 581, Bl. 21.

2 Interrogation of a witness by the East Berlin investigative police, 28.5.1962, in: StA Berlin, Az. 27 Js 152/90, Bd. 1, Bl. 151–154.

3 See "Bericht [des MfS]/HA IX/Morduntersuchungskommission, 28.5.1962," in: BStU, MfS, AS 185/66, Bl. 123–126.

4 See "Rapport Nr. 147 des PdVP Berlin/Operativstab, 28.5.1962," in: PHS, Bestand PdVP-Rapporte, n. pag.; "Spitzenmeldung des MdI/Bepo/1.GB (B)/III. Grenzabteilung betr. versuchter Grenzdurchbruch mit Schusswaffengebrauch, 27.5.1962," in: BArch, VA-07/8371, Bl. 3, also "Einzel-Information Nr. 337/62 [des MfS-] ZAIG über einen verhinderten Grenzdurchbruch am Alexanderufer, in der Nähe des KPP Invalidenstrasse, am 27.5.1962, 28.5.1962," in: BStU, MfS, ZAIG Nr. 581, Bl. 23–25.

5 See Isabel Atzl/Volker Hess/Thomas Schnalke (eds.), *Zeitzeugen Charité. Arbeitswelten der Psychiatrischen und Nervenklinik 1940–1999*, Münster, 2005, p. 38.

6 See "Bericht der West-Berliner Polizei, 5.6.1962," in: StA Berlin, Az. 27 Js 152/90, Bd. 1, Bl. 43.

7 See "Urteil des Landgerichts Berlin vom 26.3.1996," in: Ibid., Bd. 5, Bl. 110–126.

Axel Hannemann

born on April 27, 1945

shot dead on June 5, 1962
in the Spree River near the Reichstag building
at the sector border between
Berlin-Mitte and Berlin-Tiergarten

Axel Hannemann was born in Buchhain, Lusatia, in April 1945, just a few days before the war in Europe came to an end. He grew up with three siblings in Cottbus where his father worked in a general store. He was 17 years old, living with his parents and soon to begin an apprenticeship when he was shot and killed at the Wall while trying to leave East Germany on June 5, 1962. Later, in an account of her memories, his mother wrote that the news of his death was totally unexpected and deeply pained his parents and siblings.[1]

They did not know what had led him to escape. They had not even known that he was planning to escape. Wolfgang Hannemann later said that he did not think it was for political reasons – his younger brother just wanted to have a better life and live differently.[2] His brother Jürgen thought that he might have been planning to go to his grandparents' home in West Berlin.[3] In a farewell note that Axel Hannemann left his relatives, he asked them to try to understand his unexpected actions and added as a form of justification: "I have no other choice. I'll explain my reasons to you when I have made it. But for now I can say that I have done nothing wrong."[4]

Axel Hannemann took a train from Cottbus to East Berlin on June 5, 1962. Upon reaching the city center he headed towards the Marschall Bridge, not far from the sector border which crosses the Spree River between Schiffbauerdamm and Reichstagsufer. This is where cargo ships with authorization to pass through East Germany went through customs control before proceeding to the West Berlin environs. It was 5 p.m. when the young man jumped from the bridge onto a barge that had already passed through the customs control and was heading to the West.[5] But the ship captain refused to take the fleeing man with him. He instead stopped the ship and notified the customs and border guards. Axel Hannemann got into a scuffle with the captain but was able to free himself. He jumped into the river and tried to swim to the West Berlin riverbank when two border policemen fired at him from close range. Just meters away from his goal, he was fatally hit and sank beneath the water's surface. According to the autopsy report, he died from a bullet through his skull. It could not be determined with certainty how many bullets had hit him and how many had entered and exited his body.[6]

Two hours later East Berlin firemen pulled his dead body from the water. These events took place right behind the Reichstag building, which was situated on West Berlin territory. West Berlin police and members of the press soon arrived at the scene and photographed the body as it was retrieved and taken away. The next day West Berlin newspapers ran headlines such as "Murder of Fugitive at the Reichstag" and "Fugitive Shot and Killed in the Spree."

The strong reaction to Axel Hannemann's death reflected the tense situation in the divided city in the summer of 1962. Incidents at the Berlin Wall were occurring in rapid succession, while the tone of the propaganda war between the East and West was growing increasingly aggressive. Military files show that the East German leadership investigated the victim and his family, hoping to be able to use the case for its own interests. Unable to find anything damaging on Axel Hannemann, they were confirmed in their suspicion that he had been attempting to "flee the republic." He had not been a "roamer," nor had he drawn negative attention to himself or attracted the attention of the East German police. Cottbus informed East Berlin that he had even taken dancing lessons.[7] Nonetheless, the East German minister of the interior Karl Maron wrote a press release stating that the "criminal" had died of his injuries after trying violently to break through the "state border."[8] The East German press published the minister's words, reinforcing the government's efforts to demonize the fugitive.[9]

Meanwhile in West Berlin, the police and public prosecutor's office had begun an investigation of the border guards who had shot Axel Hannemann and they made the case public. The Chief of Police offered a reward of 3,000 German marks for tips leading to the identification of the perpetrator. A similar search had taken place once before when Roland Hoff was shot in the Teltow Canal on August 29, 1961. Again the wanted posters were directed mostly at the border guards on the other side of the barrier. Posters were hung along the Wall at places clearly visible to the border guards.[10] The West Berlin authorities were hoping that this drastic measure would appeal to the guards' sense of responsibility and make it quite clear to them that they should at some point expect to be held accountable for shooting a fugitive.

Once again it would take another thirty years before the gunmen could be legally prosecuted. By then, however, the former border guard identified as responsible for the deadly shots had already died. The second guard who had also aimed shots at the young man was, however, found guilty of joint manslaughter in September 1993 and sentenced to two years in prison, commuted to probation. The verdict stated that he had acted in complicity with his guard leader and had to be held accountable for "his last deadly shot at Axel Hannemann, understood as a shared effort by the two guards."[11]

Christine Brecht

1 See Charlotte Hannemann, "In schwerer Zeit," in: Werner Filmer/ Heribert Schwan, *Opfer der Mauer. Die geheimen Protokolle des Todes*, Munich, 1991, pp. 102–103.

2 See "Der Finger am Abzug," TV documentary by Heribert Schwan und Werner Filmer, WDR, 1991.

3 Letter from Jürgen Hannemann to Maria Nooke, 4.11.2008.

4 "Report [des MdI/Bepo/1.GB/III. Grenzabteilung] zur Vorlage bei Minister Maron, 6.6.1962," in: BArch, VA-07/8461, Bl. 29.

5 See "Bericht des MdI/Bepo/1.GB/III. Grenzabteilung zum versuchten Grenzdurchbruch im Abschnitt der 2. Kompanie der III. Grenzabteilung am 5.6.1962, 5.6.1962," in. BArch, DY 30/IV 2/12/76, Bd. 3, Bl. 9–11, also "Einzel-Information Nr. 361/62 [des MfS-ZAIG], 6.6.1962," in: BStU, MfS, ZAIG Nr. 581, Bl. 30–31.

6 See "Obduktionsbericht des IGM der HU, 6.6.1962," in: StA Berlin, Az. 2 Js 153/90, Bd. 1, Bl. 103–112.

7 See "Bericht [des MdI/Bepo/1.GB/III. Grenzabteilung] zur Vorlage bei Minister Maron, 6.6.1962," in: BArch, VA-07/8461, Bl. 29–30.

8 See "Mitteilung der Pressestelle des MdI, o. D.," in: Ibid., Bl. 20–21.

9 See, for example, "Grenzverletzer gestellt," in: *Berliner Zeitung*, 7.6.1962.

10 See, for example, "Grenzrapporte Nr. 160/62 und 161/62 des MdI/Kommando/Bepo/Op. Diensthabender, 10.6.1962 und 11.6.1962," in: BArch, VA-07/4739, Bd. 5, n. pag.

11 "Urteil des Landgerichts Berlin vom 29.9.1993," in: StA Berlin, Az. 2 Js 153/90, Bd. 2, Bl. 232–255, quote Bl. 244, excerpts printed in: Klaus Marxen/ Gerhard Werle/ Toralf Rummler/ Petra Schäfter (eds.), *Strafjustiz und DDR-Unrecht, Bd. 2: Gewalttaten an der deutsch-deutschen Grenze*, Berlin, 2002, pp. 217–238.

Erna Kelm

born on July 21, 1908

drowned on June 11, 1962
in the Havel River
on the outer ring between Sacrow (Potsdam city district)
and Berlin-Zehlendorf

In the early morning hours of July 11, 1962, a fisherman on the West Berlin side of the Havel River noticed the body of a woman floating in the water. He notified the police, who brought the body to land by boat a short time later. At this spot south of Nikolskoe, the border to East Germany ran through the middle of the river. The West Berlin district of Zehlendorf was situated on the one side; Sacrow, which belonged to the East German district of Potsdam, on the other. It was soon learned that the dead woman came from Sacrow. Her East German identification card, hidden in her sock, identified her as Erna Kelm from Sacrow, 53 years old. She was born on July 21, 1908 in Frankfurt (Oder). Everything suggested that she had tried to swim across the Havel to West Berlin. She was carrying other documents in a plastic bag on her body and was also wearing a life jacket under her clothes.[1]

The West Berlin investigation came to the following conclusions: "Because Frau Kelm was wearing a life jacket under her clothes it has been determined that she was attempting to flee to West Berlin by swimming across the river. According to the autopsy report, the cause of death was drowning. Upon the request of her living kin in Potsdam, her body was sent there."[2]

There was no trace of the body after it was transported to Potsdam. Nothing is known about the relatives of Erna Kelm or where she is buried. Even the West Berlin investigation, which documented the retrieval of the body from the water, was closed shortly thereafter and the file was sent to the Central Registry Office in Salzgitter. When the case was re-opened 30 years later, the original investigation findings were confirmed.[3]

Erna Kelm, who had last worked as the director of a special care facility, had lived in the West before the Wall was built. She moved from Potsdam to Lübeck in August 1947 without bothering to obtain the necessary permit issued by the occupying powers at that time. She worked as a nurse in Lübeck. In March 1948 she moved to West Berlin, where she had a position as nurse's assistant in a children's home for refugees. Because she often left West Berlin to visit her children in Potsdam, she was, according to police data, "suspected of engaging in intelligence activities," but this accusation remained unconfirmed.[4] It did, however, lead to her being interrogated in November 1953 after which she moved back to Potsdam because, in her own words, she missed her children.

Besides the files in the Central Registry Office in Salzgitter, the fate of Erna Kelm is otherwise only documented by a few newspaper reports. On June 13, 1962, the West Berlin newspaper "Tagesspiegel" reported on numerous incidents that had occurred at the Berlin Wall over the 1962 Whitsun holidays. One of the incidents involved the body of a woman retrieved from the lower Havel on Whitsum Monday, who was believed to have drowned while trying to flee.[5] The main focus of the report, however, was on the general concern over the rising tensions in Berlin. The Warsaw Pact members had submitted a statement over the holiday weekend announcing their plan to sign a separate peace treaty with East Germany if American-Soviet talks were not able to "normalize" the situation in West Berlin and remove the "occupying regime." The Soviet Union even sent a note of protest to the three western Allies, strongly criticizing the involvement of West Berlin police in border incidents at the Wall.[6] The mayor of West Berlin, Willy Brandt, used strong words to firmly dismiss the Soviet protest. "We will never be able to accept the Wall as something human or just," he declared. "As long as shots are fired at the Wall, as long as Germans who want to go from one side of the city to the other are called criminals and killed, it will not be possible to expand trade."[7]

On the first anniversary of the Berlin Wall, the Federal Ministry of All-German Affairs published a brochure taking stock of the unconstitutional crimes that occurred at the Wall. The document also mentioned Erna Kelm's fatal escape attempt,[8] which led to her name being added to the official lists of registered fatal victims. In this way the memory of the 53-year-old woman who drowned at the border to West Berlin was preserved.[9]

Christine Brecht

---

1 See "Bericht der West-Berliner Polizei [Abschrift des Tatbefundberichtes des KRes S-Bereitschaftsdienst], 11.6.1962," in: StA Berlin, Az. 27 AR 63/91, Bl. 10–11; "Vermerk der West-Berliner Polizei, 13.6.1962," in: Ibid., Bl. 12; "Vermerk der West-Berliner Polizei, 20.6.1962," in: Ibid., Bl. 13.

2 "Schlussvermerk der West-Berliner Polizei, 20.6.1962," in: Ibid.

3 See "Verfügung der Staatsanwaltschaft II bei dem Kammergericht Berlin [6 AR 63/91], 30.4.1991," in: Ibid., Bl. 15.

4 "Vermerk der West-Berliner Polizei, 13.6.1962," in: Ibid., Bl. 12.

5 See *Der Tagesspiegel*, 13.6.1962.

6 See "USA sehen ermutigende Anzeichen. Washington nimmt Moskauer Berlin-Erklärung 'nicht ungünstig' auf," in: *Frankfurter Rundschau*, 13.6.1962; "Brandt: Berlin lässt sich nicht schrecken," in: *Telegraf*, 13.6.1962.

7 *Der Tagesspiegel*, 13.6.1962.

8 See Bundesministerium für Gesamtdeutsche Fragen (ed.), *Verletzungen der Menschenrechte. Unrechtshandlungen und Zwischenfälle an der Berliner Sektorengrenze seit Errichtung der Mauer*, Bonn/Berlin, 1962, p. 25.

9 See, for example, "Aufstellung über die bei Fluchtversuchen an der DL getöteten u. verletzten Personen, o.D. (July 1962)," in: BArch, B 137, Nr. 15650, n. pag., and the list "Opfer der Mauer" of the senator for security and order of 10.8.1964, in: LAB, B Rep 002, Nr. 3660, n. pag.

Wolfgang Glöde

born on February 1, 1949

shot dead on June 11, 1962
in the "Sorgenfrei" garden settlement
at the sector border between
Berlin-Treptow and Berlin-Neukölln

An East Berlin schoolboy was killed in an accident that occurred on June 11, 1962 in a garden settlement in Berlin-Treptow. The settlement, called "Sorgenfrei" and meaning "carefree" in German, is located right at the border of the West Berlin district of Neukölln. The grounds had been heavily guarded ever since the inner-city sector border was sealed off on August 13, 1961. To prevent escape attempts in the outer areas near the border, armed guards patrolled the pathways between the garden allotments twenty-four hours a day; even on Whitsun Monday 1962. On this day two border policemen accidently fired a shot while showing their machine pistols to children in the complex. The 13-year-old Wolfgang Glöde was fatally injured.[1]

Wolfgang Glöde was born on February 1, 1949 in East Berlin and grew up in the "Sorgenfrei" garden settlement at Kiefholzstrasse in Treptow. His family had lived there since 1930. He had two older siblings. His father worked as a metal worker for the Berlin Machine Repair Center. His mother was a housewife. Because there was still a housing shortage after the war, the Glöde family, like so many others families in the neighborhood, moved permanently into its leased garden property.[2] The lives of the residents' who lived here were dramatically altered after the Wall was built. Before August 13, 1961, a number of paths led from the settlement into Neukölln, but afterwards they were all cut off from the neighboring district. Over time a military border regime with guard posts, watchdogs, barbed wire, barriers and observation towers was established around them. "Unauthorized people" were denied access to the allotment gardens. The "border population" was expected to adjust to this oppressive situation and this is why the communist regime engaged in patronizing propaganda to win over the residents while at the same time strongly distrusting them.[3] The permanent presence of armed border police posed a security hazard to them but was tacitly accepted by the military leadership.

On June 11, 1962 Wolfgang Glöde had spent the entire day with Horst und Peter W., friends his age from the garden settlement. In the afternoon they went to see the soccer games at the local field. Around 6 p.m. two border policemen came by. They had been assigned patrol duty at the nearby border grounds that Whitsun Monday. Although it was against the rules, the two 19-year-old privates engaged in a conversation with the children. Wolfgang Glöde and his friends wanted to know how the machine pistols the border guards carried worked. The men gave in to their pleas and showed the boys their weapons. Without removing the magazine, Private K. released the safety of his Kalashnikov, causing the accident. While loading the gun, K. mistakenly set off the trigger and a shot was fired, hitting Wolfgang Glöde at close range. He was shot through a lung and died shortly thereafter.[4]

Startled by the sound of the shot, Wolfgang Glöde's parents rushed to the site of the accident. We can only imagine what tragic scene took place when they saw their son dying on the ground. The files of the border police and Ministry of State Security do not reveal how the residents reacted. What is documented, however, is how the East German authorities attempted to nip all hostility and criticism in the bud. The border police, in cooperation with the Treptow Communist Party district leadership, passed a series of measures "to prevent the events from being falsely presented to the population."[5] These included the deployment of additional guards and meetings with parents and teachers of Wolfgang Glöde.

The military leadership determined that Private K. was responsible for Wolfgang Glöde's death. The commander of the 5th Border Division stressed in his investigation report that both border guards had been advised by their supervisors on the correct way to handle and use their weapons before they went on duty. He thus concluded "that the events were caused by blatant negligence on the part of Private K."[6] In another passage he wrote that the accident proved that certain guards did not handle their weapons responsibly. This required that "strong disciplinary and legal measures be taken."[7]

Private K. was arrested on the spot and interrogated by a military attorney who immediately opened an investigation of negligent homicide.[8] It is not known whether K. was tried by a military court or what his punishment was.[9]

News of Wolfgang Glöde's death quickly spread to West Berlin where authorities initially assumed that the information was false and that the boy was more likely shot while trying to escape.[10] This was suggested in a press release that the Senate published on June 15, 1962.[11] Over the following days newspapers ran headlines such as "Pankow Border Guards Shoot [...] East Berlin Schoolboy" and "Wolfgang in Mortal Agony for an Hour."[12] Even Chancellor Adenauer and the mayor of Berlin, Willy Brandt, mentioned the name of Wolfgang Glöde in speeches they held on June 17, 1962, the Day of German Unity, both strongly condemning the shots fired at fugitives fleeing at the Wall.[13] Sometime the following year the law enforcement agency in the West learned that the boy was indeed killed by accident, after which his name was removed from the list of Wall victims.[14]

A quiet funeral took place in the presence of his family at the Baumschulenweg Cemetery in Treptow. The tombstone bears the inscription: "Here rests our dear son, brother and brother-in-law Wolfgang Glöde, *1.2.1949, killed on 11.6.1962. Our hearts will always be with you until our final days."

Christine Brecht

1 See "Bericht des MdI/Bepo/1.GB/V. Grenzabteilung über den fahrlässigen Schusswaffengebrauch mit tödlichem Ausgang, 11.6.1962," in: BArch, DY 30/IV 2/12/76, Bd. 3, Bl. 90–93.

2 See conversation conducted by Christine Brecht with Gisela K., Wolfgang Glöde's sister, 20.6.2007.

3 See Dirk Keil, "Nichts blieb, wie es war. Vierundsiebzig Tage im Jahr 1961," in: Falk Blask (ed.), *Geteilte Nachbarschaft. Erkundungen im ehemaligen Grenzgebiet Treptow und Neukölln,* Berlin, 1999, pp. 61–74.

4 See "Bericht des MdI/Bepo/1.GB/V. Grenzabteilung über den fahrlässigen Schusswaffengebrauch mit tödlichem Ausgang, 11.6.1962," in: BArch, DY 30/IV 2/12/76, Bd. 3, Bl. 90–93, also "Informationsbericht [des MfS]/HA IX/Mord- und Branduntersuchungskommission, 12.6.1962," in: BStU, MfS, AS Nr. 185/66, Bl. 101–104.

5 "Bericht des MdI/Bepo/1.GB/V. Grenzabteilung über den fahrlässigen Schusswaffengebrauch mit tödlichem Ausgang, 11.6.1962," in: BArch, DY 30/IV 2/12/76, Bd. 3, Bl. 93.

6 Ibid., Bl. 92.

7 "Grenzrapport des MdI/Bepo/1.GB (B)/OpD, 12.6.1962," in: BArch, VA-07/4752, Bd. 3, Bl. 116.

8 See "Informationsbericht des [MfS]/HA IX/Mord- und Branduntersuchungskommission, 12.6.1962," in: BStU, MfS, AS Nr. 185/66, Bl. 101–104.

9 No corresponding documents could be found in the Military Archive Freiburg or in the BStU Archive.

10 See *Der Tagesspiegel,* 16.6.1962; *Berliner Morgenpost,* 16.6.1962; *Die Welt,* 16.6.1962.

11 See "Mitteilung der Pressestelle des Innensenators, 15.6.1962," in: LAB, B Rep 002, Nr. 7059, n. pag.

12 See *Der Tagesspiegel,* 16.6.1962; *Der Kurier,* 16.6.1962.

13 See *17. Juni – Reden zum Tag der Deutschen Einheit. Schriftenreihe der Bundeszentrale für politische Bildung,* Bonn, 1964.

14 See letter from the Senator for Security and Order to the Federal Ministry of All-German Affairs regarding communist crimes committed at the demarcation line, 20.8.1963, in: BArch, B 137, Nr. 15650, n. pag., and the list of Wall victims, 21.2.1963, in: Ibid.

Siegfried Noffke

born on December 9, 1939

shot dead on June 28, 1962
at Heinrich-Heine-Strasse 49
at the sector border between
Berlin-Mitte and Berlin-Kreuzberg

Two unidentified people laid a wreath in the West Berlin district of Kreuzberg, not far from the Heinrich-Heine-Strasse border crossing, in the summer of 1962. They were mourning Siegfried Noffke, who was shot and killed on the other side of the Wall two days earlier during a tunnel escape operation. The ribbon decoration bore the inscription: "To our dear Siegfried Noffke as a final farewell from his friends. – He died a victim of the Wall."[1] The twenty-two-year-old West Berliner and two other men were hoping to help their families escape from the other side of the city. Contrary to the rumors spread in East Germany that "armed terrorists had invaded," what happened was far from what they called "a job commissioned by western agents." It was a private undertaking.[2] The tunnel builders were ambushed while opening the tunnel on June 28, and, although they were unarmed, the East German agents ruthlessly fired at them. Stasi files later revealed that an informer within the group had betrayed their plans quite early on.[3]

Siegfried Noffke was born in 1939 in Berlin and grew up in the Soviet sector. The trained bricklayer fled to the western side of the city in the 1950s, lived in the Kreuzberg district and worked as a driver. In May 1961, after his son was born, he married the mother, Hannelore, who lived on the other side of the sector border in Prenzlauer Berg. The newlyweds had probably presumed that the wife and child would be allowed to move to the west side of the city after the wedding. But the East Berlin authorities refused to grant them an exit permit and consequently, when the border was later sealed, they found themselves unexpectedly separated.[4] Like many East-West couples, they had no choice over the following weeks and months but to meet secretly at the border grounds where they could occasionally see and speak to each other briefly across the barrier. This situation continued for almost a year until, at one of these meetings, Siegfried Noffke met a West Berliner who was in the same situation and who invited him to join a tunnel escape project to get their wives over to West Berlin.[5] Siegfried Noffke, Dieter H. and Dieter G. had made considerable progress digging their tunnel, which began in a basement on Sebastianstrasse, a street in Kreuzberg located directly on the border of the East Berlin district of Mitte.

99

The year 1962 is considered the heyday of tunnel-building. A number of people were able to escape through more than a dozen tunnels running beneath the Berlin Wall that year, but it was a thin line between success and failure, and arrests and fatalities were common.[6] Heinz Jercha, a native of West Berlin, was killed by Stasi agents while leading people through a tunnel. In mid-June, when the excavations on Sebastianstrasse were moving forward slowly, the East German border guard Reinhold Huhn died from shots fired by a West Berlin tunnel builder. After that East German propaganda became more openly hostile to "criminal intruders" and the Stasi increased its behind-the-scenes measures to prevent escape operations.

It was only through a coincidence that the East German secret police was able to track down Siegfried Noffke and his fellow tunnel builders. Not aware that her brother was a Stasi informer, one of the East Berliners, who was planning to flee through the tunnel, told him about the tunnel project. The brother, under the alias "Pankow," immediately informed the East Berlin Stasi district administration.[7] Thus, even before Siegfried Noffke had joined the project, the agent mission "Maulwürfe" (moles) was underway with the aim of spying on all the people involved and arresting them all at once when the underground escape route was completed.[8] To achieve this, the informant "Pankow" infiltrated the group by pretending to be someone who wanted to flee. He participated in the preparations without anyone seeing through his duplicity. The betrayer was even present when the tunnel was opened on the afternoon of June 28, 1962. He helped the three tunnel builders break through to the basement where the Stasi agents were expecting them.[9]

According to accounts from surviving tunnel builders, shots were fired as soon as Siegfried Noffke and Dieter H. entered the basement.[10] Stasi files document that one of the Stasi men got rattled and, contrary to the plan to arrest the escape helpers, began shooting.[11] Siegfried Noffke was fatally wounded and Dieter H. suffered major injuries. The informant "Pankow" and another Stasi man also suffered gunshot injuries. Even after the collapse of the East German state, the former Stasi informant Jürgen H. and the man believed to have fired the deadly bullet refused to speak about what had happened. Consequently, the legal proceedings that were opened on the basis of Stasi files in the 1990s had to be discontinued without arraignment due to a lack of sufficient proof.[12]

Although he was critically wounded, Siegfried Noffke was interrogated on the spot so that the Stasi, to quote one of their reports, could squeeze a "confession" out of him.[13] The twenty-two-year-old father seems to have died from his injuries on the way to the hospital. His wife was arrested along with all the other East Berliners who were planning to escape through the tunnel. The informant "Pankow" was also arrested for appearance's sake. They were convicted by the Berlin-Mitte city court in November 1962 of "attempting to leave East Germany illegally" and handed down prison sentences ranging from one to two years. After his arrest Dieter H. was brought to a Stasi prison hospital. In October 1962 he was tried for "state-endangering acts of violence" and for "tempting people to leave East Germany." He was found guilty and sentenced to nine years in prison.

Christine Brecht

1　"Funkmeldung der West-Berliner Polizei, 17.7.1962," in: PHS, Bestand Grenzvorkommnisse, n. pag.

2　See reporting in *Neues Deutschland*, 8.7.1961, and a counter view "Pankow meldet die Erschiessung eines West-Berliners," in: *Der Tagesspiegel*, 8.7.1962.

3　See Bernd Eisenfeld/Roger Engelmann, 13.8.1961. *Mauerbau, Fluchtbewegung und Machtsicherung*, Berlin, 2001, pp. 102–105, and Rainer Hildebrandt, *Es geschah an der Mauer*, 20th edition, Berlin 2003, p. 111.

4　See *Bild-Zeitung*, 9.7.1962; *Der Kurier*, 9.7.1962; *Berliner Morgenpost*, 8.7.1962.

5　See "Bericht der West-Berliner Polizei, 10.6.1965," in: StA Berlin, Az. 2 Js 169/90, Bd. 1, Bl. 89.

6　For context, see Marion Detjen, Ein *Loch in der Mauer. Die Geschichte der Fluchthilfe im geteilten Deutschland 1961–1989,* Munich, 2005, also Dietmar Arnold/Sven Felix Kellerhoff, *Die Fluchttunnel von Berlin*, Berlin, 2008.

7　See "[MfS-] report on a meeting with GI "Pankow," 4.6.1962," in: BStU, Ast. Berlin, AIM 3870/91, Bd. 2, Bl. 1–4.

8　See "Massnahmeplan der VfS Gross-Berlin/Büro des Leiters betr. Beabsichtigter Tunnelbau im Grenzgebiet Heinrich-Heine-Strasse, 5.6.1962," in: BStU, MfS, HA I Nr. 6086, Bl. 221–223; "Massnahmeplan der VfS Gross-Berlin betr. Abschluss des Operativvorgangs 'Maulwürfe,'" 22.6.1962," in: BStU, Ast. Berlin, AIM 3870/91, Bd. 2, Bl. 56–60, also "Ergänzung zum Maßnahmeplan der VfS Gross-Berlin, 22.6.1962," in: Ibid., Bl. 61–63.

9　On the course of events, see especially the report from the VfS Gross-Berlin, 28.6.1962, in: BStU, MfS, HA I Nr. 6086, Bl. 211, 249–250. In contrast, a document apparently manipulated for propaganda purposes: "Einzel-Information Nr. 432/62 des MfS/ZAIG über Aufdeckung eines unterirdischen Stollens in Berlin-Mitte, Heinrich-Heine-Straße 48/49, 30.6.1962," in: BStU, MfS, ZAIG Nr. 619, Bl. 2–6.

10　On testimony from Dieter G., who escaped to West Berlin uninjured, see transcript of West Berlin police witness hearing of a resident of the building from which the tunnel was dug, 28.6.1962, in: StA Berlin, Az. 2 Js 169/90, Bd. 1, Bl. 13–14. Dieter H. testified both after his release from prison in 1971 and in 1994. See "Niederschrift der Zeugenvernehmung eines ehemaligen Tunnelbauers durch die West-Berliner Polizei, 8.11.1972," in: Ibid. Bl. 137, and "Niederschrift der Zeugenvernehmung eines ehemaligen Tunnelbauers durch die Berliner Polizei, 25.1.1994," in: Ibid., Bd. 2, Bl. 274–280.

11　See "[MfS-]Schlussbericht zum Operativvorgang 'Maulwürfe,'" 28.6.1962, in: BStU, MfS, AOP 9745/65, Bd. 1, Bl. 418–510, here Bl. 507; see also report from VfS Gross-Berlin, 28.6.1962, in: BStU, MfS, HA I Nr. 6086, Bl. 211, 249–250, and "Schlussbericht der VfS Gross-Berlin/BdL/AG Staatsgrenze betr. Operativvorgang 'Maulwürfe', 28.6.1962," in: Ibid., Bl. 251–263.

12　See "Verfügung der Staatsanwaltschaft II bei dem Landgericht Berlin, 25.11.1994," in: StA Berlin, Az. 2 Js 165/90, Bd. 2, Bl. 344–346, and ibid., 21.1.1997, in: Ibid., Bd. 3, Bl. 127–136, here Bl. 135.

13　See "[MfS-] Bericht, 28.6.1962," in: BStU, MfS, HA I Nr. 6086, Bl. 283.

Peter Fechter

born on January 14, 1944

shot dead on August 17, 1962
on Zimmerstrasse near the Friedrich / Zimmerstrasse
border crossing ("Checkpoint Charlie")
at the sector border between
Berlin-Mitte and Berlin-Kreuzberg

T he atmosphere in Berlin had been very tense all summer long in 1962. An observer remarked in June of that year that sheet lightning was flashing at the
Wall more often than ever.[1] Hardly a day or a week passed without a bloody incident occurring. Demonstrations on August 13, the first anniversary of the Berlin
Wall, showed that the West Berlin population was increasingly less willing to toler-
ate the ongoing division of the city and the violence against people trying to flee.
Moreover, the events that led to the death of Peter Fechter on August 17, 1962
triggered outrage in West Berlin and kept the city on edge for days.

It was early afternoon when shots were fired on Zimmerstrasse, where the Wall
cut right through the neighborhood that had once been Berlin's lively newspaper
quarter. The West Berlin police received the first dispatches at 2:12 p.m.[2] It soon
became clear that the border guards' shots were aimed at two teenagers who had
tried to flee over the Wall between Charlottenstrasse and Markgrafenstrasse. One
of them, the 18-year-old construction worker Helmut K., was able to make it
through the hail of bullets to the West. But his friend Peter Fechter, also eighteen,
was hit and remained on the ground right in front of the border wall. Many people
on both sides of the barrier witnessed the tragedy that followed. The badly wounded
young man was screaming loudly for help, but no reaction was taken for a long
time on the East Berlin side. Standing on a ladder, West Berlin police officers asked
him his name and threw bandages to him over the Wall. But they did not want to
endanger themselves by climbing over the Wall to help him. Members of the American military police from the nearby Checkpoint Charlie also did not want to risk
stepping on East Berlin territory because, given the ongoing conflict over responsibility for the divided city, they feared it might trigger a military conflict. "It's not
our problem," one of them was quoted as saying. As a consequence, 50 long minutes passed before Peter Fechter's screams eventually ceased. Finally East German
border troops carried him away behind an artificially produced veil of fog. He was
officially declared dead a short time later in the East Berlin People's Police Hospital. His death was announced on East German radio that night.[3]

At the same time, pictures taken by western photographers and camera crews of the young man dying were shown around the world.[4] They turned Peter Fechter's agonizing death into a symbol of the East German border regime's inhumanity.[5] Today, no chronicle of the 20th century or review of Cold War history omits the name Peter Fechter. The inscription on his gravestone, "remembered by all," sadly proved itself true.

Peter Fechter, who died so publicly and painfully on that August 17, 1962, was a quiet, inconspicuous East German teenager. Born during the war in 1944 in Berlin, he grew up with two older sisters in humble conditions in the Weissensee district. His father worked as an engine builder; his mother was a salesclerk. Their only son left school at the age of 14 and began an apprenticeship as a bricklayer, a vocation that was in high demand during the reconstruction period following the war. His oldest sister was married and lived on the west side of the city. Her parents and siblings had visited her regularly before the Wall was built.[6] Before passing his qualification exam, Peter Fechter met Helmut K., who was doing an apprenticeship in the same company. In early 1962 they were both involved in rebuilding the former Kaiser-Wilhelm-Palais, a palace on the Unter den Linden boulevard.[7] Helmut K. later put on record in West Berlin that the two of them had been thinking about fleeing for a long time and were looking for a good opportunity to explore the border grounds, but that they did not yet have a concrete plan, nor had they begun any specific preparations.[8] The investigation that the Stasi staff conducted after his death found "no evidence of a prepared border breach."[9]

It appears that the two youths had hardly discussed with each other their reasons for wanting to flee. They knew that they were both unable to identify with the existing political situation and dreamed of a better life in the West. A Stasi file also revealed that Peter Fechter's company had denied him a trip to West Germany and this may have played a role in his decision to flee. But his work evaluation was impeccable. "Colleague F. is a willing and hard-working craftsman. Loafing and absenteeism are not a problem with him."[10] Helmut K. also spoke of him as "a good colleague, cordial and honest, and that is why I hung out with him. He was a good acquaintance of mine, although we were not really friends."[11] One day, Helmut K. explained, while wandering about, they noticed a dilapidated building on Schützenstrasse that had once housed a carpentry workshop. Its back windows faced Zimmerstrasse and extended almost to the Wall. During their lunch break two days later, they spontaneously agreed not to return to the construction site and to check out the building instead.

The two young men were able to reach the back of the building from the carpenter workshop without being noticed. They found a window in the storage room that had not been bricked up. When they heard voices a little later they feared that they might be discovered and hastily jumped out the window. Having taken off their shoes earlier, they ran in their socks to the Wall, just a few meters away. When the first shots were fired, Helmut K. said Peter Fechter remained motionless as if he were rooted to the ground. "I had reached the Wall by then, jumped up and forced myself through the barbed wire on the top of the Wall. I don't know why Peter didn't climb up. He should have been at the Wall before me. He didn't say anything and I had the feeling when the shots were fired that Peter Fechter was in a state of shock. I called out loudly to him: 'Come on, come on, hurry up!' But he didn't move."[12]

The border troop files reveal that the two fugitives were shot at from both sides without warning. Four border guards fired a total of 35 shots. Peter Fechter, hit as he jumped up on to the Wall, fell backwards and leaned against the Wall support.[13] The report claimed that he had already given up his flight at this point, but instead of arresting the defenseless young man, the border guards took up a new position and continued firing until he collapsed to the ground. When he began screaming loudly for help, the guards took cover, supposedly because they felt threatened by the West Berlin police officers on the other side who were pointing their guns at them.

In the East mistakes were later admitted and followed up with demands that "in this kind of case [...] an injured person should be removed directly from the border grounds because the enemy should not be provided with any argument for getting riled up."[14] Official East German reports, however, continued to present the view that the conduct of the West Berlin police, photographers and camera teams was responsible for causing delays in the retrieval of the injured fugitive. The chief propagandist, Karl-Eduard von Schnitzler, went so far as to justify the border guards' brutality as being good for and in the interest of the state. In his commentary he dishonored the victim with the following words: "And when this kind of element [...] is wounded directly on the border and not retrieved immediately – then a huge fuss is made. [...] The life of each one of our brave young men in uniform is more important to us than the life of a lawbreaker. By staying away from our state border – blood, tears and screams can be avoided."[15]

This commentary was broadcast on the East German radio program "Schwarzer Kanal" on the same day that Peter Fechter's funeral took place at the cemetery of the Resurrection Congregation in Berlin-Weissensee. In addition to the painful loss of their only son, the family of the deceased was subjected to reprisals from the East German government for decades. In July 1990 Peter Fechter's sister pressed charges that opened preliminary proceedings and that ultimately ended in the conviction of two guards. Found guilty of manslaughter, they were sentenced to 20 and 21 months in prison, a sentence that was commuted to probation.[16] During the main proceedings, Ruth Fechter, the victim's younger sister who served as a joint plaintiff in the trial, expressed herself through her attorneys. They explained that she thought it important to speak out, to no longer be "damned by passivity and inactivity" and to get out of "the objectified role that she had been put in until then." She movingly described how she and her family experienced the tragic death of her brother and had felt powerless to act against his public defamation. They had been sworn to secrecy, an involuntary obligation that put the family under tremendous pressure. "We were ostracized and experienced hostile encounters daily. They were not born of our personal desire, but were instead imposed on us by others, becoming a central element in the life of the Fechter Family." After all those years, participating in the trial as a joint plaintiff offered Ruth Fechter an opportunity to participate in the effort to explain, research and evaluate the circumstances of her brother's death. And she added that the legal perspective occasionally overlooks the fact that in this case "world history fatally intersected with the fate of a single individual."[17]

Christine Brecht

1 Sebastian Haffner, "Auf der Flucht erschossen. Will Chruschtschow den Ulbricht zügeln?," in: *Christ und Welt*, 22.6.1962, p. 5.

2 "Funkmeldung der West-Berliner Polizei, 17.8.1962," in: PHS, Sammlung Peter Fechter, n. pag.

3 See "Ereignismeldung der West-Berliner Polizei, 18.8.1962," in: PHS, Bestand Ereignismeldungen der West-Berliner Schutzpolizei, n. pag.

4 See Christoph Hamann, "Schnappschuss und Ikone. Das Foto von Peter Fechters Fluchtversuch 1962," in: *Zeithistorische Forschungen/Studies in Contemporary History*, Online-Ausgabe, 2 (2005), H. 2, URL: http://www.zeithistorische-forschungen.de/16126041-Hamann-2-2005.

5 See Roman Grafe, "'Ein Akt barbarischer Unmenschlichkeit'. Der Tod des Mauerflüchtlings Peter Fechter vor 40 Jahren," in: *Deutschland Archiv* 35 (2002), pp. 793–798.

6 See "Ermittlungsbericht [des MfS/]KD Berlin-Weissensee betr. Peter Fechter, 18.8.1962," in: BStU, MfS, ZKG Nr. 7610, Bl. 9–10, and "Aktenvermerk [des MfS]HA V/2 betr. Feststellung der Zusammenhänge des Grenzdurchbruchs von Peter Fechter und deren ehem. Verbindungen, 11.1.1963," in: Ibid., Bl. 11–14.

7 See "Ermittlungsbericht der VfS Gross-Berlin/Abt. III/3 betr. Peter Fechter, 18.8.1962," in: Ibid., Bl. 3–4, and personnel record card from Peter Fechter, 2.8.1961, in: Ibid., Bl. 25–26.

8 "Niederschrift der Zeugenvernehmung des Mitflüchtlings von Peter Fechter durch die West-Berliner Polizei, 21.8.1962," in: LAB, B Rep 002, Nr. 3660, n. pag.

9 "Bericht [des MfS]/Abt. VII/1 betr. vollendeten und versuchten Grenzdurchbruch an der Staatsgrenze, 18.8.1962," in: BStU, MfS, ZKG Nr. 7610, Bl. 1–2, quote Bl. 2.

10 "Entwurf des Prod.-Abschn.-Ltr/VEB Ingenieurhochbau Berlin betr. Beurteilung des Koll. Peter Fechter, zwecks Reisegenehmigung nach Westdeutschland, 13.6.1962," in: Ibid., Bl. 32.

11 "Niederschrift der Zeugenvernehmung des Mitflüchtlings von Peter Fechter durch die West-Berliner Polizei, 21.8.1962," in: LAB, B Rep 002, Nr. 3660, n. pag.

12 Ibid.

13 See "Bericht des MdI/1.GB (B)/Kommandeur zum versuchten Grenzdurchbruch in Verbindung mit einem vollzogenen Grenzdurchbruch am 17.8.62, 17.8.1962," in: BArch, VA-07/16930, Bl. 2–5.

14 "Einzel-Information Nr. 539/62 des MfS/ZAIG über den schweren Grenzdurchbruch in der Zimmerstrasse am 17.8.1962, 18.8.1962," in: BStU, MfS, ZAIG Nr. 581, Bl. 40–43, here Bl. 43.

15 Schwarzer Kanal, DDR-Fernsehen, 27.8.1962.

16 See "Urteil des Landgerichts Berlin vom 5.3.1997," in: StA Berlin, Az. 27 Js 83/90, Bd. 6, Bl. 120a–120g, here Bl. 120a–120b. Excerpts printed in: Klaus Marxen u.a. (eds.), *Strafjustiz und DDR-Unrecht, Bd. 2: Gewalttaten an der deutsch-deutschen Grenze*, Berlin, 2002, pp. 239–248.

17 Uwe Ewald, Schlussvortrag für die Nebenklägerin Ruth Fechter. Urteil gegen ehemalige Angehörige der DDR-Grenztruppen im Fechter-Prozess, in: *Neue Justiz* 51 (1997), pp. 407–408.

Hans-Dieter Wesa

born on January 10, 1943

shot dead on August 23, 1962
at the Bornholmer Strasse S-Bahn station
at the sector border between
Berlin-Prenzlauer Berg and Berlin-Wedding

In April 1962 the transport police officer Hans-Dieter Wesa's unit was transferred from Leipzig to Berlin to guard the border stations and railroad facilities. The 19-year-old man was assigned duty as a border guard at the Berlin Wall. On August 23, 1962 he was on duty at the Bornholmer Strasse S-Bahn station, located near the border to the West Berlin district of Wedding.[1] He and the 18-year-old Adolf B. were assigned to a post at the "ghost station" beneath the Böse Bridge, where trains passed by without stopping. They quickly began talking because Hans-Dieter was acquainted with B. from the days when they had served together in the Leipzig transport police. B. later recounted a conversation where Wesa said, as if in jest, that his sister in West Germany would certainly be surprised when he showed up there.[2] B. had not taken the comment seriously because Wesa was considered a reliable comrade. He only became suspicious after dark when Wesa, on the pretense that he had to turn on the lights on the other side of the track, disappeared.

As soon as B. began looking for him, he realized that Wesa had climbed over the border fence to West Berlin. When Wesa ignored his order to come back, he "made use of his firearms," as the official reports euphemistically put it, although Wesa was already past the sector border and had reached West Berlin territory.[3] B. described what happened: "I ordered Wesa to stop. Wesa turned around and when he saw me he tried to run away. I fired a burst of about six shots at him, after which he fell to the ground and remained there motionless. I then fired another burst of fire, about six shots at him."[4] Hans-Dieter Wesa probably died immediately. Criminal and forensic investigations in West Berlin conducted soon after his death revealed that he was shot in the thigh in such a way that he must have fallen to the ground before B. approached the fence from the other side and shot him again from close proximity in the face and body, killing him.[5]

The West Berlin Chief of Police pressed charges against an "unknown Soviet zone transport police officer" although in the divided city even a case with such overwhelming evidence had little chance of bringing a perpetrator to justice.[6]

After East Germany collapsed, the Berlin public prosecutor's office opened the investigation again, which led in 1990 to criminal proceedings against B. When the accused tried to evade police questioning, he was placed in temporary detention in November 1993. He was ultimately charged with manslaughter in June 1994.[7] But the case never came to trial because Adolf B. took his own life in September 1994.[8] He never revealed what reasons or circumstances led him to shoot down his comrade.

Hans-Dieter Wesa grew up in Trebitz near Wettin. His parents came from Galicia. His father was a carpenter and had had his own workshop in his hometown in Ukraine. After the Second World War began, the family was resettled "back home to the Reich" as part of Nazi policy. After the Polish population was expelled from the Warthegau, the family was assigned a farm lot. Hans-Dieter Wesa was born there in January 1943 in a town called Schlewen in the rural district of Gostingen. He was the youngest of four siblings. His father was taken prisoner of war by the Russians rather early in the war. The mother and four children fled westward, away from the Red Army in 1945. After arriving in the Soviet zone of occupation, the local authorities assigned them to Trebitz. When the father returned from captivity in 1949 and began looking for work as a carpenter again, the parents decided to remain in the small community northwest of Halle an der Saale. As devout Christians, they harbored reserve towards the communist regime. They were active in the Protestant Church, where the mother was a member of the church consistory. They supported their eldest son's decision in 1954 to make a new life for himself in Baden-Württemberg in West Germany.[9]

His brother reported that after finishing school, Dieter began an apprenticeship with the railroad company in Halle. After that, in September 1960, just before the Wall was built, he signed up for five years of service with the transport police as a way to advance his career. He was powerless against the transfer to the Berlin sector border and did not like the fact that he had to wear a "different" uniform, especially because he personally rejected the idea of having to shoot at people. The transfer to East Berlin must have brought Hans-Dieter Wesa into a moral conflict. His brother believed that this may have been the ultimate reason why he risked deserting. He did not leave behind an explanation, nor did he in any way indicate that he was planning to escape when he spent his vacation with his parents in Trebitz a few days before he tried to flee. Evidently neither his supervisors nor his comrades had any idea of his intentions. Wesa appeared completely at ease with his situation. He was friendly and open and was regarded as an "exemplary officer of the East German Police." Just a few weeks before his escape attempt, in July 1962, he supposedly even helped hinder a "border breach," which is why he was prematurely advanced to head constable.[10] In his final report, the commander of the 1st Border Brigade wrote that the trust "that was invested in him, through his promotion and assignment to the open position at the state border to West Berlin" was absolutely justified. For lack of any other explanation, he concluded that "despite his good service and participation in politics class, the deserter did not have a strong class consciousness and deceived his supervisors and comrades."[11]

In West Berlin the brutal act of violence against Hans-Dieter Wesa – just days after Peter Fechter's death – triggered strong feelings of disgust, but there was also concern that mass protests might erupt again. The press reported that Mayor Willy

Brandt and Senator Klaus Schütz visited the death strip that very evening. Over the next few days the mayor and the senator, along with other politicians, tried to express their sympathies in a way that would prevent emotions from flaring up even more.

When Hans-Dieter Wesa's brother in Eybach, in Baden-Württemberg, read in the newspaper about what had happened in Berlin, he immediately contacted the West Berlin authorities and arranged for his brother's body to be sent to his residence so that he could be buried there. The deputy commander of the West Berlin uniformed police gave the funeral eulogy.[12] A number of West Berlin police officers also attended the official memorial service that had taken place in Berlin two days earlier on August 25, 1962. They wanted to pay their last respects to their East German colleague.

Christine Brecht

1 See "Bericht des [MfS] / HAVII / 7 betr. besondere Vorkommnisse an der Staatsgrenze in Berlin am 23.8.1962 gegen 20.15 Uhr, 24.8.1962," in: BStU, MfS, AP 20359 / 62, Bl. 5 – 9; "Bericht des MdI / 1.GB (B) / Kommandeur über die Fahnenflucht des VF-Oberwachtmeisters Hans-Dieter Wesa, 23.8.1962," in: BArch, DY 30 / IV 2 / 12 / 77, Bd. 4, Bl. 84 – 85, and "Abschlussbericht des MfNV / Stadtkommandantur Berlin / 1.GB / Der Kommandeur über die Fahnenflucht des Owm. Hans-Dieter Wesa, 1. / II.GA, am 23.8.1962 am S-Bahnhof Bornholmer Strasse, 3.9.1962," in: BArch, VA-07 / 17152, Bl. 539.

2 See "Handschriftlicher Bericht des Grenzpostens und Todesschützen betr. Fahnenflucht des Oberwachtmeisters der Trapo Hans-Dieter Wesa, 23.8.1962," in: BStU, MfS, AP 20359 / 62, Bl. 10 –13, here Bl. 10. It was, in fact, not one of his sisters, but actually an older brother who lived in West Germany.

3 See "Bericht des [MfS] / HAVII / 7 betr. besondere Vorkommnisse an der Staatsgrenze in Berlin am 23.8.1962 gegen 20.15 Uhr, 24.8.1962," in: BStU, MfS, AP 20359 / 62, Bl. 6. This report shows that Wesa had already reached West Berlin territory when he was discovered by B., but other military and Stasi reports disguised the true facts, claiming that Wesa was just about to climb over the border fence when he was discovered. See, for example, "Bericht des MdI / 1.GB (B) / Kommandeur über die Fahnenflucht des VF-Oberwachtmeisters Hans-Dieter Wesa, 23.8.1962," in: BArch, DY 30 / IV 2 / 12 / 77, Bd. 4, Bl. 86.

4 "Handschriftlicher Bericht des Grenzpostens und Todesschützen betr. Fahnenflucht des Oberwachtmeisters der Trapo, Hans-Dieter Wesa, 23.8.1962," in: BStU, MfS, AP 20359 / 62, Bl. 11.

5 See "Bericht der West-Berliner Polizei, 23.8.1962," in: StA Berlin, Az. 27 / 2 Js 54 / 90, Bd. 1, Bl. 27; "Schlussbericht der West-Berliner Polizei, 29.8.1962," in: Ibid., Bl. 55.

6 See "Strafanzeige des West-Berlin Polizeipräsidenten / Abt.I / I1-KJ1 wegen Totschlags von Hans-Dieter Wesa gegen Unbekannt, 24.8.1962," in: Ibid., Bl. 28. See also "Wieder ein Deutscher von Deutschen niedergeschossen. Flüchtling einwandfrei auf West-Berliner Gebiet getötet", in: *Die Welt,* 24.8.1962.

7 See "Anklageschrift der Staatsanwaltschaft bei dem Kammergericht Berlin (27 / 2 Js 54 / 90), 29.6.1994," in: Ibid., Bl. 154 –178.

8 "Mit zwei Flaschen Schnaps: Mauerschützen-Selbstmord," in: *Berliner Morgenpost,* 17.12.1994.

9 Conversation conducted by Christine Brecht with E. Wesa, Hans-Dieter Wesa's brother, 13.11.2007.

10 See "Abschlussbericht des MfNV / Stadtkommandantur Berlin / 1.GB / Der Kommandeur über die Fahnenflucht des Owm. Hans-Dieter Wesa 1. / II.GA am 23.8.1962 am S-Bahnhof Bornholmer Strasse, 3.9.1962," in: BArch, VA-07 / 17152, Bl. 538.

11 Ibid., Bl. 546 – 547.

12 See "Hans-Dieter Wesa beigesetzt," in: *Berliner Morgenpost,* 28.8.1962.

Ernst Mundt

born on December 2, 1921

shot dead on September 4, 1962
at the Sophien Cemetery,
Bernauer Strasse / Bergstrasse
at the sector border between
Berlin-Mitte and Berlin-Wedding

T he cemetery of the East Berlin Sophien Parish bordered Bernauer Strasse, which belonged to the western part of the city. After the Wall was built, access to these grounds was highly restricted. Border guards patrolled between the rows of graves and checked all visitors' papers before they could enter the cemetery. On the afternoon of September 4, 1962, two gun shots interrupted the peacefulness of the cemetery. A man, fatally wounded, fell down from the cemetery wall between the graves.[1] On the other side of Bernauer Strasse, West Berlin residents opened their windows and saw border guards carry a lifeless body away on a stretcher. Many of the eyewitnesses remembered the fugitive as the "man with the cap"[2] because when he fell, his hat flew off and landed on the west side of the Wall. Forensic investigations later found that the hat had a hole in it, bearing evidence that the victim had been shot in the head.[3]

Ernst Mundt was 40 years old when he was killed trying to escape. He was born on December 2, 1921 in Bad Polzin in Eastern Pomerania. In 1950 the carpenter moved from Falkensee to East Berlin in search of work. He worked on the construction of the Friesen Stadium, a socialist prestige project that was erected very quickly on Dimitroffstrasse, now known as Danziger Strasse. The stadium was officially opened in 1951. Ernst Mundt had to give up his profession due to poor health.

When the Berlin Wall was erected, the bachelor, who received a disability pension and lived in a studio apartment in Prenzlauer Berg, was separated from his relatives on the west side of the city. Since visits were no longer possible, his mother maintained contact with him by mail and regularly sent him packages with food and other necessities. She did not know that her son was planning to flee or why he decided to do so. The East German authorities never found out what had motivated him. Staff members of the Ministry of State Security who questioned Ernst Mundt's neighbors after his escape attempt only learned that he had openly criticized the fact that the sector border had been sealed off.[4]

Ernst Mundt traveled by bike from his apartment to the Sophien Cemetery on the afternoon of September 4, 1962. He parked his bike on Bergstrasse, where the path was blocked by barbed wire. He climbed on top of the cemetery wall that was covered with pieces of broken glass to prevent intruders and ran along the top towards the sector border. Eyewitnesses reported that when cemetery visitors and border guards demanded that he get down, he answered: "I won't get down. I am on duty."[5] He had almost reached the border when two transport police officers who were posted approximately a hundred meters away on the grounds of the Nordbahnhof station noticed him fleeing. One of them fired a warning shot and then quickly fired a shot at him. Ernst Mundt was hit in the head and killed immediately. Thirty years later, when the guard who fired the shot faced charges in court, he justified his actions by claiming that he was only following orders.[6]

At the time the guard received immediate approval for his actions from the border troop leadership. That very day the East Berlin commander Helmut Poppe awarded him a bonus and the "Medal for Exemplary Service at the Border." In his final report the commander of the 1st Border Brigade concluded that Sergeant M. "handled his weapon superbly and put it to use masterfully."[7]

The quick removal of the deceased was also praised as a military success. The border troop leader praised the border guards involved for successfully removing the "injured criminal before the West Berlin police, press and camera crews could arrive."[8] They had taken the right measures according to Order 56/62, which had been passed in reaction to the death of Peter Fechter fourteen days earlier. The order was designed to ensure that fugitives who were killed or injured at the Wall be removed as quickly as possible to make sure that the western public had nothing to see.

Ernst Mundt's relatives in West Berlin had great difficulty in finding out what had happened to him. His mother's request for information from the East German authorities remained unanswered, but private investigations from East Berlin relatives were able to confirm her fear that the fugitive who was killed was her son Ernst. In early November the younger son traveled from Krefeld to Berlin in order to find out the facts once and for all.[9] As a West German, he was allowed to travel to East Berlin. His mother was not. Stasi files show that his unexpected visit put the East German authorities under pressure. After he refused to be sent away, an East Berlin state prosecutor eventually told him tersely that his brother had been injured during a "border provocation" and died from his injuries.[10] The family was told that the urn was buried in the Baumschulenweg Cemetery. The Stasi had already had the body cremated and buried anonymously.[11]

Ernst Mundt was the third fugitive in three weeks to be killed at the Berlin Wall. Anger and disgust grew in West Berlin in response to the frequency of such fatal incidents. The police had to break up a group of angry demonstrators on Gartenstrasse, who, according to one report, "were adopting a threatening attitude toward the Grepo [border police] and Trapo [transport police] positioned near the sector border."[12] There were also clear expressions of public mourning and sympathy for the fate of those killed as well. A cross was erected at the corner of Bernauer Strasse and Bergstrasse and decorated by passersby with flowers and wreaths.[13] A year later the Wedding district office replaced the cross with a monument made of logs and barbed wire. Today a sidewalk plate with the inscription "To the unknown victims of the shameful wall, † 4. 9. 1962" still marks the site where Ernst Mundt died.

Christine Brecht

1 See "Spitzenmeldung des MfNV/ Stadtkommandantur Berlin/ 1.GB/ Stabschef betr. versuchten Grenzdurchbruch am 4.9.1962 um 14.20 Uhr mit Schusswaffengebrauch, 4.9.1962," in: BArch, VA-07/ 8461, Bl. 48 – 49; "Bericht des [MfS]/ HA I/ Abteilung Aufklärung (B) betr. verhinderten Grenzdurchbruch am 4.9.1962 am Friedhof Berg-/ Gartenstrasse, 4.9.1962," in: BStU, MfS, AS 754/ 70, Bd. 2, Nr. 2, Bl. 17–18, and "Bericht der West-Berliner Polizei betr. vermutlicher Mord an einem männl. Flüchtling aus dem SBS, Bernauer-/ Bergstr., 5.9.1962," in: PHS, Bestand Grenzvorkommnisse, n. pag.
2 Interview conducted by Maria Nooke with Günter and Ursula Malchow, who were residents of Bernauer Strasse at the time, 7.4.2002.
3 See "Untersuchungsbericht der Kriminaltechnischen Untersuchungsstelle der West-Berliner Polizei, 12.9.1962," in: StA Berlin, Az. 2 Js 88/ 90, Bd. 1, Bl. 62.
4 See "Einzel-Information [des MfS-ZAIG] Nr. 584/ 62 über einen versuchten Grenzdurchbruch im Bereich der III. Grenzabteilung, Unterabschnitt 1. Kompanie, 5.9.1962," in: BStU, MfS, ZAIG Nr. 581, Bl. 44 – 47, and "Ermittlungsbericht der VfS Gross-Berlin/ Abt. VIII, 4.9.1962," in: BStU, AS 754/ 70, Bd. 2, Nr. 2, Bl. 78 – 80.
5 "Bericht über die Zeugenvernehmung einer Anwohnerin der Bernauer Strasse durch die West-Berliner Polizei betr. Grenzzwischenfall am 4.2.62 gegen 14.15 Uhr an der Grenzmauer der Sophienkirchgemeinde, 4.9.1962," in: StA Berlin, Az. Js 88/ 90, Bd. 1, Bl. 37.
6 See "Protokoll der Vernehmung des mutmasslichen Todesschützen M. durch die Berliner Polizei, 12.2.1992," in: Ibid., Bl. 233 – 252, here Bl. 233. The Berlin district court convicted M. of manslaughter on 4.7.1994, handing down a two-year suspended prison sentence. See "Urteil des Landgerichts Berlin vom 4.7.1994," in: Ibid., Bd. 4, Bl. 224 – 244, here Bl. 224 – 225.
7 "Bericht des MfNV/ Stadtkommandantur Berlin/ 1.GB/ Kommandeur betr. Auswertung eines besonderen Vorkommnisses im Abschnitt der III. Grenzabteilung, 6.9.1962," in: BArch, VA-07/ 16930, Bl. 27– 31, here Bl. 29.
8 "Bericht des MfNV/ Stadtkommandantur Berlin/ 1.GB/ Kommandeur zum versuchten Grenzdurchbruch am 4.9.1962, 4.9.1962," in: BArch, VA-07/ 8461, Bl. 52 – 57, here Bl. 56.
9 See "Niederschrift der Zeugenvernehmung der Schwester von Ernst Mundt durch die West-Berliner Polizei, 30.10.1962," in: StA Berlin, Az., 2 Js 88/ 90, Bd. 1, Bl. 74 – 22, and "Niederschrift der Zeugenvernehmung des Bruders von Ernst Mundt durch die West-Berliner Polizei, 9.11.1962," in: Ibid., Bl. 76.
10 "Bericht [der Verwaltung für Staatssicherheit Gross-Berlin/ Abt. IX], 6.11.1962," in: BStU, MfS, AS 754/ 70, Bd. 2, Nr. 2, Bl. 72 – 75, here Bl. 73.
11 See "[MfS-]Aktenvermerk über die Bestattungskosten für Ernst Mundt, 27.9.1962," in: Ibid., Bl. 11.
12 "Ereignismeldung der West-Berliner Schutzpolizei, 6.9.1962," in: PHS, Bestand Ereignismeldungen der West-Berliner Schutzpolizei, n. pag.
13 See "Ereignismeldung der West-Berliner Schutzpolizei, 7.9.1962," in: Ibid.

Anton Walzer

born on April 27, 1902

shot dead October 8, 1962
in the Spree River near the Oberbaum Bridge
at the sector border between
Berlin-Friedrichshain and Berlin-Kreuzberg

Anton Walzer was 60 years old when he tried to flee from East Berlin to West Berlin in October 1962. Born on April 27, 1902 in Weiler, located in Upper Swabia near Ravensburg, he had lived with his first wife in Berlin-Weissensee since the mid-1920s. They had two daughters. The father, a trained paint refiner, worked for many years for a paint company in Weissensee called Warnecke & Böhm. He saw the business 'aryanized' under the Nazis and witnessed Jewish slave laborers being forced to work there.[1] After 1945 the company, which was now located in the Soviet-occupied sector of Berlin, was expropriated and nationalized. It was during this time that Anton Walzer married a second time. Like so many skilled workers, in 1955 he turned his back on East Germany and fled with his second wife and their children to West Germany. They settled in Offenbach am Main, but when Anton Walzer's mother-in-law became seriously ill, his wife wanted to be by her and in 1958 the family moved back to East Berlin.[2]

This move caused Anton Walzer tremendous difficulties. The East German authorities considered so-called repatriates to be politically unreliable and this suspicion affected his professional life directly. He was allowed to work for the same company he had worked for previously, but not in a position that corresponded to the skills and abilities that he had acquired as a master paint refiner. He felt compelled to take on a poorly paid position for which he was overqualified. This form of humiliation was especially hard for Anton Walzer to endure and he turned increasingly to alcohol. The relationship with his wife also fell apart. A date for the divorce had already been set when he attempted to flee to West Berlin on the evening of October 8, 1962. After drinking alcohol to boost his courage, the sixty-year-old man approached the sector border on the Oberbaum Bridge in the East Berlin district of Friedrichshain. He entered the premises at the Spreeufer unnoticed and climbed onto a barge that was attached there. Protected by the darkness, he jumped from the ship into the water at around 10:15 p.m. and began swimming to the West Berlin bank on the other side.[3]

The East German border troops had an observation site not far away. The two guards in charge of keeping surveillance on the embankment and river immediately noticed the escape attempt. When Anton Walzer jumped in the water the head guard was said to have called out: "Someone is taking off over there,"[4] and both border guards opened fire. A number of shots hit the West Berlin riverbank (Gröbenufer). The people there had just barely enough time to take cover. Finding himself in danger, a West Berlin police officer on duty returned the fire. At the same time a boat with East German border troops was approaching the fugitive in the Spree at a place that belonged entirely to East Berlin. His arrest was inevitable, but the guard leader on the bank did not stop shooting. He fired a total of 18 shots at the man. One bullet hit Anton Walzer in the back of his head, killing him immediately. He sank into the water.[5]

Moments after the shots were heard, a crowd of Kreuzberg residents gathered on the riverbank. They expressed their disgust with calls of "Murderer, murderer!" while the border soldiers searched the Spree for the dead man. The next day the water police and firemen continued the search under the gaze of many West Berliners. When the body was found and pulled out of the water at around 8:30 a.m., boats were positioned in front of the divers to obstruct the West Berliners' view. Ever since the pictures of the dying Peter Fechter had been seen around the world in August 1962, the East German leadership placed great importance on keeping the dead fugitives out of view of the western public. This time the western photographers were not even able to get a picture of the dead man. One newspaper commented: "Vopo murderers don't want any eyewitnesses."[6] The West did not immediately learn the name of the deceased, although soon after they retrieved the body the East German authorities were able to identify the sixty-year-old man as Anton Walzer.

Protest demonstrations took place on Gröbenufer for days after the shooting. Udo Düllick had died at the same spot just a year earlier. A wooden cross and a memorial stone still preserved the memory of his failed escape. Two young teenagers erected another wooden cross next to it. Other West Berlin protesters unrolled a banner with the words "death penalty for Ulbricht and his murderous helpers" written in large letters. The young teenagers who put up the cross wanted to disassociate themselves from this attitude. They wanted to try to put a stop to the spiral of violence and came up with their own slogan: "We can also be strong without violence."[7]

The East German authorities declared the shooting of Anton Walzer to be an "armed provocation of the enemy" in which a "border violator" received covering fire from the west side.[8] This version of the situation also found expression in the reports of the border troop leadership which fully justified the conduct of the marksmen. The East Berlin commander Poppe commented that, "in spite of the shots fired at them by the enemy," the guards had shown "strong initiative and responded tactically, thereby fulfilling the assigned combat mission in an exemplary fashion."[9]

Thirty years later, when the violent acts at the Berlin Wall were prosecuted in court, the head guard who had been on duty at the time confessed to the act. He testified that he found himself in a moral conflict with which he could no longer live,[10] although he denied having aimed his shots directly at the man, claiming that he had merely fired shots to try to get the victim to turn back. In August 1994 the

Berlin district court found Arno O. guilty of manslaughter and sentenced him to one and a half years in prison which was commuted to probation. The opinion of the court indicates that it found mitigating circumstances in the fact that the defendant showed remorse, but that there was no doubt about his personal responsibility for the death of Anton Walzer: "The killing of a clearly defenseless person, swimming, who posed in no way a threat to the gunman, only to the interests of the East German state, is so blatantly in breach of elementary principles of humanity and justice to which East Germany [...] – at least verbally – has pledged itself, that the legal wrong before us should have been apparent to anyone and recognizable to most."[11]

Christine Brecht

1   See Bezirksamt Pankow von Berlin (ed.), *Zwangsarbeit und "Arisierung". Warnecke & Böhm – ein Beispiel*, Berlin, 2004.

2   See "Niederschrift der Zeugenvernehmung der Tochter von Anton Walzer durch die Berliner Polizei, 17.3.1992," in: StA Berlin, Az. 2 Js 41/90, Bd. 1, Bl. 98–102, and "Niederschrift der Zeugenvernehmung der Ehefrau von Anton Walzer durch die Berliner Polizei, 25.3.1992," in: Ibid., Bl. 144–150.

3   See "Bericht der NVA/1.GB/IV. Grenzabteilung/Stv. Kdr. über den verhinderten Grenzdurchbruch einer männlichen Person, 8.10.1962," in: BArch, VA-07/16930, Bl. 36–40.

4   "Anklageschrift der Staatsanwaltschaft bei dem Kammergericht Berlin [Az. 2 Js 41/90], 5.2.1993," in: StA Berlin, Az. 2 Js 41/90, Bd. 2, Bl. 68–87, here Bl. 69.

5   See "Urteil des Landgerichts Berlin vom 12.8.1994," in Ibid., Bd. 3, Bl. 57a–57y, here Bl. 57h–57i.

6   *Berliner Morgenpost*, 10.10.1962.

7   See *Berliner Morgenpost*, 11.10.1962; *Der Kurier*, 12.10.1962.

8   "Rapport Nr. 281 des PdVP Berlin/Operativstab, 9.10.1962," in: PHS, Bestand PdVP-Rapporte, n. pag.

9   "Bericht der NVA/Stadtkommandant Poppe über den verhinderten Grenzdurchbruch am 8.10.1962, 9.10.1962," in: BStU, MfS, HA XX Nr. 5310, Bl. 6–8, here Bl. 8.

10 See "Niederschrift der Vernehmung eines Beschuldigten durch die Berliner Polizei, 18.3.1992," in: StA Berlin, Az. 2 Js 41/90, Bd. 1, Bl. 103–120.

11 "Urteil des Landgerichts Berlin vom 12.8.1994," in: Ibid., Bd. 3, Bl. 57a–57y, here Bl. 57o.

Horst Plischke

born on July 12, 1939

drowned on November 19, 1962
in the Havel River north of the Glienicker Bridge
on the outer ring between
Potsdam and Berlin-Zehlendorf

On November 19, 1962, Horst Plischke, 23 years old, tried to flee from Potsdam to West Berlin. He entered the Havel River north of the Glienicker Bridge in the early morning hours with the intention of swimming to the West Berlin embankment on the other side. The East German border soldiers noticed the escape attempt at around 3:30 a.m. According to West Berlin press reports, a number of shots were fired, after which the water and the eastern bank of the Jungfernsee, a lake extending from the river, were searched.[1] The search operation continued the following day.[2] But Horst Plischke could not be found.

Four months later the border soldiers made a gruesome discovery: At around 6:45 in the morning on March 10, 1963, they discovered the dead body of a young man in the lake, Jungfernsee. It had risen to the surface when the water thawed.[3] They found an ID card and a draft notice for military service on the body, which made it possible to identify him as Horst Plischke from Potsdam, born on July 12, 1939 in Bernau.[4] Further investigations led the East German authorities to conclude that Horst Plischke was the fugitive that had been shot early in the morning on November 19, 1962. He had drowned in the lake without having been hit by any of the border guards' bullets.

Despite news reports on the shooting in the Jungfernsee, the West knew nothing of Horst Plischke's fate during the East German era. His death was not registered with any agency and his name did not appear on any list of victims. But when the violent acts at the Wall were being criminally prosecuted, records that documented Horst Plischke's failed escape attempt and the retrieval of the body were found in the files of the East German border troops in November 1994. Further investigations confirmed that the 23-year-old had drowned and had not been shot. Consequently, the guards involved could not be legally prosecuted and the Berlin public prosecutor's office dismissed the case on May 3, 1995.[5] Up to now, no archival documents or newspaper articles have been found providing information about who Horst Plischke was or why he wanted to flee.

Christine Brecht

1 See *Berliner Morgenpost*, 20.11.1962; *Der Tagesspiegel*, 20.11.1962.

2 "Vopo-Boote setzen Suche nach Flüchtling fort," in: *Der Tagesspiegel*, 21.11.1962.

3 See "Bericht des VPKA Potsdam/Aufklärung-Meldewesen für die Zeit vom 1.3.–29.3.1963, 29.3.1963," in: BLHA, Bez. Pdm. Rep. 405, 15.1, Nr. 590, Bl. 70–71.

4 See "Sofortmeldung der NVA/1.GB über den Fund einer Leiche, 10.3.1962," in: BArch, VA-07/8462, Bd. 2, Bl. 213, and "Operative Tagesmeldung Nr. 69/63 der NVA/1.GB, 11.3.1963," in: BArch, VA-07/4755, Bd. 1, Bl. 256.

5 See "Bericht der ZERV, 18.4.1995," in: StA Berlin, Az. 27 AR 726/94, Bl. 27; "Mitteilung der Staatsanwaltschaft II bei dem Landgericht Berlin, 3.5.1995," in: StA Berlin, Az. 27 AR 726/94, n. pag.

Otfried Reck

born on December 14, 1944

**shot dead on November 27, 1962
at the corner of Invalidenstrasse and Gartenstrasse
near the sector border between
Berlin-Mitte and Berlin-Wedding**

O tfried Reck was 17 years old when he tried to flee from East to West Berlin with his friend Gerd P. Their plan was to reach the other side of the city by following the underground tracks of the north-west railroad. They knew of a ventilation shaft at the corner of Invalidenstrasse and Gartenstrasse, not far from the border grounds near the closed Nordbahnhof station that followed the so-called "cellar line." Gerd P. later reported that they had grown up together in the Mitte district and when they were children used to play on the railroad grounds, and that they had occasionally climbed through the shaft to the tracks.[1] This time they planned to use a red-painted flashlight to wave down a passing train headed for West Berlin. The fact that the opening had been blocked off with a grid to prevent escapes did not deter them.[2] Early on the evening of November 27, 1962 they set off with a plan to remove the grid with a crowbar. Their friend Michael M., who did not want to flee with them, acted as a lookout.

According to official reports, they were noticed at 6 p.m.[3] A border soldier positioned beneath the S-Bahn tracks heard a noise, reported it and a search party was set in motion. The teenagers, sensing that something was not right, sent Michael M. to check out the situation. When he did not come back, Otfried Reck and Gerd P. became suspicious and decided to give up the plan for the day. This is when they first noticed their pursuers and started to run to avoid arrest. Later Gerd P. said that it never occurred to them that the border soldiers might shoot at them at the skating rink, one of their favorite hangouts. K., second lieutenant, however, did not hesitate to use his weapon to stop the assumed "border violators." A bullet hit Otfried Reck in his back. Badly injured, the 17-year-old was brought to the People's Police Hospital where he died three hours later.[4]

The fact that he was shot down quite a distance from the border fortifications remained unmentioned in the border troop and Stasi files. Contrary to the usual practice, no sketches were made to document the site where the events occurred. When the gunman K. was found guilty of manslaughter in 1995, the Berlin district court concluded, on the basis of eyewitness accounts, that at the time he "used his weapon frivolously because he should have recognized that the escape attempt had already failed" and that the shots fired at the youths "could in no way be justified, not even in light of the regulation on the use of firearms."[5]

Even before his tragic failed escape attempt, Otfried Reck, whom his friends called Otti, had experienced the severity with which the East German authorities went after insubordinate youths. He was born in November 1944 in Berlin, the only child of Otto and Margit Reck, and lived with his parents on Torstrasse, which had been renamed Wilhelm-Pieck-Strasse in 1951 in honor of the first president of the East German state. Like many Berliners, the family had relatives on the other side of the city and was not supportive of the communist regime. His father was trained as a tailor, but worked as a night watchman for a state-owned company. His mother, who came from Austria, worked on the buffet staff of the State Opera House on Unter den Linden. Consequently, their son had contact with the world of opera from an early age. He attended performances as often as possible and dreamed of one day becoming an opera singer, even though his friends were typically more into rock and roll and pop music and teased him about his taste in music. Apparently Otfried Reck had no difficulty finishing his schooling and received the secondary school level certificate, after which he began an apprenticeship as a gas station attendant. He spent most of his free time with other young people his age. The skating rink in his neighborhood, where he was later hit by a deadly bullet on November 27, 1962, and the "Helmut Just" youth club in the cultural house across the street were their favorite hangouts. When the sector border was still open they also spent a lot of time on the west side of the city. According to his friend Gerd P., they never let an opportunity pass to make fun of East German policemen. In the eyes of the police, however, these teenage cliques were susceptible to falling under the bad influence of the western class enemy.[6]

There was no open conflict with the state authorities, however, until after the Wall was built. After this the authorities responded with rigorous counter measures to every form of protest against the border fortifications and hundreds of people were arrested for merely expressing resentment.[7] Otfried Reck's activities caught up with him on September 12, 1961 when he was arrested on Gartenstrasse for being part of a crowd that had gathered at the sector border and was supposedly condemning the border fortifications. Such conduct was considered "state-endangering agitation" and, with no consideration for his young age, Otfried Reck was found guilty and sentenced to one and a half years in prison.[8] He served his sentence in the youth penitentiaries of Dessau and Torgau until he was released on parole in August 1962. His mother later said that the state had "obstructed" his future with this.[9] After he was released, his fear of being arrested again was so great that he wanted to escape the state's grasp by fleeing to the West. He placed his trust in his friend Gerd P., who was three years older and had already spent time in West Berlin before the Wall was built. Reck decided straight away to join forces with him.

Today, Gerd P. still believes that they were betrayed by someone. He was initially able to get away when the shots were fired, but was arrested the next day along with Michael M. and sentenced to three years in prison. His interrogators left him in the dark for weeks about what had happened to his friend Otfried. At the same time the Stasi ordered an "investigation plan" that makes very clear that the preliminary proceedings were conducted with immense biases. The investigation was to prove "that the criminal elements were put up to RF [flight from the republic] by RIAS and other western publication organs." Moreover, "the criminal past" and their "disinclination to work" required further investigations "to prove just what kinds of elements are taken in by western propaganda."[10] That teenagers like Otfried Reck and his friends might have had their own reasons for wanting to escape the pressure to conform in East Germany is an idea that had no place in this ideological world view.

Christine Brecht

1 See conversation conducted by Christine Brecht with Gerd. P., Otfried Reck's friend who fled with him, 21.1.2008.

2 See "Vermerk der Deutschen Reichsbahn/Reichsbahndirektion Berlin/Der Vizepräsident A zum Auftrag vom 26.3.1962 über Absicherung des Nord-Süd-S-Bahntunnels, 30.3.1962," in: LAB, C Rep. 303-26-02, Nr. 1289, n. pag., and "Bericht der Trapo/Abschnitt Berlin betr. Sicherungsmässiger Zustand der Notausstiege auf der Nord-Süd-Bahnstrecke, 12.4.1962," in: Ibid.

3 See "Bericht der NVA/1.GB/III. Grenzabteilung zum versuchten Grenzdurchbruch im Unterabschnitt I am 27.11.62, 27.11.1962," in: BArch, VA-07/8461, Bl. 66–69.

4 See ibid. and "Bericht des Leiters der Abteilung für Sicherheitsfragen im ZK der SED, 28.11.1962," in: BArch, DY 30/IV 2/12/77, Bd. 4, Bl. 175.

5 "Urteil des Landgerichts Berlin vom 14.11.1995," in: StA Berlin, Az. 2 Js 166/90, Bd. 1, Bl. 171–186, here Bl. 185. K. was sentenced to two years in prison, commuted to probation, a slightly more severe penalty than most of the sentences handed down in the "Wall sniper" trials.

6 See Thomas Lindenberger, *Volkspolizei. Herrschaftspraxis und öffentliche Ordnung im SED-Staat 1952–1968*, Köln, 2003, especially Chapter Nine on the East German police and teenager "rowdiness."

7 See Bernd Eisenfeld/Roger Engelmann, *13. August 1961: Mauerbau, Fluchtbewegung und Machtsicherung*, Bremen, 2001, pp. 73–79.

8 See "Strafnachricht, o. D. [1962]," in: BStU, MfS, JAK Speicher XII/01, n. pag.

9 See "Protokoll der VPI Mitte/Abt. K-Dauerdienst betr. Grenzdurchbruch mit Schusswaffengebrauch, 27.11. 1962," in: BStU, MfS, Ast I AR 289/62, Bl. 1–2. According to the protocol documents the questioning of Otfried Reck's parents who, because Gerd P. had not yet been captured, were supposedly under suspicion of collusion and were thus not yet informed of their son's death. According to a file note of the administration of the State Security Service in Greater Berlin, another two days passed before his parents received notice of his death, see ibid., Bl. 3.

10 "Untersuchungsplan [der VfS Gross Berlin], o. D. [28.11.1962]," in: BStU, MfS, AU 13009/63, Bd. 1, Ermittlungsverfahren, Bl. 26–29, here Bl. 26. See Dorothee Wierling, Der Staat, die Jugend und der Westen. Texte zu Konflikten der 60er Jahre, in: Peter Becker/Alf Lüdtke (eds.), *Akten, Eingaben, Schaufenster. Die DDR und ihre Texte*, Berlin, 1997, pp. 223–238.

Günter Wiedenhöft

born on February 14, 1942

drowned on the night of December 5, 1962
in Griebnitz Lake
on the outer ring between
Potsdam-Babelsberg and Berlin-Zehlendorf

Günter Wiedenhöft was twenty years old when he tried to flee from Potsdam to West Berlin in December of 1962. A few days earlier an East Berlin court had sentenced him to an eight-month prison sentence for "illegally attempting to leave East Germany." He had been arrested in October of the previous year at the inner-city sector border.[1] Before he had to begin his prison term, however, the young man again tried to get through the border fortifications. He died on the night of December 5, 1962 while trying to escape.

Born in Berlin on February 14, 1942, Günter Wiedenhöft spent his first years in a children's home. His mother retrieved him when he was six years old and he went to live with her and his younger sister in Berlin-Treptow. After eight years of schooling he began an apprenticeship as an electrician and was hired by the company that had trained him. Like so many East Berlin teenagers, before the Wall was built he had spent much of his free time in the western part of the city where friends of his lived. After the border was closed off, he stayed in contact with them through letters. Without knowing it, Günter Wiedenhöft was suspected of espionage when one of his letters was intercepted by the post office surveillance office, but the Stasi investigation was unable to confirm the suspicion.[2]

Günter Wiedenhöft first came into conflict with the East German authorities when he was arrested on October 11, 1962 for exploring the border grounds along the West Berlin district of Kreuzberg.[3] After he was arrested he admitted to wanting to flee, explaining in the interrogation that he was constantly fighting with his mother and that his conscription into the National People's Army was imminent. He was also quoted in the interrogation protocol as having said: "Before 13.8.61 I was often in West Berlin where I met other people my age and their parents. I am still in contact with various people in West Berlin today. But in all my letters I never spoke about wanting to cross the border. I didn't tell my mother or my sister about my intentions; even when we had conflicts I never spoke about it."[4]

That Günter Wiedenhöft would have spoken about his true motivations during his police interrogation is highly unlikely: In the precarious situation of an arrest, what was important was that the fugitive get a short sentence and protect others by eliminating the impression that the escape had been planned far in advance or that anyone else knew about it. With this in mind, it makes sense to assume that during the interrogation before the Treptow district court on November 27, Günter Wiedenhöft showed insight and claimed that his actions had been foolish.[5] He was still sentenced to eight months in prison but the East German authorities evidently had no reason to assume that he would try to escape again. They even granted him a few weeks time before he had to go to prison.[6] Günter Wiedenhöft used this remaining time to plan his second escape attempt.

He traveled from Potsdam to Berlin on December 5, 1962 and at dusk approached the embankment of Griebnitz Lake. Half of the water extension to the Havel River belonged to the East German district of Potsdam. The other half was part of the West Berlin outer district of Zehlendorf. Parts of the lake near the embankment had already frozen over that cold winter, but to prevent escapes the East German border troops kept a channel open. Why Günter Wiedenhöft chose to escape through the difficult border waters is not known. Evidence showed that three layers of barbed wire fence that blocked access to the bank had been cut at a number of places. Having reached the embankment, he must have set off on the ice at around midnight. This is when two border guards heard something, first a cough and then later the loud crack of ice breaking.[7] The guards could not see anyone in the dark, but they were certain that it had to be a fugitive.[8] They ordered him to come back, fired a warning shot and after back-up arrived, let off curtain fire parallel to the bank. The search for the fugitive that followed was unsuccessful. There was no trace of him except for the pincers, coat and scarf that he had left behind on the riverbank.[9] After hearing the shots, the West Berlin police also assumed that someone had tried to escape and wanted to offer the fugitive assistance, but West Berlin police and press reports show that they did not find anyone either.[10]

Günter Wiedenhöft must have fallen through the ice on Griebnitz Lake and drowned that December night without being hit by any of the guards' bullets. When his body was found in the Havel River the following spring it bore no signs of a bullet wound.[11] Border soldiers discovered the body in the water on March 25, 1963 in the so-called "Babelsberger Enge." The papers found on him made it possible to identify the deceased immediately as Günter Wiedenhöft.[12] During investigations the East German authorities also learned that he was the fugitive that had been shot at on the night of December 5 at Griebnitz Lake.[13] When Günter Wiedenhöft's mother was presented with the scarf and coat left behind on the riverbank, she was able to recognize them as clothes belonging to her missing son. Conflicting sources make it difficult to determine exactly when Günter Wiedenhöft died that night. Since the escape occurred around midnight, the exact date of his death is not certain. Evidence suggests that he died early on December 6, 1962: According to one report of the East German border troops, the wristwatch that was found on the body had stopped ticking at fourteen minutes past midnight.[14]

Christine Brecht

121

1 "Urteil des Stadtbezirksgerichts Treptow, 29.11.1962," in: BStU, MfS, A-SKS 117036, Bl. 35–38, here Bl. 35.
2 See "Abschrift [des MfS]-Berichts betr. Günter Wiedenhöft, 26.3.1962," in: BStU, MfS, AP 15846/62, Bl. 8–10, and "Handschriftlicher Schlussvermerk [des MfS]/Verwaltung Gross-Berlin/KD Treptow," in: Ibid., Bl. 13.
3 See "Anzeige bei der VPI-Treptow/Abt. K [gegen Günter Wiedenhöft] durch einen Gefreiten der NVA/1.GB/V. Abt., 11.10.1962," in: BStU, MfS, A-SKS 117036, Bl. 2.
4 "Niederschrift der Vernehmung von Günter Wiedenhöft durch die VPI-Treptow/Abt. K, 11.10.1962," in: BStU, MfS, A-SKS 117036, Bl. 10–12, here Bl. 12.
5 See "Handschriftliches Protokoll der Verhandlung der Strafkammer 812 des Stadtbezirksgerichts Treptow gegen Günter Wiedenhöft, 27.11.1962," in: Ibid., Bl. 29–33.
6 See "Urteil des Stadtbezirksgerichts Treptow vom 29.11.1962," in: Ibid., Bl. 35–38.
7 See "Operative Tagesmeldung Nr. 101/62 der NVA/Stadtkommandantur Berlin/Operative Abteilung, 6.12.1962," in: BArch, VA-07/4726, Bd. 4, Bl. 599–601.
8 See "Niederschrift der Beschuldigtenvernehmung eines der ehem. Grenzposten durch die Berliner Polizei, 29.4.1993," in: StA Berlin, Az. 27 Js 133/91, Bd. 1, Bl. 144–157, and "Niederschrift der Beschuldigtenvernehmung eines der ehem. Grenzposten durch die Berliner Polizei, 29.7.1993," in: Ibid., Bl. 165–175. The investigation of the border soldiers involved in the case was suspended in 1995. See "Einstellungsverfügung der Staatsanwaltschaft II bei dem Landgericht Berlin (27/2 Js 133/91), 9.6.1955," in: Ibid., Bd. 2, Bl. 88–89.
9 See "Operative Tagesmeldung Nr. 102/62 der NVA/Stadtkommandantur Berlin/Operative Abteilung, 7.12.1962," in: BArch, VA-07/4726, Bd. 4, Bl. 605.
10 See "Bericht der West-Berliner Polizeiinspektion Zehlendorf betr. Schüsse an der Zonengrenze, 6.12.1962," in: PHS, Bestand Grenzvorkommnisse, n. pag.; "Schüsse bei Kohlhasenbrück. Polizei fand keine Spur von Flüchtlingen," in: *Der Tagesspiegel,* 7.12.1962; "Schüsse an der Grenze," in: *Nacht-Depesche,* 6.12.1962.
11 See "Meldung des PdVP Berlin/Abt. Strafvollzug betr. Strafsache gegen Günter Wiedenhöft, 23.5.1963," in: BStU, MfS, A-SKS 117036, Bl. 46, and "Schlussbericht der ZERV, 23.5.1995," in: StA Berlin, Az. 27 Js 133/91, Bd. 2, Bl. 60.
12 See "Funkspruch Nr. 265 [des VPKA Potsdam], 25.3.1963," in: BArch, VA-07/8462, Bl. 212.
13 See "Operative Tagesmeldung Nr. 84/63 der NVA/Stadtkommandantur Berlin/Operative Abteilung, 26.3.1963," in: BArch, VA-07/4731, Bd. 2, Bl. 186, and "Operative Tagesmeldung Nr. 85/63 der NVA/Stadtkommandantur Berlin/Operative Abteilung, 27.3.1963," in: Ibid., Bl. 191.
14 See "Funkspruch Nr. 265 [des VPKA Potsdam], 25.3.1963," in: BArch, VA-07/8462, Bl. 212.

Hans Räwel

born on December 11, 1941

**shot dead on January 1, 1963
in the Spree River near the Oberbaum Bridge
at the border grounds between
Berlin-Friedrichshain and Berlin-Kreuzberg**

"**H**e was celebrating with his girlfriend at Zenner, near the Oberbaum Bridge on 1.1.63, and never came back." These were the words Hans Räwel's mother wrote in her private notes to describe the loss of her youngest son. He had been missing since the morning of January 1, 1963. She also noted that in the following days of uncertainty, she received "the unfathomable news that Hans had been found on the state border, where he had drowned."[1] But his mother had been lied to. In truth East German border soldiers had shot and killed her son while he was trying to swim across the Spree River to West Berlin.

Born during the war in 1941 in Stralsund, Hans Räwel grew up with three older siblings on Rügen, an island in the Baltic Sea. His parents ran their own bakery where their children also worked from an early age. In 1957 the family moved to East Berlin, where the parents took over a bakery in Rahnsdorf, Köpenick. Following his father's wish, after he finished his schooling, Hänschen, as he was called by his parents and siblings, trained to become a baker. His sister recalled that her brother was very musical and often played the harmonica or accordion in the bakery. But their family life in East Berlin became increasingly overshadowed by the division of Germany. The oldest brother moved to West Germany in 1954. The other sisters and Hans Räwel's father also moved to the West before the Wall was built. His sister Renate was the last to go in December 1960. They could not bear the constant political patronizing any longer, she remembered.[2] She knew that Hans was also determined to leave East Germany as soon as he finished his pastry chef training. The closure of the border on August 13, 1961 put an end to his plans. After that an escape to the West involved major difficulties and risks. He would have had to leave his mother behind, alone for a time – it was not clear for how long. This was why Hans Räwel hesitated at first. Weeks and months passed, lending the impression that he had come to terms with the new situation. Even on New Year's Eve, 1962, he gave no sign of what he was planning. He spent the evening with a friend in the dance café "Plänterwald" in Berlin-Treptow, where they stayed until early in the morning. When they went their separate ways at around 4 a.m., nothing suggested that he was planning to flee to West Berlin just hours later.[3]

It was an unusually cold New Year's morning with temperatures more than ten degrees below zero when Hans Räwel entered the freezing cold water of the Spree near the Oberbaum Bridge. For a good swimmer, trying to reach the West Berlin bank on the other side was not necessarily a futile undertaking. Any number of fugitives had been able to swim across the Spree between the Friedrichshain und Kreuzberg districts without anyone's noticing. In fact, Berlin police reports documented that someone had managed to escape that very morning just a short way up the river.[4] Hans Räwel, however, was not able to evade the gaze of the guards. As soon as he entered the water he was noticed by the crew of a boat belonging to the East German border guards. When the border guards began pursuing him at around 6:15 a.m., he dove between the wooden posts that were placed in the middle of the river to hinder access.[5] Consequently, his pursuers had to maneuver around the so-called "Dalbenreihe" that blocked off an area longer than 300 meters between the Oberbaum Bridge and Osthafensteg.[6] In the end they caught up with him and opened fire at close range until Hans Räwel, fatally injured, sank beneath the water's surface. "The border violator," one of the guards wrote in the protocol, "was situated at this point ca. 35 meters away from the western embankment."[7]

Two police officers on the West Berlin embankment heard the border soldiers' shots. According to their own account, they returned the fire because they felt threatened. Their shots hit the boat, slightly injuring the coxswain.[8] This incident triggered a strong political reaction. In the West use of firearms by the police was deemed justified when the officer in question found himself in physical danger.[9] East Germany saw this as a "confrontational attack of fire" from the West Berlin police.[10]

The East German Defense Ministry used the ADN press agency to spread its characterization of Hans Räwel's escape attempt as a "prepared border provocation" and claimed that "forces hostile to peace and understanding" in West Berlin were using these kinds of murderous attacks on East German border security forces to try to "poison the international climate."[11] In contrast, the American Berlin commander, James H. Polk, spoke of a "regrettable start of a new year in Berlin." He condemned the shots at the defenseless fugitive as a "particularly irresponsible, provocative and frivolous misuse of firearms."[12]

In April 1994 three former East German border soldiers were charged with joint manslaughter.[13] All three of the men had been on the boat when it began the pursuit. It was determined that two of the soldiers had fired shots. The mother and sister of the victim attended the trial before the Berlin district court. Having been left in the dark by the East German authorities about the circumstances of Hans' death, they hoped to finally learn what had happened that night. Regrettably, they found the guards to be disinterested and without any signs of remorse.[14] The court was unable to ascertain with certainty which of the men had fired the deadly shot. Consequently, both of the gunmen were found guilty of the charges against them in March 1996. It was the opinion of the court that, "had they given a bit of thought to the validity of the orders issued to them, they would have recognized that they were unjust. Given that the killing of a completely defenseless person swimming in ice cold water is in glaring violation of the fundamental principles of humanity, the violation of the law should have been recognizable to anyone."[15]

Christine Brecht

1 Handwritten note by Hans Räwel's mother, undated, privately owned.
2 See conversation conducted by Christine Brecht with Renate N., Hans Räwel's sister, 26.1.2007.
3 See "Niederschrift der Zeugenvernehmung der Freundin von Hans Räwel durch die Berliner Polizei, 4.5.1993," in: StA Berlin, Az. 27/2 Js 103/90, Bd. 2. Bl. 278–283.
4 See "Bericht der West-Berliner Polizeiinspektion Kreuzberg betr. Sowjetsektoraler Grepo schiesst auf zwei Polizeibeamte, die Grundstück nach vermutlichem Flüchtling absuchen, 1.1.1963," in: PHS, Bestand Grenzvorkommnisse, n. pag.
5 See "Bericht der NVA/1.GB/V. Grenzabteilung/Der Stabschef über den verhinderten Grenzdurchbruch durch Anwendung der Schusswaffe, 1.1.1963," in: BArch, VA-07/16930, Bl. 54–56.
6 "Dalben" are posts or groups of posts that are rammed into the ground of the harbor, and usually used to fasten boats. In this case, however, they were part of the border fortifications, set up as a barrier, and continually expanded over the following years. See "Bericht des Wasserstrassenhauptamts Berlin, 7.7.1962," in: LAB, C Rep 311, Nr. 5, n. pag.
7 "Abschrift des Berichts eines der Grenzposten und Schützen zum verhinderten Grenzdurchbruch am Osthafen, 1.1.1963," in: BStU, MfS, HA I Nr. 5862, Bl. 14.
8 According to the People's Police Hospital report of 2.1.1963, it was a small injury on the skin's surface at the back of the neck. See "Gutachten des Krankenhauses der Vopo über die Verletzung des Gen. Uffz., 2.1.1963," in: Ibid., Bl. 27.
9 See "Bericht der West-Berliner Polizeiinspektion Kreuzberg betr. Sowjetsektoraler Grepo schiesst auf zwei Polizeibeamte, die Grundstück nach vermutlichem Flüchtling absuchen, 1.1.1963," in: PHS, Bestand Grenzvorkommnisse, n. pag., and "Stellungnahme der West-Berliner Polizei zum Schusswaffengebrauch am 1.1.1963, 3.1.1963," in: Ibid.
10 *Neues Deutschland*, 3.1.1963.
11 "ADN-Mitteilung des DDR-Verteidigungsministeriums [Abschrift], o.D. [Januar 1963]," in: PHS, Bestand Grenzvorkommnisse, n. pag.
12 "In der Spree erschossen?", in: *Telegraf*, 3.1.1963.
13 See "Anklageschrift der Staatsanwaltschaft II bei dem Landgericht Berlin (27/2 Js 103/90), 13.4.1995," in: StA Berlin, Az. 27 Js 103/90, Bd. 3, Bl. 90–117.
14 See conversation conducted by Christine Brecht with Renate N., Hans Räwel's sister, 26.1.2007.
15 "Urteil des Landgerichts Berlin vom 6.3.1996," in: StA Berlin, Az. 27Js 103/90, Bd. 6, Bl. 1–47, here Bl. 40.

Horst Kutscher

born on July 5, 1931

shot dead on January 15, 1963
near Rudower Strasse
at the sector border between
Berlin-Treptow and Berlin-Neukölln

The instructions given to the 2nd Platoon of the 4th Border Company were unambiguous. The border guards were informed that the following day the VI Communist Party Congress was to begin under the leadership of Walter Ulbricht and each one of them should "consider it his personal duty" to ensure that no border breaches take place.[1] Moreover, the number of deployed patrol guards was to be increased. Horst Kutscher and Joachim F. had no idea of the difficult conditions under which they were planning their escape. They made a spontaneous decision to flee to West Berlin on the night of January 15, 1963. It cost Horst Kutscher his life.

Horst Kutscher, born on July 5, 1931 in Berlin-Treptow, was the youngest of thirteen children born to a mechanical engineer and flower-seller in Berlin-Adlershof. According to information he provided about himself, he quit school at the age of 14 and began training as an auto mechanic, but for company reasons had to discontinue his apprenticeship after six months.[2] After that Horst Kutscher worked as a cleaner at construction sites and in September 1954 began working for various coal merchants in the district. He was a member of the FDGB trade union in the 1950s, but was not politically active. In March 1952, at the age of 21, Horst Kutscher got married. He fathered six children with his wife.

Horst Kutscher first got into trouble with the East German law as a teenager. He was convicted of numerous crimes such as theft, burglary and assault. He was sentenced to a number of prison terms over the years.[3] In February 1956 the East German police inspection recruited Horst Kutscher as a secret informant.[4] He agreed – possibly under pressure – to cooperate with the criminal investigation department and to provide information about criminal activities in his surroundings.[5] But Horst Kutscher did not appear at the agreed meeting places and spoke openly about his informant activities and was subsequently released from his obligation after only two months.[6]

In April 1956 he fled to West Germany – at first without his wife and children. His wife told the East German police that he left because of marital conflicts.[7] It appears, however, that his wife followed a short time later. In Bochum she gave birth to their fourth child. For reasons that are unknown, Horst Kutscher moved with his family from Bochum back to Berlin-Treptow a year later. The family initially registered their address as his parents' home. The investigation report by a state border work group shows that after his return to the East, he worked as a so-called "border-crosser" in the West until the border was closed on August 13, 1961.[8] Horst Kutscher's ongoing alcohol problem led to his divorce in November 1962. At that point he had been living separately from the family at his father's home in Berlin-Adlershof for two and a half years.[9] Problems also arose at his new job with a coal merchant in East Berlin. When Horst Kutscher and Joachim F., a colleague at work, began drinking on the job on December 14, 1962, they were both fired immediately. Apparently they were not aware of having done anything wrong and took legal action against their dismissal. But the Treptow district court rejected the case on January 14, 1963.[10] Both men began drinking in the early afternoon of that day to get over their disappointment about the negative result of their claim. They went into a number of bars and, after becoming quite intoxicated, decided to flee to West Berlin that very evening. Joachim F., who survived the failed escape attempt, later testified during an interrogation with the East German police that the lost court case was the main reason they fled.[11]

On January 14, 1963, at around 10 p.m., Horst Kutscher and Joachim F. went to the border area at Semmelweissstrasse with the intention of crossing the frozen Teltow Canal to West Berlin. But once they got there they realized that the border area all around the canal was brightly lit so they decided to try their escape at another place in Berlin-Treptow. This time they tried to cross the border along the garden settlement between Wrede Bridge and the duck pond at Rudower Strasse. They crossed an open field and slid under a barbed wire fence. They watched the border guards and waited for them to move away before they began crawling through the security trenches toward the border. At about ten minutes past midnight and with only 25 meters between them and the border to West Berlin, two shots were suddenly fired. Horst Kutscher and Joachim F. threw themselves on the ground to seek protection.[12] The border guards arrested Joachim F. and dragged Horst Kutscher, who had been wounded, into the communication trench. They transported him by truck to their base where medics declared him dead.[13]

Although the East German secret police tried to prevent the fatal escape attempt from becoming public, information about the death of Horst Kutscher reached West Berlin. In the remand prison on Kissingenstrasse in Berlin-Pankow, Joachim F, who was convicted of fleeing the republic, told another prisoner about the escape attempt. A short time later this prisoner managed to get to West Berlin and reported the incident to the police in October 1963.[14] Horst Kutscher's father moved to West Berlin to be close to his family in November of the same year. In March 1965 he received a subpoena from the West Berlin police. He told them that he had not been allowed to see his dead son before he was buried, nor was he permitted to attend the funeral.[15]

After the collapse of East Germany, Horst Kutscher's ex-wife was questioned as a witness in the trial against the guard who pulled the trigger. He was sentenced on August 27, 1997 to a year and three months on probation.[16] She recalled that

14 days after the funeral she visited Horst Kutscher's gravesite at Baumschulenweg Cemetery. It was only with the help of the cemetery attendant that she was able to find the unidentified gravestone marking where Horst Kutscher and two other people were buried.[17]

Lydia Dollmann

1   "Anklageschrift der Staatsanwaltschaft II bei dem Landgericht Berlin, 22.5.1996," in: StA Berlin, 27 Js 71/90, connected with 2 Js 855/92, Bd. II, p. 11.

2   See "Handschriftlicher Lebenslauf von Horst Kutscher, 3.2.1956," in: BStU, MfS, AOG 431/60, Bl. 5.

3   See "Ermittlungsbericht der Arbeitsgruppe Staatsgrenze über Horst Kutscher, 15.1.1963," in: BStU, MfS, AS 754/70, Bd. 11, Nr. 2, Bl. 39.

4   See "Vermerk der VPI/K Treptow/RKSt/K 235 zur Anwerbung von Horst Kutscher als GI, 17.11.1955," in: BStU, MfS, AOG 431/60, Bl. 33.

5   See "Handschriftliche Verpflichtungserklärung von Horst Kutscher, 3.2.1956," in: Ibid., Bl. 35.

6   See "Vermerk der VPI/K Treptow/RKSt/K 235, 14.4.1956," in: Ibid., Bl. 39.

7   See "Bericht der VPI Treptow/Revier 235 über die Republikflucht von Horst Kutscher, 9.5.1956," in: Ibid., Bl. 42.

8   See "Ermittlungsbericht der Arbeitsgruppe Staatsgrenze, 15.1.1963," in: BStU, MfS, AS 754/70, Bd. 11, Nr. 2, Bl. 39–40.

9   See ibid. Horst Kutscher's mother died in July 1959.

10 See "Spitzenmeldung der VPI Treptow, 15.1.1963," in: Ibid., Bl. 16; "Ladung des Stadtbezirksarbeitsgerichts Treptow, 8.1.1963," in: Ibid., Bl. 57.

11 See "Spitzenmeldung der VPI Treptow, 15.1.1963," in: Ibid., Bl. 16.

12 See "Niederschrift der Beschuldigtenvernehmung von Joachim F. durch die VPI Treptow/Abteilung K, 15.1.1963," in: Ibid., Bl. 19–23.

13 See "Einzel-Information Nr. 30/63 des MfS/ZAIG über einen verhinderten Grenzdurchbruch mit tödlichem Ausgang für den Grenzverletzer im Abschnitt Berlin-Altglienicke am 15.1.1963, 15.1.1963," in: BStU, MfS, ZAIG Nr. 696, Bl. 4–5.

14 See "Auszugsweise Abschrift der Zeugenaussage von Karl-Heinz M. bei der West-Berliner Polizei, 3.10.1963," in: StA Berlin, 27 Js 71/90, connected with 2 Js 855/92, Bd. 1, Bl. 16 a; "Strafanzeige der West-Berliner Polizei gegen Unbekannt, 25.10.1963," in: Ibid., Bl. 16.

15 See "Niederschrift der Zeugenvernehmung des Vaters von Horst Kutscher durch die West-Berliner Polizei, 23.3.1965," in: Ibid., Bl. 24.

16 See "Urteil des Landgerichts Berlin vom 27.8.1997," in: Ibid., Bd. 3, Bl. 1–2.

17 See "Niederschrift der Zeugenvernehmung der geschiedenen Ehefrau von Horst Kutscher durch die Berliner Polizei, 7.4.1992," in: Ibid., Bd. 1, Bl. 124–125.

Peter Kreitlow

born on January 15, 1943

shot dead on January 24, 1963
on the outer ring between
Niederneuendorf (Nauen district)
and Berlin-Spandau

Five teenagers set off from Hennigsdorf on the night of January 23 to break through the border grounds to West Berlin. They had happened to meet at a youth club that evening and spontaneously decided to leave East Germany together.[1] Bernd K. was the only one from Hennigsdorf; the others were from East Berlin and had come to the small town in the northwest of the city that evening to attend a dance. They followed Bernd K., who knew his way around the area, and slithered across the frozen Havel Canal between Hennigsdorf and Niederneuendorf. Then they turned into a snow-covered forest, avoiding streets and paths as they cautiously approached the border. But two soldiers hindered their escape long before the teenagers reached their goal. The soldiers, part of a Soviet military unit stationed in Niederneuendorf, were responsible for guarding the area close to the border. It was never determined exactly when they noticed the fugitives and began chasing them. Just why the soldiers opened fire in the wooded area approximately 2,000 meters from the border fortifications also remains unclear. These shots cost Peter Kreitlow, age twenty, his life. He was hit a number of times, including a shot to the head, and died shortly after midnight.[2]

It was decided that an autopsy was not necessary since the cause of death was obvious.[3] This departure from the usual practice suggests that Peter Kreitlow's death was a delicate matter for the East German leadership. If the population learned that a Soviet border patrol had shot and killed an East German youth, it might cause increased resentment towards the occupying power. An investigation of the soldiers' conduct or an attempt to punish them was not only out of the question out of respect for the Soviet Union, but also because no legal basis existed for doing this. Instead the border troop leadership and East German secret police left no doubt in their reports that the shots were completely justified. One Stasi report that reached Walter Ulbricht and Erich Honecker stated: "The Soviet border patrols made use of their firearms because the accused tried to escape arrest."[4] Moreover, it was established "that this was a planned and serious border breach."[5]

A border guard, who later fled to the West, reported that the conduct of the Soviet soldiers was explained to the East German border troops with similar arguments and approval.[6] Convicting the perpetrators in court, however, remained impossible even after the East German archives were made accessible. Berlin's public prosecutor's office opened an investigation, but found that even after the collapse of East Germany there was no legal foundation to demand that the Russian authorities reveal the name of the soldiers so that they could be tried in Germany.[7]

Peter Kreitlow is the only East German fugitive known to have been shot and killed at the Berlin Wall by members of the Soviet occupying forces between 1961 and 1989. He was born in Berlin during the Second World War in January 1943. His mother is believed to have died before the war ended. His father, who worked for the state-owned company "Bergmann-Borsig" after the war, remarried, but Peter Kreitlow did not get along with his stepmother. This caused fighting at home and as soon as Peter Kreitlow turned 18, his father threw him out. The Wall was built the same year, putting an end to his visits to the western part of the city that had been a welcome diversion from the daily routine in East Germany. After the Wall went up, Peter Kreitlow's life was marked by trouble with his parents and conflicts with his supervisors at work. After training to become a baker, he eked out a living as a part-time worker at various industrial plants. He last worked at an industrialized building site in Schwedt, but continued to sublet an apartment in East Berlin.[8] Apparently there was nothing keeping the young man in East Germany. It seems likely that Peter Kreitlow and his friends dreamed of a better life in the West without having any concrete plans to escape.[9] Stasi reports polarized these desires and hopes and came to the conclusion that the teenagers wanted to flee to West Berlin "because they were hostile to the social conditions in East Germany."[10]

Peter Kreitlow and his three friends drove to Hennigsdorf on January 23, 1963. They met Bernd K. there, whom Peter Kreitlow knew from previous visits to Hennigsdorf. Bernd K. had already been convicted of planning an escape in February 1962 and had been sentenced to a seven-month prison term. The Stasi files stated that he had spent a lot of time in West Berlin before the Wall was built.[11] Bernd K. knew that Peter Kreitlow and his friends were on his wavelength. When they started talking, he told them that he intended to flee and invited them to join him. One of the youths admitted during a Stasi interrogation that after an initial hesitation, Peter Kreitlow and his friends let themselves be talked into fleeing.[12] Another one said that K.'s description had been tempting, but he did not tell the Stasi interrogator what his motives had been for leaving: "I didn't have any reason and I don't think the others did either. For me it was about getting to West Berlin because [K.]'s description excited me. Apparently it was the same for the others. No one had any real reasons for taking this step."[13] The Stasi interrogator put on record that, unlike the others, K. had envisioned what a good life he would have in West Berlin since he would be able to live with his grandmother and could get away from home, where he no longer felt comfortable. He barely spent any time at home anymore because of his bad relationship with his father. Peter Kreitlow and his friends also wanted to get away. The friend said "that he didn't care about anything and was happy to give up his apartment in Berlin. He acted as though he had nothing more to lose here. Kreitlow agreed [...] and said that it wouldn't be because of him if they failed to go through with the plan."[14] That is how they came to agree to risk an escape and set off towards the border at around 11 p.m.

During a closed hearing on May 20, 1963, the city court of greater Berlin found Peter Kreitlow's friends guilty of "leaving illegally" and inciting such action and sentenced them to ten months and 18 months in prison.[15] Because of the shooting of Peter Kreitlow, the East Berlin district administration deemed it necessary "to exclude the public in the interest of the security of the state."[16] Nonetheless, the Stasi was not able to prevent the news that Peter Kreitlow had been shot by Soviet soldiers from spreading among neighbors and colleagues and even reaching the West Berlin authorities.[17]

The victim's funeral was organized by a Stasi agent who employed every conspiracy method in the book. It was noted that "Comrade H. took it upon himself to purchase the urn site at the Berlin-Pankow III Cemetery without allowing the cause of death to be known there." Moreover, at the cemetery it was announced "that the father did not want other family members to be informed of the date of the burial. The cemetery administration agreed to honor this frequently-requested wish."[18] The memorial service for Peter Kreitlow finally took place on March 5, 1963. On request of his father, the urn was buried next to his mother's grave.

Christine Brecht

1   See "Niederschrift der Vernehmung eines Mitflüchtlings von Peter Kreitlow durch das MfS, 24.1.1963," in: BStU, MfS, AU 16072/63, Bd. 2 (Untersuchungsvorgang), Bl. 36–42, here Bl. 38–39, and "Niederschrift der Vernehmung eines Mitflüchtlings von Peter Kreitlow durch das MfS, 13.3.1963," in: Ibid., Bd. 3 (Untersuchungsvorgang), Bl. 93–100, here Bl. 93–97.

2   See "Tatortbefundbericht des VPKA-Oranienburg/RKST-Oranienburg zum vers[uchten] Grenzdurchbruch in der Nacht 24.1.1963 in Niederneuendorf, 24.1.1963," in: BStU, MfS, AS 754/70, Bd. 10, Nr. 1, Bl. 4–7.

3   See "Bericht der VfS Gross-Berlin/Abt. IX betr. Leichenvorgang Peter Kreitlow, 7.2.1963," in: Ibid., Bl. 28–30.

4   "Einzel-Information Nr. 60/63 [des MfS-ZAIG], 25.1.1963," in: BStU, MfS, ZAIG Nr. 696, Bl. 9–12, here Bl. 11. See also "Bericht der NVA/2.GB/Stabschef an den Stadtkommandanten Berlin betr. verhinderter schwerer Grenzdurchbruch unter Anwendung der Schusswaffe durch eine sowj. Kontrollstreife, 24.1.1963," in: BArch, VA-07/8462, Bl. 237–238, and "Spitzenmeldung des VPKA Oranienburg/Abt. Kriminalpolizei/Stützpunkt an die BDVP Potsdam/Aufklärungs und Meldewesen, 24.1.1963," in: BStU, MfS, AU 16072/63, Bd. 3 (Untersuchungsvorgang), Bl. 30–31.

5   "Bericht der NVA/Stadtkommandant Berlin an den Minister für Nationale Verteidigung betr. verhinderter schwerer Grenzdurchbruch unter Anwendung der Schusswaffe durch eine sowj. Kontrollstreife, 25.1.1963," in: BArch, VA-07/6002, Bl. 219–220, here Bl. 220.

6   See "Auszug aus einem Bericht vom 19.2.1963 über die Zeugenvernehmung eines geflüchteten Grenzsoldaten durch die West-Berliner Polizei, 20.2.1963," in: StA Berlin, Az. 27/2 Js 73/90, Bd. 1, Bl. 33.

7   See "Schlussvermerk der ZERV, 18.7.1995," in: Ibid., Bd. 2, Bl. 10, and "Verfügung der Staatsanwaltschaft II bei dem Landgericht Berlin (27/2 Js 73/90), 15.7.1996," in: Ibid., Bl. 54–58.

8   See "Bericht [des MfS]/Verwaltung Gross-Berlin/Abt. IX betr. Grenzdurchbruch im Raum Niederneuendorf, 25.1.1963," in: BStU, MfS, AU 16072/63, Bd. 3 (Untersuchungsvorgang), Bl. 71.

9   See ibid., Bl. 67–74. According to the Stasi investigation findings on the teenagers, three friends that Peter Kreitlow was with that evening came from families with divorced parents or with a father who had not returned from the war. Their daily life was strongly affected by generational conflicts. Two of the youths had worked on the west side of the city before the Wall was built.

10 "Bericht [des MfS]/Verwaltung Gross-Berlin/Abt. IX betr. Grenzdurchbruch im Raum Niederneuendorf, 25.1. 1963," in: Ibid., Bl. 74.

11 See ibid., Bl. 69.

12 See "Niederschrift der Vernehmung eines Mitflüchtlings von Peter Kreitlow durch das MfS, 13.3.1963," in: Ibid., Bl. 94 – 96.

13 "Niederschrift der Vernehmung eines Mitflüchtlings von Peter Kreitlow durch das MfS, 24.1.1963," in: Ibid., Bd. 2 (Untersuchungsvorgang), Bl. 24.

14 "Niederschrift der Vernehmung eines Mitflüchtlings von Peter Kreitlow durch das MfS, 13.3.1963," in: Ibid., Bd. 3 (Untersuchungsvorgang), Bl. 95 – 96.

15 "Urteil des Stadtgerichts von Gross-Berlin vom 20.5.1963," in: Ibid., Bd. 5 (Gerichtsakte), Bl. 271–272.

16 "Kurzmitteilung [des MfS] an den GStA Gross-Berlin/Abt. I zum Verfahren, 23.3.1963," in: BStU, MfS, AU 16072/63, Bd. 3 (Untersuchungsvorgang), Bl. 119.

17 See "Auszug aus einem Bericht der West-Berliner Polizei über eine informatorische Vernehmung des am 16.1.1963 im Gebiet um Stolpe Süd geflüchteten ehem. Soldaten, 20.2.1963," in: StA Berlin, Az. 27/2 Js 73/90, Bd. 1, Bl. 33, and "Bericht der West-Berliner Polizei, 22.2.1973," in: Ibid., Bl. 109.

18 "Bericht der VfS Gross-Berlin/Abt. IX betr. Leichenvorgang Peter Kreitlow, 7.2.1963," in: BStU, MfS, AS 754/70, Bd. 10, Nr. 1, Bl. 28 – 30, here Bl. 30.

Wolf-Olaf Muszynski

born on February 1, 1947

drowned in the Spree River in February 1963
probably near the Oberbaum Bridge
at the sector border between
Berlin-Friedrichshain and Berlin-Kreuzberg

The 16-year-old Wolf-Olaf Muszynski had been reported missing from the East Berlin district of Friedrichshain since February 6, 1963. This led the East German police headquarters to contact the western side of the city on March 18 to inquire whether a young boy had "arrived for registration," or in other words, whether he had escaped to the West.[1] Given that relations between the East and West governments had been largely cut off since the Wall had been built, this kind of request was quite unusual.[2] In West Berlin the search for Wolf-Olaf Muszynski at the Marienfelde refugee center for East German fugitives and other places remained fruitless.[3] Information from his grandmother in West Berlin was also unhelpful. She told the West Berlin police on March 27 that in the past her grandson had expressed a desire to flee. She also gave the following description of the boy: "apparent age 18, approx. 177 cm. tall, slender, ash-blond hair, blue eyes."[4]

On the morning of April 1, 1963, residents found Wolf-Olaf Muszynski's body not far from the Oberbaum Bridge on the West Berlin Spree riverbank. All evidence suggested that he had drowned while trying to escape, unnoticed by East German borders guards. Under the headline "16 Year-Old Drowned Fugitive Washed Ashore," the "Tagesspiegel" reported the following details the next day: "According to the West Berlin police, the young boy could be immediately identified because his identification papers had been attached to his back under his shirt."[5] The corpse, it continued, did not bear any physical injuries, but its condition suggested that the deceased must have drowned quite some time ago.

An autopsy was requested in order to determine the exact cause of death. The examination found that neither sickness nor violence had played a role in the death, which was caused by drowning.[6] With no reason to believe a second party was involved in the death, the police investigation was closed.[7] When the case reopened in the 1990s, the results were confirmed again without the unearthing of any new information about the life of Wolf-Olaf Muszynski or why he had decided to flee.

Christine Brecht

133

1 "Auszug aus dem Fernschreiben des PdVP/Berlin 31 an die West-Berliner Polizei betr. vermisste Person, 18.3.1963," in: StA Berlin, Az. 7 AR 224/92, Bl. 3.

2 For context, see Gerhard Kunze, *Grenzerfahrungen. Kontakte und Verhandlungen zwischen dem Land Berlin und der DDR 1949–1989,* Berlin, 1999.

3 "Vermerk der West-Berliner Polizei, 19.3.1963," in: StA Berlin, Az. 7 AR 224/92, Bl. 3.

4 "Niederschrift der Zeugenaussage der Grossmutter von Wolf-Olaf Muszynski durch die West-Berliner Polizei, 27.3.1963," in: Ibid., Bl. 4–5, here Bl. 5.

5 *Der Tagesspiegel,* 2.4.1963.

6 See "Obduktionsbericht des West-Berliner Instituts für gerichtliche und soziale Medizin der FU Berlin, 2.4.1963," in: StA Berlin, Az. 7 AR 224/92, Bl. 12–14.

7 See "Vermerk der West-Berliner Polizei, 29.5.1963," in: Ibid., Bl. 17.

Peter Mädler

born on July 10, 1943

shot dead on April 26, 1963
in the Teltow Canal on the outer ring between
Kleinmachnow (Potsdam county district)
and Berlin-Zehlendorf

P eter Mädler was 18 years old when the border between West and East Berlin was sealed off on August 13, 1961. Born on July 10, 1943 in Opperau near Breslau, today's Wrocław, he was presumably separated from his biological parents as a young child during the chaos of the war. The Mädlers, a married couple living in Hoyerswerda, adopted him in 1950. The father worked as a storekeeper; the mother was a housewife. According to a report from a childhood friend, Peter Mädler learned in the early 1960s that his biological parents lived in West Germany. This was probably why he began thinking about an escape plan that he could use after he finished his schooling, but the Berlin Wall foiled his plans.[1] Peter Mädler put the plan aside for a while, but in April 1963 he was ready to take action. He wanted to try to escape to West Berlin.

Peter Mädler grew up with his adoptive parents in Hoyerswerda, where he attended school until the 8th grade. In 1958 he began an apprenticeship as an electrician in the company training school of the nearby Lauta power station in Lauterberg. He successfully completed his training on August 30, 1961. His childhood friend recalled that Peter Mädler had drawn attention to himself through his appearance during his vocational training: He was among the first teenagers in East Germany to dye his hair platinum blond. He was a good student – more interested in girls than politics. He did not join the FDJ youth association during his vocational training. Shortly after the Wall was built, he and the other trainees of the power station were expected, as an FDJ contingent, to commit themselves to serving in the National People's Army. The teenagers were clearly averse to this idea. Along with the other apprentices, Peter Mädler refused to sign the agreement form put before him. After he completed his training he worked as an electrician in the Lübbenau power station until he transferred to the industrial plant, "Teltower Geräte und Reglerwerk," in December 1961.[2] It is not known whether this change in location and workplace precipitated his plan to flee to West Berlin. From the roof of the company compound he could see the Kleinmachnow border grounds at the Teltow Canal. He had not mentioned anything about his plans to flee to his colleagues at work or to his foster parents.[3]

On the night of April 26, 1963, under the cover of darkness, the young man approached the border security grounds not far from the Erlenweg at the Teltow Canal. He used a side cutter to break through the two lower wires of the barrier fence. When he reached the canal, he left his clothes on the embankment. He tied a leather belt around his body and attached the side cutter and a plastic bag containing his wallet and identification papers to it. Then he entered the Teltow Canal and began swimming to West Berlin. It took a great effort to get through the obstacles placed along the canal. He cautiously swam along the northern bank towards the harbor entrance that was located close to a watchtower. It was 4:45 a.m. The border guards on duty at the tower had only a few more minutes left on their shift when they noticed the swimmer. He was approximately ten meters from the border when one of the guards ordered him to get out of the water. Peter Mädler called out to the border guards: "Don't shoot!" and continued swimming to West Berlin. Without setting off a warning shot, the guard fired 30 bullets in his direction. Peter Mädler was not injured and dived under the water, still trying to reach the border. The second border soldier climbed down from the watchtower and looked for the fugitive from the embankment. Peter Mädler came to the surface right before the border that ran through the waterway. The border guard fired three single shots directly at him. Peter Mädler was hit and sank beneath the water's surface. One of the guards climbed over the fence to wait for the fugitive to resurface, but he did not reappear. Following an extensive search the fire department finally found the body near the entrance to the Teltow Harbor on the afternoon of April 26, 1963 at 4:46 p.m.[4] That same day the commander of the border division commended the border guards for their correct and determined action. They were awarded the "Medal for Exemplary Service at the Border."[5]

It took another 32 years before the guards were prosecuted. The Potsdam district court found the guards who had been on duty at the time guilty of manslaughter and sentenced them to a year and three months probation. The court found it immaterial that the shots from the one border soldier did not hit Peter Mädler since he too had tacitly accepted the death of the fugitive.[6]

On the West Berlin side of the canal, residents of the Teltow dockyard heard the guards' gunshots in the early morning hours, but they were not witness to the escape attempt. One of the residents saw the dead fugitive being retrieved from the water in the afternoon and thought he recognized a uniform on the body which led the West Berlin police and press to report that the dead man had been a border soldier.[7] Other residents thought they had seen border guards searching for the fugitive near the embankment on West Berlin territory.[8] The West Berlin press reported on the incident a few days later and criticized the inaction of the West Berlin police who, according to the residents, had paid little attention to the events.[9] The Berlin CDU also looked into the matter and made a "small query" in parliament: It wanted to know whether the criticism expressed in the press was valid and what the Senate planned to do about it.[10] In reaction to the incident, more patrols were put on duty at the Teltow dockyard and disciplinary action was taken against the West Berlin police officers involved.[11]

According to a childhood friend, Peter Mädler was buried in an urn grave on the Waldfriedhof, a cemetery in Hoyerswerda. The grave was later leveled and no longer exists.[12] Yet the unknown fugitive who had died was not forgotten in West Berlin. A commemorative cross was erected to him at the Steinstücken triangle on the tenth anniversary of the Wall's construction.[13] Today a memorial stone in Kleinmachnow is dedicated to the victims of divided Germany, in particular to fugitives like Peter Mädler who died at the border in Kleinmachnow.

Lydia Dollmann

1 See conversation conducted by Lydia Dollmann with Rainer Walther, 25.1.2008.

2 See ibid.

3 See "Urteil des Landgerichts Potsdam vom 19.6.1995," in: StA Neuruppin, Az. 61 Js 29/94 (= StA Berlin, Az. 22 Js 174/90), Bd. 3, Bl. 553.

4 See "Urteil des Landgerichts Potsdam vom 19.6.1995," in: Ibid., Bl. 552–554.

5 See ibid., Bl. 554.

6 See ibid., Bl. 545, 559.

7 See "Strafanzeige der West-Berliner Polizei gegen namentlich nicht bekannten Angehörigen der sowjetzonalen Grenztruppen, 29.4.1963," in: Ibid., Bd. 1, Bl. 1.

8 See "Schlussbericht der West-Berliner Polizei, 17.5.1963," in: Ibid., Bl. 75.

9 See, for example "Neuer Vopo-Mord an der Grenze," in: *BZ,* 30.4.1963; "Polizei zum Vopo-Mord am Teltow- kanal: Zustand bleibt unverändert," in: *BZ,* 2.5.1963.

10 See "Vermerk 'Kleine Anfrage' der CDU, 2.5.1963," in: PHS, Bestand Grenzvorkommnisse, n. pag.

11 See "Kurzbericht der West-Berliner Polizei-Inspektion Zehlendorf, 7.5.1963," in: PHS, Bestand Grenzvorkomm- nisse, n. pag.

12 Conversation conducted by Lydia Dollmann with Rainer Walther, 25.1.2008.

13 See the photo of the memorial cross for the unidentified fugitive at Gleisdreieck Steinstücken, in: BStU, MfS, HA I Nr. 3637, Bl. 43.

Klaus Schröter

born on February 21, 1940

shot on November 4, 1963, causing him to drown
in the Spree River near the Reichstag building
at the sector border between
Berlin-Mitte and Berlin-Tiergarten

"I wore black for a whole year to express my opposition."[1] The silent protest of Klaus Schröter's mother was directed at the East German authorities who had treated her badly: They did not tell her that border soldiers had shot her son and were responsible for his death. They pressured her to agree to a cremation burial – and, what is more, they even told her that it was no longer fashionable to wear black. "What an interest they took in my private affairs!" she exclaimed after she emigrated from East Germany. "That should give pause for thought, and it is all proof of what was done."[2]

Klaus Schröter came from Friedersdorf near Bitterfeld, where he was born in February 1940. He grew up there with two brothers. His parents had a little house in a settlement that later gave way to coal mining.[3] Interested in technology at a young age, he did an electrician apprenticeship with the Agfa film factory in nearby Wolfen. At the age of 18, his company sent him to the Hanno Günther School of Engineering in Velten, in Brandenburg, to study electrical engineering. After completing his studies, he began working as an electrical engineer in East Berlin in September 1961. At this time, just a few weeks after the Wall was built, such a move required a special moving permit, but this was not difficult for the young electrical engineer to acquire since he now worked for the state-owned heavy current plant on Schlegelstrasse in Berlin-Mitte. Klaus Schröter had a successful career in Berlin. He soon began pursuing an additional degree and working on the side as a lecturer at Pankow's adult education center.[4]

But in April 1963 Klaus Schröter handed in his resignation. He was disappointed that his company had refused him the new position for which he had been hoping. The company leadership refused to accept his decision and forced him to take back his resignation.[5] Klaus Schröter's friends and colleagues believed that it was this experience that tipped the scale for him, leading him to pursue his plan to flee, one he had long been considering. Although during his studies he had been a part of the engineering school's FDJ leadership, the twenty-three-year-old engineer was not at all committed to socialism. His mother said that he never made a secret of his disapproval of the Communist Party and its regime when he spoke to her.[6]

138

A colleague of his, who managed to flee to the West three years after Klaus Schröter died, recalled that "we were both unhappy with the political situation in East Germany and began to discuss ways to escape after the Wall was built."[7]

Klaus Schröter had good reasons for not telling anybody about the concrete details of his plan. Even a friend whom he had visited the evening before he tried to escape had no idea: "I knew that at some point he planned to flee to West Berlin, but that he was going to do it the following night, that didn't come up. Klaus didn't want me to know the exact date because he didn't want to make things difficult for me."[8]

Klaus Schröter carefully planned his escape long in advance. He planned his route under the water across the Spree River and acquired all the necessary equipment over time. He sold his television set so that he could buy a scuba outfit. He had compressed air tanks delivered to his apartment. He sewed himself a diving suit that he weighed down with lead weights. Finally, before sunrise on the morning of November 3, 1963, he biked with all his equipment to Berlin-Mitte. He left his bike on the Marschall Bridge that crossed the Spree not far from the sector border between Reichstagsufer and Schiffbauerdamm. Beneath the bridge Klaus Schröter cut through the barbed wire fence that blocked access to the water. He descended the staircase in the embankment wall and entered the water. A border soldier on duty in the watchtower at the corner of Reichstagsufer and Ebertstrasse noticed him doing this. He and two other border guards tried to stop the escape by opening fire as soon as the fugitive dove under water.[9] A bullet grazed the back of Klaus Schröter's head; he lost consciousness and drowned.[10] Following a long search, his body was pulled out of the Spree at 7:45 a.m. An East Berlin fire boat hung out a water curtain to block the view of observers on the west side.

Hence the West Berlin police could only surmise "that a fugitive was shot by the Soviet sector 'Grepo' (border police) and later retrieved from the Spree."[11]

Thirty years later the circumstances that led to Klaus Schröter's death were finally made known. The guards that were brought to court in 1994 denied their guilt, claiming that they had only fired into the water without aiming so that they would not be punished for refusing to obey orders.[12] But the judges believed that at least one of them had acted with a degree of intent to kill, and he was declared guilty.[13]

At the time of Klaus Schröter's death East Germany denied that he had been shot and killed by border guards.[14] The East Berlin Stasi agent that brought his mother the news told her that her son had been found dead in the Spree and that he had drowned after suffering a brain contusion.[15] The Stasi man presented himself as a state prosecutor and pressured the mother to agree to a cremation. "I was so wiped out and so scared that I did everything he asked. He presented me with the letter, gave me a pen [and] dictated."[16]

Klaus Schröter's colleagues at work were also left in the dark about the true circumstances of his death. When the Stasi learned that "rumors were spreading that Schröter had been shot while trying to break through the border," Stasi employees, with the help of the company leadership, organized a "get-together" to put a stop to the rumors.[17] It was announced at the meeting that Klaus Schröter suffered a brain contusion while trying to leave East Germany illegally with a diving apparatus and that this caused him to drown."[18] It was stated that as an engineer he should have known that trying to dive under the Spree was an act of suicide and that anyone in the company who had known about Schröter's intentions bore "a certain degree of responsibility for the result of his undertaking."[19] His colleagues did not believe the official announcement. They thought it more likely that Klaus Schröter had been shot by border guards. They had heard on the news from a West Berlin radio station that shots had been fired that morning on the Reichtagsufer.[20]

No amount of intimidation could stop his friends and colleagues from going to Friedersdorf for the funeral on December 14, 1963. Klaus Schröter's father placed the urn in the grave. The minister did not mention the circumstances of the death. For his sermon he chose a bible verse from the Epistle to the Romans. "For thy sake we are killed all the day long; we are accounted as sheep for the slaughter. Nay, in all these things we are more than conquerors through him that loved us."[21]

Christine Brecht

1 "Niederschrift der Zeugenvernehmung der Mutter von Klaus Schröter durch die Bielefelder Polizei, 12.12.1966," in: StA Berlin, Az. Js 86/90, Bd. 1, Bl. 84–92, here Bl. 92.

2 "Abschrift eines Schreibens der Mutter von Klaus Schröter an den Untersuchungsausschuss Freiheitlicher Juristen, 7.11.1966," in: Ibid., Bl. 69–72, here Bl. 71.

3 See LStU Sachsen-Anhalt (ed.), *Tod in der Spree. Zur Erinnerung an Klaus Schröter, erschossen auf der Flucht am 4.11.1963,* Magdeburg, 2001.

4 See "Ermittlungsbericht [des MfS]/KD Berlin-Mitte, 5.11.1963," in: BStU, MfS, AS 754/70, Bd. 2, Nr. 4, Bl. 15–16.

5 See ibid.

6 See "Niederschrift der Zeugenvernehmung der Mutter von Klaus Schröter durch die Bielefelder Polizei, 12.12.1966," in: StA Berlin, Az. Js 86/90, Bd. 1, Bl. 85–87.

7 "Niederschrift der Zeugenvernehmung eines Freundes von Klaus Schröter durch die West-Berliner Polizei, 15.11.1966," in: StA Berlin, Az. Js 86/90, Bd. 1, Bl. 74–75, here Bl. 74.

8 "Niederschrift der Zeugenvernehmung eines Freundes von Klaus Schröter durch die Berliner Polizei, 29.10.1991," in: Ibid., Bl. 155–159, here Bl. 156.

9 See "Bericht der NVA/1.GB/GR 33 zum versuchten Grenzdurchbruch am 4.11.1963 gegen 4.00 Uhr am Reichstagsufer im Abschnitt des GR 33, 4.11.1963," in: BArch, VA-07/16931, Bl. 27–30.

10 See "Obduktionsbericht des IGM der HU, 5.11.1963," in: BStU, MfS, AS 754/70, Bd. 2, Nr. 4, Bl. 33–39.

11 "Schlussbericht der West-Berliner Polizei, 13.1.1964," in: StA Berlin, Az. Js 86/90, Bd. 1, Bl. 42.

12 See "Mauer-Tod: Abrechnung nach 31 Jahren", in: *Super-Illu,* 15.11.1994.

13 See "Urteil des Landgerichts Berlin vom 17.11.1994," in: StA Berlin, Az. Js 86/90, Protokollband, Bl. 1–34.

14 See "Bericht der VfS Gross-Berlin/Abt. IX zur Leichensache, 6.11.1963," in: BStU, MfS, AS 754/70, Bd. 2, Nr. 4, Bl. 4–6, here Bl. 5, and "[MfS-]Abschlussvermerk, 8.11.1963," in: Ibid., Bl. 46.

15 Ibid.

16 "Abschrift eines Schreibens der Mutter von Klaus Schröter an den Untersuchungsausschuss Freiheitlicher Juristen, 7.11.1966," in: StA Berlin, Az. Js 86/90, Bd. 1, Bl. 69.

17 "II. Bericht der VfS Gross-Berlin/Abt. IX zur Leichensache Klaus Schröter," in: BStU, MfS, AS 754/70, Bd. 2, Nr. 4, Bl. 42.

18 See "[MfS-]Bericht über die Grenzverletzung durch den Betriebsangehörigen des VEB Starkstromanlagenbau Berlin, 10.12.1963," in: Ibid., Bl. 25–28.

19 Ibid., Bl. 27.

20 See "Niederschrift der Zeugenvernehmung eines Freundes von Klaus Schröter durch die West-Berliner Polizei, 15.11.1966," in: StA Berlin, Az. Js 86/90, Bd. 1, Bl. 75.

21 LStU Sachsen-Anhalt (ed.), *Tod in der Spree. Zur Erinnerung an Klaus Schröter, erschossen auf der Flucht am 4.11.1963,* Magdeburg, 2001, p. 32.

Dietmar Schulz

born on October 21, 1939

fatally injured on November 25, 1963

on the S-Bahn tracks north of the Bornholmer Strasse station

at the sector border between

Berlin-Prenzlauer Berg and Berlin-Wedding

On the evening of November 25, 1963, East German border soldiers found a critically injured young man on the grounds of the S-Bahn north of the Bornholmer Strasse station. It was Dietmar Schulz, age 24, who lived in the nearby East Berlin district of Pankow. He had been hit by a moving train while crossing the tracks in an attempt to reach the West Berlin district of Wedding on the other side. Unconscious and covered in blood, he was transported to the People's Police Hospital where he died from his injuries a short time later.[1]

Evidently, Dietmar Schulz, who was born on October 21, 1939, had been harboring thoughts of escaping for a long time. He confided in a young West German that he met in an East Berlin bar in April 1963 that he was opposed to the Communist Party regime and planned to take off to the West someday. His fiancée was also aware that he wanted to escape from East Germany. She believed he feared being conscripted into the National People's Army.[2] When Dietmar Schulz left the apartment they shared on November 25, 1963 at around 7 p.m., nothing indicated that he was planning to go through with his plan that evening.

His apartment on Gaillardstrasse in Pankow was only a few minutes away from the sector border that ran along the S-Bahn tracks between the Bornholmer Strasse and Wollankstrasse stations. The Bornholmer Strasse station had been closed down when the Wall was built and West Berlin S-Bahn trains were only permitted to pass through the "ghost station" without stopping. The East Berlin north-south line ran directly parallel to the west line on a new two-track route that was situated within the border area, a 100-meter-wide prohibited zone. This special zone had been created on order of the East German Defense Ministry in June 1963[3] with the official explanation that the measure would serve "to protect the state border between East Germany and West Berlin." In truth, however, it was designed to prevent escape attempts at an early stage by making it more difficult to reach the border barriers at the Wall.

Dietmar Schulz was not completely sober when he entered the railway grounds in the border area that November evening, but evidently nobody noticed him. Contradictory reports exist about how the young man was able to enter the prohibited zone and how the fatal accident occurred. One report from the East Berlin command stated that a male person jumped from a moving S-Bahn train south of Maximilianstrasse at 9:20 p.m. It concluded succinctly: "The person was delivered to the VP hospital with a fractured skull and remained there."[4] But the transport police that was responsible for further investigations came to the conclusion that Dietmar Schulz had walked from his apartment to the railroad embankment where he was run over by an S-Bahn train under unknown circumstances. The Trapo report did not mention that it involved an escape attempt, and instead classified the incident as a "personal accident with fatal consequences."[5]

The victim's fiancée was mistrustful of the official information provided by the authorities and refused to believe that Dietmar Schulz had died in an accident. She was certain that he had been shot and killed. After the funeral, which took place on December 2, 1963 in East Berlin, she contacted the young West German whom her fiancé had met a half year earlier. He passed her information on to the West German authorities. In response the Central Registry Office in Salzgitter opened an investigation in April 1964 to determine whether an escape attempt by an East German, age 24, was thwarted by force of arms.[6] The Berlin public prosecutor's office reopened the case after the East German archives were made accessible, but the theory that Dietmar Schulz had been shot by border soldiers could not be confirmed.[7]

Christine Brecht

1   See "Verfügung der Staatsanwaltschaft bei dem Kammergericht Berlin (2 Js 132/91), 29.1.1992," in: StA Berlin, Az. 2 Js 132/91, Bl. 163, and "Trapo-Rapport Nr. 330/63, 26.11.1963," in: PHS, Bestand Trapo-Rapporte, n. pag.

2   See "Niederschrift der Zeugenvernehmung eines Brieffreundes von Dietmar Schulz durch die Polizei in Karlsruhe, 9.4.1964," in: Ibid., Bl. 28–31, and the conversation conducted by Christine Brecht with Ingo S., a penpal of Dietmar Schulz, 28.6.2007.

3   See "'Verordnung über Massnahmen zum Schutz der Staatsgrenze zwischen der Deutschen Demokratischen Republik und Westberlin' des DDR-Ministerrates, 21.6.1963," and "Anordnung über die Ordnung im Grenzgebiet an der Staatsgrenze der Deutschen Demokratischen Republik zu Westberlin' von DDR-Verteidigungsminister Hoffmann, 21.6.1963," in: Gesetzblatt der DDR, 1963, part. II, pp. 381–384.

4   "Operative Tagesmeldung Nr. 329/63 der NVA/Stadtkommandantur Berlin/Operative Abteilung, 26.11.1963," in: BArch, VA-07/6025, Bl. 339.

5   "Trapo-Rapport Nr. 330/63, 26.11.1963," in: PHS, Bestand Trapo-Rapporte, n. pag.

6   See "Schreiben des Landeskriminalamts Baden-Württemberg an die Zentrale Erfassungsstelle der Landesjustizverwaltungen Salzgitter, 14.4.1964," in: StA Berlin, Az. 2 Js 132/91, Bl. 27.

7   See "Verfügung der Staatsanwaltschaft bei dem Kammergericht Berlin (2 Js 132/91), 29.1.1992," in: Ibid., Bl. 163–164.

Dieter Berger

born on October 27, 1939

shot dead on December 13, 1963
at the Teltow Canal near the Wrede Bridge
in Berlin-Johannisthal at the sector border
between Berlin-Treptow and Berlin-Neukölln

D ieter Berger from Glienicke in the Oranienburg district was 24 years old when
he entered the East Berlin border area not far from his workplace in December
1963. Neither archival documents nor eyewitness reports provide conclusive evidence as to why he ended up there. According to border troop and Stasi files, he
was trying to cross the border grounds, but his relatives thought it was more likely
that after consuming alcohol he had wandered around aimlessly and unknow-
ingly entered the border grounds. But after careful analysis of the facts, there is
little to indicate that Dieter Berger had attempted an escape on the afternoon of
December 13, 1963. Neither the life situation of the young family man nor the
course of events that led to his death supported the idea of an escape attempt.

Dieter Berger, a bricklayer, was working in Adlershof at a construction site of
the East Berlin Academy of Sciences that had established its natural science technology institute in the southeast of the city. He had been married for over a year
and was the father of a little girl. Dieter Berger was born on October 27, 1939 in
Polkau, Silesia. He never met his biological father, who died as a soldier in the
Second World War. He grew up with his younger half-brother, his mother and
stepfather. After the war, in 1947, his family left Silesia and settled in Glienicke, a
northern suburb of Berlin located in the Soviet sector. He attended school here
from 1947 to 1955, after which he did an apprenticeship as a bricklayer in a state-
run company in East Berlin.[1] He married Gerda, who was five years younger than
he, in 1962. She had also grown up in Silesia and moved as a child with her family
to Glienicke. They moved into a small house with a garden not far from their parents and in-laws, with whom they got along well. After his death his widow commented that politics had not interested her husband, who was crazy about motorcycles. They had never discussed fleeing. As far as she knew, he had no reason to
leave his family.[2] His parents, like his wife, did not think that he had attempted to
flee. His mother wrote in a letter to relatives in West Germany that "Dieter did not
intend to leave us, nor did he have reason to do so. He was apparently drunk and
lost his sense of direction [...]."[3] The investigations conducted by Stasi staff after
his death confirmed this theory. The local East German police described Dieter

Berger "as a highly regarded citizen who was not opposed to our system. Aside from the fact that he listened to loud popular western music in his house, there is nothing negative to report." He was always friendly and courteous and everything suggests that his marriage was harmonious.[4]

December 13, 1963 was a Friday. That morning Dieter Berger drove to work in Berlin-Adlershof as usual. According to Stasi files, during his lunch break he got drunk with a colleague and left the construction site later that afternoon.[5] After that he presumably walked to Johannisthal, the next bordering district. Two guards watched him approach the border grounds at the bank of the Teltow Canal at around 3 p.m.[6] They were in a communication trench within the prohibited strip and assumed that he was a fugitive. When they ordered him to halt, the man insulted them and continued to try to climb the fence. Later one of the guards testified before the court that the young man's conduct had disconcerted them.[7]

In response to their warning shots, Dieter Berger climbed down from the fence and raised his hands in the air as they demanded. Workers and employees of the West Berlin cement asbestos plant on the other side of the canal became aware of what was happening. They also assumed that the fugitive had attempted to flee and was being arrested. Then they observed the supposed fugitive take a step away from the border grounds and witnessed his being shot by the border guards.[8] The East German border troop reports described the situation differently. They claimed that the West Berlin eye-witnesses engaged in a "provocation" by insulting the guards. The "border violator" tried to take advantage of this by escaping into the hinterland.[9]

Dieter Berger died from his injuries on the way to the People's Police Hospital. He did not have any papers on him so it took the East German authorities a number of days to identify him.[10] The day after his death the West Berlin press reported: "Like hired assassins the members of the communist border police struck down a fugitive with his hands raised at the sector border in Johannisthal yesterday just after 3:30 p.m."[11]

His wife had to identify the body at the forensic institute of Charité Hospital on December 16, after which an autopsy was performed.[12] The East Berlin coroners established that Dieter Berger had collapsed after being hit by a bullet in his thigh and was already lying on the ground when the fatal shots hit him. They also stressed that Dieter Berger was heavily intoxicated, which led them in the autopsy report to conclude that "at the time of his death, the person in question was no longer capable of recognizing the danger of his actions, nor could he act accordingly."[13]

After reunification two border soldiers were arraigned, but the main hearing never took place because the gunman had already suffered two strokes and was unable to stand trial. The man who had been his guard leader at the time was acquitted on November 1, 1995. The court found it was not evident that he had fired shots or ordered the shooting.[14]

Christine Brecht

1   See "Arbeitsbuch von Dieter Berger, ausgestellt vom Rat des Landkreises Oranienburg / Arbeit u. Berufsausbil-dung / Arbeitskraftlenkung, 8. 6. 1955," privately owned.

2   See the conversation conducted by Christine Brecht with Gerda L., Dieter Berger's wife at the time, 9. 7. 2007.

3   "Leseabschrift eines Briefs der Mutter von Dieter Berger, 25. 12. 1963," in: StA Berlin, Az. 2 Js 66 / 90, Bd. 1, Bl. 102.

4   "Ermittlungsbericht der [MfS] / Verwaltung Gross-Berlin / Abt. VIII, 17. 12. 1963," in: BStU, MfS, AS 754 / 70, Bd. 2, Nr. 1, Bl. 9.

5   See "[MfS-]Bericht über die Identifizierung des unbekannten männlichen Grenzverletzers, 16. 12. 1963," in: Ibid., Bl. 4 – 8, here Bl. 4 – 5.

6   See "Bericht der NVA / 4.GB / Kommandeur über den versuchten Grenzdurchbruch im Bereich der 1. Grenzkom-panie des Grenzregiments 42, 13. 12. 1963," in: BArch, VA-07 / 6003, Bl. 14 – 17.

7   See "Urteil des Landgerichts Berlin vom 1. 11. 1995," in: StA Berlin, Az. 2 Js 66 / 90, Bd. 4, Bl. 149 – 171.

8   See "Funkspruch des West-Berliner Polizeireviers 221 betr. Schussabgabe auf vermutl. Flüchtling, 13. 12. 1963," in: PHS, Bestand Grenzvorkommnisse, n. pag.

9   See "Bericht der NVA / 4.GB / Kommandeur über den versuchten Grenzdurchbruch im Bereich der 1. Grenzkom-panie des Grenzregiments 42, 13. 12. 1963," in: BArch, VA-07 / 6003, Bl. 15.

10 See "[MfS-]Bericht über die Identifizierung des unbekannten männlichen Grenzverletzers, 16. 12. 1963," in: BStU, MfS, AS 754 / 70, Bd. 2, Nr. 1, Bl. 4.

11 "Vopo schoss Flüchtling nach Festnahme MP-Garbe in den Rücken," in: Telegraf, 14. 12. 1963. See also "Wehr-loses Opfer von hinten erschossen," in: BZ, 14. 12. 1963; "Wieder ein Opfer des Mord-Befehls!", in: Bild-Zeitung, 14. 12. 1963; "Flüchtling hinterrücks niedergeschossen," in: Spandauer Volksblatt, 14. 12. 1963.

12 See "[MfS-]Bericht über die Identifizierung des unbekannten männlichen Grenzverletzers, 16. 12. 1963," in: BStU, MfS, AS 754 / 70, Bd. 2, Nr. 1, Bl. 6 – 8.

13 "Obduktionsbericht des IGM der HU, 19. 12. 1963," in: Ibid., Bl. 22 – 31, here Bl. 31.

14 See "Urteil des Landgerichts Berlin vom 1. 11. 1995," in: StA Berlin, Az. 2 Js 66 / 90, Bd. 4, Bl. 149 – 171.

Paul Schultz

born on October 2, 1945

shot dead on December 25, 1963
on the corner of Melchiorstrasse and Bethaniendamm
at the sector border between
Berlin-Mitte and Berlin-Kreuzberg

Paul Schultz was shot and killed at the Berlin Wall on Christmas Day 1963. The eighteen-year-old from Neubrandenburg in Mecklenburg and his friend Hartmut D. had tried to break through the border between the Mitte and Kreuzberg districts that day. They had just scaled the wall, which was covered with barbed wire along the top, when border guards opened fire. Hartmut D. jumped down to the other side uninjured, but Paul Schultz was fatally hit by a hail of bullets before he could fall to the ground on the West Berlin side. A police constable on duty at the nearby Mariannenplatz rushed to the aid of the fugitive. Paul Schultz uttered in pain to him that he had been hit in the back.[1] He died that very night in the Bethanien Hospital in Kreuzberg from a bullet through his lung.[2]

The violent death of the 18-year-old fugitive not only overshadowed the Christmas celebrations, but also set off angry political protests. In December 1963, a "border pass agreement" had been negotiated allowing West Berliners to visit relatives on the east side of the city for the first time since the Wall had gone up. Now the political change that the Senate had worked so hard to achieve, and which everyone hoped would lead to an easing of tensions between the East and West, was suddenly called into question.[3] Everywhere doubts were raised as to whether it was right to engage in negotiations with the representatives of the East German communist regime who were responsible for the shots fired at the Wall. The vice chancellor and FDP politician, Erich Mende, said that it was unfathomable "that on the Christmas holiday shots were aimed and fired at a young person who wanted to do in a big city what is totally normal in a civilized society: go from one side of the city to the other without weapons and without luggage."[4] There were protest demonstrations for days at Mariannenplatz. Opponents of the East German communist regime erected a wooden cross with a photo of Paul Schultz at the site where he was shot and began a fasting campaign to denounce the East German leadership's disregard for human rights.[5]

Paul was his best friend, Hartmut D. told the West Berlin police.[6] He fell into a state of shock when he realized that his friend had died right next to him. Later he said that it took him many years to get over this experience.[7] They had grown up together in Neubrandenburg. Paul Schultz, the youngest of three brothers, had been born there in October 1945. He never knew his father, who had fallen in the Second World War. He and Hartmut D. both left school upon receiving the secondary school certificate at the end of 10th grade. Paul became an apprentice to a private electrician in September 1962. Hartmut and Paul were almost exactly the same age and had celebrated their 18th birthdays together in October 1963. Hartmut D. later recalled that they began to discuss their plan to escape to West Berlin that evening. They had planned to go from there to West Germany. They knew that what they were planning was risky and that they might be shot at the Wall, but they said "it's all or nothing."[8]

The two boys left their homes early in the morning on Christmas Day, telling their parents that they were going to visit friends. Hartmut D. reported that they took a train from Neubrandenburg to East Berlin and walked for hours along the inner-city security grounds, looking for a good place to flee. When dawn broke they decided on a spot at the corner of Melchiorstrasse and Bethaniendamm because it seemed like the security strip there was narrower. They stopped a while, observing the border guards patrolling back and forth along the area and waited for the right moment. Then they climbed the interior fence and tried to run through the barriers as quickly as possible. "We heard the Soviet zone border guards cry out, 'Halt!' just as we were trying to get through the last fence before the Wall," Hartmut D. said. The guards started shooting immediately.[9]

The border troop and Stasi files show that at the very moment when the two boys entered the security strip, two additional guards appeared who happened to be patrolling between the individual border sections. The guards did not hesitate before opening fire.[10] They were later commended for their actions by the NVA city commander Poppe and awarded with a briefcase and a wristwatch.

In 1995 the Berlin district court found that both guards were determined to use their firearms to prevent the escape and had willfully accepted the death of the two fugitives. At the time of the hearing one of the gunmen had already passed away, but the second one was found guilty of joint manslaughter and sentenced to 18 months probation.[11]

As soon as Paul Schultz's mother and brothers heard about his death from the RIAS West Berlin radio station, they came under East German secret police surveillance.[12] But the East German secret police were unable to find anything that could be held against the boys or their relatives. The Stasi files show that investigators used ideological biases and unproven assumptions to explain the boys' actions: "Constantly listening to western radio" had "negatively influenced" Paul Schultz. The Stasi believed that Hartmut D. had been the "initiator of the border breach," and that Paul Schultz had allowed himself to be talked into fleeing.[13] East German media also presented the "facts" to suggest that the teenage fugitives had not acted of their own free will, but had been seduced by RIAS, western television and western politicians.[14]

The West Berlin authorities contacted the family of the deceased in East Germany to arrange to have the body transferred to them. The Stasi was aware of this because it had the family under surveillance, but it did not interfere.[15] On December 28, a West Berlin police escort accompanied the hearse to the border crossing at Heinrich-Heine-Strasse. West Berlin residents also joined in the murdered fugitive's "final trip."[16] But the public was excluded from the funeral in Neubrandenburg that took place two days later.[17] The local Stasi district office and the Communist Party district leadership made sure that Paul Schultz's friends and colleagues were not permitted to attend the memorial service.

Christine Brecht

1 See "Niederschrift der Zeugenvernehmung eines West-Berliner Polizeiwachtmeisters durch die West-Berliner Polizei, 27.12.1963," in: StA Berlin, Az. 27/2 Js 159/90, Bd. 1, Bl. 15.

2 See "Protokoll über eine Leichenöffnung im Sektionsraum des Leichenschauhauses Berlin-West, 27.12.1963," in: Ibid., Bl. 75–77, and "Bericht der West-Berliner Polizei, 6.1.1964," in: Ibid., Bl. 46.

3 For context, see Heinrich Potthoff, *Im Schatten der Mauer. Deutschlandpolitik 1961 bis 1990,* Berlin, 1999, and Gerhard Kunze, *Grenzerfahrungen, Kontakte und Verhandlungen zwischen dem Land Berlin und der DDR 1949–1989,* Berlin, 1999.

4 "Drei Tage fasten am Gedenkkreuz," in: *Bild-Zeitung,* 30.12.1963.

5 See ibid.; *Die Welt,* 27.12.1963; *Telegraf,* 29.12.1963.

6 See "Niederschrift der Zeugenvernehmung des Mitflüchtlings von Paul Schultz durch die Berliner Polizei, 25.12.1963," in: StA Berlin, Az. 27/2 Js 159/90, Bd. 1, Bl. 6–7, and ibid., 26.8.1964, in: Ibid., Bl. 102.

7 See "Niederschrift der Zeugenvernehmung des Mitflüchtlings von Paul Schultz durch die West-Berliner Polizei, 15.12.1992," in: Ibid., Bl. 196–202, here Bl. 202.

8 Ibid.

9 "Niederschrift der Zeugenvernehmung des Mitflüchtlings von Paul Schultz durch die West-Berliner Polizei, 25.12.1963," in: StA Berlin, Az. 27/2 Js 159/90, Bd. 1, Bl. 7.

10 See "Einzel-Information Nr. 801/63 [des MfS-ZAIG] über einen gewaltsamen Grenzdurchbruch am 25.12.1963 vom Demokratischen Berlin nach Westberlin, 26.12.1963," in: BStU, MfS, ZAIG Nr. 699, Bl. 40–41; "Bericht der NVA/Stadtkommandant Poppe an Erich Honecker betr. Grenzdurchbruch im Abschnitt des GR-35, [27.] 12.1963," in: BArch, VA-07/6003, Bl. 6–8, and "Bericht der NVA/1.GB/Grenzregiment 35/Kommandeur, 25.12.1963," in: Ibid., Bl. 10–12.

11 See "Urteil des Landgerichts Berlin vom 4.9.1995," in: StA Berlin, Az. 27/2 Js 159/90, Bd. 4, Bl. 1–46, here Bl. 1–2, 38.

12 See "Einzel-Information Nr. 8091/63 [des MfS-ZAIG] über einen gewaltsamen Grenzdurchbruch am 25.12. 1963 vom demokratischen Berlin nach Westberlin, 28.12.1963," in: BStU, MfS, ZAIG Nr. 699, Bl. 42–46.

13 Ibid., Bl. 44, 46.

14 See, for example "Provokation am Schutzwall," in: *Neues Deutschland,* 27.12.1963.

15 See "Aktenvermerk des [MfS]/HA V/Einsatzgruppe, 27.12.1963 und 28.12.1963," in: BStU, MfS, ZKG Nr. 13077, Bl. 57–58.

16 See "Ereignismeldung der West-Berliner Polizei/Kommando der Schutzpolizei, 29.12.1963," in: PHS, Bestand Ereignismeldungen der West-Berliner Schutzpolizei, n. pag.

17 See "Mitteilung des Informationsbüros West, 6.1.1964," in: BArch, B 137, Nr. 6429, n. pag., and "Ulbricht befahl Stille," in: *Berliner Morgenpost,* 7.1.1964.

Walter Hayn

born on January 31, 1939

shot dead on February 27, 1964
on Kiefholzstrasse
at the sector border between
Berlin-Treptow and Berlin-Neukölln

A section of the sector border along the Kiefholzstrasse in the East Berlin district of Treptow was fenced in on both sides by garden plots. The small garden settlement "Sorgenfrei" ('Carefree') was located on the East Berlin side. The last barbed wire fence marked the border to the "Neuköllnische Wiesen" garden colony on the West Berlin side. On the evening of February 27, 1964, residents on the West Berlin side heard gunshots and tried to find out what was going on behind the fence. Their view was blocked by a hedge, but they could clearly hear the voices of border guards a few meters away. One of them called out, "Grab him!" Another one threatened in a harsh tone, "Stop you bastard or I'll wipe you out."[1] Based on this information the West Berlin police had no doubt that firearms had been used to prevent an escape, but it was not known whether the fugitive had been hit by the shots fired. Finally, after the East German archives were opened, the events of that evening came to light: Border soldiers had shot and killed 25-year-old Walter Hayn while he was trying to escape to West Berlin. For "security reasons," the East German authorities did not reveal the circumstances of his death at the time, not even to the victim's relatives.[2]

Walter Hayn was born in 1939 in Breslau. After the family was expelled from Silesia at the end of the Second World War, they resettled in Ebersbach, a community near Dresden in the Grossenhain district of Saxony. His father had remained missing since the war and the mother raised the four children alone and under difficult circumstances. The eldest brother turned his back on the newly founded East German state in 1950 and settled in West Germany. Walter Hayn, the second youngest brother, left school after eight years and began agricultural training. He worked for a time in construction before enlisting with the East German police force in 1958 – not so much out of conviction as in the hope that it would improve his career prospects. He was sent to East Berlin with the army, where, according to information provided by his brother, he served his duty on the inner-city sector border.[3] Walter Hayn was no longer serving in the East German police force when he became acquainted with the border regime that was established after the Wall. He was discharged from police duty in June 1961 and worked as a transport and construction worker.[4] By this time he was married and lived with his wife and their son in the Lichtenberg district until they divorced in September 1963. What led him to risk his life a few months later by attempting to escape is not known. His brother thought he wanted a better life. In the investigations conducted after his death the Stasi was unable to find any motive for his escape attempt. All they found out was that Walter Hayn was not, as they had first suspected, a "slacker at work" or a "drinker." He went to work regularly, paid child support, his financial situation was stable and his neighbors found him to be friendly and courteous.[5]

Whatever his reasons may have been, it must not have been easy for him to embark on this dangerous undertaking. Before entering the border area Walter Hayn boosted his courage with a few drinks in a bar on the grounds of the "Sorgenfrei" garden settlement.[6] He had his identification card, employment record, divorce papers and his brother's address in West Germany in his pocket. He then set off, climbing over the interior fence into the security strip and tried to reach the three rows of border fence behind which the West Berlin garden settlement was located. It was 10:20 p.m. when he was noticed by the two guards who were patrolling this section of the border. When he failed to stop, they shot at him. The guards were assisted by another guard on duty nearby who also opened fire from the watchtower.[7] A total of 17 shots were fired. Two bullets hit Walter Hayn right in front of the fence; one of them killed him.

During the era of East Germany, the three guards were commended for "preventing a border breach." In 1995 they were indicted for joint manslaughter. During the main hearing all three men claimed that they had only shot into the air.[8] The court, however, concluded that at least two of them were determined to use all means to stop Walter Hayn from escaping and thus willingly accepted his death. It could not be determined which one was responsible for the fatal shot, but the court assumed that the two former border soldiers had acted together and their orders and insults that had been overheard that February night implicated them. For this reason the deadly shot could be attributed to either of them. Given the complicated legal position and in consideration of all the mitigating factors, they were sentenced to one year and nine months and one year and six months in prison with the sentence being commuted to probation. The court decision stated that one of the defendants was to "be punished more severely since he was personally responsible for hitting the victim with at least one bullet."[9] The third guard was acquitted because the court could not disprove his claim that he intentionally shot off target.

Walter Hayn's brother, who pressed charges in 1991 and followed the trial closely, found the light sentences unfair. He remembered well how the East German authorities had pressured him and his mother after his brother died. Neither of them had believed the official claim that Walter Hayn had drowned at the "state border." Internally the East Berlin Stasi district administration justified their deceptive maneuver with the "Hayn family's connections to the West." They tried to intimidate the relatives by warning them "that they are liable to prosecution if they spread rumors about this affair."[10] Nevertheless, the Stasi was not able to prevent a "certain agitation" from spreading in Walter Hayn's hometown of Ebersbach after his mother filed a complaint with the local police.[11] Walter Hayn's brother, however, did not leave it at that. He drove to East Berlin and began his own investigation but was unable to find any evidence. When a state prosecutor told him that everyone has to know what happens to a fugitive at the border, he became certain that his brother had been shot.[12]

Christine Brecht

1   See "Bericht der West-Berliner Polizei, 27.2.1964," in: StA Berlin, Az. 27/2 Js 93/90, Bd. 2, Bl. 5 – 6, here Bl. 5.

2   See "[MfS-]Abschlussvermerk zur Leichensache Walter Hayn, 4.3.1964," in: BStU, MfS, AS 754/70, Bd. 2, Nr. 5, Bl. 40.

3   Conversation conducted by Christine Brecht with P. Hayn, Walter Hayn's brother, 3.7.2007.

4   "Bericht der VfS Gross-Berlin/Abt. IX über die Grenzverletzung in Berlin-Treptow, "Kolonie Sorgenfrei", Dammweg durch eine männliche Person, 28.2.1964," in: BStU, MfS, AS 754/70, Bd. 2, Nr. 5, Bl. 4 – 6, and "Arbeitsbuch von Walter Hayn, ausgestellt vom Rat des Kreises Grossenhain/Abt. Arbeit und Berufsausbildung, 27.9.1954," in: Ibid., Bl. 44.

5   "Ermittlungsbericht der VfS Gross-Berlin/Abt. VIII/Referat 2 an die Arbeitsgruppe Staatsgrenze, 28.2.1964," in: Ibid., Bl. 10 –12.

6   See "Einzel-Information [des MfS-ZAIG] Nr. 167/64, 29.2.1964," in: BStU, MfS, ZAIG Nr. 836, Bl. 7.

7   See "Bericht der NVA/1.GB/Der Kommandeur über das besondere Vorkommnis vom 27.2.64, 20.20 Uhr, im Abschnitt 5/GR-37 Kleingartenanlage Sorgenfrei, 27.2.1964," in: BArch, VA-07/16933, Bl. 191–193.

8   See "Schlagader zerrissen – aber keiner will getroffen haben," in: *Die Welt am Sonntag,* 14.1.1996.

9   "Urteil des Landgerichts Berlin vom 22.1.1996," in: StA Berlin, Az. 27/2 Js 93/90, Bd. 3a, Bl. 1–38, here Bl. 37.

10 "Bericht der VfS Gross-Berlin/Abt. IX zum Leichenvorgang Walter Hayn, 5.3.1964," in: BStU, MfS, AS 754/70, Bd. 2, Nr. 5, Bl. 18 – 20, here Bl. 20.

11 See "Bericht der VfS Gross-Berlin/Abt. IX zum Leichenvorgang Walter Hayn, 5.3.1964," in: Ibid., Bl. 18 – 20, and "[MfS-]Abschlussvermerk zur Leichensache Walter Hayn, 4.3.1964," in: Ibid., Bl. 40.

12 Conversation conducted by Christine Brecht with P. Hayn, Walter Hayn's brother, 3.7.2007.

Adolf Philipp

born on August 17, 1943

shot dead on May 5, 1964
on the outer ring between
Berlin-Spandau and Falkenhagen
(Nauen district)

An announcement from the East German news agency ADN on May 5, 1964 caused horror and dismay in West Berlin. It reported that the 20-year-old West Berliner Adolf Philipp had been shot that night while attacking a border guard in the area of Staaken.[1] The next day the East Berlin chief state prosecutor had the body sent to the authorities on the west side of the city, leaving no doubt that Adolf Philipp had died from bullet wounds, but a number of unanswered questions remained. The Senate press chief announced on RIAS that West Berlin investigations were unable to find any damage done to the barbed wire fence on the border to Staaken, nor had any shots been heard during the time in question.[2] The East German archives that are now accessible reveal that the East German authorities had kept the western authorities guessing as to the exact location of the incident. But the theory that the supposed "attack" may have had to do with an operation to help people escape had already been proven false during the Cold War.[3]

Adolf Philipp came from Bavaria and had just recently moved to West Berlin. His younger sister remembered him as a thoughtful young man with high ideals who was highly regarded by everyone for his friendly and helpful manner. Born in 1943 in Ziemetshausen near Augsburg as the oldest of four children, he grew up happy and sheltered in humble conditions.[4] The father had a small radio shop and the mother contributed to the family income with a job at the nearby press plant. Their only son was a very good and hard-working student with a special interest in math and technology. He completed school with the secondary school level certificate and did an apprenticeship as a radio and television technician. After completing his examination with very good marks he had the employment office arrange a job for him in West Berlin in the summer of 1963. Skilled laborers had become rare in Berlin after the sector border was sealed. Anyone willing to move to the walled-in half-city could expect to receive a number of benefits, but Adolf Philipp's main reason for moving there was that as a West Berliner he could not be drafted into the military.

Adolf Philipp began his new job in Berlin-Schöneberg as a radio and television technician in August 1963 and moved into a furnished room on the Kurfürstendamm. He wrote letters to his parents and sister describing in detail what he experienced: "Believe me, there is so much going on here, I have plans for the next half year," he reported shortly after he arrived.[5] At first it was the many leisure and cultural activities in the big city that captivated him. He went to the movies, theater and a radio show, he watched the six-day bike race in the Deutschlandhalle stadium and raved about the Chubby Checker rock and roll concert in the Sportpalast. But over time he became increasingly preoccupied with the Berlin Wall. He visited tourist attractions such as the Brandenburg Gate, and reported that it looked magnificent at night, "but the Wall [and] barbed wire in front of it are disturbing."[6] He repeatedly rode his bike along the sector border and to the city limits and spent a lot of time "studying," as he called it, the border grounds. Despite all the warning signs, he did not refrain from entering no-man's-land, those areas that, seen from West Berlin, were situated between the actual border line and the East German barricades. He described that on one of his Sunday bike tours in the Grunewald woods, he entered into "at least 50 meters of eastern territory" because the barbed wire was set far back there. "Two Grepos appeared promptly. They stared at me as if I were the 8th world wonder. I was holding my camera in my hand, but since they did not say anything [...], I refrained from taking a snapshot, although it would have been a good picture. These guys have the habit of staring at you through binoculars even from close up. They have to complete a report and write a personal description of every unusual incident."[7]

Adolf Philipp made no secret of his contempt for the border regime that the East German leadership had erected at the Berlin Wall. His sister recalled that during his visits to Ziemetshausen and in his letters he told relatives, neighbors and friends about the situation at the Wall and about families he knew that were separated. He described the situation at Bernauer Strasse as "dreadful." "The border runs right through the buildings on the other side of the street. Doors and windows are walled up. Shards of broken glass have been strewn over the top of the Wall. There is a church there that no one can visit. A cemetery with the graves of West Berliners lies deserted; there are four memorial plaques to people who died there trying to escape."[8] He could not understand West Berliners who had come to accept the division of the city. It is always the same, he once wrote: "When you say to them that they are really indifferent to the Wall they say, 'Well what else should we do?' As if there was nothing to do."[9] After his death colleagues reported that he had sought out people who felt the same way as he did, people involved in organizing escapes, so that he could become active himself.[10] He also attended some of the daily protest rallies against moving the Wall at the memorial to Peter Fechter that made the headlines in April 1963. Notes that he left behind in his apartment confirm that he was planning something, but they do not reveal exactly what.

Hence only the official reports of the border troops and East German Ministry of State Security provide information as to how Adolf Philipp died on the night of May 4, 1964.[11] They document that two border soldiers from the 2nd Company of Border Regiment 34, responsible for guarding the East German Nauen district bordering the West Berlin Spandau district, saw footprints on the border strip during their evening rounds. Assuming that these were tracks from a fugitive, they ran to a ground bunker to report it. When they got there, they were surprised to find Adolf Philipp threatening them with a pistol. Sergeant G. opened fire without hesitation. Adolf Philipp was hit a number of times and presumably died immediately. The Stasi investigation found that the weapon he had on him was only a gas pistol that could not fire real bullets. In 1991, after the East German archives were opened, Berlin's public prosecutor's office opened a new investigation. The two border guards involved in the case were identified through military and Stasi files. They both confessed to the fact that Sergeant G. had fired the deadly shots at that time. His claim that he had felt threatened by Adolf Philipp and had acted in self-defense was confirmed by the other guard and could not be disproved. Hence, he was not arraigned and the investigation was ended.[12]

Adolf Philipp was buried in his hometown of Ziemetshausen on May 11, 1964 amidst strong public sympathy. His mourning relatives received many letters of condolence from teachers, colleagues and acquaintances. His landlady in Berlin wrote: "I know it is not much of a comfort, but this young man was exactly the way my deceased husband would have wanted his son, who died in the war, to have been."[13] The Spandau district office erected a wooden cross in memory of Adolf Philipp.[14] It was dedicated in August 1964 as the third anniversary of the Berlin Wall's construction approached and still stands at the site where Adolf Philipp left his bike before he entered East German territory that night. His sister recalled that his relatives found his death "unfathomable, but not meaningless. He wanted something to change at the Wall and, after this cruel murder, all of Germany was looking at Berlin."[15]

Christine Brecht

1   See "Mordüberfall auf Grenzposten der DDR," in: *Neues Deutschland,* 6.5.1964.
2   See "Stellungnahme von Senatspressechef Egon Bahr im RIAS Berlin, 6.5.1964," in: *Deutschlandradio, Die Zeit im Funk,* 6.5.1964.
3   See "Schlussbericht der West-Berliner Polizei, 10.6.1964," in: StA Berlin, Az. 2 Js 150/91, Bd. 1, Bl. 98–99, and "Vermerk der West-Berliner Polizei zu den Angaben der am 11.12.65 nach West-Berlin geflüchteten ehemaligen Angehörigen der "NVA", 4.1.1966," in: Ibid., Bl. 138–139.
4   See the letter from Adolf Philipp's youngest sister to Christine Brecht, 16.4.2007.
5   Letter from Adolf Philipp to his parents, 29.8.1963," privately owned.
6   Letter from Adolf Philipp to his brothers and sisters, 18.9.1963," privately owned.
7   Letter from Adolf Philipp to his parents, 21.10.1963," privately owned.
8   Letter from Adolf Philipp to his parents, 22.9.1963," privately owned.
9   Letter from Adolf Philipp to his parents, 14.9.1963," privately owned.
10 See "Bericht der West-Berliner Polizei, 6.5.1964," in: StA Berlin, Az. 2 Js 150/91, Bd. 1, Bl. 38–43, and "Bericht der West-Berliner Polizei, 8.5.1964," in: Ibid., Bl. 55–56.
11 See "Bericht der NVA/2.GB/Der Kommandeur betr. Untersuchungsbericht zum versuchten Grenzdurchbruch Westberlin-DDR am 5.5.1964 gegen 1.35 Uhr durch 1 Person, 5.5.1964," in: BArch, VA-07/8371, Bl. 221–226, here Bl. 225; "Einzel-Information [des MfS-ZAIG] Nr. 370/64, 5.5.1964," in: BStU, MfS, ZAIG Nr. 863, Bl. 12–14.
12 See "Verfügung der Staatsanwaltschaft bei dem Kammergericht Berlin (2 Js 150/91), 19.2.1993," in: StA Berlin, Az. 2 Js 150/91, Bl. 354–356.
13 Letter from Adolf Philipp's West Berlin landlord to his family, 8.5.1964, privately owned.
14 See "Meldung der West-Berliner Polizei betr. Errichtung eines Mahnmals im Spandauer Stadtforst, 12.8.1964," in: PHS, Bestand Grenzvorkommnisse, n. pag.
15 Letter from Adolf Philipp's youngest sister to Christine Brecht, 16.4.2007.

Walter Heike

born on September 20, 1934

shot dead on June 22, 1964
on the grounds of the Invaliden Cemetery
at the sector border between
Berlin-Mitte and Berlin-Tiergarten

W alter Heike was 29 years old when he was shot on June 22, 1964 while try-ing to get past the Berlin Wall. The bachelor had been living at the time with his mother in Bad Freienwalde and had resumed work in his old profession as a painter. He had been living in East Berlin and working for the East German cus-toms administration just a few months before, but had been dismissed from his job there on February 5, 1964 because he had supposedly met a woman from West Berlin while on duty at the border customs office at Friedrichstrasse.[1] The information provided by the available files is not conclusive, but the abrupt end to his professional career was no doubt a turning point in Walter Heike's life and must have played a role in his decision to leave East Germany. Nonetheless, he sounded confident in a résumé that he wrote a short time later: "My social ac-tivities include singing in a choir, painting wall news sheets, club rooms, wall charts [...] I am also keen on learning and further education. I have many diverse cultural interests."[2]

Walter Heike was born in 1934 in Taurage (Tauroggen), Lithuania. He was the first of two children born to the carpenter Rudolf Heike and his wife, Marie. The family belonged to a small German minority that had lived in the Baltic States for many generations. Walter Heike's childhood was strongly affected by changes that had occurred as a consequence of the Second World War: His family was forced to move under troubling circumstances, which included expulsion, flight and resettle-ment. After resettling in German-occupied Poland, returning to Tauroggen and fleeing from the Red Army to Stettin, he finally reached Brandenburg with his mother and sister in July 1945 and settled in Wriezen, southeast of Berlin. His fa-ther never returned from the war and was registered as missing after 1945.[3] Walter Heike left school at the age of 16 without graduating. He worked for a time for a company that did painting for theaters and advertising in Strausberg and he trained as a painter. In early 1955 he enlisted for five years of service in the East German Garrisoned Police that became the National People's Army of East Germany the following year. During this time, before the draft was introduced, the state and party engaged in a strong propaganda campaign to recruit people into the mili-

155

tary.[4] Although the population was strongly opposed to rearmament, many young men enlisted for a number of years in the hope that it would improve their job prospects. For Walter Heike it seemed like his service had paid off. After leaving the National People's Army, he immediately received a position working for the East Berlin customs administration.[5]

The available files do not provide information as to when Walter Heike began thinking about escape or whether, as the East German authorities claim, he wanted to be with the West Berlin woman who caused him to lose his job at the customs service. But there are strong indications that he had planned his escape in advance: During his last visit in early June 1964, he suggested to his sister that inquiries would soon be made about him.[6] Walter Heike was carrying personal documents and cash on him when he escaped, suggesting that it was not a spontaneous act. Moreover, he left behind a notebook in which he had carefully listed the names of all the books he had to leave behind. He approached the border at a spot where construction was taking place – a plot on Scharnhorststrasse in Berlin-Mitte that ran parallel to the Spandauer Schifffahrts Canal near the Sandkrug Bridge.[7]

A member of the Stasi guard regiment that was responsible for guarding the entrance to the government hospital next door was the first to notice Walter Heike when he entered the border grounds there on the morning of June 22, 1964. The watch guard ordered him to halt and fired two warning shots, but Walter Heike did not stop. He climbed the wall of the Invaliden Cemetery and ran towards the canal bank. According to military files, he was then noticed by four border soldiers at 5:30 a.m. – two guards who were on duty on what is now known as the Peter Göring Tower, and two guards in a vehicle who were about to replace the other guards on duty. Sergeant L. set off after the fugitive who had just reached the last obstacle and was trying to pull himself over the Wall in front of the canal embankment. Absolutely determined to stop the man from fleeing, the border guard knelt down, released the safety on his Kalashnikov and opened fire from a distance of 25 to 30 meters.[8] A bullet hit Walter Heike in his abdomen causing internal injuries and he presumably died immediately. The fact that the "enemy" on the other side of the canal was unable to observe the events was evaluated by the border troops as a success.[9] The West Berlin police officers on the other side had heard gunshots and seen a seemingly lifeless person being carried away on a stretcher but they were unable to see what had happened behind the Wall.[10]

Two days later the victim's mother and sister were paid a visit by a Stasi agent and questioned. When Walter Heike's sister demanded to know the reason for the questioning, she was told that her brother "had been fatally wounded in Berlin as a consequence of his own actions." The relatives were not told that he had died on the "state border" because the Stasi feared that they might have contact with relatives in the West. Walter Heike's sister was not satisfied with this meager information, but her efforts to find out from the East Berlin attorney general where and how the supposed accident occurred were in vain.[11] The East German authorities were apparently also not pleased when Walter Heike's last employer inquired about a death certificate. The state prosecutor in charge of the case informed him that the family had no claim to death benefits since the burial costs had been paid for by the state.[12] In truth, however, Walter Heike's burial had been paid for with the cash that he had on him when he died.[13]

Christine Brecht

1 See "Bericht der VfS Gross-Berlin/Abt. IX über Grenzprovokation am KPP Invalidenstrasse mit tödlichem Ausgang, 22.6.1964," in: BStU, MfS, AS 754/70, Bd. 2, Nr. 6, Bl. 7–10.

2 "Handschriftlicher Lebenslauf von Walter Heike, o.D. [1964]," in: ibid., Bl. 71.

3 See "Handschriftlicher Personalbogen von Walter Heike, 1964," in: ibid., Bl. 72.

4 See Torsten Dietrich/Rüdiger Wenzke, *Die getarnte Armee. Geschichte der Kasernierten Volkspolizei der DDR 1952 bis 1956,* Berlin, 2002.

5 See "Arbeitsbuch für Walter Heike vom Rat des Kreises Strausberg, 1.2.1960," in: BStU, MfS, AS 754/70, Bd. 2, Nr. 6, Bl. 51, and "Sozialversicherungsausweis für Walter Heike vom AZKW/BV Berlin/Finanzen, 26.3. 1962," in: ibid., Bl. 50.

6 See "Abschlussbericht der VfS Gross-Berlin/Abt. IX zum versuchten Grenzdurchbruch des Walter Heike mit tödlichem Ausgang, 30.6.1964," in: ibid., Bl. 30–32, here Bl. 30.

7 See "Fotodokumentation der NVA/1.GB/Grenzregiment 33, betr. bildliche Darstellung des Annäherungsweges beim versuchten Grenzdurchbruch am 22.6.1964, 5.55 Uhr, 22.6.1964," in: BArch, VA-07/16933, Bl. 78–80.

8 The former guard was sentenced for manslaughter in 1995 to a youth sentence of one year and three months, commuted to probation. See "Urteil des Landgerichts Berlin vom 29.6.1995," in: StA Berlin, Az. 2 Js 121/90, Bd. 3, Bl. 30–63.

9 See "Bericht der NVA/1.GB/Grenzregiment 33 zum versuchten Grenzdurchbruch im Abschnitt des Grenzregimentes 33, 4. Kompanie zwischen Invalidenfriedhof und Regierungskrankenhaus am 22.6.64, 5.40 Uhr, 22.6.1964," in: BArch, VA-07/16933, Bl. 72–77, and "Bericht der NVA/Stadtkommandant Poppe an Erich Honecker, 22.6.1964," in: BArch, VA-07/6005, Bl. 25–26.

10 See "Tatortbericht der West-Berliner Polizei, 22.6.1964," in: StA Berlin, Az. 2 Js 121/90, Bd. 2, Bl. 8–9, sowie "Flüchtling vermutlich erschossen", in: *Der Tagesspiegel,* 23.6.1964; "Schüsse am Invaliden-Friedhof. Neue Bluttat der Vopo an der Mauer," in: *Der Kurier,* 22.6.1964; "Fluchtversuch gescheitert," in: *Telegraf,* 23.6.1964.

11 See "Schreiben der Schwester von Walter Heike [MfS-Abschrift], 30.6.1964," in: BStU, MfS, AS 754/70, Bd. 2, Nr. 6, Bl. 37.

12 "Schreiben des VEB Ausbau Nord Frankfurt/Oder Sitz Angermünde betr. Sterbeurkunde Walter Heike, 27.7. 1964," in: StA Berlin, Az. 2 Js 121/90, Bd. 1, Bl. 29, and "Antwortschreiben der Staatsanwaltschaft (I A AR 169.64), 26.9.1964," in: ibid., Bl. 30.

13 See "Kostenaufstellung [des MfS] für die Bestattung von Walter Heike, o.D. [Juni 1964]," in: BStU, MfS, AS 754/70, Bd. 2, Nr. 6, Bl. 43.

Norbert Wolscht

born on October 27, 1943

drowned on July 28, 1964
in the Havel River
on the outer ring between
Potsdam-Babelsberg and Berlin-Zehlendorf

N orbert Wolscht and Rainer Gneiser had been planning and preparing their escape from East Germany for months. In July 1964 the two 20-year-olds from
Freiberg in Saxony set off for Potsdam. Equipped with oxygen tanks, flippers, and
diving suits, they planned to cross the Havel River to West Berlin on the night of
July 28. The next day members of Border Regiment 48 pulled Norbert Wolscht's
body from the river. The time and place were documented in the East German
border troop's daily reports.[1] A week later the body of Rainer Gneiser was also
found on the Babelsberger embankment of the Havel River.[2] The West was unaware of the fate of Norbert Wolscht and Rainer Gneiser at the time.

After the collapse of East Germany, friends and relatives of the deceased drew
attention to the case. Criminal investigations were opened in the early 1990s to
determine the circumstances of their deaths and confirmed the theory that the two
friends had fallen victim to a tragic accident while trying to escape.[3] Norbert Wolscht and Rainer Gneiser grew up in Freiberg. They had known each other since
their school days. Norbert Wolscht was born in October 1943 in Greiffenberg in
Silesia, the second child of Benno Wolscht and his wife Charlotte. His sister Barbara was a year older than he. In 1947, when the father was still in captivity as a
prisoner of war, the mother had to leave Greiffenberg, which now belonged to
Poland. The grandmother, mother and children packed up their belongings and
moved. Norbert Wolscht's sister recalled that, although they were quite young at
the time, the war and expulsion had been important events in their childhood.[4]
After they were definitively expelled from Silesia their mother hoped to go to the
British zone because she had brothers there living in Düsseldorf. But the refugee
camp near Görlitz, where they were first taken in, was so overcrowded that she
pushed hard to get a permit to move to relatives in nearby Freiberg and the family
ended up settling in Saxony.

Norbert Wolscht left school upon receiving the secondary school level certificate after which he completed an apprenticeship as a lathe operator in a Freiburg
company for high-precision mechanics. Although he did not have any obvious
problems at school or in training, his sister believed that he had a hard time subor-

dinating himself and adjusting to the ideological demands of the East German state. A friend with whom he had maintained a long mail correspondence remembered that he had always said that he would someday immigrate to South Africa. Nonetheless, he first followed the advice of a friend and completed his apprenticeship and started to learn English. When the Berlin Wall was built, Norbert had not yet celebrated his 18th birthday. The Wall seemed to ruin his plans for the future, but he did not completely give up his dream of living at the other end of the world. In the summer of 1963 he joined forces with Rainer Gneiser who had already failed to escape once before and who was now even more determined to give it a second try and turn his back on East Germany for good. They began to practice long-distance swimming and learned how diving equipment was built.[5] Norbert Wolscht was very athletic and a good swimmer.

The next summer they were ready to put their plan into action. They did not inform their friends or relatives of the details. Pretending that they were going on a camping trip, the two boys set off from Freiberg on a motorcycle on July 25. They probably went straight to Potsdam and spent a few days checking out the situation there. It is not known at what time and where on the riverbank they entered the water of the Havel on the night of July 28. The place where Norbert's body was discovered suggested that they began their escape attempt at Tiefen See, the section of the Havel River between Potsdam and Babelsberg. They had probably wanted to swim underwater to the north and pass through the Babelsberger Enge on their way to the West Berlin embankment of the Havel, but they drowned in unexplained circumstances. The autopsy of Norbert Wolscht determined that he died at around two in the morning on July 28. It also stated that he died as a consequence of a faulty breathing apparatus.[6] The last sign of life that he left behind was a waybill addressed to his parents documenting that he had sent his camping equipment from Potsdam to Freiberg on July 27.[7]

Since his death had been an accident, the Ministry of State Security was not notified of the case. The Potsdam police district office took charge of processing the "occurrences." Norbert Wolscht's parents were informed the same evening and drove to Potsdam the next day.[8] They were presented with an identity card and neck pouch as proof that the deceased was their son. The parents requested and were permitted to see the body of their son. To understand exactly what caused the death, Norbert Wolscht's father turned to the doctor in charge who gave him explicit assurances that no external wounds had been found. According to the doctor it was far more likely "that death occurred as a consequence of inhaling carbon dioxide toxins. Apparently the self-made diving equipment's dioxide absorption filter had not functioned properly."[9]

Norbert Wolscht was buried in the Donatsfriedhof, a cemetery in Freiberg, on August 1, 1964. His parents wrote in the obituary that he died in a tragic accident, although they did not conceal from relatives and friends that their son had died while trying to escape.[10]

Christine Brecht

1   See "Operative Tagesmeldung Nr. 210/64 der NVA/Stadtkommandantur Berlin/Operative Abt., 29.7.1964,"
    in: BArch, VA-07/6028, Bl. 104; "Tagesmeldung Nr. 24/VII/64 des MNfV/Operativer Diensthabender, 29.7.
    1964," in: BArch, VA-01/5088, Bl. 32; "Handschriftliche Lagemeldungen [der NVA/Stadtkommandantur Ber-
    lin], 28.7.1964 und 29.7.1964," in: BArch, VA-07/18612, Bl. 35–36, 41–42.

2   See "Operative Tagesmeldung Nr. 216/64 der NVA/Stadtkommandantur Berlin/Operative Abt., 6.8.1964," in:
    BArch, VA-07/6028, Bl. 135, and the biographical text about Rainer Gneiser in this book.

3   See "Verfügung der Staatsanwaltschaft II bei dem Kammergericht Berlin (27/2 Js 72/91), 7.10.1993," in: StA
    Berlin, Az. 27 Js 72/91, Bl. 131–132.

4   Conversation conducted by Christine Brecht with Barbara B., Norbert Wolscht's sister, 2.10.2007.

5   See "Handschriftliche Erklärung eines Freundes von Rainer Gneiser gegenüber der Berliner Polizei, 12.7.1993,"
    in: StA Berlin, Az. 27 Js 72/91, Bl. 100–101.

6   See "Abschrift des Sektionsbefunds zum Sterbefall Norbert Wolscht des Städtischen Krankenhauses Potsdam-
    Babelsberg, o.D. [28.7.1964]," privately owned.

7   See "Handschriftliche Lagemeldungen [der NVA/Stadtkommandantur Berlin], 28.7.1964," in: BArch, VA-07/
    18612, Bl. 35–36.

8   "Schreiben der Mutter von Norbert Wolscht an die ZERV, 29.7.1993," in: StA Berlin, Az. 27 Js 72/91, Bl. 117.

9   Letter from the municipal hospital in Potsdam-Babelsberg to Norbert Wolscht's father, 25.8.1964, privately
    owned.

10 See "Handschriftliche Erklärung eines Freundes von Norbert Wolscht an die ZERV, 19.8.1993," in: StA Berlin,
    Az. 27 Js 72/91, Bl. 110–111.

Rainer Gneiser

born on January 10, 1944

drowned on July 28, 1964
in the Havel River
on the outer ring between
Potsdam-Babelsberg and Berlin-Zehlendorf

Rainer Gneiser was born on January 10, 1944 in Kreuzburg, Silesia. He was the son of Wilhelm Gneiser and his wife, Ruth, and had an older sister. They probably ended up in Freiberg, Saxony after being expelled from Silesia, which fell to Poland after the Second World War. Rainer Gneiser grew up in the Soviet-occupied zone and in East Germany. He left school after the tenth grade with the secondary school level certificate and completed a technical apprenticeship. In the spring of 1962, at the age of 18, he tried for the first time to flee from the walled-in East German state. He had wanted to reach the West via the Baltic Sea, but was arrested on April 16, 1962 for "attempting to illegally exit East Germany" and sentenced by the Freiberg district court to ten months in prison.[1] After serving his sentence he returned to Freiberg but was still determined to go to the West. A friend of Rainer Gneiser stated many years later that he had told him back then that under no circumstances did he want to stay in East Germany.[2] He found a like-minded friend in Norbert Wolscht, who was the same age and whom he had known since his school days. The two had apparently been planning and preparing their escape through the Havel River from Potsdam to West Berlin since the summer of 1963.[3] A year later, equipped with oxygen tanks and diving suits, they embarked on their plan. They drowned on the night of July 28, 1964 under unexplained circumstances.[4]

Norbert Wolscht was found the same day, but Rainer Gneiser remained missing for several days. His body was not found until August 5. Members of Border Regiment 48 on duty in this area pulled his body out of the Havel River at the Babelsberger embankment.[5] According to information from the East German border troops, he was found in Tiefen See, a section of the Havel situated between Potsdam and Babelsberg. The corpse, "identified as Rainer Gneiser from Freiberg/ Sa. G., was wearing self-made diving equipment."[6] The East German border troops also noted what the deceased was carrying on him: In addition to the diving equipment with oxygen bottles and a breathing filter, there were a compass, watch, flashlight and a waterproof pouch containing Rainer Gneiser's identity card, military card and employment book.[7]

On August 18, 1964, Rainer Gneiser was buried at the Donatsfriedhof in Freiberg, the same cemetery where his friend Norbert Wolscht had been buried two weeks earlier. The obituary that his parents placed in the local newspaper stated that "he died in a tragic accident in Potsdam."

Christine Brecht

1 See "[MfS/]Abt. XII/Zentralarchiv, Strafnachricht zu Rainer Gneiser, 15.5.1962," in: BStU, MfS, SKS-Akten, Speicher XII/01, Strafnachricht.

2 See "Handschriftliche Erklärung eines Freundes von Rainer Gneiser an die Berliner Polizei, 12.7.1993," in: StA Berlin, Az. 27 Js 72/91, Bl. 100–101.

3 See ibid.

4 Investigations conducted by the public prosecutor's office after East Germany ceased to exist confirm that it must have been an accident. See "Verfügung der Staatsanwaltschaft II bei dem Kammergericht Berlin (27/2 Js 72/91), 7.10.1993," in: Ibid., Bl. 131–132.

5 See "Operative Tagesmeldung Nr. 216/64 der NVA/Stadtkommandantur Berlin/Operative Abt., 6.8.1964," in: BArch, VA-07/6028, Bl. 135; "Handschriftliche Operative Tagesmeldung Nr. 216/64 [der NVA/Stadtkommandantur Berlin/Operative Abt.] vom 28.7.1964 von 00.00–24.00 Uhr, o.D. [29.7.1964]," in: BArch, VA-07/18583, Bl. 24, and "Einschätzung der BdVP Potsdam über die Lage in den Grenzkreisen – Monat August 1964," in: BArch, VA-07/6019, Bl. 263.

6 "Einschätzung der BdVP Potsdam über die Lage in den Grenzkreisen – Monat August 1964," in: BArch, VA-07/6019, Bl. 263.

7 See "Handschriftliche Lagemeldungen [der NVA/Stadtkommandantur Berlin], 5.8.1964," in: BArch, VA-07/181612, Bl. 91.

Hildegard Trabant

born on June 12, 1927

shot dead on August 18, 1964
on the closed-off S-Bahn tracks between
Schönhauser Allee and Gesundbrunnen
at the sector border between
Berlin-Prenzlauer Berg and Berlin-Wedding

The S-Bahn tracks between the Schönhauser Allee and Gesundbrunnen stations were closed down after the Berlin Wall was built. The track grounds in Prenzlauer Berg on the east side of the city ran parallel to Kopenhagener Strasse in the direction of West Berlin and belonged to the security area that was off-limits to unauthorized people. An escape attempt was prevented within this 'dead area,' as it was referred to in border troop jargon, on August 18, 1964. Border soldiers noticed a woman in the "wooden bridge" patrol area at around 6:50 p.m. She had been hiding behind an elderbush on the untended grounds. When one of the guards ordered her to come out of her hiding place, the woman jumped up and ran away. But she did not run towards the border grounds that divided her from West Berlin. A sketch drawn up by one of the East German border troops showed that she headed in the opposite direction.[1] Nevertheless one of the guards released the safety of his machine gun and, after firing a warning shot, fired directly at her back. She died an hour later in the People's Police Hospital. The border regiment's deputy commander certified that the guard had engaged in "exemplary behavior."[2]

The woman who died was Hildegard Trabant. She was born as Hildegard Pohl on June 12, 1927 in Berlin. Documents show that she joined the Communist Party in 1949, the year the East German state was founded, and was valued as an active party member. She married in 1954 and lived with her husband in Friedrichshain in East Berlin. She held a managerial position in a municipal housing administration. Her husband was a member of the East German police force, employed in the passport and registration division.[3] Whatever led the 37-year-old woman to attempt to flee in August 1964 was probably of a private nature. Hildegard Trabant and her husband had had serious conflicts in the past. Her husband, the police officer, was questioned by his supervisor about this in February 1964.[4]

On August 19, 1964, the day after Hildegard Trabant died, a Stasi agent informed her husband that his wife had been shot and killed while "attempting a border breach."[5] The director of his work division was also present at the meeting. During the talk, the husband was apparently unable or unwilling to give information about why his wife undertook the escape attempt. In the end he had to agree in writing to remain silent about the fact that Hildegard Trabant was shot at the Wall. The statement that he was required to sign stated: "I have been instructed that I am only to tell my supervisor about the cause of death. To all other people I will only speak of a fatal accident."[6]

The Stasi's methods were aimed at keeping the number of informed people low and decisive details, such as the place and time of the event, secret so that no information would leak to the West. The Stasi lieutenant in charge noted that "All officers involved in this affair maintained the usual security measures to ensure that particulars concerning the site of the incident were not made known."[7] This also meant that the Stasi took responsibility for arranging the cremation and urn burial of the deceased that took place on August 23 at the Frieden-Himmelfahrt Cemetery in Berlin-Niederschönhausen. The East German authorities, however, were not able to completely suppress all undesirable reactions. The news of the party comrade's death led to a discussion among the Friedrichshain Communist Party district leadership that caused the Stasi to consult with higher-ranking party leadership "to avoid this sort of thing in the future."[8] Another annoyance occurred when the widower paid a visit to the East Berlin attorney general to apply for a death certificate to submit for an insurance claim. When the state prosecutor informed him that he had no claim to death benefits, he responded that by now it was generally known in what manner his wife had died. Her company had been informed by the Communist Party district leadership the day after her death and this had led to the spread of "certain rumors," even in their neighborhood.[9]

In West Berlin the brutal death of Hildegard Trabant went completely unnoticed. A legal investigation of the incident did not begin until October 1990, when the East Berlin files from 1964 were handed over to the German federal judiciary.[10] The trial against the guard involved in this case dragged on despite the overwhelming evidence against him because the accused insisted that he was not the perpetrator. In 1997, and in consideration of the fact that he was only 20 years old at the time of the offence, he was arraigned by the juvenile division of the criminal court.[11] The former border guard finally made a confession during the main hearing. He was found guilty on June 10, 1998 of manslaughter and sentenced to a year and nine months in prison. The court commuted the sentence to probation.[12] The court found that, based on the available documents, it was clear that when the shots were fired, Hildegard Trabant "was no longer trying to flee over the border and had instead run into the hinterland merely to avoid arrest."[13]

Christine Brecht

1 See "Skizze [der NVA/1.GB/Grenzregiment 31/Stellvertreter des Kommandeurs/Leiter der Polit-Abt. GR 31] zum versuchten Grenzdurchbruch am 18.8.1964, 18.53 Uhr, o.D. [18.8.1964]," in: BArch, VA-07/6012, Bl. 96.

2 See "Bericht [der NVA/1.GB/Grenzregiment 31/Stellvertreter des Kommandeurs/Leiter der Polit-Abt. GR 31] zum versuchten Grenzdurchbruch mit Anwendung der Schusswaffe, 18.8.1964," in: BArch, VA-07/6012, Bl. 93–95, here Bl. 94.

3 See "Information der VfS Gross-Berlin, 18.8.1964," in: BStU, MfS, AS 754/70, Bd. II, Nr. 7, Bl. 4.

4 See "Bericht der VfS Gross-Berlin über Grenzverletzung mit tödlichem Ausgang, 19.8.1964," in: Ibid., Bl. 5–6.

5 See "Bericht der VfS Gross-Berlin/Abt. IX über Grenzverletzung mit tödlichem Ausgang vom 18.8.1964, 21.8.1964," in: Ibid., Bl. 9–10.

6 "Erklärung des Ehemannes von Hildegard Trabant, 19.8.1964," in: Ibid., Bl. 24.

7 "Bericht der VfS Gross-Berlin/Abt. IX über Grenzverletzung mit tödlichem Ausgang vom 18.8.1964, 21.8. 1964," in: Ibid., Bl. 10.

8 "Handschriftlicher Nachtrag [der VfS Gross-Berlin/Abt. IX], o.D. [21.8.1964]," in: Ibid., Bl. 11.

9 "Vermerk des Generalstaatsanwalts von Gross-Berlin (I A AR 1 83.64), 4.9.1964," in: StA Berlin, Az. 27/2 Js 69/90, Bd. 1, Bl. 6.

10 See "Verfügung des Generalstaatsanwalts bei dem Kammergericht Berlin, 30.10.1990," in: Ibid., Bd. 1, Bl. 21–22.

11 See "Anklageschrift der Staatsanwaltschaft II bei dem Landgericht Berlin (27/2 Js 69/90), 18.4.1997," in: Ibid., Bd. 2, Bl. 180–198.

12 See "Urteil des Landgerichts Berlin vom 10.6.1998," in: Ibid., Bd. 3, Bl. 22 a–22 h.

13 Ibid., Bl. 22 f.

Wernhard Mispelhorn

born on November 10, 1945

shot on August 18, 1964
in the "Schönholz" garden settlement
at the sector border between
Berlin-Pankow and Berlin-Reinickendorf
died from his bullet wounds on August 20, 1964

A number of shots were fired shortly past midnight in the East Berlin "Schön-holz" garden settlement on August 18, 1964. The grounds directly bordered the Reinickendorf district in the western half of the city. West Berlin police officers tried to observe what was taking place behind the East Berlin barrier. They identified two border soldiers with a stretcher, but they could not see that a critically injured young man was being carried away.[1] The man's name was Wernhard Mispelhorn, age 18. He had been shot in the head while trying to cross the sector border and died in an East Berlin hospital two days later.[2]

Born on November 10, 1945 in Berlin, Wernhard Mispelhorn grew up with three older siblings in his parents' house in Berlin-Buchholz. The fact that their home was located in the Soviet sector hardly affected the family in the first years following the war. His brother remembered visiting relatives in the western sector regularly when they were children and how much they liked it when their grand-mother in Berlin-Wedding gave them money for the cinema. The parents were rather lax with their two sons, which is why they were mischievous children. After the parents divorced, they stayed with their mother in Buchholz and their older sisters went out on their own. One of them studied biology in East Berlin; the other one followed her boyfriend to West Berlin in 1960 and settled in Hanover. After he left school, Wernhard Mispelhorn completed an apprenticeship with a private company as a gas and water pipe fitter and later worked as a metalworker outside of Berlin.[3]

Wernhard Mispelhorn was 15 years old when the Wall went up. Like so many East Berlin youths of his generation, he experienced the loss of freedom and movement as a major change in his life. He and his friends did not care much about "building socialism." They preferred listening to the American radio station, AFN, wearing jeans and raving about western-brand motorcycles and cars. Sometimes they discussed whether it would be better to take off for the West, but given the danger involved in escaping, these conversations remained mere talk.[4] It was not only a general dissatisfaction with the conditions in East Germany that led the 18-year-old to risk his life in August of 1964, but also the fact that his girlfriend had recently moved to West Berlin, apparently one of the rare cases in which the East German authorities permitted a family to be reunited.[5] Wernhard Mispelhorn confided to his brother that he wanted to risk an escape across the security grounds so that he could be with her. His brother tried in vain to talk him out of it.

Wernhard Mispelhorn spent the evening of August 17, 1964 with his friends Hans and Dieter in a bar in the Prenzlauer Berg district. They did not know that he wanted to go to the West because of the girl. They had always insisted it was a spontaneous idea that had developed over the course of the evening and after a number of beers. They decided to drive to Schönholz together that very night. Hans R. recalled hearing a rumor that you could get across the border there without difficulty. They just wanted to check out the area and were not seriously considering fleeing. Having arrived in the garden colony, they found a place where they could lift up the back fence so that Wernhard Mispelhorn could crawl under it and get a look at the border strip. They were completely surprised when he suddenly stood up and ran off. When they heard the gun shots, they panicked and ran away.[6]

Wernhard Mispelhorn was seen by two auxiliary border soldiers patrolling the interior security grounds. One Stasi report noted that the area was known as a "focal point for border violator advances."[7] They continued to shoot at the fugitive until he collapsed in front of the border fence. The East Berlin commander immediately reported the "deterrence of a border breach" to Erich Honecker, who at that time was the East German secretary of the National Defense Council. The border guards were honored with the usual awards.[8] The fate of the fugitive, who died from his critical injuries two days later, played no role in these reports. Nor was anyone interested in who had fired the fatal shot.[9]

While Wernhard Mispelhorn was lying in mortal agony, the Stasi began asking questions about him in his neighborhood and work place. This formed the basis for a long report in which the state authorities vented their bias against the young people there because of their western lifestyle and accused the fugitive of many things, including "hooliganism."[10] The Stasi did not notify his mother until the investigation was over. Her son was fatally injured at the border, they told her, but she was not allowed to see him. After he died she was forced to agree to remain silent about what had happened and not to investigate the matter herself. These methods of intimidation were aimed at keeping the relatives in the dark about the details of the escape attempt so that information would not leak to the West. The Stasi officer in charge noted in the file: "As usual, the offices (forensic medicine, hospital, registry office, crematorium) were not provided with any information on the location of the incident."[11]

In order to avoid conflict with the authorities, the relatives maintained the official "rule of silence" and spoke of his death as an accident in the obituary and at the funeral. Wernhard Mispelhorn's two friends kept quiet out of fear that they might be punished as accessories in helping a fugitive to "flee the republic." Letters from his oldest sister in East Berlin that were personally delivered to Hanover show that within the family it was not a taboo to acknowledge that their youngest son and brother was shot while trying to escape. "It was a serious 'accident' caused by our special Berlin situation," she explained with unambiguous clarity.[12] In another passage she asked her sister to keep her letters, which she wrote so that "the little that we know can be documented in writing. [...] Even if it won't bring him back I don't think we should just accept his death!"[13]

Christine Brecht

1 See "Funkspruch der West-Berliner Polizei, 18.8.1964," in: PHS, Bestand Grenzvorkommnisse, n. pag., and *Der Tagesspiegel*, 19.8.1964.

2 See "Schlussbericht der ZERV, 16.6.1993," in: StA Berlin, Az. 27/2 Js 91/90, Bd. 2, Bl. 246.

3 Conversation conducted by Christine Brecht with H. Mispelhorn, Wernhard Mispelhorn's brother, 13.4.2007.

4 Conversation conducted by Christine Brecht with Hans R., Wernhard Mispelhorn's friend, 19.3.2007.

5 See Ludwig A. Rehlinger, *Freikauf. Die Geschäfte der DDR mit politisch Verfolgten 1963–1989,* Berlin/Frankfurt am Main, 1991.

6 See "Niederschrift der Zeugenvernehmung eines Mitflüchtlings von Wernhard Mispelhorn durch die Berliner Polizei, 17.2.1997," in: StA Berlin, Az. 27/2 Js 91/90, Bd. 3, Bl. 588–593, and "Niederschrift der Zeugenvernehmung eines Mitflüchtlings von Wernhard Mispelhorn durch die Berliner Polizei, 28.2.1997," in: Ibid., Bl. 608–613.

7 "Sofortmeldung [des MfS/]HA I/Abwehr B/Unterabt. 1.GB/31.GR betr. Verhinderung eines Grenzdurchbruches unter Anwendung der Schusswaffe, 18.8.1964," in: BStU, Ast. Berlin, 9016/91, Bl. 11–13, here Bl. 12.

8 See "Meldung der NVA/Stadtkommandant Poppe an Erich Honecker betr. Anwendung der Schusswaffe gegen Grenzverletzer mit Verletzung, 18.8.1964," in: BArch, VA-07/6005, Bl. 36–37.

9 This question could also not be clarified during the criminal investigation of the former guards. The investigation of the one guard was suspended; the other guard was convicted of attempted manslaughter and given a suspended sentence of 15 months. See "Urteil des Landgerichts Berlin vom 16.9.1998," in: StA Berlin, Az. 27/2 Js 91/90, Bd. 4, Bl. 36–43.

10 See, for example "Ermittlungsbericht des MfS/Verwaltung Gross-Berlin/Abt. VIII/Referat II, 18.8.1962," in: BStU, Ast. Berlin, 9016/91, Bl. 32–36.

11 "Bericht der VfS Gross-Berlin/Abt. IX über Grenzprovokation mit tödlichem Ausgang vom 18.8.1964, 21.8.1964," in: Ibid., Bl. 3–4, here Bl. 4.

12 "Briefkarte der Schwester von Wernhard Mispelhorn an die Schwester in Hannover, 22.8.1964," in: StA Berlin, Az. 27/2 Js 91/90, Bd. 1, Bl. 55–56, here Bl. 56.

13 "Brief der Schwester von Wernhard Mispelhorn an die Schwester in Hannover, 13.11.1964," in: Ibid., Bl. 57–62, here Bl. 60.

Hans-Joachim Wolf

born on August 8, 1947

shot dead on November 26, 1964
in the Britzer-Zweig Canal
at the sector border between
Berlin-Treptow and Berlin-Neukölln

Hans-Joachim Wolf, age 17, was last seen by his parents at around 8 o'clock in the morning on November 25, 1964. His parents had left for work. Hans-Joachim Wolf was supposed to go to his vocational school, but he never arrived there. Instead he rented a room in the Hotel Adlon.[1] He had a briefcase with him containing an umbrella, pills, and a rope. The Hotel Adlon was situated very close to the border fortifications at the Brandenburg Gate. Apparently Hans-Joachim Wolf had considered crossing the border to West Berlin by climbing down a rope there. His parents were already very worried and reported him missing to the police that night.[2]

The next day Hans-Joachim Wolf decided against this escape plan. He put his briefcase in a locker at Alexanderplatz.[3] That evening he tried to escape to West Berlin from another location. He approached the border in Berlin-Treptow from Baumschulenstrasse. He went through the "Silberlinde" garden settlement and climbed over the approximately 2.5-meter-high barbed wire fence east of the Heidekampgraben on the southern bank of the Britzer Zweig Canal.[4] It was 6:30 p.m., already dark and the air temperature was four degrees Celsius when Hans-Joachim Wolf jumped into the canal. He probably thought that the border soldiers would not be expecting an escape through the ice cold water at this time of year and would therefore be less attentive. But the border guards stationed not far from the bank saw him and without warning, began shooting. Hans-Joachim Wolf was aware of the danger he was in. He called out to the guards that they should stop shooting, but the two guards ignored his effort to abandon his escape attempt. They fired a total of 61 shots at Hans-Joachim Wolf. One hit him in the chest and killed him.[5]

The shots were heard on the West Berlin side of the canal. Given the intense shooting, the West Berlin police felt compelled to close the nearby border crossing at Sonnenallee from 6:30 to 7 p.m. so that the West Berliners who were waiting for senior citizens to arrive from East Berlin would not be endangered. The next day newspapers reported that an unknown fugitive was killed in a hail of bullets.[6]

Hans-Joachim Wolf was living in Berlin-Friedrichshain with his parents and was working as a gas station attendant and a salesclerk when he tried to escape. He had begun an apprenticeship at a cable plant in Berlin-Köpenick in September 1964. After his death his mother suggested that he may have fled because he had been denied the apprenticeship he wanted as a radio and telecommunications technician, although he had good grades and was active in the state-run youth associations.[7] A Stasi report on Hans-Joachim Wolf stated: "W. has a good reputation. He is polite, friendly and cooperative in his neighborhood. He is characterized as a very clean and orderly young person with a distinct dress style. He does not roam about and is characterized as a loner. [...] He is not sympathetic toward our Worker and Peasant State. If the border were still open he would have fled the republic long ago."[8] His sister thought that it was probably his escape plans that had turned Hans-Joachim Wolf into a loner. She remembered her brother as a very friendly and cheerful person who had a number of close friendships and also maintained a number of letter correspondences. His relationship with his parents was also very good and open.[9] In discussions with his parents, Hans-Joachim Wolf had articulated his view that the living conditions in West Berlin and West Germany were better than in East Germany, although he never specifically expressed thoughts about fleeing.[10] He probably wanted to spare his parents repercussions from the Stasi that they would have been subjected to had they known of his plans. Moreover, he would not have wanted them to worry since his sister, who was four years older than he, had already fled to West Berlin in 1961 and was still suffering from health problems as a consequence. Only to his grandmother did he mention in the summer of 1964 "that he could try to get to West Berlin from the bank of the Reichstag."[11] Hans-Joachim Wolf probably began preparing his escape in November 1964. His mother saw her son sort out his belongings and burn all the letters he had received from friends in West Berlin.[12]

Hans-Joachim Wolf had already tried to escape once before on December 9, 1963. He had wanted to reach West Berlin by train. When he was caught at the Friedrichstrasse station, he claimed that he had boarded the wrong train by mistake. Evidently they believed him because he was not criminally prosecuted.[13]

His parents did not learn of their son's death until two days after his failed escape attempt. They were told that he had accidentally drowned while "violating the state border."[14] The exact location was not disclosed to them. They were not allowed to see their son's body, nor were they permitted to have a large memorial service. Hans-Joachim Wolf was cremated in the crematorium in Berlin-Baumschulenweg. The urn burial took place in the Parochial Cemetery in Berlin-Friedrichshain.

Hans-Joachim Wolf's parents did not believe the story they had been told by the Stasi. They knew that their son was a good swimmer. Moreover, the father found blood stains on his son's watch when it was returned to him.[15] The mother contacted a cousin living in West Berlin to try to find out how her son really died.[16] Joachim Wolf's sister in Munich also tried to get information. Her mother sent her letters telling her what had happened. She shared her parents' belief that her brother had not drowned but had been shot while trying to escape. The sister informed the human rights organization "Liberal Jurists Board of Inquiry" in Berlin about the case and made a statement to the Munich police in February 1965, which she revoked a short time later: She feared that it might cause problems for her parents who were living in East Germany.[17]

Exactly what happened to Joachim Wolf was not clarified until 1994 when the guards involved were tried by the Berlin district court. The case against one of the former border guards was discontinued when he died in March 1996. That same year the court sentenced the other defendant to a year and a half in prison for manslaughter.[18] The prison sentence was commuted to probation. By then Joachim Wolf's parents had passed away.[19]

Lydia Dollmann

1 See "Bericht der VfS Gross-Berlin / Abt. VIII über die Überprüfung des Gästebuches im Hotel Adlon, 27.11.1964," in: BStU, MfS, HA IX Nr. 18287, Bl. 26; Kopie der Hotelrechnung, in: Ibid., Bl. 46.

2 See "Anzeige über eine vermisste Person [Hans-Joachim Wolf] bei der Volkspolizei-Inspektion Friedrichshain/ VPR 91, 26.11.1964," in: Ibid., Bl. 15–18.

3 See "Niederschrift der Zeugenvernehmung der Mutter von Hans-Joachim Wolf durch die Kriminalpolizeiinspektion Ingolstadt, 20.3.1981," in: StA Berlin, Az. 27 Js 87/90, Bd. 1, Bl. 83; "Bericht der West-Berliner Polizei, 9.12.1964," in: Ibid., Bl. 50.

4 See "Bericht des MfS/HA I/Abwehr/U. Abt. 1./GB/GR 37 über einen verhinderten Grenzdurchbruch am 26.11.1964, 26.11.1964," in: BStU, MfS, HA IX Nr. 18287, Bl. 10–11.

5 See "Urteil des Landgerichts Berlin vom 27.9.1996," in: StA Berlin, Az. 27 Js 87/90, Bd. 6, Bl. 6–7; "Sektionsbericht in der Leichensache Hans-Joachim Wolf, 28.11.1964," in: BStU, MfS, HA IX Nr. 18287, Bl. 52–66.

6 See *Nacht-Depesche,* 27.11.1964.

7 See "Niederschrift der Zeugenvernehmung der Mutter von Hans-Joachim Wolf durch die Kriminalpolizeiinspektion Ingolstadt, 20.3.1981," in: StA Berlin, Az. 27 Js 87/90, Bd. I, Bl. 87. Hans-Joachim Wolf's mother settled in West Germany in 1977 as a pensioner and testified to the Ingolstadt police in 1981 concerning the death of her son.

8 "Ermittlungsbericht der VfS Gross-Berlin / Abt. VIII / Referat II, 28.11.1964," in: BStU, MfS, HA IX Nr. 18287, Bl. 27.

9 Letter from Hans-Joachim Wolf's sister to Hans-Hermann Hertle, August 2008.

10 See "Ergänzungsbericht der VfS Gross-Berlin / Abt. IX zur Grenzprovokation mit tödlichem Ausgang, 30.11.1964," in: BStU, MfS, HA IX Nr. 18287, Bl. 75.

11 "Bericht der West-Berliner Polizei, 8.12.1964," in: StA Berlin, Az. 27 Js 87/90, Bd. 1, Bl. 48.

12 See ibid., Bl. 47.

13 See "Strafkartei-Überprüfung Hans-Joachim Wolf betreffend, 27.11.1964," in: BStU, MfS, HA IX Nr. 18287, Bl. 25.

14 See "Ergänzungsbericht der VfS Gross-Berlin / Abt. IX zur Grenzprovokation mit tödlichem Ausgang, 30.11.1964," in: Ibid., Bl. 75.

15 See "Niederschrift der Zeugenvernehmung der Mutter von Hans-Joachim Wolf durch die Kriminalpolizeiinspektion Ingolstadt, 20.3.1981," in: StA Berlin, Az. 27 Js 87/90, Bd. 1, Bl. 83.

16 See "Kopie des handschriftlichen Briefes der Mutter von Hans-Jürgen Wolf, 28.11.1964," in: Ibid., Bl. 44–45.

17 See "Niederschrift der Zeugenvernehmung der Schwester von Hans-Joachim Wolf durch die Polizeiinspektion München, 3.2.1965," in: Ibid., Bl. 59; "Niederschrift der Zeugenvernehmung der Mutter von Hans-Joachim Wolf durch die Kriminalpolizeiinspektion Ingolstadt, 20.3.1981," in: Ibid., Bl. 84.

18 See "Urteil des Landgerichts Berlin vom 27.9.1996," in: Ibid., Bd. 6, Bl. 1–13.

19 Hans-Joachim Wolf's father died in 1966, his mother in 1987. See "Niederschrift der Zeugenvernehmung der Mutter von Hans-Joachim Wolf durch die Kriminalpolizeiinspektion Ingolstadt, 20.3.1981," in: Ibid., Bd. 1, Bl. 85; "Anfrageschreiben der Schwester von Hans-Joachim Wolf an die Staatsanwaltschaft beim Landgericht Berlin, 4.8.1992," in: Ibid., Bd. 5, Bl. 1.

Joachim Mehr

born on April 3, 1945

shot dead on December 3, 1964
near Bergfelde on the outer ring
between Hohen Neuendorf (Oranienburg district)
and Berlin-Reinickendorf

Two young men attempted to escape from the north of Berlin on the night of December 2, 1964. Firearms were used to stop them. According to West Berlin police and press reports, customs officers on duty in Frohnau in Reinickendorf heard shots fired and saw flares fly through the air at 2:20 in the morning. The newspaper reported the next day: "Customs officers noticed the two fugitives in the glow of light. They were lying down flat in the death strip."[1] The customs officers tried to get as close to the barbed wire fence as possible in order to establish contact. One of the fugitives indicated that they were injured and had to give up their escape attempt. Then more shots were fired.[2] The observers on the west side could not see what happened next. A smoke screen had been set off on the other side of the fence to obstruct the view from the west side when the two fugitives were carried off.[3] The 23-year-old Hans-Jürgen K. was delivered to the Henningsdorf Hospital with bullet wounds in both legs. Joachim Mehr, age 19, died immediately.

Joachim Mehr was born in Belgard, Pomerania, in April 1945 as the second child. He grew up in the Prenzlauer Berg district of East Berlin. His father was a master carpenter and had his own workshop and the son had followed in his father's footsteps. He completed a carpenter apprenticeship in a state-run company and after passing his final exam he began working in his father's workshop. He moved into his own apartment on Sonnenburger Strasse when he turned 18, but continued to take his meals at his parents' house. After they learned of their son's violent death, the parents were harassed by Stasi investigators and accused of harboring a "negative attitude" towards the East German state. In the eyes of the Stasi, Joachim Mehr was an unknown quantity. They were unable to identify western influences or thoughts of escape in the young man.[4]

According to the Stasi interrogation protocol, the father said that his son worked until 5 p.m. on December 2, 1964, as he did every day, and that he had dinner with his parents. After that he visited the Christmas market at Alexanderplatz with some of his friends. His girlfriend was also part of the group.[5] After bringing her home, Joachim Mehr stopped by the "Mila-Eck" bar where he met

Hans-Jürgen K., whose younger brother was a good friend of his. K. was three years older and had successfully escaped to the West in 1962, but had later returned to East Berlin. They began talking and K. told him how he had managed to escape from the edge of the city back then. As they talked, they agreed to drive there that very night. Hans-Jürgen K. later asserted to the Stasi that it was a spontaneous decision that they made together on his suggestion.[6] When the bar closed they drove a moped out of the city to Hohen Neuendorf, a northern suburb on the border of the West Berlin district of Frohnau. They left the moped there and went by foot to the border area between Hohen Neuendorf and Bergfelde. The border here ran straight through the woods and the border strip was brightly lit. They climbed over the interior wall, and, careful to stay in the dark, watched the border guards for a while. Then K. gave a sign and they ran off towards the last obstacle, the three rows of barbed wire fence.

During the trial against the border guards in the Potsdam district court in 1994, it became clear that the two fugitives had been seen by two border soldiers who were stationed in a watchtower 160 meters away.[7] The guard leader opened fire from the tower. Apparently the other guard's gun had jammed. Joachim Mehr and Hans-Jürgen K. were injured and collapsed to the ground shortly before reaching the barbed wire fence. The border guards had left the tower by then and ordered the two youths to remain on the ground where they were. Despite their injuries, they continued to crawl on their stomachs until they reached the barbed wire fence, but then they agreed to give up their flight. At that point Sergeant K., who was on border patrol, arrived at the scene. Although both men were lying on the ground just 100 meters away from him and were already hopelessly entangled in the barbed wire, he fired more shots at Joachim Mehr when he moved. The youth, who had not had life-endangering wounds until then, was fatally hit. The court found the former border troop sergeant guilty of manslaughter and sentenced him to 18 months probation. The guard leader who first shot at Joachim Mehr and Hans-Jürgen K. received the same sentence for attempted manslaughter on two counts.

The East German authorities did not show clemency or leniency towards either Hans-Jürgen K., who suffered permanent damage as a result of his bullet wounds, or towards Joachim Mehr's relatives. Although he was seriously injured, the twenty-three-year-old was transferred from a Stasi prison hospital to Berlin-Hohenschönhausen just one day after the failed escape attempt. After sitting many months in pre-trial confinement, the city court of greater Berlin sentenced him in August 1965 to three years in prison, a sentence that he served almost in its entirety.[8] During the investigation, Joachim Mehr's parents were left in the dark about what had happened to their son. As soon as they received the news of his death, they were forced to sign a written statement claiming that he had "died from injuries that he brought upon himself during a border violation."[9] They were also obliged to pretend that their son had died in a traffic accident. Although they engaged an attorney, they were not permitted to see their son's body. When Joachim Mehr's father refused to accept this, he was subjected to a "talk" with the state prosecutor in charge of the case and an interrogation by the staff of the East Berlin Stasi district administration.[10]

Despite this pressure, the parents did not refrain from referring to the death of their son as a "tragic accident" in a local newspaper. The funeral took place on December 30, 1964 in the municipal cemetery in Berlin-Weissensee.

Christine Brecht

1 "Tragödie im Todesstreifen," in: *BZ,* 4.12.1964.

2 See "Bericht der West-Berliner Polizei/Inspektion Reinickendorf betr. vermutlichen Fluchtversuch von zwei NVA-Angehörigen in Uniform, 3.12.1964," in: PHS, Bestand Grenzvorkommnisse, n. pag.

3 See "Operative Tagesmeldung Nr. 338/64 der NVA/Stadtkommandantur Berlin/Operative Abteilung, 4.12. 1964," in: BArch, VA-07/6030, Bl. 148–152.

4 See "Ergänzungsbericht der VfS Gross-Berlin/Abt. IX zur Grenzprovokation mit tödlichem Ausgang im Grenzgebiet Bergfelde, Krs. Oranienburg, 11.12.1964," in: BStU, Ast. Berlin, 9017/91, Bl. 113–119, here Bl. 116.

5 See "Niederschrift der Vernehmung des Vaters von Joachim Mehr [durch das MfS], 16.12.1964," in: Ibid., Bl. 109–112. See establishment of the facts concerning circumstances of events in: "Urteil des Landgerichts Potsdam vom 27.9.1994," in: StA Neuruppin, Az. 60/1 Js 6/93, Bd., 4, Bl. 408–437, here Bl. 417–422.

6 See "Niederschrift der Beschuldigtenvernehmung des Mitflüchtlings von Joachim Mehr [durch das MfS], 10.12.1964," in: BStU, Ast. Berlin, 9017/91, Bl. 28–30.

7 See "Urteil des Landgerichts Potsdam vom 27.9.1994," in: StA Neuruppin, Az. 60/1 Js 6/93, Bd. 4, Bl. 408–437, here Bl. 422.

8 See "Anklageschrift der Staatsanwaltschaft Potsdam (60/1 Js 6/93), 26.7.1993," in: StA Neuruppin, Az. 60/1 Js 6/93, Bd. 3, Bl. 122–156, here Bl. 146–147.

9 "Statement" forced from Joachim Mehr's mother by the Stasi, 11.12.1964, in: BStU, Ast. Berlin, 9017/91, Bl. 105.

10 See "Bericht der VfS Gross-Berlin/Abt. IX, 15.12.1964 zur Leichensache Joachim Mehr," in: Ibid., Bl. 134–137, and "Niederschrift der Vernehmung des Vaters von Joachim Mehr [durch das MfS], 16.12.1964," in: Ibid., Bl. 109–112.

Unidentified Fugitive

drowned on January 19, 1965

in the Spree River

at the sector border

between Berlin-Friedrichshain

and Berlin-Kreuzberg

I t was about 5:30 p.m. on January 19, 1965 when two employees of a company situated directly on the Spree River in the West Berlin district of Kreuzberg heard cries for help. They followed the direction of the calls and saw a man, approximately 30 years old, swimming in the ice cold river toward the embankment. Since the entire width of the Spree here belonged to East Berlin, they had no doubt that he was a fugitive fleeing to the West. They called out to the man, who was only a few meters from the riverbank, and told him to swim towards them so that they could help him out of the water. But the man apparently lost all energy and they watched as he drowned before their very eyes. A West Berlin police report summarized what they had seen: "The fugitive, about 10 meters away from the West Berlin bank, suddenly went under, probably as a consequence of hypothermia and not due to the involvement of a third party."[1] The attempted escape was also noticed on the other side of the river. Border soldiers shot off flares and drove by boat to the site where the man had sunk. Divers also joined the search, but by midnight they gave up without success.

Reports from the East Berlin border troops also documented the fatal escape attempt of the young man whose identity remained unknown. They reported that he was noticed by a border soldier who had illuminated the water's surface with a flood light. The border guard apparently was unable to see the swimmer clearly, but heard him calling for help before he went under. Investigators found evidence on the East Berlin bank that confirmed their suspicion that the man had been trying to escape. With the help of a tracking dog, they were able to determine that the fugitive approached the river from a lot on Mühlenstrasse and had then crawled beneath the security fence. He left a briefcase behind that contained a shirt, magazines, an empty fountain-pen case and an open-faced sandwich wrapped in newspaper that had been printed in the Halle district in East Germany and was dated September 21, 1964.

But there was no information as to the identity of the man. The investigation results led the commander of Border Regiment 35 to conclude that the "border violator had duly reconnoitered the border segment, patrol duty, and grounds in preparation for his criminal undertaking."[2] Further investigations in both the East and the West did not lead to any new findings.

In the nineties research on the case was resumed as part of the legal proceedings against violent acts at the Wall. But having been unable to find any new evidence, the public prosecutor's office in Berlin dismissed the unsolved case in 1995.[3] The theory that the unidentified corpse discovered in the Spree on July 8, 1965 may have belonged to the unknown man who died on January 19 of that same year could neither be proven nor disproven.

Christine Brecht

1 "Auszugsweise Abschrift der Ereignismeldung der West-Berliner Polizei vom 20.1.1965 für den Senat von Berlin, 20.1.1965," in: BArch, B 137, Nr. 6429, n. pag.
2 "Bericht der NVA/1.GB/GR35/Kommandeur über den versuchten Grenzdurchbruch im Abschnitt 4./GR-35 Mühlenstrasse, 19.1.1965," in: BArch, VA-07/16934, Bl. 225–230, here Bl. 228.
3 See "Verfügung der Staatsanwaltschaft II bei dem Kammergericht (7 AR 390/92), 27.6.1995," in: StA Berlin, Az. 7 AR 390/92, Bl. 24.

Christian Buttkus

born on February 21, 1944

**shot dead on March 4, 1965
near Stahnsdorfer Damm / Teerofendamm
on the outer ring between
Kleinmachnow (Potsdam county district)
and Berlin-Zehlendorf**

C hristian Buttkus received his conscription order for the National People's Army (NVA) at the end of February 1965. He was told that he should report to the Chemical Defense Battalion in Eggesin, Mecklenburg on May 1, 1965.[1] Christian Buttkus had known with certainty for a while that he did not want to serve in the NVA. He did not regard East Germany as his fatherland and hence did not want to take the oath of allegiance that every new conscript must take during the swearing-in ceremony. Christian Buttkus and his fiancée, Ilse P., had planned to flee to West Berlin in the summer, but when he was drafted sooner than expected, they decided to move their plans forward.[2]

Christian Buttkus, who had many relatives and friends living in West Berlin, had been thinking about escaping every day since the border had been closed on August 13, 1961. His fiancée later stated during an interrogation with the Stasi that he had been opposed to the sealing of the border because he felt it limited his personal freedom.[3] Christian Buttkus had wanted to pursue his career in West Berlin and study chemical engineering so that he could establish a livelihood there with his fiancée.

Christian Buttkus, who was born in Tilsit on February 21, 1944, experienced flight for the first time as a child. His birthplace was heavily bombed and declared a city on the battle front of the war in the fall of 1944. A large part of the population living in Tilsit was forced to evacuate. The city was captured by Soviet troops on January 1945 and, in accordance with the Potsdam Agreement, was granted to the Soviet Union. The remaining German population had to leave the city by 1947. The Buttkus family must have left Tilsit by then at the very latest. They found a new home in Berlin-Niederschönhausen. The father died in 1950 and Christian Buttkus, the younger of two children, grew up with his mother. He completed secondary school with the secondary school certificate in 1960 and immediately began training as a chemical expert in the state-owned chemical plant in Berlin-Adlershof. After completing his training he was hired by the same company. Christian Buttkus and Ilse P. became engaged in April 1964 at which point they immediately began planning their joint escape to West Berlin.[4]

Christian Buttkus started building his own diving equipment in August 1964. The couple's original plan was to leave East Germany in the summer of 1965 by way of the Teltow Canal in Kleinmachnow. The chemical expert built an underwater vehicle to enable them to get through the water escape route as quickly as possible. The young couple tested it in their laundry room and in the nearby waters and realized that the vehicle did not work. Since diving suits were not available for purchase in East Germany, the couple decided to make their own. Christian Buttkus took the taped diving pants to a shop in Prenzlauer Berg to have them vulcanized on March 1, 1965,[5] but then decided against the plan to leave East Germany by way of water. When Christian Buttkus heard the weather forecast on March 3, 1965, he thought that the predicted snow and strong winds might offer them good conditions for reaching West Berlin unnoticed by land. That very evening the couple made the decision to cross the border later that night in Kleinmachnow. Ilse P. had grown up there and knew the area well. Carrying a briefcase containing money, documents, two pliers and two white aprons as a disguise, the couple took the S-Bahn at around 10:30 p.m. and then transferred to a bus going to Kleinmachnow. They got off at the Schleusenkrug bus stop, crossed the Teerofendamm and Stahnsdorfer Damm where they attached the money and documents to their bodies, put on the white aprons and buried the briefcase in the snow. The weather report was accurate: It was a cold night with heavy snowfall. Christian Buttkus and Ilse P. approached the border grounds through the nearby woods. Everything was going according to plan. They crossed the so-called "anti-vehicle trench." It was 1:15 a.m. when they triggered an acoustic signal alarm that was installed there. Now they had to move fast. The couple quickly ran over a ten-meter-wide deforested area that consisted of the border patrol path and security strip. They had only the three layers of barbed wire fence left to get through. But two guards who had been on duty since 10 p.m. at the "Dreibirken-Durchschub" border area at Stahnsdorfer Damm near the transit highway, as well as another set of guards, had been alerted by the triggered signal. The first guards fired warning shots; the border guards on the control strip aimed directly at the fugitives.[6] Before the fleeing couple could use their pliers to get through the fence, Christian Buttkus was hit by 25 bullets on the right side of his chest. He died immediately from internal injuries.[7] One of the 199 bullets fired grazed Ilse P.'s left calf. A short time later the injured young woman was driven to the border company headquarters. The border soldiers first carried Christian Buttkus' body back to the anti-vehicle trench.[8] They wanted to prevent people in the West from seeing what had taken place. The body was transported to the company headquarters hours later and then delivered to the forensic institute of Charité Hospital in Berlin for an autopsy.

The border soldiers involved in preventing the escape were honored with awards and a few were even promoted.[9] Ilse P., after being released from the hospital and serving pre-trial confinement in the Stasi prison in Potsdam, was tried by the Potsdam district court and found guilty of violating paragraph 8 of the passport law. She was sentenced to a year and eight months in prison on June 1, 1965.[10] She did not learn that her fiancé had died until the proceedings. Ilse P.'s prison sentence became unbearable after that. Apparently the district court was sympathetic to this and approved the district attorney's request to have the remainder of her prison sentence suspended to probation. She was released on November 11, 1965.[11]

Four days after the failed escape, Christian Buttkus' mother was informed by the Stasi "that her son had died from injuries he received during a self-inflicted border breach at the state border on March 4, 1965."[12] She was made to understand that her son's death was to be portrayed as an accident and that she must keep silent about the actual circumstances. Christian Buttkus' corpse had already been cremated on March 10, 1965 in the Baumschulenweg Crematorium. The files do not clarify whether the mother's request to have the urn buried at the cemetery in Berlin-Pankow was honored.[13] Although the Stasi tried to keep the circumstances of his death a secret, the news that he was shot and killed at the border quickly spread around the mother's neighborhood and at Christian Buttkus' former workplace.[14]

In West Berlin Christian Buttkus' death first became known through his relatives living there. In July 1965 they notified the "Liberal Jurists Board of Inquiry" in the hopes of finding out more about the true circumstances of his death.[15]

The border soldiers who shot Christian Buttkus were not investigated until the 1990s. The former border guard who fired the shots was convicted by the Potsdam district court of manslaughter in coincidence with attempted manslaughter and sentenced to a year and six months probation on December 22, 1994.[16]

A memorial stone commemorating the victims of divided Germany was placed in Kleinmachnow in 1999. Memorial services are conducted here every year but a wooden cross that was erected on the edge of Berlepschstrasse in Berlin-Zehlendorf in honor of Christian Buttkus was removed in 1999 and has been missing ever since.

Lydia Dollmann

1 See "Niederschrift der Zeugenvernehmung der Verlobten von Christian Buttkus durch die Berliner Polizei, 5.3.1992," in: StA Berlin, Az. 27 Js 76/95, Bd. 1, Bl. 106–107.

2 See "Urteil des Landgerichts Potsdam vom 22.12.1994," in: StA Potsdam, Az. 61 Js 40/94 (= StA Berlin Az. 27 Js 96/90), Bd. 2, Bl. 245.

3 See "Information [des MfS]/HA IX/9, 5.3.1965," in: BStU, Ast. Potsdam, AU 9764/65, Bd. 1, Untersuchungsvorgang, Bl. 62–63.

4 See "Ergänzungsbericht der VfS Gross-Berlin/Abt. IX zum Bericht der HA I/Abwehr (B) U. Abt. 4. Brigade/GR 46, 10.3.1965," in: BStU, MfS, AS 754/70, Bd. 11, Nr. 1, Bl. 57–61.

5 "Handschriftliche Stellungnahme von Ilse P., o.D.," in: BStU, Ast. Potsdam, AU 9764/65, Bd. 2, Gerichtsakte, Bl. 88–97.

6 See "Urteil des Landgerichts Potsdam vom 22.12.1994," in: StA Potsdam, Az. 61 Js 40/94 (= StA Berlin Az. 27 Js 96/90), Bd. 2, Bl. 245–250.

7 See "Ergänzungsbericht der VfS Gross-Berlin/Abt. IX, zum Bericht der HA I/Abwehr (B) U. Abt. 4. Brigade, GR 46, 10.3.1965," in: BStU, MfS, AS 754/70, Bd. 11, Nr. 1, Bl. 59–60; "Einzel-Information Nr. 206/65 des MfS-ZAIG über einen verhinderten Grenzdurchbruch mit tödlichem Ausgang für einen der Grenzverletzer im Raum Dreilinden/Potsdam am 4.3.1965, 8.3.1965," in: BStU, MfS, ZAIG Nr. 1159, Bl. 2.

8 See "Abschlussbericht [des MfS/]HA I/Abwehr (B)/U. Abt. 4 Brigade/GR 46 über einen verhinderten Grenzdurchbruch am 4.3.65, 4.3.1965," in: BStU, MfS, AS 754/70, Bd. 11, Nr. 1, Bl. 11.

9 See ibid., Bl. 13.

10 See "Urteil des Bezirksgerichts Potsdam vom 1.6.1965," in: BStU, Ast. Potsdam, AU 9764/65, Bd. 2, Gerichts-
    akte, Bl. 200.

11 See "Beschluss des Bezirksgerichts Potsdam vom 29.11.1967," in: Ibid., Bl. 215.

12 "Ergänzungsbericht der VfS Gross-Berlin/Abt. IX zum Bericht der HA I/ Abwehr (B) U. Abt. 4. Brigade, GR 46,
    10.3.1965," in: BStU, MfS, AS 754/70, Bd. 11, Nr. 1, Bl. 60.

13 See ibid., Bl. 61.

14 See "Vermerk des DDR-Generalstaatsanwalts von Gross-Berlin zur Leichensache Christian Buttkus, 30.3.1965,"
    in: Ibid., Bl. 64; Vermerk [der VfS Gross-Berlin/Abt. IX], in: Ibid., Bl. 65.

15 See "Schreiben des Untersuchungsausschusses Freiheitlicher Juristen an die Zentrale Erfassungsstelle der
    Landesjustizverwaltungen die Vorermittlung gegen Unbekannt wegen Tötung des Christian Buttkus betreffend,
    8.7.1965," in: StA Berlin, 27 Js 76/95, Bd. 1, Bl. 72.

16 The accompanying border patrol guard died in the 1980s. The other former border soldier facing trial was
    acquitted because the court was of the opinion that preconditions for a joint crime did not exist. See "Urteil
    des Landgerichts Potsdam vom 22.12.1994," in: Ibid., Bd. 2, Bl. 234–235, 270–271.

Ulrich Krzemien

born on September 13, 1940

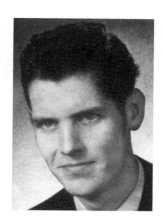

drowned on March 25, 1965
in the Spree near Osthafen
at the sector border between
Berlin-Kreuzberg and Berlin-Friedrichshain

An unidentified man entered the Spree from the west bank between the Kreuzberg and Friedrichshain districts and swam towards the east side at around 9:30 p.m. on March 25, 1965.[1] Twenty meters in front of the East Berlin riverbank near the Osthafen paper mill, the man, "presumably under the influence of alcohol" – as it was noted in a border troop report – asked the border guard for help. He did not have any strength left apparently. The guard may not have recognized the seriousness of the situation or perhaps he thought that he should not recognize it while on duty. In any case, he did no more than to point out to the swimmer "places at the bank wall where it was possible to exit."[2] Following his advice, the swimmer tried to climb the steep bank of the Spree and reach land, but he fell back into the water just five meters away from the watchtower. He went under right before the eyes of the border guard, who remained passive.[3]

Only then did the guard take action; he "fired five shots in the air with his service weapon to alarm the border patrol boat." He also set off a red flare. In response a number of boats arrived and using hooks searched the water for the sunken man. They gave up the search at around 10:30 p.m. Having been alarmed by the shots an hour earlier, West Berlin fire trucks arrived at the scene. They were joined by police cars and two water rescuers in diving suits. Between 80 and 100 West Berliners watched the events from the west bank. The commander of the 1st Border Brigade who had rushed to the scene gave the order from the east bank: "If divers from the west side attempt to enter the water then you are to open fire. Border violators [are] to be exterminated."[4] The presence of the West Berlin police was proof enough to the East Berlin side that they were dealing with "a planned provocation from the enemy."[5]

Nineteen days later, on April 13, 1965, a body was discovered floating downstream between the Brommy Bridge and the Schilling Bridge. The Stasi was certain that this must have been the man who had died on March 15. The Berlin investigating authorities came to the same conclusion in the 1990s. The identity card found on the dead man's body belonged to Ulrich Krzemien.

Ulrich Krzemien was born in Berlin on September 13, 1940, the fourth of six children.[6] His father, a Wehrmacht soldier, never returned home from the Second World War. The mother provided for the large family alone during the difficult post-war years. After completing 8th grade, Ulrich trained as a bricklayer with a state-owned building company in Berlin and in 1958 began working for a number of different East Berlin building companies. One day in the summer of 1959 he did not return home to his mother's apartment in Berlin-Treptow and she reported him missing to the East German police. At that time Ulrich Krzemien had been looking for an apartment and a job on the west side of the city. After a few weeks the nineteen-year-old sent his mother a letter explaining that from now on he planned to live in the West.

He visited his mother often in the eastern part of the city as long as the sector border was still open.[7] That is where he was arrested in July 1961 and charged with "exiting democratic Berlin illegally and slandering the state in coincidence with resistance against state authority."[8] The Berlin-Treptow district court sentenced him to a year and two months in prison in early August. He served his sentence in Berlin-Rummelsburg and in the Bützow-Dreibergen prison and was released on September 29, 1962 – but he was not permitted to return to his residence and workplace in West Berlin. He was forced to remain against his will on the east side of the city[9] and was given a job working for a state-owned company, "VEB Kühl-automat." The city's sector borders were closed and walled up by then, but Ulrich Krzemien did not let this deter him. He succeeded in escaping to West Berlin again by mid – October 1962. He wrote his mother that he had fled through the Teltow Canal. She received mail regularly from her son on the west side of the city. She learned that he was soon engaged to be married, but the relationship only lasted six months and was over by the end of 1964. The man, now 24 years old, may not have gotten over his broken engagement.

One day after the body was found, Ulrich Krzemien's mother was interrogated by a Stasi agent and informed of her son's death. She was told that he died during a border provocation and she should pretend that the death was an accident. She was handed a death certificate dated March 25, 1965, but she was not permitted to send it to his residence and workplace in West Berlin. She was also not permitted to see his body and was pressured to agree to a cremation and burial at the Berlin-Baumschulenweg Cemetery. The memorial service was only to be for "the immediate family."[10]

An autopsy was conducted on the body on April 15. The autopsy report and expert opinion recorded the death date as March 31, 1965. Evidently a Stasi agent had directed the autopsy examiners to do this.[11] The body's decomposition made it impossible to identify the body as that of Ulrich Krzemien based on the photos in the passport that he had on him. But a comparison of the autopsy results with the information on Ulrich Krzemien's identifying features that the mother and sister had provided on May 10 showed that almost everything matched up.[12]

At the end of 1990, one of Ulrich Krzemien's sisters, who lived in East Berlin, wrote a letter to the Berlin Senate stating that she believed her brother was shot on the inner-city border between Rudow and Johannisthal near the Massante Bridge and that the body had been retrieved from the Teltow Canal on April 15, 1965. An

"East German state prosecutor" – that was usually how Stasi agents presented themselves to the relatives of people who died at the Wall – had provided her with this information at the time of her brother's death. Upon her insistence the agent had admitted that her brother had been shot and killed, but he forbade her from speaking about it.[13]

The sister filed charges against unknown persons and requested an investigation. When she was questioned about the case in October 1991, she said that this "state prosecutor" had told her that the identifying features of her brother that she had provided corresponded exactly to those of the body found in the Teltow Canal. To this day, she added, she does not know "whether my brother Ulrich drowned by accident or whether he was shot and killed for violating the border." The "prosecutor" at that time had not provided any additional information.[14]

A short time later the investigation initiated by the Berlin public prosecutor's office was dismissed due to a lack of probable cause. The investigating authorities agreed with the autopsy report and the expert opinion on alcohol consumption, and they concluded that Ulrich Krzemien had died "an unnatural death by drowning," facilitated by a high level of intoxication. No indication of physical violence from another party was found.[15]

What ultimately led Ulrich Krzemien – if indeed he was the swimmer found on March 25 – to swim in the Spree from West Berlin to East Berlin in the cold month of March, completely dressed and under the extreme influence of alcohol, was a secret he took with him to his grave.

Martin Ahrends / Hans-Hermann Hertle

1 See "Bericht [der VfS Gross-Berlin/Abt. IX] zur Grenzprovokation am 25. März 1965 im Bereich der 1. Grenzbrigade in Berlin zur Staatsgrenze nach Westberlin, 19.4.1965," in: BStU, MfS, AS 754/70, Bd. 2, Nr. 10, Bl. 100–106; "Meldung der NVA/Der Stadtkommandant der Hauptstadt der DDR/Generalmajor Poppe an SED-Politbüromitglied Erich Honecker über die Vorbereitung einer Provokation des Gegners im Abschnitt der 4./GR-35, 26.3.1965," in: BArch, VA-07/8373, Bl. 17–19.

2 "Meldung des NVA-Stadtkommandanten Poppe an SED-Politbüromitglied Erich Honecker über die Vorbereitung einer Provokation des Gegners im Abschnitt der 4./GR-35, 26.3.1965," in: BArch, VA-07/8373, Bl. 17.

3 Ibid.

4 Ibid., Bl. 18.

5 Ibid.

6 See "Protokoll der Vernehmung der Mutter von Ulrich Krzemien [durch die VfS Gross-Berlin/Abt. IX], 14.4.1965," in: BStU, MfS, AS 754/70, Bd. 2, Nr. 10, Bl. 36–42.

7 See ibid., and "Ermittlungsbericht der VfS Gross-Berlin/Abt. VIII zu Ulrich Krzemien, 14.4.1965," in: BStU, MfS, AS 754/70, Bd. 2, Nr. 10, Bl. 14–17.

8 "Auskunft des DDR-Generalstaatsanwalts aus dem Strafregister zu Ulrich Krzemien, 26.4.1965," in: BStU, MfS, AS 754/70, Bd. 2, Nr. 10, Bl. 26.

9 See "Protokoll der Vernehmung der Mutter von Ulrich Krzemien [durch die VfS Gross-Berlin/Abt. IX], 14.4.1965," in: BStU, MfS, AS 754/70, Bd. 2, Nr. 10, Bl. 40.

10 See "statement" handwritten by the responsible Stasi agent of Abt. IX of the VfS Gross-Berlin, Lieutenant Meissner, and signed by Ulrich Krzemien's mother, 14.4.1965, in: BStU, MfS, AS 754/70, Bd. 2, Nr. 10, Bl. 43; see also "Bericht [der VfS Gross-Berlin/Abt. IX] zur Grenzprovokation am 25. März 1965 im Bereich der 1. Grenzbrigade in Berlin zur Staatsgrenze nach Westberlin, 19.4.1965," in: BStU, MfS, AS 754/70, Bd. 2, Nr. 10, Bl. 100.

11 "Obduktions-Gutachten zu Ulrich Krzemien, 15.4.1965," in: BStU, MfS, AS 754/70, Bd. 2, Nr. 10, Bl. 76–85.

12 See "[VfS Gross-Berlin/Abt. IX], Merkmale zur Identifizierung der Leiche Krzemien, Ulrich, 19.5.1965," in: BStU, MfS, AS 754/70, Bd. 2, Nr. 10, Bl. 108–109.

13 See "Schreiben der Schwester von Ulrich Krzemien an den Regierenden Bürgermeister von Berlin, Walter Momper, 30.11.1990," in: StA Berlin, 2 Js 14/91, Bl. 5.

14 "Zeugenbefragung der West-Berliner Polizei, 25.10.1991," in: StA Berlin, 2 Js 14/91, Bl. 39.

15 See "Schlussvermerk der West-Berliner Polizei, 29.10.1991," in: StA Berlin, 2 Js 14/91, Bl. 43–46.

Peter Hauptmann

born on March 20, 1939

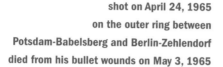

shot on April 24, 1965
on the outer ring between
Potsdam-Babelsberg and Berlin-Zehlendorf
died from his bullet wounds on May 3, 1965

Saturday, April 24, 1965: It was a warm evening in Potsdam-Babelsberg when Peter Hauptmann, who was born on March 20, 1939 in Gittersee near Dresden, met two seamen from the East German navy in the restaurant "Waldschlösschen." Both men were captains and worked on a salvage tug as machine operators. Their brigade was competing for the title "socialist work collective." The award required that they engage in cultural activities and this is why they were taking a weekend sightseeing trip to Berlin, the "capital of East Germany." Since hotels in East Berlin were completely booked, the sailors had moved into a pension in Babelsberg.[1] After enjoying a number of different alcoholic beverages, the men began talking and when the restaurant closed they took a bottle of spirits with them and headed towards the local man's home.

Peter Hauptmann lived with his wife and their four children on Stahnsdorfer Strasse, which was located within the border area. He had often had problems with the border soldiers because he resented having to show his ID every time he came and went. Sometimes the guards recognized him as a local resident and would greet him and wave him through, but when a young recruit was on duty, he was often required to show his ID before he could enter his own house or leave to go to work. Peter Hauptmann had been a police officer himself for many years and was later employed by the East German police force and by the customs office. That may explain why he did not like having his ID checked at his own doorstep. He was a policeman and did not like being treated as a potential "border violator." Moreover, he did not always take the inexperienced border guards seriously. Serious conflicts occurred on occasion when he repeatedly refused to show his ID. Once he even threatened to hit a guard and was arrested and dismissed from duty. After that he changed jobs frequently before finding a position as a driller for a company in Teltow.[2]

On that fatal evening in April 1965, the fight with the border guards came to a head. When Peter Hauptmann was heading home with his guests, he encountered border guards who knew him. After a brief exchange they let them pass.[3] They had probably agreed that the guests should leave his house before the replacements arrived on duty, but they ended up leaving later. When he bid farewell to the men at 3 a.m., new guards had already begun their shift. The sailors' IDs were checked and they were detained temporarily because they were not in possession of an "entry pass" into the border area. Peter Hauptmann watched this take place from his doorstep and became angry. He approached the border guards with the words: "Let these people go, I was the one who let them in. I am the one responsible." All this achieved was that they now demanded to see his identity papers as well.[4] Although he possessed valid documents for the border area, he was temporarily detained for "smuggling unauthorized people into the border area."[5]

This went too far for Peter Hauptmann, a former policeman. Deciding to put an end to this commotion, he turned around and headed towards his house. "Stop! Don't move, or I will make use of my weapon!" the guard called after him.[6] This apparently caused Peter Hauptmann to boil over. He turned around, walked toward the guard and grabbed the barrel of his machine pistol. The guard warned him again. The ex-policeman used his other hand and a skirmish followed as they wrangled for the gun. Then the guard put an end to it: He later claimed to have first fired a warning shot and then aimed at the man standing just a few steps away. Two short shots. Then he let go. Peter Hauptmann swayed backwards and collapsed, fatally wounded. The guard fired the signal "Help. Urgent" and ordered the second man, who until then had been in charge of guarding the sailors, to administer first aid. Peter Hauptmann's wife, startled by the shots, hurried outside and brought towels to help bandage her husband's wound.

The ambulance was taking too long to arrive so the border guards laid the injured man on a stretcher and drove him with a military truck to the Drewitz Army Hospital. He was operated on that very night because he was in too critical a condition to be transported to a civilian hospital. When his condition had stabilized by April 28 he was transferred to the Berlin-Buch clinic. His right kidney had to be removed in another operation. But just days later his left kidney also stopped functioning and Peter Hauptmann died from his injuries early in the morning of May 3.[7] The Buch doctors told the victim's wife that he had died because he had lost too much blood as a consequence of the delayed rescue measures.[8]

Two days later the widow pressed charges against the East German border troops for negligent homicide. Her father-in-law, a captain in the East German police, supported her efforts in this and also submitted a complaint to the Ministry of Interior.[9] But all their attempts to bring those responsible to justice were in vain.

In the summer of 1993 the Central Investigating Agency for Governmental and Party Crimes opened an investigation but it was dismissed in December 1996 because from the viewpoint of the Berlin public prosecutor's office, the man who pulled the trigger had "acted in self-defense, justifying his actions."[10] The widow, who never heard a single warning shot but did hear a series of repeated shots fired together, was never questioned for the investigation.[11] Nor were the neighbors who had been roused from their sleep by the arguments, shots and cries of pain and who had secretly witnessed the events from their balcony. They could have given testimony as to how long it had taken before the critically wounded man was "seized by his arms and legs," thrown onto a truck and transported away.[12]

Peter Hauptmann's father asserted in 1965 that there had been no urgent need for the guard to use his weapon. The border soldiers knew his son and had checked and confiscated his ID so that his "personal data had been established and Peter Hauptmann could not have avoided being held accountable."[13] His wife was of the opinion that her husband had been shot from behind. She had found him lying face down. The doctor's in the army infirmary confirmed her theory that he had been shot in the back.[14] According to the medical information, which the Stasi naturally kept secret, Peter Hauptmann was shot by six bullets: three in his upper arm, two that had grazed his lower arm and a deadly shot to his back.[15]

Martin Ahrends / Udo Baron / Hans-Hermann Hertle

1   See "Vernehmung eines Zeugen (des Kapitäns) durch das VPKA Potsdam, 24.4.1965," in: BStU, Ast. Potsdam, AU 1474/65, Bd. 1, Bl. 44–47, here Bl. 45.

2   See "Abschlussbericht der NVA/4. Grenzbrigade/Der Kommandeur über einen Verstoss gegen die Grenzordnung mit tätlichem Angriff auf den Grenzposten und Anwendung der Schusswaffe durch den Grenzposten, 24.4.1965," in: BStU, Ast. Potsdam, AU 1474/65, Bd. 1, Bl. 22–29.

3   See "Vernehmung eines Zeugen (des Kapitäns) durch das VPKA Potsdam, 24.4.1965," in: BStU, Ast. Potsdam, AU 1474/65, Bd. 1, Bl. 46.

4   See "NVA/2. GK/GR 48, Bericht des Postenführers [und Todesschützen, d. Verf.], 24.4.1965," in: BStU, Ast. Potsdam, AU 10781/65, Bl. 50/51, here Bl. 50.

5   Ibid., Bl. 50. The statement that Peter Hauptmann was in possession of valid border papers came from the guard leader who had checked his papers (see ibid.). In reports of the border troops, it was wrongly claimed that one reason for his arrest had been that he "did not possess a valid stamp for this quarter authorizing entry into the border grounds." See "Abschlussbericht der NVA/4. Grenzbrigade/Der Kommandeur über einen Verstoss gegen die Grenzordnung mit tätlichem Angriff auf den Grenzposten und Anwendung der Schusswaffe durch den Grenzposten, 24.4.1965," in: BStU, Ast. Potsdam, AU 1474/65, Bd. 1, Bl. 23/24.

6   See "Abschlussbericht der NVA/4. Grenzbrigade/Der Kommandeur über einen Verstoss gegen die Grenzordnung mit tätlichem Angriff auf den Grenzposten und Anwendung der Schusswaffe durch den Grenzposten, 24.4.1965," in: BStU, Ast. Potsdam, AU 1474/65, Bd. 1, Bl. 22–29, here Bl. 24.

7   See "Schreiben der NVA/Lazarett Potsdam an den Militärstaatsanwalt beim Stab der 4. Grenzbrigade, 6.5.1965," in: BStU, Ast. Potsdam, AU 1474/65, Bd. 1, Bl. 61/62, and "VfS Gross-Berlin/Abt. XX, Bericht, 7.5.1965," in: BStU, Ast. Potsdam, AU 1474/65, Bd. 1, Bl. 63/64.

8   See conversation conducted by Hans-Hermann Hertle and Lydia Dollmann with Peter Hauptmann's wife at that time, 8.9.2008.

9   See "Bericht der VfS Gross-Berlin/Abt. XX, 7.5.1965," in: BStU, Ast. Potsdam, AU 1474/65, Bd. 1, Bl. 63/64.

10 "Verfügung der Staatsanwaltschaft II bei dem Landgericht Berlin, 10.12.1996," in: StA Berlin, Az. 27 Js 30/94, Bd.1, Bl. 245–248, here Bl. 247.

11 See conversation conducted by Hans-Hermann Hertle and Lydia Dollmann with Peter Hauptmann's wife at that time, 8.9.2008.

12 See conversation conducted by Hans-Hermann Hertle with Peter Hauptmann's neighbor at that time, 7.9.2008.

13 "Bericht der VfS Gross-Berlin/Abt. XX, 7.5.1965," in: BStU, Ast. Potsdam, AU 1474/65, Bd. 1, Bl. 63/64.

14 See conversation conducted by Hans-Hermann Hertle and Lydia Dollmann with Peter Hauptmann's wife at that time, 8.9.2008.

15 See "Bericht der VfS Gross-Berlin/Abt. XX, 7.5.1965," in: BStU, Ast. Potsdam, AU 1474/65, Bd. 1, Bl. 63. In contrast, a possibly manipulated "investigation report," which was demanded by the Stasi following the charges of negligent homicide brought forth by the widow, written by a 'major medical specialist' from the Drewitz Army Hospital stated: "The powder residue indicated that the bullets entered the front side of the body [...]." He noted explicitly, however, that his report was not to be used as an expert opinion in court. See "Schreiben der NVA/Lazarett Potsdam an den Militärstaatsanwalt beim Stab der 4. Grenzbrigade, 6.5.1965," in: BStU, Ast. Potsdam, AU 1474/65, Bd. 1, Bl. 61/62, here Bl. 61.

Hermann Döbler

born on October 28, 1922

**shot dead on June 15, 1965
on the Teltow Canal near the Dreilinden
border crossing
on the outer ring between
Berlin-Zehlendorf and Potsdam**

T he West Berlin businessman Hermann Döbler was shot and killed by an East German border soldier in the early afternoon of June 15, 1965 because he crossed the invisible border line in the Teltow Canal with his motorboat. The use of armed force against the forty-two-year-old entrepreneur from Berlin-Steglitz and his companion, Elke Märtens, who survived the shooting with serious wounds, was unanimously condemned in West Berlin. Detailed reports were printed in the newspapers about the couple and what had happened to them. Berlin's mayor, Willy Brandt, referred to the act as "cold-blooded murder" and demanded that the guilty people in East Germany be held accountable.[1]

On the other side of the Wall, East German authorities tried to justify the shots by claiming that the border guards had been provoked by the two passengers on the boat.[2] The Stasi organized a malicious smear campaign against Hermann Döbler, who had lived in East Germany before the Wall was erected.[3] The East German head propagandist, Karl Eduard von Schnitzler, spread rumors that Döbler had a criminal record for theft and assisting flight from the republic and that he was long known to them as an agitator who had engaged in organized attacks on the East German state border.[4] Hermann Döbler had in fact helped his wife and children to escape from East Germany, but there was no direct connection between his former activities and the circumstances under which he was killed that June afternoon.

Hermann Döbler was born in 1922 in a small town named Roderbeck in what at that time had been the Pomerania district of Greifenhagen, south of Stettin. He was conscripted into the Wehrmacht at the age of 18 and experienced the end of World War II in Berlin. Destitute and without vocational training, he was able to find a place to stay in the eastern section of the city during the chaotic years after the war. He worked for a time as a messenger and clerk, but soon became a successful independent businessman. He met his future wife in 1949 in Görlitz and they married a year later. The determined and attractive man quickly won her over with his charm, Irene Döbler later remembered.[5] They had three children together. In the mid-fifties, with the active support of his wife, Hermann Döbler founded a shipping company in Eberswalde near Berlin. A few years later the family moved to Karlshorst on the outskirts of East Berlin where the couple ran its own auto repair shop.

The company was thriving and business operations were not subjected to any restrictions from the East German authorities, hence he and his wife had no reason to consider leaving East Germany at that time. This did not change even when he was sentenced to six months in prison in 1958 for spontaneously helping a young man whom he had given a ride to in his car to flee from East Berlin to West Berlin.[6] A little later his business operations required that he cross the border regularly. In 1960 he took over a block of garages on Rothenburgstrasse in West Berlin's Steglitz district. Hermann Döbler was spending more and more time at the other end of the city while his wife ran the company in Berlin-Karlshorst and lived there with their children. He was at his secondary residence in West Berlin on August 13, 1961 when the Wall went up and completely separated the family. Hermann Döbler tried to stay in contact with the family. He sent money and packages and set up meetings with the wife and children at the border fortifications. He was finally able to organize an escape for his family in May 1962. They hid in a truck that was traveling to West Berlin. After a few weeks in the West his wife realized that their marriage was finished and she returned with the children to East Germany without considering that the East German authorities would accuse her of having "fled the republic." They were divorced in May 1965, but Hermann Döbler stayed in contact with his children through letters and paid child support regularly. After he was killed, his children suffered tremendously from the public hostility and smear campaign against their father. They even had to endure having their teacher present him to the whole class as a criminal.

Hermann Döbler was accompanied by the 21-year-old Elke Märtens on June 15, 1965.[7] He had invited the young woman to take a daytrip with him on his motorboat. It was beautiful weather when they set off on the open boat along the River Havel and headed towards Wannsee. They reached Griebnitzsee and at the Kohlhasen Bridge turned into the Teltow Canal which, at the farthest southwestern edge of the city, bordered directly on East Germany at certain spots. The line of the border in this section of the canal was difficult to recognize and poorly marked. The first section of the waters belonged completely to West Berlin, then in the middle they were divided evenly between West Berlin and East Germany, and finally, behind the highway bridge that led to the nearby Dreilinden border crossing, the entire width of the canal belonged to East Germany. Elke Märtens later told the West Berlin police that they were sitting behind the steering wheel when they drove under the highway bridge. She had noticed a water barrier after the bridge that blocked off the entire width of the canal and she pointed this out to her companion, but Hermann Döbler reassured her that they could continue up to the water barrier.[8] Neither was aware that the east-west boundary lay 100 meters in front of this barrier or that they had already entered an area where the boundary was in the middle of the canal.

The couple on the boat was observed by the two border soldiers stationed on the watchtower at the southern bank of the canal. The guards evidently felt provoked by Hermann Döbler and Elke Märtens, possibly because they had waved to them. The border troop commander in charge wrote in his report: "After crossing the state border," the two boat passengers had turned provocatively back towards the guard tower, after which the guard decided "to use his weapon to annihilate the border violators."[9] He opened fire immediately and when Elke Märtens turned the boat around and headed towards the West Berlin bank, he aimed directly at the boat and its occupants. Hermann Döbler was hit four times: on his knee, torso and head. He died immediately. A bullet grazed Elke Märtens' head and she was transported in critical condition to a West Berlin hospital. She survived but sustained permanent damage from her injuries. Hermann Döbler was buried on June 22, 1965 in the municipal cemetery on Bergstrasse in Berlin-Steglitz. His death was accompanied by tremendous public sympathy. More than 1,000 people paid him their last respects.[10]

After the East German state collapsed, the guard who had shot the couple, the border soldier who had stood by him on the tower without shooting, as well as the head guard who had given the orders that day, were held accountable for this brutal act. The Berlin district court was convinced that the gunman had acted with premeditation and convicted him of murder in coincidence with attempted murder. He was sentenced to six years in prison, one of the harshest punishments ever handed down to a border guard.[11]

Christine Brecht

---

1 See the statement from Mayor Willy Brandt on RIAS, 15.6.1965, in: Archiv Deutschlandradio, Sendung: Die Zeit im Funk, Reporter: Helmut Fleischer, Gerd Meyer, Gerd Hente. On media coverage the following day, see "Vopo-Mord an Westberliner. Wassersportler kaltblütig erschossen", in: Telegraf, 16.6.1965; "West-Berliner bei Grenzzwischenfall getötet," in: Frankfurter Allgemeine Zeitung, 16.6.1965; "East German Police Shoot West Berlin Boaters," in: The New York Times, 16.6.1965.

2 See "Grenzverletzung am Teltowkanal," in: Neues Deutschland, 16.6.1965, sowie "Organisierte Grenzprovokation," in: Neues Deutschland, 17.6.1965.

3 See "Schreiben [des MfS-ZAIG]/Abt. Agitation, 17.6.1965," in: BStU, MfS, ZAIG Nr. 10717, Bl. 263; "Bericht [des MfS-ZAIG]/Abt. Agitation zur Grenzprovokation am Teltow-Kanal vom 15.6.1965, 17.6.1965," in: Ibid., Bl. 264–265, and "Ermittlungsergebnisse [des MfS-ZAIG] zur Person des Grenzverletzers Hermann Döbler, 17.6.1965," in: Ibid., Bl. 212–214.

4 See Karl-Eduard von Schnitzler, Gedanken zu einem Bild, in: Neues Deutschland, 18.6.1965; ders., Bestellte Aktion, in: Berliner Zeitung, 17.6.1965; ders., Der Fall Döbler, in: Visite, Heft 8, 1965, pp. 44–45.

5 See conversation conducted by Christine Brecht with Irene Döbler, Hermann Döbler's former wife, 20.4.2007.

6 See ibid., and "Urteil des Stadtbezirksgerichts Mitte vom 3.7.1958," in: BStU, MfS, ZAIG Nr. 10717, Bl. 98–101.

7 See "Niederschrift der Zeugenvernehmung von Elke M. durch die Berliner Polizei, 27.2.1992," in: StA Berlin, Az. 2 Js 161/90, Bd. 2, Bl. 49–51.

8 See ibid., and "Niederschrift der Zeugenvernehmung von Elke M. durch die West-Berliner Polizei, 28.6.1965 bzw. 12.7.1965," in: Ibid., Bd. 1, Bl. 105 bzw. Bl. 124.

9 See "Bericht der NVA/4.GB/Der Kommandeur betr. Abschlussbericht über die Verletzung des DDR-Territoriums mit provokatorischem Charakter durch ein westberliner Sportboot, 15.6.1965," in: BArch, VA-07/6007, Bl. 32–37, here Bl. 33, and "Bericht [des MfS]/HA I Abwehr (B)/Unterabteilung 4. Brigade über die Anwendung der Schusswaffe gegen zwei Grenzverletzer mit Motorsportboot bei der Verletzung des DDR-Territoriums mit provokatorischem Charakter, 15.6.1965," in: BStU, MfS, ZAIG Nr. 10717, Bl. 184–188.

10 See "Letztes Geleit für Vopo-Opfer," in: Der Kurier, 23.6.1965.

11 See "Urteil des Landgerichts Berlin vom 16.11.1993," in: StA Berlin, Az. 2 Js 161/90, Bd. 5, n. pag.

Klaus Kratzel

born on March 3, 1940

fatally injured on August 8, 1965
in the S-Bahn tunnel north of
the Bornholmer Strasse station
at the sector border between
Berlin-Pankow and Berlin-Wedding

"I am only coming if my chances are good," Klaus Kratzel wrote from East Berlin to his in-laws in the western section of the city in early August 1965.[1] He had already suggested in other letters that he had written in the previous weeks that he wanted to flee to West Berlin. But he avoided using the word "escape" so that the East German authorities would not become suspicious when they read his mail. Instead he spoke in a roundabout way about moving to a new apartment. But his relatives understood his message clearly. Klaus Kratzel, who had recently left his wife and children and moved from West Berlin to East Berlin, was now looking for an opportunity to return to his family.[2]

Born in Berlin on March 3, 1940, Klaus Kratzel grew up with four siblings in the Weissensee district of East Berlin. After completing school he trained to become a bricklayer and later worked in that field. He met his future wife at a fair in Berlin-Stralau when he was 18. Their wedding took place in April 1961 after their first daughter was born, but the young married couple's life changed abruptly when the Wall was built. Klaus Kratzel's father-in-law was a Social Democrat. He worried that after sealing off the border between the East and West, the East German communist regime would go after political dissenters and their relatives more harshly. Hence he insisted that they flee to the West. Leaving all their possessions behind, Klaus Kratzel, his wife, their young daughter and his in-laws were able to get through the barriers on August 18, 1961.[3]

They registered at the Marienfelde Refugee Camp and, like hundreds of other East German refugees who had fled to West Berlin after the Wall went up, they spent a difficult time in various refugee camps.[4] After living for a year in destitution, they finally found their own apartment and the second daughter was born soon after that. Klaus Kratzel's wife recalled that he was a good father who enjoyed looking after the children. But he had difficulties resisting the temptations of western consumerism and by January 1965 was once again facing financial straits. This caused a fight with his wife, which led him to leave their apartment, drive to the Friedrichstrasse S-Bahn station and apply at the border crossing for the right to return to East Germany. He had to go through a reception camp in the East

Berlin district of Blankenfelde after which he was able to move in with his mother again.[5] The letters to his in-laws show that it was not long before Klaus Kratzel regretted his decision and wanted to risk escaping to West Berlin again.

The twenty-five-year-old was found dead in an S-Bahn tunnel north of the closed down Bornholmer Strasse station on August 8, 1965 at around 11:30 p.m. S-Bahn trains traveling regularly between the Schönhauser Allee and Pankow stations passed through this tunnel, which was situated within the border grounds. All signs indicated that Klaus Kratzel, who had mustered up his courage with alcohol, was hit by a train while trying to cross the track grounds to the Wedding district in West Berlin.[6] The East German authorities were puzzled by how he had managed to enter the heavily-guarded border grounds unnoticed. There had already been a few successful escapes in this rather confusing area of the border. Sometimes passengers pulled the emergency brakes while the train was passing through the border grounds and jumped out of the S-Bahn train at a good spot.[7] In the case of Klaus Kratzel, however, the East German border troops' investigation was unable to find any clues to his "approach path." There was some thought that his accident may have had something to do with the escape of another young man that had also taken place that night in the same border area, but this could not be confirmed. The only certain thing was that Klaus Kratzel was accidentally killed while trying to reach West Berlin. The report written by the regiment commander in charge stated: "Site of accident, time and circumstances justify the theory that the fatally injured man was trying to break through the state border towards Grüntaler Strasse (West Berlin)."[8]

The border troop investigation findings were categorized as military secrets and not disclosed to Klaus Kratzel's relatives. His mother wrote to West Berlin that all she had learned was that he had been involved in a fatal accident "on the tracks."[9] The East German authorities did not let her know where the accident had occurred. She was also denied her request to see her dead son's body. He was buried on August 18, 1965 in East Berlin.

The non-transparent conduct of the authorities made the bereaved family members mistrustful, particularly since everyone in the family knew that the deceased had been intending to flee. For years rumors spread in the family that Klaus Kratzel had been shot at the Wall, a theory that after the East German archives were made accessible was ruled out by the Berlin public prosecutor's office during its investigation in the 1990s.[10]

Christine Brecht

1 "Handschriftlicher Brief von Klaus Kratzel, o.D.[August 1965]," in: StA Berlin, Az. 27 Js 197/91, Bl. 49.

2 See "Schreiben des Untersuchungsausschusses Freiheitlicher Juristen an den Polizeipräsidenten von Berlin betr. Sowjetzonales Gewaltverbrechen an der Sektorengrenze, 24.8.1965," in: Ibid., Bl. 45.

3 See conversation conducted by Christine Brecht with Renate D., Klaus Kratzel's wife at that time, 19.6.2007.

4 See Katja Augustin, Im Vorzimmer des Westens. Das Notaufnahmelager Marienfelde, in: Bettina Effner/Helge Heidemeyer (eds.), Flucht im geteilten Deutschland, Berlin, 2005, pp. 135–151.

5 See conversation conducted by Christine Brecht with Renate D., Klaus Kratzel's wife at that time, 19.6.2007.

6 See "Verfügung der Staatsanwaltschaft bei dem Kammergericht Berlin (27/2 Js 197/91), 25.11.1993," in: StA Berlin, Az. 27 Js 197/91, Bl. 104.

7   At least one person managed to escape this way on the S-Bahn route between Pankow-Schönhauser Allee in 1964. See "Analyse der NVA/Stadtkommandantur Berlin/Operative Abt. über Grenzdurchbrüche im Zeitraum 1.1.–1.12.1964 und 1.1.–31.8.1965, 2.9.1965," in: BArch, VA-07/6004, Bl. 134–148, here Bl. 137.

8   "Bericht der NVA/Grenzregiment 31/Kommandeur zum Grenzdurchbruch im Abschnitt der 4. GK/GR-31 am 8.8.1965, gegen 23.50 Uhr durch eine männliche Person, 12.8.1965," in: BArch, VA-07/16934, Bl. 76–82, here Bl. 80.

9   See "Handschriftlicher Brief der Mutter von Klaus Kratzel, 12.8.1965," in: StA Berlin, Az. 27 Js 197/91, Bl. 50–53.

10 See "Verfügung der Staatsanwaltschaft bei dem Kammergericht Berlin (27/2 Js 197/91), 25.11.1993," in: Ibid., Bl. 104–105.

Klaus Garten

born on July 19, 1941

shot dead on August 18, 1965
near the Philipp-Müller-Allee in Seehof
on the outer ring between
Teltow (Potsdam county district)
and Berlin-Steglitz

Klaus Garten, who was born on July 19, 1941 in Radeberg, Saxony, was three years old when he lost his father in the Second World War. He grew up in his hometown with his mother and stepfather, a Communist Party functionary.[1] The trained bodywork technician completed his military service with the National People's Army in Stahnsdorf at the southwest edge of Berlin from 1959 to 1962.

He met his future wife during reserve training in Oranienburg and after finishing his military service moved with her into a garden house in their hometown.[2] Klaus Garten got a position working as a metalworker with the Hennigsdorf steel plant. As a skilled worker he took on extra tasks to make his contribution in helping to fulfill the expectations of the economic plan. He was a member of the Communist Party and designated his company's party group organizer,[3] but this responsibility caused him increasing uneasiness. Only a very few of the 50 staff members in his division belonged to the party, and he sensed that his colleagues "looked down" on him because of his political role.[4] An East German secret police report noted "manifestations of resignation among the party members in this division of the company."[5]

As he became increasingly isolated at work, he considered quitting his job and opening a restaurant, but he also began to think about fleeing to the West. He spoke to his wife about it in July 1965.[6] Klaus Garten had been living with his wife in their one-room garden house for a year and half. They had moved in there together with the hope of establishing a dignified home over time. But the young husband became increasingly demoralized by the impossibility of ever obtaining building material.[7] As a childless couple they had little chance of being allotted another apartment. Klaus Garten tried to obtain a car, probably to transport building material, but used cars were absurdly expensive. They could cost three times as much as a new car for which he would have had to wait at least ten years.

Klaus Garten began looking for a car that had been in an accident and was damaged: As a body mechanic he was confident he could get it into tiptop shape again. During his vacation in 1965, the young couple drove on August 17 to East Berlin, "the capital of East Germany," in the hope of somehow getting a suitable junk car. In Pankow he was told to go to the "German trade office" in Teltow. His wife returned home by S-Bahn and he embarked on the long trip which entailed taking the train and bus via Schönefeld and driving around the west side of the city.[8] But when he reached the "German Trade Office" in Teltow the people there were unable to help him. Although they sold discarded company vehicles, there was an endlessly long waiting list to obtain one. Additionally, the people on the list were often bypassed anyway because new arrivals were often sold for cash under the table. This was one more disappointment to add to Klaus Garten's other bad experiences that year and may have been what tipped the scales for him and his faith in East German socialism. The young man, who until then had been active as a Communist Party comrade and a long-standing servant of his state, must have finally recognized the hard and fast truth that he could not get ahead in East Germany. At this point he decided to leave East Germany.

He was familiar with the Stahnsdorf area because he had spent his time in the military there. At around 9 p.m. a border guard watched as the 24-year-old climbed over a wire mesh fence on a lot on Paul-Gerhard-Strasse in Teltow-Seehof that was located very close to the border. The border strip was only 20 meters wide there. A guard positioned about 200 meters away opened fire before the fugitive could even begin running towards West Berlin. Three shots were fired from the machine gun and the fugitive fell off the fence.[9] After a short search the border guards found him in the anti-vehicle trench to which he had dragged himself. His thigh was wounded and he was bleeding heavily. Two additional border soldiers who had been called to the scene also arrived, but instead of bandaging the man's wounds or transporting him away, the four guards ducked into the trench to stay out of view. Policemen who were close by on the West Berlin side had begun searching the border grounds with hand-held lamps. More and more residents gathered on the west side of the border, trying to identify something in the darkness.[10] The West Berlin police registered that six border guards wrapped an injured man in a tarpaulin at about 9:50 p.m.[11]

The border guards, however, did not know that they had been seen pulling the man out of the trench. "Our actions were carried out under cover and could not be witnessed by the enemy,"[12] one of them reported. And he added: "We transported the border violator on our backs as we crawled on all fours."[13] It is clear that they took a considerable detour in order to avoid being seen by the people on the west side when they transported the injured man through the anti-vehicle trench to the observation tower where they hastily bandaged him. Almost an entire hour had passed before he received any medical aid at all. When Klaus Garten was finally taken away he had already lost a tremendous amount of blood. Nevertheless, they did not take him to the church-run hospital a kilometer away, but to the Stasi Prison Hospital in Hohenschönhausen, which took at least an hour to reach. Klaus Garten died from his injuries later that night.[14]

Thirty-five years later the Berlin public prosecutor's office opened an investigation on Klaus Garten's case. But in 1995 the case was dismissed again because the man suspected of having pulled the trigger claimed to have only fired a warning shot and the court was unable to prove otherwise.[15]

The morning after his death, a member of the East German secret police paid

Klaus Garten's wife a visit and brought her to Oranienburg to be interrogated. She was questioned about her marriage, her husband's problems at work and his plans to escape, but was not informed that her husband had died while attempting to flee until a few days later. She later learned more details from a newspaper clipping from the "BZ" that a relative in West Berlin had sent her. It was dated August 18, 1965 and reported on her husband's fatal escape attempt.[16]

In order to ensure that the circumstances of Klaus Garten's death remained secret, the East German secret police demanded that the widow only tell the truth of how he died to her next of kin. She was to tell everyone else that Klaus Garten had died in a motorcycle or car accident.[17]

Klaus Garten's body was cremated in the Berlin-Baumschulenweg Crematorium on August 20, 1965. The remains were buried in the Schmachtenhagen Cemetery.

Martin Ahrends / Udo Baron

1 See "Ermittlungen der VfS Gross-Berlin/Abt. IX zur Leichensache Klaus Werner Garten, 20.8.1965," in: BStU, MfS, AS 754/70, Bd. 10, Nr. 3, Bl. 22–23.

2 See "Protokoll der Vernehmung der Ehefrau von Klaus Garten durch das MfS, 18.8.1965," in: BStU, MfS, AS 754/70, Bd. 10, Nr. 3, Bl. 12–16, here Bl. 13.

3 See "Beurteilung des Kollegen Klaus Garten durch den VEB Stahl- und Walzwerk "Wilhelm Florin", 19.8.1965," in: BStU, MfS, AS 754/70, Bd. 10, Nr. 3, Bl. 11.

4 See "Protokoll der Vernehmung der Ehefrau von Klaus Garten durch das MfS, 18.8.1965," in: BStU, MfS, AS 754/70, Bd. 10, Nr. 3, Bl. 14.

5 "Ermittlungen der VfS Gross-Berlin/Abt. IX zur Leichensache Klaus Werner Garten, 20.8.1965," in: BStU, MfS, AS 754/70, Bd. 10, Nr. 3, Bl. 21.

6 See "Protokoll der Vernehmung der Ehefrau von Klaus Garten durch das MfS, 18.8.1965," in: BStU, MfS, AS 754/70, Bd. 10, Nr. 3, Bl. 14.

7 See "Ermittlungen der VfS Gross-Berlin/Abt. IX zur Leichensache Klaus Werner Garten, 20.8.1965," in: BStU, MfS, AS 754/70, Bd. 10, Nr. 3, Bl. 21.

8 See "Zeugenvernehmung von E. V., verwitwete Garten, durch die Berliner Polizei, 11.3.1991," in: StA Berlin, Az. 27 Js 90/90, Bd. 1, Bl. 20.

9 See "Einzel-Information Nr. 754/65 des MfS/ZAIG über einen verhinderten Grenzdurchbruch im Abschnitt Teltow-Seehof/Potsdam am 17.8.1965, 19.8.1965," in: BStU, MfS, ZAIG Nr. 1159, Bl. 11–12.

10 See "Handschriftlicher Bericht des Grenzsoldaten K. über die Bergung des Grenzverletzers am 17.8.1965," 18.8.1965, in: BStU, MfS, AOP 6505/66, Bl. 17.

11 See "Strafanzeige der Berliner Polizei wegen Verdachts des versuchten Totschlages gegen unbekannte Angehörige der 4. Grenzbrigade, 46. Rgt. der sogen. NVA-Grenztruppen, 18.8.1965," in: StA Berlin, Az. 27 Js 90/90, Bd. 1, Bl. 70.

12 "Handschriftlicher Bericht des Grenzsoldaten K. über die Bergung des Grenzverletzers am 17.8.1965, 18.8.1965," in: BStU, MfS, AOP 6505/66, Bl. 17.

13 Ibid.

14 See "Einzel-Information Nr. 754/65 des MfS/ZAIG über einen verhinderten Grenzdurchbruch im Abschnitt Teltow-Seehof/Potsdam am 17.8.1965, 19.8.1965," in BStU, MfS, ZAIG Nr. 1159, Bl. 12.

15 See "Verfügung der Staatsanwaltschaft Berlin, 20.10.1995," in: StA Berlin, Az. 27 Js 90/90, Bd. 2, Bl. 389–390.

16 See "Zeugenvernehmung von E. V., verwitwete Garten, durch die Berliner Polizei, 11.3.1991," in: StA Berlin, Az. 27 Js 90/90, Bd. 1, Bl. 20–21.

17 See "Bericht der VfS Gross-Berlin/Abt. IX über die Leichensache Klaus Garten, 20.8.1965," in: BStU, MfS, AS 754/70, Bd. 10, Nr. 3, Bl. 25.

Walter Kittel

born on November 21, 1942

shot dead on October 18, 1965
at Stammbahn 53
on the outer ring between
Kleinmachnow (Potsdam county district)
and Berlin-Zehlendorf

A sentence handed down by the Potsdam district court in one of the Border Guard Trials in December 1992 drew special attention. A former border guard was found guilty of manslaughter and sentenced to six years in prison on the basis of the East German criminal code.[1] The following year the Federal Court of Justice in Berlin increased the penalty on appeal to ten years in prison for murder.[2] The judge sentenced the former border soldier to the highest prison term possible with the explanation that the thirty shots that the defendant fired at the fugitive Walter Kittel after he had already surrendered were comparable to an execution.

Walter Kittel's murderer was not prosecuted in East Germany. In fact the commander of the group division in Kleinmachnow was awarded honors and promoted to staff sergeant. The other guards involved were also praised and each received a wristwatch as a bonus for his good work.[3]

On the evening of October 17, 1965, Walter Kittel, who was 22 years old at the time, and Eberhardt K., who was two years younger, happened to meet at the "Libelle" bar in Teltow-Seehof. The two young men knew each other vaguely, but when they began talking, they quickly realized that they had something in common: They were both planning to flee to West Berlin. They left the bar at around midnight and took a bus to Kleinmachnow. It was Walter Kittel who suggested that they carry through with their escape plans that very night. Since he lived near the border grounds he had been observing the border strip and the border guards' movements for quite some time. He also knew exactly where they should make their escape. Eberhardt K. agreed with the plan and accompanied Walter Kittel to his apartment where he had prepared a sketch of the escape route and had the tools needed to break though the barriers.[4] By 2:45 a.m. the two young men had reached the garden property at "An der Stammbahn 53" in Kleinmachnow and proceeded towards the one-and-a-half-meter-high interior fence that closed off the property from the border grounds. They made it through the fence, crossed the border patrol route and the anti-vehicle trench within the border grounds and crawled towards the border fence. They paused when they reached the chained-dog run. A watchdog approached them but did not sniff them out. Walter Kittel

197

and Eberhardt K. were just a few steps from the last border fence when they were noticed by two border guards. The guards fired a signal flare and ordered the fugitives to move toward the guard path with their hands in the air. Walter Kittel and Eberhardt K. realized by then that their escape had failed. They went to the guard path as they were told to do at which point a verbal conflict flared up between them and the guards during which one of the border soldiers fired three shots at the captured fugitives. Eberhardt K. was hit in the foot. Walter Kittel and Eberhardt K. sought protection from the trigger-happy guards by climbing into the anti-vehicle trench. Yet the border guards continued shooting. Eberhardt K. was hit again and critically wounded in his upper arm and pelvis. At this point the commander of the group division, who had been alerted by the flare, arrived and took charge.[5] He ordered the fugitives to leave the trench. Unlike Eberhardt K., Walter Kittel had not yet been injured and was able to obey the order. After leaving the protection of the trench the commander fired 30 shots at him from a distance of 15 meters while screaming: "I swore to myself that no one would get out of here alive!"[6] Walter Kittel was hit in the chest and stomach and fell to the ground. He died immediately from internal injuries.

To prevent people on the West Berlin side from seeing what was happening the border guards immediately brought Walter Kittel's body and the injured Eberhardt K. to the back area of the border grounds.[7] One of the border guards contemptuously knocked the corpse of Walter Kittel with his foot and said: "This bastard is dead but that dog there is still alive!"[8] They were loaded onto a truck and taken away. An autopsy was carried out on Walter Kittel's body at the forensic medicine department of Humboldt University. Eberhardt K. was first taken to the Kleinmachnow Hospital and later to the People's Police Hospital on Scharnhorststrasse in Berlin.[9]

Walter Kittel's father was a member of the Communist Party and worked as a technical director for a state-owned company. The Stasi informed him the following day of his son's death and had him sign a statement in which he agreed "not to inform a third party" about what had happened.[10] He also had to allow the state to organize the burial. A Stasi report stated that he was deeply pained by the news of his son's death. He did not question the escape attempt since his son had fled to West Berlin once before in September 1959.[11] The family – Walter Kittel, his father and two siblings – had moved from Kölleda in Thuringia to Kleinmachnow just a few weeks earlier, after a number of close relatives in Walter Kittel's family had all died within a few years.[12]

Walter Kittel, born on May 21, 1942, grew up and attended school in Kölleda. In 1957 he began an apprenticeship as an auto mechanic in nearby Gutmannshausen. After he fled to West Berlin he had to live in a refugee camp. Three months later his father picked him up there and brought him back to Kleinmachnow.[13]

It is not known why Walter Kittel decided to return to East Germany, but after his "repatriation" he seemed to have become politically active. He founded a marching band within his local FDJ youth group, joined the "writing workers" circle and became a member of the FDJ county leadership in Jüterbog, and later in Nauen. After completing his apprenticeship in Kleinmachnow in 1961, Walter Kittel volunteered to join the National People's Army but was not accepted for health reasons. He attended the FDJ district school in Schwante for eight weeks the following year.[14] It was during this time that he met a young woman with whom he later had a child.[15] In August 1961 he was hired by the "Milchader," a milk production company in the Nauen district, and in 1964 worked for the Melioration Construction Company in Potsdam.[16]

By 1964, Walter Kittel's political activities had started to subside.[17] He also drew public attention to himself around this time. In a drunken state he railed against Walter Ulbricht to an East German police officer. He also compared the methods of the East German police and his father's parenting to those of the SS.[18] As a consequence, Walter Kittel was convicted in May 1964 of "criminal intoxication in connection with slander against the state" and sentenced to nine months in prison commuted to two years probation.[19] His statements were an indication of how unhappy Walter Kittel was with the political conditions in East Germany, but they also shed light on his family problems. The reasons for his second escape attempt were probably both political and personal.

Eberhardt K., who had fled with Walter Kittel, was convicted in December 1965 by the Potsdam district court of violating the passport law and sentenced to two years in prison. After spending nine months in a hospital he was transferred to the Berlin-Rummelsburg Penitentiary.[20] He told fellow-prisoners there about the failed escape attempt and Walter Kittel's death. Two years later two of these prisoners made it to West Berlin where they made an official statement to the police.[21] Their report confirmed the suspicion long held by the West Berlin police that a fugitive had died on the sector border in Kleinmachnow on the night of October 18, 1965. A West Berlin policeman and a customs officer in the neighboring district of Berlin-Zehlendorf had heard shots fired that night, but they had been unable to see if anyone was arrested or if a body had been carried away from the border area.[22] The next day the press reported on a failed escape attempt in Kleinmachnow.[23] The West Berlin police placed charges against an unidentified member of the 4th Border Brigade of the 46th Regiment on October 25, 1965.[24] A few days later information leaked to West Berlin that a fugitive named Walter Kittel had died that night.[25]

Since 1999 a memorial stone at Adam-Kuckhoff-Platz in Kleinmachnow has commemorated the victims of the German division who, like Walter Kittel, died on the border in Kleinmachnow.

Lydia Dollmann

1   Three former border soldiers were tried. One of the defendants was acquitted for legitimate reasons. Another defendant was convicted of attempted manslaughter and received a suspended prison sentence of two years. See "Urteil des Bezirksgerichts Potsdam vom 9.12.1992," in: StA Neuruppin, 60 Js 12/92 (= StA Berlin, Az. 2 Js 100/90) Bd. 5, Bl. 537–575. On the Walter Kittel case trial, see also Roman Grafe, *Deutsche Gerechtigkeit. Prozesse gegen DDR-Grenzschützen und ihre Befehlsgeber,* München, 2004, pp. 260–261.

2   See "BGH-Urteil betr. Revision [5 StR 473/93], 20.10.1993," in: StA Neuruppin, Az. 60 Js 12/92 (= StA Berlin, Az. 2 Js 100/90) Bd. 5, Bl. 732–758.

3   See "Urteil des Bezirksgerichts Potsdam vom 9.12.1992," in: Ibid., Bd. 5, Bl. 567–568.

4   Another person also considered fleeing, but according to Eberhardt K., he became scared and changed his

mind. See "Bericht der DDR-Generalstaatsanwaltschaft über die Befragung des Beschuldigten Eberhardt K., 20.10.1965," in: BStU, Ast. Potsdam, AU 1684/66, StA 3077, Bl. 22–23.

5 See "Urteil des Bezirksgerichts Potsdam vom 9.12.1992," in: StA Neuruppin, 60 Js 12/92 (= StA Berlin, Az. 2 Js 100/90), Bd. 5, Bl. 541–543.

6 "Urteil des Bezirksgerichts Potsdam vom 9.12.1992," in: Ibid., Bl. 553.

7 See "Anklageschrift der Staatsanwaltschaft Potsdam vom 4.8.1992," in: Ibid., Bd. 4, Bl. 264–272.

8 "Urteil des Bezirksgerichts Potsdam vom 9.12.1992," in: Ibid., Bd. 5, Bl. 555.

9 See ibid., Bl. 557.

10 "Statement" forced from Walter Kittel's father by the Stasi, 19.10.1965, in: BStU, MfS, AS 754/70, Bd. 2, Nr. 9, Bl. 65.

11 See "[MfS-]Abschlussbericht zum Leichenvorgang, 25.10.1965," in: Ibid., Bl. 67–68.

12 Walter Kittel's biological mother had died in 1953. His father remarried a year later. In the spring of 1958 the grandmother who lived with the family also died, and in the fall the father's second wife died in fatal accident. He remarried once more in 1959. See letter from Walter Kittel's sister to Lydia Dollmann, 4.9.2008.

13 See "Niederschrift der Vernehmung von Walter Kittel durch die Trapo/Amt Wustermark/Abt. K/Oranienburg, 22.3.1964," in: BStU, MfS, B-SKS 16976, Bl. 11–12.

14 See "Urteil des Kreisgerichts Nauen gegen Walter Kittel vom 30.5.1964," in: Ibid., Bl. 35–36.

15 Letter from Walter Kittel's sister to Lydia Dollmann, 4.9.2008.

16 See "Niederschrift der Vernehmung von Walter Kittel durch die Trapo/Amt Wustermark/Abt. K/Oranienburg, 22.3.1964," in: Ibid., Bl. 11–12.

17 See "Urteil des Kreisgerichts Nauen gegen Walter Kittel vom 30.5.1964," in: Ibid., Bl. 35–36.

18 See "Niederschrift der Vernehmung von Walter Kittel durch die Trapo/Amt Wustermark/Abt. K/Oranienburg, 22.3.1964," in: Ibid., Bl. 5–7.

19 "Urteil des Kreisgerichts Nauen gegen Walter Kittel vom 30.5.1964," in: Ibid., Bl. 35.

20 Eberhardt K. suffered his entire life from consequences caused by his bullet wound. See "Niederschrift der Zeugenvernehmung von Eberhardt K. durch die ZERV, 12.12.1991," in: StA Berlin, Az. 2 Js 940/92, Bd. 1, Bl. 152–153.

21 See "Vorermittlungen gegen Unbekannt durch die Zentrale Erfassungsstelle der Landesjustizverwaltungen in Salzgitter, 31.8.1967," in: Ibid., Bl. 78–92.

22 See "Meldung der West-Berliner Polizei über Schüsse an der Demarkationslinie, 18.10.1965," in: Ibid. Bl. 45.

23 See Der Tagesspiegel, 19.10.1965.

24 See "Strafanzeige der West-Berliner Polizei gegen namentlich nicht bekanntgewordene Angehörige der NVA, 25.10.1965," in: StA Berlin, Az. 2 Js 940/92, Bd. 1, Bl. 43.

25 See "Niederschrift der Zeugenaussage eines Anwohners des Grenzgebietes bei der West-Berliner Polizei, 29.10.1965," in: Ibid., Bl. 50.

Heinz Cyrus

born on June 5, 1936

seriously injured from a jump or fall out
of the building at Gartenstrasse 85
while under fire on November 10, 1965
on the sector border between
Berlin-Mitte and Berlin-Wedding
died from his injuries on November 11, 1965

B erlin-Mitte, November 10, 1965, just past 9 p.m.: Heinz Cyrus was slowly moving towards the border fortifications near the Nordbahnhof station. A watchdog caught the scent of the fugitive and attacked. Two guards reported the incident immediately. East German policemen were called in and sealed off the back border grounds. After the guards allegedly called out to him to surrender, and he refused, they opened fire from three sides. The young man remained uninjured and rescued himself from the hail of bullets by entering a nearby building at Gartenstrasse 85. His pursuers surrounded the building and began a search. Heinz Cyrus climbed from one level to the next, his situation increasingly hopeless. Finally, in an act of desperation, he climbed out the hallway window on the fourth floor, clutched the rain pipe and crashed down into the courtyard below. He was transported to the People's Police Hospital in Berlin-Mitte at around 9:30 p.m. with a fractured skull and a number of broken bones.[1] Doctors performed an emergency operation that night but he died from his injuries in the early morning.[2]

Heinz Cyrus, the illegitimate child of a nurse in Greifswald, was born on June 5, 1936 and spent his first years in a children's home.[3] He was adopted by foster parents in 1943 and grew up in the small town of Dreschvitz on the island of Rügen. After completing elementary school he trained to become a dairy worker and worked at a number of state-owned farms on Rügen. He married in 1954 and had four children. A school buddy described Heinz Cyrus as a well-behaved, strong man and able worker who was perhaps a "little wild."[4] In October 1956 he was imprisoned for beating up an East German policeman. He was released early from the prison work camp and in April 1957 he and his wife took over a single farm in Teschvitz with eight hectares of land. The couple joined the local agricultural production cooperative (LPG) "New Life" two years later. Heinz Cyrus was soon appointed deputy LPG chairman and was responsible for the production cooperative's cattle.

The young man caught the attention of the East German secret police in October 1959 when an informant reported that he had gotten into a drunken fight with the LPG chairman and said: "You communist pigs, the day will come when you will hang from trees!"[5] He was arrested by the Stasi in March 1960 – a time when the forced collectivization and the "class struggle" in agriculture was intensifying.[6] The Rostock district court sentenced him during a public trial in June 1960 to seven years in prison for supposedly engaging in "harmful activities." Heinz Cyrus, the cattle breeder and dairy worker, was presented in the arraignment as a dangerous criminal. It was claimed that he disrupted the establishment of socialism in the countryside and "through his crimes had aligned himself with warmongers."[7] He was accused of having improperly fed the cattle of his LPG and improperly cared for them, causing considerable damage during the year 1959. Furthermore he was accused of pilfering animal feed and instigating rampant agitation against Communist Party members. During the trial the wives of LPG farmers in his village claimed that he had made advances towards them. Heinz Cyrus vehemently denied these and all the other accusations. But no fewer than ten "witnesses" and three so-called experts incriminated the accused. It remained unclear whether they acted voluntarily or under pressure from the East German secret police who had led the investigation and had also arranged the outcome. Heinz Cyrus was left alone with his argument that the animals' food stock that he had taken over was insufficient from the start and the animal feed inadequate. The organizers of the show trial did not allow any witnesses for the defense. At the end of the trial, Heinz Cyrus' counsel did not even object to the state prosecutor's excessive demand for a seven year prison sentence. According to the protocol he instead asked the court for an "appropriate punishment" for his client.[8] Heinz Cyrus had to speak the last word himself, but his plea was made in vain: "I did not act as an enemy of East Germany and had no intention of harming it. I appeal for a mild sentence." The 24-year-old father was transferred in the summer of 1960 from the Rostock Stasi remand prison to the Torgau penal facility.

An amnesty decree passed by the East German state council in September 1964 facilitated his early release.[9] He was divorced by then and found work with a field crop brigade at a state-owned farm in Güttin (Rügen). In July of 1965 the county court of Rügen sentenced him for assault to six months in prison with a two year probation period. In early November 1965 the East German police on Rügen investigated him again. This time he was accused – whether falsely or not is unknown – of committing a violent crime. It was probably the threat of once again being put in prison that led him to decide to flee to West Berlin. He had four siblings living in West Germany.[10]

Members of the East German secret police visited Heinz Cyrus' foster mother five days after his failed escape attempt to inform her of his death. They learned from her that on the evening of November 9 her foster son had said that he was "taking a few days vacation and was going on a 'trip.'" He did not say where he was going. His foster mother inquired "whether the incident had taken place at the state border and whether he had been shot," which led East German secret police agents to surmise that she must have known about his plan to escape.[11] The Stasi told her and later also his ex-wife that he had fled from an identification check in Berlin-Mitte under the influence of alcohol, run into a building and jumped out of an upper-story window. Even the local East German police division representative in Heinz Cyrus' hometown of Dreschvitz on Rügen and the deputy director of the state-owned farm in Güttin were not told the truth about the escape attempt. Instead they were told that he had been in an accident. A Stasi report explained that this was done "to prevent possible rumors from spreading in his hometown and workplace."[12]

Heinz Cyrus was buried on January 5, 1966 in the Protestant cemetery in Samtens on Rügen in the presence of his close family and friends.[13] The Stasi paid for his cremation with the money they had stolen from the dead man's pocket.[14]

At the end of 1990 the Berlin public prosecutor's office opened an investigation of the case. The West Berlin police had already placed official charges against unknown members of the National People's Army on suspicion of manslaughter in 1965. Shots had been heard on the West Berlin side and a person was seen being carried away on a stretcher. In 1993 the public prosecutor's office came to the conclusion that the members of the border troops had acted "in accordance with their official instructions" and thus were "not guilty." The investigation was closed on October 6, 1993 because the accused had evidently not violated the law and that "at least from a subjective viewpoint, the preconditions for criminal prosecution" were lacking.[15] The hounding of Heinz Cyrus and his death were never punished by law.

Martin Ahrends / Udo Baron / Hans-Hermann Hertle

1 See "Bericht des MfS/HA I über die Festnahme eines Grenzverletzers vom 10.11.1965," in: BStU, MfS, AS 754/70, Bd. 2, Nr. 8, Bl. 9–11.

2 See "Zwischenbericht der West-Berliner Polizei, 9.9.1991," in: StA Berlin, Az. 2 Js 85/90, Bd. 2, Bl. 9–11.

3 On this and the following see Heinz Cyrus' defense plea ("Protokoll der öffentlichen Sitzung des I. Strafsenats des Bezirksgerichts Rostock, 28. Juni 1960," in: BStU, Ast. Rostock, AU 42/60, Bd. 2, Bl. 314–316).

4 Telephone conversation between Hans-Hermann Hertle and H. D., 5.2.2009.

5 "[MfS-]KD Rügen, Betr.: Einschätzung des LPG-Mitgliedes Heinz Cyrus, Teschvitz (Abschrift), Bergen, 23.10.1959," in: BStU, Ast. Rostock, AOP 110/60, Bl. 11.

6 See Jens Schöne, "Frühling auf dem Lande". Die Kollektivierung der DDR-Landwirtschaft, Berlin, 2005.

7 "Urteil des I. Strafsenats des Bezirksgerichts Rostock in der Strafsache gegen Heinz Cyrus (I Bs 63/60), 29.6. 1960," in: BStU, Ast. Rostock, AU 42/60, Bd. 2, Bl. 394–408, here Bl. 408.

8 "Protokoll der öffentlichen Sitzung des I. Strafsenats des Bezirksgerichts Rostock, 28. Juni 1960," in: BStU, Ast. Rostock, AU 42/60, Bd. 2, Bl. 361.

9 See "Ergänzungsbericht der VfS Gross-Berlin/Abt. IX zur Leichensache Heinz Cyrus, 16.11.1965," in: BStU, MfS, AS 754/70, Bd. 2, Nr. 8, Bl. 56–61.

10 See "Abschlussvermerk [der VfS Gross-Berlin/Abt. IX] über die Leichensache Cyrus, Heinz, vom 30.12.1965," in: BStU, MfS, AS 754/70, Bd. 2, Nr. 8, Bl. 105–106.

11 See "Ergänzungsbericht der VfS Gross-Berlin/Abt. IX zur Leichensache Heinz Cyrus, 16.11.1965," in: BStU, MfS, AS 754/70, Bd. 2, Nr. 8, Bl. 58/59.

12 Ibid., Bl. 60.

13 Letter from Minister Ohm, Lutheran Ministry of Altefähr, 26.1.2009.

14 See "Abschlussvermerk [der VfS Gross-Berlin/Abt. IX] über die Leichensache Cyrus, Heinz, 30.12.1965," in: BStU, MfS, AS 754/70, Bd. 2, Nr. 8, Bl. 105–106.

15 "Vermerk der Staatsanwaltschaft Berlin bei dem Kammergericht über die Einstellung des Verfahrens in der Strafsache gegen Unbekannt wegen Totschlags, 6.10.1993," in: StA Berlin, Az. 2 Js 85/90, Bd. 2, Bl. 163.

Heinz Sokolowski

born on December 17, 1917

shot dead on November 25, 1965
between the Reichstag Building
and the Brandenburg Gate
on the sector border between
Berlin-Mitte and Berlin-Tiergarten

Heinz Sokolowski was 47 years old when he was shot and killed by an East German border guard while trying to flee from East Berlin to West Berlin early in the morning on November 25, 1965. West Berlin police heard the gun shots and saw the badly injured fugitive being carried away.[1] The dead man's name and his tragic fate were also soon known in the West. In early December a writer living in West Berlin let a ministry official in Bonn know that his friend Heinz Sokolowski had written to him in October saying "that he wanted to try to reach the west side of the city because he could no longer bear living in East Berlin. He wanted to try and reach freedom near the Brandenburg Gate. One of his friends in East Berlin let me know that he was shot and killed at around 5 o'clock in the morning while trying to escape on November 25. [...] As soon as we read the press reports that another fugitive had been shot down near the Brandenburg Gate we feared that it might be Heinz Sokolowski. Unfortunately it was. We were quite shocked."[2]

The author of those lines, Herbert Stargaard, had met the journalist Heinz Sokolowski in the early 1960s when they were both serving time in the Waldheim prison in East Germany.[3] Heinz Sokolowski had been serving the rest of a ten-year prison term that a Soviet military tribunal had sentenced him to in 1953 for supposedly engaging in espionage. An East German secret police report stated that even during the time when they were in prison together, Heinz Sokolowski had made no secret of the fact "that he wanted to go to West Germany after his release because he had no chance of making a living in East Germany."[4]

Heinz Sokolowski, who was born during the First World War in Frankfurt an der Oder and grew up in modest conditions in the Weimar Republic, was 15 years old when the National Socialists came to power in Germany. His tragic life was marked by the Second World War, Russian captivity and the political persecution he experienced during the post-war period. This was at least the impression made by the description of his life that he wrote after he was released from East German imprisonment.[5] He also wrote that he did a tailoring apprenticeship after completing elementary school and had attended a business school in order to qualify for the final secondary school examination. When he was offered the chance to work as an editing intern at the "Frankfurter Oderzeitung" in 1936, he gave up the idea of attending university and instead decided to pursue a career in journalism. Drafted into the army two years later, he served as a Wehrmacht soldier at various war locations during the Second World War, serving both as a war reporter and as a private on the eastern front. He was taken into Russian captivity at the age of 26, went through anti-fascist training and, like so many Wehrmacht soldiers, allowed himself to be won over by the communist cause for a time.

After returning to Germany he settled in 1946 in the Soviet-occupied sector of Berlin and worked during the following years as an independent journalist for radio and press on the east side of the city. He married in 1947 and lived with his wife and their daughter in Prenzlauer Berg until they were divorced in 1951. Although he was not a member of the party, he worked for the Soviet occupying powers' communist-controlled media during this time. In early 1953, a breach occurred but the files do not indicate what led Heinz Sokolowski to distance himself from his political work or why he fell out of favor with the communists. What is certain is that he was arrested in East Berlin on February 12, 1953 and sentenced by a Soviet military tribunal on April 27, 1953 to twenty years in prison for supposedly having spied for the West and for possessing anti-Soviet literature.[6] After the prison sentence was reduced to ten years by the court of appeals, Heinz Sokolowski was sent directly to the Soviet Union to serve out the sentence. After spending three years in a work camp he was returned to East Germany in 1956 as part of the final repatriation of German war and civilian prisoners, but he was labeled a so-called "non-amnesty prisoner" and consequently had to serve the rest of his sentence in East Germany.[7] He spent time in various East German penitentiaries, including Bautzen, Brandenburg and Waldheim, where he contracted tuberculosis in early 1960, and was finally released in February 13, 1963. But contrary to what he had hoped, he was not released to the West but to his last place of residency, East Berlin.

With no contact with his family, in poor health and degraded to the job of elevator operator for an industrial company, Heinz Sokolowski tried to obtain an exit permit from East Germany with the explanation that he had distant relatives in the West. He must soon have realized that the East Berlin authorities were not prepared to let him go at any price.[8] His contact with a former political prisoner on the west side caused the state authority again to take an interest in him in March 1964.[9] It appeared that he also had problems at his workplace in May of the following year. According to a Stasi report he was "dismissed without notice for refusing to work in response to the company's new regulation of the work norm."[10] Heinz Sokolowski began to prepare his escape a short time later. He searched for a suitable spot along the border grounds, equipped himself with ropes and blankets to climb over the wall and barbed wire, and gradually sold his personal belongings. He told his friends on the west side about his plans.

He approached the inner-city border grounds from Clara-Zetkin-Strasse, today's Dorotheenstrasse, on November 25, 1965 at around 5 o'clock in the morning. Although it was still dark outside a border guard posted on a watchtower on the corner of Clara-Zetkin-Strasse and Ebertstrasse noticed him. Heinz Sokolowski continued undeterred towards his goal even after the guard fired warning shots.

He triggered an alarm signal which alerted two other border soldiers who were on duty near the site of his escape attempt. He had already reached the border wall that was covered on top with barbed wire when one of the men began shooting at him.[11] Hit by a bullet in his abdomen, Heinz Sokolowski died a short time later from his injuries while on his way to the municipal hospital in Berlin-Mitte.

In the spring of the following year, the association "Working Group 13th of August" erected a three-meter-high wooden cross at the corner of Scheidemann-strasse and Ebertstrasse in honor of Heinz Sokolowski.[12] The inscription read, "after serving seven years in East German prisons he was shot while trying to flee," and made clear that he had been a twofold victim of communist injustice – as a political prisoner and as a Wall fugitive.

Christine Brecht

1 See "Bericht des Bundesministers der Finanzen/II A/5-03051-77/65, 25.11.1965," in: BArch, B 137, Nr. 6429, n. pag., and "Schlussbericht der West-Berliner Polizei, 21.12.1965," in: StA Berlin, Az. 27/2 Js 84/90, Bd. 1, Bl. 59 – 60.

2 Copy of letter from Herbert Stargaard, writer and friend of Heinz Sokolowski, to the Ministerial Director of the "Federal Ministry of Berlin" [the Ministry of All-German Affairs is probably meant], 3.12.1965," in: BArch, B 137, Nr. 15650, n. pag. The author of the letter wrote a number of popular and historical novels under the pseudonym Herbert Gabriel Stargaard.

3 See "Bericht der West-Berliner Polizei betr. Ermittlungsverfahren gegen bisher unbekannte "NVA"-Angehörige wegen vermutlichen Totschlags einer bisher unbekannten Person am 25.11.65, 8.1.1965," in: StA Berlin, Az. 27/2 Js 84/90, Bd. 1, Bl. 57– 58.

4 "Auszug aus der [MfS-]Haftakte von Heinz Sokolowski, 18.7.1963," in: BStU, MfS, AOP 7559/65, Bd. 1, Bl. 74.

5 See "[MfS-]Abschrift des Lebenslaufs von Heinz Sokolowski, 5.11.1963," in: Ibid., Bl. 77.

6 See "Auszug aus der [MfS-]Haftakte von Heinz Sokolowski, 18.7.1963," in: Ibid., 74. From 1945 to 1955, as the communist regime was being established in the Soviet zone of occupation and in East Germany, between 30,000 and 40.000 German civilians were convicted by the Soviet occupying judiciary. The average sentence was 25 years in a work camp. A large number of death sentences were also given and executed. See Andreas Hilger/Mike Schmeitzer/Ute Schmidt (eds.), Sowjetische Militärtribunale, Bd. 2: Die Verurteilung deutscher Zivilisten 1945 bis 1955, Köln, 2003.

7 See references to prisoner Heinz S. in Andreas Hilger/Jörg Morré, SMT-Verurteilte als Problem der Entstalini-sierung. Die Entlassung Tribunalverurteilter aus sowjetischer und deutscher Haft, in: Ibid., pp. 685–756, here pp. 732, 743.

8 See "Bericht der VfS Gross-Berlin/Abt. IX/XX, 25.11.1965," in: BStU, MfS, AOP 7559/65, Leichensache 7/65, Bl. 3–9, here Bl. 6–8.

9 See "Operativplan der VfS Gross-Berlin/KD Prenzlauer Berg, 14.1.1964," in: BStU, MfS, AOP 7559/65, Bd. 1, Bl. 12–14.

10 "Bericht der VfS Gross-Berlin/Abt. IX/XX, 25.11.1965," in: BStU, MfS, AOP 7559/65, Leichensache 7/65, Bl. 3–9, here Bl. 6.

11 See "Urteil des Landgerichts Berlin vom 21.2.1997," in: StA Berlin, Az. 27/2 Js 84/90, Urteilsband, n. pag. The border soldiers involved in the case were identified in the 1990s. The guard who fired the shot was ar-rested and sentenced to a youth sentence of 16 months on parole for manslaugher on 21.2.1997.

12 See "Meldung der West-Berliner Polizei betr. Aufstellung eines Mahnkreuzes im Sicherheitsraum, 26.3.1966," in: PHS, Bestand Grenzvorkommnisse, n. pag.

Erich Kühn

born on February 27, 1903

shot on November 26, 1965
on Kiefholzstrasse
on the sector border between
Berlin-Treptow and Berlin-Neukölln
died from his injuries on December 3, 1965

I t was already dark when Erich Kühn tried to flee on the evening of November 26 from Kiefholzstrasse in the East Berlin district of Treptow to West Berlin. A large area had been blocked off around the grounds of the deserted tracks that ran across Kiefholzstrasse between the Treptower Park and Sonnenallee stations. Two border soldiers were posted on the bridge but they could not see Erich Kühn, who had approached the cordoned off area from beneath the railroad embankment. They were first alerted of his presence by a noise coming from the embankment slope. In the darkness they were unable to tell whether it was a fugitive and they were reluctant to intervene. So the guard leader contacted the company head guard by phone. When he ordered him to take action he demanded that the other guard shoot. The second guard released the safety of his Kalashnikov and fired "hastily into the shrubbery." This was reported by the press three decades later when the three border soldiers were taken to court.[1] Erich Kühn was hit, badly injured and brought to the People's Police Hospital. A bullet through his stomach caused the man to die at the age of 62.

He evidently did not leave behind any relatives to grieve for him. At least the East German authorities were unable to find anybody to take care of his funeral. Hence the urn was buried in an anonymous grave in the Baumschulenweg Cemetery.[2] Erich Kühn's fate did not become public until after the East German archives were opened. The public was very interested in the trial of the three former border soldiers who were held responsible for his death in 1995. The Berlin district court found them guilty of manslaughter and inciting manslaughter and sentenced them each to a one year prison sentence on probation.

Only fragments of Erich Kühn's life could be reconstructed on the basis of official documents. They show that he was living an unsettled life full of problems and conflict, and that he was lonely, sick and poor when he decided to flee to West Berlin. Erich Kühn was born on February 27, 1903 in Landsberg an der Warthe, which now belongs to Poland. When he was nine years old he moved to Berlin where he spent most of his life. Not having any trained skills, he managed to make a living doing odd jobs and, according to Stasi files, he came into conflict with the law quite early in life. A police file of the East Berlin criminal investigation division revealed that at age 14 Erich Kühn served his first sentence, four weeks in prison, for theft.[3] That was in 1917, when Germany was still a monarchy and fighting in the First World War. During the Weimar Republic and Nazi era he was sentenced to prison and penal institutions a number of times for theft and falsifying documents. The last time was in January 1942. After the Second World War the authorities in the Soviet sector of Berlin first became aware of him due to his black-market dealings. Then, on November 16, 1953, he was convicted to six years and three months in a penitentiary for "fornication with children."[4] Erich Kühn was said to have had sex with a 13-year-old who evidently bore him a child.[5]

Erich Kühn was 56 years old when he was released from prison in June 1959. His life in the years that followed was dominated by personal and health problems, as well as a frequent change of jobs. After divorcing his second wife he married a third time in 1960, but this marriage also failed and he divorced four years later. His work situation also remained precarious. Before the Wall was erected, he apparently became a 'border-crosser,' a term used for someone who crossed the border daily to work in West Berlin. His employment record, which he had on him when he tried to escape, showed that he had been working for a number of companies in East Berlin as a transport and warehouse worker since February 1963.[6] His employment book also showed that he had spent the last weeks before his escape attempt in the hospital. Following a long stay in the Protestant Queen Elizabeth Hospital he was transferred to the Herzberg Municipal Hospital, a mental institution, on September 27.[7] He was sent home for a two-day leave on November 13 but never returned.[8] Documents found in his apartment suggested that he had found himself in a financial crisis: On November 18 he wrote an unsent letter to his last employer in which he refused to accept his dismissal. He was evidently being threatened with compulsory enforcement of alimony claims at that time as well.[9] He took a suit to a pawn shop on November 24.[10] All of this suggested that Erich Kühn had hoped to free himself of his problems by fleeing to West Berlin.

After his "arrest" on November 25, the wounded fugitive was operated on that night in the People's Police Hospital. He was evidently conscious over the next few days but the condition of the 62-year-old deteriorated noticeably. The serious bullet wound had caused peritonitis, an inflammation of the abdominal lining, causing Erich Kühn to die on the evening of December 3, 1965.[11]

Christine Brecht

1 See "Mauerschütze: Blindlings ins Gebüsch gefeuert," in: *Die Welt am Sonntag*, 19.2.1995, and "Urteil des Landgerichts Berlin vom 24.2.1995," in: StA Berlin, Az. 2 Js 67/90, Bd. 3, Bl. 102–123, here Bl. 108–109. Excerpts published in: Klaus Marxen/Gerhard Werle et al. (eds.), *Strafjustiz und DDR-Unrecht, Bd. 2: Gewalttaten an der deutsch-deutschen Grenze*, Berlin, 2002, pp. 445–479.

2 See "Abschlussvermerk [des MfS] zur Leichensache Erich Kühn, 28.1.1966," in: BStU, MfS, AU 3948/71 (Staatsanwaltschaftsakte), Bl. 16–17.

3 See "Aktenvermerk des [MfS] zur Leichensache Erich Kühn, 8.3.1966," in: BStU, MfS, AU 3948/71 (Staatsanwaltschaftsakte), Bl. 24–25.

4 Ibid., Bl. 24.

5   See "[MfS-]Information, 27.11.1965," in: BStU, MfS, AU 3948/71 (Ermittlungsverfahren), Bl. 8–10; "[MfS-] Abschlussvermerk, 28.1.1966," in: Ibid.

6   See "Ausweis für Arbeit und Sozialversicherung für Erich Kühn, ausgestellt vom VEB Grossdrehmaschinenbau "7. Oktober" in Berlin-Weissensee, 8.2.1963," in: BStU, MfS, AS 754/70, Bd. 5, Nr. 2, Bl. 37.

7   See "Obduktionsbericht des IGM der HU in der Leichensache Erich Kühn, 7.12.1965," in: BStU, MfS, AU 3948/71 (Staatsanwaltschaftsakte), Bl. 6–13. Whether and why he received pyschological treatment, as claimed by the Stasi, is not revealed by the documents reviewed.

8   See "Erlaubnisschein zum Verlassen des Städtischen Krankenhauses Herzberge, Berlin-Lichtenberg, 13.11.1965," in: BStU, MfS, AU 3948/71, Bl. 72.

9   See "Aktenvermerk [des MfS] zur Leichensache Erich Kühn, 27.1.1966," in: BStU, MfS, AU 3948/71 (Staatsanwaltschaftsakte), Bl. 15.

10 See "Information [des MfS] zum versuchten Grenzdurchbruch am 26.11.1965 in Höhe der Gartenkolonie "Eintracht" in Berlin-Treptow, 27.11.1965," in: BStU, MfS, AU 3948/71 (Ermittlungsverfahren), Bl. 8–10.

11 See "Urteil des Landgerichts Berlin vom 24.2.1995," in: StA Berlin, Az. 2 Js 67/90, Bd. 3, Bl. 110, and "Totenschein für Erich Kühn, ausgestellt vom Krankenhaus der Volkspolizei/Berlin, 4.12.1965," in: in: BStU, MfS, AS 754/70, Bd. 5, Nr. 2, Bl. 23.

Heinz Schöneberger

born on June 7, 1938

shot dead December 26, 1965
on the Heinrich-Heine-Strasse border crossing
at the sector border between
Berlin-Mitte and Berlin-Kreuzberg

Heinz Schöneberger was born on June 7, 1938 in Wagten, East Prussia, but had to leave his home after the Second World War. He was able to reach West Germany with his mother and three brothers.[1] The family settled in the Harz mountains in the West, where Heinz Schöneberger attended school and trained to become a construction worker. After this he managed to get through life with different temporary jobs. He married and moved to East Germany with his wife in June 1961, probably to escape a prison sentence for driving without a license. He tried to find work as a construction worker there but eventually returned to West Germany before the Wall was built. He was planning to bring his wife over later, but when the Wall was erected on August 13, 1961, it appeared that the couple would be separated permanently.

But Heinz Schöneberger had devised a plan: On October 17, 1961 he left the transit highway going to West Berlin to pick up his wife in Karl-Marx-Stadt – today Chemnitz – so that he could bring her with him to the West. Before they could even begin planning their escape, however, Heinz Schöneberger was arrested and sentenced to one year in prison for "fleeing the republic" in the summer and for illegally re-entering the country. After he was released from prison, an East German court convicted him again in 1962, this time to thirteen months in prison for "violating the border." While in prison he was sentenced to an additional prison term of eight months for trying to escape and for "mutiny." Heinz Schöneberger's wife divorced him while he was serving his various sentences in East German prisons.[2] He was finally released to West Germany on August 1, 1964. A week after he arrived there a warrant for his arrest caught up with him and he had to spend two months in the Wolfenbüttel prison in West Germany for driving without a license.

After his release Heinz Schöneberger worked with his brother Horst in West Berlin at various construction sites. During their time off the brothers often drove to East Berlin with colleagues from work. They met Monika P. and Christel R. in a dance hall in East Berlin and began dating them regularly. The two women were determined to leave East Germany and Heinz and Horst Schöneberger wanted to help them.[3] At around 5 a.m. on Christmas Day, 1965, the brothers drove in a Ford Taunus 17 M to East Berlin to pick up the women and take them to the West. The car had continuous front and back seats and their plan was to have Monika P. hide behind the back seat of the car and Christel R. to hide behind the front seat. Should they be discovered at the border, they agreed that the driver should hit the gas and break through the border as fast as possible.[4]

The four set off shortly before midnight. At a remote area the two women went into their hiding places in the car. They reached the border crossing at Heinrich-Heine-Strasse at half past midnight on December 26 and lined up in the exit lane. When the brothers reached the front of the line they were asked to get out of their vehicle. A border soldier discovered Monika P. behind the backseat and called out: "Apprehend her!" At this point Heinz Schöneberger jumped into the driver's seat, locked the doors and drove as fast as he could toward the border through the zigzag concourse of concrete barriers and swiped another car. The border officials sounded the alarm. The last barrier before passing through the Wall to West Berlin was closed. Heinz Schöneberger tried to break through it but the zigzag concourse had made it impossible for him to accelerate the car beyond 40 kilometers per hour. The car came to a halt. Bullets from the tower next to the border barrier were fired at the door on the driver's side, but Heinz Schöneberger was only hurt on his calf. When the tower gunman stopped firing, Heinz Schöneberger tore open the door, ran around the broken barrier and ran the last ten meters in a stooped position to the border. A second guard came out of the guard house next to the barrier, pulled out his pistol, knelt down and shot at the fleeing man from behind.[5] Five meters from the border a bullet hit him in his back and penetrated his cervical artery. Heinz Schöneberger reached West Berlin territory but died soon thereafter from excessive blood loss.[6] His body was transported to Dortmund on December 30, 1965 and was buried there.[7]

Policemen, customs officials and passersby from West Berlin witnessed the incident and that night angry protests against the brutal behavior of the East German border guards broke out. Repeated demonstrations took place on the West side of the border crossing over the following days.[8]

Horst Schöneberger and the two women were arrested by the East German border guards and brought to the Stasi prison in Berlin-Hohenschönhausen. The brother of the deceased was quickly convicted in a summary proceeding in December 1965. He was sentenced by the Potsdam district court to twelve years in prison for "jointly executed state-endangering acts of violence."[9] Six and a half years later Horst Schöneberger was finally released from the Bautzen Penitentiary and sent to the West.[10] Monika P. was sentenced on June 26, 1966 to two years and six months in prison. She married in 1972 and moved to West Berlin with her husband a year later.[11] Christel R. was sentenced to two years in prison and ended up serving a year and nine months of the sentence. In 1975 she received permission to immigrate to West Germany.[12]

Immediately following the incident at the Heinrich-Heine-Strasse border crossing, the West Berlin police opened an investigation of manslaughter against unknown members of the East German National People's Army,[13] but the case was dismissed in 1967 because they were unable to identify the man who had shot and killed Heinz Schöneberger.

The case was re-opened in the early 1990s and on March 31, 1995 the border guards involved were charged with manslaughter. The Berlin press reported with great interest on the trial about the "escape helper who acted out of love."[14] The Berlin district court came to the conclusion in its decision of February 28, 1997 that the charges against the accused "could not be proven with sufficient certainty to justify a conviction."[15] All the defendants were acquitted.

Martin Ahrends / Udo Baron

1 On this and the following see "Bericht der West-Berliner Polizei, 3.2.1966," in: StA Berlin, Az. 27 Js 158/90, Bd. 1, Bl. 198–200; "Niederschrift der Zeugenvernehmung des Bruders von Heinz Schöneberger durch die Kriminalpolizei in Hamm, 24.7.1971," in: StA Berlin, Az. 27 Js 158/90, Bd. 2, Bl. 45.

2 See ibid.

3 See "Niederschrift der Zeugenvernehmung des Bruders von Heinz Schöneberger durch die Kriminalpolizei in Hamm, 24.7.1971," in: StA Berlin, Az. 27 Js 158/90, Bd. 2, Bl. 45.

4 See "Einzel-Information Nr. 1151/65 [des MfS-]ZAIG über die Verhinderung eines gewaltsamen Grenzdurchbruches an der Grenzübergangsstelle Heinrich-Heine-Strasse, 27.12.1965," in: BStU, MfS, ZAIG Nr. 1159, Bl. 26–27.

5 See "Ereignismeldung des Kommandos der West-Berliner Schutzpolizei über missglückten Fluchtversuch am Übergang Heinrich-Heine-Strasse/Prinzenstr. (SBS), 16.12.1965," in: PHS, E-Meldung 26.12.1965, n. pag.; "Einzel-Information Nr. 1151/65 [des MfS-]ZAIG über die Verhinderung eines gewaltsamen Grenzdurchbruches an der Grenzübergangsstelle Heinrich-Heine-Strasse, 27.12.1965," in: BStU, MfS, ZAIG Nr. 1159, Bl. 24–25.

6 See "Ereignismeldung des Kommandos der West-Berliner Schutzpolizei S1 über missglückten Fluchtversuch am Übergang Heinrich-Heine-Strasse/Prinzenstrasse (SBS), 16.12.1965," in: PHS, E-Meldung 26.12.1965, n. pag.

7 See "Bericht der West-Berliner Polizei über Totschlag, versuchten Totschlag und anderes am 26.12.1965, gegen 01.00 Uhr, am Sektorenübergang Heinrich-Heine-Strasse, 29.12.1965," in: StA Berlin, Az. 27 Js 158/90, Bd. 1, Bl. 95.

8 See "Bericht der West-Berliner Polizei über missglückten Fluchtversuch durch Sperrmauer am 26.12.1965, 26.12.1965," in: PHS, E-Meldung 27.12.1965, n. pag.; "Eilmeldung der West-Berliner Polizei über Ansammlung von Personen am Grenzübergang Prinzen-/Heinrich-Heine-Strasse am 26.12.1965," 27.12.1965, in: PHS, E-Meldung 27.12.1965, Bl. 18.

9 "12 Jahre Zuchthaus für Provokateur," in: *Neues Deutschland,* 31.12.1965.

10 See "Niederschrift der Zeugenvernehmung des Bruders von Heinz Schöneberger durch die Berliner Polizei, 24.11.1992," in: StA Berlin, Az. 27 Js 158/90, Bd 2, p. 192.

11 See "Niederschrift der Zeugenvernehmung von Monika P. durch das Amtsgericht Berlin-Tiergarten, 1.8.1975," in: StA Berlin, Az. 27 Js 158/90, Bd. 2, Bl. 79–80.

12 See "Niederschrift der Zeugenvernehmung von Christel R. durch die Berliner Polizei, 2.2.1993," in: StA Berlin, Az. 27 Js 158/90, Bd. 3, Bl. 253, 256.

13 See "Strafanzeige der West-Berliner Polizei gegen Angehörige des 35. Regiments der 1. Grenzbrigade, 27.12.1965," in: StA Berlin, Az. 27 Js 158/90, Bd. 1, Bl. 1.

14 "Keiner will getroffen haben," in: *BZ,* 22.1.1997.

15 "Urteil des Landgerichts Berlin vom 28.2.1997," in: StA Berlin, Az. 27 Js 158/90, Bd. 5, Bl. 55.

Dieter Brandes

born on October 23, 1946

shot on June 9, 1965
on the grounds of the Nordbahnhof station
near Feldstrasse at the sector border between
Berlin-Mitte and Berlin-Wedding
died from his injuries on January 11, 1966

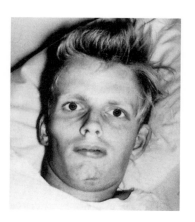

Dieter Brandes was born in Frankfurt an der Oder on October 23, 1946 and grew up in East Germany. His childhood and youth were spent in an odyssey of state educational facilities. He lived for the first sixteen years of his life in various children's homes and later moved into a home for young people in Bad Freienwalde.[1] He evidently tried to escape in June 1964 at the age of 17, but without success and as punishment was committed to a "youth work yard" in Sömmerda, Thuringia. East Germany used such facilities to try to re-educate non-conformist and delinquent teenagers and get them to accept the values and norms of the socialist state.[2] After Dieter Brandes was released at the end of 1964, he moved in with his father and stepmother in Frankfurt an der Oder and got a job as an untrained concrete worker. When he did not come home on June 9, 1965, his parents presumed that he had tried once again to make it to the West. According to Stasi files, they assumed that he was repeating his behavior of the previous year and planning to go to his biological mother in Hamburg with whom he corresponded by mail.[3]

Dieter Brandes did, in fact, travel to East Berlin on that June day. He was noticed in the evening by East German border soldiers on the grounds of the Nordbahnhof station in the Mitte district while trying to get through the border fortifications. The East German border troops noted that "fire arms were utilized to prevent a border breach." The soldiers and their superiors were commended for their conduct.[4] Dieter Brandes was badly injured and suffered from his bullet wounds for six months before he died in January 1966 in an East Berlin hospital.

During his escape the 18-year-old had triggered a signal alarm in the patrol station of Border Regiment 33 at 9 p.m. A sergeant of the East German border troops responsible for checking on the other border guards in the surveillance area was alerted. The sergeant opened fire when the young man did not stop running even after he had ordered him to halt and had fired a warning shot. Dieter Brandes collapsed a few meters from the last barrier.[5]

Startled by the shots, West Berlin residents from the neighboring Ernst Reuter housing development watched from their windows and balconies as the badly wounded man was carried away by border soldiers. They saw his arms and legs dangling lifelessly.[6] On the basis of this information the West Berlin police concluded that a young man had been caught trying to escape and that he was "at least wounded, perhaps even killed."[7] The press reported on the failed escape the following day.[8] That evening a wooden cross was erected on Gartenstrasse.[9] The West Berlin police chief issued official charges against unknown individuals of Border Regiment 33. The incident was also entered into the Central Registry Office in Salzgitter.[10] This formed the basis for the investigation that the Berlin public prosecutor's office re-opened in October of 1990. But the perpetrator could not be identified even after the East German archives were opened and the proceedings were dismissed on May 29, 1996.[11]

West Berlin observers presumed that Dieter Brandes had died immediately, but this was not the case. A bullet had shattered his breast cage and his lung was badly injured. After he regained consciousness following an operation conducted in the People's Police Hospital, he was paralyzed.[12] Although he had not yet recovered, he was transferred on June 12 from the People's Police Hospital – where fugitives injured at the Wall were usually delivered so that they remained concealed from the public – to the municipal clinic in Berlin-Buch. A medical evaluation of his condition conducted on August 31 stated: "The pat.[ient] is strongly altered psychologically, apathetic towards his treatment and his future. For this reason the pat.[ient] is not currently in a position to appear before the VP or speak with VP representatives. The patient, if he is still alive in six months, will not be able to endure prison in this condition."[13] After the doctors repeatedly ascertained that he was unable to withstand transport and could not be interrogated, the routine investigation over his "illegal attempt to leave" East Germany was discontinued on October 5, 1965.[14] Dieter Brandes' condition continued to worsen until his circulatory system failed and he died on January 11, 1966.[15]

A note made in the file two weeks after his death sheds light on the Stasi's methods. It stated that the hospital staff in his station had collected money for the young patient and given him a Christmas present. The Stasi lieutenant in charge went to great efforts to counter the "impression that Brandes was a 'poor victim.'" He tried to portray him instead as a "criminal and asocial element". He even went so far as to claim "that Brandes had employed violence during his attempted border breach and injured border soldiers."[16] It is not known whether the hospital staff believed this fabrication.

The East German judiciary authority files show that Dieter Brandes' father was informed that his son had incurred major bullet wounds while trying to escape.[17] He was also permitted to see him in the hospital. After his son's death, he signed a statement under pressure from the Stasi, waiving his right to have the urn sent to his hometown. The Stasi had Dieter Brandes' human remains buried anonymously in a grave in the Baumschulenweg Cemetery.[18]

Christine Brecht

1 See "Sachstandsbericht der VfS Gross-Berlin/Abt. IX, 31.8.1965," in: BStU, MfS, Ast. Berlin, AP 3198/66, Bd. 1, Ermittlungsverfahren, Bl. 28–30, and "Schreiben [des MfS] an den Generalstaatsanwalt von Gross-Berlin," 30.9.1965, in: Ibid., Bl. 61–63.

2 See Verena Zimmermann, *Den neuen Menschen schaffen. Die Umerziehung von schwererziehbaren und straffälligen Jugendlichen in der DDR (1945–1990)*, Köln, 2004.

3 See "Sachstandsbericht der VfS Gross-Berlin/Abt. IX, 31.8.1965," in: BStU, MfS, Ast. Berlin, AP 3198/66, Bd. 1, Ermittlungsverfahren, Bl. 28–30.

4 "Bericht der NVA/Stadtkommandant Poppe an Erich Honecker betr. Verhinderung eines Grenzdurchbruchs durch Anwendung der Schusswaffe, 10.6.1965," in: BArch, VA-07/8372, Bl. 28–29.

5 See "Bericht des MfS/HA I/Abwehr B/UA 1.GB/Operativgruppe GR 33 über Verhinderung eines Grenzdurchbruches mit Anwendung der Schusswaffe, 9.6.1965," in: BStU, MfS, Ast. Berlin, AP 3198/66, Bd. 1, Ermittlungsverfahren, Bl. 6–8.

6 See "Bericht der West-Berliner Polizeiinspektion Wedding betr. vereitelte Flucht aus SBS, 10.6.1965," in: PHS, Bestand Grenzvorkommnisse, n. pag.

7 See "Bericht der West-Berliner Polizei betr. vermutlicher Totschlag zum Nachteil einer unbekannten männlichen Person, 10.6.1965," in: Ibid.

8 See "Flüchtling erschossen!," in: *BZ*, 10.9.1965; "Wieder ein Flüchtling niedergeschossen," in: *Der Tagesspiegel*, 11.9.1965.

9 "Zeichen für Flüchtlingsschicksal," in: *Die Welt*, 12.6.1965. See also "Bericht der West-Berliner Polizeiinspektion Wedding betr. Aufstellung eines Gedenkkreuzes in der Gartenstrasse, 15.6.1965," in: PHS, Bestand Grenzvorkommnisse, n. pag.

10 See "Strafanzeige des West-Berliner Polizeipräsidenten in Berlin wegen Verdacht des Totschlags gegen unbekannte Angehörige der 1.GB/33 Grenzregiment der NVA Grenztruppen, 9.6.1965," in: StA Berlin, Az. 27/2 Js 95/90, Bd. 1, Bl. 59; "Verfügung der Zentralen Erfassungsstelle der Landesjustizverwaltungen in Salzgitter (IAR-ZE 698/65), 20.12.1967," in: Ibid., Bl. 110.

11 See "Verfügung der Staatsanwaltschaft II bei dem Kammergericht Berlin (27/2 Js 95/90), 29.5.1996," in: Ibid., Bd. 3, Bl. 157–158.

12 See Schlussbericht der ZERV (27/2 Js 95/90), 3.1.1995, in: StA Berlin, Az. 27/2 Js 95/90, Bd. 2, Bl. 387.

13 "Ärztliche Bescheinigung des Städtischen Klinikums Berlin-Buch, 31.8.1965," in: BStU, ASt. Berlin, AP 3198/66, Gerichtsakte, Bl. 52–53.

14 See "Einlieferungsanzeige des MfS, 10.6.1965," in: Ibid., Bl. 4, and "[MfS-]Vermerk, 5.10.1965," in: Ibid., Bl. 8.

15 See "Schlussbericht der ZERV (2772 Js 95/90), 3.1.1995," in: StA Berlin, Az. 27/2 Js 95/90, Bd. 2, Bl. 387.

16 "Aktenvermerk [des MfS]/Abt. IX zur Leichensache Dieter Brandes, 28.1.1966," in: BStU, ASt. Berlin, AP 3198/66, Bd. 1, Gerichtsakte, Bl. 124.

17 See "Aktenvermerk des Generalstaatsanwalts von Gross-Berlin/Abt. IA, 28.9.1965," in: StA Berlin, Az. 27/2 Js 95/90, Bd. 1, Bl. 20.

18 See BStU, MfS, AS 754/70, Bd. XI, Nr. 3, Bl. 121; "Rechnung des Städtischen Bestattungswesen, 21.1.1966," in: Ibid., Bl. 120, and "Abschlussvermerk [des MfS] zur Leichensache Dieter Brandes, 29.1.1966," in: BStU, ASt. Berlin, AP 3198/66, Gerichtsakte, Bl. 125.

Willi Block

born on June 5, 1934

shot dead on February 7, 1966
near the Staaken border crossing
on the outer ring between
Staaken (Nauen district) and Berlin-Spandau

W illi Block, born on June 5, 1934 in Berlin, trained to become a construction worker and served in the East German border police from 1954 to 1959. During these years he attended sergeant school, became a tank commander and in the end worked as an instructor in Wismar. By the time he was released he had acquired the rank of staff sergeant and was a member of the Communist Party. As an active member of a worker's militia, he was also involved in building the Berlin Wall in 1961.

His internal knowledge of the border police was no doubt helpful to him in planning his three escape attempts. He fled the first time to West Berlin on January 13, 1962, five months after the Wall was built. He returned to East Germany a month later to pick up his wife. He was arrested, but got off relatively lightly. He was put in a re-education and work camp, but was released after six months thanks to the intervention of his father who was a devout communist, apparently with influence.[1] In the camp he agreed to cooperate with the Stasi as a secret informant (GI) and was expected to deliver reports from the Blankenfelde repatriation camp, but evidently he refused to take on concrete spy missions.[2] On August 18, 1962 he fled a second time to West Berlin. He informed the authorities there of his recruitment by the Stasi and that he had provided the Stasi with information about the refugee camp in West Berlin. Consequently, the (West) Berlin superior court of justice charged him with violating the freedom protection law.[3]

Willi Block returned to East Germany again in December 1962 when he learned that his wife wanted a divorce. He had not suffered any legal consequences for his first escape attempt, but this time he was considered a traitor and was arrested under the charge that he had engaged in espionage for the western secret service. In April 1963 he was sentenced to five years in prison, a term he served in Bautzen.[4] He was released early in November 1965 and was forced to accept a job that the state assigned to him at the Staaken concrete plant located near the border. There was often friction between him and his supervisors.[5]

On February 7, 1966 Willi Block got so drunk during his shift that he was not allowed to continue working. The last time a colleague from work saw him, he was sleeping on a cot in the lounge at around 3 p.m.[6] He must have made the decision to flee again to West Berlin a short time later. He set off in broad daylight and, unnoticed, was able to pass the interior security fence and a dog run at a site near the border crossing to the West Berlin district of Spandau. The watchdogs did not attack him. In fact it looked more like they were greeting an old acquaintance again.[7] He continued toward the anti-vehicle trench. Two border soldiers on a watchtower noticed him at around 3:45 p.m. They shot a flare and curtain fire. Bullets hit the ground in front of Willi Block, but he was undeterred and tried to crawl beneath the three rolls of barbed wire that separated him from West Berlin. When his clothing got entangled in the second roll of wire, he was unable to move and remained stuck, lying on his stomach, beneath the barbed wire.

Meanwhile customs officials and police arrived on the West Berlin side with an ambulance. They tried to establish contact with the fugitive. Willi Block called out to them that he was injured. He also mentioned the name of his brother who lived in West Berlin and told them to send him his regards. When Willi Block asked them to provide him covering fire they explained that he had to reach West Berlin first, to which Block responded: "Then I'll just have to go to jail."[8] As more and more border guards appeared on the east side with their machine pistols ready to fire, the West Berlin police began loading their weapons and taking cover behind the trees. By this time photo reporters had also arrived at the site on the west side. On the east side the six border guards were joined by the commander of the border regiment. When Willi Block raised his hand, they shouted: "Stay down, don't move." An officer called out from the anti-vehicle trench: "Come back!" The man caught in the wire answered: "I can't."

It was a strange situation: Before the eyes and ears of the armed western police, Willi Block, encircled by East German border guards with their guns ready to fire, was firmly caught in the barbed wire. Nothing happened for a few minutes: The police on the west side were unable to intervene and Block was unable to move either forward or backward. The regiment commander, the highest ranking soldier among the border guards, appeared overwhelmed by the task of freeing the fugitive from the barbed wire and arresting him. "Shoot me already, you dogs," Willi Block called out to the border guards and tried one more time to free himself from the barbed wire, shifting forward, toward West Berlin.[9] He managed to move just a few centimeters when suddenly a hail of bullets flew at him. A number of border guards opened fire, including the regiment commander who fired his pistol until the magazine was empty. Since his shots missed the fugitive he demanded a machine pistol. A guard gave him his Kalashnikov and the regiment commander fired from a distance of 15 meters at the defenseless man lying on the ground. A total of seventy-two shots were fired. Four bullets hit Willi Block; one of them was fatal.

The border guards had to use a wire cutter to disentangle the body from the barbed wire and bring it to the regiment headquarters by ambulance. Two border soldiers on their way to their barracks caught a glimpse of Willi Block's blood-covered body lying on the truck and spontaneously decided to flee. They did not want to find themselves in a situation where they would have to shoot at a fugitive.[10] That very evening they escaped together to West Berlin and reported on the incident. For days the West Berlin media reported in depth on the shots fired in Staaken.[11]

Three days later a Potsdam state attorney informed the victim's father that his son "had died during a self-inflicted border breach attempt," and forced him to sign a statement agreeing to keep the circumstances of his son's death a secret and to accept an urn burial on the Baumschulenweg Cemetery. Only then did he receive his son's personal possessions.[12]

In 1993 the chief of staff, two border guards and the commander of the 34th Border Regiment were charged with attempted manslaughter. The chief of staff and the two border guards were acquitted by the Berlin district court in January 1995. Although the judges had their doubts about their version of the events – they claimed to have only fired warning shots or intentionally aimed to miss the fugitive – it was not possible to prove "that they had aimed their shots at the victim or acted jointly with the gunman."[13] Even in the separate trial against the regiment commander, the court failed to determine who had fired the fatal shots although it was assumed with a high degree of probability that he was the gunman. He was first convicted of attempted manslaughter, but upon objection of the public prosecutor, the Federal Court of Justice ultimately sentenced him as the direct perpetrator, accomplice or sole perpetrator of manslaughter to three years in prison without probation.[14] The Berlin district report stated that his conduct at the scene of the crime bore the "character of an (attempted) execution."[15]

Martin Ahrends / Udo Baron / Hans-Hermann Hertle

1 See "Anklageschrift der Berliner Staatsanwaltschaft bei dem Kammergericht gegen Karl B., Heinz K., Hans-Jürgen S. und Dietmar H., Az. 2 Js 71/91, vom 21.4.1993," in: StA Berlin, Az. 2 Js 71/91, Bd. 4, Bl. 59–60.

2 See "Bericht der West-Berliner Polizei vom 27.10.1992," in: StA Berlin, Az. 2 Js 71/91, Bd. 3, Bl. 60–61.

3 See "Schlussbericht der West-Berliner Polizei vom 4.3.1966," in: StA Berlin, Az. 2 Js 71/91, Beiakte, Bl. 44–50, here Bl. 48.

4 See "Einzel-Information Nr. 110/67 des MfS/ZAIG über einen verhinderten Grenzdurchbruch DDR-West im Abschnitt Staaken/Bez. Potsdam unter Anwendung der Schusswaffe mit tödlichem Ausgang, 8.2.1966," in: BStU, MfS, ZAIG Nr. 1306, Bl. 4–7.

5 See Hannelore Strehlow, *Der gefährliche Weg in die Freiheit. Fluchtversuche aus dem ehemaligen Bezirk Potsdam,* Potsdam, 2004, p. 56 ff.

6 On the following see "Anklageschrift der Berliner Staatsanwaltschaft bei dem Kammergericht gegen Karl B., Heinz K., Hans-Jürgen S. und Dietmar H., Az. 2 Js 71/91, vom 21.4.1993," in: StA Berlin, Az. 2 Js 71/91, Bd. 4, Bl. 59–60, and "Urteil des Landgerichts Berlin in der Strafsache gegen Karl B., Az. 2 Js 71/91, vom 1.2.1995," in: StA Berlin, Az. 2 Js 71/91, Bd. 5, Bl. 59 a–59 z, (pp. 1–48). On the trial see Roman Grafe, *Deutsche Gerechtigkeit. Prozesse gegen DDR-Grenzschützen und ihre Befehlsgeber,* München, 2004, pp. 285–289.

7 "Anklageschrift der Berliner Staatsanwaltschaft bei dem Kammergericht gegen Karl B., Heinz K., Hans-Jürgen S. und Dietmar H., Az. 2 Js 71/91, vom 21.4.1993," in: StA Berlin, Az. 2 Js 71/91, Bd. 4, Bl. 60.

8 Ibid., Bl. 65.

9 See "Einzel-Information Nr. 110/67 des MfS/ZAIG über einen verhinderten Grenzdurchbruch DDR-West im Abschnitt Staaken/Bez. Potsdam unter Anwendung der Schusswaffe mit tödlichem Ausgang, 8.2.1966," in: BStU, MfS, ZAIG Nr. 1306, Bl. 4–7; see also "Vernehmung des West-Berliner Zollassistenten Manfred J. vom 14.2.1966," in: StA Berlin, Az. 2 Js 71/91, Beiakte, Bl. 27–31.

10 See Hannelore Strehlow, *Der gefährliche Weg in die Freiheit. Fluchtversuche aus dem ehemaligen Bezirk Potsdam,* Potsdam, 2004, p. 58.

11 See *Der Tagesspiegel, Die Welt* und *Der Kurier,* 8. und 9.2.1966.

12 "Statement" forced from Willi Block's father by the Stasi, 10.2.1966, in: BStU, Ast. Potsdam, AP 1114/76, Bl. 10.

13 See "Urteil des Landgerichts Berlin in der Strafsache gegen Heinz K., Hans-Jürgen S. und Dietmar H., Az. 2 Js 71/91, vom 13.1.1995," in: StA Berlin, Az. 2 Js 71/91, Bd. 5, Bl. 8a–8e.

14 See "Urteil des Landgerichts Berlin in der Strafsache gegen Karl B., Az. 2 Js 71/91, vom 1.2.1995," in: StA Berlin, Az. 2 Js 71/91, Bd. 5, p. 46.

15 See "Urteil des Landgerichts Berlin in der Strafsache gegen Karl B., Az. 2 Js 71/91, vom 1.2.1995," in: StA Berlin, Az. 2 Js 71/91, Bd. 5, Bl. 59a–59z, (pp. 1–48); "Urteil des Bundesgerichtshofs in der Strafsache gegen Karl B., Az. 5 StR 494/95, vom 4.3.1996," in: StA Berlin, Az. 2 Js 71/91, Bd. 5, Bl. 154–163; "Urteil des Landgerichts Berlin in der Strafsache gegen Karl B., Az. 2 Js 71/91, vom 23.4.1997," in StA Berlin, Az. 2 Js 71/91, Bd. 6, Bl. 181aff.

Jörg Hartmann

born on October 27, 1955

shot dead on March 14, 1966
on Kiefholzstrasse near the "Sorgenfrei" garden settlement
on the sector border between
Berlin-Treptow and Berlin-Neukölln

On March 14, 1966, border guards shot two children, aged 10 and 13, who had managed to enter the border area in the East Berlin district of Treptow unnoticed after dark. Thirty years later the guard who fired the shots explained that he had seen a shadow from his watchtower and only opened fire because he thought it was his duty.[1]

Jörg Hartmann, the ten-year-old, died immediately. His thirteen-year-old friend, Lothar Schleusener, was brought to the People's Police Hospital in Berlin-Mitte and died there from his injuries that same night. Both boys were born in East Berlin and had grown up in the Friedrichshain district. East Germany covered up what actually happened that night because the politicians and military leaders did not want to admit that children had been shot at the Wall. The relatives were led to believe that Jörg Hartmann and Lothar Schleusener died in an accident. The evidence was destroyed; consequently, only a few documents exist today that record the violent crime. The staff of the Central Investigating Agency for Governmental and Party Crimes was nonetheless able to bring the facts to light in the 1990s[2] because the gunshots that killed the young boys had also been heard in the neighboring West Berlin district of Neukölln.[3]

According to western investigation files, a "reliable source" in the East Berlin People's Police Hospital at the time had informed the West that the bullets had hit two children.[4] In March 1966, the news was publicized on the radio and in the press that children trying to reach West Berlin near the Plänterwald S-Bahn had been seen and immediately shot at with machine pistols.[5] Even the name of one of the victims reached the West through unknown channels and was put on record: Jörg Hartmann.[6]

Jörg Hartmann and his two younger siblings lived with their grandmother on Schreinerstrasse in Berlin-Friedrichshain. He left the small apartment in the rear building on March 14, 1966 to buy fresh rolls and disappeared without a trace. Ursula Mörs, Jörg Hartmann's third grade teacher at the elementary school on Rigaer Strasse, recalled that when the RIAS radio station reported that two children had been shot at the Wall, she immediately became apprehensive.[7] Alarmed by the radio news, she began asking around in her class. One of Jörg's classmates said that Jörg had wanted to see his father in West Berlin. To learn more, she paid a visit to the boy's grandmother and learned that Jörg had never met his father but had indirectly inquired about his address on the west side of the city shortly before he disappeared.

Jörg Hartmann's mother was mentally ill and unable to care for her children herself so the siblings grew up with their grandmother.[8] When Jörg did not return home, his grandmother began to worry. She notified the East German police that very evening that her grandson was missing but was not given any information about what had happened to him. When the grandmother heard that two children had been shot and killed at the Wall she became very fearful, but she did not know that Jörg had been with Lothar Schleusener that day. The two boys had known each other since they were small children because they used to live in the same neighborhood before Jörg and his siblings moved to his grandmother's.

It was about 7:15 p.m. when the two boys were noticed by border soldiers that evening near the garden colony "Sorgenfrei." This was stated in a report that the East Berlin city commander gave to the Communist Party Politburo member Erich Honecker, who, as head of the Communist Party's security division and secretary of the East German National Defense Council, was responsible for the "state border."[9] The report stated that the border guards "recognized as silhouettes two people who had passed the interior barrier." When they did not respond to the warning shots, the guards opened fire.

The grandmother received the news of Jörg Hartmann's death two weeks later. The East Berlin attorney general told her that her grandson had drowned and that his body showed signs of boat propeller abrasions when it was retrieved from a lake in Köpenick on March 17. The grandmother, however, remained mistrustful of this information for the rest of her life.

Ursula Mörs did not believe the official version of his death, either. When the teacher tried to find out more, she was pulled aside by the school director and instructed to discontinue her inquiry. This experience motivated her to expedite her own escape to the West and she succeeded in fleeing that same year.

Jörg Hartmann's corpse was cremated and buried anonymously in the Baumschulenweg Cemetery in Berlin-Treptow before the relatives were even notified of his death. Later the grandmother was able to have the urn reburied and the new grave site marked with a tombstone.

Ursula Mörs remembered Jörg Hartmann as a quiet, shy child, small and thin with blond hair and light blue eyes. He had had a hard time meeting the demands of school, and therefore was very pleased when he was praised. To preserve the memory of her student she supported the efforts to have a monument erected in his honor. It was dedicated in 1999, on Kiefholzstrasse.

In November 1997 the Berlin district court declared the former border soldier guilty of manslaughter in the death of Jörg Hartmann and Lothar Schleusener and sentenced him to twenty months probation.[10] The defendant had confessed that he and another border guard, who had passed away by then, had shot at the children on March 14, 1966.[11]

Christine Brecht

1   See Karl-Heinz Baum, "'Pflichtgefühl' kostet zwei Kindern das Leben," in: *Frankfurter Rundschau,* 20.11.1997.

2   See Zentrale Ermittlungsstelle für Regierungs- und Vereinigungskriminalität (ed.), *Jahresbericht* 1997, Berlin, 1998. See also Barbara Zibler, Kinder als Opfer der Mauer, in: Falk Blask (ed.), *Geteilte Nachbarschaft. Erkundungen im ehemaligen Grenzgebiet Treptow und Neukölln,* Berlin, 1999, pp. 75–81, and the film documentary *"Geboren* 1955 – *Erschossen* 1966. *Der Tod eines Zehn-Jährigen an der Berliner Mauer",* directors: Simone Warias and Friedrich Herkt, Vidicon/MDR 2001.

3   See "Bericht der West-Berliner Polizei/R 217 betr. Schüsse im SBS, 15.3.1966," in: PHS, Bestand Grenzvorkommnisse, n. pag., and "Schlussbericht der West-Berliner Polizei, 1.4.1966," in: StA Berlin, Az. 27/2 Js 568/92, Bd. 1, Bl. 21–22.

4   See "Bericht der West-Berliner Polizei betr. Grenzzwischenfall vom 14.3.1966 gegen 19.00 Uhr in Berlin-Neukölln, Höhe Sackführerdamm, 16.3.1966," in: Ibid., Bl. 17.

5   "Schüsse auf Kinder," in: *Frankfurter Allgemeine Zeitung,* 17.3.1966.

6   See "Bericht der West-Berliner Polizei, 21.6.1966," in: StA Berlin, Az. 27/2 Js 568/92, Bd. 1, Bl. 38–39.

7   See conversation conducted by Christine Brecht with Ursula Mörs, Jörg Hartmann's classroom teacher, 7.9.2006.

8   See "Niederschrift der Zeugenvernehmung des Bruders von Jörg Hartmann durch die Berliner Polizei, 19.10.1992," in: StA Berlin, Az. 27/2 Js 568/92, Bd. 1, Bl. 105–111.

9   See "Meldung der NVA/Stadtkommandant Poppe an SED-Politbüromitglied Erich Honecker betr. Verhinderung eines Grenzdurchbruches durch Anwendung der Schusswaffe, 14.3.1966," in: BArch, VA-07/8373, Bl. 101–102.

10 See "Urteil des Landgerichts Berlin vom 19.11.1997," in: StA Berlin, Az. 27/2 Js 568/92, Bd. 5, Bl. 197–219, here Bl. 198.

11 See "Niederschrift der Vernehmung von Siegfried B. durch die Polizei in Aschersleben, 1.2.1996," in: StA Berlin, Az. 27/2 Js 568/92, Bd. 3, Bl. 556–557.

Lothar Schleusener

born on January 14, 1953

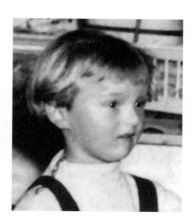

shot dead on March 14, 1966
on Kiefholzstrasse
near the "Sorgenfrei" garden settlement
on the sector border between
Berlin-Treptow and Berlin-Neukölln

I n November 1997 the Berlin district court pronounced a former border guard
guilty of manslaughter in the deaths of Jörg Hartmann und Lothar Schleusener
and sentenced him to 20 months probation.[1] The defendant had confessed that he
and another border guard, who had passed away by then, had shot at the children
on March 14, 1966.[2] From where he was stationed on the observation tower in an
area known as "Grenzknick," he had noticed a human shadow and thought he
saw a person who was trying to get out of the anti-vehicle trench but who kept
slipping back down into it. In order to stop the suspected fugitive, he ordered the
other guard to climb down from the tower to "secure" the grounds and then he
opened fire because he did not know what else to do and felt this was his duty. He
fired a total of forty bullets. The guard later explained that when he stopped shooting and descended from the tower and saw the children, he was "totally shattered"
and knew immediately that it had been wrong to shoot like crazy.[3]

The only existing official document recording what happened that evening states
that the injured victims "were retrieved and transported to the People's Police
Hospital by ambulance. One of the two border violators died from his injuries; the
other one was interrogated in the People's Police Hospital and said that he came
from the Friedrichshain district."[4] Nowhere does the report acknowledge that the
victims were children. It does not mention their names or the fact that Lothar
Schleusener, the older of the two boys and the one who was supposedly capable of
being interrogated, died the same night.

Lothar Schleusener was born in East Berlin in 1953 and grew up with his older
sister in the Friedrichshain district. His father was an electrician; his mother worked
as a seamstress for the state-owned company "Fortschritt" (Progress) in Berlin-
Lichtenberg. The parents were divorced in 1965, but were still living in the same
apartment in March 1966 when their son died. Lothar Schleusener's sister recalled
that their mother had occasionally worked on the west side of the city before the
Wall was erected.[5] They had relatives there that used to send them "west packages" at Christmas time during the first years after the border was closed. The area
where they lived was a poor neighborhood, called "Hinterland" or rear area. The

people who lived in the so-called "Vorderland," (front area) were mostly party members and better off. Since both parents worked, Lothar and his sister were often left to themselves. They enjoyed spending time in the family's garden house where they had animals and even spent the night there sometimes in summer.

Lothar Schleusener had been missing for days before his mother was officially informed that he had died from an electric shock in Espenhain near Leipzig. A death certificate from the Leipzig registry office apparently certified this.[6] In private Lothar Schleusener's parents doubted whether the information provided by the authorities was true. They could not explain how their son had ended up in Leipzig, but because they feared reprisals, they did not dare express their mistrust openly.[7] Lothar Schleusener's sister said that their mother basically knew that she had been lied to. Her mother knew that western radio had reported that two children were shot at the Wall on the day her son had disappeared. Out of grief and fear she never spoke about the death of her son and asked her daughter not to speak of it or ask any questions.

Because the mother had been given a falsified death certificate, the Berlin public prosecutor's office, in addition to prosecuting the border guards, tried to introduce proceedings for false certification. But the case was dismissed without results in August 1997 because no documents could be found providing information on a possible perpetrator in the files of the border troops, Communist Party or Stasi.[8]

Informer reports, however, show that after the incident, the Stasi kept surveillance on the border guards who had been on duty at the time. It was criticized that "the attempted border breach of the children at 'Grenzknick' was not kept as secret as had been desired. It had already spread around our unit [...] before the guards involved were sworn to secrecy. Afterwards there was all kinds of talk in our room." It was said that the two guards had "wept." Had they been more attentive, "the border breach could have been prevented without the use of fire arms."[9]

Lothar's sister later remembered that her brother had been particularly fond of animals. He was a friendly and caring young boy who had badly wanted to be big and strong. He liked to imagine how he would drive his grandmother around in a car when he was older. Shortly before he disappeared he confided to his sister that he wanted to go to West Berlin with a friend to visit relatives. He promised to bring her back something nice from over there. At the time she had not taken his words seriously. Only after the Wall fell did she realize how serious he had been.[10]

Lothar Schleusener was buried at the cemetery on Friedensstrasse in Berlin-Friedrichshain. Only his parents, grandparents and sister were present at the funeral.

Christine Brecht

1 See "Urteil des Landgerichts Berlin vom 19.11.1997," in: StA Berlin, Az. 27/2 Js 568/92, Bd. 5, Bl. 197–219, here Bl. 198.

2 See "Niederschrift der Vernehmung von Siegfried B. durch die Polizei in Aschersleben, 1.2.1996," in: StA Berlin, Az. 27/2 Js 568/92, Bd. 3, Bl. 556–557.

3 See "Niederschrift der Vernehmung von Siegfried B. durch die Polizei in Aschersleben, 12.2.1996," in: Ibid., Bl. 574–587.

4 "Meldung der NVA/Stadtkommandant Poppe an SED-Politbüromitglied Erich Honecker betr. Verhinderung eines Grenzdurchbruches durch Anwendung der Schusswaffe, 14.3.1966," in: BArch, VA-07/8373, Bl. 101.

5   Conversation conducted by Christine Brecht with I. Schleusener, Lothar Schleusener's sister, 2.4.2007.

6   See "Mitteilung des Standesamts Leipzig an den Polizeipräsidenten in Berlin/ZERV, 14.12.1992," in: StA Berlin, Az. 27/2 Js 568/92, Bd. 1, Bl. 162.

7   See "Niederschrift der Zeugenvernehmung der Mutter von Lothar Schleusener durch die Berliner Polizei, 2.12. 1992," in: StA Berlin, Az. 27/2 Js 568/92, Bd. 1, Bl. 155–159.

8   See "Verfügung der Staatsanwaltschaft II bei dem Landgericht Berlin (30 Js 350/96), 4.8.1997," in: StA Berlin, Az. 30 Js 350/96, Bl. 100–101.

9   "Handschriftlicher Bericht des GI "Grosche" [an das MfS], 5.4.1966," in: BStU, MfS, AIM 7999/66, Teil A, Bl. 12.

10 Conversation conducted by Christine Brecht with I. Schleusener, Lothar Schleusener's sister, 2.4.2007.

Willi Marzahn

born on June 3, 1944

shot dead or committed suicide on March 19, 1966
near Steinstücken / Kohlhasenbrück
on the outer ring between
Potsdam-Babelsberg and Berlin-Zehlendorf

Willi Marzahn, born on June 3, 1944 in Jüterbog, studied to become a locomotive mechanic after he finished school. He had lived with his wife and child in Schwedt an der Oder since 1964 and had worked as an engine fitter in the central workshop of the crude oil refinery there.[1]

That same year he enlisted for three years as a soldier in the East German National People's Army and began his military service on November 3, 1964. He was politically discreet and regarded as a loner in his "barracks collective."[2] Assurances were made to him when he enlisted that he would be placed in an armored unit close to his home after he completed his basic training, but this did not happen. Instead he was sent as a weapons master to a mobile guard unit in Stahnsdorf, southwest of Berlin. At that time the trip from there to Schwedt by public transportation took almost a day; this meant that he was unable to see his family when he had time off.

He made a number of transfer requests because he was concerned that his marriage might fall apart under these conditions, but his requests were either left unanswered or rejected. Then Willi Marzahn tried to reverse his three year military commitment. He wrote a letter in February 1966 requesting to be released from duty: "My basic military service comes to an end in April and now my wife says that if I don't come home she is going to divorce me. [...] Since I enlisted under preconditions that differ from those that currently exist, I do not think it is right to require me to continue. This is why I am distancing myself from my commitment. I am married and have a child and if my marriage suffers or breaks up because of this commitment then my service does not make much sense."[3]

The army brushed off this petition as "dismissal psychosis."[4] His supervisors paid no attention to Willi Marzahn's problems although they were clearly serious. They ignored his complaints about chronic headaches after suffering a concussion and an operation on his inner ear, his constant use of painkillers and sleeping pills and even a suicide threat.

In early March 1966, quite unexpectedly and without explanation, he wrote a letter to his wife asking her for a divorce.[5] He may have really meant it, but it may also have been a deceptive maneuver to prevent his wife from being accused of having known of his plans: Apparently the 21-year-old was already thinking of fleeing.

The two sergeants, Willi Marzahn and Eberhard M., both had time off on March 18, 1966 and were permitted to leave the barracks until 6 o'clock the next morning. They had discussed their escape plan the previous week and now were ready to go through with it. They spent the evening together at a bar in Potsdam and returned to their barracks in Stahnsdorf at around 3 a.m. Willi Marzahn entered the building alone and took the key to the armory, supposedly to do a weapons check. He then opened the window of the armory and handed Eberhard M. two "Kalashnikov" machine pistols, three "Makarov" pistols and some ammunition. They took the weapons and ammunition to the fence and the two soldiers signed out again for the rest of their time off. They put their weapons through a hole in the barracks fence and then picked them up. Then they walked for a few hours through the woods, sometimes along a road, towards the border strip near Kohlhasenbrück / Griebnitzsee.

They reached the wooded border grounds unnoticed and crawled under a signal fence near Steinstücken at around 6 a.m. Although they set off an alarm, the guards on duty did not react immediately. Eberhard M. shot one watchdog and choked another within the security strip. As they continued they touched a wire on the signal device, setting off a flare. Leaving the protection of the woods, the two soldiers then ran through the death strip to a spot that was 250 and 500 meters away from the next watchtowers. Only then were they seen by the border guards on duty.[6] There was an exchange of fire between the fugitives and the border guards. Eberhard M. was able to climb over an anti-tank obstacle, get through the last barbed wire barrier and reach West Berlin territory,[7] but Willi Marzahn was found in front of a tank trap wall with a bullet through his head. He was retrieved at around 6:30 a.m. and brought to the nearby Drewitz Army Hospital.[8] He died from his injuries at 8 in the morning without ever having recovered consciousness.[9]

The residents of the West Berlin exclaves Steinstücken and Kohlhasenbrück were startled by the gunshots fired in the early morning. One bullet hit an open window casement of a nearby house.[10] One witness heard someone call from the death strip in between shots, "Help, you're going to shoot me dead."[11] The Stahnsdorf Mobile Guard Battalion made a statement on April 13, 1966 that said: "Marzahn got the punishment he deserved when he paid for his crime with his life."[12]

Willi Marzahn was buried in the presence of his family and under the surveillance of the East German secret police on March 23, 1966 at the cemetery in his hometown of Jüterbog. A memorial cross with the inscription: "Willi Marzahn, 19.3.1966, shot while trying to escape" was later erected in the Berlin district of Zehlendorf to commemorate the dead fugitive.

Neither the East German military state prosecutor, nor the East German secret police, nor the Berlin public prosecutor after 1990 was able to determine who had shot Willi Marzahn. The guards saw Willi Marzahn collapse after they fired shots. The autopsy first declared that a Kalashnikov bullet shot from a distance was the cause of death but a second examination called for by the Stasi came to the "reliable assumption" that his death was caused by a "very close shot" from a Makarov pistol that was found lying next to the dead man.[13] Since the border troops failed to conduct an "orderly investigation of the crime scene" and neither fingerprints on the weapon nor footprints were secured,[14] it remained ambiguous whether Willi Marzahn was shot or whether he may have committed suicide as the Stasi insisted.

Due to the conflicting witness accounts the public prosecutor's office in Berlin was unable to determine with certainty after 1990 whether the border guards or the fugitive had fired the first shot.[15] Consequently the case against the accused border soldiers was dismissed in 1992 according to the principle "in dubio pro reo."

Udo Baron / Hans-Hermann Hertle

1 "Bericht des MfS/HA I/MB V/Unterabteilung 1. MSD, 19.3.1966," in: BStU, MfS, HA I Nr. 5756, Teil 2 von 2, Bl. 194–200.

2 See "Abschlussbericht der NVA/Kommando des Militärbezirkes V/Untersuchungskommission über die Gruppenfahnenflucht der Unteroffiziere Willi Marzahn und E.M. vom III. MSB des MSR-2 am 19.3.1966, 20.3.1966," in: BStU, MfS, U 83/88, Bl. 77–85, here Bl. 77/78.

3 "Entpflichtungsgesuch von Uffz. Willi Marzahn (Abschrift)," in: BStU, MfS, AF 431/78, Bd. 1, Bl. 110.

4 See "Abschlussbericht der NVA/Kommando des Militärbezirkes V/Untersuchungskommission über die Gruppenfahnenflucht der Unteroffiziere Willi Marzahn und E.M. vom III. MSB des MSR-2 am 19.3.1966, 20.3.1966," in: BStU, MfS, U 83/88, Bl. 78.

5 "Zwischenbericht des Militärstaatsanwalts Potsdam-Eiche, 3.5.1966," in: BStU, MfS, U 83/88, Bl. 98–101, here Bl. 101.

6 See "Vernehmung des Fluchtbegleiters von Willi Marzahn durch die West-Berliner Polizei vom 23.3.1966," in: StA Berlin, Az. 2 Js 134/91, Bd. 3, Bl. 20–23.

7 See "Bericht der West-Berliner Polizei vom 19.3.1966," in: StA Berlin, Az. 2 Js 134/91, Bd. 3, Bl. 13–14.

8 See "Abschlussbericht der NVA/4. Grenzbrigade/Der Kommandeur über den Grenzdurchbruch des Uffz. E.M. und die Verhinderung des Grenzdurchbruchs des Uffz. Marzahn, Willi, 19.3.1966," in: BArch, VA-07/17895, Bl. 12–21.

9 See "Abschlussbericht der NVA/Kommando des Militärbezirkes V/Untersuchungskommission über die Gruppenfahnenflucht der Unteroffiziere Willi Marzahn und E.M. vom III. MSB des MSR-2 am 19.3.1966, 20.3.1966," in: BStU, MfS, AU 83/88, Bl. 77–85, here Bl. 81.

10 See "Schlussbericht der West-Berliner Polizei, 4.4.1966," in: StA Berlin, Az. 2 Js 134/91, Bd. 3, Bl. 29–30, here Bl. 30.

11 Ibid., Bl. 30.

12 "Stellungnahme der Angehörigen des III. MSB/MSR-2 zum Verbrechen der ehemaligen Unteroffiziere M. und Marzahn, 13.4.1966," in: BStU, MfS, AF 431/78, Bl. 17.

13 "Institut für Gerichtliche Medizin der Humboldt-Universität zu Berlin, Ermittlungssache Marzahn, Willi," in: BStU, MfS, U 83/88, Bl. 13.

14 "Zwischenbericht des Militärstaatsanwalts Potsdam-Eiche, 3.5.1966," in: BStU, MfS, U 83/88, Bl. 98–101, here Bl. 100.

15 See "Verfügung der Staatsanwaltschaft Berlin vom 10.12.1992," in: StA Berlin, Az. 2 Js 134/91, Bd. 2, Bl. 68–72.

Eberhard Schulz

born on March 11, 1946

shot dead on March 30, 1966
near the Rudower Woods
on the outer ring between
Grossziethen (Königs Wusterhausen district)
and Berlin-Neukölln

Eberhard Schulz was born on March 11, 1946 in Glasow, Brandenburg. After his parents separated, he lived with his mother and four siblings in Brusendorf, south of Berlin. After completing school he worked as an unskilled farmhand on a state-owned farm in Boddinsfelde.[1] He often spoke with his friend Dieter K., who worked for the same company, about the different living conditions in the East and West. Eberhard Schulz was able to compare them because one of his brothers lived in West Berlin and managed very well there. Without making any concrete plans, the two young men occasionally discussed the possibility of fleeing to the West, with Dieter K.'s special knowledge playing a key role. In 1964/65, houses in Grossziethen that were situated close to the border stood in the way of the security strip. When they were torn down Dieter K. had been involved in removing the construction debris. At that time this temporary section of the border grounds consisted merely of rolls of barbed wire and a mesh-wire fence. That is how Dieter K. remembered the border and he thought it would be easy to get through.[2]

When he spoke about this among a larger group one evening over a beer, a few of the young men present decided they wanted to try to flee, but the two friends thought this was too risky. They wanted to flee together but without the others. By the end of March 1966 their plans had become more concrete. They set their escape date for the night of March 30. Late in the evening on March 29 they took a bolt-clipper from the company workshop and began the trek by bike from Brusendorf to Grossziethen, a distance of almost twenty kilometers.[3]

On March 30, at around 3 a.m., they parked their bikes close to the border and continued by foot, orienting themselves to the illuminated highrises on the west side. They lost the bolt-clipper somewhere along the way and thus had to continue their escape without any tools, and the border facility they encountered was no longer as primitive as Dieter K. had remembered its being. This section of the border now contained 64 signal devices, ten watchdogs and a functioning signal fence; the death strip was a good 250 meters wide and illuminated by arching lights.[4] Dieter K. managed to crawl under the interior fence but triggered an alarm soon after that. Flares suddenly shot into the air. Petrified, the men ducked into the grass. Dieter K. was already on the other side of the first fence, but Eberhard Schulz was still in front of it. Apparently he had lost his nerve and had not followed his friend through the fence. Neither of them dared move. Dieter K. did not stand up until three border guards were standing in front of him and ordered him to get up with his hands in the air. Eberhard Schulz thought the order was directed at him as well, so he got up. But the guards had not yet noticed him. He appeared from behind the fence within the border grounds as a dim silhouette in the dark about 15 meters away.[5]

There are two versions of what happened next: one from Dieter K. and one from the border guards. Dieter K. said a border guard began shooting from the hip at Eberhard Schulz without calling out or firing a warning shot. Then a second guard called out "stop shooting!"[6] In the soldiers' version, both "border violators" had been "extremely confrontational and stubborn" and had engaged in "passive resistance."[7] They claimed that Eberhard Schulz suddenly ducked, reached for something in his jacket pocket and began to run, after which the guards aimed automatic fire at him, supposedly to "prevent a possible attack on a guard or an escape."[8] What is certain is that two shots hit Eberhard Schulz in his face and neck and that he was dead immediately.[9]

The border guards' version is not very plausible. The escape attempt had failed and both fugitives, having been noticed and confronted with the superiority of three armed guards and more approaching, stood rooted to the ground in fear.[10] Why would Eberhard Schulz have tried to continue his escape or evade arrest in this hopeless situation after having voluntarily surrendered to the border guards?

Eberhard Schulz' body was retrieved and transported to the forensic institute in Charité Hospital about twenty minutes later. The East German secret police informed his mother of her son's death the next day. Dieter K. was arrested and brought to the Stasi remand prison in Potsdam. The Potsdam district court resided upon by Judge Wohlgethan found him guilty of "a collective attempt to illegally leave East Germany" and sentenced him on June 1, 1966 to two years in prison which he served in the Stasi prison in Berlin-Hohenschönhausen.[11]

While conducting research in the Military Interim Archive in Potsdam in 1991, the Berlin police came upon border troop documents concerning the incident on March 30, 1966. Preliminary proceedings were opened the same year against the East German border guards involved. Despite extensive research and interrogations, the police were unable to clarify without a doubt the exact circumstances under which the shots were fired. Statements by the border soldiers and by Dieter K. stood in direct opposition to one another and sometimes contradicted the border troop and Stasi reports written at the time. The public prosecutor's office concluded to the benefit of the suspected border guard – who denied having had any intention of killing – that "he must have acted out of putative self-defense." Dieter K.'s presentation of the facts did not justify a conviction.[12] The case was dismissed in November 1996 and the shooting of the 20-year-old Eberhard Schulz remained unpunished by law.

Udo Baron

1 See "Bericht des MfS/HA IX/4, 1.4.1966," in: BStU, MfS, AS 146/69, Bd. 8a, Bl. 167.

2 See "Protokoll der Vernehmung von Dieter K. durch die BVfS Potsdam, 30.3.1966," in: BStU, Ast. Potsdam, AU 1180/66, Bd. 1, Bl. 44.

3 See "Protokoll der Zeugenvernehmung von Dieter K. durch die Berliner Polizei, 30.6.1992," in: StA Berlin, Az. 27 Js 432/91, Bd. 1, Bl. 96–97.

4 "Abschlussbericht der NVA/4. Grenzbrigade/Grenzregiment 42/Der Kommandeur über den versuchten schweren Grenzdurchbruch von zwei männlichen Personen am 30.3.1966, 4.4.1966," in: BArch, VA-07/17895, Bl. 76–80.

5 See "Bericht des MfS/HA I/Abwehr (B), Unterabteilung, 4. Brigade, über den verhinderten Grenzdurchbruch unter Anwendung der Schusswaffe am 30.3.1966, 30.3.1966," in: BStU, MfS, AS 146/69, Bd. 8a, Bl. 160–161.

6 See "Protokoll der Zeugenvernehmung von Dieter K. durch die Berliner Polizei, 30.6.1992," in: StA Berlin, Az. 27 Js 432/91, Bd. 1, Bl. 99, 101.

7 "Bericht der NVA/Grenzregiment 42/Der Kommandeur über den versuchten schweren Grenzdurchbruch von zwei Personen, 30.3.1966," in: BArch, VA-07/6014, Bl. 72–74, here Bl. 73; "Bericht des MfS/HA I/Abwehr (B), Unterabteilung, 4. Brigade, über den verhinderten Grenzdurchbruch unter Anwendung der Schusswaffe am 30.3.1966, 30.3.1966," in: BStU, MfS, AS 146/69, Bd. 8a, Bl. 160, 161.

8 Ibid., Bl. 161.

9 See ibid.; "Obduktionsbericht des Instituts für Gerichtliche Medizin der Humboldt-Universität zu Berlin, 30.3.1966," in: BStU, Ast. Potsdam, AP 1112/76, Bl. 23–32, here Bl. 32.

10 See "Protokoll der Zeugenvernehmung von Dieter K. durch die Berliner Polizei, 30.6.1992," in: StA Berlin, Az. 27 Js 432/91, Bd. 1, Bl. 98; "Protokoll der Zeugenvernehmung von Dieter K. durch die Berliner Polizei, 30.10.1995," in: StA Berlin, Az. 27 Js 432/91, Bd. 7, Bl. 104.

11 See "Urteil des Bezirksgerichts Potsdam in der Strafsache gegen Dieter K., 1.6.1966," in: BStU, Ast. Potsdam, AU 1180/66, Bl. 49; "Meldung der BVfS Potsdam/Abt. IX über den Abschluss des Strafverfahrens gegen D.K., 30.8.1966," in: BStU, Ast. Potsdam, AU 1180/66, Bd. 1, Bl. 135.

12 See "Verfügung der Staatsanwaltschaft II bei dem Landgericht Berlin vom 12.11.1996," in: StA Berlin, Az. 27 Js 432/91, Bd. 7, Bl. 252–258, here Bl. 257.

Michael Kollender

born on February 19, 1945

**shot dead on April 25, 1966
at the Teltow Canal in Johannisthal
on the sector border between
Berlin-Treptow and Berlin-Neukölln**

I t was a mild night in late April. The border guards on the Teltow Canal were in good spirits because they were going to be discharged in a couple of days and only had an hour left of the shift that evening. Although it was against the rules they stood together and chatted. The young men were expressing their relief over the fact that no attempted escapes had occurred while they were on duty and that they had not had to make use of their weapons.[1] At about 3:45 in the morning the flare signal "5 star white" was suddenly set off near the watchtower at Wrede Bridge. They saw the shadow of a fugitive in the light of the flare. One of the border soldiers thought he recognized fatigue clothes, the summer uniform of the National People's Army. A moment later he realized that the fugitive was holding a gun in his hand.

The fugitive was the NVA soldier Michael Kollender, who had duty on the night of April 24 at the former Hentschel factory halls in Berlin-Johannisthal, where his unit's combat equipment was housed. He fled during his duty shift while in uniform and ran with his loaded machine pistol across the grounds of the former Johannisthal landing strip towards the border grounds. He had already passed through the interior security fence.

Michael Kollender, born on February 19, 1945 in Silesia, grew up in a Catholic family as the oldest of three children in Oberlungwitz, Saxony. He worked as a tractor driver in the machine and tractor station of a neighboring town. He was drafted into the National People's Army in early November 1965 where he was trained as a gunner in the anti-aircraft missile regiment of the air force. He was scheduled to participate in the May Day Parade in East Berlin on May 1, 1966.[2] This could not have pleased the Catholic soldier, who was regarded by his supervisors as "pigheaded." In one report it stated that he was "extremely undisciplined," engaged in "discussions over orders" and carried out "his duty grudgingly."[3] Kollender had thought about fleeing ever since he had joined the army. He evidently had once confided in his younger brother that "he was going to cross the border to West Berlin illegally if he ever had the chance."[4]

When they saw the fugitive, the four guards removed their machine guns from their shoulders and set the safety lever on automatic fire. They pursued him and encircled him, firing scores of salvos into the air to try to get him to surrender, but Kollender continued crawling through the security strip and had only one more barrier to cross – the triple barbed wire fence. The bank slope of the Teltow Canal behind it already belonged to West Berlin. As they caught up with the fugitive, the border guards fired curtain fire parallel to the border to prevent him from getting farther away. "Man, stay down!" a guard called out to him.[5] Michael Kollender was only a few meters away from the border line and continued crawling forward. No less than 109 shots were fired by the border guards. They were not poor marksmen and could have hit him had they wanted to do so. The shots could be heard from quite a distance. The crew of a barge on the canal was so startled that they lay down on the floor of their cabins.[6] A shot hit Michael Kollender in his head. It may have been aimed directly at him, or it could have ricocheted off the concrete post of the border fence. He remained on the ground motionless two or three meters from the barbed wire fence. The border soldiers dragged the injured man into the trench, administered first aid and notified their headquarters. Michael Kollender had not fired a single shot from his unlocked machine pistol.

A half hour later he was wrapped in a sheet, pushed beneath a medical truck that had arrived and loaded onto the side that was out of view from the West so that no one on the West Berlin side could see him being transported away. Michael Kollender was brought to the People's Police Hospital in Berlin-Mitte where he died at around six o'clock in the morning.

That same day one of the border guards was awarded the "Medal for Exemplary Service at the Border." Each of the other three was awarded a gold wristwatch.[7] The NVA city commander Poppe reported to Communist Party Politburo member Erich Honecker that the border soldiers had exhibited "correct," "consistent" and "exemplary" conduct.[8]

In the fall of 1995 the guard presumed responsible for the fatal shot was acquitted by the Berlin district court because "desertion is a legal wrong that is criminally prosecuted in accordance with the rule of the law." By deserting, Michael Kollender had allowed for a "legitimate legal claim to prosecution by the responsible East German organs."[9] Hence the border guard did not act in a manner contrary to the law.[10] Shooting NVA deserters was legitimized by the highest judicial authority during proceedings on appeal before the Federal Court of Justice: The court stated that according to the East German military law of 1962, military desertion was regarded as a crime. Killing a deserter was therefore excusable because, in this "special case," the illegality of the marksmen's action could not have been evident to them.[11]

Two days after his death, NVA officers informed Michael Kollender's parents that he had been shot and killed while trying to escape.[12] They did not learn any details but were "advised" to keep quiet about the circumstances of their son's death. The files that the family had concerning his military service were confiscated.

Michael Kollender was buried in his hometown in the presence of his immediate family and under the watchful eyes of the Stasi.

Martin Ahrends / Udo Baron / Hans-Hermann Hertle

1   On the establishment of facts concerning circumstances of events see: "Urteil des Landgerichts Berlin vom 12.9.1995," in: StA Berlin, Az. 2 Js 79/91, Bd. 3, esp. Bl. 226–240.

2   See "Einzel-Information Nr. 327/66 des MfS/ZAIG über eine verhinderte Fahnenflucht mit tödlichem Ausgang im Abschnitt Berlin-Johannisthal, Wredebrücke am 25.4.1966, 27.4.1966," in: BStU, MfS, ZAIG Nr. 1305, Bl. 21–23, here Bl. 22.

3   Ibid., Bl. 23.

4   "Zeugenvernehmung des Bruders von Michael Kollender durch die Polizeidienststelle Amberg vom 9.7.1979," in: StA Berlin, Az. 27 Js 46/95, Bd. 1, Bl. 137.

5   See "Urteil des Landgerichts Berlin vom 12.9.1995," in: StA Berlin, Az. 2 Js 79/91, Bd. 3, here Bl. 236.

6   Ibid., Bl. 237.

7   Ibid., Bl. 239.

8   "Meldung von NVA-Stadtkommandant Poppe an SED-Politbüromitglied und NVR-Sekretär Erich Honecker, betr.: Verhinderung eines Grenzdurchbruchs durch Anwendung der Schusswaffe am 25.4.1966 im Abschnitt 1./ GR 42, 25.4.1966," in: BArch, VA-07/8373, Bl. 109–110.

9   "Urteil des Landgerichts Berlin vom 12.9.1995," in: StA Berlin, Az. 2 Js 79/91, Bd. 3, Bl. 254.

10 Ibid., Bl. 255.

11 "Urteil des Bundesgerichtshofs (5 StR 137/96) vom 17.12.1996," in: StA Berlin, Az. 2 Js 79/91, Bd. 4, Bl. 87–95, here Bl. 93. The first judicial verdict of the Berlin district court from 12.9.1995 and the verdict on appeal by the Federal Court of Justice from 17.12.1996 are documented in: Klaus Marxen/Gerhard Werle (eds.), *Strafjustiz und DDR-Unrecht. Band 2/1. Teilband: Gewalttaten an der deutsch-deutschen Grenze*, Berlin/New York, 2002, pp. 249–281.

12 On this and the following see "Zeugenvernehmung eines Bruders von Michael Kollender durch die Polizeidienststelle Amberg vom 9.7.1979," in: StA Berlin, Az. 27 Js 46/95, Bd. 1, Bl. 138.

Paul Stretz

born on February 28, 1935

shot dead on April 29, 1966
in the Spandauer Schifffahrts Canal
near Invaliden Cemetery
at the sector border between
Berlin-Tiergarten and Berlin-Mitte

Paul Stretz, born on February 28, 1935 in Luitpoldshöhe, Bavaria, lived in Ottensoos near Nuremberg with his wife. The couple suffered a severe blow in October 1960 when their first daughter, Karin, died at the age of three months. Paul Stretz's wife left him because of his drinking problem in November 1961, shortly before their second daughter was born. He continued to live in Ottensoos for a time, but did not maintain contact with his family or pay child support.[1] Then he moved to West Berlin, but did not have a permanent residence there. His last job was working in the warehouse of a shipping company.[2] The divorce was settled in January 1966.

On April 29, 1966 Paul Stretz was working with other colleagues at the Spandauer Schifffahrts Canal where the border ran along the West Berlin canal embankment. It was a hot day and Paul Stretz had quenched his thirst with beer. He was more than a little drunk when at around 3:30 p.m. he came up with the idea of taking a swim in the canal.[3] He descended the steps in the canal wall and splashed in the water. His colleagues, watching from above, warned him that the waterway belonged to the east side of the city and that swimming there was dangerous.

Paul Stretz did not take any notice of this. He got undressed and swam a few meters out to the middle of the canal. A customs official also tried to get him to come back, but also failed to stop him from enjoying his swim. A number of witnesses reported his last words: "Snipers? Who cares. The water is so warm!!"[4]

The strong current began to cause him difficulty when he was ready to swim back. He swam behind a boat and when it passed, he came into view of two border guards posted on the watchtower who thought he was an East German fugitive who had almost reached the West. The watchtower was about 250 meters away. The swimmer would not have heard a warning call. Both border guards began to shoot at Paul Stretz who dove under the water in an effort to evade the shots.

His work colleagues took cover from the flying bullets. When one of the guards was unable to prevent his machine gun from shaking under automatic fire, they exchanged weapons and continued to shoot. Two other border soldiers who were on patrol heard the shooting and ran to the watchtower and saw the swimmer and what was going on. They rushed to the canal bank and began shooting directly at him from there. A ricochet bullet hit one of the guards in the arm and he stopped firing.[5] A total of 176 bullets were fired. They hit the West Berlin side, striking a window of the Reichstag building, a VW bug and an educational institution.[6] Four bullets hit Paul Stretz in the back of the head, chest and upper arm. He died immediately and sank into the canal.[7] A short time later an East German border troop boat arrived to retrieve the body from the water. Angry West Berliners began throwing stones at the boat.[8] The search was discontinued until nighttime. At around 11:15 that night, East German divers, unnoticed by anyone on the west side, found the body and brought it to the forensic institute of Charité Hospital for an autopsy.[9]

In 1997 the guards who shot Paul Stretz were sentenced by the Berlin district court to one year in prison commuted to probation.[10]

The death of Paul Stretz and the shooting on the Spreebogen, in the heart of the city, caused quite an uproar. West Berlin police, firemen, customs officials and British military police arrived at the scene soon after the shooting. The incident received considerable political and media attention as a consequence of the ongoing talks between the East German Communist Party and West German Social Democrats concerning a planned exchange of speakers.[11] West Berliners organized a number of protest actions against the shootings at the Wall. A banner was put up at the site where Paul Stretz died with the inscription: "Murder! Should the world point its finger at us Germans again?"[12] In contrast, the East Berlin press depicted the incident as a "provocation against the East German state border."[13] Paul Stretz was presented as a victim of an "organized, targeted-oriented (political) attack"[14] by West Germany against East Germany.

Although the East had learned from western newspaper articles the name of the man who was shot, he was buried as "the unidentified dead man" at the municipal cemetery in Berlin-Marzahn in early May 1966.[15] All efforts to have the human remains delivered to his mother in his hometown failed.[16]

Martin Ahrends / Udo Baron

1 See letter from Paul Stretz' ex-wife to Hans-Hermann Hertle, 5.12.2008.

2 See "Schreiben der Gemeinde Ottensoos an die West-Berliner Polizei, 9.5.1966," in: StA Berlin, Az. 27 Js 169/90, Bd. 1, Bl. 45.

3 See establishment of facts concerning circumstances of events in: "Urteil des Landgerichts Berlin vom 27.1. 1997," in: StA Berlin, Az. 27 Js 169/90, Bd. 5, Bl. 13–18.

4 "Bericht der West-Berliner Polizei über den Totschlag an der Sektorengrenze in Berlin-Tiergarten, Spandauer Schifffahrtskanal, 29.4.66," in: Ibid., Bl. 8.

5 See "Urteil des Landgerichts Berlin vom 27.1.1997," in: StA Berlin, Az. 27 Js 169/90, Bd. 5, Bl. 14–17.

6 See "Bericht der West-Berliner Polizei über den Totschlag an der Sektorengrenze in Berlin-Tiergarten, Spandauer Schifffahrtskanal, 29.4.66," in: StA Berlin, Az. 27 Js 169/90, Bd. 1, Bl. 6–7.

7 See "Urteil des Landgerichts Berlin vom 27.1.1997," in: StA Berlin, Az. 27 Js 169/90, Bd. 5, Bl. 17.

8 See "Bericht der NVA/1. Grenzbrigade zum versuchten Grenzdurchbruch im Abschnitt des GR 33, 29.4.1966," in: BArch, VA-07/19876, Bl. 15.

9 See "Bericht des MfS/HA I/Abwehr B/UA 1. Grenzbrigade/Operativgruppe GR 33 über versuchten Grenzdurchbruch einer männlichen Person mit tödlichem Ausgang, 29.4.1966," in: BStU, MfS, ZAIG Nr.10747, Bl. 103.

10 See "Urteil des Landgerichts Berlin vom 27.1.1997," in: StA Berlin, Az. 27 Js 169/90, Bd. 5, Bl. 1–3.

11 See *Die Welt am Sonntag,* 1.5.1966; *Berliner Morgenpost,* 1.5.1966; *Frankfurter Allgemeine Zeitung,* 2.5. 1966.

12 "Bericht des MfS/HA I/Abwehr B/UA 1. Grenzbrigade/Operativgruppe GR 33 über die Aufstellung eines Hetz- plakates durch das "SAS", 30.4.1966," in: BStU, MfS, ZAIG Nr.10747, Bl. 102.

13 "Erneute Provokation gegen die Staatsgrenze der DDR," in: *Neues Deutschland,* 30.4.1966.

14 "Bestellte Provokation," in: *Neues Deutschland,* 1.5.1966.

15 See "Schreiben des DDR-Generalstaatsanwalts an das Städtische Bestattungswesen in Ost-Berlin, 4.5.1966," in: StA Berlin, Az. 27 Js 169/90, Bd. 3, Bl. 166.

16 See "Schreiben der Gemeinde Ottensoos an die West-Berliner Polizei, 9.5.1966," in: StA Berlin, Az. 27 Js 169/90, Bd. 1, Bl. 45.

Eduard Wroblewski

born on March 3, 1933

shot dead on July 26, 1966
on the outer ring between
Mahlow (Zossen district) and Berlin-Tempelhof

T hree very different worlds intersected in the south of Berlin one summer evening in July 1966 during an escape attempt that ended in the death of a fugitive. Plagued with worries and problems, the 33-year-old family man Eduard Wroblewski, who came from an area near the Lutheran town of Wittenberg, was looking for a way to escape East Germany. Five border soldiers, aged 18 to 22, opened fire on him with their machine pistols to hinder his escape. Residents of the nearby West Berlin district of Lichtenrade, who were eating in their gardens or watching the semi-final of the World Cup championship between England and Portugal on television, became involuntary witnesses to one of the most brutal shootings to have ever taken place at the Wall. The border guards fired no less than 274 bullets in quick succession.[1] Twelve shots hit Eduard Wroblewski from behind, killing him immediately.

The residents on the West Berlin side of the Wall watched as his lifeless body was hastily carried away and they yelled loudly at the border guards, calling them "murderers" and "pigs." There was also strong outrage because a number of bullets flew to the West Berlin side, hitting houses, rooftops, windows and even a living room wall.[2] The Minister of the Interior Heinrich Albertz and the American city commander John Franklin both condemned the brutal and reckless use of firearms.[3] As part of its campaign "Studio at the Barbed Wire," the West Berlin Senate produced posters with the words: "Soldier, that was murder! Did you think about his mother?"

The West German authorities received information about the man who was killed a short time later. Eduard Wroblewski's brother, who lived in Hamburg, had learned of the killing from relatives in East Germany and was certain that his brother was the man shot at the Wall that July evening.[4] His brother had been living in Zahna, a town in the Wittenberg district, halfway between Berlin and Halle. Born in 1933 in Wutschdorf, previously the Prussian district of Züllichau-Schwiebus, he came from a large family that settled in the Fläming Heath before the Second World War. Eduard Wroblewski left school at the age of 14 and found work on a farm. He was evidently not an enthusiastic supporter of socialism, neither as a teenager and nor as an adult. This probably had to do with the fact that his older brother had been caught in the wheels of the arbitrary justice system and had been convicted of supposedly engaging in espionage and sent to the Soviet Union to serve his sentence. Eduard Wroblewski tried to flee to West Germany in 1952 when he was 19 years old but, like so many young East Germans who tried their luck in the West without any job skills or support from relatives, he was unable to gain a foothold.[5] This remained a short interlude and after nine months he returned to East Germany.

He worked as a trackman for the East German railroad company for a time. Later he found jobs in agriculture and construction. His first marriage, in 1956, ended in divorce. He married his second wife in 1962 and they had a son and a daughter.[6] But he soon began having problems with his supervisors and the authorities, which put a strain on the marriage.[7] He was dismissed from another job in July 1966. When he left the house on the morning of July 26, 1966, his wife thought he was going to work in the Zahna mosaic plate factory. In truth, however, he headed for Mahlow, a suburb in the south of Berlin, without giving his family any explanation. He probably had had a few drinks to boost his courage before he entered the border area early in the evening at the closed-down S-Bahn tracks that once led from Mahlow to Lichtenrade. He came within 100 meters of the last three-tiered barbed wire fence unnoticed. Then suddenly, without any warning, the first shots were fired. He ran and was able to get past the first two rows of fences before he was hit from behind and collapsed in the barbed wire.

After the incident the border troop leadership and Stasi not only investigated the victim and his relatives, but also put the border guards involved under immediate surveillance.[8] At the same time the border guards were awarded the usual honors for acting "with determination" and in a "tactically correct" way to ensure the "inviolability of our state border."[9] Poor marksmanship and excessive use of munitions was criticized but not questioned.[10]

The guards' conduct remained unchallenged in East Germany, but Eduard Wroblewski was publicly denigrated in the East after he died. The East Berlin newspaper "Berliner Zeitung" claimed on July 29, 1966 that a "social deviant" had been stopped at the "state border." It reported that he was a foreign legionary and wanted in the Halle district for major crimes. That he had committed a crime was a rumor without foundation. No evidence was found to confirm the claim that he had joined the foreign legion as a teenager during his short stay in the West. Eduard Wroblewski's son recalled that the libel and slander continued to have effect years later.[11] How his father died was an open secret in his hometown, but out of shame and fear of reprisals, the circumstances and background of his death remained a taboo within the family. His son first learned the truth when a fellow classmate taunted him by saying that his father was a "criminal" who had been shot at the Wall. He later realized that this "blemish" had accompanied his every step in other ways as well. The Stasi files show that in 1982, when the son was serving his military duty, he was denied training as a radio operator because his father was on file as a so-called "border violator."

The criminal proceedings against the perpetrators that were introduced after the collapse of the East German state showed that not all of the guards had hit or even aimed at Eduard Wroblewski. Once again it became evident that the border soldiers displayed very different attitudes and conduct. The Potsdam district court found evidence that of the six conscripts involved in the incident, one did not shoot at all, another intentionally shot off-target, and two had aimed but missed. Two of the former border guards were held accountable for the fatal shots that killed Eduard Wroblewski. They were sentenced in August 1996 to 18 months probation for manslaughter.[12]

Christine Brecht

1   See "Bericht der NVA/4.GB/Der Kommandeur betr. Bericht über verhinderten Grenzdurchbruch unter Anwendung der Schusswaffe im Abschnitt 2. GK/GR 44, 26.7.1966," in: BArch, VA-07/17895, Bl. 47–50, here Bl. 49, and "Bericht des [MfS]/HA I/Abwehr (B)/Unterabteilung 4. Brigade, 26.7.1966," in: BStU, Ast. Potsdam, AP 1115/76, Bl. 64–68.

2   See "Bericht der Polizeiinspektion Tempelhof vom 26.7.1966," in: PHS, Bestand Grenzvorkommnisse, n. pag., and "Bericht des Bundesfinanzministers an den Bundesminister des Innern, 28.7.1966," in: Politisches Archiv des AA, B 38, Nr. 166, Bl. 302.

3   See *Der Kurier,* 27.7.1966; *Die Welt,* 27. and 28.7.1966; *Telegraf,* 28.7.1966; *Berliner Morgenpost,* 28.7. 1966; *Der Tagesspiegel,* 28.7.1966.

4   See "Schreiben des Bruders von Eduard Wroblewski an den Untersuchungsausschuss Freiheitlicher Juristen, 23.10.1966," in: StA Berlin, Az. 26 Js 13/96, Bd. 3, Bl. 115, and "Niederschrift der Zeugenvernehmung des Bruders von Eduard Wroblewski durch die Hamburger Polizei, 8.11.1966," in: Ibid., Bl. 125–128.

5   See Volker Ackermann, *Der "echte" Flüchtling. Deutsche Vertriebene und Flüchtlinge aus der DDR 1945–1961,* Osnabrück, 1995.

6   Conversation conducted by Christine Brecht with R. Wroblewski, Eduard Wroblewski's son, 27.10.2006.

7   See "Bericht [der BVfS Potsdam], 2.8.1966," in: BStU, Ast. Potsdam, AP 1115/76, Bl. 32–33.

8   See "Bericht der NVA/4.GB/Der Kommandeur betr. Bericht über verhinderten Grenzdurchbruch unter Anwendung der Schusswaffe im Abschnitt 2. GK/GR 44, 26.7.1966," in: BArch, VA-07/17895, Bl. 50; "Bericht der HA I/Abwehr (B)/UA 4. Brigade über den versuchten Grenzdurchbruch im Bereich des GR 44, 2. Kp am 26.7. 1966, 26.7.1966," in: BStU, Ast. Potsdam, AP 1115/76, Bl. 68.

9   "Bericht der NVA/Stadtkommandant Poppe an das SED-Politbüromitglied Kurt Hager betr. verhinderter Grenzdurchbruch im Abschnitt des GR-44 am 26.7.1966, 27.7.1966," in: BArch, VA-07/8373, Bl. 119–120, here Bl. 120.

10 See "Teileinschätzung der NVA/4.GB/Der Kommandeur für das Ausbildungsjahr 1965/66 zur Militärratsvorlage, 15.9.1966," in: BArch, VA-07/6050, Bl. 161–183, here Bl. 163.

11 Conversation conducted by Christine Brecht with R. Wroblewski, Eduard Wroblewski's son, 27.10.2006.

12 See "Urteil des Landgerichts Potsdam vom 21.8.1996," in: StA Neuruppin, Az. 61 Js 2/95 [zuvor StA Berlin Az. 27 Js 231/91], Bd. 5, Bl. 975–1015.

Heinz Schmidt

born on October 26, 1919

shot dead on August 29, 1966
in the Spandauer Schiffahrts Canal
on the sector border between
Berlin-Tiergarten and Berlin-Mitte

Heinz Schmidt was born on October 26, 1919 in Berlin. He married in 1949 and lived with his wife and their three children in the West Berlin district of Wedding until 1962. As he got older, his mental health deteriorated.[1] He became an alcoholic and was unemployed. He repeatedly came into conflict with the law for minor offenses, such as drunkenness, theft and fraud, and had to spend time in prison and pay a number of fines. In 1962, the Berlin-Wedding local court labeled him "mentally frail" and a lawyer was appointed as his caretaker. He came into conflict with East German border guards in September 1965 when he began insulting them loudly as he crossed the sector border at the Oberbaum Bridge from the West Berlin district of Kreuzberg.[2]

After living apart from his family for a few years, he was divorced in April 1966. In mid-July he moved into a homeless shelter in Wedding. On August 29, 1966, Heinz Schmidt was rebuffed by the social welfare office when he asked them for money. He met his father that afternoon, but his father was unable to help him. A short time later the 46-year-old man turned up on the southern bank of the Nordhafen Harbor in the Tiergarten district. Highly intoxicated, he took off his clothes and entered the water in his underwear. Two fishermen called out to him that he was swimming in the border waters and that he should get out right away. Heinz Schmidt, however, continued to swim across the Spandauer Schiffahrts Canal, which in this area belonged in its entirety to East Berlin.

Two border guards noticed him near a former loading ramp. The fishermen had notified the West Berlin police and British military police and they had both arrived at the scene by then. When the East German border guards fired a warning shot, the West Berlin police called out: "Don't shoot. He jumped in from our side and is a little drunk!"[3] The border guards opened fire anyway – at the man who, because of his illness, did not know what he was doing. He swam to the east bank among a hail of bullets and sought cover where a wall of the loading ramp projected slightly outward. A policeman ordered him to take cover and stay there.[4] But after a short rest Heinz Schmidt went back into the water and tried to swim under the water back to the western embankment. He had to come up for air a number of times and came under fire from border guards posted on the roof of a former ice cream factory and in a bunker in the Invaliden Cemetery. Although he was hit by five bullets, Heinz Schmidt managed to reach the west bank. Firemen pulled him out of the water at 1:45 p.m. and brought him to the Rudolf Virchow Hospital where the doctors could do no more than determine that he was dead. A bullet had shattered his cervical spine. Heinz Schmidt was buried on September 8, 1966 in the St. Pauli Cemetery in Wedding.

Many people on both the west and east side of the canal had watched the events unfold. In the East a brewery worker was arrested for insulting the border soldiers. Cries of "murderers!" were called across the canal from the west side.[5] A number of bullet holes were later found on the outer wall of the Nordhafen Harbor warehouse in West Berlin. One bullet even hit the balcony window of an apartment located 1.5 kilometers from the canal.[6] When a family in West Berlin was driving nearby, the car door on the left side was hit by a ricochet bullet. The western press reported in detail on the shooting in the Nordhafen Harbor. A speaker of the Senate called the "murder of a person, who was not completely sane, particularly tragic, cruel and inhuman."[7] The three Allied city commanders condemned the incident as an example of "cruel disregard for human life."[8] In "Neues Deutschland," the Communist Party paper in East Germany, the incident was referred to as a "new provocation." It stated that "in order to secure the inviolability of the state border, it had been necessary for the border guards of the NVA to use their firearms."[9]

The West Berlin police officers present at the scene faced charges for failing to assist a person in danger because they had not provided Heinz Schmidt with covering fire, but they were defended by the mayor and by the interior minister, Heinrich Albertz: The officers could not have noticed the bullets since they struck 150 meters away from the police car. A police labor union press release stated: "Even the tragic situation at the Wall cannot allow police officers to let their actions be led by their emotions."[10]

In 1991, the Central Investigating Agency for Governmental and Party Crimes opened preliminary proceedings against the East German guards suspected of having shot Heinz Schmidt. The East German border troop files do not indicate clearly who fired the shots. In the 1990s none of the former border guards was able or willing to remember. The border soldier who received the "Medal for Exemplary Service at the Border" – his three comrades were awarded the "Badge of Merit" – refused to incriminate himself by testifying on his use of his weapon. He insisted that it remained a mystery to him why he received the medal. Because of this wall of silence, at the end of the investigation there was no one "who could prove with certainty that he had fired a shot or many shots at Heinz Schmidt – perhaps with the intention to kill, and this proof would be necessary for an arraignment."[11] Consequently, the public prosecutor's office had to close the case without a verdict on July 25, 1997.

Martin Ahrends / Udo Baron

1 See *Berliner Morgenpost,* 30.8.1966.

2 See "Bericht der West-Berliner Polizei über den am 29.8.1966 getöteten Heinz Schmidt, 30.8.1966," in: StA Berlin, Az. 27 Js 146/91, Bd. 1, Bl. 14–16, here Bl. 15.

3 *Berliner Morgenpost,* 30.8.1966.

4 On this and the following see "Schlussbericht der West-Berliner Polizei, 23.9.1966," in: StA Berlin, Az. 27 Js 146/91, Bd. 1, Bl. 61–65.

5 *Berliner Morgenpost,* 30.8.1966.

6 See "Schlussbericht der West-Berliner Polizei, 23.9.1966," in: StA Berlin, Az. 27 Js 146/91, Bd. 1, Bl. 61–65.

7 *Der Tagesspiegel,* 31.8.1966.

8 *Berliner Morgenpost,* 30.8.1966.

9 *Neues Deutschland,* 30.8.1966.

10 *Der Tagesspiegel,* 3.9.1966; *Spandauer Volksblatt,* 3.9.1966.

11 "Einstellungsverfügung der Staatsanwaltschaft II bei dem Landgericht Berlin, 25. Juli 1997," in: StA Berlin, Az. 27 Js 146/91, Bd. 4, Bl. 244–246, here Bl. 244.

Andreas Senk

born 1960

drowned on September 13, 1966
in the Spree near the Oberbaum Bridge
on the sector border between
Berlin-Kreuzberg and Berlin-Friedrichshain

September 13, 1966 was a hazy late summer day. That morning between 10 and 12 o'clock, six year-old Andreas Senk was pushed into the Spree by a playmate of the same age who, shocked by his own actions, ran away.[1] When the six-year-old – the only son of his 25-year-old mother Renate Senk – fell into the water at this spot, he fell from the west side of the city to the east side since the entire width of the Spree here belonged to the Soviet sector. The East regarded the border here to be an official state border and kept it heavily guarded, although the guards here focused their attention primarily on the east side. Either the guards posted on the Oberbaum Bridge watchtower about 200 meters away did not notice the incident, or they did not consider it a serious "border violation." The same was true of the East German border boats that were patrolling along the middle of the river, approximately 80 meters from the western riverbank. For hours no effort was made to save or retrieve Andreas Senk from the water.

The East German border boat did not register the presence of four West Berlin fire trucks until 2 p.m.: "Firemen on the western bank began searching the Spree with long poles. At 2:30 p.m. a child, approximately 5 years old, was pulled out of the water and quickly transported into the western hinterland. Afterwards all the forces withdrew to the western hinterland without further action."[2] Andreas Senk was brought to the Bethanien Hospital where he was declared dead.

"Six-Year-Old Dies Before the Very Eyes of the Border Police" ran the headline in the West Berlin "BZ" the next day.[3] The same day the speaker of the West Berlin Senate condemned the behavior of the East German border guards on the patrol boat, accusing them of having hampered and even prevented the rescue operation. The Berlin Christian Democrats requested that the public prosecutor's office at the Central Registry of State Judicial Administrations in Salzgitter "immediately open an investigation against the zone border guards who were partially responsible for a six-year-old's death."

It is not clear whether the border guards even noticed that the boy had fallen into the water. There is no note of it in the files. Two days after the accident, after firemen involved in the rescue operation had been questioned, the claim that the patrol boat had prevented the rescue was toned down. A chief fire inspector reported that when the firemen had arrived at the riverbank, the boat had reached the rescue site from a distance of about 30 meters. "He had called out to the zone soldiers: 'We have to search here. Apparently someone has fallen in.' A soldier answered: 'Okay, but don't come too far out into the water.' The border guards stood on the deck the whole time with their machine pistols in ready position, but otherwise they did not do anything."[4] But they also did not do anything to help find the boy as they had been asked to do by the western side.

Does this make Andreas Senk a victim at the Berlin Wall? The fact that the fire department was notified so late was not political. Andreas Senk could only have been rescued alive if he had been retrieved from the water within a maximum of eight minutes after his fall. But the chances that he could have been rescued at this site in particular were very low and this was definitely because of political reasons: "There were no passersby at the Berlin death strip that could have quickly become rescuers," wrote one commentator. "And even if they had been there, wouldn't they have expected to be shot when they jumped in the East Berlin waters?"[5]

Another four children fell – from West Berlin to East Berlin – into the Spree here at the Gröbenufer in Kreuzberg and died between 1972 and 1975. The fact that they could not be rescued and were retrieved under awkward conditions had to do with the border situation. Finally, in the fall of 1975, a new agreement to prevent these kinds of accidents from occurring in the future was reached between the government offices in East and West Berlin and was implemented in the spring of 1976: Rescue posts with a light on all sides, which was also visible from the East German border watchtowers, were installed on the West Berlin side along six kilometers of the water border.

Martin Ahrends

1 See "Ereignismeldung der West-Berliner Polizei, 14.9.1966, p. 4/5," in: PHS, Bestand Grenzvorkommnisse; see also *BZ*, 19.9.1966.
2 "Operative Tagesmeldung der NVA/Stadtkommandantur Berlin Nr: T 256/66, 14.9.1966," in: BArch, VA-07/6037, Bl. 129.
3 *BZ*, 14.9.1966.
4 Ibid.
5 Günter Matthes, Ein Grenzfall, in: *Der Tagesspiegel*, 15.9.1966.

Karl-Heinz Kube

born on April 10, 1949

shot dead on December 16, 1966
near the Teltow Harbor
on the outer ring between
Kleinmachnow (Potsdam county district)
and Berlin-Zehlendorf

"**Y**our son participated provocatively in a border breach, was injured and died from his injuries." These words came as a serious blow to Helmut and Martha Kube shortly before the 1966 Christmas celebration. The words were spoken at police headquarters in Kleinmachnow. "I will never forget that sentence," the father wrote in January 1990, a good 23 years later, to Eberhard Diepgen, then mayor of Berlin.[1] They did not learn more about the circumstances of their son Karl-Heinz Kube's death at that time or at any later date. The father inquired at the mayor's office in West Berlin whether his son was commemorated with a memorial cross, perhaps bearing the inscription "unknown." A year later, when Helmut Kube wrote yet another letter, he was told to contact the association "Working Group 13th of August."[2] Since the death was not registered in the West, the association advised him to place charges with the police in Berlin against persons unknown.[3] After trying for a year to get more information about his son's death, Helmut Kube wrote that he was "back to square one" and followed the advice.[4] The subsequent police investigation carried out in March 1993 led to the indictment of the guards believed to have killed his son.

Karl-Heinz Kube, born on April 10, 1949, grew up with four siblings in a town called Ruhlsdorf near Teltow in the south of Berlin. After attending school in Stahnsdorf, in November 1964 he began working in the state-owned Ludwigsfelde industrial plant. He had begun work there as an electric trolley driver in April 1966.[5]

Karl-Heinz Kube was 17 years old in the fall of 1966 when he began making plans to flee to West Berlin with his 18-year-old friend Detlev S.[6] They first considered swimming across the Teltow Canal or ramming through the border with a stolen car. They even thought of escaping with a glider. In the end they agreed to try to escape from the area around Kleinmachnow. Stasi reports show that "Kalle," as he was known to his friends, had some political issues with his surroundings. Stasi documents reveal that he discouraged young people from joining the FDJ, the Communist Party's youth organization, and that he spoke out against donations for the communist Vietcong in the Vietnam War.[7] The things that he and his friends did like were the very things that his state rejected: western rock music, especially the Beatles, a group which the East German authorities derided at the time as "deadbeats" and subsequently banned. His insubordinate attitude offended the Communist Party leadership at the company where he worked. They even threatened to have him committed to a "youth work yard," a prison-like facility for young people, for political reasons.[8] His friend felt that his career chances in East Germany were ruined: He wanted to be a ship's cook, but his applications were repeatedly rejected – probably because his father and brother lived in the West. Instead of traveling on the sea, he had to take a training position in the state-run Stahnsdorf guest house.

On the evening of December 16, 1966 the two teenagers drove with a "Berlin" model scooter from Ruhlsdorf to the border area at Erlenweg in Kleinmachnow, not far from Teltow harbor.[9] They thought that just before the holidays a large number of border soldiers would already be on Christmas leave and the border would not be as heavily guarded – this turned out to be a fateful error. Karl-Heinz Kube prepared for the escape by acquiring two wire cutters from the Konsum department store in Potsdam. These were needed to cut through the wire obstacles. The two young men managed to get passed the first wall, the trip wires and a barbed-wire barrier, and to enter the 12-to-15-meter-wide death strip. At about 9:45 p.m., when they had reached a trench obstacle and were only separated from Berlin by a two-and-a-half-meter-high iron mesh fence, they were seen by border soldiers and came under fire. The two men gave up their escape and sought shelter in a trench that offered them cover and a chance to run back but, as they ran away from one set of guards, they ran into the line of fire of a second group of guards who opened automatic fire on them. Both fugitives ran back and forth in the trench trying to avoid the bullets, but Karl-Heinz Kube was fatally hit by two bullets in the head and chest. Detlev S., uninjured, was arrested and delivered to the Stasi remand prison in Potsdam.

When he was interrogated by the Stasi in prison, Detlev S. put on record his and Karl-Heinz Kube's belief "that it was a violation of the principles of humanity that the citizens of East Germany be forbidden by the 'Wall' from visiting their relatives in the other part of Germany. I find this kind of measure to be inhumane. I reject it because I feel that it puts limits on my personal freedom."[10] While in prison he wrote a hand-written report on their "arrest," stating that Karl-Heinz Kube was carried "up to the 'Wall' that was about 1.5 meters high by two border guards and was thrown over it, and that he got caught with his belongings in the barbed wire and for that reason fell awkwardly. It should also be noted that he had lost a lot of blood and was unconscious. [...] After a while my friend was thrown onto a truck and I was taken by truck to the border watch station. I was accompanied by the words 'you bastards, someone should punch you in the face.'"[11]

When Detlev S. wrote the report he did not know that Karl-Heinz Kube had been killed; for weeks the Stasi kept this information from him in prison. On March 2, 1967 the Potsdam city district court, presided over by the notorious "people's judge" Hermann Wohlgethan, charged him with a "collaborative attempt to break through the border in coincidence with the collective offense committed in violation of the decree to protect the state border" and sentenced him to a year and eight months in prison.[12] Karl-Heinz Kube's scooter was confiscated as a "crime weapon." After he was released from prison, Detlev S. was branded by his escape attempt and discriminated against professionally until East Germany collapsed.

The East German secret police also refrained from telling Karl-Heinz Kube's parents the details of his death. His father, Helmut Kube, was coerced into signing the following statement at the Kleinmachnow police headquarters on December 21, 1966: "I was informed today by representatives of the Potsdam state prosecutor's office that my son died during a self-inflicted border breach. I agree to have my son cremated. I was also informed that this would be carried out in the Berlin-Baumschulenweg Crematorium."[13] The parents were not permitted to see their son a final time. The urn containing his ashes was sent to them by mail. The uncertainty of what truly happened to their son, whether he suffered and how he died, preoccupied his mother for the rest of her life. She died in December 1983 at the young age of 54, just before the anniversary of her son's death.[14]

The four border soldiers, who together fired 40 shots at Karl-Heinz Kube and Detlev S., were awarded either the "Medal for Exemplary Service at the Border" or the "Border Troop Merit of Honor" and invited to a cold buffet.[15] In March 1993, they were charged with committing joint manslaughter and attempted manslaughter. A youth court of the Potsdam district court acquitted them of these charges. The court decision stated that it could not be determined with certainty during the main proceedings which of the accused had fired the fatal shots.[16] There was no indication that in regard to the killing of Karl-Heinz Kube the defendants had "consciously and willingly acted together." The court followed the claim of the former border soldiers that they had not intended to kill and hence had only fired "warning shots" in order to make it appear that they were meeting the demands of the order to shoot. The defendants' defense plea was "comprehensible" and could "not simply be dismissed as a mere attempt to justify their conduct."[17] The court did not deem it important that, when the deadly shots were fired, Karl-Heinz Kube and Detlev S. had already given up their attempt to flee and were strongly outnumbered. Nor was it considered that the four border soldiers should have been able to arrest the two unarmed, defenseless fugitives without using their weapons.

Karl-Heinz Kube's younger sister commented on the sentence, noting that the acquittal did not remove the defendants' guilt: "They said they did not intend it and that they did not know about it. But they shot at them! They said that they did not aim. But they hit them! And every one of them knew that if they hit someone, they could kill him. And they did kill."[18]

In the winter of 1966 the youth of Ruhlsdorf wanted to ensure that Karl-Heinz Kube would not be forgotten. But when the East German secret police found out that his friends wanted to hang a picture of Karl-Heinz Kube in the Ruhlsdorf youth clubhouse and attend his funeral as a group, the Stasi went to great efforts to hinder this.[19]

Nonetheless, they could not prevent a teacher at a school conference from asking how she should conduct herself in regard to Karl-Heinz Kube's death – which meant that all the teachers in the region of Teltow-Stahnsdorf learned that he had been killed while trying to escape.[20]

An inconspicuous wooden cross was placed on the edge of Berlepschstrasse in Berlin-Zehlendorf to commemorate Karl-Heinz Kube, who was killed at the age of 17 merely because he wanted to go from East Germany to West Germany.

Hans-Hermann Hertle

1 "Schreiben von Helmut Kube an den Regierenden Bürgermeister von Berlin, Eberhard Diepgen, 28.1.1990," in: StA Neuruppin, Az. 60/1 Js 146/92, Bd. 1, Bl. 3–6, here Bl. 4.

2 "Schreiben der CDU-Fraktion des Abgeordnetenhauses von Berlin an Helmut Kube, 2.1.1991," in: StA Neuruppin, Az. 60/1 Js 146/92, Bd. 1, Bl. 7.

3 "Schreiben von Helmut Kube an die Arbeitsgemeinschaft 13. August, 6.2.1991," in: StA Neuruppin, Az. 60/1 Js 146/92, Bd. 1, Bl. 8; "Schreiben der Arbeitsgemeinschaft 13. August an Helmut Kube, 13.2.1991," in: Ibid., Bl. 9.

4 "Schreiben von Helmut Kube an den Polizeipräsidenten von Berlin, 24.2.1991," in: StA Neuruppin, Az. 60/1 Js 146/92, Bd. 1, Bl. 10–11.

5 See "Information des MfS/HA IX/9, 18.12.1966," in: BStU, MfS, HA IX Nr. 12464, Bl. 11 f.

6 See "Urteil des Kreisgerichts Potsdam-Stadt in der Strafsache gegen Detlev S., Az. S 48/67 St., 2.3.1967," in: BStU, Ast. Potsdam, AU 477/67, StA 3063, Bd. 2, Bl. 29–34.

7 See "Einzel-Information Nr. 977/88 des MfS/ZAIG über einen verhinderten schweren Grenzdurchbruch im Raum Kleinmachnow/Hafen Teltow/Potsdam am 16.12.1966, 19.12.1966," in: BStU, MfS, ZAIG Nr. 1307, Bl. 33–36, here Bl. 35.

8 Ibid.

9 On the course of events see "Urteil des Bezirksgerichts Potsdam in der Strafsache gegen Werner H., Helmut K., Horst M. und Helmut L., Az. 60/1 Js 146/92, vom 1.9.1993," in: StA Neuruppin, Az. 60/1 Js 146/92, Bd. 2, Bl. 452–455; "Abschlussbericht des Kommandeurs der 2. Grenzbrigade über die Verhinderung eines schweren Grenzdurchbruchs mit Anwendung der Schusswaffe, 17.12.1966," in: BArch, VA-07/6016, Bl. 9–14.

10 "Protokoll der Vernehmung von Detlev S. [durch die BVfS Potsdam/Abt. IX], 21.12.1966," in: BStU, Ast. Potsdam, AU 474/67, Bd. 1, Bl. 26–28, here Bl. 28.

11 "Handschriftlicher Bericht von Detlev S. über die Behandlung bei seiner Festnahme, Potsdam, den 21.12.1966," in: BStU, Ast. Potsdam, AU 474/67, Bd. 1, Bl. 60.

12 "Urteil des Kreisgerichts Potsdam-Stadt in der Strafsache gegen Detlev S., Az. S 48/67 St., 2.3.1967," in: BStU, Ast. Potsdam, AU 477/67, StA 3063, Bd. 2, Bl. 29–34.

13 "Statement" forced from Karl-Heinz Kube's father by the Stasi, 21.12.1966, in: BStU, Ast. Potsdam, AP 1111/76, Bl. 40–41.

14 Karola Linow, Soll ihr Schuldbewusstsein die einzige Strafe sein?, in: *Märkische Allgemeine Zeitung*, 8.9.1993.

15 See "Medaille, kaltes Buffett – und kein Wort drüber!," in: *Märkische Allgemeine Zeitung*, 20.8.1993.

16 "Urteil des Bezirksgerichts Potsdam in der Strafsache gegen Werner H., Helmut K., Horst M. und Helmut L., Az. 60/1 Js 146/92, vom 1.9.1993," in: StA Neuruppin, Az. 60/1 Js 146/92, Bd. 2, Bl. 455.

17 Ibid., Bl. 458.

18 Karola Linow, Soll ihr Schuldbewusstsein die einzige Strafe sein?, in: *Märkische Allgemeine Zeitung*, 8.9.1993.

19 "Bericht des MfS/KD Potsdam über Diskussionen in Ruhlsdorf zum Ableben des Grenzverletzers Kube, Karl-Heinz, Potsdam, 6.1.1967," in: BStU, Ast. Potsdam, AU 474/67, Bd. 1, Bl. 67–69.

20 Ibid., Bl. 69.

Max Sahmland

born on March 28, 1929

shot and drowned on January 27, 1967
in the Teltow Canal near Kanalstrasse
on the sector border between
Berlin-Treptow and Berlin-Neukölln

Max Sahmland, born in Berlin on March 28, 1929, was 16 years old at the end of the war and evidently had a hard time finding his niche in post-war Germany. After finishing school he worked in agriculture and as a blacksmith in the Wildau heavy equipment construction company. According to a West Berlin police report, he resettled in West Berlin in January 1961 without his wife and their two children.[1] Little is known about why he made this move or what led him to return to East Germany a few months later. He told the East German police that marriage problems had been the reason,[2] and, in fact, his marriage did fall apart a short time later. He repeatedly came into conflict with the law as a consequence of alcohol problems. He had to serve an 18-month prison sentence for causing a traffic accident in 1964.[3] In early January 1967, the district court of Königs Wusterhausen sentenced him to six months in prison for assault; this was followed by hospitalization in a detoxication center. He was said to have beaten his fiancée while intoxicated and to have insulted the policemen who came to her assistance.[4] Because Max Sahmland did not want to spend any more time in prison, he decided to flee to West Berlin – with his fiancée.[5] She had a cousin living in West Berlin and Max Sahmland had a sister in West Germany.[6]

They had already tried to escape twice and failed. On the day before the next planned escape, Max Sahmland and his fiancée told a mutual friend about their plans to try and cross the border one more time. She spontaneously decided to join them. In a drunken state the three of them set off shortly before midnight on January 26, 1967 and drove with stolen bicycles to the Zeuthen train station where they took the S-Bahn train to Berlin-Adlershof.[7] They walked to the border area that Max Sahmland was familiar with from when he had worked in a sewage treatment plant nearby.[8] They moved slowly towards one of the trenches. It was a stormy night, not cold, but rainy, and the poor visibility was to their advantage. Sahmland left the women back in the trench a few meters from the first fence so that he could cut an opening with a wire-cutter. "Be brave," he said to his fiancée and started to creep forward.[9] The women were supposed to follow him a few minutes later or, if they sensed danger, to withdraw. They stayed put until, startled by the sound of machine gun fire, they ran back from where they had come. They were able to reach their homes unnoticed.[10]

Max Sahmland tried to get past the signal fence at about 2 : 30 a.m. When he set off an alarm, guards at the Wredebrücke observation tower opened fire on him.[11] A letter from the NVA city commander to Erich Honecker, who at the time was secretary of the National Defense Council, stated that the "border violator" showed "strike effects, but was nonetheless able to get past the wire barrier."[12] Injured, Max Sahmland continued to flee, crawled under the barrier and was able to reach the bank of the Teltow Canal, which he then attempted to swim across. The border guards pursued him and continued to shoot at him even after he had reached West Berlin territory.[13] Max Sahmland was hit by a number of bullets. One bullet went into his right lung.[14]

Two workers from the nearby cement asbestos plant on the west side were alarmed by the shots and ran to the riverbank to help the fleeing man who was still a few meters away from the bank. But they had to take cover because he was still under fire and eventually Max Sahmland sank into the canal.[15] Police and emergency medical services arrived on the West Berlin side, but the West Berlin firemen who were assisted by divers were unable to find Max Sahmland in the area of the west bank. The West Berlin water police did not find his body until March 8, 1967, six weeks later. His body was retrieved from the Teltow Canal and could be identified from the identity card he had on him.[16] In February 2000, the man suspected of having shot Max Sahmland was acquitted by the Berlin district court because it was unable to disprove his claim that he had fired in the direction of the fleeing man but had intentionally tried to miss him by a few meters.[17]

Max Sahmland's fiancée was arrested on January 28, 1967 and sentenced to two years and eight months in prison for trying to flee the republic and for "enticing" her friend to join her. She served twenty months of her sentence in the Stasi prison in Potsdam and in the Hoheneck prison for women. Her friend was also sentenced to a year and seven months for trying to flee.[18]

Max Sahmland's mother, who lived in East Berlin, was prevented from bidding farewell to her dead son. Letters to her sister show that she was not informed of the possibility of having the body sent to East Berlin.[19] Consequently, Max Sahmland was buried on April 5, 1967 in the Park Cemetery in the West Berlin district of Neukölln.[20] To hinder the mother from attending her son's funeral, the East German secret police imposed a travel ban on the seventy-year-old woman until the end of April 1967.[21]

Martin Ahrends / Udo Baron

1 See "Bericht der West-Berliner Polizei über die Bergung einer männlichen Leiche, 8.3.1967," in: StA Berlin, Az. 27 Js 162/90, Bd. 1, Bl. 67–69.

2 See "Protokoll des VPKA Königswusterhausen/Abt. K/Komm. I, 5.12.1966," in: BStU, Ast. Potsdam, AU 1546/67, Bd. 1, Bl. 204.

3 See "Protokoll der Zeugenvernehmung der ehem. Verlobten von Max Sahmland durch die West-Berliner Polizei, 14.11.1969," in: StA Berlin, Az. 27 Js 162/90, Bd. 1, Bl. 137.

4 See "Einzel-Information Nr. 87/67 des MfS/ZAIG über einen Grenzdurchbruch im Abschnitt Wredebrücke in Berlin-Johannisthal am 27.1.1967, 28.1.1968," in: BStU, MfS, ZAIG Nr. 1321, Bl. 3.

5 See "Protokoll der Zeugenvernehmung der ehem. Verlobten von Max Sahmland durch die West-Berliner Polizei, 14.11.1969," in: StA Berlin, Az. 27 Js 162/90, Bd. 1, Bl. 137–138.

6 See "Befragungsprotokoll des VPKA Königswusterhausen, 27.1.1967," in: BStU, Ast. Potsdam, AU 1546/67, Bd. 1, Bl. 22–24.

7 See ibid., Bl. 138; "Anklageschrift der Staatsanwaltschaft bei dem Landgericht Berlin, 20.10.1999," in: StA Berlin, Az. 27 Js 162/90, Bd. 4, Bl. 229, 231 a.

8 See "Einzel-Information Nr. 87/67 des MfS/ZAIG über einen Grenzdurchbruch im Abschnitt Wredebrücke in Berlin-Johannisthal am 27.1.1967, 28.1.1968," in: BStU, MfS, ZAIG Nr. 1321, Bl. 4.

9 "Befragungsprotokoll [des VPKA Königswusterhausen], 28.1.1967," in: BStU, Ast. Potsdam, AU 1546/67, Bd. 1, Bl. 95–100, here Bl. 99.

10 See "Protokoll der Zeugenvernehmung der ehem. Verlobten von Max Sahmland durch die West-Berliner Polizei, 14.11.1969," in: StA Berlin, Az. 27 Js 162/90, Bd. 1, Bl. 138–139.

11 See "Anklageschrift der Staatsanwaltschaft bei dem Landgericht Berlin, 20.10.1999," in: StA Berlin, Az. 27 Js 162/90, Bd. 4, Bl. 230.

12 "Meldung des NVA-Stadtkommandanten der Hauptstadt der DDR/Berlin an Erich Honecker, 27.1.1967," in: BArch, VA-07/8374, Bl. 19.

13 See "Einzel-Information Nr. 87/67 des MfS/ZAIG über einen Grenzdurchbruch im Abschnitt Wredebrücke in Berlin-Johannisthal am 27.1.1967, 28.1.1968," in: BStU, MfS, ZAIG Nr. 1321, Bl. 1–2.

14 "Anklageschrift der Staatsanwaltschaft bei dem Landgericht Berlin, 20.10.1999," in: StA Berlin, Az. 27 Js 162/90, Bd. 4, Bl. 231–231 a.

15 See "Ereignismeldung des Kommandos der Schutzpolizei/S1, 27.1.1967," in: PHS, Bestand Ereignismeldungen der West-Berliner Schutzpolizei, Bl. 1–2; see also *Der Tagesspiegel*, 28.1.1967; *Die Welt*, 28.1.1967; *Telegraf*, 28.1.1967.

16 See "Ereignismeldung 37 zu 29 (erschossener Flüchtling) der West-Berliner Schutzpolizei, 8.3.1967," in: PHS, Bestand Ereignismeldungen der West-Berliner Schutzpolizei, n. pag.; see "Ereignismeldung 56 der West-Berliner Schutzpolizei, 9.3.1967," in: Ibid.

17 See "Urteil des Landgerichts Berlin vom 9.2.2000", in: StA Berlin, Az. 27 Js 162/90, Bd. 5, Bl. 1–3.

18 See "Protokoll der Zeugenvernehmung der ehem. Verlobten von Max Willi Sahmland durch die West-Berliner Polizei, 25.11.1969," in: StA Berlin, Az. 27 Js 162/90, Bd. 1, Bl. 141–142.

19 See letter from Max Sahmland's mother to her sister in West Berlin, 3.4.1967, in: StA-Berlin, Az. 27 Js 162/90, Bd. 1, Bl. 116; "Vermerk der West-Berliner Polizei I/A/KJ1, 4.4.1967," in: Ibid., Bl. 115. A file note of the East German state prosecutor suggests that the mother did not want the body sent over. See "Schreiben des Staatsanwalts des Stadtbezirkes Berlin-Friedrichshain an den DDR-Generalstaatsanwalt, 23.3.1967," in: BStU, MfS, ASt G IA (a) 27/67, Bd.1, Bl. 24.

20 See "Schlussbericht der West-Berliner Polizei I/A/KI1, 18.4.1967," in: StA Berlin, Az. 27 Js 162/90, Bd. 1, Bl. 120–123.

21 See "Vermerk [der DDR-Generalstaatsanwaltschaft], 23.3.1967," in: BStU, MfS, ASt G IA (a) 27/67, Bd.1, Bl. 5.

Franciszek Piesik

born on November 23, 1942

drowned on October 17, 1967
in the Niederneuendorfer Lake
on the outer ring between
Hennigsdorf (Nauen district) and Berlin-Spandau

Franciszek Piesik was a Polish boatman with a rank equivalent to that of a captain. He probably knew the course of the border in northwest Berlin better than most East German residents. Polish freight traffic heading westward (to Holland, Belgium and West Germany) traveled across the Oder-Havel Canal and through East German border grounds near Hennigsdorf, just a few meters from West Berlin. Piesik had a sketch of the boundary line in this region and a side-cutter on him when he undertook his escape attempt on the evening of October 17, 1967.[1]

Two days earlier he had crossed the Oder River and the border between Poland and East Germany at night unnoticed in a row boat. Although an immediate search warrant for him was issued he was able to reach the Berlin area without being identified.[2] His escape had been carefully planned and revealed a special knowledge of the local surroundings. Near Hennigsdorf, in the harbor of the "building mechanics' company sports club," Piesik stole a motorboat that had once been used by the border unit responsible for guarding this section of the border. This suggests that the company sports club was on good terms with the border guards: civilians who lived close to the border were often enlisted as "voluntary helpers" in the border troops.[3] Franciszek Piesik initially traveled south in the boat. To reach the lake and cross the border, it was necessary for him to maneuver around a headland. It is possible that he was recognized as a fugitive here and thus had to change his original plan. In any case, Piesik docked on the headland that divided the canal from the Niederneuendorfer Lake and formed a dangerous marsh to anyone not familiar with the terrain.

The NVA daily report stated succinctly: "After passing the island, he swam across the Havel Lake."[4] He left everything that would have hindered his swimming, including a jacket and briefcase, on the riverbank. Why would he have carried a bag with personal documents with him if he had planned to escape this way? It is more likely that the man had not intended to leave his boat and enter the water to reach the safe bank of West Berlin. The border ran through the middle of the lake here. Piesik had to cover a distance of about 200 to 300 meters and in mid-October the water was hardly more than 10 degrees Celsius. The NVA daily report set the time of the "border breach" at 6:15 p.m. By then East German border troops must have noticed Piesik's escape or discovered the things he had left behind on land; they may even have seen him swimming to the West. During an evaluation of the incident the NVA city commander criticized the "non-adherence to existing directives" and the "non-use of firearms to arrest or annihilate the enemy." He disapproved of one more thing: their "blind confidence."[5] The border guards probably had not initially suspected that Piesik was a fugitive; because of his boat they probably thought that he was a trustworthy member of the water sports club.

The West Berlin police report stated that "We are not aware of firearms being employed by the NVA during the period of time in question."[6] What took place that evening in the Niederneuendorfer Lake? Had someone followed him or searched for him? Had he tried to hide from the border guards under water, in the swampy reeds? Franciszek Piesik probably drowned as a consequence of hypothermia and exhaustion. When his body was found in West Berlin eleven days later, it was found that his respiratory tracts were filled up to his lungs with sludge. There was no indication of any externally applied force.[7]

Long and drawn out negotiations with the Polish authorities began over the body of the fugitive. Two and a half months passed before the Polish military mission provided fingerprints and a personal description. Only then could the dead man be identified with certainty.[8] Franciszek Piesik was buried at the Berlin-Heiligensee Cemetery six months after he died.[9]

Since there was no indication of third-party negligence, the Berlin public prosecutor's office refrained from opening a preliminary investigation in mid-1996. What led the 24-year-old man to flee and the exact circumstances of his death remain unknown.

Martin Ahrends / Udo Baron

1 See "Bericht der West-Berliner Polizei, 31.10.1967," in: StA Berlin, Az. 27 AR 56/95, Bd. 1, Bl. 41.

2 See "Tagesmeldung Nr. 289/67 der NVA/Kommando der Grenztruppen/ODH, 14./15.10.1967," in: BArch, GT 1755, Bl. 174/75.

3 On this and the following see "Operative Tagesmeldung Nr. T 290/67 der NVA/Stadtkommandantur Berlin/Abteilung Operativ, 17.10.1967," in: BArch, VA-07/6042, Bl. 31–32.

4 Ibid., Bl. 31.

5 Ibid., Bl. 32.

6 "Bericht der West-Berliner Polizei vom 13.12.1967," in: StA Berlin, Az. 27 AR 56/95, Bd. 1, Bl. 97.

7 "Bericht der West-Berliner Polizei vom 31.10.1967," in: StA Berlin, Az. 27 AR 56/95, Bd. 1, Bl. 99.

8 See "Bericht der West-Berliner Polizei vom 16.1.1968," in: StA Berlin, Az. 27 AR 56/95, Bd. 1, Bl. 101.

9 See "Vermerk der West-Berliner Polizei vom 18.4.1968," in: StA Berlin, Az. 27 AR 56/95, Bd. 1, Bl. 103.

Elke Weckeiser

born on October 31, 1945

shot dead on February 18, 1968
across from the Reichstag building,
near Kronprinzen Bridge
at the sector border between
Berlin-Mitte and Berlin-Tiergarten

Dieter Weckeiser

born on February 15, 1943

shot on February 18, 1968
across from the Reichstag building,
near Kronprinzen Bridge
at the sector border between
Berlin-Mitte and Berlin-Tiergarten
died from his bullet wounds on February 19, 1968

Dieter Weckeiser, born on February 15, 1943 in Rhodebach/East Prussia, was only 25 years old when he was shot and killed by border guards in mid-February 1968. His short life was dominated by flight.[1] After his father fell on the eastern front in 1943, his mother fled with the young boy to West Prussian Elbing in 1944. When the Red Army approached in January 1945, they again fled westward. The Weckeisers spent a few years in different places in the Soviet zone of occupation before they finally reached West Germany in 1949. Once there they lived in various refugee centers and homeless shelters. The family was finally able to settle permanently in Warendorf, Westphalia, when the mother remarried in 1954.

The young boy had suffered from tuberculosis while he was growing up. At the age of seven he spent half a year in a sanatorium where his mother was not allowed to visit him. After finishing school Dieter Weckeiser trained to become a furniture upholsterer. During this period he met Renate G. who had arrived in Warendorf from East Germany in March 1961. He wanted to marry her, but his mother and stepfather were opposed to the relationship. Later his mother testified to the Berlin public prosecutor's office that the family conflicts intensified after that.

Without telling their parents, Dieter Weckeiser and his pregnant girlfriend moved to West Berlin in July 1962 and tried, unsuccessfully, to gain a foothold there. On the insistence of his girlfriend, he agreed to resettle in East Germany, in Fürstenwalde/Spree, where Renate G.'s parents lived. The couple married there in 1962 and had three children. Dieter Weckeiser worked in various jobs, including as an interior designer and as a co-driver. They divorced in 1966 and shortly after that Dieter Weckeiser became seriously ill.[2] It was during this period that he met the twenty-year-old Elke Möbis, who, after completing an apprenticeship as a textile twister, had found work as a kitchen assistant in a company cafeteria in Fürstenwalde. They married in late November 1966. The next year Dieter Weckeiser saw his mother for the first time since he had hastily fled from Warendorf. Since she was not allowed to travel to Fürstenwalde they met every day for an entire week in East Berlin, which his mother was able to visit on a one-day visa from West Berlin. During their last meetings Dieter Weckeiser told his mother that he had come under political pressure after he had used his experience in the West to try and revise the official image of West Germany as the class enemy. He also expressed a desire to return "home" to the West.[3]

The temperatures had reached almost freezing on the evening of February 18, 1968 when the young couple attempted to cross the border to West Berlin. They chose to flee from the Spree in the city center, diagonally across from the Reichstag building, a spot that was heavily guarded and secured. After getting past the barbed wire and watchdog run, they had to climb over a three-meter-high expanded metal fence and then swim across the ice-cold Spree. The bank on the west side consisted of a wall that they had to pull themselves up and over, which was practically impossible without tools or help from someone. Guards stationed on a tower noticed them crawling under the first barbed wire at about 11 p.m. and immediately began to shoot at them without warning. A total of seventeen shots were fired from the tower. Elke Weckeiser was hit in the chest and thigh. A bullet went through Dieter Weckeiser's skull.

An ambulance brought the critically injured couple to the nearby People's Police Hospital. The young woman died there from her injuries that very night. An emergency operation was conducted on her husband, but he died the next day.

The border soldiers were commended and awarded the "Medal for Exemplary Service at the Border." One of them was promoted ahead of time to private. Thirty years later they faced charges from the Berlin district court for the shots fired at Elke and Dieter Weckeiser. The guard who fired the shots was sentenced in 1997 to a probation term of one year and nine months for "a less serious case" of manslaughter. His supervisor, who referred to the dead couple in front of the court as "two border violators who intentionally endangered themselves," was acquitted because the court decided that he could not be held legally responsible for the "excesses" of the gunman.[4] The majority of the officers and soldiers who were stationed at the border had already stated during their police interrogation that, from an objective viewpoint, the use of firearms had not been necessary.[5]

To conceal the circumstances under which the young couple had died, the East German secret police created a "legend," a false version of events, which entailed a purposeful character assassination of them.[6] It was decided that Dieter Weckeiser's debts should be paid for by the state treasury in order to prevent "creditors […] from conducting their own inquiry and learning of the concrete circumstances of the Weckeisers' death."[7] Dieter Weckeiser's ex-wife was told by the East German secret police that her former husband had died with his new wife in a traffic accident with a stolen car. The mail of the dead couple's relatives was monitored and confiscated. Consequently, Dieter Weckeiser's mother, who had inquired in vain to the East German police, did not learn that her son had died while trying to escape until a year later when the minister of her hometown in the West had established direct contact with the minister in Fürstenwalde in the East.[8]

The urn containing the ashes of Elke Weckeiser was buried in her mother's grave in Fürstenwalde on May 7, 1968. Her half-sister had to first assure the Stasi that she would refrain from having a "ceremonial burial" or placing a death notice in the newspaper.[9] The urn with the ashes of Dieter Weckeiser was withheld from his relatives by order of the East German secret police and buried at the Baumschulenweg Cemetery in Berlin-Treptow.

Martin Ahrends / Udo Baron

1   On the lives of Dieter and Elke Weckeiser described here, see "Zeugenvernehmung von Margarete G. [der Mutter von Dieter Weckeiser] durch die West-Berliner Polizei, 13.4.1993," in: StA Berlin, Az. 27 Js 106/90, Bd. 2, Bl. 55–58; "Zeugenvernehmung von Margarete G. [der Mutter von Dieter Weckeiser] durch das Amtsgericht Warendorf, 20.3.1997," in: StA Berlin, Az. 27 Js 106/90, Bd. 8, Bl. 37–42.

2   See ibid., sowie "Fernschreiben Nr. 286 [des MfS]/KD Fürstenwalde an die VfS Gross-Berlin/Abt. IX, 19.2. 1968," in: BStU, MfS, AS 198/69, Nr. 1, Bl. 49.

3   "Zeugenvernehmung von Margarete G. [der Mutter von Dieter Weckeiser] durch das Amtsgericht Warendorf, 20.3.1997," in: StA Berlin, Az. 27 Js 106/90, Bd. 8, Bl. 37–42, here Bl. 40.

4   See "Urteil des Landgerichts Berlin vom 18.4.1997," in: StA Berlin, Az. 27 Js 106/90, Protokoll-/Urteilsakte, Bl. 84–137. On the trial in the case of Elke and Dieter Weckeiser see also Roman Grafe, *Deutsche Gerechtigkeit. Prozesse gegen DDR-Grenzschützen und ihre Befehlsgeber,* München, 2004, pp. 281–284.

5   See "Urteil des Landgerichts Berlin vom 18.4.1997," in: StA Berlin, Az. 27 Js 106/90, Protokoll-/Urteilsakte, Bl. 84–137, here Bl. 106.

6   See "Vorschlag der VfS Gross-Berlin/Abt. IX zum Inhalt des Gesprächs, das mit der westdeutschen Bürgerin [Name geschwärzt] im Zusammenhang mit dem Tod ihres Sohnes geführt werden soll, 30.4.1968," in: BStU, MfS, AS 198/69, Nr. 1, Bl. 264–267.

7   "Vorschlag der VfS Gross-Berlin/Abt. IX, 7.5.1968," in: BStU, MfS, AS 198/69, Nr. 1, Bl. 271–274, here Bl. 272.

8   Letter from the minister of the Lutheran Ministry of Fürstenwalde/Spree, Kieselbach, to his fellow colleague in Warendorf, 22.1.1968" [Weckeiser family private archive].

9   "Handschriftliche Erklärung der Halbschwester von E.W. gegenüber der Stasi, 26.2.1968," in: BStU, MfS, AS 198/69, Nr. 1, Bl. 18.

Herbert Mende

born on February 9, 1939

shot on July 8, 1962
at the Glienicke Bridge
on the outer ring in Potsdam
died from his bullet wounds on March 10, 1968

Herbert Mende was born on February 9, 1939 to Anastasia and Franz Mende. He grew up with two older sisters in Steinaugrund, Silesia, which is now Ligota Tulowicka in Poland. In 1945 his mother fled with the children to Zieran in the Altmark, where the father joined them after he was released from British captivity. In 1957 the family, which by this time had also taken in a foster child of Ana Mende's brother, moved to Potsdam. After completing an apprenticeship at the state-owned company "Ausbau Potsdam," Herbert Mende worked in Potsdam as a floor technician and mason.[1]

Herbert Mende went out dancing on the first Saturday in July 1962. He traveled all the way from the West of Potsdam to the eastern edge of the city where the youth clubhouse "John Scheer" was located. From there it was not far to the death strip and the Glienicke Bridge, which was heavily guarded and only accessible to Allied military personnel. West Berlin was situated on the other side – and had remained off-limits to Potsdam residents ever since the Wall was built. The young man left the youth club just past midnight in order to catch the last bus back home. The East German customs head assistant saw "a male civilian" approaching him at about ten past twelve. He moved toward Herbert Mende at which point the young man, intoxicated and not without a touch of irony, asked him: "Uncle, can you tell me where the bus to Potsdam departs?" After the customs officer gave him directions, Herbert Mende walked toward the bus stop – and away from the border. He apparently looked back a number of times and called to him: "You can put down your damn gun and change your opinion, too."[2]

It all might have ended well if a guard patrol of the East German police force had not arrived at that moment and caught up with the young man in order to check his identification papers. Herbert Mende did not have his ID with him and was only able to show his military service registration card. The policemen decided to take him with them to the East German police district office "to do a further check."[3] They escorted him to a guard house that was situated right at the Glienicke Bridge barrier where they planned to have him picked up.[4] That was practically the same as a preliminary arrest, but the 23-year-old apparently did not know this at the time. Herbert Mende was told to wait outside the building. When, a few minutes later, the bus he had been waiting for arrived at its final destination and turned around to begin its return tour, the young man asked the policemen whether they still wanted anything from him. When he did not receive an answer, he ran off to catch his bus.[5] Herbert Mende later told his father that one of the policemen came out of the guardhouse and called out to two other border guards who were patrolling close by: "Shoot him! Shoot him!"[6] After firing a warning shot, one of the border guards fired two shots at the young man from a distance of 30 meters.[7]

From his hospital bed a week later, Herbert Mende presented the events from his point of view in an accident report for his insurance company: "Had been dancing in a youth clubhouse from 7.7.–8.7., 12:20 a.m. Had consumed alcohol and wanted to go home on the bus at 12:20 a.m. While looking for the bus stop, two policemen came up and asked me where I was going; I answered: to the bus stop. When the policemen demanded to see my ID I realized that I had forgotten it. The police took me with them up to the barrier in the prohibited zone and made phone calls; they had already demanded from me my personal data and written everything down. When I saw the bus coming, I ran, thinking that they were through with me and I wanted to catch my bus. I saw the bus in front of me and then shots were fired and I collapsed. Before I lost consciousness I only heard one voice that said: 'That bastard hasn't gotten enough.'"[8]

Herbert Mende was brought to the district hospital in Potsdam. It is thanks to the resolute insistence of the head doctor there that the seriously injured young man was not transferred the following day to the army hospital in Drewitz. For months he was only barely able to withstand the pain from his injuries. The bullet wounds in his pelvis and abdomen had turned him into an invalid. He was awarded 124 marks a month pension in early 1963.[9]

The East German police and border police admitted to his parents that an "accident" had occurred. The father was even permitted to review the files on the incident. He gathered from them that the East German police had made an error in bringing his son into the prohibited zone.[10] An internal investigation report of the East German Ministry of the Interior, which at the time was still responsible for the border police, criticized the "poor tactics" and the "unsatisfactory coopera-tion between the forces" and concluded that the use of firearms had "not been necessary."[11]

The armed forces lacked this openness towards Herbert Mende and his family. The "VP officer present at the accident bears no guilt," the district authorities of the East German police in Potsdam told the Mende family's attorney. He was told that he should instead contact the military state prosecutor of the 2nd Border Bri-gade in Gross Glienicke.[12] But the military state prosecutor H. also denied to the family that the marksman had made himself culpable through his actions. Hence he did not open a preliminary investigation and saw no reason to provide them with the name of the border soldier in question.[13]

In 1960, before the incident, Herbert Mende had taken out a combination ac-cident and sick pay insurance with the "Deutsche Versicherungs-Anstalt" (DVA), an East German insurance company. After the shooting, he and his parents were involved in a struggle for years over receiving the benefits of this insurance. It did not end until a settlement was reached in June 1966 in which the DVA agreed to pay the legal and trial costs. He was also awarded 10,000 marks compensation for pain and suffering and 16,000 marks disability payments.

After 1990 Herbert Mende's father had a preliminary investigation opened against the man who had shot his son. He argued that the border guards could not possibly have mistaken the young man for a "border violator" since he was not moving towards West Berlin but in the direction of Potsdam. But the case was dismissed in the fall of 1996 because the public prosecutor was unable to prove without a doubt that the gunman had had the intention to kill.[14] The case was reopened again following a complaint filed by the father. This time, in his defense, the gunman claimed that he had not intended to shoot Herbert Mende, but only wanted to give him a scare, and had pointed his weapon to the ground when he started shooting from the hip. Consequently, the public prosecutor concluded "that with near certainty, he had not recognized the danger of his actions, not to speak of taking them seriously."[15] In a letter dated February 25, 1997, the case was closed in favor of the perpetrator for the second time. Nonetheless, Franz Mende once again filed a complaint, underscoring the fact that in the case of his son it did not entail an escape attempt that could have "justified any use of firearms."[16] The attorney general of the state of Brandenburg was of a different view. He wrote to Franz Mende that it could not be disproved that the guard "erroneously presumed that your son was a so-called 'border violator.' Nor could it be determined that he willingly accepted the death of your son – that is to say that he had killed with intent."[17] He continued to explain that the public prosecutor's office only brings charges against an individual when a conviction is highly likely, not however, when the outcome of the case is uncertain and there is only the mere possibility of a conviction. The events "are extraordinarily tragic and I can imagine the pain you have," he wrote, but due to a lack of prospects for a conviction he rejected pressing charges.[18]

After remaining in the hospital continuously for two years, Herbert Mende was sent home as an invalid in the summer of 1964. His mother had to give up her work to care for her son.[19] After a long and painful period of suffering, Herbert Mende died on March 10, 1968 in the St. Josef's Hospital in Potsdam – one month after his 29th birthday.

Hans-Hermann Hertle

1 Conversation conducted by Hans-Hermann Hertle with Erika Neumann, Herbert Mende's sister, 6.10.2008.

2 "Untersuchungsbericht des DDR-Ministeriums des Innern/Bereitschaftspolizei/2. Grenzbrigade (b) zum Schusswaffengebrauch mit schwerer Körperverletzung am 8.7.1962 gegen 00.20 Uhr im Abschnitt der 1./I./2. Grenzbrigade an der Brücke der Einheit, 9.7.1962," in: BArch, DY 30/IV 2/12/76, Bd. 3, Bl. 286–290, here Bl. 286/87.

3 Ibid., Bl. 287.

4 Ibid., Bl. 287.

5 See "Vermerk der Staatsanwaltschaft Potsdam über eine Vorsprache von Franz Mende, 18.6.1991," in: Franz Mende's estate.

6 "Protokoll der Zeugenvernehmung von Franz Mende durch die Berliner Polizei vom 8.4.1992," in: Franz Mende's estate.

7   "Verfügung der Staatsanwaltschaft Neuruppin, 16.10.1996," in: Franz Mende's estate.

8   "Unfallschaden-Anzeige von Herbert Mende an die Deutsche Versicherungs-Anstalt, 16.7.1962," in: Franz Mende's estate.

9   See "Rentenbescheid für Herbert Mende ab 7.1.1963," in: Franz Mende's estate.

10 "Protokoll der Zeugenvernehmung von Franz Mende durch die Berliner Polizei, 8.4.1992," in: Franz Mende's estate.

11 "Untersuchungsbericht der MdI-Bereitschaftspolizei, 9.7.1962," in: BArch, DY 30/IV 2/12/76, Bd. 3, Bl. 286–290.

12 "Schreiben der BdVP Potsdam an den Rechtsvertreter von Franz Mende, Rechtsanwalt Günter B., 9.10.1963," in: Franz Mende's estate.

13 "Schreiben des Militärstaatsanwalts H. (Gross Glienicke) an den Rechtsvertreter von Franz Mende, Rechtsanwalt Günter B., 21.10.1963," in: Franz Mende's estate.

14 "Verfügung der Staatsanwaltschaft Neuruppin, 16.10.1996," in: Franz Mende's estate.

15 "Verfügung der Staatsanwaltschaft Neuruppin, 25.2.1997," in: Franz Mende's state.

16 "Beschwerde von Franz Mende gegen die Einstellungsverfügung der Staatsanwaltschaft Neuruppin vom 25.2. 1997, 1.4.1997," in: Franz Mende's estate.

17 "Schreiben des Generalstaatsanwalts des Landes Brandenburg an Franz Mende, 27.2.1998," in: Franz Mende's estate.

18 Ibid.

19 Conversation conducted by Hans-Hermann Hertle with Erika Neumann, Herbert Mende's sister, 6.10.2008.

Bernd Lehmann

born on July 31, 1949

drowned on May 28, 1968
in the Spree
on the sector border between
Berlin-Treptow and Berlin-Kreuzberg

E arly in the evening of June 28, 1968, a man's sports jacket, a sweater, a pair of pants, socks and a pair of shoes were found in the bushes near the Soviet monument in Berlin-Treptow. An identity card with personal data on Bernd Lehmann was found in the side pocket of the jacket. Five days later a border soldier discovered the dead body of a man wearing only a bathing suit and a green turtleneck sweater. The dead man was Bernd Lehmann.[1]

Bernd Lehmann, a native of Berlin, had already come into conflict with the East German law as a young boy. A report of the East German police inspection of Berlin-Friedrichshain stated that "correctional measures of different sorts including placement in a special home are being taken."[2] Bernd Lehmann had to serve a number of prison sentences for theft, fraud and forgery.

He developed his first escape plan at the age of fifteen: He planned to drive to the inner-German border in a stolen car and force his way across the border with a weapon. According to an East German police report, however, before he could go through with his plan he was "held to account for preparing to leave East Germany illegally."[3] Stasi files do not indicate whether his conduct was criminally prosecuted or whether it was addressed in connection with his incarceration in the Berlin I Penal Institution that occurred that same year.[4] In the youth cell there, inmates discussed daring ways of escaping. Bernd Lehmann began working on a new escape plan. He planned to steal an airplane from the "Society for Sports and Technology" at the airfield near Falkenrehde in Havelland. A fellow-inmate had told him that the airfield was situated deep in a forest and guarded only by a single watchman. While in prison, he asked a fellow-prisoner to find a weapon for him.[5] Bernd Lehmann did not meet this acquaintance again until February 1968. After that the East German police and the Stasi were well-informed about Bernd Lehmann's escape plans. His supposed friend was an informant for the Stasi and passed on to the relevant offices all the information that he could get out of Bernd Lehmann during their meetings.[6]

Bernd Lehmann was absolutely determined to flee. After he was released from his last prison term for burglary in December 1967, he was assigned to a job that he did not like. The 18-year-old was employed as a lathe operator at the state-owned electric appliances plant in Treptow. He still had to pay compensation which left him little of his meager earnings. Bernd Lehmann was not allowed to change jobs. The staff of the internal affairs division warned him "to show some respect for the caring efforts of the state organ and to make his contribution to achieving a structured life."[7] The young man, however, dreamed of a future as a sports teacher. To reach this goal, he planned to acquire the qualification of a 10th grader at the adult education center. His mother, who had worked in East Berlin as a swimming teacher, served as his role model.[8] He evidently did not see any chance of realizing these plans in East Germany. He had difficulty getting rid of the habits that repeatedly led him into conflict with the East German laws. In May 1968 the Stasi informant reported that Bernd Lehmann had given up on his plans to escape with an airplane and only considered this as a last resort. He also regarded escaping across the border grounds to West Berlin to be too dangerous because the grounds appeared to be too strongly secured. Instead he figured that he was more likely to succeed across the inner-German border. One just had to know where the mine fields were and then make it into the five-kilometer zone unnoticed.[9]

It was perhaps a rash and spontaneous decision that ultimately led Bernd Lehmann to flee across the border to West Berlin. He had gotten into an argument with his family on the evening before he fled. He admitted to his mother that he had not shown up for work for days and was planning to start a job as a waiter. His mother worried that he would get into trouble again with the law if he were to handle large sums of money and expressed her concern to him. She threatened to report his skipping work to the internal affairs division. Bernd Lehmann tried unsuccessfully to change his mother's mind.

Bernd Lehmann left the apartment late that night. Evidently there was nothing keeping him in East Berlin anymore. Without further ado he entered the Spree and began swimming from Treptow Park towards Osthafen, where he probably hoped to cross the border to West Berlin near the Flutgraben channel. He did not know that barbed wire was installed in the water[10] and became caught in the underwater obstacles in the Osthafen Harbor about 20 meters away from the channel and drowned painfully.

Lydia Dollmann

1 See "Protokoll des PdVP Berlin/Abteilung K/Dez. III, 3.6.1968," in: BStU, MfS, AOP 8027/68, Bl. 53.

2 "Bericht der VP-Inspektion Berlin-Friedrichshain/Kommissariat I über den Verdacht der Vorbereitung der Republikflucht, 22.3.1968," in: BStU, MfS, AOP 8027/68, Bl. 34.

3 Ibid., Bl. 34.

4 See "Bericht [des MfS]/KD Friedrichshain, 5.3.1968," in: BStU, MfS, AOP 8027/68, Bl. 37.

5 See "Bericht der VP-Inspektion Friedrichshain/Kommissariat I über die nochmalige Befragung des IM "Heinz Schmidt", 5.3.1968," in: BStU, MfS, AOP 8027/68, Bl. 23–24.

6 See "Eröffnungsbericht der VP-Inspektion Friedrichshain/Kommissariat I zur KA "Flugzeug", 3.3.1968," in: BStU, MfS, AOP 8027/68, Bl. 16–17; "Information der VP-Inspektion Friedrichshain/Kommissariat I vom 1.3.1968," in: BStU, MfS, AOP 8027/68, Bl. 20–21.

7 "Bericht der VPI Friedrichshain/Kommissariat VII über eine Aussprache mit dem Haftentlassenen Bernd Lehmann, 28.12.1967," in: BStU, MfS, AOP 8027/68, Bl. 43–44.

8   See ibid., and "Kontrollbericht der VP-Inspektion Friedrichshain/VPR 83/Abteilung K über Bernd Lehmann, 31.1.1968," in: BStU, MfS, AOP 8027/68, Bl. 45 – 46.

9   See "Aktenvermerk [des MfS]/KD Friedrichshain, 18.5.1968," in: BStU, MfS, AOP 8027/68, Bl. 48.

10 On this and the following see "Schlussbericht [des MfS]/KD Friedrichshain, 5.7.1968," in: BStU, MfS, AOP 8027/68, Bl. 58 – 59.

Siegfried Krug

born on July 22, 1939

shot dead on July 6, 1968
on Pariser Platz in front of the Brandenburg Gate
on the sector border between
Berlin-Mitte and Berlin-Tiergarten

Siegfried Krug, born in Stettin on July 22, 1939, was expelled from his home during the war and fled to Erfurt with his parents and sister in February 1945. After finishing school he trained to become a high-voltage current electrician there. The East German secret police considered him to be oriented toward the West. It was said that he tore up his pioneer ID as a child. He was passionate about bike riding and had undertaken bike trips from Austria to Italy.[1] He fled to West Germany shortly before the Wall was built.[2] His married sister, who also fled East Germany, lived near Marburg. When his mother joined them a little later the family was reunited in the West.

Siegfried Krug was drawn to the big city and moved to Frankfurt am Main where he appeared to have been successful. Every time he visited his mother and sister in Marburg, he left an even better impression: He was both well-nourished and well-dressed. Sometimes he even came with his boss's Mercedes. He worked for a publishing company, he said, but did not tell his relatives that he was employed in Frankfurt as a "pusher," someone who sold newspaper subscriptions door to door.[3] He also had a girlfriend and was engaged to be married, an intention he soon announced publicly. The couple was planning to get married in Frankfurt in the summer of 1968.

In early July 1968 Siegfried Krug left his fiancée, telling her that he was going to Berlin. He would be back, he said, but he did not know when.[4] He told his sister that he did not want to get married and was going to disappear for a long time.[5] He flew from Frankfurt to West Berlin on July 5, 1968 and spent the night in the "Hotel am Bahnhof Zoo." The following evening, July 6, he took the S-Bahn to the Friedrichstrasse station. He passed the border crossing at 6:30 p.m. and an hour later got out of a taxi in front of the Brandenburg Gate, which was only a ten-minute walk from the train station.[6] It was not possible to get very close to the Brandenburg Gate from the East Berlin side. The border grounds began about 300 meters in front of it. A barrier and warning signs kept everyone back who did not want to be arrested for violating the border.

Carrying in his hand a white briefcase that contained, among other things,

1,100 West German marks in large bills,[7] Siegfried Krug walked along the left sidewalk of the Unter den Linden boulevard towards the border and ducked beneath the barrier. He continued to walk across Pariser Platz towards the Brandenburg Gate. He did not move quickly or slowly. He walked as if what he was doing was the most natural thing in the world. What motivated Siegfried Krug to engage in this precarious act when he could have returned to the west side of the city legally at any time? Where did he go with the taxi from the Friedrichstrasse train station before arriving at the Brandenburg Gate? Where he had obtained the money that he had with him and what was it for? All these questions remain a mystery to his relatives and are still unanswered today.[8]

He was the only civilian on the spacious plaza and was immediately noticed by border guards who called out to him: 'Can't you read? You aren't allowed to go any farther. This is the state border to East Germany.' It is reported that Siegfried Krug answered "I don't care. I want to go to the Brandenburg Gate."[9] In a walking pace he passed by the guard unperturbed and was warned again. When Krug also ignored this warning, the guard fired a warning shot in the air. Alarmed by the shots, two other border guards ran to the scene to stop Krug from continuing any farther. They blocked his way with their guns clearly in view. Siegfried Krug found himself surrounded by a triangle of guards. One guard stood behind him and two stood in front of him, yet he walked on.[10]

Pariser Platz lay in the middle of the divided city and was highly visible from many sides. From the point of view of the East German leaders, it was a very unsuitable setting for a border conflict since this kind of incident would do damage to the impression they strove to achieve: the city as a peaceful capital. The border guards stationed here had been instructed accordingly. One of the guards standing in front of Siegfried Krug warned the approaching man that he would make use of his weapon if he did not stop. "You guys aren't shooting,"[11] Krug answered calmly and continued along, slipping between the two guards who were standing in his way. Evidently, he was confident that he would not be hindered forcefully or shot at while walking from the East to the West at this very visible public site.

The guard standing behind him fired warning shots in the air. Krug stood still and then turned around. He had covered about 50 meters and had another 250 to go before reaching the Brandenburg Gate. After hesitating a moment, Siegfried Krug turned back in the direction that he had come – and walked directly towards the guard who had fired the last shots in the air. The guard called out that he should stop and give himself up for arrest or voluntarily go to the building headquarters that were located in the former Hotel Adlon. Krug did not respond and continued walking towards the guard. Krug was unarmed and outnumbered by the guards. But the guards had never had to deal with a situation like this before and were probably not prepared for it. The guard gripped the handle of his Kalashnikov and pointed it – with one hand – at Krug. When the young man with the white briefcase came within a few meters of him, the guard aimed his gun at Krug and fired. One burst of fire and all three shots hit Siegfried Krug in his stomach, chest and upper arm.[12] He was quickly removed from view and brought to the People's Police Hospital where he died an hour later.

The guard who fired the shots was, as usual, promoted and awarded a medal.[13] But some of the soldiers who knew what had taken place protested. A lieutenant colonel of the border troops concluded in his report that because the border guards had a great advantage over the perpetrator, the guard "should have acted differently."[14] The guard in question did not learn that he had killed Krug until he was interrogated by the police in 1992.[15] The Berlin district court convicted him of manslaughter and sentenced him to two years probation. The court decision stated that he had "simply shot and killed an obviously unarmed and defenseless intruder who was not dangerous."[16] A case against members of the East German secret police and East German military state prosecutor for perverting justice and serving as an accessory to the fact was dismissed by the Berlin public prosecutor's office in mid-1998 due to a lack of probable cause.[17]

In July 1968, the West Berlin Senate and the federal government of West Germany criticized the shooting: The West Berlin "Studio at the Barbed Wire" set up a poster at the Brandenburg Gate with a warning to the border guards: "Those who praise you today will disown you tomorrow!"[18]

The incident was observed on both sides of the Brandenburg Gate but nobody knew that the man who was killed had not been an East German fugitive but a citizen of West Germany – except the Stasi, of course. This provided them with an ideal opportunity to have the dead man cremated and then make him disappear. The Stasi made sure that any inquiries from the East German authorities concerning the dead man remained unanswered.[19] Consequently, Siegfried Krug was buried anonymously in Treptow in gravesite P 1 R – 229. Neither his fiancée in Frankfurt am Main nor his mother and sister in Marburg ever received information from the East German authorities about his fate.[20] Siegfried Krug was considered missing for years and his relatives continued to hope for his return.[21] They did not find out about his death until 1991.

Martin Ahrends / Udo Baron

1   See "Telegramm der KD Erfurt an die VfS Gross-Berlin/Abt. IX, 7.7.1968," in: BStU, MfS, AS 199/69, Bd. 2, Nr. 1, Bl. 131–132.

2   See "Information der VfS Gross-Berlin/Abt. IX, 7.7.1968," in: BStU, MfS, AS 199/69, Bd. 2, Nr. 1, Bl. 80.

3   See letter from Siegfried Krug's sister to the Berlin district court, 20.3.1993, in: StA Berlin, Az. 2 Js 92/90, Bd. 3, Bl. 157, 160.

4   See letter from Siegfried Krug's fiancé to his mother, 8.10.1968, in: StA Berlin, Az. 2 Js 92/90, Bd. 3, Bl. 163.

5   See "Anklageschrift der Staatsanwaltschaft bei dem Kammergericht Berlin vom 3.12.1992," in: StA Berlin, Az. 2 Js 92/90, Bd. 3, Bl. 12.

6   See "Information der VfS Gross-Berlin/Abt. IX, 7.7.1968", in: BStU, MfS, AS 199/69, Bd. 2, Nr. 1, Bl. 78–80.

7   See "Vermerk [der VfS Gross-Berlin/Abt. IX], 7.7.1968," in: BStU, MfS, AS 199/69, Bd. 2, Nr. 1, Bl. 157.

8   See conversation conducted by Udo Baron with Siegfried Krug's brother-in-law and nephew, 27.9.2007 and 30.9.2007.

9   "Urteil des Landgerichts Berlin vom 30.3.1993," in: StA Berlin, Az. 2 Js 92/90, Bd. 4, p. 16.

10 See ibid., p. 16.

11 Ibid., p. 16.

12 See ibid., pp. 17–18.

13 See "Verfügung der Staatsanwaltschaft Berlin, 12.2.1996," in: StA Berlin, Az. 28 Js 26/96, Bd. 1, Bl. 2.

14 "Anklageschrift der Staatsanwaltschaft bei dem Kammergericht Berlin vom 3.12.1992," in: StA Berlin, Az. 2 Js 92/90, Bd. 3, Bl. 18.

15 See "Urteil des Landgerichts Berlin vom 30.3.1993," in: StA Berlin, Az. 2 Js 92/90, Bd. 4, p. 22.

16 See ibid., p. 55.

17 See "Verfügung der Staatsanwaltschaft Berlin, 26.6.1998," in: StA Berlin, Az. 28 Js 26/96, Bd. 2, Bl. 306–314.

18 See *Die Welt,* 9.7.1968.

19 See "Vermerk [der VfS Gross-Berlin/Abt. IX], 10.7.1968," in: BStU, MfS, AS 199/69, Bd. 2, Nr. 1, Bl. 285.

20 See "Rechnung des Krematoriums Treptow, 8.7.1968," in: BStU, MfS, AS 199/69, Bd. 2, Nr. 1, Bl. 390.

21 See letter from Siegfried Krug's sister to the Berlin district court, 20.3.1993, in: StA Berlin, Az. 2 Js 92/90, Bd. 3, Bl. 158–16.

Horst Körner

born on July 12, 1947

shot dead on November 15, 1968

in the Babelsberg Palace Park

on the outer ring between

Potsdam-Babelsberg and Berlin-Zehlendorf

Horst Körner, born on July 12, 1947 in Wolfen, completed secondary school and then attended a vocational school of the state-owned film factory in Wolfen. He had qualified as a mechanic and had his high school degree in his pocket in the summer of 1967, but instead of serving in the military, something he may have wanted to avoid, he became a candidate for the Criminal Police division of the East German police district office in Bitterfield.[1] He was promoted within a year to sergeant.

One of his main responsibilities was to address property crime cases, but this did not interest him and, in early March 1968, he requested to be released from his police duty. At the same time he applied to an advanced college in Beichlingen where he hoped to study veterinary medicine. His superiors at the East German police probably convinced him that his application would be hopeless without their approval. In any case, under pressure, he withdrew his release request and instead agreed to pursue a "development plan" that would allow him to work towards the position of officer within the Criminal Police.

At the age of twenty he was a promising police officer as well as a member of the Communist Party. His superiors were pleased with him. In early September 1968 he was sent to participate in a seminar at a school for criminological basic training and further education run by the East German Ministry of the Interior in Potsdam. It seemed as if he had come to accept his situation. But a farewell letter he wrote to his parents, which he had with him during his escape, clearly revealed that the 21-year-old had by no means come to terms with his professional situation. "This may be my last greeting to you. I am almost at the border. [...] I have caused you much distress, but believe me, I stopped living a long time ago."[2]

On November 15, Horst Körner had to substitute for a comrade on short notice and guard the Potsdam criminal police school between 9 p.m. and 11 p.m. He had told his roommate about a quarrel that he had with his girlfriend a few days earlier and this may have been the deciding factor that led him to try to flee. It seemed he had been presented with an unexpected opportunity:[3] He asked to be stationed on the outer position and managed to leave his station armed and unnoticed. He reached the nearby train tracks of the Deutsche Reichsbahn, the East German railroad company, where he left his steel helmet, his munitions bag and an empty gun magazine. Then he walked along the tracks across the Havel Bridge to the Potsdam City train station. He probably traveled from there across Alt Nowawes through the Babelsberg Palace Park towards Klein Glienicke.

Here, at the spot across from the famous Glienicke Bridge, the border became very tricky. In order to get close to the death strip from here, Horst Körner would have had to pass the heavily guarded bridge that runs across the Teltow Canal into the enclave Klein Glienicke; alternatively, he could have entered the water of the canal or Havel River, which was very cold at this time of year. It is not clear whether Horst Körner thought he had an advantage here with special internal police knowledge of the area or whether the local border here was completely unfamiliar to him.

His absence was noticed at 11 p.m. when the next guard came to replace him and a group of guards began looking for him on the grounds of the police school. They thought he might have gotten on one of the Allied military trains that often stopped at a signal not far from the school.

At the same time Horst Körner was unexpectedly noticed by two border guards on control duty in a Trabant "Kübel." They saw him standing behind a tree in a police uniform and initially thought he was the police officer in charge of this section of the border. According to the investigation results of the East German secret police, when the border soldiers turned around and Horst Körner realized he had been seen, he opened fire on the army vehicle.[4] He fired continuously at the driver, Private Rolf Henniger, through the windshield. The driver was hit by a number of bullets in his chest and head, and collapsed behind the steering wheel. The other soldier in the passenger seat had jumped out of the vehicle and shot at Horst Körner with numerous bursts of ammunition from his machine pistol. He died immediately.

The border guards found an envelope in one of his uniform bags upon which he had written words of farewell to his parents. "I would rather die than let myself be caught."[5] Rolf Henniger, the man whose life he claimed with his own, happened to be a border soldier who had also been thinking about escaping.[6]

The next day the East German secret police searched Horst Körner's parents' apartment. They were told that their son had been shot and killed after he had killed another border soldier while trying to escape.[7] The East German secret police ordered that the body of Horst Körner be cremated. The funeral took place in the presence of his immediate family at the cemetery in Greppin near Bitterfeld.

The East German authorities kept the policeman's identity a secret from the public. The Communist Party-controlled media only spoke of an "armed agitator" and "murderer." Nothing else was revealed.[8] Rolf Henniger, the private whom he killed, was elevated to the status of a hero and buried amidst a major propaganda campaign in his hometown of Saalfeld in Thuringia.[9] The West Berlin mayor, Klaus Schütz, spoke of two victims of inhumanity that showed "that we must not forget how unnatural the Wall, barbed wire and the order to shoot fugitives is for Germany."[10]

In 1992 the case was opened by the Berlin public prosecutor's office against the guard who shot at Horst Körner, but was dismissed in 1994 because it was recognized that his use of firearms had been justified by self-defense.[11]

Martin Ahrends / Udo Baron / Hans-Hermann Hertle

1 On this and the following see "MfS / KD Potsdam / Abt. VII, versuchter Grenzdurchbruch unter Anwendung der Schusswaffe mit Todesfolge," in: BStU, MfS, AS 34 / 70, Bl. 34 – 38, here Bl. 34 / 35; see also: "Information des MfS / Hauptabteilung IX / 9, 17. 11. 1968," in: BStU, MfS, AS 34 / 70, Bl. 28 – 33, here Bl. 29.

2 Copy of farewell letter, in: BStU, MfS, AS 34 / 70, Bl. 37.

3 "Information des MfS / HA IX / 9, 17. 11. 1968," in: BStU, MfS, AS 34 / 70, Bl. 28 – 33, here Bl. 30.

4 "Schreiben des NVA-Stadtkommandanten an Erich Honecker, 16. 11. 1968," in: BArch, VA-07 / 8374, Bl. 60 – 64, here Bl. 61.

5 Copy of farewell letter, in: BStU, MfS, AS 34 / 70, Bl. 37.

6 According to testimony from Rolf Henniger's relatives to the Neuburg investigative police, 16. 1. 1969 and 28. 8. 1969, in: StA Berlin, Az. 27/2 Js 131/91, Bd. 1, Bl. 26, 44.

7 See "Schreiben der Polizeistation Wolfen an die ZERV vom 12. 11. 1992," in: StA Berlin, Az. 27/2 Js 131/91, Bd. 1, Bl. 165 – 166.

8 See *Neues Deutschland,* 17. 11. 1968.

9 See *Neues Deutschland,* 22. 11. 1968.

10 See *Berliner Morgenpost,* 17. 11. 1968; *Frankfurter Allgemeine Zeitung,* 18. 11. 1968.

11 See "Vermerk der Staatsanwaltschaft Berlin bei dem Kammergericht, 25. 1. 1994," in: StA Berlin, Az. 27/2 Js 131/91, Bd. 3, Bl. 114 – 117.

Johannes Lange

born on December 17, 1940

shot dead on April 9, 1969
near Fritz-Heckert-Strasse
on the sector border between
Berlin-Mitte and Berlin-Kreuzberg

Johannes Lange, born on December 17, 1940 in Dresden, trained to become a decorative painter. Before he got into trouble with the law, he had been a volunteer for the East German police. He fled to West Germany on March 31, 1959.[1] Two years later, after the Wall had been erected, he returned to East Germany. He explained to the East German authorities that he wanted to evade having to serve in the West German army, but they did not excuse his previous flight from East Germany. In 1962 an East German court sentenced him to a year in prison for evading the East German military registration by "illegally leaving the Republic" two years earlier. An East German secret police report claimed that after he was released from prison he was "expelled from his parents' house." He moved to Dresden to live with his girlfriend and her children.[2]

In the summer of 1968, when his relationship with his girlfriend, with whom he had a child, ended and his conscription into the National People's Army was imminent, Johannes Lange once again decided to flee. He tried to cross the Czechoslovakian border to West Germany in early August. The Czechoslovakian border guards arrested him and handed him over to East Germany, where he was given a year and three month suspended sentence in October. After that a general travel ban was imposed on him. He worked as an unskilled laborer for a building combine in Dresden and lived in the company's bachelor dormitory. He was seen there for the last time on March 30, 1969.

Ten days later, on April 9, 1969, border soldiers observed Johannes Lange as he inspected the border grounds to West Berlin at the corner of Adalbertstrasse and Fritz-Heckert-Strasse near the Berlin-Mitte Hospital and then backtracked.[3] It was almost dark when he returned at around 10 p.m. He climbed over the interior fence and the anti-tank obstacles unnoticed, but when he climbed over the signal fence he triggered an alarm. Colored flares shot off, helping the border guards on the watchtower to identify the location of the fugitive.

Shots were fired at him from two watchtowers and duty replacements, who had just arrived on duty, also fired at the fugitive. Eight border soldiers fired a total of 148 shots at Johannes Lange. Right before he reached the last obstacle, the three-and-a-half-meter-high concrete wall, he was hit by five bullets in the back of his head, neck and thigh and died immediately.

The guards rushed to the site and quickly dragged the dead man behind one of the watchtowers so people on the West Berlin side could not see anything. A report from a Stasi informant revealed that a paramedic from the nearby hospital in Mitte had wanted to administer first aid but was "very gruffly sent away."[4] A few days later the guards involved were awarded medals and promoted. Each of three soldiers received a wristwatch as a "gift." Almost 30 years later, one of the guards was tried by the Berlin district court for attempted manslaughter and sentenced as a youth to a year and three months on probation. The court was unable to prove that the other guards had aimed their shots at Johannes Lange. The man who was convicted had been 19 years old at the time of the shooting. The incident had deeply affected him psychologically, leading him to seek professional medical care. Later, in 1985, when he was frustrated by the lack of free speech, the strong state presence in their lives and the poor living conditions in East Germany, he and his wife applied for an exit visa to leave the country. He was allowed to move to the West with his family in May 1989.[5]

Alarmed by the sounds of bullets, a number of people on the east and west sides observed the shooting that night. Patients in a nearby hospital in Berlin-Mitte insulted the border guards as "scallywags, criminals and murderers."[6] The East German secret police later tried to find out which patients "had thrown insults from the hospital."[7] A number of bullets hit both sides of the curved border there. In the East Berlin hospital in Mitte, a window shattered and a bullet landed on a table in the nurses' staff room. The West Berlin Bethanien Hospital in the Kreuzberg district was also hit and windows of nearby apartments were shattered. The East German secret police registered all the bullet shots and concluded that "bodily injury did not occur during the entire action."[8]

One day after the fatal shots that killed Johannes Lange were fired, West Berliners set up a wooden cross and laid a wreath at the site. The inscription read: "We free citizens grieve for you. You will not be forgotten."[9] The "Studio at the Barbed Wire" put up signs in clear view of the border guards that read: "Soldier, you are alone in your guilt." A citizen of West Germany filed charges of murder against the border guards with the East German military state prosecution. He did not expect to have any success with it he told the Central Registry Office in Salzgitter, but the East German leaders should at least be made aware of "how these acts are regarded in the Federal Republic."[10] The shooting was condemned by the federal government and the Berlin Senate and the three Allied city commanders criticized "this case of merciless cruelty and disrespect for human life."[11]

Johannes Lange's body was cremated in the Baumschulenweg Crematorium on April 15, 1968 and buried in his father's urn site a short time later at the Neustädtische Cemetery in Dresden.[12]

Udo Baron

1 See "Abschlussbericht der VfS Gross-Berlin/Abt. IX, Berlin, 2.5.1969," in: BStU, MfS, AS 754/70, Bd. 6, Nr. 4, Bl. 81–86.

2 Ibid., Bl. 83.

3 On this and the following see "Urteil des Landgerichts Berlin vom 1.12.1998," in: StA Berlin, Az. 27 Js 80/92, Protokoll- und Urteilsband, Bl. 64 a – 64 o.

4 "Information der VfS Gross-Berlin/Abt. VII/2, 2.5.1969," in: BStU, MfS, AS 754/70, Bd. 6, Nr. 4, Bl. 8.

5 See "Urteil des Landgerichts Berlin vom 1.12.1998," in: StA Berlin, Az. 27 Js 80/92, Protokoll- und Urteilsband, Bl. 64 a – 64 o.

6 "Einzel-Information Nr. 355/69 des MfS/ZAIG über einen verhinderten Grenzdurchbruch mit tödlichem Ausgang für den Grenzverletzer im Bereich der Staatsgrenze Berlin-Mitte, Abschnitt Fritz-Heckert-Strasse, am 9.4.1969, 11.4.1969," in: BStU, MfS, ZAIG Nr. 1779, Bl. 1– 4, here Bl. 2.

7 "Massnahmeplan des MfS, 10.4.1969," in: BStU, MfS, AS 754/70, Bd. 6, Nr. 4, Bl. 45.

8 "Bericht des MfS/HA I/Abwehr/Unterabteilung 1. Grenzbrigade, 10.4.1969," in: BStU, MfS, AS 754/70, Bd. 6, Nr. 4, Bl. 33 – 36, here Bl. 36.

9 See "Telegramm der West-Berliner Polizei vom 11.4.1969," in: StA Berlin, Az. 27 Js 80/92, Bd.3, Bl. 78; *BZ*, 11.4.1969.

10 See "Schreiben von Dieter W. an die DDR-Militärstaatsanwaltschaft und die Zentrale Erfassungsstelle in Salzgitter, 12.4.1969," in: StA Berlin, Az. 27 Js 80/92, Bd. 3, Bl. 3 and 4.

11 *Berliner Morgenpost,* 10.4.1969.

12 See "Abschlussbericht der VfS Gross-Berlin/Abt. IX, Berlin, 2.5.1969," in: BStU, MfS, AS 754/70, Bd. 6, Nr. 4, Bl. 84.

Klaus-Jürgen Kluge

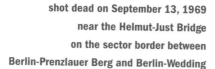

born on July 25, 1948

shot dead on September 13, 1969
near the Helmut-Just Bridge
on the sector border between
Berlin-Prenzlauer Berg and Berlin-Wedding

Klaus-Jürgen Kluge, born on July 25, 1948 in Schönow near Bernau, attended the secondary school in his hometown and graduated following the tenth grade. He successfully completed an apprenticeship as a pattern maker in spring 1969.[1]

The older he became, the more critical he was of East Germany. A Stasi informant reported that Klaus-Jürgen Kluge had often commented "negatively about the lack of provisions" in East Germany and compared "everything with the 'good development' in West Germany."[2] Thus, the Stasi considered him one of those people who did not fit in with the image of the "new people" living in "real-life socialism": "Klaus Jürgen is not in a party. He is not engaged in organizations. His attitude towards our state is negative. [...] His physical appearance, long hair, pants with wide bell-bottoms and fly appear decadent."[3] In November 1969, just after an acquaintance of Klaus-Jürgen Kluge had successfully fled to the West,[4] he was supposed to begin his service in the detested NVA. At this point, at the very latest, he seemed to believe his only way out was to escape to West Berlin.

Klaus-Jürgen Kluge left his parents' house in the afternoon of September 13, 1969. He said he was going to attend a dance.[5] In truth, however, he drove to East Berlin where, at around 8:40 p.m., he entered the border grounds in the former S-Bahn-Gleisdreieck, south of the border crossing at Bornholmer Strasse.[6] Near the Helmut-Just Bridge, he was able to get past the first border facilities unnoticed, but when he climbed over the signal fence he triggered an alarm.[7] In response a border soldier left his watchtower, but he intentionally moved slowly: He feared having to shoot at somebody and secretly hoped that an animal had set off the alarm as had often happened in the past. Having reached the bottom of the tower, the border soldier fired a flare in the air that temporarily blinded him. The guard leader, who was still in the tower, saw Klaus-Jürgen Kluge at the Wall. When the guard down below did not react to his order to arrest the fugitive, he stormed down from the tower. He ran to the Wall and, without calling out or firing a warning shot and while still running, he fired two shots from the hip from a distance of about 60 meters directly at the fugitive, who had already flung his upper body over the Wall.[8] Two bullets hit him in the chest and head causing Klaus-Jürgen Kluge to fall down. He died from his wounds within minutes.

His body was brought to the observation tower a short time later and was taken from there to the People's Police Hospital in Berlin-Mitte. To the satisfaction of the East German secret police, by the time the local and French military police arrived on the West Berlin side to illuminate the area and take pictures, the body had already been removed. The border guards involved in the shooting were awarded medals and bonuses by the regiment commander the following day.[9] In 1997, in unified Germany, the man who killed Klaus-Jürgen Kluge was tried by the Berlin district court and convicted as a youth to a one-year-and-four-month suspended sentence. The guard under his supervision was acquitted.[10] The gunman's supervisors also stood trial two years later for accessory to manslaughter. The former regiment commander was sentenced to a year and three months in prison and the man who had served as chief of staff was sentenced to a year in prison.[11]

Klaus-Jürgen Kluge's parents were not informed by the East German secret police of their son's death until his body had been cremated. The Stasi demanded that they tell their relatives and friends that their son died in an accident in Berlin.[12] The urn with Klaus-Jürgen Kluge's ashes was buried in the cemetery in Schönow under the surveillance of the East German secret police on October 8, 1969.[13]

Udo Baron

1 See "Information des MfS/HA IX/9 über einen Grenzdurchbruch am 13.9.1969, 16.9.1969," in: BStU, MfS, AS 754/70, Bd. 5, Nr. 1, Bl. 14.
2 "Abschrift der mündlichen Einschätzung von Klaus Kluge durch den IM "Karl Martin", 16.9.1969," in: BStU, MfS, AS 754/70, Bd. 5, Nr. 1, Bl. 105.
3 Ibid.
4 See "Ermittlungsbericht der MfS/KD Bernau über Klaus-Jürgen Kluge, 15.9.1969," in: BStU, MfS, AS 754/70, Bd. 5, Nr. 1, Bl. 102.
5 See "Information der VfS Gross-Berlin/Abt. IX über Klaus-Jürgen Kluge, 23.9.1969," in: BStU, MfS, AS 754/70, Bd. 5, Nr. 1, Bl. 169.
6 See "Bericht der VfS Gross-Berlin/Abt. IX, 14.9.1969," in: BStU, MfS, AS 754/70, Bd. 5, Nr. 1, Bl. 10.
7 See "Information der VfS Gross-Berlin/Abt. IX über Klaus-Jürgen Kluge, 23.9.1969," in: BStU, MfS, AS 754/70, Bd. 5, Nr. 1, Bl. 165.
8 See "Urteil des Landgerichts Berlin vom 7.11.1997," in: StA Berlin, Az. 27 Js 94/90, Bd. 2, Bl. 8–9.
9 See ibid., Bl. 10–11.
10 See ibid., Bl. 1–2.
11 See "Urteil des Landgerichts Berlin vom 12.7.1999," in: StA Berlin, Az. 27 Js 80/97 Bd. 2, Bl. 95–96.
12 See "Handschriftliche Erklärung der Eltern von Klaus-Jürgen Kluge, 24.9.1969," in: BStU, MfS, AS 754/70, Bd. 5, Nr. 1, Bl. 156.
13 See "Schreiben der [MfS]Abt. XIV über eingeleitete Massnahmen bei der Urnenfeier vom 6.10.1969," in: BStU, MfS, AS 754/70, Bd. 5, Nr. 1, Bl. 175; "Rechnung des Städtischen Bestattungswesens, 17.9.1969," in: Ibid., Bl. 186.

Leo Lis

born on May 10, 1924

shot dead on September 20, 1969
near the Nordbahnhof station
on the sector border between
Berlin-Mitte and Berlin-Wedding

Leo Lis was 45 years old when he was shot and killed while trying to escape in Berlin-Mitte on September 20, 1969. Born on May 10, 1924 in Beuthen, Upper Silesia, today Bytom in Poland, he lived with his wife and seven children in Hennersdorf in Saxony. He worked there as a dairy milker for an agricultural production cooperative (LPG).[1] It is not known what led him to want to flee East Germany.

Leo Lis left his family and took a train to East Berlin on September 19, 1969. One day later, at about 8 p.m. on September 20, 1969, he entered the border area near the Nordbahnhof station. He managed to get around a dog run, but when he climbed beneath a signal fence, he set off an alarm. A border guard descended the tower to arrest him, but Leo Lis had already moved beyond the signal fence and the guard was unable to find him in the dark. It appears that the guards on the two adjacent towers could see more because "wild shooting" erupted from the towers, leading the guard on the border strip to run for cover under an overturned lorry.[2] One of the guards on the tower also had to take cover when he was mistakenly fired at. "Cease fire!" a border guard cried, but his order went unheard.[3] The other guards continued to shoot until the fugitive, who had meanwhile passed the patrol road, security strip and anti-tank obstacles, remained motionless on the ground.[4] Leo Lis was critically injured in the chest. A paramedic declared him dead before he was transported from the border strip.[5]

The border guards fired a total of 78 shots at him. One bullet hit the window of an apartment building on the West Berlin side, just barely missing a retired couple that was sitting near it, watching television. The senior citizens later filed charges against unknown individuals for "damage to property and unauthorized possession of a weapon."[6]

A number of residents on both the east and west side heard the shots and watched from their windows. Cries of "murderer" and "you are shooting your own countrymen" were hurled at the guards.[7] On September 21, 1969, as an act of protest against the shots fired at the fugitive, West Berlin teenagers threw stones onto the border grounds with the words "communist pigs" and "dirty swine" written on them.[8] The West Berlin and West German press reported in detail on the events and the reaction of the French city commander, who fiercely condemned the border shooting at the sector border to Wedding and viewed it "as another example of disrespect for human dignity."[9]

The border soldiers involved were awarded the "Medal for Exemplary Service at the Border."[10] More than thirty years later, when they had to answer for their actions before a court, the Berlin public prosecutor accepted that they had acted in the belief that the orders they had followed were lawful and the case was dismissed in early April 1997.[11]

Leo Lis' wife was not notified of her husband's death until September 27, 1969, after his body had already been cremated. An East German secret police agent, who introduced himself as an employee of the state prosecutor's office, informed her that her "husband was fatally injured while trying to leave East Germany illegally."[12] Without further explanation, she was handed the death certificate and a few personal possessions that Leo Lis had had on him when he fled.

She was also required to agree in writing to inviting only the immediate family to attend the funeral service and to refrain from printing an obituary.[13] The Lis family's mail was examined by the East German secret police regularly thereafter and Stasi informants were asked to record the mood and reaction of the Hennersdorf residents to the incident.[14]

Leo Lis' ashes were buried in an urn in Kamenz on October 29, 1969. The funeral was attended by his widow and children and by Leo Lis' stepmother, who traveled from West Germany, as well as his sister and a small delegation from his LPG. The East German secret police noted with satisfaction that no "negative discussion" had taken place.[15]

Udo Baron

1 See "Information der VfS Gross-Berlin/Abt. IX über den vom DDR-Bürger Leo Lis am 20.9.1969 versuchten Grenzdurchbruch, 21.9.1969," in: BStU, MfS, AS 754/70, Bd. 7, Nr. 1, Bl. 6.

2 See "Vermerk der Staatsanwaltschaft Berlin über die Einstellung des Verfahrens gegen die ehemaligen Grenzposten, 3.6.1997," in: StA Berlin, Az. 27 Js 70/90, Bd. 2, Bl. 272.

3 Ibid., Bl. 272.

4 See ibid., Bl. 270–279.

5 See "Information der VfS Gross-Berlin/Abt. IX über den vom DDR-Bürger Leo Lis am 20.9.1969 versuchten Grenzdurchbruch, 21.9.1969," in: BStU, MfS, AS 754/70, Bd. 7, Nr. 1, Bl. 7.

6 "Strafanzeige gegen Unbekannt wegen Sachbeschädigung und unbefugtem Waffenbesitz bei der West-Berliner Polizei, 20.9.1969," in: StA Berlin, Az. 27 Js 70/90, Bd. 1, Bl. 57.

7 "Bericht des MfS/HA I/SKB Abwehr/UA 1. Grenzbrigade/Op.-Gruppe GR 33 über einen versuchten und mit der Schusswaffenanwendung verhinderten Grenzdurchbruch DDR-WB einer männlichen Person am 20.9.69 im Grenzabschnitt Nordbahnhof, 20.9.1969," in: BStU, MfS, AS 754/70, Bd. 7, Nr. 1, Bl. 3.

8 See ibid.

9 "Flüchtling wurde brutal niedergeschossen," in: *Die Welt,* 22.9.1969; "An der Mauer niedergeschossen," in: *Berliner Morgenpost,* 21.9.1969; "Neuer Beweis von Menschenverachtung," in: *BZ,* 22.9.1969.

10 See "Vermerk der Staatsanwaltschaft Berlin über die Einstellung des Verfahrens gegen die ehemaligen Grenzposten vom 3.6.1997," in: StA Berlin, Az. 27 Js 70/90, Bd. 2, Bl. 271.

11 See ibid., Bl. 281.

12 "Schreiben der BVfS Dresden/KD Kamenz über die Benachrichtigung der Frau Lis vom Tod ihres Mannes an die BVfS Dresden/Leiter der Abt. IX, 29.9.1969," in: BStU, MfS, AS 754/70, Bd. 7, Nr. 1, Bl. 53.

13 See BStU, MfS, AS 754/70, Bd. 7, Nr. 1, Bl. 55.

14 "Vermerk der VfS Gross-Berlin/Abt. IX über die Sprachregelung gegenüber der Ehefrau von Leo Lis, 26.9.1969," in: BStU, MfS, AS 754/70, Bd. 7, Nr. 1, Bl. 51.

15 "Aktenvermerk des MfS/KD Kamenz über die Urnenbeisetzung von Leo Lis, 10.11.1969," in: BStU, MfS, AS 754/70, Bd. 7, Nr. 1, Bl. 81.

Christel Wehage

born on December 15, 1946

Eckhard Wehage

born on July 8, 1948

committed suicide on March 10, 1970
after a failed hijacking attempt
at the East Berlin-Schönefeld airport

Eckhard Wehage was born on July 8, 1948 in Berssel. When he was fifteen, he tried to flee to the West with a friend in a boat across the Baltic Sea, but the boys aroused suspicion before they had even cast off. They were arrested by the East German police on May 10, 1963 and sent back to their parents.

The same year, on August 21, Eckhard Wehage made a second attempt to leave East Germany, this time alone. His plan was to take a train to Czechoslovakia and to flee from there to West Germany. But this attempt also failed and he was arrested in Adorf, Vogtland. The first time he was arrested, the East German authorities had taken his young age into account and had refrained from opening an investigation. Following his second attempt, however, charges were filed against him for "fleeing from the republic." The court responsible for juvenile cases sentenced Eckhard Wehage, age 16, to eight months probation on October 18, 1963.[1] A "protective chaperone" was also assigned because of "considerable errors in his upbringing by his parents."[2] The court explained that he should realize that "it is in his own interest that the worker and peasant state not allow him to cross over from a socialist state to an exploiter state."[3]

After this Eckhard Wehage seemed to have accepted the conditions in East Germany. By 1967 he had joined the East German Marines and enlisted for ten years as a professional soldier. He graduated from the non-commissioned officer school in Stralsund, after which he was assigned to a de-mining boat as chief petty officer.[4]

It was during this time that he met Christel Zinke, born on December 15, 1946 in Wolmirstedt. She worked as a psychotherapist in her hometown's district hospital.[5] They soon married and tried to start a family, but were confronted with the restrictions and regimentation of adult life in East Germany: Residents of East Germany were unable to choose their own place of work or residency. The state delegated where graduates worked and lived. For years the couple did everything to acquire an apartment together in an area where they both could work. In the farewell letters that they wrote to their parents, they explained in detail their reasons for their joint escape attempt. The apartment dilemma played a central role in their justification: If they had had children then, after waiting for an indefinite period of time, they might have been "provided" with common living quarters. "But we cannot afford to have children under the current uncertain circumstances. That would only make the dilemma greater."[6]

The Wehages did not want to spend their young lives waiting. In spring 1970, when their hopes of being allocated an apartment together were dashed, the couple resolved to flee to West Germany by hijacking an airplane. Eckhard Wehage was able to get into the armory of his unit and remove two pistols and ammunition before he took off on a short leave from duty. He met his wife in East Berlin. The couple booked two seats on a scheduled flight from East Berlin to Dresden on March 9, 1970.[7] When the flight was cancelled they tried again. They purchased two tickets on a flight from East Berlin to Leipzig that was scheduled to depart the following day. They spent the night in the hotel at the Schönefeld airport. Their parents received the farewell letters that they had written to them from there.[8] In his letter, Eckhard Wehage acknowledged the possible consequences of a third escape attempt: "All we want is to live our own lives the way we would like. [...] Should our plan fail, Christel and I are going to depart this life. [...] Death is then the best solution."[9]

On the morning of March 10, 1970, just before 8 o'clock, the young couple and 15 other passengers boarded the AN-24 airplane to Leipzig run by the East German airline, Interflug. Shortly after take-off, Eckhard Wehage held his pistol in front of him and ordered the stewardess to establish contact with the pilots and tell them to fly to an airport in Hanover. The stewardess passed the information on to the cockpit using the secret code for an emergency. When there was no response from the cockpit, Eckhard Wehage shot at the lock on the door until it opened. But another door still blocked his entry to the cockpit and despite all his efforts, it could not be opened. While the stewardess tried to convince the desperate couple that a lack of fuel made it necessary to land in Berlin-Tempelhof instead of Hanover, the crew in the cockpit was able to watch through a peep hole and turn the plane back.

Seconds before the plane landed a passenger called out in surprise that they were back in Schönefeld. When Christel and Eckhard Wehage looked out the window, they realized that their escape attempt had failed. The couple went back to their seats while the plane landed. Then the shots were fired. Christel and Eckhard Wehage had killed themselves.[10] Their bodies were cremated in East Berlin and later buried at a cemetery in Magdeburg in the presence of their close family circle.[11]

After this the parents of the victims became the focus of a secret police investigation. A "counter measure plan" from March 15, 1970 stated that "operative techniques in the apartments and mail inspections are to be engaged in."[12] Their apartments were searched and "bugged," they were kept under surveillance during their daily activities, and they were interrogated with regard to possible "complicity." The secret police was able to "convince" both sets of parents to cooperate in disguising the true circumstances of their children's death. Relatives, friends and work colleagues were told that Eckhard and Christel Wehage had been driving in a company car on their way to Rostock where they were going to look at an apartment when they crashed into a tree and died. "In response to any possible curious inquiries, both couples will explain that the accident was the result of driving at too high a speed along icy roads and that there were not any witnesses."[13] Stasi informants were also told to record and influence the mood of the people in the area where the parents lived.[14]

Despite all the efforts on behalf of the Stasi to conceal the truth, rumors connecting the death of the two young Wehages to the failed hijacking of an airplane in Berlin-Schönefeld could not be silenced.[15]

During an elaborate celebration on March 26, 1970, the crew of the hijacked Interflug plane was granted the NVA Gold Medal of Merit, awarded to them personally by Stasi minister Erich Mielke. The minister also gave the pilot a stereo radio, the co-pilot a tape recorder, the mechanic a rug and the stewardess a knitting machine.[16]

A quarter of a century later a former citizen of East Germany contacted the Central Investigating Agency for Governmental and Party Crimes and reported on the Wehage's fatal escape attempt. In response, the public prosecutor's office opened an investigation in October 1996. But the case was dismissed in June 1997 because no evidence of criminal action on the part of the East German authorities could be found. Charges against Christel and Eckhard Wehage for any crime they may have committed were made gratuitous by their deaths.[17]

Martin Ahrends / Udo Baron

1 See "Urteil des Kreisgerichts Halberstadt gegen Eckhard Wehage vom 21. Oktober 1963," in: BStU, MfS, HA IX Nr. 10389, Bl. 230–233.

2 Ibid., Bl. 234.

3 Ibid.

4 See "Protokoll der Zeugenvernehmung des Vorgesetzten von Eckhard Wehage bei der DDR-Volksmarine durch das MfS, Wolgast, 13.3.1970," in: BStU, MfS, HA IX Nr. 10388, Bl. 204.

5 See "Information des MfS/HA IX, 10.3.1970," in: BStU, MfS, HA XIX Nr. 1956, Bl. 8.

6 Handwritten farewell letter from Christel Wehage to her parents, undated [postmark 10.3.1970], in: BStU, MfS, HA IX Nr. 10389, Bl. 221.

7 See "Information des MfS/HA IX, 10.3.1970," in: BStU, MfS, HA XIX Nr. 1956, Bl. 11.

8 Ibid.

9 Handwritten farewell letter from Eckhard Wehage to his parents, undated [postmark 10.3.1970], in: BStU, MfS, HA IX Nr. 10389, Bl. 83–85.

10 See "Information des MfS/HA IX, 10.3.1970," in: BStU, MfS, HA XIX Nr. 1956, Bl. 8–10; handwritten transcript of questioning of two passengers by the MfS, 10.3.1970, in: BStU, MfS, HA IX Nr. 10388, Bl. 335–339.

11 See "IM-Bericht des MfS/Kreisdienststelle Wolmirstedt, 17.4.1970," in: BStU, MfS, HA IX Nr. 10391, Bl. 143–145.

12 "Massnahmeplan des MfS/HA IX zur weiteren Aufklärung der versuchten Flugzeugentführung vom 10.3.1970, 16.3.1970," in: BStU, MfS, HA IX Nr. 10387, Bl. 156.

13 "Bericht über das Gespräch eines Militärstaatsanwalts und eines MfS-Mitarbeiters mit den Eltern von Christel und Eckhard Wehage," in: BStU, MfS, HA IX Nr. 10391, Bl. 168.

14 See "Massnahmeplan des MfS/HA IX zur weiteren Aufklärung der versuchten Flugzeugentführung vom 10.3. 1970, 16.3.1970," in: BStU, MfS, HA IX Nr. 10387, Bl. 156.

15 See "IM-Bericht des MfS/Kreisdienststelle Wolmirstedt, 17.4.1970," in: BStU, MfS, HA IX Nr. 10391, Bl. 143–145.

16 See "Festveranstaltung anlässlich der Auszeichnung von Mitarbeitern der Interflug am 26.3.1970 im Klub der Interflug," in: BStU, MfS, HA XIX Nr. 1956, Bl. 123–127.

17 See "Verfügung der Staatsanwaltschaft II bei dem Landgericht Berlin, 4.6.1997," in: StA Berlin, Az. 27 Js 175/96, Bd. 1, Bl. 66–68.

Heinz Müller

born on May 16, 1943

shot dead on June 19, 1970
near the Schilling Bridge
at the sector border between
Berlin-Kreuzberg and Berlin-Friedrichshain

Heinz Müller was born on May 16, 1943 in Rostock. He was raised by foster parents in Medebach in Sauerland, West Germany. It has not been possible to reconstruct when and how he came to the west zone or West Germany, but once there, he trained to become a commercial clerk and after completing his training found a temporary position in a department store in West Berlin. His foster father later told the West Berlin police that his son enjoyed spending his weekends in East Berlin. He visited acquaintances there and often dined in restaurants.[1]

On June 18, 1970, Heinz Müller spent the afternoon hours on a viewing platform in front of the Wall in the Kreuzberg district. Residents on the East Berlin side in the Friedrichshain district watched as he stood with a bottle in his hand and gesticulated demonstratively towards East Berlin. No one could understand the words he called out.[2] The East German border soldiers registered the "agitator." In the middle of the night, at around 1:50 a.m., Müller, intoxicated, either fell or climbed over the Berlin Wall – or he may have been pushed by someone. He probably did not realize what had happened until he found himself in the glaring light of the security grounds. Disoriented, he began walking around within the border grounds. A border guard in a nearby watchtower on the Schilling Bridge noticed him and fired two shots in his direction from a distance of 200 meters. Heinz Müller was hit in the hip and collapsed. He cried out in agonizing pain for help. When the border soldiers approached him, he screamed: "You swine!" Witnesses watching the incident from their nearby apartments in East Berlin called out to the border guards: "You murderers! Help him!"[3]

When an officer arrived, Heinz Müller was dragged to a nearby bunker and given first aid. Another hour passed before he was taken to the People's Police Hospital in an army vehicle. Heinz Müller died from his injuries at 4:50 a.m.[4]

His body was cremated on July 31, 1970 in Berlin's Baumschulenweg Crematorium and the urn was buried in the Baumschulenweg Cemetery. The man who fired the shots was soon commended for his actions and awarded the Border Troop Badge of Merit. The other border guards involved received gifts and extra vacation time. They were not told that Heinz Müller had died.[5]

The Berlin public prosecutor's office brought charges against the gunman in November 1991. The Berlin district court sentenced him as a young offender to a two-year prison sentence that was commuted to probation.[6] The verdict came into force on April 19, 1994, after the Federal Court of Justice rejected the appeal.

At the time of the shooting, nobody in West Berlin knew that Heinz Müller had died in June 1970. When he did not show up for work three days in a row, he was fired.[7] A colleague reported him missing on July 3, which led the West Berlin police to have firemen force open the door to Heinz Müller's apartment, where all they found was a tidy room.[8]

Heinz Müller's foster parents began to search for him but he remained missing without a trace. Over the following weeks and months, his foster father repeatedly inquired with the police on the progress of the investigation. He feared that his foster son might have been arrested in East Berlin.[9] But the West Berlin police could not find out anything because the East German authorities remained silent on the matter. Inquiries suggesting that Heinz Müller may have shown up in East Berlin were refuted by authorities there.[10] Consequently, no information about the real reasons for his absence could be attained. Only after German reunification did it become known what really happened to Heinz Müller on the night of June 1970.[11]

The death certificate issued by East Germany for Heinz Müller listed an East German address.[12] The secret police presumably created a "legend," a false identity for the victim, and pretended that he was a citizen of East Germany so that the inquiries from the West would be fruitless.[13]

Udo Baron

1 See "Handschriftliches Schreiben des Pflegevaters von Heinz Müller an die West-Berliner Polizei, 30.10.1970," in: StA Berlin, Az. 2 Js 97/90, Beistück, n. pag.

2 On the course of events see "Urteil des Landgerichts Berlin vom 28.10.1992," in: StA Berlin, Az. 2 Js 97/90, Bd. 2, Bl. 183 a ff. See also "Niederschrift der Zeugenvernehmung von einer Anwohnerin, die den Vorfall beobachtet hat, durch die Berliner Polizei, 12.7.1991," in: StA Berlin, Az. 2 Js 97/90, Bd. 1, Bl. 93–94; "Niederschrift der Zeugenvernehmung von einer Anwohnerin, die den Vorfall beobachtet hat, durch die Berliner Polizei, 4.7.1991," in: Ibid., Bl. 90–91.

3 "Urteil des Landgerichts Berlin vom 28.10.1992," in: StA Berlin, Az. 2 Js 97/90, Bd. 2, Bl. 183 q.

4 See "Bericht des MfS/HA I/Grenzkommando Berlin, Aufklärung/UA-Vorfeld über die Festnahme eines Grenzverletzers Westberlin/DDR in Abschnitt des Grenzregiments 35, 19.6.1970," in: BStU, MfS, HA I Nr. 3974, Bl. 7–9.

5 See "Urteil des Landgerichts Berlin vom 28.10.1992," in: StA Berlin, Az. 2 Js 97/90, Bd. 2, Bl. 183 s–183 t.

6 See ibid., Bl. 183 a–183 b.

7 See "Bericht der West-Berliner Polizei über Heinz Müller, 26.8.1970," in: StA Berlin, Az. 2 Js 97/90, Beistück, n. pag.

8 See "Bericht der West-Berliner Polizei über angeblich vermisste männliche Person, 3.7.1970," in: Ibid., n. pag.

9 See "Handschriftliches Schreiben des Pflegevaters von Heinz Müller an die West-Berliner Polizei, 30.10.1970," in: Ibid.

10 See "Bericht der West-Berliner Polizei über den Verbleib von Heinz Müller, 8.7.1970," in: Ibid.

11 See "Vermerk der Berliner Polizei über die Ermittlung zur Einäscherung und Grabstätte von Heinz Müller, 19.7.1991," in: StA Berlin, Az. 2 Js 97/90, Beistück, n. pag.

12 See "Totenschein von Heinz Müller, 22.6.1970," in: Ibid.

13 See "Bericht der VfS Gross-Berlin/Abt. IX über die Anwendung der Schusswaffe bei einem Grenzdurchbruch von Westberlin in die Hauptstadt der DDR, 19.6.1970," in: BStU, MfS, AS 288/74, Bd. 5, Bl. 458–460.

Willi Born

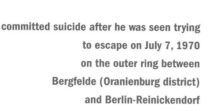

born on July 19, 1950

committed suicide after he was seen trying
to escape on July 7, 1970
on the outer ring between
Bergfelde (Oranienburg district)
and Berlin-Reinickendorf

Willi Born, who had six younger siblings, spent his early childhood years in Klein-Marzehns in the Belzig district.[1] His mother passed away when he was still young and when he was 13 he lived for a time in a children's home in the Königswusterhausen district. Later he returned to live with his father, who had remarried. The large family found a new home in Lindow in the Mark Brandenburg region.

Willi Born completed an apprenticeship as a farm machine mechanic and then worked as a tractor operator in the local agricultural production cooperative (LPG) in Lindow where his father also worked.

In 1969 Willi Born married. The young couple moved a short time later to Velten, a northern suburb of Berlin.[2] But they had only a short time to build a life together because the 19-year-old had to serve his military duty in the armored rifle division in Oranienburg, a troop unit of the National People's Army's 1st Armored Rifle Division of Potsdam.[3] In the early morning hours of July 7, 1970, three weeks before his 20th birthday, Willi Born left his unit unnoticed. By the time his absence from the barracks was noticed, he had entered the border territory near Bergfelde, north of Berlin, in broad daylight. A search for Willi Born was ordered and all the border guards were told to be on special alert. At around 10:30 in the morning a guard noticed the fugitive and fired a warning shot. Hunted by a number of border soldiers, Willi Born took cover in a patch of woods. He was found there, but before a guard could arrest him, Willi Born fired a bullet through his own head. He died immediately.[4]

Willi Born's family buried him on the cemetery in Lindow. The parents believed that private problems were the reason for his flight and suicide.[5]

The greeting card Willi Born's parents had sent him for his 20th birthday was returned and kept by his stepmother in his memory.

Udo Baron / Maria Nooke

1 On this and the following see "Kreismeldekartei Oranienburg und Personalausweisantrag vom 20.11.1968," in: Oberhavel district archive, and conversation conducted by Maria Nooke with Willi Born's relatives, May 1, 2010.

2 "Standesamt Velten, Eintragung im Heiratsbuch Nr. 3/1969," in: Oberhavel district archive.

3 On this and the following see: "Abschlussbericht der NVA/Grenzregiment 36/Der Kommandeur über den verhinderten Grenzdurchbruch mit Selbsttötung des Grenzverletzers am 7.7.1970 gegen 10.45 Uhr im GR-36, 7.7.1970," in: BArch, VA-07/17904, Bl. 26–30.

4 See "Standesamt Hohen Neuendorf, Sterbeeintrag Nr. 117/1970," in: Oberhavel district archive.

5 See conversation conducted by Maria Nooke with Willi Born's relatives, May 1, 2010.

F riedhelm Ehrlich, born on July 11, 1950 in Nägelstedt in Thuringia, grew up
with his parents in Gräfentonna as an only child. He trained to become a ma-
chinist and was drafted into the National People's Army in May 1969. In early
August 1970 he was serving the last weeks of his duty in the Glienicke/Nordbahn
border company of the Schildow border regiment.[1] A report written by the secret
police after his death stated that Friedhelm Ehrlich's duty supervisor regarded the
young man as showing "satisfactory work," but that there had also been signs of
a "lack of military discipline."[2] His "unstable conduct in basic ideological issues"
was regarded as a consequence of the fact that he read "western literature, glorified beat groups" and listened to "enemy radio stations."[3]

Friedhelm Ehrlich was close to his parents and wrote to them regularly. They
even received a letter from him on the day he died. Later his parents reported to
the Berlin state prosecutor that their son did not really like being a soldier, but
nothing had suggested that he was planning to flee, not even his last letter.[4]

Friedhelm Ehrlich was scheduled for time off in Schildow on a warm summer
afternoon on August 2, 1970, but the approval for his leave was delayed: Due to a
"minor lack of discipline" he was assigned to "barrack cleaning" although it was
not his turn.[5] Later that evening, when he met up with other members of his unit
at a bar, he was noticeably revved up. He began bar hopping with his barrack
comrade, who had completed the cleaning chores with him. Since they were both
up for release from the military soon they no longer took the official rules very
seriously; perhaps they were eager to avenge the humiliation to which they had
been subjected.[6]

On the way home Friedhelm Ehrlich suddenly ran off, leaving his comrade,
who assumed that his friend was in a hurry to get back to the barracks.[7] In truth,
however, Friedhelm Ehrlich had entered the border grounds at around 10:15 that
night. But he did not behave like a fugitive. The drunken 20-year-old broke the
wooden slats of the interior fence[8] and whistled loudly[9] as he moved towards the
guard road. Border guards heard him and ordered him to stop. He obeyed the
second time they called out to him, was arrested and led back away from the border.

He was forced to lie face down on the street. Two other guards who had been notified arrived on motorcycle and took over. The fugitive was flinging around insults common among NVA members ("you badger, you red ass"), but which were usually reserved for the new arrivals in the barracks when they were initiated by soldiers about to be released.

The two guards stood about five meters away with locked guns and kept an eye on the man lying face-down on his stomach on the unlit street. It was so dark that Private T. repeatedly asked his sergeant if he could shine the light on the man.[10] At this point Ehrlich is said to have suddenly sat up and threatened: "Go on, go ahead and shoot, or I will shoot," and stretched his hand out to a hip pocket. The Stasi report stated: "This gesture from Ehrlich and his excited comment" led Private T. "to conclude that the border violator had a weapon and was about to use it on him."[11] The private released the safety on his gun and fired a shot at the man on the ground. He hit the man's thigh and the main artery of his left leg. The sergeant examined the injured man, determined that he did not have a weapon on him and took his papers from him. He did not, apparently, administer any first aid. The ambulance arrived 20 minutes later. Friedhelm Ehrlich was brought to the People's Police Hospital where he died a short time later. He had bled to death.[12]

The Stasi's presentation of the facts leaves a few questions unanswered: How was Private T. able to see what Private Ehrlich was doing when he was lying on the ground in the dark? Should he not have known that a private could not possibly take a weapon with him when he had time off from the barracks? Why was no first aid administered to the injured man? The extensive bleeding that ultimately led to his death could have been stopped immediately with a bandage. If Ehrlich, who was soon to be released from his duty, had intended to flee, would it not have made more sense for him to have done so when he was stationed at the border?

Neither the letters to his parents nor conversations with his army comrades gave any indication that Friedhelm Ehrlich was planning an escape. In retrospect, his relatives and friends agreed that it was not likely that he would have attempted to escape when he only had three months left of his military service. They suspected that the 20-year-old had merely wanted to provoke the border guards or that he had perhaps lost his way. The barracks were located only 100 meters away from the border.[13]

A military state prosecutor informed Friedhelm Ehrlich's parents of his death on August 3, 1970 and handed them the death certificate and his personal documents. The next evening two men appeared claiming to be members of the NVA. They gave the parents information concerning the delivery of the dead body, as well as an advance payment of 250 marks for the burial costs that the NVA would cover. Although the official version was that an "attempted desertion had been thwarted," the parents' apartment, where the son had also lived, was not searched and the parents were not interrogated as was usually done in such cases. This unusually gentle treatment puzzled the parents. Over the following years they tried to find out the circumstances of their son's death but all they were told was that the case was closed. This did not satisfy them.

In late 1990 the public prosecutor's office in Berlin filed charges and demanded that the circumstances of the death be investigated.[14] The investigation that followed was dismissed in mid-June 1994 because the court accepted the defense's claim that the man who had pulled the trigger, former Private T. – who also happened to be an informant for the East German secret police – had mistakenly acted in self-defense. The public prosecutor was of the opinion that although, objectively speaking, Friedhelm Ehrlich had not posed a physical threat to Private T., this had not been clear to the soldier at the time.[15]

West Berlin residents had been aware of the events that took place that night. At the time of the shooting, border guards of the border regiment in Schildow were confronted with cries of "You are all murderers, we see everything."[16]

Friedhelm Ehrlich's comrades were asked by their supervisors to provide a statement justifying the shooting. What really happened and why was not known but they nevertheless fiercely condemned his supposed "betrayal," explaining that it was only possible because he "had succumbed to the enemy ideology. He had broken his voluntary oath […] and had thus received the punishment he deserved."[17]

The body of Friedhelm Ehrlich was transferred from Berlin to Gräfentonna on August 6, 1970. A few days later his parents were able to see their son's body in the cemetery mortuary.[18] It had been prepared so that no external injuries were visible.

Martin Ahrends / Udo Baron

1 See "Bericht des MfS/HA IX/6, 4.8.1970," in: BStU, MfS, HA I Nr. 5024, Bl. 674–675.
2 Ibid., Bl. 675.
3 Ibid.
4 See "Protokoll der Zeugenbefragung der Eltern von Friedhelm Ehrlich durch die Eisenacher Polizei, 11.8.1992," in: StA Berlin, Az. 27 Js 249/90, Bl. 97–98.
5 Ibid.
6 See "Bericht des MfS/HA IX/6, 4.8.1970," in: BStU, MfS, HA I Nr. 5024, Bl. 675.
7 See "Bericht des MfS/HA IX/6, 4.8.1970," in: BStU, MfS, HA I Nr. 5024, Bl. 675–676; "Protokoll der Zeugenbefragung von L.M., eines Kameraden von Friedhelm Ehrlich, durch die Berliner Polizei, 18.8.1992," in: StA Berlin, Az. 27 Js 249/90, Bl. 106–108.
8 See "Bericht des MfS/HA IX/6, 4.8.1970," in: BStU, MfS, HA I Nr. 5024, Bl. 677.
9 See "Protokoll des Militärstaatsanwaltes Berlin-Treptow über die informatorische Befragung des Soldaten D., 3.8.1970," in: StA Berlin, Az. 27 Js 249/90, Bl. 25.
10 See "Bericht des MfS/HA IX/6, 4.8.1970," in: BStU, MfS, HA I Nr. 5024, Bl. 677–678.
11 Ibid., Bl. 678.
12 Ibid., Bl. 679.
13 See "Protokoll der Zeugenbefragung von L.M., eines Kameraden von Friedhelm Ehrlich, durch die Berliner Polizei, 18.8.1992," in: StA Berlin, Az. 27 Js 249/90, Bl. 110–111; "Protokoll der Zeugenbefragung der Eltern von Friedhelm Ehrlich durch die Eisenacher Polizei, 11.8.1992," in: Ibid., Bl. 98–100.
14 See "Protokoll der Zeugenbefragung der Eltern von Friedhelm Ehrlich durch die Eisenacher Polizei, 11.8.1992," in: Ibid., Bl. 99–101.
15 See "Verfügung der Staatsanwaltschaft bei dem Kammergericht Berlin, 23.6.1994," in: StA Berlin, Az. 27 Js 249/90, Bl. 261–267.
16 "Meldung der NVA/Stadtkommandant Poppe an SED-Politbüromitglied Erich Honecker, 3.8.1970," in: BArch, VA-07/8374, Bl. 140–142, here Bl. 141.
17 "Stellungnahme des Kollektivs des 2. Zuges [der NVA/Grenzregiment 38/2. Kompanie] zur versuchten Fahnenflucht des ehemaligen Gefreiten Ehrlich, o.D.," in: StA Berlin, Az. 27 Js 249/90, Bl. 37.
18 See "Protokoll der Zeugenbefragung der Eltern von Friedhelm Ehrlich durch die Eisenacher Polizei, 11.8.1992," in: StA Berlin, Az. 27 Js 249/90, Bl. 100–101.

Gerald Thiem

born on September 6, 1928

shot dead on August 7, 1970
at the corner of Kiefholzstrasse and Puderstrasse
on the sector border between
Berlin-Neukölln and Berlin-Treptow

G erald Thiem, born on September 6, 1928 in Berlin, lived with his wife and two daughters in Britz, West Berlin. The professional pipe layer worked as a foreman for a building company.

August 7, 1970 was a Friday. His wife was not concerned when he did not come home after work that afternoon. She knew that he liked to have a drink on payday, but when it got late she began to worry. He had promised to take his daughters on a steamboat on Saturday. At this point she did not know that her husband would remain missing for the rest of her life.

Gerald Thiem had had a lot to drink that evening as he walked on the east side near the Wall between Neukölln and Treptow.[1] It is not known why he was there, but it is documented that he insulted the border soldiers at 11:15 p.m. and proceeded to climb over the old and then the new Wall barrier in a rather complicated area of the border. He continued in the direction of East Berlin. When a border soldier called out to him with the intention of arresting him, he fled beneath a railway underpass which brought him right into the shine of the border lights and range of fire of two other guards who immediately began shooting. In the end six border guards fired a total of 177 bullets at Gerald Thiem from different positions until he collapsed into the anti-vehicle trench.[2]

The border guards retrieved him from the grounds and brought him to the rear border area at about 11:35 p.m. He was taken in an ambulance to the People's Police Hospital in Berlin-Mitte[3] but by the time he arrived there, shortly past midnight, he had already died from shots into and through his chest.[4]

The most zealous of the guards were awarded the "Border Troop Medal of Merit" the following day. Although Gerald Thiem could easily have been arrested without the use of weapons, all the border guards involved were given gifts as a bonus.[5] In mid-1998 two of the guards were tried as youths for joint manslaughter by the Berlin district court and sentenced to a year and three months in prison. The sentence was commuted to probation.[6]

The East German secret police was able to identify the dead man from papers he had on him. Officials in the East decided to conceal his death since no one on the west side had made a connection between his sudden absence and the shooting at the Wall. The Communist Party leadership feared that the shooting of Gerald Thiem might jeopardize the détente diplomacy that it was hoping would bring international recognition to the state. Just a few days later, on August 12, 1970, the Moscow Treaty was to going to be signed by the Federal Republic of Germany and the Soviet Union, normalizing relations and strengthening the renunciation of force. A Stasi file note written on August 10, 1970 on the "Thiem corpse issue" stated: "After examining all the circumstances it has been decided that the corpse should be treated as an unidentified body and the case closed. It has been directed that all measures be taken to keep this secret."[7] The East German secret police had a death certificate issued that listed "Berlin-Mitte" as the place of death.[8]

Under strict secrecy and Stasi surveillance, Gerald Thiem was cremated in the Baumschulenweg Crematorium as the "unknown dead man," register number 353105. His ashes, identified as Number 15, were dispersed in the grove of ashes at the neighboring cemetery on September 22, 1970.[9] Everyone involved was sworn to secrecy and monitored thereafter by the East German secret police.[10]

At the same time the search for Gerald Thiem continued in West Berlin where the shots from August 7, 1970 had also been heard. The bullets that hit West Berlin territory were examined by the criminal investigation department. The American city commander protested the use of weapons at the Wall.[11] But the West Berlin police had no reason to connect the shots that had been fired that night with the missing persons' report filed by Gerald Thiem's wife. Over the following weeks and months his wife extended the search for her husband to include East Berlin as well, but all attempts to learn anything about what had happened to him from the East German authorities were in vain. The East German attorney general only provided the information that "her husband Gerald Thiem was not within the national territory of the German Democratic Republic."[12]

The search remained unsuccessful and upon the request of his wife, Gerald Thiem was officially declared dead on June 10, 1981. His death date was set as December 31, 1975.[13]

It was not until the West Berlin criminal investigation department stumbled upon the case within the files of the East German border troops and Stasi that Gerald Thiem's daughters learned in the fall of 1994 the truth about their missing father.[14] His wife Charlotte Thiem had already passed away by then.

Martin Ahrends / Udo Baron / Hans-Hermann Hertle

1 On the establishment of facts concerning circumstances of events see: "Urteil des Landgerichts Berlin vom 16.6.1998," in: StA Berlin, Az. 27 Js 190/94, Bd. 4, n. pag. (pp. 9–11).

2 See "Bericht des MfS/HA I/Grenzkommando Berlin/Abwehr/UA 1. Grenzbrigade, 8.8.1970," in: BStU, MfS, AS 754/70, Bd. 1, Nr. 1, Bl. 3–5.

3 See "Bericht der NVA/Grenzregiment 35/Der Kommandeur zum verhinderten Grenzdurchbruch Bewegungsrichtung Westberlin – DDR am 7.8.1970 im Abschnitt des GR-35, 8.8.1970," in: BArch, VA-07/8378, Bl. 52–56.

4 See "Obduktionsgutachten des Instituts für Gerichtliche Medizin der Humboldt-Universität zu Berlin, 8.8.1970," in: BStU, MfS, AS 754/70, Bd. 1, Nr.1, Bl. 27–40, here Bl. 40.

5 "Bericht der NVA/Grenzregiment 35/Der Kommandeur zum verhinderten Grenzdurchbruch Bewegungsrichtung Westberlin – DDR am 7.8.1970 im Abschnitt des GR-35, 8.8.1970," in: BArch, VA-07/8378, Bl. 52–56.

6   See "Urteil des Landgerichts Berlin vom 16.6.1998," in: StA Berlin, Az. 27 Js 190/94, Bd. 4, n. pag. (pp. 1–19).

7   See "Aktenvermerk [der VfS Gross-Berlin]/Abt. IX, 10.8.1970," in: BStU, MfS, AS 754/70, Bd. 1, Nr.1, Bl. 55.

8   See "Totenschein ("Familienname: unbekannt"), 8.8.1970," in: BStU, MfS, AS 754/70, Bd. 1, Nr. 1, Bl. 20; see also "Sterbeurkunde ("ein unbekannter Mann, etwa 50 Jahre alt"), 11.8.1970," in: Ibid., Bl. 22.

9   See "Aktenvermerk [der VfS Gross-Berlin]/Abt. IX, 22.9.1970," in: BStU, MfS, AS 754/70, Bd. 1, Nr.1, Bl. 156.

10 "Aktenvermerk [der VfS Gross-Berlin]/Abt. IX, 12.8.1970," in: BStU, MfS, AS 754/70, Bd. 1, Nr. 1, Bl. 58.

11 See *Der Abend,* 8.8.1970; *Berliner Morgenpost,* 9.,10. und 11.8.1970; *Die Welt,* 10. and 11.8.1970.

12 See "Schreiben des DDR-Generalstaatsanwalts an die Ehefrau von Gerald Thiem, 13.11.1970," in: BStU, MfS, AS 754/70, Bd. 1, Nr. 1, Bl. 214.

13 See "Beschluss des Amtsgerichts Neukölln, 10.6.1981," in: StA Berlin, Az. 27 Js 190/94, Bd. 1, Bl. 158.

14 See *Berliner Morgenpost,* 8.10.1994; *Der Tagesspiegel,* 8.10.1994; *Berliner Zeitung,* 8.10.1994; *Die Tageszeitung,* 8.10.1994; *Bild-Zeitung,* 8.10.1994; *Berliner Kurier,* 8.10.1994.

Helmut Kliem

born on June 2, 1939

shot dead on November 13, 1970
in Falkenhöh near Pestalozzistrasse
on the outer ring between
Falkensee (Nauen district) and Berlin-Spandau

Helmut Kliem returned home from his night shift on November 13, 1970 at around 6:45 in the morning. His wife, who also worked, had already left the house with their two children, whom she dropped off at daycare on her way to work. Helmut Kliem's half-brother Bernhard had the day off and had announced that he would stop by for a visit that morning.

The brothers went to the "Volkshaus" restaurant in Staaken and had a few beers and schnapps with their lunch. They were looking forward to the upcoming weekend and planned to attend a Carnival party that evening. Both of them were relatively well-off: Three years earlier Bernhard P. had served a youth sentence in prison for "attempting to flee the republic," but now he had a well-paid position with a highway construction company. Helmut Kliem, who was born on June 2, 1939 in Ebereschenhof, had worked since 1957 as an East German police officer and, after serving guard, patrol and light duty, had recently been appointed head constable for security of the locomotive and electric technical plant in Hennigsdorf.[1] He lived with his family in Staaken, which was situated directly on the border of the West Berlin district of Spandau.

The two men set off at around 3 p.m. It had been agreed the day before that Helmut Kliem would pick up his wife from her early shift and then the children from nursery school with his motorcycle. He brought his brother with him. There was enough room for everyone in his "Touren-AWO" sidecar.

Deep in conversation with his brother, he missed the exit onto the dirt road that led to his wife's work place and to the daycare center. Instead he continued driving straight ahead and soon found himself in front of the gated entrance to the border grounds.[2] He had overlooked the signs marking the border territory and stopped about ten meters in front of the gate. He saw a border soldier behind the gate. Two guards stood on a watchtower behind him. He had clearly gone the wrong way. He turned the motorcycle around to drive back. Perhaps he did not take the border soldier seriously when he ordered the motorcycle driver to stop. Perhaps he did not hear the call or a possible warning shot over the noise of the motor. In any event, Helmut Kliem accelerated in order to leave the area quickly.

Apparently the guards on the tower did not see any reason to get involved but the guard at the gate raised his machine gun, aimed at the motorcycle tires and fired. Seven shots were set off. He later claimed that he was not aware of having set his Kalashnikov on automatic fire. In a standing position and without holding on to anything, he fired his gun at his target which was 30 meters away. Every guard was taught that a Kalashnikov tends to swerve upward and to the right of the target when set on automatic fire and this is what happened. Instead of hitting the motorcycle tires, the bullet went through Helmut Kliem's shoulder blade, hitting the upper arm artery and blood vessel. His brother was also hit in his hand, and another bullet just barely missed him. Helmut Kliem braked, got off the motorcycle and took a few steps towards the guard before he collapsed to the ground. A resident who heard the shots and rushed to the site to help Helmut Kliem was held back by the border guards who held their machine pistols in front of them.[3] Later a guard maintained that Bernhard P. had screamed excitedly to him "Go on and shoot you Saxon bastard, go ahead and shoot me, too," before he noticed his own pain and realized the severity of the bullet wound through his brother's torn leather jacket.[4] The brothers were not given any medical care until an hour later when the ambulance arrived and took them to the Staaken Hospital.[5] By then it was too late for Helmut Kliem. He bled to death from his injuries at around 4:30 p.m.[6]

Even the official regulations of the border guards did not justify using a weapon in this situation. There had been no recognizable threat of a border breach. According to the East German criminal code, the death of Helmut Kliem qualified as murder.[7] But the military prosecutor did not investigate the case. Colonel Krug, commander of the border brigade, certified that that border guard had acted according to regulation and had engaged in "exemplary, class-appropriate conduct" that was to be "evaluated" by all troop units. The city commander also informed Erich Honecker of the incident.[8] The border guards involved were awarded medals and promoted the very same day. The man who pulled the trigger was awarded the "Medal for Exemplary Service at the Border." The fact that he had fatally wounded his target was scrupulously concealed from him. He did not learn the truth until the 1990s. In 1997 the Potsdam district court tried him for manslaughter in coincidence with attempted manslaughter and sentenced him as a youth to a year and eight months in prison which was commuted to probation.[9]

Helmut Kliem's wife waited in vain for her husband to arrive at 4 p.m. on November 13, 1970. Disappointed, she picked the children up and walked home. That evening two strangers showed up at her door identifying themselves as criminal police from Potsdam. They asked her questions about her husband but did not provide her with any information. She did not find out that Helmut Kliem was dead until November 14, 1970 when she appeared at the Potsdam district authority of the East German police. They did not tell her how he had died and she was denied her request to see her husband's body. They told her that the body had already been cremated, although this was not true.[10]

At the same time her brother-in-law was being interrogated by the Stasi in Potsdam. On November 13, 1970 he was transported directly from the Staaken Hospital to the Stasi remand prison in Potsdam where preliminary proceedings for suspicion of "illegally leaving" East Germany were opened and an arrest warrant was issued. The Stasi interrogators tried unsuccessfully to force a confession out of him. The political division of the Potsdam state prosecutor's office waited 14 days before dismissing the case. Another week passed before the arrest warrant was revoked and Bernhard P. was released from prison.[11] The death of his brother was then presented to him as a regrettable accident.[12]

Both Helmut Kliem's wife and half-brother were sworn to secrecy about what had happened. In Staaken various rumors spread, but no one found out the truth. The supervisor of the "Border Work Group" of the East German police in Nauen apparently came closest to the truth: During questioning in the hospital he learned what had really happened. He was unable to reconcile the murder with his conscience and in an act of protest handed over his weapon and announced that he was quitting his service at the border.[13]

Almost three months passed before the urn with Helmut Kliem's ashes was buried on February 4, 1971 in the cemetery in Falkensee.[14]

Martin Ahrends / Udo Baron / Hans-Hermann Hertle

1 See "Telegramm der BVfS Potsdam/Abt. IX an das MfS/HA IX/8 Berlin, 16.11.1970," in: BStU, Ast. Potsdam, AU 70/71, Bd. 1, Bl. 26–28.

2 On the establishment of the facts concerning circumstances of events see: "Urteil des Landgerichts Potsdam vom 13.6.1997," in: StA Neuruppin, 61 Js 139/96, Bd. 3, Bl. 587–591.

3 See "Protokoll der Zeugenvernehmung eines Anwohners durch die Berliner Polizei, 15.11.1993," in: StA Neuruppin, Az. 61 Js 139/96, Bd. 1, Bl. 235–236.

4 In his interrogation by the Stasi on 14.11.1970 in the Potsdam remand prison, Bernhard P. protested against the border soldiers claim that he had called him a "Saxon bastard." See "Vernehmungsprotokoll der Abt. IX der BVfS Potsdam vom 14.11.1970," in: BStU, Ast. Potsdam, AU 70/71, Bd. 1, Bl. 43.

5 See "Zeugenbefragung des Halbbruders von Helmut Kliem durch die West-Berliner Polizei vom 4.8.1993," in: StA Neuruppin, 61 Js 139/96, Bd.1, Bl. 224–233.

6 See "Telegramm der BVfS Potsdam/Abt. IX an das MfS/HA IX/8, 16.11.1970," in: BStU, Ast. Potsdam, AU 70/71, Bd. 1, Bl. 26–28.

7 See "Urteil des Landgerichts Potsdam vom 13.6.1997," in: StA Neuruppin, 61 Js 139/96, Bd. 3, Bl. 594.

8 See "Schreiben des Kommandeurs der 2. Grenzbrigade, Oberst Krug, an NVA-Stadtkommandant Generalmajor Poppe vom 13.11.1970," in: BStU, Ast. Potsdam, AU 70/71, Bd. 1, Bl. 60–65, here Bl. 65; "Schreiben von NVA-Stadtkommandant Generalmajor Poppe an SED-Politbüromitglied und NVR-Sekretär Erich Honecker, 13.11.1970," in: BArch, VA-07/8374, Bl. 50–51.

9 See "Urteil des Landgerichts Potsdam vom 13.6.1997," in: StA Neuruppin, 61 Js 139/96, Bd. 3, Bl. 584–596.

10 See "Informationsbericht des MfS/KD Nauen zur Lage im Verantwortungsbereich zu dem Vorkommnis am 13.11.1970, 19.11.1970," in: BStU, Ast. Potsdam, AU 70/71, Bd. 1, Bl. 76–78.

11 The request for an arrest warrant, the prison ruling, a prison complaint from Bernhard P., the suspension of the investigation and repeal of the arrest warrant are presented in: BStU, Ast. Potsdam, AU 70/71, Bd. 1, Bl. 6, 11, 20–22.

12 See "Zeugenbefragung des Halbbruders von Helmut Kliem durch die West-Berliner Polizei vom 4.8.1993," in: StA Neuruppin, 61 Js 139/96, Bd.1, Bl. 231.

13 See "Informationsbericht des MfS/KD Nauen zur Lage im Verantwortungsbereich zu dem Vorkommnis am 13.11.1970, Nauen, 19.11.1970," in: BStU, Ast. Potsdam, AU 70/71, Bd. 1, Bl. 76–78.

14 See "Zeugenbefragung der Witwe von Helmut Kliem durch die West-Berliner Polizei vom 11.5.1993," in: StA Neuruppin, Az. 61 Js 139/96, Bd. 1, Bl. 82–84.

Christian Peter Friese

born on January 5, 1948

shot dead on December 25, 1970
on the Köllnische Heide rail embankment in Johannisthal
at the sector border between
Berlin-Treptow and Berlin-Neukölln

C hristian Peter Friese, born on January 5, 1948 in Munich, grew up as an only child with his mother in Naumburg. His mother's husband had been missing since 1944 and was officially declared dead; the name of his biological father was not recorded. After finishing school he did a motor mechanic apprenticeship in a motor vehicle company. When he had successfully completed his training he moved with his fiancée to Karl-Marx-Stadt – today's Chemnitz – but soon returned to Naumburg alone.[1] He worked there as an automobile motor mechanic for the Reichsbahn, the East German railway company, and worked as a volunteer for the "Naumburger Settlement Club," a youth center in his city. The director of the clubhouse confirmed his commitment to a "positive and high-quality club life." She also noted that he was "always a good role model" for the young people. "Because of his night classes," he had to give up his head position to a younger club member.[2] The State Security saw this differently: It claimed he had a "bad reputation" in his neighborhood, supposedly due to his "penchant" for western beat music and that he spread a "decadent view of art" and bore an "unstable attitude towards the social development in East Germany." This was the reason he had to be replaced as club leader.[3]

After Germany was unified, his mother testified to the Naumburg police in 1992 that her son had repeatedly stated that he wanted to "take off" to the West if the opportunity presented itself. The twenty-two-year-old man did not agree with the conditions in East Germany and in particular did not want to serve in the National People's Army.[4] Although a friend of his had tried to escape to West Berlin in 1968 and was caught and put in prison, this did not deter Christian Peter Friese from pursuing his own escape ambitions. "They won't catch me," he had told his mother.[5]

At the end of 1970 Christian Peter Friese was living in the same apartment building as his mother. She stopped by to pick him up on Christmas Eve, but he was not in his room. He had not said goodbye and did not leave a letter behind. But his mother noticed that a few things were missing that were important to him, including a photo album, a tape recorder and some clothing. "My first thought was that he had left for Berlin," his mother put on record in the early 1990s.[6] That evening, December 24, 1970, Christian Peter Friese was riding on a train to East Berlin. Later he hid in a small garden colony located near the border in Treptow and observed the border grounds.[7] At around midnight he climbed the interior fence unnoticed. When he crawled under the signal fence and jumped over the trip wires placed there, he triggered an alarm. The grounds there were in clear view from two watchtowers to the right and left. Moreover, an "alarm group" had been posted on the four meter high railway embankment of "Köllnische Heide" for Christmas Eve. There was good visibility and the border grounds were well lit. Five border guards fired a total of 98 bullets at the young man. He sought cover in the anti-vehicle trench, after which the shooting stopped for a moment. He then continued running and again came under fire. Just a few meters in front of the last border fence he collapsed to the ground, badly injured.[8] He had been hit by a number of bullets in his thigh and calf. Border guards testified that he called out: "My legs, my legs."[9] He died on the death strip from bullet wounds through his stomach and chest.

Twenty-eight years later the border guards involved in the shooting were acquitted by the Berlin district court because an intent to kill could not be established and because the person responsible for the actual killing could not be determined.[10]

Residents on both sides of the border were awakened by the shots. A number of bullets hit trees and building fronts on the West Berlin side. West Berliners called out to the border guards: "Murderers! Pigs!"[11] The incident caused major protests. A speaker of the West Berlin Senate explained that the incident "once again showed clearly the 'power-obsession' of a regime that does not know humanity."[12] The American city commander characterized the incident "as another demonstration of the frivolous disrespect for human life by zone organs."[13] The West Berlin police opened an investigation.

Christian Peter Friese's mother already suspected that it might have been her son who was killed when, on Christmas Day, she heard on western television that a young man had been killed at the Berlin Wall. Many days of uncertainty passed before the East German secret police informed her on January 7, 1971 that her son was dead. She was lied to about the circumstances under which he died: The Stasi agents told her that her son "died in an accident" in East Berlin while "engaging in illegal activity." They said that he crashed into a tree with a car and died from the accident. They told her that his body had already been cremated.[14] The Stasi pressured his mother to sign a statement in which she promised to tell her acquaintances that her son had died "in a car accident," and that she had requested the "state organs to argue similarly in the interest of her reputation."[15]

The urn was sent to Naumburg a month after Christian Peter Friese's death. The funeral took place on the municipal cemetery in Naumburg under Stasi surveillance.[16] A short time later his life insurance was paid out to his mother because her son had 'officially' died in a car accident.[17]

Martin Ahrends / Udo Baron / Hans-Hermann Hertle

1 See "Protokoll der Zeugenvernehmung der Mutter von Christian Peter Friese durch die Naumburger Polizei, 6.10.1992," in: StA Berlin, Az. 27 Js 68/90, Bd. 2, Bl. 242–243.

2 "Schreiben der Leiterin des Clubhauses der Jugend des Kreiskulturhauses Naumburg (Saale) an den Rat des Stadtbezirkes Süd der Stadt Karl-Marx-Stadt/Abt. Volksbildung/Referat Jugendhilfe, 2.4.1970," in: BStU, MfS, AS 754/70, Bd. 6, Nr. 3, Bl. 7.

3 See "Zwischenbericht der VfS Gross-Berlin/Abt. IX zur Grenzprovokation am 25.12.1970 in Berlin-Treptow, 29.12.1970," in: BStU, MfS, AS 754/70, Bd. 6, Nr.1, Bl. 27.

4 See "Protokoll der Zeugenvernehmung der Mutter von Christian Peter Friese durch die Naumburger Polizei, 6.10.1992," in: StA Berlin, Az. 27 Js 68/90, Bd. 2, Bl. 243.

5 See ibid.

6 Ibid., Bl. 244.

7 See establishment of the facts concerning circumstances of events in: "Urteil des Landgerichts Berlin in der Strafsache gegen Wolfgang S., Klaus Walter S. und Klaus D. vom 21.1.1998," in: StA Berlin, Az. 27 Js 68/90, Bd. 5, Bl. 12–16.

8 See "Bericht der [MfS]/HA I/Grenzkommando Mitte/Abwehr UA 1. Grenzbrigade/Grenzregiment 37 über die Verhinderung eines Grenzdurchbruches DDR-Westberlin mit Anwendung der Schusswaffe und tödlichen Verletzungen, 25.12.1970," in: BStU, MfS, AS 754/70, Bd. 6, Nr.1, Bl. 94–95; "Urteil des Landgerichts Berlin in der Strafsache gegen Wolfgang S., Klaus Walter S. und Klaus D. vom 21.1.1998," in: StA Berlin, Az. 27 Js 68/90, Bd. 5, Bl. 12–14.

9 "Urteil des Landgerichts Berlin in der Strafsache gegen Wolfgang S., Klaus Walter S. und Klaus D. vom 21.1.1998," in: StA Berlin, Az. 27 Js 68/90, Bd. 5, Bl. 16.

10 See ibid., Bl. 5, 21.

11 "Bericht des GMS "Heide" (Abschrift), o.D.," in: BStU, MfS, AS 754/70, Bd. 6, Nr. 1, Bl. 86.

12 Der Tagesspiegel, 29.12.1970.

13 Berliner Morgenpost, 29.12.1970.

14 "Abschlussbericht [der VfS Gross-Berlin/Abt. IX], 27.1.1971," in: BStU, MfS, AS 754/70, Bd. 6, Nr. 1, Bl. 23.

15 See BStU, MfS, AS 754/70, Bd. 6, Nr. 1, Bl. 29.

16 See ibid., Bl. 22–23.

17 See ibid.

Rolf-Dieter Kabelitz

born on June 23, 1951

shot on January 7, 1971
on the outer ring between
Bergfelde (Oranienburg district) and Berlin-Reinickendorf
died from his bullet wounds on January 30, 1971

Rolf-Dieter Kabelitz, born on June 23, 1951, was four years old when his mother divorced his father and re-married.[1] After this he lived in Potsdam with his mother and stepfather, a captain in the East German police. His relationship with the officer was tense. The young man rebelled against his parents, both of whom were members of the Communist Party. In their view he often displayed a lack of discipline – and his long hair was upsetting. Later, in a "talk" with his supervisor from the district authority of the East German police, the captain spoke negatively about his stepson and attributed his poor character to his biological father. This statement may have been an expression of his true feelings, but he may have feared that his family would be held responsible for the actions of his stepson.

After Rolf-Dieter Kabelitz quit his lathe operator apprenticeship at the state-owned locomotive plant "Karl Marx" in Potsdam-Babelsberg, his parents got him a job at the Warnow shipyard in Rostock in August 1969. But he chose not to adapt to the socialist work routine there and gave notice to leave his job on January 10, 1971. He wanted to find work near his hometown. This caused a fight with his stepfather that completely spoiled the family's New Year's celebration. The young man left his parent's house early in the morning of January 4, 1971, saying he was going to Rostock to work the late shift there.

It is not known where Rolf-Dieter Kabelitz spent the next three days. On January 7 he took the S-Bahn to Oranienburg.[2] There was a lot of snow on the ground when he walked from the last stop on the S-Bahn line back along the tracks through Birkenwerder to Hohen Neuendorf, where the tracks curved toward the border grounds. In the darkness of the early evening he left the tracks and walked by Bergfelde toward the border. He set off a "signal device with firearm character" at 7:55 p.m. when he tried to pass the first barriers and the border guards were notified of his presence.

The 19-year-old continued in the direction of West Berlin. When he realized that the border guards were pursuing him with tracking dogs, Rolf-Dieter Kabelitz turned around and ran back towards the S-Bahn tracks. He dropped his bag containing a shirt, sweater, toiletry bag and other personal belongings so that he could run better. But his pursuers had no difficulty following his tracks in the snow. He tried to hide in the hilly grounds but one of the border guards found him standing behind a tree at 9:45 p.m. Although the fugitive was surrounded and was no longer moving towards the border but away from it, a lieutenant, supposedly after calling out, fired in his direction. Two bullets hit Rolf-Dieter Kabelitz in his pelvis and thigh and he collapsed to the ground.

He was in critical condition when he arrived at the Friedrich Wolf Hospital in Hennigsdorf. Once there, he was entrusted to the care of the doctors, but he remained under the control of the East German secret police.

Rolf-Dieter Kabelitz was physically and psychologically weakened from the loss of blood and shock that he had endured and was not totally conscious. Nonetheless, the East German secret police began to interrogate him right after he arrived at 2 a.m. The doctors reported that the patient was in a life-threatening condition due to a wound through his intestines, but the Stasi and the Oranienburg district court director W. were not deterred from appearing on January 9 to present an arrest warrant to the patient who had just been operated on and was sporadically unconscious. They conducted a judicial interrogation and took him into pre-trial confinement.

"He has been informed of his right to legal remedy," the district court director put on record in perfect form.[3] Rolf-Dieter Kabelitz was guarded by the Stasi in his hospital bed twenty-four hours a day. The hospital staff in Hennigsdorf was instructed not to permit any visitors and not to provide any information to his relatives or anyone else.[4]

Rolf-Dieter Kabelitz repeatedly claimed to his interrogators and guards that he had not wanted to flee and that he had merely lost his way. One of his guards noted in his explanation that he had "hidden behind an embankment because he had heard dogs in front of him and could see the guards behind him. He had leaned against a tree when he heard someone behind him call, "Hey, guard, guard." He claims not to have heard a warning shot but only the double shots from the MPi [machine pistol] at which point his feet were torn out from under him."[5] East German secret police, however, did not believe his version of events.

An internal infection spread through his body over the following weeks, causing him a long and painful death. He had a fluctuating high fever and spoke deliriously. The East German secret police wrote everything down that he said in his sleep and under high fever. "The man under surveillance was in a kind of half sleep during our shift and had strong dreams," the guard noted on January 8. He wrote down the following statement: "A dog squatted in front of me and then a pain, and my legs were gone."[6] Does this note suggest what really happened? Kabelitz had been hiding when he was detected. It could be that he did not leave his hiding place as ordered by the border guard and was consequently guarded by a border or tracking attack dog and hence did not dare to move.

Rolf-Dieter Kabelitz was operated on twice. His condition stabilized for a few days but then deteriorated rapidly. On the morning of January 30, the doctors diagnosed pneumonia. By evening they predicted that he would not survive. Rolf-Dieter Kabelitz fell into a fevered delirium. He died at 11:50 that night in the

Hennigsdorf Hospital as a consequence of his critical injuries. During the 23 days that he spent in the hospital he had not been allowed to see a single relative. His body was cremated and the ashes buried in an urn.

West Berlin was not aware of the incident at first. A lieutenant of the National People's Army who later fled to the West informed the West Berlin police in September 1971 about the escape attempt of January 7, 1971, but claimed that the fugitive, whose name was unknown, had been arrested without the use of weapons and had remained uninjured.[7] In July 1991 the Central Investigating Agency for Governmental and Party Crimes opened an investigation. It could not be conclusively established whether Rolf-Dieter Kabelitz had entered the border grounds by mistake, as he had told the Stasi, or whether he had planned to escape. One of the two gunmen claimed to have fired into the air, which his fellow guard confirmed. The second gunman, the lieutenant that fired the shots at Kabelitz, had died in 1986. The Berlin public prosecutor dismissed the case against the perpetrators on August 15, 1994 without an arraignment.[8]

Martin Ahrends / Udo Baron

1 On this and the following see "Protokoll über eine Aussprache in der BDVP Potsdam mit dem Stiefvater von Rolf-Dieter Kabelitz am 8. Januar 1971," in: BStU, Ast. Potsdam, AU 350/71, Bd. I, Bl. 51/52.

2 On the following see "Abschlussbericht der NVA/Grenzregiment 36/Der Kommandeur über den verhinderten Grenzdurchbruch mit Anwendung der Schusswaffe und Verletzung des Grenzverletzers am 7.1.1971, 8.1.1971," in: BArch, GTÜ-AZN 6947, Bl. 129–134; "[MfS]/KD Oranienburg, versuchter ungesetzlicher Grenzübertritt am 7.1.1971 um 19.55 Uhr im Pq. 3885/9 c DDR – WB, 8.1.1971," in: BStU, Ast. Potsdam, AU 350/71, Bl. 28–31.

3 "Handschriftliche Notiz von Kreisgerichtsdirektor W., Kreisgericht-Strafkammer Oranienburg, 9.1.1971," in: BStU, Ast. Potsdam, AU 350/71 (Vollzugs-/Erziehungs-Akte), Bl. 3.

4 See "Schreiben des leitenden Arztes der Anästhesie-Abteilung und Intensivtherapie-Station, 8.1.1971," in: BStU, Ast. Potsdam, AU 350/71, Bd. I, Bl. 123.

5 "[MfS-]Bericht über Gespräch mit Kabelitz, Rolf, am 11.1.1971," in: BStU, Ast. Potsdam, AU 350/71, Bd. I, Bl. 60/61.

6 "[MfS-]Bericht über Krankenbewachung vom 8.1.–9.1.1971 im Krankenhaus Hennigsdorf, 9.1.1971," in: BStU, Ast. Potsdam, AU 350/71, Bd. I, Bl. 54.

7 See "Bericht/Strafanzeige der West-Berliner Polizei von Amts wegen aufgrund des Verdachts des versuchten Totschlags, 8.9.1971," in: StA Berlin, Az. 27 Js 233/91, Bd. 1, Bl. 1.

8 See "Verfügung der Staatsanwaltschaft Berlin zum Verfahren 27/2 Js 233/91, 15.8.1994," in: StA Berlin, Az. 27 Js 233/91, Bd. 2, Bl. 400–402.

Wolfgang Hoffmann

born on September 1, 1942

jumped to his death on July 15, 1971
from the East German police inspection building
in Berlin-Treptow after being arrested
at the Friedrichstrasse station border crossing

Wolfgang Hoffmann was born on September 1, 1942 in Berlin. He and his brother Peter, who was five years older, grew up with their mother in Berlin-Johannisthal. Their father, a soldier in the Second World War, was reported missing in 1944.[1] Wolfgang Hoffmann was a trained lathe operator and worked as a toolmaker for the institute for measuring and testing technology at the Academy of Sciences in Berlin-Adlershof.

Like most residents of Johannisthal und Adlershof, the Hoffmann family routinely crossed the sector border and entered the neighboring West Berlin district of Neukölln to go shopping or see a movie. This ended when the Wall was built in the summer of 1961. Soon after that, on August 24, 1961, Wolfgang Hoffmann fled across the barbed wire to West Berlin with a colleague from work. He did not speak to his mother or his brother beforehand about his plans to leave or his reasons for doing so. He may have wanted to avoid having to serve in the National People's Army because, at that time, young men in the FDJ, the Communist Party youth organization, were under tremendous pressure to enlist.[2] The East German police of Berlin-Treptow investigated him in September 1961 for a "passport offence" which led to an arrest warrant a year later.[3]

Evidently Wolfgang Hoffmann adjusted quickly to life in the West. He was athletic and played soccer for the 1st FC Neukölln team. He wrote letters to his mother about his success. She was saddened to hear that he had broken up with his girlfriend, but in general the family knew little about his new life in West Berlin. Because mail was read by the Stasi it was difficult to convey any private information through letters. Later he was quoted in his interrogation as having said that he had been without a permanent residence or job since the late 1960s. He had moved into a hotel room at the Sportpalast and played his luck at roulette.[4] His relatives in East Berlin knew nothing of this.

He was almost 29 years old and had lived apart from his mother and brother for almost ten years when, on the evening of July 14, 1971, he was overwhelmed by the desire to visit his mother in East Berlin. After the Berlin border pass negotiations between the two German states failed in 1966, there was practically no way for West Berliners to travel to East Berlin. A former refugee risked being arrested even if he was only traveling through East Germany to West Germany.

Wolfgang Hoffmann stood at the control gate of the Friedrichstrasse station border crossing at 10:40 p.m. Although he did not have a visa, he demanded entry; he had probably been drinking.[5] He was sent away but continued to insist that he be allowed to visit his mother. When the border inspector demanded to see his identification, he presented it to him. Not until that moment did he seem to realize the danger that he was putting himself in here as a "fugitive of the republic." He abruptly tried to leave the checkpoint, but was followed and arrested on platform B, to which only travelers from the West had access. Numerous people watched passively as he was taken away.[6]

It was not long before the East German passport inspectors found out that Wolfgang Hoffmann had been wanted since 1962 for "fleeing the republic." The man under arrest was transported to Berlin-Treptow and subjected to an interrogation at 2 o'clock in the morning and then locked up in a basement cell. On the morning of July 15, 1971, just past 8 o'clock in the morning, a policeman escorted him to the forensic room on the second floor of the police building.[7] That is where personal data was recorded. He was supposed to wash his hands before his finger prints were taken. He was asked to stand up. Wolfgang Hoffmann suddenly climbed up onto a table, jumped head first out of the closed bay window and fell ten meters down. He suffered a basal skull fracture and a number of broken bones and remained motionless on the ground in front of the police building. He died a short time later on his way to the hospital.

The doctor on duty gave instructions to have Wolfgang Hoffmann's body delivered immediately to the kidney transplantation center of the Friedrichshain Hospital, where it could be determined whether his kidneys could be removed. But when the doctors realized that he was a West Berliner, they decided against removing his organs.[8]

For the East German police in Treptow the case was clear: Wolfgang Hoffmann had not known that he was on the second floor when he tried to escape. He had probably thought that he could hold on to the tree outside the window. A suicide was deemed out of the question and hence the incident was established as a fatal accident.[9] Peter Hoffmann argued that his brother may very well have known exactly where he was since, as a boy, he had passed by the East German police building for years on his way to school.[10]

The arrest of the West Berliner, and the fact that he had jumped to his death while in East Berlin police custody, was to be kept secret. It was deemed particularly important that it not be leaked to the West. The Four Allied Powers were currently negotiating the Berlin Treaty and the two German states were engaged in a dialogue over a basic treaty and measures to facilitate travel. East German officials feared that the circumstances of his death might disrupt the political climate. The East German secret police arranged to have all information blocked. Everyone involved in the events of July 14 and 15 was sworn to secrecy. This included the staff of the kidney transplant center, the Friedrichshain Hospital morgue, the Johannisthal emergency rescue office, the East German police inspection of Treptow, the

Treptow district state prosecutor's office and the attorney general of Greater Berlin. All these individuals were examined and thereafter their mail was checked.[11] The Stasi neutralized the death certificate that had been issued identifying the place of death as the East German police inspection of Treptow and the cause of death as a "fall from window." Instead a new death certificate was created that stated the place of death as "Berlin-Mitte (Transport)" and cause of death as a "basal skull fracture."[12]

The Stasi waited a number of days to see if their measures of secrecy were successful. Wolfgang Hoffmann had claimed during his late night interrogation that he did not have family in West Berlin. He had acquaintances there but no girlfriend or relatives.[13] To the satisfaction of the Stasi, nothing had been leaked to the western press. In West Berlin neither Wolfgang Hoffmann's disappearance, nor his almost public arrest, not even his death, was made public.

Only then, eight days later, did the Stasi summon Wolfgang Hoffmann's mother to their headquarters. A "legend" had been created for her about the failed existence of a man who ultimately committed suicide. In truth, his gambling debts had been minimal and the level of alcohol in his blood at the time of his death was zero. The Stasi lied to the mother, telling her that her son had accumulated considerable debt as a consequence of his "deviant moral conduct" and his "passion for gambling" which had "caused a psychological depression, leading him to commit suicide […] under the heavy influence of alcohol."[14] The Stasi's strategy was to not provide the mother and brother with any details so that at a "later point in time – should they learn the true circumstances of Wolfgang Hoffmann's death– it would be possible to provide new information without getting tangled in contradictions."[15]

His mother seemed to accept that her son may have committed suicide under the circumstances presented to her – at least the documents of the East German secret police leave this impression. She was informed of his death while in the offices of the East Berlin general state prosecutor. In a state of shock, she agreed to have her son cremated and buried anonymously. Given the location, she probably thought the Stasi agent was from the state prosecutor's office. She promised not to speak to anyone about her son's death[16] after she was perfidiously reminded that otherwise "the people her son owed money to might demand that she pay his debt."[17] When the conversation was over the Stasi agent handed her the false death certificate.

The mother notified her son Peter, who returned from vacation early.[18] She was intimidated by the threats from the Stasi, and consequently, he only learned from her that his brother was dead and that she had sworn herself to secrecy about it. He was also summoned to speak with the "general state prosecutor." Peter Hoffmann was brought to an office on the fifth floor of the building on Littenstrasse and told of his brother's supposed debts, but the Stasi had also thought up an extra lie for him: A man who introduced himself by name informed him that his brother had been found dead in the border territory. He did not provide any details. Peter Hoffmann was in a state of shock when he left the building. The thought that "they shot my brother" kept running through his head as he remained in a trance-like state. Later, when he was able to think clearly again, he had many questions.

He returned to the office and asked to speak to the man he had spoken to previously, but was told that no one by that name worked at the general state attorney's office.

From the very beginning Peter Hoffmann had doubts about the version of his brother's death that had been presented to him. The lack of information about the cause of death had made him suspicious. His mother died in 1986 and the brother tried as early as 1990 to find out the truth, first from the East German general state prosecutor's office and then from the Berlin public prosecutor.[19] Peter Hoffmann turned to the district offices of Mitte, Tiergarten and Kreuzberg; he requested information from Charité Hospital, the Central Registry Office in Salzgitter, the association "Working Group 13th of August," the federal statistics office and the Gauck Authority, responsible for Stasi files. He wrote to the mayor of Treptow and to the minister of internal affairs and the minister of justice. He found it unbelievable that his brother could have disappeared from West Berlin without a trace in 1971 and died under unknown circumstances and that no one in divided Germany or in reunited Germany was interested in looking into the case or felt responsible for it.

He finally learned how his brother allegedly died from the Stasi files and documents of the Berlin state prosecutor's office. The Berlin public prosecutor ultimately dismissed the case because neither the autopsy records nor the police investigation conducted in the 1990s indicated any legally relevant third party negligence in the death of Wolfgang Hoffmann.[20]

Wolfgang Hoffmann's body was cremated in 1971 in the Baumschulenweg Crematorium as "secret official business." His mother and brother were not permitted to identify the body or bid Wolfgang Hoffmann farewell. At the funeral they were presented with an urn supposedly containing his ashes. The East German secret police also interfered with the memorial service on August 20, 1971: They only permitted a small number of guests to attend, and observed them with suspicion at the cemetery.

The Four-Power Treaty on Berlin went into effect in June 1972 and the Berlin Senate and East German government signed an agreement over the facilitation of travel and visitor traffic. East Germany granted an official pardon to all people who had left the country before January 1, 1972.[21]

This amnesty came almost exactly 15 months too late for Wolfgang Hoffmann and his family.

Martin Ahrends / Udo Baron / Hans-Hermann Hertle

---

1 Conversation conducted by Hans-Hermann Hertle with Peter Hoffmann, 29. September 2008.

2 See "Bericht der VfS Gross-Berlin/Abt. IX über den unnatürlichen Todesfall eines festgenommenen, zur Zeit in Westberlin aufenthältlichen DDR-Bürgers in der Volkspolizei-Inspektion Berlin-Treptow, 16.7.1971," in: BStU, MfS, AS 754/70, Bd. 15, Nr. 1, Bl. 60–64.

3 See "Zweiter Bericht der VfS Gross-Berlin/Abt. IX über den unnatürlichen Todesfall des Hoffmann, Wolfgang, 20.7.1971," in: BStU, MfS, AS 754/70, Bd. 15, Nr. 1, Bl. 150–154.

4 "VP-Inspektion Treptow/Abteilung K, Vernehmungsprotokoll des Beschuldigten Hoffmann, Wolfgang, 15.7.1971, Beginn: 2.00 Uhr," in: BStU, MfS, AS 754/70, Bd. 15, Nr. 2, Bl. 46–51. See also "Ermittlungsbericht der VPI

Treptow/Dez. II/Komm. TK in der Todesermittlungssache Wolfgang Hoffmann, 15.7.1971," in: BStU, MfS, AS 754/70, Bd. 15, Nr. 1, Bl. 7–8.

5   See "VP-Inspektion Treptow/Abteilung K, Vernehmungsprotokoll des Beschuldigten Hoffmann, Wolfgang, 15.7. 1971, Beginn: 2.00 Uhr," in: BStU, MfS, AS 754/70, Bd. 15, Nr. 2, Bl. 50.

6   See "Bericht der VfS Gross-Berlin/Abt. IX über den unnatürlichen Todesfall eines festgenommenen, zur Zeit in Westberlin aufenthältlichen DDR-Bürgers in der Volkspolizei-Inspektion Berlin-Treptow, 16.7.1971," in: BStU, MfS, AS 754/70, Bd. 15, Nr. 1, Bl. 61.

7   The following description is based solely on East German police and Stasi documents or material witnesses. See "Bericht der VfS Gross-Berlin/Abt. IX über den unnatürlichen Todesfall eines festgenommenen, zur Zeit in Westberlin aufenthältlichen DDR-Bürgers in der Volkspolizei-Inspektion Berlin-Treptow, 16.7.1971," in: BStU, MfS, AS 754/70, Bd. 15, Nr. 1, Bl. 62. See also "Protokoll der Vernehmung des damaligen Offiziers für Kriminaltechnik der VPI Berlin-Treptow durch die ZERV vom 5.7.1994," in: StA Berlin, Az. 2 Js 122/90, Beistück, Bl. 162–175.

8   See "Bericht der VfS Gross-Berlin/Abt. IX über den unnatürlichen Todesfall eines festgenommenen, zur Zeit in Westberlin aufenthältlichen DDR-Bürgers in der Volkspolizei-Inspektion Berlin-Treptow, 16.7.1971," in: BStU, MfS, AS 754/70, Bd. 15, Nr. 1, Bl. 60–64.

9   See "Ermittlungsbericht der VPI Treptow/Dez. II/Komm. TK in der Todesermittlungssache Wolfgang Hoffmann, 15.7.1971," in: BStU, MfS, AS 754/70, Bd. 15, Nr. 1, Bl. 7–8.

10 Conversation conducted by Hans-Hermann Hertle with Peter Hoffmann, 29. September 2008.

11 See "Bericht der VfS Gross-Berlin/Abt. IX über den unnatürlichen Todesfall eines festgenommenen, zur Zeit in Westberlin aufenthältlichen DDR-Bürgers in der Volkspolizei-Inspektion Berlin-Treptow, 16.7.1971," in: BStU, MfS, AS 754/70, Bd. 15, Nr. 1, Bl. 60–64.

12 Both death certificates are presented in: BStU, MfS, AS 754/70, Bd. 15, Nr. 1, Bl. 92 and 94.

13 See "VP-Inspektion Treptow/Abteilung K, Vernehmungsprotokoll des Beschuldigten Hoffmann, Wolfgang, 15.7. 1971, Beginn: 2.00 Uhr," in: BStU, MfS, AS 754/70, Bd. 15, Nr. 2, Bl. 49.

14 "Dritte Information zum unnatürlichen Todesfall des Hoffmann, Wolfgang, 23.7.1971," in: BStU, MfS, AS 754/70, Bd. 15, Nr. 1, Bl. 160–163, here Bl. 162.

15 "Zweiter Bericht der VfS Gross-Berlin/Abt. IX über den unnatürlichen Todesfall des Hoffmann, Wolfgang, 20.7.1971," in: BStU, MfS, AS 754/70, Bd. 15, Nr. 1, Bl. 150–154, here Bl. 154.

16 See the "statement" forced from Wolfgang Hoffmann's mother by the Stasi, 23.7.1971, in: BStU, MfS, AS 754/70, Bd. 15, Nr. 2, Bl. 21.

17 "3. Information zum unnatürlichen Todesfall des Hoffmann, Wolfgang, 23.7.1971," in: BStU, MfS, AS 754/70, Bd. 15, Nr. 1, Bl. 160–163, here Bl. 162.

18 On the following, see the conversation conducted by Hans-Hermann Hertle with Peter Hoffmann, 29. September 2008.

19 See "Schreiben des Bruders von Wolfgang Hoffmann an die Staatsanwaltschaft bei dem Landgericht Berlin, 30.7.1991," in: StA Berlin, Az. 2 Js 122/90, Bd. 1, Bl. 44–45.

20 The autopsy findings of the Charité Institute for Forensic Medicine from 16.7.1971 state that "indications of violence by a third party" could not be established (BStU, MfS, AS 754/70, Bd. 15, Nr. 2, Bl. 25–28, here Bl. 27). See "Verfügung der Staatsanwaltschaft Berlin, 17.9.1991," in: StA Berlin, Az. 2 Js 122/90, Bd. 1, Bl. 76–78.

21 On the agreements, rules and laws resulting from the détente policies of the 1970s, see: Bundesministerium für innerdeutsche Beziehungen (ed.), *Zehn Jahre Deutschlandpolitik. Die Entwicklung der Beziehungen zwischen der Bundesrepublik Deutschland und der Deutschen Demokratischen Republik 1969–1979. Bericht und Dokumentation,* Bonn, 1980.

Werner Kühl

born on February 10, 1949

shot dead on July 24, 1971
near the bridge at Britzer Allee / Baumschulenweg
on the sector border between
Berlin-Neukölln and Berlin-Treptow

Werner Kühl was born on February 10, 1949 in West Berlin. He attended school until 1963 and then worked as a gardener for various companies. His parents were separated and his permanent address was registered with his father, but his mother looked after him. Werner Kühl led an unsettled life and was repeatedly unemployed and homeless. He met Bernd Langer, who was his same age, in a dormitory of a youth welfare agency in 1968–69. Bernd Langer was born in East Berlin, but in 1966 had been allowed to resettle in West Berlin, where his father lived, as part of the official East German policy to reunite families. But he soon yearned for East Berlin and wanted to go back to his grandmother's, where he had grown up. As a child he had been in a motorcycle accident with his father and suffered ever since from an impaired consciousness and neural disease.[1] In July 1971 Werner Kühl and Bernd Langer were hired for a few days as transport workers and lived together in an inn.

They began to speak often about resettling in East Germany, where they thought they could have a better life. Later on, this explanation for their actions would earn them little sympathy, not in the West, and surprisingly, not in the East.

The two young men left the West Berlin hotel with their luggage on July 24, 1971. It was a warm Saturday. That afternoon they took the S-Bahn to Neukölln and walked to the Britzer Zweigkanal. It was warm and there was a bathing area there. Once they arrived at their destination, Kühl told his friend about what was perhaps his spontaneous plan to cross the border grounds to East Berlin there. Bernd Langer objected to the idea, insisting that it was much too dangerous and that they could simply use the border crossing at the Friedrichstrasse station or at Sonnenallee, which was close by, but Werner Kühl dismissed his doubts. He convinced him that his idea was possible, and his friend let himself be talked into it.[2] The two men crossed the small canal, camped out right next to the stretch metal fence of the border grounds and waited for it to get dark.

At 11:30 at night they threw their blankets over the metal fence to protect themselves from the sharp edges and climbed over it. They left most of their luggage on the west side. Then they ran towards East Berlin, towards the garden settlement

"Gemütlichkeit III." A former East German policeman was sitting with his wife in a garden there and noticed the two West Berliners as they were crossing the security grounds. Dutifully, he walked through "Harmonie," the neighboring garden settlement, to the nearest watchtower and reported the incident. The guards soon found the two young men in the border strip and, believing them to be East German fugitives, shot at them. Bernd Langer, hit in the thigh, arm and shoulder, crawled back to the fence that he had just gotten past. Werner Kühl reached the border gate on the East Berlin side uninjured but was unable to open it. When he turned around and ran back in the direction from which he had come a bullet hit him in the shoulder, rupturing his pulmonary lung, feed pipe and two arteries before exiting on the other side. Bernd Langer saw Kühl "turn like a spiral" and collapse into the anti-vehicle trench.[3] He crawled back to his friend, gave him a shake, called out to him and then lay down next to him on the ground and waited. Werner Kühl bled to death within minutes.

A drunken first lieutenant of the border troops who had the evening off had watched everything from an acquaintance's garden. Although he was not in uniform he intervened, employing the familiar commanding tone to quickly get the dead man and the injured man out of view of the West. Later he had to formally apologize for his violation of duty regulations.[4]

Policemen, customs officers and civilians on the west side watched as Werner Kühl's body and the injured Bernd Langer were taken away. They assumed falsely that they were both East German fugitives and that the drunken officer in civilian dress was their third man. The dead body was brought to the People's Police Hospital in Berlin-Mitte and a fire department ambulance brought Bernd Langer to the prison hospital of the East German secret police. The investigative division of the East Berlin Stasi district opened an investigation against him on July 24, 1971; two days later a warrant for his arrest was issued.[5]

Lieutenant General Peter, head of the East German border troops, attested in a letter to the Communist Party general secretary, Erich Honecker, that the two guards involved in the shooting had "acted tactically correct." They were soon awarded the "Medal for Exemplary Service at the Border."[6] In May 2000 one of the gunmen was sentenced as a youth to a year and two months probation for complicity in manslaughter; the other guard had already passed away.[7] It remained unclear who had shot how many bullets and with which weapon that night. Since investigators had failed to conduct a forensic analysis of the weapon and projectiles and did not examine Werner Kühl's clothing at the time, it was difficult for the Berlin district court to determine the responsibility of each individual border soldier. Because the Communist Party leaders and functionaries had been given legally binding mild sentences, the court felt itself limited in its ability to "make the defendant understand the injustice of his actions through a criminal sentence."[8]

It was 1971 and the victims became a pawn in the Cold War conflict. Politics at the time were aimed at a policy of détente. The four major powers were struggling to agree on a treaty for Berlin and the two German states were engaged in negotiations to facilitate travel and visitor traffic between East Germany and West Berlin, as well as between East Germany and West Germany. The East German order to shoot fugitives at the border made the negotiations in West Germany very controversial. The Socialist-Liberal government coalition and the conservative CDU/CSU-opposition hotly debated the decision to engage in talks with the Communist Party leadership. A few weeks earlier Erich Honecker had succeeded Walter Ulbricht as Communist Party general secretary in East Germany; the new leader had been the architect of the Berlin Wall and called for a celebration of the 10th anniversary of the "anti-fascist protective wall." The dead man and his injured friend agitated both sides and were used as tools to manipulate the opponent.

Without conducting its own investigation, the West Berlin police released eyewitness reports to the press that claimed that a hail of bullets had prevented three East German citizens from escaping to the West. The information created a furor in the western media. The West German federal government and the West Berlin Senate protested the shooting. The American city commander pointed out that the "inhuman incident [...] is in no way beneficial to the negotiations that are intended to improve the lives of people in Germany."[9]

ADN, the East German press agency, responded the same day in "Neues Deutschland": It clarified that the incident had not involved three East German fugitives, but that two West Berliners had been "injured" after engaging in a "severe provocation" at the border. The Communist Party newspaper did not mention the death of Werner Kühl and accused the "Springer Corporation's West Berlin press of publishing reports contrary to the truth in order to heat up the mood of the people against any negotiations and efforts towards détente."[10] The West Berlin Senate promptly repudiated this version of the incident.[11] At the same time the West Berlin police requested by cable more information from the East German police about the two supposed West Berliners, but received no answer. After the international press also condemned East Germany for the shooting, the East German leadership, ten days after the border incident had occurred, decided to publicize a new explanation. It published the names and addresses of the two West Berliners. It also admitted for the first time that Werner Kühl was shot and killed and it attacked the West for encouraging a "massive hate campaign against East Germany" over what "Neues Deutschland" called a "border provocation."[12]

The West Berlin police felt compelled to withdraw their false version of the facts. An investigation of the personal data revealed that Werner Kühl was known to the criminal investigation department for various offenses, including stealing cars, defamation and joint theft. Bernd Langer had a police record for coercion and resistance; it was also known that he suffered from a neural disease. The West Berlin police released all this information to the press and, based on "additional information" that was not more narrowly specified, presented a new version of the incident: Werner Kühl and Bernd Langer had wanted to help a friend in East Berlin flee to the West.[13]

During this war of propaganda, the East German secret police quickly developed "a counter measure plan." It first planned to have Bernd Langer, who was a firsthand witness of the events, disappear in the psychiatric division of the Waldheim Hospital in a "special facility for people with secret information."[14] A feverish and creative effort was made to think up a justification for the deadly shots fired at the West Berliner. One suggestion was to claim that the telephone number of a "terrorist organization," – meaning the "Association for the Victims of Stalinism" – had been found on Kühl, but someone commented in the margins that this idea was "too heavy-handed."[15] They needed to "create more evidence suggesting a criminal invasion into the territory of East Germany."[16] The Stasi agents considered finding evidence to suggest that "Kühl had been carrying either a gun, dynamite or a detonator [...]."[17] They also planned to find a legal basis for not having to "return the body." They cited "generally accepted issues of hygiene" that were set in the "Cremation Law of 10.8.1938" and still valid in East Germany.[18] In agreement with the East German general state prosecutor's office, the Stasi finally decided to have Werner Kühl cremated "in order to prevent West Berlin from making a political demonstration of his body."[19]

Little remained of the other plans. In information provided to Erich Honecker, the Stasi came to the conclusion that "the two border violators are not particularly well suited for presentation to the public as major agitators."[20] They lacked real backers, such as a secret service or agent headquarters. Hence Honecker provided the solution in a handwritten note to the Stasi: "Bernd Langer should be deported to West Berlin if that is what he wants."[21]

Bernd Langer was released from pre-trial detention on August 30, 1971 and handed over to the West Berlin police at the Sandkrug Bridge border crossing by Wolfgang Vogel, the East Berlin attorney and confidant of Honecker. Bernd Langer soon clarified that there had been no fiancée or girlfriend in East Berlin and that he had nothing to do with an escape attempt or any group providing escape assistance, nor had he pursued any political motives.[22] Vogel also handed over the urn with Werner Kühl's ashes along with his death certificate and identification card.[23]

The documents and papers found on Werner Kühl were kept in East Berlin as evidence since they had been "contaminated by the bullet wounds." To avoid contradicting the ADN report, a false death certificate was issued for Werner Kühl stating that he died on July 26, 1971 at 11:50 p.m.[24]

Werner Kühl's family buried him in the St. Johannes Cemetery on the northern bank of the Plötzensee in Berlin-Wedding.

Martin Ahrends / Udo Baron / Hans-Hermann Hertle

1 On this and the course of events see "Untersuchungsbericht der NVA/Grenzkommando Mitte/Kommandeur über einen verhinderten Grenzdurchbruch durch Grenzposten des Grenzregiments 42, 25.7.1971," in: BArch, GT 6488, Bl. 27–33, as well as the establishment of facts in: "Urteil des Landgerichts Berlin in der Strafsache gegen Peter O. vom 12.5.2000," in: StA Berlin, Az. 27 Js 145/91, Bd. 3, pp. 6/7.

2 "Urteil des Landgerichts Berlin in der Strafsache gegen Peter O. vom 12.5.2000," in: StA Berlin, Az. 27 Js 145/91, Bd. 3, p. 7.

3 Die Welt, 1.9.1971.

4 See "Bericht des Oberstleutnants [Name geschwärzt] über das von mir getätigte besondere Vorkommnis am 24.7.1971 im Grenzabschnitt des GR 42, O.U., 26.7.1971 (Abschrift)," in: BStU, MfS, AS 754/70, Bd. 12, Nr. 1, Bl. 200–202.

5 See "Information Nr. 744a/71 des MfS über die Grenzprovokation in Berlin-Johannisthal am 24.7.1971, 29.7.1971," in: BStU, MfS, ZAIG Nr. 1990, Bl. 7. The entry "ZAIG did not distribute inf.[ormation]" was added handwritten on this document – as well as handwritten comments from Erich Honecker. See below for more on this.

6   "Meldung des Chefs der Grenztruppen, Generalleutnant Peter, an den 1. Sekretär des SED-Zentralkomitees, Erich Honecker, 25.7.1971," quoted from: StA Berlin, Az. 27 Js 145/91, Bd. 1, Bl. 141–144, here Bl. 143.

7   "Urteil des Landgerichts Berlin in der Strafsache gegen Peter O. vom 12.5.2000," in: StA Berlin, Az. 27 Js 145/91, Bd. 3, pp. 1–16.

8   Ibid., p. 15.

9   *Die Welt,* 26.7.1971; see also *Frankfurter Allgemeine Zeitung,* 26.7.1971; *Berliner Morgenpost,* 26.7.1971.

10 "Westberliner verübten schwere Grenzprovokation", in: *Neues Deutschland,* 27.7.1971.

11 See *Der Tagesspiegel,* 27.7.1971; *Berliner Morgenpost,* 27.7.1971. On 28.7.1971 the West Berlin newspaper *Der Abend* characterized the actions of the West Berlin authorities as "amateur" and "politically inept."

12 "Grenzprovokation Vorwand für grossangelegte Hetzkampagne gegen DDR," in: *Neues Deutschland,* 3.8.1971.

13 See z.B. *Der Abend,* 3.8.1971; *Der Tagesspiegel,* 4.8.1971; *Süddeutsche Zeitung,* 4.8.1971; *Telegraf,* 4.8.1971; *Die Welt,* 4.8.1971; *Spandauer Volksblatt,* 4.8.1971; *Berliner Morgenpost,* 4.8.1971.

14 "Erster Entwurf der 2. Information der VfS Gross-Berlin/Abt. IX zur Grenzprovokation am 24.7.1971 in Berlin-Johannisthal, Berlin, 27.7.1971," in: BStU, MfS, AS 754/70, Bd. 12, Nr. 1, Bl. 350.

15 "2. Information der VfS Gross-Berlin/Abt. IX zur Grenzprovokation am 24. Juli 1971 in Berlin-Johannisthal, Berlin, den 27.7.1971," in: BStU, MfS, AS 754/70, Bd. 12, Nr. 1, Bl. 340.

16 Ibid., Bl. 342.

17 "Erster Entwurf der 2. Information der VfS Gross-Berlin/Abt. IX zur Grenzprovokation am 24. Juli 1971 in Berlin-Johannisthal, Berlin, den 27.7.1971," in: BStU, MfS, AS 754/70, Bd. 12, Nr. 1, Bl. 349.

18 "Vorschlag der VfS Gross-Berlin/Abt. IX zur Durchführung der Abschlussmassnahmen im Vorgang L./Kühl, Berlin, den 17.8.1971," in: BStU, MfS, AS 754/70, Bd. 12, Nr. 1, Bl. 442.

19 "Dritter Entwurf der 2. Information der VfS Gross-Berlin/Abt. IX zur Grenzprovokation am 24. Juli 1971 in Berlin-Johannisthal, Berlin, den 27.7.1971," in: BStU, MfS, AS 754/70, Bd. 12, Nr. 1, Bl. 356–370, here Bl. 370.

20 "Information Nr. 744a/71 des MfS über die Grenzprovokation in Berlin-Johannisthal am 24.7.1971, 29.7.1971," in: BStU, MfS, ZAIG Nr. 1990, Bl. 15.

21 Ibid., Bl. 20.

22 See *Berliner Morgenpost,* 31.8.1971.

23 See *DPA,* 30.8.1971; *AP,* 30.8.1971; *Der Tagesspiegel,* 31.8.1971; *BZ,* 31.8.1971; *Spandauer Volksblatt,* 31.8.1971; see also "Bericht der West-Berliner Polizei, Betr.: Entlassung des Bernd L. nach West-Berlin und Übernahme der Urne des bei dem Zwischenfall am 24.7.1971 erschossenen Werner Kühl, 31.8.1971," in: StA Berlin, Az. 27 Js 145/91, Bd. 1, Bl. 112–113.

24 See "Anlage der VfS Gross-Berlin/Abt. IX zum Abschlussbericht, o.D. [17.8.1971]," in: BStU, MfS, AS 754/70, Bd. 12, Nr. 1, Bl. 452.

Dieter Beilig

born on September 5, 1941

shot dead on October 2, 1971
near the Brandenburg Gate
on the sector border between
Berlin-Tiergarten and Berlin-Mitte

Dieter Beilig was born in Berlin and grew up in the western part of the city. He was 20 years old when the sector borders were sealed off in August 1961. Like so many West Berliners of his generation, he was not willing to passively accept that his city had been brutally divided. He went out onto the streets to protest against the East German border regime. His protest activities throughout the early 1960s repeatedly attracted attention in West Berlin. Only many years later did it become known that Dieter Beilig, a committed opponent of the Wall, had himself died at the Berlin Wall in October 1971. East Germany kept secret what had happened to Dieter Beilig after he climbed onto the Wall near the Brandenburg Gate on October 2, 1971.

Since childhood, Dieter Beilig had lived in the Kreuzberg district, which belonged to the American sector. He grew up under modest circumstances and never knew his father, who had fallen as a soldier in Second World War. His mother did not have an easy time raising her only child, but she always remained an important person in his life.[1] Her son quit a baker's apprenticeship and later found work as an unskilled laborer at the federal printing office. He moved into an apartment on Köpenicker Strasse, near the Kreuzberg bank of the Spree River that bordered the East Berlin district of Friedrichshain. It was not far from the Oberbaum Bridge, which, until August 13, 1961 had been a busy crossing point between the East and the West. Dieter Beilig had probably personally experienced how border guards shot at fugitives here and he continually thought up new ways to express his outrage. On occasion he got into trouble with the West Berlin police. In July 1962, for example, he was arrested temporarily for throwing smoke bombs over the Wall.[2] A month later a picture of the red-headed, freckle-faced young man was published in a number of newspapers after he had participated in the front row of demonstrations that took place in August 1962, one year after the Wall had been built and Peter Fechter had been killed. He was carrying a large wooden cross bearing the inscription: "We condemn it." Later Beilig explained what had been meant by it: "I went through West Berlin on August 13, 1962 carrying a wooden cross that I placed at the site where Peter Fechter was murdered. After all it was murder. [...]

He had a right to be offered assistance. [...] I did not break the law. I merely pro-tested against this pointless murder. [...] I am a worker and despise every form of totalitarian dictatorship, be it Hitler or the present one. I love freedom and human dignity."[3]

The young West Berliner was sitting in an East German prison when he wrote these lines. He had fallen into the clutches of the Stasi in April 1964 under un-known circumstances.[4] At the time West Berliners believed that Dieter Beilig had been kidnapped and taken to East Berlin.[5] But Stasi files claim that he had driven to the Friedrichstrasse station border crossing in a drunken state on April 29, 1964, had identified himself at the passport control office and stated that he wanted to get into contact with the Stasi.[6] After his arrest Dieter Beilig was subjected to end-less interrogations and remained in pre-trial detention for many months. In the end his anti-Wall activities led to his indictment by the East Berlin city court for "seditious propaganda and incitement" and for "seditious acts of violence." He was sentenced to twelve years in prison in December 1964.[7] In January 1965 he was serving time in the Brandenburg Penitentiary, sometimes in solitary confine-ment because he rebelled against the guard staff and was said to have been in-volved in escape plans.[8] After many weeks of uncertainty, his mother in West Ber-lin finally learned what had happened to him and hired an attorney. The political prisoner was redeemed by the Federal Republic of Germany in 1966 and released to the West by the East German authorities in September, well before his sentence had expired.

Dieter Beilig moved back to Berlin-Kreuzberg after his release. He probably remained true to his political convictions even though he kept quiet after he was let out of prison. The mood in West Berlin had changed fundamentally during this time. A large part of the population began to view the continued division of the city as an unalterable reality and was supportive of Willy Brandt's policy of détente.[9] One consequence of this political change was the Four Powers Treaty of Septem-ber 1971. A month later, on October 2, Dieter Beilig climbed on top of the Berlin Wall at the Brandenburg Gate. It is not known whether his action that Saturday morning was supposed to be an expression of support or opposition to the "new east policies" pursued by the former mayor of Berlin. When he ran along the Wall, West Berlin policemen demanded that he get down. Instead, he jumped down to the other side of the Wall, unrecognized, while calling out "freedom for Germany, Willy is the greatest."[10]

The western observers were unable to see what happened next on East Berlin territory. According to border troop and Stasi reports, Dieter Beilig was immedi-ately arrested and identified from his identity card.[11] In the 1970s, these kinds of incidents, regarded by East Germany as "illegal border crossings" and "enemy agitations" were not uncommon at prominent sites such as the Brandenburg Gate.[12] To avoid negative headlines, East Germany usually arrested the undesired intruder, conducted an interrogation and then sent him back to West Berlin without a fuss. After his arrest, Dieter Beilig was brought to the command point of the border troop regiment that was located in the Academy of Arts building on the nearby Pariser Platz. On the way there he tried to break free of his captors but was caught again. After arriving at the command post he was guarded by two border soldiers and forced to take a seat in a small room and wait. According to the border guards' version of the events, he again tried to flee and was shot at close range without warning. The East German border troops reported that, at 9:43 a.m., the "border violator" attempted to flee through the window. "The head guard" reacted by "using his firearm" and "injured the person in his upper body with a bullet from his MPi."[13] Dieter Beilig probably died immediately.[14]

Given the large number of visitors to both sides of the Brandenburg Gate, the Stasi initially expected that it would be impossible to conceal the death. Nevertheless, to be on the safe side, the Stasi went to the trouble of making it look as if the guard had acted in self-defense. The Stasi file noted that after Dieter Beilig's death, his fingerprints were put on the weapon to create "evidence" to make it look as if he had "wanted to disarm a member of the border troops, making the use of firearms necessary."[15] When it became clear that, besides the border guards involved in the incident, there had been no other eyewitnesses on either side of the Wall, the Stasi began efforts to completely conceal Dieter Beilig's death from the public. They did not answer any requests for information from authorities and relatives in the western side of the city. A West Berlin attorney, hired by Dieter Beilig's mother, tried in vain to contact the relevant offices in East Germany. Dieter Beilig's mother died in 1988 without ever learning what had happened to her son.[16]

After the collapse of East Germany in 1989, the crime and its cover-up were discovered during the investigation of the man responsible for shooting him. But it turned out that the gunman, a former border troop officer, could not face trial because he had already passed away.[17] At the same time the law-enforcement authorities tried to open a preliminary investigation against eleven former members of the East German Ministry of State Security and judicial authority. They were charged with participating in an attempt to conceal the circumstances of Dieter Beilig's death. Three former Stasi members were ultimately tried. The Berlin public prosecutor charged them, saying they had aided the gunman by creating false evidence. But in the main trial before the Berlin state court, the defendants refused to provide any information to clarify the circumstances of the manipulation. They were acquitted in June 1999 because the charge of accessory to the fact could not be sufficiently proven.[18]

Dieter Beilig's fate became public in 2003 when the Academy of Arts was being refurbished.[19] Markings on the floor inside the re-opened building show the location of the border troop command post where he died. It is still not known where the Stasi buried Dieter Beilig's human remains after his body was cremated at the Baumschulenweg Crematorium in Berlin-Treptow.

Christine Brecht

---

1   See BStU, MfS, AS 754/70, Bd. XVI, Nr. 3, Bl. 152–159, and *Berliner Zeitung,* 11.8.2003. Photos of his mother were among the few things that Dieter Beilig had on him at his death on October 2, 1971. See ibid., Nr. 4, Bl. 3.

2   See "Bericht der West-Berliner Polizeiinspektion Kreuzberg betr. vorläufige Festnahme wegen Werfens eines Rauchkörpers über Grenzmauer in SBS, 26.7.1962," in: PHS, Bestand Grenzvorkommnisse, n. pag., and

"Vermerk der West-Berliner Polizeiinspektion Kreuzberg betr. vorläufige Festnahme wegen Werfens eines Wurf-körpers über die Grenzmauer in den SBS, 15.8.1962," in: Ibid.

3 "Handschriftlicher Brief von Dieter Beilig aus dem Zuchthaus Brandenburg an DDR-Generalstaatsanwalt Streit, o. D. [um 1965/66]," in: BStU, MfS, 5040/65, Gefangenenakten, Bl. 86–87, here p. 87.

4 See "Ereignismeldung der West-Berliner Schutzpolizei, 19.6.1964," in: PHS, Bestand Ereignismeldung der West-Berliner Schutzpolizei, n. pag.

5 See *Bild-Zeitung*, 19.6.1964.

6 See "Festnahmebericht [des MfS/]HA Passkontrolle-Fahndung/KPP Bhf.-Friedrichstrasse/Arbeitsgruppe 1, 30.4.1964," in: BStU, MfS, 5040/65, Ermittlungsakten, Bl. 31, and "Information der VfS Gross-Berlin/Abt. IX, 30.4.1964," in: Ibid., Bl. 37–41. Since the Stasi was eager to present Beilig as a ringleader, it strongly exaggerated his anti-Wall activities in its files, a fact made evident when they are compared to the West Berlin reports.

7 See "Urteil des Stadtgerichts von Gross-Berlin vom 11.12.1964," in: BStU, MfS, 5040/65, Gerichtsakten, Bl. 258.

8 See "Handschriftliches Protokoll [eines Mitarbeiters des Strafvollzugs], Brandenburg, 20.4.1965," in: Ibid. Gefangenenakte, Bl. 62–63, und "Handschriftlicher Aktenvermerk [eines Mitarbeiters des Strafvollzugs], Brandenburg, 11.8.1965," in: Ibid., Bl. 66.

9 For context, see Heinrich Potthoff, *Im Schatten der Mauer. Deutschlandpolitik 1961 bis 1990*, Berlin, 1999, and Hans Georg Lehmann, Mit der Mauer leben? Die Einstellungen zur Berliner Mauer im Wandel, in: *Aus Politik und Zeitgeschichte*, B 33–34 (1986), pp. 19–34.

10 See *Berliner Morgenpost*, 3.10.1971; *Der Tagesspiegel*, 3.10.1971; *Spandauer Volksblatt*, 3.10.1971.

11 On the course of events see "Information Nr. 972/71 des MfS-ZAIG," in: BStU, MfS, ZAIG Nr. 1992, Bl. 3–6, and "Information der VfS Gross-Berlin/Abt. IX zur Grenzprovokation in Berlin-Mitte, Brandenburger Tor am 2.10.1971, 2.10.1971," in: BStU, MfS, HA IX, Nr. 17687, Bl. 44–51.

12 For data on West-East border transfers for training year 1970/71 see "Information Nr. 11/71 der NVA/Grenz-kommando Mitte, 4.12.1971," in: BArch, GT 2152, Bl. 70–76.

13 "Tagesmeldung Nr. 233/71 der NVA/Kommando der Grenztruppen/Operativer Diensthabender, 3.10.1971," in: BArch, GT 6376, Bl. 111–114, here Bl. 111–112.

14 One witness, who at the time was called in as a medic, put on the record in West Germany in 1978 that the injured man showed no signs of life when medical assistance arrived. See "Niederschrift der Zeugenverneh-mung eines Augenzeugen durch die westdeutsche Grenzpolizei in Mellrichstadt, 27.2.1978," in: StA Berlin, Az. 27 Js 62/92, Bd. 1, Bl. 2–3.

15 "Information der VfS Gross-Berlin/Abt. IX zur Grenzprovokation in Berlin-Mitte, Brandenburger Tor am 2.10.1971, 2.10.1971," in: BStU, MfS, HA IX Nr. 17687, Bl. 50; see also "Massnahmeplan [des MfS] betr. Anruf von Genossen Major Wolf/HA IX/9 am 4.10.71, o. D. [4.10.1971]," in: BStU, MfS, AS 754/70, Bd. XVI, Nr. 3, Bl. 251.

16 On the unsuccessful efforts undertaken by the East German lawyer, Wolfgang Vogel, and others, see "Befragungs-protokoll des damaligen Rechtsanwalts von Dieter Beilig durch die ZERV, 23.10.1992," in: StA Berlin, Az. 27/2 Js 62/92, Bd. 1, Bl. 93–134.

17 See "Verfügung der Staatsanwaltschaft II bei dem Landgericht Berlin (27/2 Js 62/92), 28.2.1996," in: Ibid., Bd. 2, Bl. 139–140.

18 See "Urteil des Landgerichts Berlin vom 8.6.1999," in: StA Berlin, Az. 28 Js 22/96, Bd. 5, Bl. 164a–164j, and "Stasi-Offiziere sollen Tötung vertuscht haben," in: *Frankfurter Rundschau*, 7.5.1999.

19 *Pressemitteilung der Akademie der Künste*, 10.8.2003; see also "Mauermord in der Akademie," German tel-evision program "Kulturzeit", 3SAT, 11.8.2003.

Horst Kullack

born on November 20, 1948

shot on December 31, 1971
on the outer ring between
Grossziethen (Königs Wusterhausen district)
and Berlin-Tempelhof
died from his bullet wounds on January 21, 1972

H orst Kullack was 23 years old when he was shot by the East German border troops on December 31, 1971. He was born on November 20, 1948 and grew up as the oldest of five siblings in Grossziethen, a village near the border, southeast of Berlin. He did poorly in school and quit after the eighth grade. Lacking vocational training, Horst Kullack got a job as a transport worker in Zeesen and helped out on the family subsidiary farm by looking after the cattle and garden. According to a Stasi report, the residents of Grossziethen said he "received more beatings than food" as a child.[1] His mother believed the many beatings were the reason for his mental sluggishness and for his loneliness.[2] He did not have many friends and the villagers did not take him very seriously. An uncle and grandmother lived in West Berlin.

In 1967, at the age of 21, Horst Kullack tried to escape for the first time, which according to a statement made by his father, earned him a fine.[3] After that he often caught the attention of the state authorities. He was investigated in 1968 for "slandering the state" because he supposedly insulted a border soldier, calling him a "pig, criminal and murderer."[4] After having a few drinks in a bar, he spoke of wanting to flee to his grandmother in West Berlin and was dragged to a soldiers' barracks as a consequence. But a psychological evaluation determined that he was not certifiably sane and so he was spared arrest. After speaking with his mother, the East German secret police noted that the 23-year-old man, often beaten and picked on, was said to have suffered from depression and even spoke occasionally of suicide.[5]

On the last day of 1971, Horst Kullack headed towards the border after dark. His father later surmised that he may have been planning to visit his relatives in the West Berlin district of Neukölln.[6] At around 10 p.m. he knocked on the window of a house that was situated within the security grounds and inquired whether he was already at the border. When he was asked what he wanted there, he responded by saying "that he was taking off for West Berlin."[7] The resident of the house, a member of the Communist Party, reported Kullack's plan to the responsible East German police division and the border guards were informed.

Horst Kullack nonetheless managed to climb the interior security fence and creep towards the front wall in a hunched over position before he was suddenly caught in the spotlight. Without calling out to Kullack in advance, each of the border guards aimed and fired two shots at him. One of the bullets hit him in the stomach and the young man collapsed.

Before treating his wounds, the border soldiers hid Kullack, who was bleeding severely, in the anti-vehicle trench. He was not provided medical care until after he was transported to the rear border area in a Trabant "Kübel." The New Year's Eve fireworks had drowned out the sound of the shots and the guards were intent on preventing anyone on the West Berlin side from seeing the incident.[8] The final report to the commander of the border troops stated that "the well-organized action resulted in ensuring that the struggle against and retrieval of the border violator was not noticed by the enemy."[9]

The two gunmen were rewarded: One received a badge of marksmanship and the other was promoted to private.[10]

The hospital staff initially denied that he was there when Horst Kullack's father tried to visit his son in the hospital. Only after he protested loudly did the doctors tell him that his son had been wounded and permitted him to visit him at his bedside. One of them quietly expressed his disgust over the shots fired at the fugitive.[11] The Kullack family's home was searched by the East German secret police a short time later.[12]

An East German secret police report written after Horst Kullack's failed escape attempt stated that "in the past numerous psychological evaluations had determined that K. is not certifiably sane [...]."[13] Due to "constant pathological disturbance in his mental ability," the Stasi dismissed the charges of "attempted flight from the republic" on January 4, 1972 and suggested "committing him to a long period of treatment in a psychiatric hospital after he recovers."[14]

Although doctors in the Königs Wusterhausen District Hospital operated on him five times in an effort to heal his inner injuries, Horst Kullack died on January 21, 1972. He was buried at the cemetery in Grossziethen in the family grave in the presence of a small group of friends and family on January 29, 1972. His relatives in the West could not attend the funeral because they were denied an entrance visa to East Germany.

Horst Kullack's death became known in the West in February 1972, shortly after he was buried, when his uncle in West Berlin issued charges against unnamed members of the border troops. His brother had sent him a letter informing him of the shooting of his nephew.[15] More than 23 years later, on November 1, 1995, the two men responsible for shooting him were charged with joint manslaughter and both sentenced by the Potsdam state court to a youth sentence of one year and three months probation.[16] One of them had the courage to apologize to the father of the victim for his act and the suffering that he caused the family.[17]

For many decades a memorial cross has stood in commemoration of Horst Kullack on Wittelsbacher Strasse in the Lichtenrade district, on the West Berlin side of the area where he had attempted his escape.

Martin Ahrends / Udo Baron / Hans-Hermann Hertle

1   See "Laufende Einschätzung über die Sicherung der Schwerpunkträume im Verantwortungsbereich [Fragment eines Dokumentes], undatiert," in: BStU, Ast. Potsdam, AU 1195/75, Bd. 1, Bl. 39.

2   See "Geführte Aussprache mit der Mutter des Kullack, Horst, in der [MfS-]KD Königs Wusterhausen, 4.1.1972," in: BStU, Ast. Potsdam, AU 1195/75, Bd. 1, Bl. 35/36, here Bl. 36.

3   See "Urteil des Landgerichts Potsdam vom 1.11.1995," in: StA Berlin, Az. 2 Js 39/95, Bd. 2, Bl. 1–28 (Duplikatsakte).

4   "Schreiben des VPKA Königs Wusterhausen an die BDVP Potsdam/ODH, Betr.: Staatsverleumdung, 10.8.1968," in: BStU, Ast. Potsdam, AU 1195/75, Bd. 1, Bl. 26.

5   See "Geführte Aussprache mit der Mutter des Kullack, Horst, in der [MfS-]KD Königs Wusterhausen, 4.1.1972," in: Ibid., Bl. 35/36, here Bl. 36.

6   See conversation conducted by Udo Baron with Willi Kullack, 27.9.2007.

7   See "Geführte Aussprache mit [Name geschwärzt], wohnhaft Grossziethen, in der [MfS-]KD Königs Wusterhausen, 2.1.1972," in: BStU, Ast. Potsdam, AU 1195/75, Bd. 1, Bl. 21.

8   See "Bericht der NVA/Grenzregiment 42/Der Kommandeur über Anwendung der Schusswaffe bei Verhinderung eines Grenzdurchbruches am 31.12.1971, 22.30 Uhr, im Abschnitt Lichtenrader Strasse, 1.1.1972," in: BStU, Ast. Potsdam, AU 1195/75, Bd. 1, Bl. 6–8.

9   Ibid., Bl. 8.

10 See "Urteil des Landgerichts Potsdam vom 1.11.1995," in: StA-Berlin, Az. 2 Js 39/95, Bd. 2, Bl. 17.

11 See ibid.

12 See ibid.

13 "Telegramm der BVfS Potsdam/Abt. IX an das MfS/HA IX/8, 3.1.1972," in: BStU, Ast. Potsdam, AU 1195/75, Bd. 1, Bl. 22–23.

14 "Verfügung des Leiters der BVfS Potsdam, 4.1.1972," in: Ibid., Bl. 38.

15 See "Bericht/Strafanzeige der West-Berliner Polizei, 4.2.1972," in: StA Berlin, Az. 2 Js 39/95, Bd. 1, Bl. 3.

16 See "Urteil des Landgerichts Potsdam vom 1.11.1995," in: Ibid., Bd. 2, Bl. 1–28.

17 See conversation conducted by Udo Baron with Willi Kullack, 27.9.2007.

Manfred Weylandt

born on July 12, 1942

shot and drowned on February 14, 1972
near the Schilling Bridge
in the Spree between
Berlin-Friedrichshain and Berlin-Kreuzberg

Manfred Weylandt, born on July 12, 1942 in Berlin, grew up with his mother and two sisters. He left school after seventh grade and eked out a living as an unskilled worker. He also served various prison sentences between 1957 and 1970 for different offenses. When he married a second time in the fall of 1970, he seemed to have gained a degree of stability in his life. After this he worked as an assistant stoker for a filter and gasification plant located right at the Berlin Wall near the Ostbahnhof station in the Friedrichshain district. He underwent training as a boiler attendant and an East German secret police report noted that "after this he attended to his work with discipline."[1] But in December 1972 the Friedrichshain city court sentenced him again to two years in prison "for theft to the detriment of Socialist property."[2] He expected to be arrested at any moment. A Stasi agent cited statements from his wife that he began drinking alcohol to counter his fear and taking pills for his insomnia.[3]

He received the news by mail on February 13, 1972 that he was to begin his sentence on March 1 at the Rummelsburg Penitentiary. Manfred Weylandt did not want to go back to prison. Over the last few months he had often spoken to his wife about escaping to the West and now this seemed the only option left to him.[4] He got into a fight with his wife on February 14 after he had spent the last of their money on alcohol and a guitar. Drunk, Manfred Weylandt stormed from their home in Berlin-Adlershof at 9:30 p.m. He was last seen in the state-run bar called "Gemütliche Ecke" (Cozy Corner) in Berlin-Friedrichshain at 10:30 p.m. He left with the words "I am planning something that the world can only dream of."[5]

He biked to the company where he worked.[6] When he got there he managed to reach the fence that blocked off the grounds from the border without his colleagues' on the night shift noticing. He climbed onto the roof of a shack and slid down a heating pipe that landed him in a dog run within the border grounds, but no dog attacked. The East German secret police later found out that at that very moment the company staff was feeding the dogs.[7] Manfred Weylandt apparently knew that he did not have to worry about the dogs. He took off his jacket and scarf, and crossed the border grounds up to the bank wall of the Spree where he entered the ice cold water and began swimming towards West Berlin. Two border guards noticed him at around 11:30 at night, after he was halfway across the river. When he failed to respond to their shouts, they opened fire and shot from the hip at the fugitive until he disappeared from view. A bullet hit him in the back of his head and Manfred Weylandt sank into the Spree and drowned.[8]

The search for him soon began, but the divers did not find his body near the Schilling Bridge until the next day. They were able to conceal the retrieval of his body by fastening the corpse to the bottom of the boat so that no one on the West Berlin riverbank could see it. Other distractions were also created to make it look like the "divers were searching for some objects."[9]

The gunmen were awarded the "merit award of the East German border troops" the very same day and a bonus of 150 marks. In their testimonies they later claimed that they were not informed about the fate of the fugitive. Twenty-one years later they were indicted by the Berlin district court for joint manslaughter and sentenced as youths to a year and ten months in prison, which was commuted to probation.[10]

Manfred Weylandt did not have any papers on him when he fled but the Stasi was able to identify him two days after his death from his finger prints. His wife, however, was not informed about his whereabouts. The Stasi agents first wanted to find out who knew about his plans to flee so that his death could be kept as secret as possible. They intended to fabricate a different version of his death. Initially, the wife was only to be informed that "her dead husband was retrieved from Berlin waters."[11] The conditions for concealing the truth appeared propitious Although people on the West Berlin side had heard the shots, all they had seen was a patrol boat searching the Spree.

Manfred Weylandt's wife reported her husband's absence to the East German police on February 15, 1972. Her missing persons' report was not registered for another six days. She looked for her husband at various hospitals and prisons without success and became increasingly worried that he may have followed through on his occasionally expressed thoughts about committing suicide because he feared his impending imprisonment.[12] His relatives waited in uncertainty for many weeks. The East German secret police used the time to investigate his circle of friends and acquaintances, as well as his work place and close relatives. Meanwhile they had Manfred Weylandt's body cremated at the Baumschulenweg Crematorium on March 13, 1972. At that point they were certain that neither his friends nor colleagues at work had learned the reason for his disappearance.[13]

The following day the widow was informed that the body of her husband had been pulled out of the Spree near the Museum Island and that he had already been cremated at public expense. The death certificate noted the time of death as February 15, 1972, 5:30 p.m., which is when the autopsy was conducted. Although she was not told how he died, according to a Stasi report, the widow appeared calm when she received the news from the East German secret police.[14] She probably felt confirmed in her suspicion that her husband may have taken his own life. The family did not find out the truth for another twenty years.

The urn containing Manfred Weylandt's ashes was buried in the East Berlin

Baumschulenweg cemetery on March 21, 1972. His relatives were not present at the funeral.

Martin Ahrends / Udo Baron

1 "2. Information der VfS Gross-Berlin / Abt. IX zur Grenzprovokation am 14. Februar 1972 an der Spree in Berlin-Friedrichshain, Stralauer Platz, 17.2.1972," in: BStU, MfS, AS 754/70, Bd. 16, Nr. 1, Bl. 50–54, here Bl. 53.

2 Ibid., Bl. 53.

3 See "Bericht der VfS Gross-Berlin, 21.2.1972," in: BStU, MfS, AS 754/70, Bd. 16, Nr. 1, Bl. 87–92, here Bl. 87.

4 See "Urteil des Landgerichts Berlin vom 17.6.1993," in: StA Berlin, Az. 2 Js 55/91, Bd. 2, Bl. 144–185, here Bl. 154.

5 See "Abschlussbericht der VfS Gross-Berlin / Abt. IX zur Grenzprovokation am 14.2.1972 an der Spree in Berlin-Friedrichshain, Stralauer Platz, 3.4.1972," in: BStU, MfS, AS 754/70, Bd. 16, Nr. 1, Bl. 123–125, here Bl. 124.

6 On the establishment of the facts concerning circumstances of events see "Urteil des Landgerichts Berlin vom 17.6.1993," in: StA Berlin, Az. 2 Js 55/91, Bd. 2, esp. Bl. 153–162.

7 "Information des [MfS] / KD Friedrichshain über Diskussionen im VEB Vergaser- und Filterwerke Werk III zum Vorkommnis am 14.2.1972," in: BStU, MfS, AS 754/70, Bd. 16, Nr. 1, Bl. 79.

8 "Obduktionsbericht des Instituts für Gerichtliche Medizin der Humboldt-Universität zu Berlin, 15.2.1972," in: BStU, MfS, AS 754/70, Bd. 16, Nr. 1, Bl. 207–215, here Bl. 212.

9 "Information der VfS Gross-Berlin / Abt. IX zur Grenzprovokation am 14. Februar 1972 in Berlin-Friedrichshain, Stralauer Platz, 16.2.1972," in: BStU, MfS, AS 754/70, Bd. 16, Nr. 1, Bl. 105–107, here Bl. 105.

10 See "Urteil des Landgerichts Berlin vom 17.6.1993," in: StA Berlin, Az. 2 Js 55/91, Bd. 2, Bl. 144–185. One defendant appealed the verdict to the Federal Court of Justice (BGH-Urteil vom 26.7.1994, AZ. 5 StR 167/94), which rejected it. Consequently, the appeal of this entered as an institutional issue introduced by the Federal Constitutional Court but was also rejected (BVerfG-Beschluss vom 24.10.1996, Az. 2 BvR 1852/94). In response the European Court of Human Rights took on the case, deciding in 2001 that the killing of Manfred Weylandt was also a crime at the time that it was committed. The verdicts concerning the Weylandt case are documented in: Klaus Marxen / Gerhard Werle (eds.), *Strafjustiz und DDR-Unrecht. Band 2/1. Teilband: Gewalttaten an der deutsch-deutschen Grenze,* Berlin/New York, 2002, pp. 157–215. See also Roman Grafe, *Deutsche Gerechtigkeit. Prozesse gegen DDR-Grenzschützen und ihre Befehlsgeber,* München, 2004, pp. 261–264.

11 "2. Information der VfS Gross-Berlin / Abt. IX zur Grenzprovokation am 14. Februar 1972 an der Spree in Berlin-Friedrichshain, Stralauer Platz, 17.2.1972," in: BStU, MfS, AS 754/70, Bd. 16, Nr. 1, Bl. 50–54, here Bl. 54.

12 See "Bericht der VfS Gross-Berlin, 21.2.1972," in: BStU, MfS, AS 754/70, Bd. 16, Nr. 1, Bl. 87–92, here Bl. 89.

13 See "Abschlussbericht der VfS Gross-Berlin / Abt. IX zur Grenzprovokation am 14.2.1972 an der Spree in Berlin-Friedrichshain, Stralauer Platz, 3.4.1972," in: BStU, MfS, AS 754/70, Bd. 16, Nr. 1, Bl. 124.

14 Ibid., Bl. 124; Sterbeurkunde von Manfred Weylandt, 9.3.1972, in: BStU, MfS, AS 754/70, Bd. 16, Nr. 1, Bl. 135.

Klaus Schulze

born on October 13, 1953

shot dead on March 7, 1972
near Falkenhöh, across from the Eiskeller exclave
on the outer ring between
Falkensee (Nauen district) and Berlin-Spandau

K laus Schulze was born on October 13, 1953 in Falkensee, which borders West Berlin. He had tried unsuccessfully to flee to West Berlin when he was 14 years old, but charges were not made against him since he was still a minor at the time.[1] The difficult circumstances under which he was raised may have been the reason for his escape attempt. Klaus Schulze attended the Geschwister-Scholl Schule, a school in Falkenhöh, from 1960 to 1968, but he fell behind in his school work. He later quit his vocational training as a cattle breeder and eked out a living as an unskilled worker.[2] He had no professional aspirations in the area where he grew up. He spent most of his time with a clique of young people his own age that the Stasi considered "a bunch of loafers" and a "negative group of teenagers."[3] This group was typical of many young people in East Germany at this time who wanted many things, but did not want to live like their parents did. The kids in these groups thought having a steady job was square.

But in East Germany anyone without a "steady job" was bound to get into trouble with the state. After Klaus Schulze and his friend Dieter Krause quit their jobs at the state-owned Hennigsdorf steel mill in the summer of 1971 and had not worked for three weeks, they were reprimanded by the Falkenssee city council and encouraged to find work immediately. This was their last chance to "remain upright citizens and engage in decent work," they were told.[4] On March 5, 1972 Klaus Schulze was again reprimanded for "absenteeism."[5] A year had passed since the East German authorities had threatened to commit him and Dieter Krause to a re-education work camp and hence they were both eager to leave East Germany as soon as possible.[6]

They had a friend whose property in nearby Falkenhöh was situated right on the border. The two young men had taken a look at the border area there once during the day and once at night and then began preparing their flight. They realized that the border strip was probably visible from a watchtower about 300 meters away, but recognized that the overgrown vegetation would provide cover and that a light in the control strip was out.[7]

In the late afternoon of March 7, 1972, Klaus Schulze and Dieter Krause stopped by a number of bars in Falkensee. At about 10 p.m. they headed for Falkenhöh. After crossing a number of properties located near the border they reached the interior wire mesh security fence that bordered on their friend's plot. He was not present at the time and was not informed about their escape plan. They found a 2.7-meter-long ladder in the shed. They pushed it through the bent fence before entering the border grounds. They were able to get over the signal fence with the ladder, but without realizing it, they had set off an alarm. Klaus Schulze, running behind one end of the ladder in a crouched position, stumbled over a trip wire. Dieter Krause was the first to reach the last fence, a 2.5-meter-high stretch metal fence set on an adjoining steep concrete slope, and placed the ladder on it. The head guard began firing his gun continuously; the other guard joined in the shooting shortly after this. Dieter Krause managed to get over the last fence amid a hail of bullets.[8] Klaus Schulze, who had fallen behind after he tripped, was hit by a bullet in his chest that shattered his major artery and lung.[9]

In the spring of 1991 Klaus Schulze's siblings requested that the Berlin justice minister investigate the death of their brother.[10] In the fall of 1994 the investigation led to charges being filed against the two guards. The case against the head guard was ultimately dismissed due to his permanent inability to stand trial. The second gunman on trial claimed that he had intentionally shot over the ladder. He was acquitted in early 1997 because the Potsdam district court was unable to prove either an intention to kill or his involvement in joint manslaughter.[11]

Klaus Schulze's sister was summoned by the authorities to an interrogation the day after her brother died. She was informed only that her brother had died under "dishonorable" circumstances.[12] Three days after the events of March 7, 1972, a state public prosecutor and member of the East German secret police informed Klaus Schulze's parents that their son had "died in a fatal, self-inflicted accident during an attempted border breach."[13] They were pressured into agreeing to a cremation. Their son's personal possessions were returned to them against a receipt: "One pair of black men's loafers."[14] Stasi informants were also assigned to keep an eye on the family. Their mail was read so that "any possible negative reactions" that emerged could be suppressed.[15]

An urn containing the ashes of Klaus Schulze was buried in the cemetery in Falkensee on April 3, 1972.[16] The teenagers in Falkensee were not informed of the funeral's date: They had wanted to use his funeral to organize a demonstration against the order to shoot fugitives at the border.[17]

Martin Ahrends / Udo Baron / Hans-Hermann Hertle

---

1 See "Bericht des MfS/HA IX/4 über ein Vorkommnis im Bereich des 34. Grenzregimentes im Raum Falkensee/Ortsteil Falkenhöh, 9.3.1972," in: BStU, MfS, HA IX Nr. 1038, Bl. 159–163, here Bl. 161.

2 On this and the following, see "Abschlussbericht des MfS/KD Nauen zur VAO "Leiter", 13.6.1973," in: BStU, Ast. Potsdam, AU 777/73, Bd. 2, Bl. 41–52, here Bl. 46.

3 "Sachstandsbericht des MfS/KD Nauen zum OVA "Leiter", 30.8.1972," in: BStU, Ast. Potsdam, AU 777/73, Bd. 2, Bl. 5.

4 "Schreiben des Rates der Stadt Falkensee/Abt. Inneres an den VEB Quarzschmelze, 12.8.1971," in: StA Neuruppin Az. 61 Js 39/94 (vormals StA Berlin, Az. 27 Js 134/90), Sonderheft, Bl. 33.

5   See "Abschlussbericht des MfS/KD Nauen zur VAO "Leiter", 13.6.1973," in: BStU, Ast. Potsdam, AU 777/73, Bd. 2, Bl. 44.

6   See "MfS-Vernehmungsprotokoll des Beschuldigten Dieter K., 5.5.1974," in: BStU, Ast. Potsdam, AU 485/75, STA 1645, Bd. 1, Bl. 45–46. After his arrest in 1974, in his "explanation of the crime" Dieter Krause stated that his reasons for fleeing were both personal and political. Some of them can be deemed typical of his generation: Ongoing difficulties with his step-father; problems at his workplace, where he was misused as a gofer; rejection of the obligatory military service in the NVA, "since I could never shoot at a person;"; eagerness for a better life in West Berlin or West Germany; wanting to be closer to his biological father, who lived in West Berlin. ("Dieter Krause, Stellungnahme zur Straftat, Potsdam, 31.7.1974," in: Ibid., Bl. 93).

7   See ibid., Bl. 46–47.

8   See ibid., Bl. 47–48. Dieter Krause had a difficult time gaining a foothold in the West. Two years after his escape to West Berlin, he was overwhelmed by the desire to see his mother again; he had not developed close or regular contact to his father and his second wife. On May 4, 1974, with the intention of "testing out" a one-day visit to East Berlin, he was arrested by the Stasi at the Friedrichstrasse station border crossing. The Nauen district court convicted him on September 19, 1974 of "fleeing the republic" and sentenced him to three years and six months in prison. The Federal Republic of Germany paid for his release in 1975. After that he continued to travel frequently from West Berlin to East Berlin, where he fell in love with 24-year-old Marlis Varschen in November 1975. He visited her no fewer than 240 times in East Berlin in 1976. They became engaged in the middle of the year. Officially, West Berliners were only permitted to enter East Germany on 30 days of the year, but at this time the East German authorities were apparently not strictly enforcing this rule. In August 1976 Marlis Varschen submitted to the Pankow city district council a request to marry Dieter Krause and move her residency to West Berlin. Suddenly, in December 1976, the East German authorities imposed an entry and transit ban on Dieter Krause. The couple was separated but managed to meet a few times in Poland until Dieter Krause was sent back and a short time later his fiancée's identification card was retracted. Dieter Krause appealed to the East German Ministry of the Interior and the chancellor of West Germany – but it did not look like help would come in the near future. The couple could not bear being separated. In later February 1977 he managed to attain a transit visa for East Germany using a visa for Poland issued by the Polish military mission in West Berlin. He exited the train in East Berlin and sought out his fiancée. The couple was distraught and saw no way out of their dilemma. Together they committed suicide. Marlis Varschen was five months pregnant and left behind an 8-year-old son from her first marriage. See the television program "Kennzeichen D," ZDF, 22.3.1977, typoscript in: BStU, MfS, HA IX Nr. 15591, Bl. 184–188; "Bericht des MfS/HA IX/7 über den Stand der Untersuchungen zum Selbstmord der DDR-Bürgerin Varschen, Marlis, und des Bürgers von Berlin (West) Krause, Dieter, Berlin, 14.3.1977," in: BStU, MfS, AS 420/80, Bd. 1, Bl. 266–272.

9   See "Bericht des MfS/HA IX/4 über ein Vorkommnis im Bereich des 34. Grenzregimentes im Raum Falkensee/Ortsteil Falkenhöh, 9.3.1972," in: BStU, MfS, HA IX Nr. 1038, Bl. 159–160; "Obduktionsgutachten des Instituts für Gerichtliche Medizin der Humboldt-Universität zu Berlin zu Klaus Schulze, Potsdam, 9.3.1972," in: BStU, Ast. Potsdam, AP 1113/76, Bl. 18–19.

10 See "Schreiben des Bruders von Klaus Schulze an die Berliner Justizsenatorin Jutta Limbach, 21.4.1991," in: StA Neuruppin, Az. 61 Js 39/94 (vormals StA Berlin, Az. 27 Js 134/90), Bd. 1, Bl. 82–84.

11 "Urteil des Landgerichts Potsdam vom 5.2.1997," in: StA Neuruppin, Az. 61 Js 39/94 (vormals StA Berlin, Az. 27 Js 134/90), Bd.1, Bl. 373.

12 See "Schreiben des Bruders von Klaus Schulze an die Berliner Justizsenatorin Jutta Limbach, 21.4.1991," in: StA Neuruppin, Az. 61 Js 39/94 (vormals StA Berlin, Az. 27 Js 134/90), Bd. 1, Bl. 83.

13 "Statement" forced from Klaus Schulze's parents by the Stasi, Potsdam, 10.3.1972, in: BStU, Ast. Potsdam, AP 1113/76, Bl. 40.

14 Ibid.

15 "Bericht des MfS/HA IX/4 über ein Vorkommnis im Bereich des 34. Grenzregimentes im Raum Falkensee/Ortsteil Falkenhöh, 9.3.1972," in: BStU, MfS, HA IX Nr. 1038, Bl. 163.

16 See "Grabstellen-Ausweis für Klaus Schulze," in: StA Neuruppin Az. 61 Js 39/94 (vormals StA Berlin, Az. 27 Js 134/90), Bd. 1, Bl. 87.

17 See "Bericht des MfS/KD Nauen zum Vorkommnis an der Staatsgrenze am 7.3.1972 und die dazu bemerkten Diskussionen, 8.4.1972," in: BStU, Ast. Potsdam, AU 777/73, Bd. 2, Bl. 155.

Cengaver Katranci

born in 1964

drowned on October 30, 1972
in the Spree near the Oberbaum Bridge
on the sector border between
Berlin-Kreuzberg and Berlin-Friedrichshain

C engaver Katranci was born in 1964 and lived with his mother, who came from Turkey, and his three siblings in the West Berlin district of Kreuzberg.[1]

It was October 30, 1972, shortly before 1 p.m. The eight-year-old Turkish child was playing with a friend on the Spree embankment at the Gröbenufer in Kreuzberg, which was located about 100 meters from the Oberbaum Bridge border crossing. The two boys were standing on the narrow quay wall feeding the swans when Cengaver Katranci suddenly lost his balance and fell into the cold water.[2] His friend screamed and ran off to get help. A nearby fisherman tried to figure out what had happened. When he finally understood the boy's pleas, he sent him to the nearby control post to get help and ran to the site of the accident. As he started to undress, he realized that the entire width of the Spree here belonged to East Berlin and that if he tried to save the boy he would risk being shot by East German border guards. He decided against jumping into the water to save the drowning child.

In the meantime the West Berlin customs officials had notified the police and fire department and had arrived at the Spree bank. A tanker was traveling on the river, accompanied by an East German fire boat. The customs officials called out to the crew, using gesticulation to persuade the crew of the boat to turn around and rescue the child. The fire boat stopped briefly and then continued on its way.

A West Berlin police car arrived at about 1:30 p.m. The police began negotiating with an officer of the border troops on the Oberbaum Bridge about retrieving the drowned boy from the water. A short time later the West Berlin firemen arrived at Gröbenufer and two divers got ready to enter the water. They stood on the quay wall waiting for authorization to jump into the border waters to no avail.

An East Berlin water police boat stopped in the middle of the river near the site of the accident. The East German water police required a special permit from the border guards before getting any closer to the western bank. The people on the western bank called out to the crew, beckoning to them and the boat moved hesitantly towards the western bank but then turned back before a border guard speed boat quickly caught up with it. The boat had moved beyond the middle of the river into the forbidden zone that was off-limits to the crew.

A crowd that, according to police estimates, numbered more than a hundred people, had gathered at Gröbenufer. They were witnesses to a situation of humiliating helplessness. The West Berlin police had been negotiating with the border troop soldiers on the Oberbaum Bridge border crossing for almost an hour and a half. The West Berlin firemen, who were prepared with divers and rescue equipment, were never permitted to take action.[3]

At about 2:30 p.m. an East Berlin lifeboat arrived and began to search for the child. After half an hour a diver with a dead child was seen climbing out of the water close to the bank. The stretcher was ready; the dead child could have been handed over, but instead of swimming to the West Berlin riverbank, the divers carried the body back to the border troop boat. It was hardly fathomable to the onlookers on the Gröbenufer, but every move the diver made toward the western bank with the young boy would have been regarded by the border guards as an attempt to escape.

That evening Cengaver Katranci's mother was permitted to travel to East Berlin accompanied by two relatives. She had to identify her son in the forensic institute of Charité Hospital after which the body was transferred to West Berlin. The mother requested that her child be buried in Ankara.[4]

The death of the eight-year-old-boy led the Berlin Senate to announce that it would negotiate a treaty with East Germany over assistance measures that could be employed should future accidents occur in the border waters.[5] It took many rounds of negotiations and the deaths of three more children in the Spree before terms could be settled on in 1975.

Udo Baron

1 The West Berlin police registered the name of the drowned child mistakenly as Cengiz Koc, the last name of his uncle. It was later corrected by the *Berliner Morgenpost* and confirmed by the police. See *Berliner Morgenpost*, 2.11.1972, and "Vermerk der West-Berliner Polizei, 2.11.1972", in: LAB, Bestand Abgeordnetenhaus.
2 See *Berliner Morgenpost*, 31.10.1972; *BZ*, 31.10.1972.
3 See *Die Welt*, 31.10.1972.
4 See *Berliner Morgenpost*, 2.11.1972.
5 See "Plenarprotokolle des Abgeordnetenhauses von Berlin, 6. Wahlperiode, 37. Sitzung vom 9.11.1972," pp. 1294–1295.

Holger H.

born in 1971

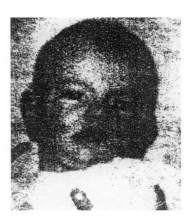

suffocated to death while fleeing with his parents on
January 22, 1973
at the Drewitz border crossing /
Dreilinden command post ("Checkpoint Bravo")
on the outer ring between
Potsdam-Babelsberg and Berlin-Zehlendorf

L ittle is known about why Ingrid and Klaus H. wanted to flee.[1] They had met in Moscow on a youth travel program. After their son was born they began their adult life together and were certain that they did not want to spend their life in East Germany: As a consequence of Klaus H.'s first escape attempt, which he undertook across the Baltic Sea with friends when he was 17, he had very limited career opportunities in East Germany. He was permanently marked as a "republic fugitive." Ingrid H. was probably tormented as a young teacher by the political patronizing she encountered, which was so typical of East Germany. They wanted to escape for themselves but also for their son: They did not want him to grow up under the constrictions that they had experienced as children and under which they suffered as young adults.

On a January night a truck belonging to a West Berlin acquaintance stopped on the parking lot of the transit highway. The couple climbed onto the back of the truck with their 15-month-old son and hid in large empty crates: The 23-year-old father was in one crate and the 20-year-old mother and child were in another. The truck stopped at the Drewitz border crossing. "The inspection at the Drewitz checkpoint took longer than usual," the driver of the truck later told the Berlin police.[2]

The nerves of the fleeing couple were extremely on edge when the child began to cry. The mother tried in vain to quiet him and in panic held his mouth shut. Little Holger was suffering from an inflammation of the middle ear and bronchitis. The infection had probably also blocked his nasal passageway. His mother did not realize that he was unable to breathe through his nose. The escape was a success; the family made it through without being discovered. The truck drove another 300 meters and then the crates were opened. "My child," Ingrid H. cried out immediately and held her motionless child out to the helpers on the western command post. Holger H. was not breathing anymore and all attempts to revive him failed.

The 15-month-old Holger H. was buried in Berlin-Marienfelde.

Martin Ahrends / Udo Baron

1   On the following see "Tragisches Ende einer Flucht mit dem Lastwagen – Kind erstickte während der Kontrolle in den Armen seiner Mutter," in: *Berliner Morgenpost*, 24.1.1973; "15monatiges Kind erstickte bei Flucht der Eltern nach Berlin," in: *Der Tagesspiegel*, 24.1.1973; "Kind starb auf der Flucht in den Westen," in: *Die Welt*, 24.1.1973; "Bei der Flucht nach West-Berlin: Baby erstickte im Arm der Mutter," *BZ*, 24.1.1973; "Ich nehme die Flüchtlinge bei mir auf," in: *BZ*, 25.1.1973; "Wir würden das nie wieder tun," in: *BZ*, 30.1.1973.

2   *Berliner Morgenpost*, 24.1.1973.

Volker Frommann

born on April 23, 1944

seriously injured in an accident on March 1, 1973
near the Pankow S-Bahn station
on the sector border between
Berlin-Pankow and Berlin-Wedding
died from his wounds on March 5, 1973

Volker Frommann was born on April 23, 1944 in Unterpörlitz, Thuringia, not far from Ilmenau.[1] He was the only child of Marie and Heinrich Frommann. The father was a metalworker and worked as a production manager in the state-owned machine and appliance manufacturer in Langewiesen. The mother worked from her home for a doll factory. Volker Frommann grew up with his cousin in his parents' home, which they shared with his uncle. He attended school in Unterpörlitz from 1950 to 1958. Because of his good grades he switched to the middle school in Ilmenau, from which he graduated in the summer of 1960. He was supposed to begin training at the state-owned cooling system plant in Scharfenstein/ Erzgebirge on September 1, 1960.

Volker Frommann's best friend in those years was Rainer Michelidse and they spent most of their time together. Rainer's father had been the target of a denunciation in 1945. He was picked up by the Soviet secret service and interned in the Buchenwald special camp without ever receiving a sentence. The family lost all trace of him after that. Both boys were active in the Protestant youth congregation in their hometown. They were critical of the FDJ, the official youth organization in East Germany, and of the direction that East Germany was going. Neither of them trusted what they learned from the East German media and preferred to listen to western radio programs for information, as well as for the music. In 1959 both boys traveled the long 300 kilometers to East Berlin so that they could secretly visit West Berlin, which they liked better than their hometown with all its political constrictions.

On the first days of April 1960, the Unterpörlitz community was officially declared a "fully collectivized village" even though the village only had three farmers who lived entirely off the land. Farming for most of the residents was only a secondary income. But the local Communist Party regarded the successful farm collectivization as reason enough for a celebration in "Zur Sonne" and "Henne," the village's local restaurants. Volker Frommann and Rainer Michelidse were convinced that the farmers had only joined the agriculture production collective under pressure since it, in fact, had dispossessed them of their property. This is what led them to want to commit a symbolic act: When the evening party reached its climax, they left the inn unnoticed and threw an iron cow chain over the Unterpörlitz power line, causing a short circuit that left the LPG celebration in the dark. They quickly returned to the party and joined the others who, sitting in candlelight, complained about the blackout. Despite the Stasi's vigorous efforts and intense investigations, it took months for the culprits to be discovered. Finally in August 1960, the Stasi put its sights on the two boys, who were arrested on August 11, 1960.

Defenseless and at the mercy of the Stasi interrogation methods, the two 16-year-olds were played against each other and forced to "confess." On November 17, 1960, the Suhl district court sentenced them as adults to three years in prison for "seditious acts of violence." In addition they were found guilty of "stealing corporative property" – they had taken cans of pineapples from the storage room of the local cultural center – and were sentenced to an additional six months in prison.[2] The court did not accept Volker Frommann's father's view that it had been a mere youth prank. Nor did it consider that the entire damage caused amounted to no more than 320 East German marks. The "acts of violence" committed by the defendants, the court wrote in its verdict, represented "active support of reactionary forces of the German people." This kind of behavior was capable "not only of disrupting our development but also of supporting the advancement of an atomic war against the peace-loving human race since every reinforcement of the war camp helps to bolster these criminal aims."[3]

After spending almost four months in a Stasi pre-trial prison in Suhl, Volker Frommann and Rainer Michelidse were moved for a short time to prisons in Untermassfeld and Halle before being transferred on December 16, 1960 to the "Torgau Youth House," a prison exclusively for youths.[4] "I have been informed," Volker Frommann was required to confirm in writing upon arrival there, "that I am not allowed to look out the window, wave or call out and will be held responsible if I violate these rules."[5] The 16-year-old soon learned what "being held responsible" meant in this prison: When he requested a Bible he was placed in confinement for hours in a basement cell.[6] A prison director's "behavior report" on the young prisoner stated that Volker Frommann was of the view "that a number of conventions in the youth house and directives from his superiors were not reconcilable with his beliefs" and he engaged in "very many discussions." The report did not mention the prison cell punishment.[7] Like many of his fellow prisoners – including Michael Gartenschläger[8] – after serving three months in prison, Volker Frommann was appointed to prison "training" as a metalworker. In the prison library he preferred to read classical literature. He was artistically inclined, painted and drew pictures, and joined a circle of inmates with similar interests. He seemed to have let go of his initial open resistance: "Negative attitudes towards our state do not find expression in his discussions as one may have expected given the beginning of his stay here," the prison director noted in July 1962. He consequently labeled him one of the "positive youths" in the prison who could be considered for a "conditional sentence waiver."[9] After serving a total of two years in prison, Volker Frommann and Rainer Michelidse were both granted amnesty and released from the Torgau Youth Prison on August 10, 1962 with a three year probation term.[10]

After returning to Unterpörlitz, Volker Frommann resumed the metalwork training that he had begun in the state-owned glass machine construction plant in Ilmenau. But he was not particularly happy with his work. The year after his release from prison he attempted to escape from East Germany but was arrested in Czechoslovakia and handed over to East German authorities. He was again sentenced to a prison term that he served until 1964 in the Untermassfeld Penitentiary.

Volker Frommann's further development can only be briefly described. He worked as a metal fitter and later got a position at a glass painting company but neither job satisfied him. "After working for two years at my factory, it is pretty normal to go nuts, don't you think so too?" he wrote to his friend Rainer Michelidse, who had moved away from Unterpörlitz by then. "The normal daily routine, the humdrum – that was not his world," his cousin later recalled.[11] In his letters to Rainer Michelidse, Volker Frommann wrote about the philosophical works he read after work: He wrote of Schopenhauer and Nietzsche, whom he apparently admired, and said that he was investigating their connection to Strindberg, Freud and Kierkegaard. He also kept Rainer Michelidse up to date on his newly discovered sources of knowledge, including Lessing, Kant and Plato.[12] His attempt to study theology at the university failed and the Dresden Art School also rejected him.[13] Anyone with cadre files and police reports accusing them of "seditious acts" and attempted "flight from the republic" was going to have a hard time professionally in East Germany.

Both his work situation and the psychological effects of his imprisonment were increasingly taking their toll on Volker Frommann. He sought psychological treatment and learned how to do autogenic training. He wrote to Rainer Michelidse: "I have made great progress again: I am able to disconnect better than before and am even better at keeping quiet."[14]

Volker Frommann got married to a doctor in the second half of the 1960s and moved away from Unterpörlitz for a few years with his wife, but they returned together at the beginning of the 1970s. The couple lived a secluded life; Volker Frommann and Rainer Michelidse lost touch and his contact with his cousin also became rare. Neither his friend nor his cousin knew what had led Volker Frommann to once again try to escape in 1973.

On March 1, 1973 at about 12:45 in the morning, Volker Frommann jumped out of a moving S-Bahn train in East Berlin about 50 meters away from the border territory between the Pankow and Schönhauser Allee S-Bahn stations. He probably had wanted to use this passage near the border to escape to West Berlin. But he was badly injured when he jumped and remained motionless on the ground near the tracks. Unable to speak, he was seen by an East German police patrol and brought to the Berlin-Friedrichshain Hospital by ambulance.[15] The first examinations determined that he had injured his spine and that his life was in acute danger. He died from his injuries on March 5, 1973.[16]

The relatives in Unterpörlitz learned from a nurse in the Friedrichshain Hospital who had attended the same nursing school as Volker Frommann's wife and his cousin's wife that he had been found seriously injured not far from the Wall.[17] His parents traveled to East Berlin to attend the memorial service in the Baumschulenweg Crematorium. His father was able to bribe the cemetery attendant and get him to open the coffin one last time for the parents so that they could bid their son farewell before his body was cremated.[18]

Volker Frommann was buried on the cemetery in Unterpörlitz, in a gravesite that he now shares with his parents.

In the early 1990s the parents tried in vain to find out more about the exact circumstances of their son's death.

Hans-Hermann Hertle

1 On the following, in particular the biographical data on Volker Frommann, see the conversation conducted by Hans-Hermann Hertle and Gabriele Schnell with Rainer Michelidse and Manfred Göllnitz, 29.10.2008.

2 "Urteil des Bezirksgerichts Suhl vom 17.11.1960–1 BS 120/60," in: BStU, Ast. Suhl, AU 66/60, Bd. 6, Bl. 60–71, here Bl. 68.

3 Ibid., Bl. 68.

4 The "Jugendhaus Torgau" was probably the most severe youth prison in East Germany with very inhuman prison conditions. The prison's history, in contrast to the "Jugendwerkhof Torgau" (1964–1989) that was later closed down, has yet to be thoroughly researched.

5 BStU, Ast. Suhl, AU 66/60, Bd. 10 (Gefangenenakten Frommann, Volker), Bl. 109.

6 See the conversation conducted by Hans-Hermann Hertle and Gabriele Schnell with Rainer Michelidse, 29.10. 2008.

7 "Jugendhaus Torgau, Führungsbericht zur Vorlage für die Kommission gem. § 24 Abs. 2 JGG, Torgau, 5.7.1962," in: BStU, Ast. Suhl, AU 66/60, Bd. 10 (Gefangenenakten Frommann, Volker), Bl. 147.

8 Michael Gartenschläger was sentenced to life in prison in 1961 for protesting the Berlin Wall. After his release was bought by West Germany in 1971, he was shot and killed by a special Stasi command on April 30, 1976, when he was caught trying to dismantle an automatic firing device in the border grounds. See Lothar Lienicke/ Franz Bludem, *Todesautomatik. Die Stasi und der Tod des Michael Gartenschläger,* Frankfurt am Main, 2003.

9 Ibid., Bl. 148.

10 "Beschluss der Kommission zur Überprüfung der Urteile gegen Jugendliche gemäss § 24 JGG, Torgau, 9.7.1962," in: BStU, Ast. Suhl, AU 66/60, Bd. 10 (Gefangenenakten Frommann, Volker), Bl. 159/160; "Jugendhaus Torgau, Mitteilung über Entlassung von Frommann, Volker, 10.8.1962," in: BStU, Ast. Suhl, AU 66/60, Bd. 7, Bl. 75.

11 Conversation conducted by Hans-Hermann Hertle and Gabriele Schnell with Manfred Göllnitz, 29.10.2008.

12 Letter from Volker Frommann to Rainer Michelidse, o.D. [1965/1966] (privately owned by Rainer Michelidse).

13 Conversation conducted by Hans-Hermann Hertle and Gabriele Schnell with Rainer Michelidse and Manfred Göllnitz, 29.10.2008.

14 Letter from Volker Frommann to Rainer Michelidse, o.D. [1965/1966] (privately owned by Rainer Michelidse).

15 See "PdVP-Rapport Nr. 60/73, 1.3.1973, p. 2, in: PHS, Bestand PdVP-Rapporte. No Stasi documents about the incident have ever been found.

16 See "Kerblochkartei der BVfS Suhl über Volker Frommann," in: BStU, Ast. Suhl, Kerblochkarte VII.

17 Conversation conducted by Hans-Hermann Hertle and Gabriele Schnell with Manfred Göllnitz, 29.10.2008. Who officially informed the family of Volker Frommann's death and what cause of death was presented to them could not be discovered. Volker Frommann's mother died in 1997; his father died in 2004.

18 Ibid.

Horst Einsiedel

born on February 8, 1940

shot dead on March 15, 1973
at the Pankow municipal cemetery
on the sector border between
Berlin-Pankow and Berlin-Reinickendorf

Horst Einsiedel, born on February 8, 1940 in Berlin-Pankow, acquired a high school degree after he completed his metalwork apprenticeship at the "worker and farmer faculty." He studied mechanical engineering at the Technical University in Dresden and, after receiving his engineering degree, he moved with his wife and daughter to Berlin-Weissensee in 1967.[1] He worked for various East Berlin companies. His last place of work was at the state-owned productivity improvement firm in Heinersdorf.[2]

The special conditions under which East German engineers worked could be frustrating to someone with ambitions. Horst Einsiedel refused to become a member of the Communist Party and this meant he had no chance of being promoted. The "party membership" requirement often meant that his supervisors – all members of the party – were unable to hold a candle to his professional competence. He spoke about this with his wife and about the possibility of fleeing to West Berlin where his sister had moved in 1951 and his mother in 1969. But his wife felt it was too risky to flee with their daughter, who had been born in 1966. Later his wife understood his decision to flee alone as a way to avoid causing his family any unnecessary danger. She testified to the police as a witness in 1992 that he was probably planning to bring them over to the West at a later time.[3]

Horst Einsiedel said goodbye to his wife in the early morning of March 15, 1973, claiming that he was going to find an emergency dentist to treat his severe toothache. He drove with his Trabant to the Pankow Cemetery where he often went to visit his father's grave. The last fence of the cemetery was only 30 meters away from the first house on West Berlin territory. The house towered above the Wall and the border grounds here were clearly visible through the interior security fence. Horst Einsiedel had planned his escape well in advance and knew exactly what he was doing in the dark of this early March morning.[4] Using a hacksaw and a bolt cutter, he divided a chain that secured two ladders to a tool shed. He used the first ladder to climb over the interior fence and the folding ladder to get over the signal fence, but in doing so he triggered an alarm. When he leaned the folding ladder against the concrete wall and climbed to the top he was only meters and seconds away from reaching his goal. But the two guards in the watchtower 200 meters away had already noticed him and opened fire at the fugitive. Horst Einsiedel was hit in the neck and chest and fell from the ladder. He died moments later from his bullet wounds.

That very day, as the West German federal government and the West Berlin Senate were protesting the shots fired at the Berlin sector border,[5] the border guards involved in the incident were being awarded the "Medal for Exemplary Service at the Border" and granted financial bonuses.[6] In early 1999 the Berlin district court found them guilty of manslaughter in the case of Horst Einsiedel and sentenced them to a year and three months probation.[7] Their commander was also tried as an accessory because, at the beginning of their shift, he had instructed them to prevent "border violations" under all circumstances, if necessary using their firearms, and to "arrest or exterminate the border violators." But the Berlin district court dismissed the case in 2002 due to the defendant's permanent inability to stand trial.[8]

Horst Einsiedel's wife started getting nervous when her husband had not returned home by 8 a.m. She called the emergency dental service and learned that he had never been there. The next day she noticed that a number of her husband's personal documents were missing. At that moment she suddenly realized what had happened.[9]

Meanwhile the East German secret police had gathered "ideas for a legend concerning the death of the border agitator of 15.3.1973" that would prevent the "western publication organs from inciting further hate campaigns."[10] The Stasi staff practiced their creative writing skills in a number of "top secret" variations that were then presented to the Stasi chief, Minister Mielke. They invented stories to explain the mysterious disappearance of the engineer Horst Einsiedel.[11] A number of individuals knew what had really happened – 42 people in all – including the border guards, doctors, secretaries, forensic medical experts and policemen. They were listed and categorized according to their degree of reliability. The Stasi ordered all of them to keep quiet about the incident, with success.[12]

Einsiedel's wife, not yet aware that she was a widow, was repeatedly questioned by the Stasi at the Berlin Alexanderplatz police headquarters about the whereabouts of her husband. They even asked her to provide photos of her husband to facilitate the search for him. The Stasi cynically referred to this as a "masked measure" of the East German police.[13] Finally, they came to the conclusion that she did not indeed know of her husband's plan to escape. At the end of March 1973 she was informed by the East German secret police that her husband's car was found unlocked in a forest and that he probably had been the victim of a violent crime. From a fake "file of evidence," they showed her a photo of the undamaged car surrounded by small pine trees. The car that was returned to her bore no signs of a violent crime.[14]

His wife's apartment in East Berlin was tapped before Horst Einsiedel's mother paid a visit from West Berlin.[15] The Stasi wanted to know how the two women were reacting to the measures the Stasi had taken to fabricate the truth.

At the end of May 1973, more than three months after Horst Einsiedel was killed, his wife was informed by the East German secret police that her husband had drowned and that his body was discovered near Potsdam in front of a fence obstacle in the Havel river.[16] The record of death stated the cause of death as "drowning."[17] The Stasi also discouraged her from identifying the corpse, which it claimed was strongly decomposed. Naturally, the widow did not know that the body had already been cremated in Baumschulenweg Crematorium as an "operative safeguarding" measure.[18] All she was given was a false death certificate marking the death date as March 17.[19]

Preliminary proceedings were opened in 1996 against the staff of the East German secret police and a doctor who had engaged in concealing the circumstances of Horst Einsiedel's death and had engaged in false certification, a crime in the eyes of the Berlin public prosecutor. But given West Germany's lenient penal law that was applied in these cases, the perpetrators had only a commuted sentence to fear. The case was consequently dismissed in August 1997, as the offense fell under the statute of limitations.[20]

Under Stasi surveillance, the urn containing Horst Einsiedel's ashes was buried in his father's grave on July 5, 1973[21] – at the very site where Horst Einsiedel had begun his escape.

Martin Ahrends / Udo Baron

1 See "Protokoll der Zeugenvernehmung der Witwe von Horst Einsiedel durch die Berliner Polizei, 1.7.1992," in: StA Berlin, Az. 27 Js 170/91, Bd. 1, Bl. 32/33; see also "Bericht der VfS Gross-Berlin/Abt. IX, 15.3.1973," in: BStU, MfS, AS 754/70, Bd. 17, Nr. 1, Bl. 33.

2 See "Protokoll der Zeugenvernehmung der Witwe von Horst Einsiedel durch die Berliner Polizei, 1.7.1992," in: StA Berlin, Az. 27 Js 170/91, Bd. 1, Bl. 32.

3 Ibid., Bl. 33.

4 On establishment of facts concerning circumstances of events, see: "Urteil des Landgerichts Berlin vom 5.2. 1999," in: StA Berlin, Az. 27 Js 170/91, Bd. 4, Bl. 58–61.

5 See Der Tagesspiegel, 16.3.1973.

6 See "Urteil des Landgerichts Berlin vom 5.2.1999," in: StA Berlin, Az. 27 Js 170/91, Bd. 4, Bl. 62.

7 See ibid., Bl. 48–49.

8 See "Beschluss des Landgerichts Berlin vom 27.6.2002," in: StA Berlin, Az. 27 Js 7/99, Bd. 4, Bl. 79a/79b.

9 See "Protokoll der Zeugenvernehmung der Witwe von Horst Einsiedel durch die Berliner Polizei, 1.7.1992," in: StA Berlin, Az. 27 Js 170/91, Bd. 1, Bl. 34–35.

10 "Vorschlag der VfS Gross-Berlin/Abt. IX zur Legendierung des Todes des Grenzverletzers vom 15.3.1973, 16.3.1973," in: BStU, MfS, AS 754/70, Bd. 17, Nr. 1, Bl. 42.

11 See "Bericht des MfS/HA IX/9 über Massnahmen zur Legendierung des Todes des Grenzprovokateurs vom 15.3.1973, 20.3.1973," in: BStU, MfS, AS 754/70, Bd. 17, Nr. 1, Bl. 56–58, as well as the proceeding "suggestions" and "plan of action" for creating a legend," in: Ibid., Bl. 41–43 and 47–49.

12 See "Aufstellung der Mitwisser [durch die VfS Gross-Berlin/Abt. IX], 17.3.1973," in: BStU, MfS, AS 754/70, Bd. 17, Nr. 1, Bl. 27–30.

13 See "Massnahmeplan der VfS Gross-Berlin/Abt. IX zum Vorschlag über die Legendierung des Todes des Grenzverletzers vom 15.3.1973, 17.3.1973," in: BStU, MfS, AS 754/70, Bd. 17, Nr. 1, Bl. 47.

14 See "Protokoll der Zeugenvernehmung der Witwe von Horst Einsiedel durch die Berliner Polizei, 21.9.1992," in: StA Berlin, Az. 27 Js 170/91, Bd. 1, Bl. 70–71.

15 "Bericht des MfS/HA IX/9 über Massnahmen zur Legendierung des Todes des Grenzprovokateurs vom 15.3.1973, 20.3.1973," in: BStU, MfS, AS 754/70, Bd. 17, Nr. 1, Bl. 57.

16 See "Protokoll der Zeugenvernehmung der Witwe von Horst Einsiedel durch die Berliner Polizei, 1.7.1992," in: StA Berlin, Az. 27 Js 170/91, Bd. 1, Bl. 36.

17 "Totenschein für Einsiedel, Horst, 31.5.1973," in: BStU, MfS, AS 754/70, Bd. 17, Nr. 1, Bl. 140.

18 See "Bericht des MfS/HA IX/9 über Massnahmen zur Legendierung des Todes des Grenzprovokateurs vom 15.3.1973, 20.3.1973," in: BStU, MfS, AS 754/70, Bd. 17, Nr. 1, Bl. 58; "Protokoll der Zeugenvernehmung der Witwe von Horst Einsiedel durch die Berliner Polizei, 1.7.1992," in: StA Berlin, Az. 27 Js 170/91, Bd. 1, Bl. 36–37.

19 See "Sterbeurkunde für Horst Einsiedel vom 1.6.1973," in: BStU, MfS, AS 754/70, Bd. 17, Nr. 1, Bl. 143.

20 See "Verfügung der Staatsanwaltschaft II bei dem Landgericht Berlin, 13.8.1997," in: StA Berlin, Az. 29 Js 223/96, Bl. 209–210.

21 See "Vermerk [der VfS Gross-Berlin/Abt. IX], 5.7.1973," in: BStU, MfS, AS 754/70, Bd. 17, Nr. 1, Bl. 151.

Manfred Gertzki

born on May 17, 1942

shot and drowned on April 27, 1973
close to the Reichstag building
at the sector border between
Berlin-Mitte and Berlin-Tiergarten

Manfred Gertzki, born on May 17, 1942 in Danzig, lost his father and brother during the Second World War. His mother fled with him to Eisenach in 1945; they later settled in Chemnitz – known as Karl-Marx-Stadt from 1953 to 1990 – where Manfred Gertzki trained to become a sheet metal worker.[1] After completing his military service with the air force of the National People's Army, he continued his education by studying mechanical engineering. He received a position at Robotron, a state-owned research center in Karl-Marx-Stadt and in 1972 went to night school at the city's technical college, where he earned good grades and from which he graduated as an engineer. He was also a track and field athlete and between 1967 and 1973 won a number of prizes in the discus and shot put in district championship competitions.

After his mother died in 1967 his only remaining close relatives lived in West Germany. Why and when he decided to begin a new life there is not known, but he planned his escape meticulously and even sent some of his personal belongings to the West in advance of his escape. When he fled he had his most important documents with him in a briefcase.

Manfred Gertzki made himself a bullet-proof vest by riveting two-millimeter-thick metal plates into an oilcloth which he sewed into his jacket. He fastened a steel face mask that could be raised and lowered to a motorcycle helmet. The athletic engineer was carrying 50 kilograms of equipment on him when he escaped and was confident that it would protect him from any bullets.

Wearing his protection equipment, he entered the border area very close to the Reichstag building in the early evening of April 27, 1973.[2] At the time the Spree Canal was being enlarged and the border grounds were temporarily under construction. Using a steel pole, Manfred Gertzki broke the lock on the interior fence gate and, using the embankment for cover, was able to walk along the riverbank to an area very close to the Wall, which was stretch metal fence here. He was able to climb over the fence from the water side but there was a section of a few meters in which he could be viewed from the "Schallplatte" (record) watchtower located just a few meters away. (The watchtower's name referred to the state-owned German record company that used to be housed in the former palace of the Reich President). He was aware of this momentary vulnerability but was convinced that his self-made equipment would guard against any threat it posed. He probably had not calculated that another observation tower, located about 300 meters away at Kronprinzen Bridge at the corner of Reinhardtstrasse on the other side of the Spree River, would play such a decisive role in his escape.

The guards in both towers were notified through the border communication system that a fugitive had entered the grounds. As soon as he was in shooting range, both guards in the "Schallplatte" watchtower began firing at Manfred Gertzki from close range. He fell or dropped to the ground, apparently hit, but he continued to crawl forward and was able to get over the stretch metal fence, the next to last obstacle from the water side. Bullets continued to fly at him, but this time they came from the guard tower on the other side of the riverbank, three hundred meters away. Manfred Gertzki had only two more meters to go before he reached the last metal fence that would have been easy to climb. Had he made it there he would have reached the West Berlin demarcation line; instead he was hit by a bullet and collapsed at the edge of the bank. He remained motionless.

The gunshots did not go unnoticed in and around the Reichstag. Passersby, British officers and West Berlin police had gathered on the Spree bank very close to where the shooting had taken place.[3] The crowd freely vented its disgust, shouting insults at the border soldiers, but no one dared to intervene.

In light of the growing crowd of spectators, the East German border guards tried to remove the fugitive as quickly as possible. A first lieutenant tried unsuccessfully to pull him out of the "upstream territory." The crew of a customs boat from the nearby Marschall Bridge border crossing tried to secure the boat near the crime site in order to pull Manfred Gertzki aboard but was unsuccessful because there was no place to dock the boat and the current was strong. "Just throw him into the water," the boat crew called out to the first lieutenant, who had neither examined nor offered first aid to the young man who had been gunned down.[4] According to a Stasi report the border guard did, in fact, push the fugitive into the Spree to prevent "West Berlin individuals or people in uniform from retrieving the perpetrator." The weight of his steel equipment quickly pulled Manfred Gertzki down to the bottom of the waterway.[5]

About two hours later, at 7:40 p.m., East German fire department divers succeeded in retrieving Manfred Gertzki's body from the water. In order to prevent West Berlin spectators and, more importantly, press reporters from seeing and photographing the dead man, he was fastened with a rope to the outboard side of the boat and dragged away in the water.

The following day the headlines of the western press were dominated by the "murder at the Reichstag." "Visitors to Berlin witnessed the crime at the Reichstag," announced "Die Welt" newspaper, adding that the shot fugitive "was hauled off by a guard boat like an animal cadaver."[6] The incident was also reported on radio and television,[7] which, unlike newspaper reports, also reached an audience in the East. This negative attention was very untimely for the Communist Party leaders who were preparing for the World Youth Festival, which was to begin in just a few weeks. They also knew that more reports would follow after the dead man was identified.

After a time the East German secret police registered with relief that nobody in East Germany seemed to miss Manfred Gertzki and this provided the opportunity to keep his name secret. Two weeks after his death the Stasi decided that "the corpse of border agitator Gertzki" should be registered as an "unknown person" at all the official agencies. The case was closed.[8]

Under Stasi direction, the registry office of the Berlin-Mitte district issued a false death certificate on May 14, 1973 for an "unknown man, approx. 25–30 years old."[9] The "municipal burial agency" and the Baumschulenweg Crematorium were also manipulated: Manfred Gertzki was placed in a coffin and cremated as the "unknown dead man" in the Baumschulenweg Crematorium on May 15, 1973. He was buried anonymously at the urn grove of the crematorium.[10] At the same time the Stasi in Karl-Marx-Stadt secretly searched his apartment and confiscated everything that could shed light on his escape plan. The Stasi also had his company make a missing persons' report in mid-May. The report allowed the East German police, under the direction of the Stasi, to open an investigation against the killed man for illegally leaving East Germany, to issue an arrest warrant and officially declare him "wanted." The investigation also provided the legal foundation for clearing out his apartment, after which the proceeds were deposited in the national budget. Manfred Gertzki's mail was read until the end of 1973. In February 1974 the Stasi concluded with satisfaction that all official examinations led to the conclusion that "that no other people had knowledge of the occurrence."[11]

In the fall of 1997, more than 24 years after Manfred Gertzki was shot, the three gunmen, who had been commended and distinguished for their actions, were tried before a court, but the body of evidence against them was complicated. Since an autopsy had not been conducted in 1973, it remained unclear whether Manfred Gertzki had "died as a consequence of the bullet wounds he suffered or whether he had drowned."[12] It could not be sufficiently proven that the two border guards stationed at the "Schallplatte" watchtower, who had shot Manfred Gertzki at close range, had engaged in illegal conduct. Consequently, they had to be acquitted. The court accepted, to their advantage, their claim that they had shot without the intention to kill and that either both of them had missed him or only one had hit him. Only the 19-year-old border guard who had shot from the Reinhardt-strasse watchtower from a distance of 300 meters was found guilty of second-degree manslaughter and sentenced as a youth to a one-year prison sentence that was commuted to probation.

Interestingly, the East German secret police had erred in its presumption that no one knew of the "occurrence." Before embarking on his escape, Manfred Gertzki had confided to a friend all the details of his plan, thus thwarting the Stasi aim of having him anonymously disappear without a trace. Although Manfred Gertzki had been certain that his protective equipment would make his death impossible, he was well aware that his escape could fail and that he might be arrested. He wrote a letter to his relatives in the Ruhr two days before he fled and deposited it with his friend, instructing him to send the letter to them four weeks after his escape attempt if he had not heard from him by then. Gertzki's letter reached his uncle and aunt in West Germany in early July 1973. "Since I have taken the necessary measures to protect myself against guns," the dead nephew had written, "it is unlikely that I will endure any serious injury or worse."[13] The next day they received an anonymous letter from the friend, who to this day has remained unidentified, in which he stated, "Manfred is no longer among the living."[14]

Martin Ahrends / Udo Baron / Hans-Hermann Hertle

1 On this and the following see "Fernschreiben der BVfS Karl-Marx-Stadt an an die BVfS Berlin / HA IX, o.D. [vermutlich 28.4.1973]," in: BStU, MfS, AS, 754/70, Bd. 18, Nr. 1, Bl. 15/16; "Information Nr. 406/73 des MfS[-ZAIG] über einen verhinderten Grenzdurchbruch DDR-Westberlin im Bereich Berlin-Mitte, Reichstagsufer, am 27.4.1973, Berlin, 30.4.1973," in: BStU, MfS, ZAIG Nr. 2130, Bl. 16–19; "Untersuchungsbericht der NVA/ Grenzkommando Mitte/ Stabschef über den versuchten Grenzdurchbruch einer männlichen Person mit Anwendung der Schusswaffe und Tötung des Grenzverletzers, 27.4.1973," in: BStU, MfS, AS, 754/70, Bd. 18, Nr. 1, Bl. 28–33. See also the personal documents of Manfred Gertzki and the certificates and records in: BStU, MfS, AS 754/70, Bd. 18, Nr. 2, Bl. 23, 25, 28–38.
2 On the course of events see "Urteil des Landgerichts Berlin vom 3.11.1997," in: StA Berlin, Az. 27 Js 163/90, Bd. 4, Bl. 138–155.
3 See "Untersuchungsbericht der NVA/ Grenzkommando Mitte/ Stabschef über den versuchten Grenzdurchbruch einer männlichen Person mit Anwendung der Schusswaffe und Tötung des Grenzverletzers, 27.4.1973," in: BStU, MfS, AS, 754/70, Bd. 18, Nr. 1, Bl. 28–33.
4 "Strafanzeige der West-Berliner Polizei wegen des Verdachts auf Totschlag gegen Unbekannt von Amts wegen, 30.4.1973," in: StA Berlin, Az. 27 Js 163/90, Bd. 1, Bl. 1–3, here Bl. 2 [Testimony from West Berlin eye-witnesses].
5 "Bericht des MfS/ HA I/ Grenzkommando Mitte/ Abwehr Unterabteilung GR 33, 27.4.1973," in: BStU, MfS, AS, 754/70, Bd. 18, Nr. 1, Bl. 9–11, here Bl. 10.
6 *Die Welt,* 28.4.1973.
7 See also the German television program *ZDF-Magazin,* ZDF, 2.5.1973.
8 "Massnahmeplan der BVfS Berlin, 10.5.1973," in: BStU, MfS, AS, 754/70, Bd. 18, Nr. 1, Bl. 104–109, here Bl. 104.
9 See "Sterbeurkunde von Manfred Gertzki, 14. Mai 1973," in: BStU, MfS, AS, 754/70, Bd. 18, Nr. 1, Bl. 133.
10 See "Rechnung des Städtischen Bestattungswesens, 14.5.1973," in: BStU, MfS, AS 754/70, Bd. 18, Nr. 1, Bl. 141; see also "Abschlussbericht des MfS zur Grenzprovokation am 27.4.1973 in Berlin-Mitte, Reichstagsufer, 12.2.1974," in: BStU, MfS, AS 754/70, Bd. 18, Nr. 1, Bl. 155–156.
11 Ibid., Bl. 156.
12 See "Urteil des Landgerichts Berlin vom 3. November 1997," in: StA Berlin, Az. 27 Js 163/90, Bd. 4, Bl. 138–155, here Bl. 152.
13 Letter from Manfred Gertzki to his aunt and his uncle, 25.4.1973, in: StA Berlin, Az. 27 Js 163/90, Bd. 1, Bl. 45.
14 Letter from Manfred Gertzki's friend to Gertzki's uncle and aunt, 28.5.1973, in: StA Berlin, Az. 27 Js 163/90, Bd. 1, Bl. 46.

Siegfried Kroboth

born on April 23, 1968

drowned on May 14, 1973
in the Spree near the Brommy Bridge
on the sector border between
Berlin-Kreuzberg and Berlin-Friedrichshain

S iegfried Kroboth, born on April 23, 1968 in West Berlin, lived with his parents and his 13-year-old brother in the West Berliner district of Kreuzberg. The family had fled East Germany many years earlier and settled in the West.

On the afternoon of May 14, 1973, the boy was playing with a friend on the Kreuzberger Ufer, a riverbank of the Spree River near the war-damaged Brommy Bridge. They had advanced as far as the quay wall when the five-year-old boy suddenly fell into the water.[1] His friend immediately called out for help and a 12-year-old girl ran to a fire alarm box located 200 meters away and pulled the alarm at 11:55 a.m. The first West Berlin police car arrived at the scene of the accident a few minutes later. Siegfried Kroboth managed to keep himself above water and tried to hold his breath by placing his hand over his mouth. But then he ran out of energy and went under the water just before the Schilling Bridge.[2] It might still have been possible to save the child at this point,[3] but the police did not have the authority to enter the water because, in this section of the border, the entire width of the Spree belonged to East Berlin. At 12:07 a water rescue vehicle of the West Berlin fire department arrived. The divers were ready to begin their rescue operation, but had to wait until they received authorization to enter the water. They had no choice but to remain inactive on the Gröbenufer.[4]

The crew of an East German border boat had apparently also noticed the accident. When the boat approached the site of the incident, the West Berlin police called out to the border soldiers, telling them where the boy had fallen into the water and where they could probably find him. The border guards, however, did not react. The mother, who had also arrived by then, had to watch in tears as the retrieval of her son continued to be delayed.

The officer in charge of the West Berlin firemen first needed to inform an East German border officer on the Oberbaum Bridge before the East German border troops sent another boat with divers on board to the site. It was already 12:45 p.m. when the first diver entered the water; a half hour later he was joined by a second one. At 2 p.m. another boat of the East German border troops arrived to drop off a third diver. The West Berlin firemen offered their assistance but were ignored, as the border guards were forbidden from engaging in any contact with people on the west side. As they searched for the boy they followed the tips offered by the people on the west bank but did not show any other reaction. "During the rescue operation the East German boat acted in accordance with the information provided by the West Berlin police but never once did the crew respond."[5] A strange feeling of helplessness set in on the west side. The officer in charge of the West Berlin firemen spoke to the East German divers through a megaphone, asking for at least a sign that they could hear him but received no reaction. Four hours after the accident occurred, at 3:50 p.m., the East German divers pulled the body of the five-year-old boy out of the water and transported him to East Berlin.

The young boy's death, which occurred just shortly before the German-German basic treaty was to take effect on June 21, 1973, put a strain on inner-German relations, not least of all because this was the second time within six months that an incident of this nature had occurred. In West Berlin loud demands were made for a binding agreement to be made with the East German government that would allow for first aid to be issued more quickly and without complications in the future. The incident was also discussed in the Berlin parliament. One parliament representative said angrily: "It simply cannot be that for the rest of the 20th century something like this happens here that stinks to high heaven just because two sides could not agree soon enough on how to do the very minimum."[6] Kurt Neubauer, the West Berlin interior minister, pointed out that the Senate had already "engaged in preliminary talks" with the western Allies "immediately following the first incident of this kind." After receiving a green light to proceed it had also established contact with the East German government.[7] West Berlin politicians sought to find a solution through long and drawn out discussions with the Allies, who were responsible for these border issues, and through negotiations with East Berlin. If it had been up to East Germany, a second wall on the other Spree bank would have been erected, but the Allies were of the opinion that "the wall does not represent a border for us or for West Berlin."[8] Eight days after the five-year-old died, Gerhard Kunze und Joachim Mitdank, representatives of the West Berlin Senate and the East German government, met in the Schöneberg town hall for preliminary talks on how to provide prompt assistance during accidents that occurred at the Berlin sector borders.[9] It took another two weeks before Heinz Annussek, the West Berlin Senate administration councilor, and Joachim Mitdank, division head of the East Berlin Ministry of Foreign Affairs, met on June 6, 1973 to conduct official talks.[10] But another two and a half years passed before an arrangement went into effect. Rescue posts with a light on all sides, which were also visible from the border watchtowers, were finally installed in West Berlin along the entire length of the six-kilometer-long water border in the spring of 1976.

In the early morning of May 16, 1973, East German border guards handed over Siegfried Kroboth's body to his parents at the Oberbaum Bridge border crossing.[11] It was the second major tragedy to affect Siegfried Kroboth's parents. Five years earlier, to the very day, their daughter, 21 years old at the time, was murdered in East Berlin and thrown into the Spree from the other side.[12]

Udo Baron

1 See "Rapport der West-Berliner Polizei Nr. 134/74, 15.5.1973," in: PHS, Bestand Grenzvorkommnisse.

2 See *Der Tagesspiegel,* 15.5.1973.

3 See *Bild-Zeitung,* 15.5.1973.

4 See *BZ,* 15.5.1973.

5 See *Der Tagesspiegel,* 15.5.1973.

6 Speech of Dr. Haus (SPD), in: Plenarprotokolle des Abgeordnetenhauses von Berlin, 6. Wahlperiode, 50. Sitzung vom 17. Mai 1973, p. 1829.

7 Speech by Minister of Interior Kurt Neubauer (SPD), in: Plenarprotokolle des Abgeordnetenhauses von Berlin, 6. Wahlperiode, 50. Sitzung vom 17. Mai 1973, p. 1829.

8 Statement made by the U.S. liason officers to the Senate, quoted in: *Der Spiegel* Nr. 28, 8.7.1974, p. 49.

9 See *DPA,* 25.5.1973.

10 See *Berliner Morgenpost,* 13.5.1975.

11 See "Fernschreiben der PdVP Berlin, 15.5.1973," in: BStU, MfS, HA IX Nr. 4875, Bl. 4–5.

12 See ibid.

Burkhard Niering

born on September 1, 1950

shot dead on January 5, 1974
on the Friedrich- / Zimmerstrasse border crossing
("Checkpoint Charlie")
on the sector border between
Berlin-Mitte and Berlin-Kreuzberg

Burkhard Niering was born on September 1, 1950 in Halle an der Saale. He was eight years old when his parents were divorced, after which he grew up with his mother, who soon remarried. He left school early, in 1966, when he was in the 9th grade. The East German secret police noted in a report that he quit due to a "lack of interest in learning." He instead trained to become a plumber and installer.[1] The Stasi blamed the "negative influence of his parents' home" for his complete lack of participation in "social activities." He did not join the "Ernst Thälmann" pioneer organization or the "FDJ," the East German children and youth organizations.

In May 1973 he was conscripted to do his military service with the East German police. After completing his basic military training he served in the mobile squad of the 19th Unit of the East German police, which was stationed in Basdorf, a village north of Berlin. A Stasi informant reported that he regarded his military service as a "meaningless waste of his youth" and increasingly found it to be a torment.[2] His supervisors described him as unobtrusive and very fit for service and he received two distinctions. His noted leisure activities focused on literature and theater. He supposedly confided to a soldier in his barrack that he would leave East Germany at the first opportunity offered to him.

Burkhard Niering spent his Christmas leave in 1973 with his mother and step-father and when he returned to his military barrack he seemed noticeably different to his barrack comrades. He avoided conversation and appeared depressed. A Stasi report mentioned a letter to his biological father dated December 30, 1973 in which he wrote "that after his leave he had become very aware of his situation and that he was concerned with the psychological problems of men in uniform, its synchronizing effect on people" and the repression of the individual that it entailed.[3]

On the evening of January 5, 1974, Burkhard Niering was assigned to guard his barrack alone from 6:40 p.m. to 8:20 p.m. This provided him with the opportunity of leaving the guard area unnoticed with his weapon and to enter the Friedrichstrasse border crossing ("Checkpoint Charlie) at 7:35 p.m. The East German secret police later pondered how he was able to get from Basdorf to the city center so quickly. Public transportation would have taken much longer and Burkhard Niering did not have his own car. His personal food voucher was found on highway F 109, which led to the theory that he had hitched a ride. But it seems unlikely that he would have left his escape to chance and he probably had arranged for someone in the area to pick him up.

Burkhard Niering appeared at "Checkpoint Charlie" at 7:35 p.m. wearing a winter battle uniform, a fur hat, boots and a machine pistol in firing position. A U.S. Allied vehicle had just entered the control area. When the East German officer returned to the guard house he suddenly found Niering standing before him. According to the staff sergeant, who belonged to the passport control unit of the East German secret police, he was given the orders "Follow …!" and "Hands up, forward march!"[4] When the sergeant was slow to obey, Burkhard Niering fired a shot in the air. Then he pushed the sergeant in front of him through the control area towards West Berlin. By this time other passport officers had been alerted, and they had closed off the pedestrian entrance and taken position with their guns unlocked. One of them shot at Niering from behind but missed him. He then ordered his hostage to move "on the double," underscoring his words with another shot in the air.

A slalom path began about halfway into the 150 meters of border crossing he had to cover. The kidnapped passport officer looked around continuously and intentionally moved slowly. According to his own account, he asked Niering "What is it you want? Do you have any demands?" He said Niering's response was: "I want to get over there, you ox."[5] The barrier of the exit post was down and the guards, waiting for Niering and his hostage, were ready to shoot. "Guns down, guns down, get down," the fugitive was said to have screamed. The guards lay down but kept their guns in ready position. The hostage gave a nod to a guard who was hidden, trying to give him a signal to shoot. "Climb under," the fugitive ordered when they reached the barrier. The hostage dropped down at lightning speed and rolled to the side at the very same moment that two border guards fired at Niering from a covered position. He was hit in the loin and dropped to the ground. The guards quickly carried him to the watchtower to remove him from public view. This operation took no more than three minutes. A short time later an ambulance took him to the People's Police Hospital where he died from his injuries shortly after 9 p.m. A Stasi surveillance camera had recorded Burkhard Niering's escape attempt and the Stasi later used the film as training material.[6] The Stasi passport officers involved in the incident were awarded combat medals for "service to the people and fatherland."

A West Berlin customs officer and two U.S. soldiers who had just returned from a visit to East Berlin were witnesses to the events. The West German federal government, the Berlin Senate and the Allied city commanders sharply condemned the conduct of the East German guards. The U.S. city commander referred to an "extremely unfortunate start to a new year in which people all over the world had been hoping for an easing of tensions."[7] The CDU party demanded that the incident be addressed in the United Nations, to which both German states had been accepted as members on September 18, 1973.[8]

In early January 1991 Burkhard Niering's mother issued criminal charges against Erich Honecker and Erich Mielke and against the guards for inciting and committing murder to the Halle district court. The Berlin public prosecutor's office opened an investigation against the gunmen in September 1997. But in its verdict it noted that unlike the deaths at the Wall during which defenseless fugitives were shot at, in this case the violence had stemmed from Burkhard Niering. Hostage-taking and deserting the military are also punishable acts in the Federal Republic of Germany hence, even according to West German law, the gunmen would have been justified in arresting the fugitive and using their weapons.[9]

In the charges she filed in 1991, the mother argued that "to appeal to valid laws in an unconstitutional state is not right. The acts of these men were based on a disrespect for human dignity, a greed for power, unscrupulousness and a total lack of pity for young people and their families. It would be an act of justice were the guilty to receive a just punishment."[10]

But Burkhard Niering and his family were denied this justice, at least from a legal perspective.

Martin Ahrends / Udo Baron / Hans-Hermann Hertle

1 On this and the following see "Information des MfS-ZAIG über einen versuchten terroristischen Grenzdurchbruch am 5.1.1974 über die Grenzübergangsstelle (GÜSt) Friedrich-/Zimmerstrasse, 6.1.1974," in: BStU, MfS, ZAIG Nr. 2368, Bl. 1–5; "Bericht des MfS/HA IX/7 zum terroristischen Anschlag mit Geiselnahme auf die Grenzübergangsstelle Friedrichstrasse/Zimmerstrasse in der Hauptstadt der DDR am 5.1.1974, 18.2.1974," in: BStU, MfS, AS 109/77, Bl. 85–91; "Abschlussbericht des MfS zum terroristischen Anschlag mit Geiselnahme auf die Grenzübergangsstelle Friedrichstrasse/Zimmerstrasse in der Hauptstadt der DDR am 5.1.1974, 20.2.1974," in: BStU, MfS, AP 2901/75, Bd. 4, Bl. 90–95.

2 "Bericht des MfS/HA IX/7 zum terroristischen Anschlag mit Geiselnahme auf die Grenzübergangsstelle Friedrichstrasse/Zimmerstrasse in der Hauptstadt der DDR am 5.1.1974, 18.2.1974," in: BStU, MfS, AS 109/77, Bl. 88.

3 "Abschlussbericht des MfS zum terroristischen Anschlag mit Geiselnahme auf die Grenzübergangsstelle Friedrichstrasse/Zimmerstrasse in der Hauptstadt der DDR am 5.1.1974, 20.2.1974," in: BStU, MfS, AP 2901/75, Bd. 4, Bl. 94.

4 "Vernehmungsprotokoll des Zeugen D.H., Mitarbeiter der Stasi-Passkontrolleinheit, 8.1.1974," in: BStU, MfS, AP 2901/75, Bl. 38–41, here Bl. 39.

5 The exchange of dialogue was pieced together from: "Vernehmungsprotokoll des Zeugen D.H., Mitarbeiter der Stasi-Passkontrolleinheit, 8.1.1974," in: BStU, MfS, AP 2901/75, Bl. 38–41, here Bl. 40, and "Information des MfS zum versuchten gewaltsamen Grenzdurchbruch durch einen Angehörigen der VP-Bereitschaft Basdorf an der GÜSt Friedrich-/Zimmerstrasse, o.D.," in: Ibid., Bl. 15–17, here Bl. 15.

6 See the Stasi film "Operative Psychologie" (BStU, MfS, Agit/Fi/1).

7 See Der Tagesspiegel, 8.1.1974.

8 See Berliner Morgenpost, 8.1.1974.

9 See "Verfügung zur Einstellung des Verfahrens 27/2 Js 239/90 der Staatsanwaltschaft Berlin, o.D.," in: StA Berlin, Az. 27 Js 239/90, Bd. 3, Bl. 219–222.

10 "Strafantrag der Mutter von Burkhard Niering beim Bezirksgericht Halle/Saale vom 8.1.1991," in: StA Berlin, Az. 27 Js 239/90, Bd. 1, Bl. 93.

Johannes Sprenger

born on December 3, 1905

shot dead on May 10, 1974
near the Hornkleepfad in Altglienicke
on the sector border between
Berlin-Treptow and Berlin-Neukölln

Johannes Sprenger, born on December 3, 1905 in Greifenhagen, Pomerania, which today is Gryfino, Poland, was 68 years old when he was shot and killed by a border soldier on the night of May 9, 1974. At the time this father of nine children was living with his second wife in Lüttenhagen/Weitendorf in the Neustrelitz district.[1] Although he already received a pension, the trained street construction worker continued to work in Weitendorf as a cooperative worker in the farm division of the Dolgen cooperative. He had joined the KPD (Communist Party of Germany) before 1945 and was also active in the Communist Party of East Germany. Since his retirement in 1970 he had belonged to the community council of his hometown. In 1974 he again campaigned as a candidate of the National Front in the local elections and was elected on May 19, nine days after his death, a fact of which only the East German secret police were aware.

No one in Johannes Sprenger's village knew that he had lung cancer, and even he had not been given a clear diagnosis from the doctors. But by April 1974 he seemed to have noticed that his condition was serious. The 68-year-old man was transferred to a special clinic in Berlin-Buch but the doctors there chose not to operate on him because of his advanced age. Instead, they treated him with medication and radiation.[2] During a visit to his hometown three days before he died, he mentioned to his wife that he was going to return in a coffin, but he did not provide more details about his condition.[3]

On the afternoon of May 9, 1974, Johannes Sprenger visited the nearby state-run bar "Schlosskrug" with two other patients from the Buch clinic. He left the pub at around 7:30 p.m. explaining that he had to go to the bathroom and wanted to buy cigarettes at the bar. His acquaintances waited a while for him to return, but when he never came back, they went back to the clinic without him. Johannes Sprenger disappeared for five hours. When he reappeared he was at the other end of the city in the border territory between Altglienicke and West Berlin.

What happened to Johannes Sprenger during these five hours remains a mystery. Neither in 1974 nor later did anyone look for witnesses who may have had contact with him. How did the man from northern Berlin-Buch get to a border territory on the southeastern edge of the city thirty kilometers away? According to East German documents, no S-Bahn tickets were found on his person. And why did he go to the border? He did not have to flee in order to get to the West. As a retired person he was free to travel to West Germany and to West Berlin. He had already taken advantage of this privilege twice: once in 1970 and again in 1972; he had even visited his son who lived in West Germany. In 2000, when the Berlin state court was searching for an explanation, it concluded that it was most likely that Johannes Sprenger was not intending to flee but had perhaps entered the border territory to "put an end to his life through the border soldiers' predictable use of fire arms."[4] With this theory the court adopted the Stasi's own speculation that Johannes Sprenger had acted in a "depressive state" and had expected "firearms to be employed."[5] There is, however, no proof for this theory and there are considerable indications to suggest that it is false: Why would a depressive, seriously ill man, if he indeed had wanted to put an end to his life, go to such pains to do so? How Johannes Sprenger got to the border territory in Altglienicke and what motivated him to do so remains a mystery, but even more puzzling is how a physically weakened man was able to climb over the interior fence and enter the death strip.

Just after midnight, at 12:40 a.m., the border soldiers on duty on the "Entenfarm" (duck farm) watchtower noticed a man moving toward them between the interior fence and signal fence, "without making any attempt to get past any other border security obstacles."[6] According to the border soldiers on duty, when he walked through a beam of light from a border lamp, they called out to him from the watchtower, but he continued to walk towards them.[7] Johannes Sprenger was 60 to 80 meters away from the tower when the head guard ordered: "Shoot!" Without firing a warning shot, the guard fired five consecutive shots. Hit in the head and neck, Johannes Sprenger fell to the ground.[8]

Although the border soldiers could have easily arrested the 68-year-old man without employing violence, the guard and guard leader were awarded the merit badge of the border troops for their "advantageous" and "determined" action.[9]

A quarter of a century later the Berlin district court sentenced both men for joint manslaughter to a nine month prison sentence commuted to probation. The court accepted the head guard and gunman's claim that they had not wanted to kill Johannes Sprenger.[10]

With the exception of the border guards, no one on the West and East Berlin sides appeared to have noticed the shooting that night. The East German secret police saw this as a chance to conceal the circumstances of Johannes Sprenger's death and create a new "legend." A report to the Stasi chief minister, Mielke, explained that the intention of the alibi was to prevent "rumors from being spread by his relatives living in the BRD or by the people in the neighborhood; uncontrolled opinions could reach the western mass media and be used to instigate a hate campaign against the German Democratic Republic."[11] For reasons that had nothing to do with this incident, the political climate between West Germany and East Germany had reached an all time low in May 1974. The Stasi had succeeded in getting Günter Guillaume, an East German spy, to infiltrate the Bonn federal chancellery. His discovery and arrest in late April strongly influenced Chancellor

Willy Brandt's decision to step down from office. The East German leaders apparently feared that news of a shooting at the Wall would only further discredit East Germany. The border troop doctor on duty established that Johannes Sprenger was dead and accompanied him to the People's Police Hospital. The Stasi took charge of his body from there and, although he had his personal identification on him, he was "stored" as an "unidentified man" in the forensic institute of Humboldt University.[12] An autopsy was not done in order to limit the number of people who knew about the incident. An investigation of the dead man and his family was conducted and an order issued to have their mail checked.

Nine days after Johannes Sprenger was killed, Stasi men, dressed in the uniform of the East German police, informed his wife and a son that he had disappeared from the clinic on May 19, 1974 – the day of the local elections.

They questioned the relatives about his whereabouts, expressing mock concern and promising to undertake "search measures" to find him.[13] That day Johannes Sprenger was re-elected to the community council of Lüttenhagen/Weitendorf and the East German authorities acted as if he were still alive.

When one of his sons mentioned to the men disguised as "East German policemen" that their father had often expressed thoughts of suicide because of his poor health, the East German secret police changed their strategy. Until then the plan had been to simply have Johannes Sprenger disappear and buried anonymously without informing his family, but now they decided to pretend that they had found him drunk in an irrigation field or shot by his own hand. In the end, the "fabricators" of the Stasi decided on a third method of death: Disguised as criminal investigators, the Stasi agents informed the family that Johannes Sprenger had been found "strangled" in an area of woods near the Buch clinic on May 20, 1974. A "clear case of suicide," they said.[14] The family was shocked. Claiming that the corpse was strongly decayed due to exposure to the weather and because it had been lying on the ground for so long, it was not recommended that the body be transferred to the hometown. The Stasi convinced the family to agree to a cremation and to refrain from viewing the dead man.[15] A death certificate signed by a doctor from the forensic institute of Humboldt University and dated May 20 – not the true date of his death – noted the cause of death as a "clear bullet wound."[16] It was never given to the family.

A few days later the urn arrived by mail in Weitendorf; the LPG chairman brought it to the family's home.[17] Johannes Sprenger was buried on June 1, 1974 in his hometown amidst many condolences. The mourners believed he had died from a tragic suicide. His wife doubted the suicide version of his death her entire life. But the truth of how Johannes Sprenger died did not come to light until 1997, two years after his wife had passed away, when the guards who shot him were brought to trial.

Martin Ahrends / Udo Baron / Hans-Hermann Hertle

1 On this and the following see conversation conducted by Hans-Hermann Hertle with Gerhard Sprenger, 14.11.2008.

2 See "Bericht der VfS Gross-Berlin/Abt. IX zum Vorgang Sprenger, Johannes, 19.5.1974," in: BStU, MfS, AS 754/70, Bd. 19, Nr. 1, Bl. 66–71. Another version is also presented in the Stasi files, claiming that Johannes Sprenger refused an operation. See "[BVfS Neubrandenburg/]KD Neustrelitz, Bericht: Rücksprache mit Frau [Name geschwärzt] zur Aufenthaltsermittlung ihres Ehemannes, Neustrelitz, den 10.5.1974," in: BStU, MfS, AS 754/70, Bd. 19, Nr. 1, Bl. 103.

3 See "Bericht der VfS Gross-Berlin/Abt. IX zum Vorgang Sprenger, Johannes, 19.5.1974," in: BStU, MfS, AS 754/70, Bd. 19, Nr. 1, Bl. 69.

4 "Urteil des Landgerichts Berlin in der Strafsache gegen Eberhard B., Klaus D. und Peter W., 27 Js 17/95, vom 12.10.2000," in: StA Berlin, Az. 27 Js 17/95, Bl. 108 i.

5 See "Vorschlag der VfS Gross-Berlin/Abt. IX, 15.5.1974," in: BStU, MfS, AS 754/70, Bd. 19, Nr. 1, Bl. 89.

6 Ibid.

7 On the course of events see "Urteil des Landgerichts Berlin in der Strafsache gegen Eberhard B., Klaus D. und Peter W., 27 Js 17/95, vom 12.10.2000," in: StA Berlin, Az. 27 Js 17/95, Bl. 108 h ff.

8 The shots in the head and neck are clearly recognizable in the photos of the dead body, but a shot in the chest, which is referred to in the Stasi files and in the Berlin district court verdict, could not be established.

9 See "Urteil des Landgerichts Berlin in der Strafsache gegen Eberhard B., Klaus D. und Peter W., 27 Js 17/95, vom 12.10.2000," in: StA Berlin, Az. 27 Js 17/95, Bl. 108 k.

10 See ibid., Bl. 108 j, Bl. 108 p.

11 See "Vorschlag der VfS Gross-Berlin/Abt. IX, 15.5.1974," in: BStU, MfS, AS 754/70, Bd. 19, Nr. 1, Bl. 92.

12 See "Bericht der VfS Gross-Berlin/Abt. IX, 10.5.1974," in: BStU, MfS, AS 754/70, Bd. 19, Nr. 1, Bl. 72–74.

13 See "Bericht der VfS Gross-Berlin/Abt. IX zum Vorgang Sprenger, Johannes, 19.5.1974," in: BStU, MfS, AS 754/70, Bd. 19, Nr. 1, Bl. 66–71.

14 See "Abschlussbericht der VfS Gross-Berlin/Abt. IX vom 24.5.1974," in: BStU, MfS, AS 754/70, Bd. 19, Nr. 1, Bl. 155.

15 See ibid.

16 "Totenschein von Johannes Sprenger," in: BStU, MfS, AS 754/70, Bd. 19, Nr. 1, Bl. 108. The death record and death certificate (see ibid., Bl. 149) bear the false date of May 9, 1974.

17 On this and the following see conversation conducted by Hans-Hermann Hertle with Gerhard Sprenger, 14.11. 2008.

Giuseppe Savoca

born on April 22, 1968

drowned on June 15, 1974
in the Spree near the Oberbaum Bridge
on the sector border between
Berlin-Kreuzberg and Berlin-Friedrichshain

Giuseppe Savoca, born on April 22, 1968 in West Berlin, lived with his parents, Italian immigrants, and two younger sisters in the Kreuzberg district.

On June 15, 1974, a Saturday, the six-year-old boy was playing with a friend on the Gröbenufer riverbank in Berlin-Kreuzberg. His Turkish friend later explained: "We just wanted to look at the fish."[1] Giuseppe Savoca climbed under the embankment railing just past 10 a.m. and began fishing with a stick in the water a half meter under the quay wall. He may have been trying to fish a toy out of the Spree River. With his arms outstretched, he leaned farther and farther forward until he lost his balance and fell into the water. He frantically paddled in the water with his arms while his playmate ran away to get help.[2]

On the Oberbaum Bridge, 60 meters away, an East German border guard watched the events through his binoculars. He saw the child fall into the water, which belonged entirely to East Berlin in that area, and he informed the command post of the boat company of the NVA border regiment. A bit later, independently of this report, a patrol boat of the East German border troops passed right by the site of the accident. An adult who had been fetched by Giuseppe Savoca's playmate called out to the boat crew that a child had fallen into the water. The coxswain stopped for a moment and then continued to pass by with his boat. Later he justified his failure to help the child with the explanation that he did not see any air bubbles on the surface of the water and consequently surmised that the call from the West Berlin bank was merely a provocation; in any case it was illegal for anyone to cross the red-white barrier line of the Spree without receiving an explicit order from the commander of the East German border regiment and without informing the border guards on the Oberbaum Bridge border crossing in advance.[3]

After he received the explicit order, the coxswain returned with his boat to the site of the accident. At about 10:25 a.m. he began searching for the drowned boy together with another East German border troop boat. Meanwhile a large crowd of West Berliners had gathered on the bank of the river, but they remained cautious and did not try to rescue the child. Ten minutes later the West Berlin police and firemen arrived. As had been the case with previous incidents of children falling into the water at Gröbenufer, the East German border guards did not allow the West Berlin rescue teams to get involved or assist in the rescue. The boy's mother later reported to the West Berlin police that a woman had told her that a man who had wanted to rescue her son had been threatened by East German border guards with their guns.[4] The search for the child did not begin until 10:45 a.m., when a diving troop of the East German border regime arrived at the site of the accident.[5] The six-year-old was pulled out of the water almost an hour after the accident had occurred and taken to East Berlin.[6]

The young boy's parents were permitted to travel to East Berlin on the evening of June 15, 1974 to identify their child at the forensic institute of Charité Hospital. Giuseppe Savoca's body was released for burial by the East German state prosecutor's office two days later and delivered to West Berlin on June 19, 1974. "The East German government charged the parents 54.50 German marks for this service."[7]

The following day the Communist Party newspaper "Neues Deutschland" falsely claimed that "all the necessary measures" to rescue the child "had been taken without delay."[8] The West Berlin press criticized East Germany, accusing the border guards of having hindered and delayed the rescue.[9]

Although representatives of the West Berlin Senate and the East German government had been negotiating for months over how to provide immediate emergency rescue measures in similar cases, they still had not come up with a solution. One more child, Cetin Mert, would have to die before the Senate and the East German government signed an agreement on October 29, 1975 on rescue measures for accidents in the Berlin waterways. The agreement determined that when people from West Berlin "were in an acute emergency situation in border waters," rescue measures could also be taken from the West Berlin side. Before this could happen, however, rescue posts set up on the bank had to indicate to the border guards that there was an emergency.[10] These rescue posts were erected in the spring of 1976 on the water border between East and West Berlin.

Udo Baron

1 Quoted in: *Der Spiegel* Nr. 28, 8.7.1974, p. 49.

2 See "Abschlussbericht des PdVP Berlin/Abt. K zur Todesermittlungssache des italienischen Staatsbürgers Giuseppe Savoca, 19.6.1974," in: BStU, MfS, AS Nr. 109/77, Bl. 155–159; see also *Der Spiegel* Nr. 28, 8.7.1974, p. 49.

3 See "Protokoll des MfS/HA IX/Untersuchungsorgan zur Befragung des Postenführers des GÜSt-Sicherungs-regimentes Berlin [Name geschwärzt], 15.6.1974," in: BStU, MfS, AS Nr. 109/77, Bl. 164–165; "Protokoll des MfS/HA IX/Untersuchungsorgan zur Befragung des Zugführers der Bootskompanie [Name geschwärzt], 15.6. 1974," in: BStU, MfS, AS Nr. 109/77, Bl. 166–167.

4 See *BZ,* 18.6.1974.

5 See "Information des MfS/HA IX/7 zum Ertrinken eines Westberliner Kindes am 15.6.1974 an der Staats-grenze der DDR zu Westberlin, 15.6.1974," in: BStU, MfS, AS 109/77, Bl. 152–154.

6 "Abschlussbericht des PDVP Berlin, 19.6.1974," in: BStU, MfS, AS 109/77, Bl. 155–159.

7 "Der nasse Tod," in: Peter Pragal/Eckart D. Stratenschulte, *Der Monolog der Lautsprecher und andere Geschich-ten aus dem geteilten Berlin,* München, 1999, p. 59.

8 *Neues Deutschland,* 16.6.1974.

9 See *BZ,* 18.6.1974.

10 See exchange of letters between East Germany and the Berlin Senate on rescue measures for accidents at the

sector boundary from October 29, 1975, in: Bundesministerium für innerdeutsche Beziehungen (ed.), *Zehn Jahre Deutschlandpolitik*, Bonn, 1980, p. 287; see background information from the West Berlin perspective: Gerhard Kunze, *Grenzerfahrungen. Kontakte und Verhandlungen zwischen dem Land Berlin und der DDR 1949–1989*, Berlin, 1999, pp. 404–405; from the East German perspective: Joachim Mitdank, *Die Berlin-Politik zwischen 17. Juni 1953, dem Viermächteabkommen und der Grenzöffnung 1989. Erinnerungen eines Diplomaten*, Berlin, 2003, pp. 100–108.

Herbert Halli

born on November 24, 1953

shot dead on April 3, 1975
on Zimmerstrasse / at the corner
of Otto-Grotewohl-Strasse
on the sector border between
Berlin-Mitte and Berlin-Kreuzberg

T he truth was not revealed until after East Germany ceased to exist and the Stasi files were made accessible. Until then, the East German secret police had deceived Herbert Halli's family, relatives, friends and colleagues into believing that he had died in April 1975 in an accident that he alone had caused and not by bullets that were shot at him at the Berlin Wall. In 1995, twenty years after her son was killed, Herbert Halli's mother reported that she had never really believed the story that she had been told about an accident.[1]

Herbert Halli, born on November 24, 1953 in the city of Brandenburg, trained to become an electrician. He married while he was serving on duty in the National People's Army in Torgelow. A son was soon born but the marriage did not last long. At the end of 1974, before the divorce was final, Herbert Halli moved from Brandenburg to East Berlin.[2] He worked at various construction sites until he received a position at the state-owned "Bau- und Montagekombinat / Ingenieurhochbau Berlin," a construction company that was involved in building the Palace of the Republic. He moved into a worker's dormitory in Lichtenberg, where he shared a double room. He and his roommate founded a FDJ youth club in the dormitory and he became its deputy director. The twenty-one-year-old also applied for membership in the Communist Party.[3] It appears that he wanted to integrate himself quickly and thoroughly into the political conditions that existed in East Germany.[4]

Herbert Halli began work at his new job on the construction site of the Palace of the Republic on April 3, 1975. By 3 p.m. he was already celebrating his first day at work by sharing a drink with his colleagues in the worker's lounge. He left around 9 p.m., heavily intoxicated and without saying goodbye to his colleagues. Instead of driving home he took bus No. 32 towards the border in Berlin-Mitte. When the bus reached the last stop he refused to get off, or perhaps he had fallen asleep. He got into a brief scuffle with the bus driver during which he lost his wallet containing his ID and other personal documents. Herbert Halli finally got off the bus and walked towards the border. By the time the bus driver had found his wallet and handed it over to the police, Herbert Halli had already reached the security grounds near the intersection of Zimmer- and Otto-Grotewohl-Strasse.[5]

By 9:45 p.m. he had gotten past a two-meter-high metal fence and the interior wall. As he tried to approach the last obstacle – the border wall to West Berlin – he touched a signal fence and triggered an optical and acoustic alarm. A border guard on the nearby observation tower rushed down to the ground and his guard leader reported the incident to the command office before leaving the tower. The first guard fired a warning shot. Halli threw himself to the ground and in the next moment jumped up again and started running back towards the interior wall. He had clearly given up on his escape attempt. From a distance of about 100 meters, the guard leader fired a shot from his Kalashnikov from a standing position. He hit Herbert Halli in the back while he was trying to return to East Berlin. He had been climbing over the interior wall not far from what was then the House of Ministers, the former Reich Aviation Ministry that now serves as the Federal Ministry of Finance. Herbert Halli was delivered to the People's Police Hospital in Berlin-Mitte with a bullet through his abdominal cavity. He died there from his wounds at 10:45 p.m.[6]

No one on the West Berlin side of the border appeared to have noticed the incident. Due to the "political-operative situation" – a reference to the upcoming meeting of government leaders at the Conference on Security and Cooperation in Europe where the Helsinki Accords were to be signed – the Stasi felt it was appropriate to conceal the circumstances of Herbert Halli's death. It arranged with the East German police to have all entries concerning the incident erased. No written reports were to be made. It also had the date of death moved forward a day to April 4, 1975. On the death certificate the registry office noted the cause of death as an accident.[7]

The state prosecutor's office was also misled by a fake autopsy report. It reported that a certain "head constable Fritsche," a fictitious figure constructed to serve as a witness, had found Herbert Halli dead in a construction ditch without any indication of third party involvement and without any external injuries.

Four days later the guard who pulled the trigger received the "Medal for Exemplary Service at the Border" for his "exemplary readiness for action and fulfillment of his duty." He was not informed of the fatal effect of his shots.[8]

The dead man's relatives and colleagues at work were also led to believe that Herbert Halli was still alive. The East German police nonchalantly accepted the mother's missing persons' report on April 10. Two weeks later, when the authorities were completely certain that the incident had not been observed on either the east or the west side, the East German secret police informed Herbert Halli's mother and his workplace that the 21-year-old man had died. They were presented with a fabricated version of the events, claiming that Herbert Halli was very drunk and had fallen into a construction ditch near the Czechoslovakian embassy where he was found on April 4 without any ID on him. The investigation had established that his death was not caused by external factors.

Under pressure from the East German secret police, his mother refrained from viewing her son's body and agreed to have the body cremated. The family was denied any benefits from state social security or from his workplace with the explanation that their family member had been responsible for his own death. Herbert Halli was buried amidst widespread sympathy at the cemetery in Branden-burg-Plaue in the grave of his father on May 8, 1975. The false death date established by the Stasi was later carved into his gravestone.

It had been easy to conceal Herbert Halli's escape attempt because many people who knew him could not imagine that he had wanted to flee. Only a few knew of his secret thoughts about fleeing. He once pointed out the border in Berlin-Mitte to his mother and said: "It would be easy here."[9] His ex-wife was also familiar with his dreams of escaping. When she heard about Halli's disappearance, her first thought was "'Herbert went to the Federal Republic.' He had always wanted to go to his brother in Kiel." This is what she told the Berlin Police Central Investigating Agency for Governmental and Party Crimes in 1995.[10] What ultimately led the young man who was so integrated in East German society to undertake such an action remains unknown. Also unclear is the significance of a letter found in his dormitory a few days before his death. In it unidentified persons threatened to throw him out the window and kill him as they had already done to another dor-mitory resident because he had denied them entry into the youth club. Perhaps the young man wanted to escape this fate by fleeing to West Berlin.[11] A rough atmos-phere prevailed among the construction workers; Halli's roommate recalled that the dormitory was also known as the "flying school" because of the many physical fights and people falling out of windows.[12]

Apparently his colleagues at work believed the story created by the East German secret police. It did not occur to any of them that Herbert Halli might have tried to escape since they considered him to be someone who "towed the party line."[13] A little later, when a friend of his mother's, an East German policeman, mentioned in passing that she would never learn the exact circumstances of her son's death be-cause they had been manipulated, she felt confirmed in her initial doubt about the official version presented to her. The following year, when she was unexpectedly presented with the "Banner of Work" award, the mother interpreted it as a gesture by the state to "make good" over the circumstances of her son's death.[14]

In 1995, during the investigation on violent acts at the Berlin Wall, the Berlin Criminal Investigation Agency came across the censored circumstances of Herbert Halli's death. In November 1996, the Berlin public prosecutor's office filed charges against the gunman who had been unaware that he had killed someone before the investigation began. He convincingly stated before the court that he regretted the act and that it weighed on him heavily. In June 1998 he was found guilty of man-slaughter and sentenced to a year on probation.[15]

Martin Ahrends / Udo Baron / Hans-Hermann Hertle

1 See "Niederschrift der Zeugenvernehmung von Paula St. vom 2.2.1995 in Brandenburg," in: StA Berlin, Az. 27 Js 189/94, Bd. 2, Bl. 99.

2 See "Niederschrift der Zeugenvernehmung von Christa L. vom 31.1.1995," in: StA Berlin, Az. 27 Js 189/94, Bd. 2, Bl. 84–87.

3 See "Bericht der VfS Gross-Berlin/Abt. IX zur Grenzprovokation in Berlin-Mitte am 3.4.1975, Berlin, den 14.4.1975," in: BStU, MfS, HA IX Nr. 3421, Bl. 6–13.

4 Ibid.

5 Ibid.

6 See "Operative Tagesmeldung Nr. 04/IV/75 des MfNV/Operativer Diensthabender vom 3./4.4.1975," in: BArch, VA-01/32893, Bd. 1, Bl. 133.

7 See "Beglaubigte Abschrift aus dem Sterbebuch von Herbert Halli vom 20.12.1994," in: StA Berlin, Az. 27 Js 189/94, Bd.1, o.Bl.; "Bericht der ZERV vom 25.1.1995," in: StA Berlin, Az. 27 Js 189/94, Bd.2, Bl. 47–51.

8 See "Befehl Nr. 15/75 des Stellvertreters des Ministers und Chef der Grenztruppen der DDR über Kader, 7.4. 1975," in: BArch, GT 6096, Bl. 238.

9 See "Niederschrift der Zeugenvernehmung von Paula St. vom 2.2.1995 in Brandenburg," in: StA Berlin, Az. 27 Js 189/94, Bd. 2, Bl. 100.

10 "Schreiben von Monika B. an die ZERV, 31.3.1995," in: StA Berlin, Az. 27 Js 189/94, Bd. 2, Bl. 181.

11 See "Niederschrift der Zeugenvernehmung von Christa L. vom 31.1.1995," in: StA Berlin, Az. 27 Js 189/94, Bd. 2, Bl. 84–87.

12 See "Niederschrift der Zeugenvernehmung von Gerold S. am 14.3.1995," in: StA Berlin, Az. 27 Js 189/94, Bd. 2, Bl. 178.

13 See "Abschlussbericht der VfS Gross-Berlin/Abt. IX zur Grenzprovokation in Berlin-Mitte am 3.5.1975, Berlin, den 23.5.1975," in: BStU, MfS, HA IX Nr. 3421, Bl. 2–4.

14 See "Niederschrift der Tonbandvernehmung von Paula S. durch die ZERV vom 2.2.1995," in: StA Berlin, Az. 27 Js 189/94, Bd.2, Bl. 96–100.

15 See "Urteil des Landgerichts Berlin vom 26.6.1998," in: StA Berlin, Az. 27 Js 189/94, Bd. 3a, Bl. 45–51.

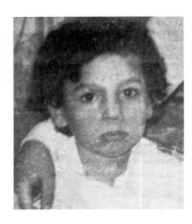

Cetin Mert
born on May 11, 1970

drowned May 11, 1975
in the Spree near the Oberbaum Bridge
on the sector border between
Berlin-Kreuzberg and Berlin-Friedrichshain

Cetin Mert was born on May 11, 1970 and lived with his Turkish parents and two brothers in the West Berlin district of Kreuzberg.

May 11, 1975 was his fifth birthday, a Sunday, and the parents planned to take their children on a picnic in the countryside. Cetin went to play ball with other children in the neighborhood on Gröbenufer until the family was ready to leave; he had just gotten new sneakers for his birthday.[1] When the ball rolled down the embankment into the Spree River, the birthday boy ran after it and tried to fish it out of the water with a stick, but he fell into the Spree, which in this stretch belonged entirely to East Berlin.

A few minutes later, at about 12:30 p.m., the West Berlin police and firemen arrived at the site of the accident. Firemen searched the bank with a rod trying to find Cetin Mert. At the same time a fire chief tried in vain to get permission from the East German authorities on the Oberbaum Bridge to have his team take rescue measures. Passersby also called out to the East German border guards, trying to draw their attention to the accident. But none of the West Berliners dared enter the heavily guarded waters. An East German border security boat did not arrive at the site until 1:10 p.m.[2] An hour later border troop divers retrieved the body of Cetin Mert from the water, just five meters away from the west bank.

Stasi files reveal something that no one at the time knew: Two border troop guards, so-called scouts, had watched as Cetin Mert fell into the water and even photographed the accident. But because they had no communication link, they did not report the incident until much later.[3]

Cetin Mert was the fourth child in three months to drown in the Spree while playing near the Oberbaum Bridge. Despite angry protests from his family and other people who had gathered at the Gröbenufer, the child's body was not brought to the West Berlin side, where he had fallen into the water. It was brought instead to the forensic institute of Charité Hospital in East Berlin.[4] Another four days passed before the dead boy was delivered to his parents.

Intense protests against the East German regime repeatedly erupted at the site of the accident over the following days. The East German secret police noted teenagers chanting in unison "murderers, murderers, child murderers!"[5] About 2,000 members of the West Berlin Turkish community demonstrated against the conduct of the East German border guards and handed out fliers with the heading "Down with the Wall of Shame – Down with Murderous Communism."[6]

To prevent any more accidents at the Gröbenufer in Kreuzberg, the West Berlin Senate took action for the first time and erected a barbed wire fence along the four entrances to the bank slope and in front of the quay wall. Large warning signs in German and Turkish were also put up.[7] The East German border troops also received the secret order to have a boat positioned downriver from the Oberbaum Bridge across from Gröbenufer from 8 a.m. until sundown so that "should the crew ascertain or be notified of an accident [...], it is to approach the accident site at once, provide immediate first aid and take the first rescue measures."[8]

The West German federal government and the Berlin Senate expressed their consternation over the conduct of the East German authorities. The federal government in particular felt duped by East Germany with regard to its efforts to achieve a better climate between the two German states. It demanded that the negotiations with East Germany over first aid measures in the area of the sector border, which had been going on for over two years by then, finally be concluded with successful results. At the beginning of the talks in June 1973, East Germany presented a treaty draft that allowed for first aid to be provided during accidents along the entire border around Berlin, but the terms were phrased in such a way as to raise the status of the sector border to a state border which, given the four-power status of Berlin, was unacceptable to the Senate and the Allies.

After the West Berlin Senate, in agreement with the Allied protective powers, rejected East Germany's proposal in 1973, subsequent negotiations remained fruitless.[9] Still more children had to drown after Giuseppe Savoca and Cetin Mert before the Senate and East German government finally signed an agreement on October 29, 1975 regarding rescue measures to be taken during accidents in the Berlin border waters. It declared that when people from West Berlin "were in an emergency situation," rescue measures could also be taken from the West Berlin side. But before this plan could take effect, rescue poles had to be erected on the bank so that the border guards would be able to recognize such situations as emergencies.[10] These rescue poles were finally installed along the water border between East and West Berlin in the spring of 1976.

The memorial service for Cetin Mert in West Berlin became a mass demonstration against the Communist Party border regime, particularly for the West Berlin Turkish community. Cetin Mert was buried in Düzce, the hometown of his Turkish parents.[11] Since then the family has held a religious ceremony for him each year on the day of his death.

Martin Ahrends / Udo Baron / Hans-Hermann Hertle

1   See "Ein Maueropfer aus dem Westen," in: *Berliner Zeitung,* 13.5.2000.

2   See "Information des MfS/HA I/Grenzkommando Mitte/Abwehr über die Bergung einer Kindesleiche aus dem Grenzgewässer, 11.5.1975," in: BStU, MfS, HA I Nr. 14878, Bl. 215–216.

3   Ibid., Bl. 216, and "Information des MfS/HA I/Grenzkommando Mitte/Abwehr über die Bergung einer Kindesleiche aus dem Grenzgewässer, 12.5.1975," in: BStU, MfS, HA I Nr. 14878, Bl. 218. This Stasi report stated flippantly that "there was no chance for the two guards to save the child" (ibid., Bl. 218). Later the two guards noted the time of the accident as 11:27, off by an hour.

4   See "Information des MfS/HA I/Grenzkommando Mitte/Abwehr über die Bergung einer Kindesleiche aus dem Grenzgewässer, 12.5.1975," in: BStU, MfS, HA I Nr. 14878, Bl. 217–218.

5   "Bericht des MfS/HA I/Grenzkommando Mitte/Bereich Aufklärung, über die Untersuchung der Provokation an der Staatsgrenze zu Westberlin im Grenzregiment 35, 14.5.1975," in: BStU, MfS, HA I Nr. 14878, Bl. 232–233.

6   "Bericht des [MfS]HA I/Grenzkommando Mitte über die Situation an der Staatsgrenze vom 19.5. bis 20.5. 1975, 20.5.1975," in: BStU, MfS, HA I Nr. 14878, Bl. 229.

7   See *Berliner Morgenpost,* 15.5.1975.

8   "Befehl Nr. 47/75 des Kommandeurs des Grenzkommandos Mitte über Massnahmen zur Rettung und Bergung von Personen aus dem Grenzgewässer im Abschnitt des Grenzregimentes 35, 8.7.1975," in: BArch, GT 5662, Bl. 256/257.

9   See *Berliner Morgenpost,* 13.5.1975.

10 See exchange of letters between East Germany and the Berlin Senate on rescue measures for accidents at the sector boundary from October 29, 1975, in: Bundesministerium für innerdeutsche Beziehungen (ed.), *Zehn Jahre Deutschlandpolitik,* Bonn, 1980, p. 287. Background information from the West Berlin perspective: see Gerhard Kunze, *Grenzerfahrungen. Kontakte und Verhandlungen zwischen dem Land Berlin und der DDR 1949-1989,* Berlin, 1999, pp. 404–405, from the East Berlin perspective: Joachim Mitdank, *Die Berlin-Politik zwischen 17. Juni 1953, dem Viermächteabkommen und der Grenzöffnung 1989. Erinnerungen eines Diplomaten,* Berlin 2003, pp. 100–108, and "Der nasse Tod," in: Peter Pragal/Eckart D. Stratenschulte, *Der Monolog der Lautsprecher und andere Geschichten aus dem geteilten Berlin,* München, 1999, pp. 58–65.

11 See "Ein Maueropfer aus dem Westen," in: *Berliner Zeitung,* 13.5.2000.

Herbert Kiebler

born on March 24, 1952

shot dead on June 27, 1975
west of Highway 96
on the outer ring between
Mahlow (Zossen district) and Berlin-Tempelhof

Herbert Kiebler was shot and killed while trying to escape on June 27, 1975. Just weeks before the final act of the CSCE (Conference on Security and Cooperation in Europe) treaty was signed in Helsinki, the Communist Party leadership did not want any negative headlines about fatal shots at the Wall. Since it appeared that no one on either side had noticed the attempted escape, the East German secret police decided to pretend the murder – which it was according to East German law – was a suicide and moved the site of the crime to a wooded area far from the border. Many people were involved in the cover-up, including foresters, policemen, civil servants, pathologists and state attorneys; the East German secret police had enough power to get all the necessary civilian institutions to cooperate with its plan. Not until the 1990s, when the public prosecutor's office opened an investigation and family members were able to view the Stasi files, did the truth of Herbert Kiebler's death come to light.

Herbert Kiebler was born on March 24, 1952 in Mahlow. He had worked since February 1975 as a presser in a semi-finished products metal plant in Berlin. His father had passed away in 1965. He lived in Mahlow, on the southern border of Berlin, with his mother and younger sister. His three older siblings had already left home.[1] On June 26, 1975, a warm summer's day, the 23-year-old-metal worker was sitting with his clique in the local Mahlow tavern. That evening a fight broke out that ended in a bad brawl, which Herbert Kiebler lost. The fight was probably about card-sharking and gambling debts. When he arrived home drunk at 10 p.m., he was in bad shape and felt hurt by his buddies, both physically and emotionally. At the time his 15-year-old sister told the East German police that he had cried in shame and even spoken of suicide. Herbert Kiebler left behind a farewell letter to his mother before leaving his parents' apartment a half hour later: "We'll meet again either in prison or in West Germany" and, "Dear mommy, if I die, I wish you all the best."[2] He told his little sister that he wanted to go "over there." She tried to hold him back and ran after him but she eventually lost sight of him.[3]

Herbert Kiebler roamed the streets through the night. His brother later found out that he had taken a bus to Drewitz, gotten off at the highway and taken the next bus back to Mahlow.[4] He passed the border signal fence near what was then Highway 96 at around 12:30 a.m. He crossed the patrol path and continued towards the anti-vehicle trench, unaware that he had set off an alarm. Two border guards set off in a Trabant "Kübel" vehicle to search for the fugitive. When they noticed markings on the ground where someone had crawled, they got into position and unlocked their weapons. As soon as Kiebler left the trench obstacle, they saw him and opened fire at the suspect from a distance of 100 meters, although they could have easily arrested him without using their weapons, which they later admitted. Herbert Kiebler was hit in his chest and upper arm and collapsed. He bled to death immediately.

The guards were awarded the "Medal for Exemplary Service at the Border" for their "determined action" and "high level of alertness." The company leader who had given them their orders was awarded the "Border Troop Merit of Honor."[5] A quarter of a century later they were tried by the Potsdam district court for manslaughter, as well as for aiding and abetting manslaughter, and were sentenced to 24 and 15 months probation.[6] One of the convicted men later became a member of the German Border Police in unified Germany. Herbert Kiebler's sister, who served as a witness at the trial, did not sense any remorse among the defendants: "On the contrary, they grinned at me maliciously."[7]

To be absolutely certain that no information about the shots that had killed Herbert Kiebler leaked beyond the border, the East German secret police intercepted the mail that the border soldiers sent to their friends and relatives. In analyzing the letters, the Stasi found cynical comments, such as "Again one less person to eat our butter" and "He just had bad luck," but also sympathy: "He was a border violator, but was it really necessary to kill him so brutally from a distance of 80 meters? There were other ways of stopping him." Someone else wrote: "Would like to know what they are going to tell his parents."[8]

Deeply alarmed by her son's farewell letter, his mother reported him missing on the morning of June 27. The Stasi began a cruel game of deception with the family. It construed a false statement made by a forester[9] and had a fake protocol on "forensic work at the crime site" written up.[10] An East German police "crime site investigation protocol" was made up "to establish a cover-up regarding the Kiebler family," the East German secret police wrote.[11] The family members were finally informed on July 3 that the dead body of Herbert Kiebler was found by a forester in a wooded area in Potsdam-West and that he had committed suicide with a knife. The state attorney of the Potsdam district was also informed of the "cover-up measures." The older brother could not make sense of why Herbert Kiebler would have gone to the trouble to travel 40 kilometers from Mahlow to Potsdam in the middle of the night in order to commit suicide. In response to his inquiry, the Potsdam state attorney repeated the story created for the family, but refused to show any photos of the body.[12] The relatives did not believe the official version. They feared that Herbert Kiebler might have fallen victim to the people who had beaten him up the night that he fled. They also could not rule out that he might have tried to escape to the West since they had heard rumors of shots being fired at the border on the night that he disappeared.[13]

Herbert Kiebler was buried in the cemetery in Mahlow on July 11, 1975; the funeral guests were monitored by State Security.[14] The Stasi naturally denied the family the opportunity to view the deceased one last time. But Herbert Kiebler's relatives wanted to bid him farewell. They secretly broke into the chapel, opened the coffin and saw the bullet wounds.[15] After that his mother repeatedly requested information from the East German police about the true circumstances of her son's death. Her daughter recalled: "The lies about Herbert's death caused our mother to perish. She received psychological treatment and died a bitter woman in 1993."

Martin Ahrends / Udo Baron / Hans-Hermann Hertle

1   See "Urteil des Landgerichts Potsdam vom 22.5.2001," in: StA Neuruppin, Az. 361 Js 14783/99, Bd. 4, Bl. 130–164; see also "Protokoll des VPKA Zossen, Betr.: Mitteilung der Mutter von Herbert Kiebler, 27.6.1975," in: BStU, Ast. Potsdam, AP 1179/76, Bl. 32, and "Ermittlungen des MfS/KD Zossen zur Familie Kiebler, 1.7.1975," in: BStU, Ast. Potsdam, AP 1179/76, Bl. 37–39.

2   "Handschriftliche Notizen von Herbert Kiebler," in: BStU, Ast. Potsdam, AP 1179/76, Bl. 15.

3   See "Urteil des Landgerichts Potsdam vom 22.5.2001," in: StA Neuruppin, Az. 361 Js 14783/99, Bd. 4, Bl. 146; see also "Bericht des VPKA Potsdam/Abt. K über die Befragung der Schwester von Herbert Kiebler, 27.6.1975," in: BStU, Ast. Potsdam, AP 1179/76, Bl. 34–36.

4   "Aktenvermerk der BVfS Potsdam/Abt. VII über ein Gespräch mit einem Bruder von Herbert Kiebler, 9.7.1975," in: BStU, Ast. Potsdam, AP 1179/76, Bl. 85–86.

5   See "Schreiben des Chefs der Grenztruppen an den Minister für Nationale Verteidigung, 27.6.1975," in: BArch, GT 6273, Bl. 115–116; "Urteil des Landgerichts Potsdam vom 22.5.2001," in: StA Neuruppin, Az. 361 Js 14783/99, Bd. 4, Bl. 147–148.

6   See "Urteil des Landgerichts Potsdam vom 22.5.2001," in: StA Neuruppin, Az. 361 Js 14783/99, Bd. 4, Bl. 130–164.

7   See Gerald Praschl, Der verlogenste Mauermord, in: Super-Illu Nr. 31, 26.7.2001, pp. 10–11.

8   "Abschriften des MfS/KD Zossen, 4.7.1975," in: BStU, Ast. Potsdam, AP 1179/76, Bl. 59–61, here Bl. 59–60.

9   See the so-called "Bericht des VPKA Potsdam/Abt. K über das Auffinden einer unbekannten männlichen Leiche im Wald von Potsdam-West am 27.6.1975, 27.6.1975," in: BStU, Ast. Potsdam, AP 1179/76, Bl. 108.

10 See the so-called "Protokoll des VPKA Potsdam/Abt. K über kriminaltechnische Tatortarbeit, 27.6.1975," in: BStU, Ast. Potsdam, AP 1179/76, Bl. 109–112.

11 See the so-called "Tatortuntersuchungsprotokoll des VPKA Potsdam/Abt. K zum unnatürlichen Tod einer unbekannten männlichen Person in Potsdam-West am 26.6.1975, 27.6.1975," in: BStU, Ast. Potsdam, AP 1179/76, Bl. 88–91.

12 See "Aktenvermerk [der Potsdamer Staatsanwaltschaft], 9.7.1975," in: BStU, Ast. Potsdam, AP 1179/76, Bl. 85.

13 See "VPKA Zossen/Abt. K, Anzeige des Bruders von Herbert Kiebler vom 22.7.1975," in: BStU, Ast. Potsdam, AP 1179/76, Bl. 63–65.

14 See "Aktenvermerk der BVfS Potsdam/Abt. IX/SK, 11.7.1975," in: BStU, Ast. Potsdam, AP 1179/76, Bl. 55.

15 On this and the following see Gerald Praschl, Der verlogenste Mauermord, in: Super-Illu Nr. 31, 26.7.2001, pp. 10–11.

Lothar Hennig

born on June 30, 1954

shot on November 4, 1975
on Weinmeisterweg in Sacrow
(Potsdam county district)
died from his bullet wounds on November 5, 1975

The village of Sacrow, not far from Potsdam, was an idyllic exclave, but it was very close to the border and, consequently, the entire area was declared border territory. Anyone wishing to enter required a special pass. There was a very strong military presence in the village and the only access road was blocked by a vehicle barrier and monitored by guards. The local residents had to show the guards their special stamp day in and day out. The officials made efforts to replace the civilian residents with "reliable citizens" or to win them over in their mission to maintain special alertness. Vigilance was a necessity in Sacrow since the Havel riverbank was not even 100 meters away from the water border and a number of people had tried to swim from there to the West Berlin side of the river.

Lothar Hennig was born on June 30, 1954 in Potsdam and grew up in Sacrow. He was very familiar with the conventions in the border territory and knew a few tricks to get around the rules. His sister remembered him as a fun-loving, crazy guy who often surprised people with his unusual ideas and behavior.[1] He was a passionate music fan and very familiar with the western music scene. He organized disco events where he enjoyed playing the recorded hits from the West, but he always managed to lead the cultural affairs authorization office into believing that he was maintaining the dictated balance of 60% East German music and 40% western music.[2] Lothar Hennig's sister was certain that he intentionally caused an accident at work in order to get out of having to serve in the army in the spring of 1973.[3] He did not particularly like his apprenticeship at the "Teltower Geräte- und Reglerwerk," a state-owned industrial plant. The work was unhealthy and his relationship to the brigade was tense.[4] The twenty-one-year-old managed to switch to PGH Auto Service in Potsdam in May 1975.[5]

Lothar Hennig had a lot of friends and he not only got along with the other residents in his hometown, but also maintained friendly contact with the border guards. His many relationships turned out to be a double-edged sword because they made him interesting to the East German secret police.[6] Why he signed on, supposedly out of conviction, as a Stasi informer (IM) in April 1975 can no longer be determined.[7] Just months after they began working together, his case officer attested to his discipline in keeping appointments and reliability in fulfilling the tasks put to him. But his reports were regarded as irrelevant and of little operative use.[8] He was apparently not willing to betray people unconditionally. One night after a summer party in the Meedehorn small garden settlement, he bumped into a man who was soaking wet who asked him and his escort how to get to West Berlin. Lothar Hennig did not report the incident and let the man flee. The Stasi agent responsible for him went into a rage over the incident and gave him a long lecture.[9]

When Lothar Hennig returned from a meeting with his Stasi case officer in downtown Potsdam on November 4, 1975,[10] there was once again a fugitive alarm in Sacrow. The bus driver, a cousin of Lothar Hennig, told him about it and warned him to be careful. The town was swarming with extra border guards who were probably on the lookout for a Soviet soldier on the run. Just how seriously he took this warning is not known. After his Stasi meeting, he went to a bar in Potsdam at around 7 p.m. and was quite drunk when he returned by bus to his hometown enclave. Since he was the only passenger on the bus, his cousin let him off at the corner of Weinmeisterweg, a few meters away from the bus stop. Lothar Hennig scrutinized his surroundings and then sprinted the last 400 meters to his parents' house, just as he always did.[11] He was not the type to resist the instructions of state organs, but he did not hear, or did not want to hear, someone calling out behind him, ordering him to halt.[12] It was late, the lighting on the street was dim and he was almost home.[13]

The man who called to him was on special duty in Sacrow on that foggy November night. He was supposed to be on the lookout for anything unusual. The border soldier was also an informer for the Stasi which meant he was on a sort of 'double-duty.'[14] The very vigilant guard watched as the man who arrived late at night looked around carefully before suddenly breaking into a sprint, which seemed like very suspicious behavior to him. Then again, whoever got off that bus had to already have had his papers checked and the young man was not running towards the border; he was running away from it. But the eager guard ran after Lothar Hennig and called out to him again, telling him to stop – at least this is what he later claimed. He then went into a squatting position and supposedly fired a warning shot that was supposed to hit the ground behind the running fugitive.[15] The second guard, who was lagging behind, saw the projectile strike sparks on the stone sidewalk. It was either the deflected bullet that hit Lothar Hennig diagonally in his back from below or a second bullet whose origins could not be explained with certainty. A forensic examination of the weapon and crime site was not conducted. The two guards performed first aid but it took another hour for a doctor to arrive.[16]

Lothar Hennig was brought to the Drewitz Army Hospital where he was declared dead at 1:30 in the morning. An autopsy report of the NVA Military Hospital in Bad Saarow later reported that he had died from internal bleeding caused by a shattered lung.[17]

On June 26, 1996 in unified Germany, the gunman who shot Lothar Hennig was tried by the Potsdam district court for bodily injury leading to death. He was sentenced as a youth to one year and two months probation. The court accepted the defendant's claim that he had not intended to kill Lothar Hennig and it considered in mitigation that he regretted the act and apologized to the family[18] – albeit not until after the judge had asked him to do so, Hennig's sisters recalled.[19]

On the afternoon of November 5, 1975, State Security agents informed Lothar Hennig's mother that her son had died.[20] A short time later a Potsdam state attorney paid a visit to his family. Lothar Hennig had "died in an accident of his own doing," he lied to them.[21] At this point talk about that night's events had already spread throughout Sacrow. Residents had heard the shots fired and the groans of the man who was hit.[22] The 21-year-old man's family openly expressed their dismay over the incident and surprised the state official with their detailed knowledge of what had transpired. Almost a month later, after Lothar Hennig had been buried on November 14, 1975 in Potsdam-Babelsberg, his mother addressed the East German minister of defense, demanding satisfactory information from him about the circumstances under which her son had died.[23] But he only referred her to the military justice organ in charge of the case.[24] The death certificate issued by Rolf Zickler, the doctor of the Potsdam Stasi district administration,[25] did not reveal the true cause of death. It merely stated that death was caused by bleeding of the aorta.[26] Lothar Hennig's family was unable to endure living in the Sacrow border territory any longer and made efforts to leave the town as soon as possible.[27]

The same day of the incident, an assembly of the Communist Party organization and National Front took place in Sacrow during which members of the border troops attempted to justify Lothar Hennig's death.[28] Although the killing of Lothar Hennig was a criminal offense according to East German law, the military state attorney refrained from opening an investigation.

It was left to the East German secret police to evaluate the local population's mood and to determine what had analytical value and what did not. Friendly relations between the population and the border troops came to an abrupt end after Lothar Hennig's death. They did not greet each other anymore, one border guard noted.[29] A resident was noted as having said that the whole thing was just a mess.[30] The Stasi also noted that, although the incident had been officially approved, there was a certain reserve among the border guards and sergeants. "Such a shame that we killed an innocent person," a staff sergeant was quoted having said. "We shot our best man in Sacrow," a border troop captain told a staff officer. "He was someone who had twice in the past given us tips on preventing a border breach."[31] From the point of view of the East German secret police the fact that Lothar Hennig had not betrayed a fugitive on one occasion probably carried more weight.

Although Lothar Hennig had not had any intention of fleeing, the rumor persisted that his death involved a supposed escape attempt and that the family members were forced to leave Sacrow against their will.

Martin Ahrends / Udo Baron / Maria Nooke

1 Conversation conducted by Maria Nooke with Lothar Hennig's sisters and brothers, 11.9.2009.

2 Ibid.

3 "SV-Buch von Lothar Hennig, Eintragung der Hauptpoliklinik Potsdam, Chirugische Abteilung zur Krankschreibung vom 24.4.1973–27.5.1973 wegen Zehenfraktur," privately owned.

4 See "Ermittlungsbericht des MfS/KD Potsdam, 21.3.1975," in: BStU, Ast. Potsdam, AIM I 1610/77, Bl. 23–25.

5 Conversation conducted by Maria Nooke with Lothar Hennig's sisters and brothers, 11.9.2009.

6 "Vorschlag zur Verpflichtung eines IM der KD Potsdam," in: BStU, Ast. Potsdam AIM I 1610/, Bl. 27–33.

7 See "Bericht zur Werbung zum IM des MfS/KD Potsdam, 30.4.1975," in: Ibid., Bl. 35–38; "Handschriftliche Verpflichtungserklärung von Lothar Hennig zur IM-Tätigkeit, 29.4.1975," in: Ibid., Bl. 34.

8 "Vorschlag des Führungsoffiziers von Lothar Hennig/KD Potsdam zur Umregistrierung des IM zum IMV, 3.9.1975," in: Ibid., Bl 39–40. As a consequence of the inadequate operative usefulness of Lothar Hennig's informations to the Stasi, the renewed registration was deferred.

9 See "Treffbericht des MfS/KD Potsdam, 19.8.1975," in: BStU, Ast. Potsdam, AIM II 1610/77, Bl. 28–34, here Bl. 29.

10 See "Treffbericht des MfS/KD Potsdam, 6.11.1975," in: Ibid., Bl. 35.

11 See "Urteil des Landgerichts Potsdam vom 26.6.1996," in: StA Berlin, Az. 27 Js 299/92 (= StA Neuruppin: 61 Js 36/95), Bd. 3, Bl. 487.

12 See "Bericht der MfS/HA I/Grenzkommando Mitte/Bereich Abwehr/UA/GR-34 über Anwendung der Schusswaffe im Grenzdienst in zwei Fällen, 6.11.1975," in: BStU, MfS, HA I Nr. 14878, Bl. 141.

13 See "Urteil des Landgerichts Potsdam vom 26.6.1996," in: StA Berlin, Az. 27 Js 299/92 (= StA Neuruppin: 61 Js 36/95), Bd. 3, Bl. 487.

14 See "Urteil des Landgerichts Potsdam vom 26.6.1996," in: StA Berlin, Az. 27 Js 299/92 (= StA Neuruppin: 61 Js 36/95), Bd. 3, Bl. 475.

15 See "Bericht der MfS/HA I/Grenzkommando Mitte/Bereich Abwehr/UA/GR-34 über Anwendung der Schusswaffe im Grenzdienst in zwei Fällen, 6.11.1975," in: BStU, MfS, HA I Nr. 14878, Bl. 141.

16 See "Urteil des Landgerichts Potsdam vom 26.6.1996," in: StA Berlin, Az. 27 Js 299/92 (= StA Neuruppin: 61 Js 36/95), Bd. 3, Bl. 488.

17 "Sektionsbericht der NVA/Zentrales Lazarett/Abteilung für Gerichtliche Medizin, Bad Saarow, 7.11.1975," in: BStU, Ast. Potsdam, AP 1180/76, Bl. 21.

18 See "Urteil des Landgerichts Potsdam vom 26.6.1996," in: StA Berlin, Az. 27 Js 299/92 (= StA Neuruppin: 61 Js 36/95), Bd. 3, Bl. 472–499.

19 Conversation conducted by Maria Nooke with Lothar Hennig's sisters and brothers, 11.9.2009.

20 See "Ergänzungsmeldung des MfS/HA I/Grenzkommando Mitte/Bereich Abwehr zum Bericht über Anwendung der Schusswaffe/Grenzregiment 34 vom 5.11.1975," in: BStU, MfS, HA I Nr. 14878, Bl. 144.

21 See "Situationsbericht des MfS/HA I/Grenzkommando Mitte/Bereich Abwehr/UA/GR-34 zum Vorkommnis über die Anwendung der Schusswaffe im Grenzdienst mit tödlichen Ausgang, 7.11.1975," in: BStU, MfS, HA I Nr. 14878, Bl. 152–153; "Bericht der BVfS Potsdam/Untersuchungsabteilung über die am 7.11.1975 durchgeführte Aussprache mit den Angehörigen des Hennig, Lothar, 7.11.1975," in: BStU, Ast. Potsdam, AP 1180/76, Bl. 36–38.

22 See "Späte Aufklärung über den mysteriösen Tod des Lothar Hennig", in: Berliner Morgenpost, 15.7.1992.

23 See "Schreiben der Mutter von Lothar Hennig an das Ministerium für Nationale Verteidigung/Armeegeneral Heinz Hoffmann, 3.12.1975," in: StA Berlin, Az. 27 Js 299/92 (= StA Neuruppin: 61 Js 36/95), Bd. 1, Bl. 120.

24 See "Schreiben des Ministers für Nationale Verteidigung an die Mutter von Lothar Hennig, 8.12.1975," in: StA Berlin, Az. 27 Js 299/92 (= StA Neuruppin: 61 Js 36/95), Bd.1, Bl. 121.

25 Dr. Rolf Zickler became head of the medical services division of the Potsdam Stasi district administration with the rank of colonel. On Zickler see also: "Mielkes Medicus," in: Focus Nr. 21, 18.5.1998.

26 "Totenschein für Lothar Hennig, 6.11.1975," in: StA Berlin, Az. 27 Js 299/92 (= StA Neuruppin: 61 Js 36/95), Bd.1, Bl. 27.

27 "Situationsbericht des MfS/HA I/Grenzkommando Mitte/Bereich Abwehr/UA GR-34 zum Vorkommnis über die Anwendung der Schusswaffe im Grenzdienst mit tödlichen Ausgang, 6.11.1975," in: BStU, MfS, HA I Nr. 14878, Bl. 147.

28 Ibid., Bl. 148.

29 Ibid., Bl. 150.

30 "Situationsbericht des MfS/HA I/Grenzkommando Mitte/Bereich Abwehr/UA/GR-34 zum Vorkommnis über die Anwendung der Schusswaffe im Grenzdienst mit tödlichen Ausgang, 7.11.1975," in: BStU, MfS, HA I Nr. 14878, Bl. 152–155, here Bl. 153.

31 "Situationsbericht des MfS/HA I/Grenzkommando Mitte/Bereich Abwehr/UA GR-34 zum Vorkommnis über die Anwendung der Schusswaffe im Grenzdienst mit tödlichen Ausgang am 5.11.1975," 7.11.1975, in: BStU, MfS, HA I Nr. 14878, Bl. 155.

Dietmar Schwietzer

born on February 21, 1958

shot dead on February 16, 1977
near Berliner Allee
on the outer ring between
Schönwalde (Nauen district) and Berlin-Spandau

D ietmar Schwietzer was born on February 21, 1958 in Magdeburg. He grew up with his parents and a sister.[1] Even as a child he had enjoyed tinkering with radios, repairing the receivers of friends and neighbors and creating his own radio station, which was unable to transmit, but could pick up international amateur radio. He did not stand out in school, but was a good pioneer and FDJ member and used the radio sport division of the pre-military youth organization, "Society for Sport and Technology," for his own purposes because he was able to transmit from there. He graduated from tenth grade and then completed an apprenticeship as a communications worker in the Magdeburg district head office of the German postal service. Dietmar Schwietzer had a few friends, but he was less interested in going to discos than the other apprentices his age and was more preoccupied with his radio equipment. The international radio network was his secret world; neither his parents, his teachers nor his trainers knew about his secret contacts.

Because he appeared to be so well-adjusted and because the Stasi was interested in him as a communications engineer, he was selected to serve in the special Stasi guard regiment "Felix Dzierzynski." He was supposed to begin his duty as a radio operator on April 1, 1977. During a ceremony on February 15, 1977 he received his trade certification and proudly showed it to his father before leaving to attend a party at the Magdeburg hotel, "International." But he only showed up there briefly and left again after drinking a glass of cola. At this point no one had any idea what the young man was planning to do on the day of his graduation. Thirty years later the parents were still wondering whether his actions were a response to the sudden death of his girlfriend earlier that year and an attempt to put everything behind him, or whether he was trying to get out of being recruited by the Stasi.

When Dietmar Schwietzer got on his motorcycle on February 15, he had all his important documents with him, including his birth certificate, his school diploma and his recently acquired trade certification card. He also had his East German savings and the 110 west marks that his grandparents in West Germany had given him.[2] He drove about 100 kilometers in almost freezing temperatures from Magdeburg to Hennigsdorf, left the bike there and continued his trip by bus. He crossed the Niederneuendorfer Canal from Schönwalde.[3] Early in the morning of February 16, he crept across a field behind the bridge until he reached the border grounds. He inspected the grounds for a long time with binoculars before proceeding beyond the interior fence through a dog run and passed a signal fence where he triggered an alarm shortly past 7 a.m. As he was running towards the final wall obstacle thirty meters away, the 18-year-old-man came under fire from two watchtowers. Four border soldiers fired a total of 91 shots of automatic fire. Three bullets hit Dietmar Schwietzer a few meters in front of the border wall; a shot to the back of his head was fatal.[4] The border guards quickly dragged him into the anti-vehicle trench and were able to prevent anyone on the West Berlin side from observing the incident. Later the border troops used the case of Dietmar Schwietzer in training as "a good example of operational readiness and advantageous alternative action" for preventing an escape. The large amount of ammunition fired was the only aspect that was criticized.[5]

Dietmar Schwietzer was buried at the Neustädter Cemetery on February 23. The East German secret police monitored the funeral and took clandestine photographs in order to ensure that critical statements and actions were nipped in the bud.[6]

The parents were shocked by the killing of their son and they vented their outrage at the highest levels. On April 10, 1977 the father submitted the original bill he received from the "VEB Grünanlagen Magdeburg," the local state-run park service, for the funeral costs to the Communist Party General Secretary Erich Honecker and demanded that his son's murderer cover the expenses.[7] The letter landed at the Magdeburg secret police office, which responded by keeping the Schwietzer family under permanent surveillance and subjecting them to countless interrogations. The family was threatened with criminal prosecution if news of the young man's death became known in West Germany.[8] As a precautionary measure to keep things quiet before the CSCE (Conference on Security and Cooperation in Europe) follow-up conference in Belgrade, the East German secret police went so far as to delay the collection procedure for the overdue funeral costs: "The Schwietzers are to cover the costs but the VEB Grünlage should postpone sending a reminder for the overdue funeral bill until after the conference in Belgrade."[9] Two months later the Magdeburg secret police "preliminarily" paid the bill for 383.40 marks, but in the end they refrained from demanding the sum from the family.[10]

As early as mid-December 1989, during the East German Peaceful Revolution, Dietmar Schwietzer's parents confronted the East German general state prosecutor's office and demanded not only that the circumstances of their son's death be clarified, but also that they be granted material compensation for the loss they suffered, just as the victims of fascism had been granted.[11] By the mid-1990s the East German military state prosecutor arranged to have the parents receive the second half of their son's life insurance policy, which had been held back at the time.[12] Their other claims for compensation, however, led nowhere.

Criminal proceedings were not opened until late 1990, first by the Berlin public prosecutor's office, then by the Neuruppin public prosecutor. One of the four accused gunmen had already passed away. Three were tried on April 10, 1995 for having jointly killed a man. At the time they had been awarded the "Merit of

Honor for Exemplary Service at the Border" and given a 150 mark bonus. Not one of them was proud of this medal, and they expressed this to the court convincingly. On November 29, 1995 they were each sentenced as youths by the Potsdam district court to a year and three months in prison for joint manslaughter. Their sentences were commuted to probation.[13]

Martin Ahrends / Udo Baron / Hans-Hermann Hertle

1 On the following see conversation conducted by Udo Baron with Dietmar Schwietzer's parents, 2.8.2007; see also "Befragungsprotokoll des Vaters von Dieter Schwietzer durch das MfS, 21.2.1977," in: BStU, MfS, AS 420/80, Bd. 1, Bl. 293–296.

2 See "Bericht des MfS/HA IX/7 zum Stand der Untersuchungen des versuchten Grenzdurchbruchs mit tödlichem Ausgang am 16.2.1977, 16.2.1977," in: BStU, MfS, AS 420/80, Bd. 1, Bl. 274.

3 On the course of events see "Urteil des Landgerichts Potsdam vom 29. November 1995," in: StA Berlin, Az. 61 Js 22/95, Bd. 2, Bl. 236–238.

4 See "Gefechtsbeispiel Nr. 1 der Grenztruppen der DDR/Grenzregiment 34, 17.2.1977," in: BArch, GT 7605, Bl. 34–37.

5 See ibid., Bl. 34–37, here Bl. 36.

6 See "Plan der BVfS Magdeburg zur operativen Absicherung der Leichenbesichtigung sowie der Erdbestattung des Schwietzer, Dietmar, 22.2.1977," in: BStU, Ast. Magdeburg, AOPK 1548/79, Bl. 111–112.

7 Quoted from "Schreiben der BVfS Magdeburg/Abt. IX an die BVfS Magdeburg/Abt. XVIII, 12.5.1977," in: BStU, Ast. Magdeburg, AOPK 1548/79, Bl. 129–130.

8 Conversation conducted by Udo Baron with Dietmar Schwietzer's parents, 2.8.2007.

9 See "Schreiben der BVfS Magdeburg/Abt. IX an die BVfS Magdeburg/Abt. XVIII, 12.5.1977," in: BStU, Ast. Magdeburg, AOPK 1548/79, Bl. 129.

10 See the corresponding file note in: BStU, Ast. Magdeburg, AOPK 1548/79, Bl. 169–172.

11 See "Schreiben der Eltern von Dietmar Schwietzer an den DDR-Generalstaatsanwalt (Abschrift), 12.12.1989," in: StA Berlin, Az. 61 Js 22/95, Bd. 1, Bl. 41.

12 See "Protokoll der Militärstaatsanwaltschaft der DDR-Grenztruppen über eine Aussprache mit der Mutter von Dietmar Schwietzer, 3.5.1990," in: StA Berlin, Az. 61 Js 22/95, Bd. 1, Bl. 42–43.

13 See "Urteil des Landgerichts Potsdam vom 29. November 1995," in: StA Berlin, Az. 61 Js 22/95, Bd. 2, Bl. 225–246.

Henri Weise

born on July 13, 1954

drowned, probably in May 1977
in the Spree
on the sector border between
Berlin-Mitte and Berlin-Tiergarten

T he border soldiers on the Marschall Bridge water border in Berlin-Mitte made a terrible discovery on July 27, 1977. When they opened the water barrier, they found a dead body jammed in it. The fire department was quickly called to the scene and finally managed to retrieve the corpse, which was then taken to the Institute of Forensic Medicine in East Berlin's Charité Hospital for an autopsy.[1] The corpse had already decomposed and was only clothed in fabric remnants suggesting that it had been in the water for about two months. The pathologist was unable to determine the cause of death but he did not find any indication of violence. The authorities were able to identify the body from an old injury on the lower jaw and dental records.[2] The dead man was Henri Weise.

Henri Weise was born on July 13, 1954 in Pössneck. He was the oldest of three sons and grew up with his parents, a driver and sales clerk, in Ranis, Thuringia. Evidently Henri Weise was unassuming and well-adjusted until he completed his vocational training. In a curriculum vitae that he wrote for an application, he stressed that he had been trusted with the position of brigade leader and deputy group chairman and was responsible for sports and cultural activities at the Ranis Secondary School.[3] Henri Weise was also a member of the FDJ.[4] When he began a toolmaker apprenticeship at the state-owned Carl Zeiss Company in Jena, he joined the FDGB and the "Society for German-Soviet Friendship." He was listed as a non-political member of the "Society for Sport and Technology."[5] His training ended in February 1974. His parents had divorced the previous year and his father moved to East Berlin. Henri Weise lived with his mother in Ranis. He first worked as a window and building cleaner, then as a rock driller and heating technician. In a later interrogation with the East German police, Henri Weise's mother described her son as a loner who did not have any friends or a girlfriend.[6]

In May 1976 Henri Weise applied for the first time for an exit permit to West Germany. He stated that he did not have any interest in working for East Germany because "it had not eliminated people's exploiting other people."[7] A few months later Henri Weise took a trip to Wittenberge. After spending time on the bank of the Elbe River, close to the border, he was arrested on the evening of August 15,

1976 under "suspicion of illegally attempting to cross the border."[8] While in prison he wrote to the East German state council, demanding that his East German citizenship be revoked and he issued a complaint regarding his imprisonment. He also informed the Permanent Mission of the Federal Republic in East Germany of his imprisonment and his plans to emigrate and requested political asylum in West Germany.[9] During an interrogation while in pre-trial confinement in Perleberg, Henri Weise denied that he had any intention of fleeing and was in fact released on October 19, 1976 from the Rudolstadt pre-trial prison to which he had been transferred.[10] At the same time he was informed that his application to leave East Germany had been rejected. Henri Weise submitted another request to leave that was definitively rejected in November 1976.[11]

After that the 22-year-old began looking into other ways of leaving East Germany. At the end of October 1976 he asked a Polish citizen at a dance in his hometown whether he could arrange for him to receive a Polish passport. The Pole immediately reported the incident to the Ranis East German police. Consequently Henri Weise did not receive a passport, but was instead charged with "suspicion of planning an illegal border crossing."[12] During the interrogation that followed, the East German police noticed that Henri Weise was carrying an invalid entry permit for a temporary visit to the border area that was issued in someone else's name. He had gotten the permit from an acquaintance, a driver whom he happened to know.[13] He again was able to convince the authorities that he had no intention of fleeing. A warrant for his arrest was not issued.[14]

In mid-1977, Henri Weise showed up once again at the Pössneck district division of internal affairs. He complained that the district council had instructed that he was not to be allowed to continue his work as heating technician and that he now had to work as a mere laborer. He pointed out that these repercussions against him were in contradiction of the UN's charter on human rights and the East German constitution. He threatened to publicize his case and his treatment by the state in the West German press if his application to emigrate was not approved.[15] In follow-up questioning by the criminal investigation department in Pössneck he stressed his intention to travel to Berlin the following day in order to bring a copy of his complaint to the West German Permanent Mission and have it added to his rejected emigration application. He mentioned that he had already been there once before in late 1976 when he had had a meeting that lasted several hours.[16]

By January 1977 at the very latest, Henri Weise was placed under intensified surveillance by the Stasi as part of an "operative investigation of the individual (OPK)." The Stasi agents assigned to watch him soon established that he was constantly expressing criticism of the politics and government of East Germany. Based on his behavior and activities, the Stasi suspected him of wanting to leave East Germany "illegally." The aim of the operative observation was to prove that he had violated article 213 of the criminal code ("illegal border crossing").[17] His visit to the Permanent Mission in East Berlin on January 21, 1977 was registered and analyzed.[18] Henri Weise told a co-worker, who was also engaged as a Stasi informant, that he had not been admitted there and was forced to leave without having achieved anything.[19]

In March 1977 Henri Weise paid a final visit to the Pössneck division of internal affairs where he was informed that his application was definitively rejected. Henri Weise demanded to have the refusal in writing. He made it clear that they would be held accountable for their actions at the CSCE follow-up conference in Belgrade in October 1977.[20] This time, however, his visit to the district council remained unsuccessful.

On May 17, 1977 Henri Weise went to East Berlin to visit his father. After a few hours he left the apartment saying that he would be back in a half hour. It is not known where he went. He probably tried to cross the Spree to West Berlin and died while doing so.[21]

His disappearance did not go unnoticed. In early June, before his body was found in the water barrier of the border crossing, Henri Weise's mother was questioned about his whereabouts by the East German police in Pössneck. She said that she was very worried but that she had no reason to believe he had tried to escape. Her apprehension became certainty when she received her son's death certificate. Her request to see her son's body was not granted.

Henri Weise was cremated in East Berlin on September 1, 1977. The urn was sent to Ranis where it was buried.[22]

In the early 1990s the Central Investigating Agency for Governmental and Party Crimes tried to clarify the circumstances that had led to Henri Weise's death. The investigation was closed on September 27, 1995 because it was not possible to "establish a conclusive cause of death or determine exactly what had happened."[23]

Lydia Dollmann

1 See "Meldung der DDR-Grenztruppen über Vorkommnisse an der Grenzübergangsstelle Marschallbrücke/Berlin-Mitte, 27.7.1977," in: BArch, GT 7013, Bl. 21–22.
2 See "Schreiben der Staatsanwaltschaft II bei dem Landgericht Berlin, 23.1.1996," in: StA Berlin, AZ 27 AR 15/95, Bl. 64–65.
3 See "Handschriftlicher Lebenslauf von Henri Weise, 14.2.1974," in: BStU, Ast. Gera, AOPK 1131/77, Bl. 125; "Meldung des VPKA Pössneck/Abt. K/Sg. V über Dauerfahndung/Vermisst/Löschung nach Henri Weise, 24.8.1977," in: Ibid., Bl. 186.
4 See "Personalbogen von Henri Weise, 14.2.1974," in: Ibid., Bl. 122; "Personalbogen von Henri Weise, 30.12.1975," in: Ibid., Bl. 140.
5 See "Sofortmeldung des VPKA Perleberg über den Verdacht des versuchten ungesetzlichen Grenzübertritts, 16.8.1976," in: Ibid., Bl. 31; "Information [des MfS]/KD Pössneck zur Person Henri Weise, 27.9.1976," in: Ibid., Bl. 44.
6 See "Protokoll des Gespräches mit der Mutter von Henri Weise im VPKA Pössneck/KP, 6.6.1977," in: Ibid., Bl. 184.
7 "Abschrift des Antrags von Henri Weise auf Ausreise in die Bundesrepublik Deutschland, 7.5.1976," in: Ibid., Bl. 20.
8 "Sofortmeldung des VPKA Perleberg über den Verdacht des versuchten ungesetzlichen Grenzübertritts, 16.8.1976," in: Ibid., Bl. 31.
9 See "Schreiben von Henri Weise an den Staatsrat der DDR, 22.9.1976," in: Ibid., Bl. 34–35; "Schreiben von Henri Weise an die Ständige Vertretung der Bundesrepublik Deutschland, 23.9.1976," in: Ibid., Bl. 36–37.
10 See "Schlussbericht der BDVP Gera/Abt. K/Dezernat II/Komm. II/Rudolstadt/VPKA Pössneck über Henri Weise, 27.9.1976," in: Ibid., Bl. 47–48.
11 See "Kurzinformation des Rates des Kreises Pössneck/Abt. Innere Angelegenheiten über den Antrag auf ÜS von Henri Weise, 19.10.1976," in: Ibid., Bl. 52.

12 "Anzeige gegen Henri Weise beim VPKA Pössneck/Abt. K, 30.10.1976," in: Ibid., Bl. 55.

13 See "Protokoll der Zeugenvernehmung des Kraftfahrers durch das VPKA Pössneck, 30.10.1976," in: Ibid., Bl. 66.

14 See "Ergänzungsmeldung des VPKA Pössneck, 31.10.1976," in: Ibid., Bl. 74.

15 See "Information des Rates des Kreises Pössneck/Abt. Innere Angelegenheiten, 19.1.1977," in: Ibid., Bl. 106.

16 See "Protokoll der Vernehmung von Henri Weise durch das VPKA Pössneck/KP, 20.1.77," in: Ibid., Bl. 107–108.

17 See "Übersichtsbogen [des MfS] zur operativen Personenkontrolle von Henri Weise, 11.1.1977," in: Ibid., Bl. 3.

18 See "Schreiben der BVfS Gera/Abt. II an die KD Pössneck, 2.2.1977," in: Ibid., Bl. 111.

19 See "Abschrift des Berichts des Führungs-IM "Ullrich" über Henri Weise, 11.2.1977," in: Ibid., Bl. 121.

20 See "Ausspracheprotokoll des Rates des Kreises Pössneck/Abt. Innere Angelegenheiten mit Henri Weise, 22.3.1977," in: Ibid., Bl. 179.

21 See "Niederschrift der Zeugenbefragung der Mutter von Henri Weise durch die KPI Jena im Auftrag der ZERV, 15.6.1995," in: StA Berlin, AZ 27 AR 15/95, Bl. 46.

22 See ibid., Bl. 46.

23 "Schlussbericht der ZERV vom 27.9.1995," in: Ibid., Bl. 47–48.

Marienetta Jirkowsky

born on August 25, 1962

shot dead on November 22, 1980
on Florastrasse, across from the Invaliden Settlement
on the outer ring between
Hohen Neuendorf (Oranienburg district)
and Berlin-Reinickendorf

M arienetta Jirkowsky was born on August 25, 1962 in Bad Saarow. She grew up in Spreenhagen, in Brandenburg, and received training in a tire combine in Fürstenwalde as a skilled textile worker. "Micki," as her friends called her, was a "small, free-spirited and fun-loving person."[1] She and her friends really "just wanted to live in peace [...], without any problems and without being forbidden to do anything," her friend Falko V. later explained.[2] Falko V. had been thinking about escaping for a long time. He and Marienetta Jirkowsky met Peter W. together in spring 1980. He, too, had not adjusted to the conditions in East Germany and had applied a number of times for an exit permit to leave the country.[3] When Marienetta Jirkowsky turned 18, the legal age of an adult under East German law, she became engaged to Peter W. They planned to move in together in the fall of 1980. This decision, however, led to major conflicts with her parents, who were opposed to their relationship and feared that they were going to lose their only child. To prevent this from happening, they succeeded in getting a police order to ban Peter W. from having any contact with their daughter.[4] After that the three were just waiting for the right moment to leave East Germany. They planned to flee together on the night of November 22, 1980. In preparation for their escape Peter W. created a folding ladder, which consisted of separate pieces, in his apartment.[5]

On November 21 the three young people took a train from Fürstenwalde to East Berlin to look for a good place to escape. They agreed that the spot they had checked out was not favorable for an escape and so they took the S-Bahn back to Hohen Neuendorf that evening. Peter W. was familiar with the border there from when he had worked as a showman. They arrived at the Hohen Neuendorf S-Bahn station at around half past midnight and worked their way across the property near the border. Without using any tools they were able to "crack" the two ladders, a so-called double ladder and a stepladder, to peer over the interior wall and get a look at the border grounds. Contrary to their original plan, the three made a spontaneous decision to flee that very night. They did not know that, thanks to this decision, the two men had just barely missed being arrested early the next morning. An informant for the East German secret police. who was a member of their group of friends, had betrayed them and reported their escape plan to the Stasi.[6]

For three hours that night the three young people observed the routine at the border while bolstering each other's courage. Then they separated the stepladder into two parts and at about 3:30 in the morning, they took one ladder element to climb over the interior wall. The two men used the double ladder to get over the 2.5 meter high signal fence and managed not to set off the alarm. But when Marienetta Jirkowsky followed them, the alarm was triggered. The men had already reached the final obstacle, the 3.5-meter-high wall facing West Berlin. Although the remaining part of the step ladder had sunk into the ground, Falko V. and Peter W. were still able to reach the top of the wall but then shots were fired at them from a watchtower located 160 meters away. Falko V. had already jumped down to the west side; Peter lay down on his stomach on top of the wall because his fiancée, who was standing on the top rung of the ladder, was too short to grasp the Wall with her hands. He reached out his hand to her to pull her up. Two additional border soldiers, who had run from their watchtower 230 meters away, also started firing at the fugitives. Marienetta Jirkowsky had already reached the top of the wall with her hands when she was struck by a bullet and fell off the ladder. Peter W. fell down onto the west side of the Wall.[7] A short time later border soldiers retrieved the young woman and provided first aid. The regiment doctor ordered her to be transported to the nearest hospital in Hennigsdorf, where an emergency operation was conducted. Marienetta Jirkowsky died there at 11:30 a.m. from a bullet through her abdomen.[8]

Fifteen years later one of the gunmen was tried for a "less serious case of manslaughter" and sentenced as a youth by the Neuruppin district court to a year and three month prison term that was commuted to probation.[9]

On behalf of all the Allied city commanders, the French city commander protested that very day against the shots fired at Marienetta Jirkowsky and demanded that East Germany finally put a stop to their "inhuman practices."[10]

The East German secret police went to great effort to prevent any information about the 18-year-old woman's death from leaking out. Under no circumstances was a photograph of the dead woman to be published and many photographs of Marienetta Jirkowsky were confiscated from her friends and relatives. The East German secret police tried to make Peter W. and Falko V. look like liars by passing a photograph of a woman who resembled Marienetta Jirkowsky on to the western media. The plan was to undermine the validity of all the reporting on the fatal escape attempt by having this photo identified as "false."[11] Another step was taken to publicly discredit the two men who had fled: Informants working for the East German secret police were supposed to win over their confidence and then try to make them look like criminals. They were to "[...] inconspicuously encourage them to spend large sums of money without deliberation, take out credit, etc, in order [...] to set the preconditions for possible criminal behavior [...]."[12] Despite these measures, Falko V. and Peter W. were able to provide detailed accounts of the case to the West. In early February 1981, they placed a cross at the site where they had escaped to honor their deceased friend. It was removed by a Stasi informant and secretly brought to the Ministry of State Security in East Berlin.[13] The Stasi also considered taking "measures to transfer the two men back to East Germany," meaning a plan to have them kidnapped.[14]

In the aftermath of Marienetta Jirkowsky's death, Falko V. became involved in spectacular acts to draw attention to the fate of his girlfriend. On February 6, 1981 he placed charges of murder against the East German minister of defense, Heinz Hoffmann, with the Central Registry Office in Salzgitter.[15] On March 2, 1981, during the CSCE follow-up conference in Madrid, he chained himself to the entrance gate of the Soviet Embassy in Madrid to denounce the East German government's violation of human rights.[16]

On the day of the fatal escape attempt, Marienetta Jirkowsky's father was summoned to the East German police in Fürstenwalde. At first all he learned there was that his daughter had been arrested at the border to West Berlin. He was not informed that she had been killed until two days later.[17] The family was not allowed to publish an obituary. Spreenhagen, the 18-year-old woman's hometown, was virtually sealed off by State Security agents when the urn containing her ashes was buried in the town's cemetery. The funeral was attended by her immediate family on December 14, 1980.

Martin Ahrends / Udo Baron

1   Interview with Falko V., in: Giordana Dunkhorst, *Hoher Preis für coole Klamotten. Jugendliche "Aussteiger" in der DDR um 1980. Eine Schülerarbeit im Rahmen des Geschichtswettbewerbs des Bundespräsidenten*, Berlin, 2007, p. 38.

2   Ibid., p. 39.

3   See "Anklageschrift der Staatsanwaltschaft Neuruppin, Az. 61 Js 109/94, vom 22.11.1994," in: StA Neuruppin, Az. 61 Js 109/94, Bd. 4, Bl. 26.

4   See "Eröffnungsbericht des MfS/KD Fürstenwalde zum Anlegen des OV "Leiter", 5.2.1980," in: BStU, Ast. Frankfurt, 1466/83 (OV "Leiter"), Bl. 31; Interview with Falko V., in: Dunkhorst, *Hoher Preis für coole Klamotten*, p. 38.

5   On this and circumstances of the escape presented in the following, see "Protokoll der Zeugenvernehmung von Peter W. durch die West-Berliner Polizei, 8.12.1980," in: StA Neuruppin, Az. 61 Js 109/94, Bd. 1, Bl. 28–32; "Protokoll der Zeugenvernehmung von Falko V. durch die West-Berliner Polizei, 22.12.1980," in: StA Neuruppin, Az. 61 Js 109/94, Bd. 1, Bl. 33–37.

6   See "Eröffnungsbericht des MfS/KD Fürstenwalde zum Anlegen des OV "Leiter", 5.12.1980," in: BStU, Ast. Frankfurt, 1466/83 (OV "Leiter"), Bl. 28–29.

7   See "Urteil des Landgerichts Neuruppin in der Strafsache gegen Detlev S. und Werner St., Az. 12 Ks 61 Js 109/94 (61/94), vom 19.12.1995," in: StA Neuruppin, Az. 61 Js 109/94, Bd. 4, pp. 77–80; "Protokoll der Zeugenvernehmung von Peter W. durch die West-Berliner Polizei, 8.12.1980," in: StA Neuruppin, Az. 61 Js 109/94, Bd. 1, Bl. 30–31.

8   "Bericht des Leiters der BVfS Potsdam über das Vorkommnis an der Staatsgrenze am 22. November 1980," in: BStU, MfS, Sekr. Neiber Nr. 263, Bl. 138–139.

9   See "Urteil des Landgerichts Neuruppin in der Strafsache gegen Detlev S. und Werner St., Az. 12 Ks 61 Js 109/94 (61/94), vom 19.12.1995," in: StA Neuruppin, Az. 27 Js 71/97, Bd. 4, Bl. 60–125.

10 See "Lagefilm des MfS/ZKG, 22.11.1980," in: BStU, MfS, Sekr. Neiber Nr. 263, Bl. 74.

11 See Hannelore Strehlow, *Der gefährliche Weg in die Freiheit*, Potsdam 2004, p. 44.

12 "Information zum Stand der operativen Bearbeitung [Name geschwärzt], 28.3.1981," in: BStU, MfS, Sekr. Neiber Nr. 263, Bl. 9.

13 See "Sachstandsbericht zu den Feindaktionen im Zusammenhang mit dem Grenzdurchbruch nach Westberlin durch [Namen geschwärzt], 3.4.1981," in: BStU, MfS, Sekr. Neiber Nr. 263, Bl.11–13; see also Hannelore Strehlow, *Der gefährliche Weg in die Freiheit*, Potsdam 2004, p. 46.

14 See "Eröffnungsbericht des MfS/KD Fürstenwalde zum Anlegen des OV "Leiter", 5.12.1980," in: BStU, Ast. Frankfurt, 1466/83 (OV "Leiter"), Bl. 35.

15 See "Schreiben von Falko V. an die Zentrale Erfassungsstelle der Landesjustizverwaltungen in Salzgitter vom 6.2.1981," in: StA Neuruppin, Az. 61 Js 108/94, Bd. 1, Bl. 48.

16 See *Die Welt*, 3.3.1981; "Sachstandsbericht zu den Feindaktionen im Zusammenhang mit dem Grenzdurchbruch nach Westberlin durch [Namen geschwärzt], 3.4.1981," in: BStU, MfS, Sekr. Neiber Nr. 263, Bl. 14.

17 On this and the following, see "Bericht über ein Gespräch der Ermittlungsgruppe der Staatsanwaltschaft bei dem Kammergericht Berlin mit den Eltern von Marienetta Jirkowsky, 15.1.1991", in: StA Neuruppin, Az. 61 Js 109/94, Bd. 1, Bl. 143–145.

Dr. Johannes Muschol

born on May 31, 1949

shot dead on March 16, 1981
near Kopenhagener Strasse in Wilhelmsruh
on the sector border between
Berlin-Reinickendorf and Berlin-Pankow

Johannes Muschol, born on May 31, 1949 in Aschau, Bavaria, was 23 years old and studying medicine when he was diagnosed with schizophrenia. He was treated for this condition for the first time in 1972 and on many occasions in the following years; nonetheless, he was still able to complete his medical degree. His illness eventually became chronic, however, and caught up with him. In May 1979 he was ascribed as having a permanent work disability.[1]

Johannes Muschol drove with a friend to West Berlin on March 14, 1981 to take part in a house-warming party.[2] He got into a fight with his companion on the transit highway because Johannes Muschol insisted on getting out of the car. Later his friend speculated that he may have wanted to visit an aunt in East Germany whom he had spoken about. As a consequence of the fight, after they arrived in West Berlin, the two men parted ways. That evening they met again at the party and agreed to meet the next morning at 11 a.m. at the Bahnhof Zoo train station to drive home together.

But Dr. Johannes Muschol never showed up at the agreed meeting place. On the evening of March 15, he was picked up at a nursing home in Treptow, a district of East Berlin, and brought back across the border to West Berlin.[3] It is not known why he was in East Berlin, how he was "returned" to the West, or where he spent the night. On the morning of March 16, he made inquiries on the west side of the Bornholmer Strasse border crossing about the security measures on the border.[4] Then he wandered around the West Berlin district of Reinickendorf, where he asked a number of residents for bread and water and for a place to wash himself. He later showed up at the sector border between Alt-Reinickendorf and the East Berlin district of Wilhelmsruh and climbed onto a viewing platform situated right next to the Wall.

It was just past 11 a.m. on March 16, a sunny day with clear skies, when Johannes Muschol climbed over the railing of the viewing platform and onto the top of the Wall. "What are you doing there, are you crazy? Come back!" an eye-witness called out to him.[5] But Johannes Muschol jumped over the Wall and ran across the death strip towards East Berlin. Two border guards saw him and one of the guards left the tower to arrest him. He thought that the strange, confused behavior of the "border violator" was due to alcohol or drugs, which later was determined not to be the case. "Halt and don't do anything foolish," the guard called to him as he tried to hold on to him by his jacket.[6] Johannes Muschol seemed to pause for a moment, but then he suddenly broke loose and ran through the anti-tank obstacles to the border signal fence, pulled the barbed wire apart and climbed through the opening. He tried a number of times without success to climb over the interior wall while the guard who followed him demanded that he surrender and allow himself to be arrested. The second border soldier, the guard leader that day, was watching the events from the tower located ten meters away. "Go on and shoot, you idiot," he called out.[7] But the guard on the ground did not shoot. Instead, he stood just a few meters away from Muschol and spoke calmly to the clearly confused man, who he believed was just about to surrender. "I do not want to shoot. Just come down and don't do anything foolish," he called to the guard leader on the tower.[8]

Although it was obvious that Muschol was unable to get over the three-meter-high wall, the guard leader shot at him from his watchtower twelve meters away. All three bullets hit Johannes Muschol and he fell to the ground. He died within seconds from a bullet that hit him in the back and went through his heart. "Are you stupid?" the other border guard called to him, horrified by what he regarded as a totally unnecessary shooting that had also put him in danger.[9]

The body was carried away hours later, under the cover of darkness, and brought to the forensic institute of the Military Medical Academy of Bad Saarow, a facility of the National People's Army, where an autopsy was conducted. The death certificate was first issued under the name Johannes Muschol, but then the same military pathologist signed a new death certificate that turned Johannes Muschol into an "unknown" dead man.[10] The military state prosecutor of the East German general state prosecutor's office was also involved in the cover-up and fake documentation. The military state prosecutor, who had ordered the autopsy under Johannes Muschol's name, later classified him as having died "an unnatural death" before releasing him to the Berlin-Mitte city district council as an "unidentified male person."[11] The Stasi did not transfer the body to the Baumschulenweg Crematorium for another 14 days and used money found on the dead man to cover the expenses.[12] After 1990, documents regarding the location of the urn could not be found in the crematorium or in the administrative offices of the Baumschulenweg Cemetery. Interrogations of people believed to have knowledge of the events turned up no new information.

The border guards were commended for their action a few days after the incident occurred. They were decorated and sent on special leave. They swore themselves to absolute secrecy to the East German secret police, which thereafter kept them under surveillance.

After March 16, 1981, the West Berlin and West German media was dominated by headlines about an unknown man who had been shot and perhaps killed at the Wall.[13] On March 17, the Permanent Mission of the Federal Republic in East Berlin tried to attain information from the East German foreign office about the identity of the man, his whereabouts and condition. An attempt was also made to establish direct contact, but the East German diplomat in charge declared that the Permanent Mission had no jurisdiction over the case and rejected the inquiry.[14]

The week after the incident, Johannes Muschol's siblings informed the Munich police department that they believed the man who had been shot might be their brother. The family filled out an official missing persons report on June 1, 1981.[15]

A number of months passed before eye-witnesses who had seen the East German border guards shoot down the man were able to positively identify the victim as Johannes Muschol.[16] "The man in the death strip was a doctor," the "Bild-Zeitung" paper reported in January 1982, and the "Berliner Morgenpost" asked: "What happened to Dr. Muschol?"[17] To find the answer, his family sought out Wolfgang Vogel, the East German negotiator for humanitarian questions. But he was certain that the person in question could not be Johannes Muschol since he would have no doubt been informed of this. The dead man's brother recalled Vogel saying that "a case like that could no longer be kept hushed up, even in East Germany."[18]

Honecker's confidant was either wrong or purposely gave inaccurate information. The deadly shots fired on March 16, 1981 came at a politically very inopportune time for the Communist Party leadership: The Leipzig Spring Convention had opened just days earlier; Rudolf Kirchschläger, the president of Austria, was paying a visit to East Germany on March 16; and the then SPD chairman, Willy Brandt, was due to arrive in East Berlin on March 17. As a result of increasing economic problems, East Germany was all the more dependent on trade with the West and believed that a good political climate was beneficial to trade relations. In order to avoid an incident like the one that had just occurred, the order to shoot fugitives at the border was explicitly toned down on March 16 and border guards were told to only shoot in cases of self-defense.[19] The leadership in East Germany decided that covering up the fatal shots fired at the Wall made more sense than admitting what had happened; and once they had started, they had no choice but to continue with the cover-up measures. The East German foreign office responded in early 1982 to further inquiries from the Permanent Mission that "no Johannes Muschol was known of in East Germany" and that he had also not turned up "as a corpse."[20]

His family was very upset by his unknown fate, but all their efforts over the years – through official channels and on their own initiative through attorneys – to understand what had happened remained unsuccessful until East Germany ceased to exist.

The shooting on March 16, 1981 violated the standard duty regulations of the border troops and was contrary to the special politically motivated orders of the day. The crime was also unlawful under East German law, yet a criminal investigation was not opened. The gunman was finally tried 15 years later. During his trial before the Berlin district court, he expressed his regret over having killed a person; he also said he had been unable to put the act out of his mind all these years.[21] But because he had shot at Johannes Muschol "without scruple or inner repulsion," although the man could have easily been arrested, the district court found him guilty of manslaughter and sentenced him to three years in prison.[22]

The public prosecutor had to drop the charges of aiding and abetting a crime and obstructing justice in 1998. The accused, including Wolfgang Schwanitz, the head of the Berlin Stasi district administration, and his then deputy and later successor, Siegfried Hähnel, either refused to testify or claimed to be unable to remember anything. Evidently any form of honor or humanity was foreign to these Chekists and their assistants. With their statements they deprived a dead man, for whose anonymous burial they were partially responsible, from receiving a dignified funeral. The investigation fizzled out because of a lack of informed witnesses who were willing to testify and who were not themselves suspect.[23]

The gravesite of Dr. Johannes Muschol has yet to be located.

Udo Baron / Hans-Hermann Hertle

1   See "Urteil des Landgerichts Berlin in der Strafsache gegen Bodo W. vom 21.6.1996," in: StA Berlin, Az. 27 Js 110/90, Bd. 8, Bl. 29.

2   On the following, see "Vernehmung eines Bekannten von Johannes Muschol durch die Münchner Polizei vom 3.12.1981," in: StA Berlin, Az. 27 Js 110/90, Bd. 2, Bl. 167–168.

3   "Anklageschrift der Staatsanwaltschaft II bei dem Landgericht Berlin gegen Bodo W., 27/2 Js 110/90 vom 27.11.1995," in: StA Berlin, Az. 27 Js 110/90, Bd. 7, Bl. 79.

4   See "Bericht der West-Berliner Polizei: Hinweis auf Grenzzwischenfall Kopenhagener Strasse, 20.3.1981," in: StA Berlin, Az. 27 Js 110/90, Bd. 2, Bl. 48.

5   "Vernehmung einer Zeugin durch die Berliner Polizei vom 10.4.1992," in: StA Berlin, Az. 27 Js 110/90, Bd. 5, Bl. 7; see also Anklageschrift der Staatsanwaltschaft II bei dem Landgericht Berlin gegen Bodo W., 27/2 Js 110/90 vom 27.11.1995," in: StA Berlin, Az. 27 Js 110/90, Bd. 7, Bl. 80.

6   "Vernehmung einer Zeugin durch die Berliner Polizei vom 10.4.1992," in: StA Berlin, Az. 27 Js 110/90, Bd. 5, Bl. 7.

7   See "Urteil des Landgerichts Berlin in der Strafsache gegen Bodo W. vom 21.6.1996," in: StA Berlin, Az. 27/2 Js 110/90, Bd. 8, Bl. 30.

8   Ibid., Bl. 35.

9   Ibid.

10 Both death certificates are preserved in: BStU, MfS, AU 90/90, Handakte Bd. 1, Bl. 4 and 6.

11 "Der Generalstaatsanwalt der DDR/Militär-Oberstaatsanwalt/Abt. IA, Anzeige eines unnatürlichen Todesfalles, Berlin, 26.3.1981," in: BStU, MfS, AU 90/90, Handakte Bd. 1, Bl. 9–10.

12 "MfS/HA IX/7, Aktenvermerk, 10.4.1981," in: BStU, MfS, AU 90/90, Handakte Bd. 2, Bl. 112.

13 See "Nach Osten über die Mauer: Niedergeschossen," in: *Berliner Morgenpost*, 17.3.1981; "Mauer: Mann sprang in Osten – Schüsse, tot?," *in: Bild-Zeitung*, 17.3.1981; "Gezielte Schüsse aus 15 Meter Entfernung vom Grepo-Wachturm," in: *BZ*, 17.3.1981; "DDR-Posten schossen Mann an der Berliner Mauer nieder," in: *Der Tagesspiegel*, 17.3.1981; "Wenig wissen wir von dem, der fliehen wollte," in: *Die Welt*, 19.3.1981.

14 "Vermerk des MfAA/HA Konsularische Angelegenheiten über ein Gespräch in der HA Konsularische Angelegenheiten am 17. März 1981, von 14.00 bis 14.25 Uhr, Berlin, 17.3.1981," in: BStU, MfS, AU 90/90, Handakte Bd. 2, Bl. 3–6.

15 See "Vermisstenmeldung der Polizei Landshut vom 1.6.1981," in: StA Berlin, Az. 27 Js 110/90, Bd. 1, Bl. 150–151.

16 See "Seit Zwischenfall an der Mauer verschollener Mann identifiziert", in: *Der Tagesspiegel*, 16.1.1982.

17 See *Bild-Zeitung*, 16.1.1982; *Berliner Morgenpost*, 16.1.1982.

18 "Gesprächsnotiz des Bruders von Johannes Muschol über die Besprechung mit Rechtsanwalt Dr. Vogel am 27.1.1982 in Ost-Berlin" (privately owned).

19 See "Urteil des Landgerichts Berlin in der Strafsache gegen Bodo W. vom 21.6.1996," in: StA Berlin, Az. 27 Js 110/90, Bd. 8, Bl. 2.

20 "Schreiben der Ständigen Vertretung der Bundesrepublik Deutschland an den Bruder von Johannes Muschol vom 2.6.1982" (privately owned).

21 See "Urteil des Landgerichts Berlin in der Strafsache gegen Bodo W. vom 21.6.1996," in: StA Berlin, Az. 27 Js 110/90, Bd. 8, Bl. 34.

22 See ibid., here Bl. 50.

23 See "Verfügung der Staatsanwaltschaft II bei dem Landgericht Berlin zu 28 Js 99/96 vom 25.6.1998," in: StA Berlin, Az. 28 Js 99/96, Bl. 211–221.

Hans-Jürgen Starrost

born on June 24, 1955

shot on April 14, 1981
on Gudrunstrasse in Sigridshorst
on the outer ring between
Teltow-Seehof (Potsdam county district)
and Berlin-Steglitz
died from his bullet wounds on May 16, 1981

H ans-Jürgen Starrost was born on June 24, 1955 in Berlin. After finishing tenth grade, he completed an apprenticeship as a skilled construction worker at the state-owned underground engineering collective combine in Berlin. He then served his military duty with the National People's Army. At the age of 22, he was a skilled construction worker who had "served" and thus had fulfilled the obligations of young East German citizens.[1] At the time he probably was not aware that this state would call upon him his entire life and, when necessary, "re-educate" him.

He changed jobs a number of times after his service in the army and at different periods of time did not work at all. He was subjected to "educational measures of various work collectives and state agencies," which he always tried to get out of.[2] In late 1979 he was sentenced to eleven months in prison for "disturbing the public order and security."[3] Hans-Jürgen Starrost had not broken any law; his crime was being "idle" and not working. Perhaps he had not found the place where he wanted to live and work, or maybe he had difficulty adjusting to his sudden "freedom" after having been patronized for 24 years. In East Germany that was reason enough to be put in prison.

He served his sentence until October 1980 in the Rüdersdorf Penitentiary, which was connected to a cement factory and a work camp, both of which were health hazards. After his release, he handed over his identity card. He was then assigned a job and had to report regularly to the "parole officer" (ABV) of the East German police.[4] But soon Hans-Jürgen Starrost stopped going to work and stopped reporting to the police as well. When he called his parole officer on April 7, 1981, he learned from the man's wife that there was a search warrant out for him because he had violated the monitoring measures and would therefore have to go back to prison. He decided to go into hiding to avoid imprisonment.[5]

The 25-year-old took a train to Berlin-Schönefeld on April 13, 1981 and took a bus from there to Teltow. He wanted to visit a friend he had met when he was in the army and he hoped he could stay with him. When he did not find him there he went into a bar and decided to try to flee across the nearby border the following night. "Under no circumstances was I going back to prison," he later said in an interrogation.[6] He stole a metal ladder from the Sigridshorst housing settlement in Teltow on his way to the border territory. When he tried to climb over the interior wall at about 1:10 a.m., two border guards heard him make a noise and, when they checked out the situation, they found the ladder and sounded the alarm. They searched for the fugitive together with their supervisor, who had joined them with his driver and an ABV. Hans-Jürgen Starrost had hidden on a nearby piece of property where he was seen by the ABV. The ABV held his cocked pistol and ordered him to surrender. Instead Hans-Jürgen Starrost tried to flee. When he was blinded by a spotlight, he ran into the arms of a border soldier who held on to him and twisted his left arm behind his back. The soldier commented: "In order to stop the male person from fleeing, I grabbed him by his left wrist and the person stopped immediately." But the soldier continued to explain: "The VP man stood with his weapon in firing position in front of the male individual."[7] In his hopeless situation, the man being detained allegedly began flinging his free right hand around. Did the policeman just lose his nerve or had Hans-Jürgen Starrost managed to break loose and attack the armed man, forcing him to act in self-defense and shoot? The files only provide the answer presented by the perpetrator who took Hans-Jürgen Starrost's life.

Three and a half hours after the events, the East German policeman testified to the Stasi. The guard, himself surprised by his actions, admitted his responsibility: "I stood right in front of the perpetrator [here and henceforth 'perpetrator' refers to the victim Hans-Jürgen Starrost – ed.] and ordered the perpetrator again to put his hands over his head and to stand still. Suddenly the perpetrator lunged at me and there was a scuffle. At that point I still had my gun in my right hand and was only repelling this attack with my left hand. I kept my right hand down and during the attack I must have tensed up and my finger pulled the trigger, causing a bullet to be suddenly fired. It is my view that at this point I no longer had any reason to use the weapon. The perpetrator was surrounded and could not have fled."[8] The Stasi's technical investigation office examined the crime weapon – a "Makarov" pistol – and tested its condition. It came to the conclusion that "when the pistol is handled correctly, a bullet cannot be fired accidentally."[9] But the bullet hit the man in his stomach at close range, shattering his left kidney and spleen, and exited through his back.[10] The man who was hit groaned: "You thugs, if you had hit it right to begin with then at least it would be done with."[11]

Hans-Jürgen Starrost was first brought to a border base. "Had the urgently needed operation been done immediately and intensive care provided, the seriously injured man would have had a chance of survival."[12] Instead, the border regiment's military doctor diagnosed a "mild injury" and had no objection to Hans-Jürgen Starrost's being questioned by an interrogation officer of the Stasi district administration of Potsdam before receiving treatment. The critical condition of the fugitive was evident even to the Stasi agent who had to interrupt the interrogation a number of times due to "necessary medical measures."[13] The Stasi interrogator recorded the interview and noted at the end: "The person in question did not take advantage of his right to listen [to the recording].[14]

After the interrogation was competed, a border troop truck took the badly injured young man to the army hospital in Potsdam where an emergency operation was conducted. An acute failure of the kidneys set in the following days and Hans-Jürgen Starrost's condition became more critical. The Drewitz Army Hospital did not have an intensive care unit. After a week had passed, the extremely sick man was transferred to the intensive care unit of the Potsdam District Hospital. Evidently the transport was delayed because the hospital was not one of the Stasi's preferred clinics for treating victims of the border. But the measures taken there came too late. Hans-Jürgen Starrost died on May 16, 1981 at 7:30 a.m. from his critical injuries.[15]

Eleven years after the fatal shots were fired, the Berlin public prosecutor brought charges against the parole officer of the East German police for attempted manslaughter. He had continued to work as an ABV until 1989 and also served under the code name "Manfred" as an informant for the East German secret police.[16] The public prosecutor accepted the perpetrator's version of the events and found that the shots had not been fired intentionally. The shot was "released" when Starrost resisted his arrest. The charges were dropped in June 1995 because the East German policeman had used his gun "without a direct or conditional intention to kill."[17]

On the day of the crime, April 14, the East German secret police decided "that regardless of how his health condition develops [...], Starrost's relatives should not be informed of what happened until after the 10th Party Congress [of the SED]."[18] On May 20, 1981 the state prosecutor and East German secret police informed Hans-Jürgen Starrost's mother and sister of the death of their son and brother. Contrary to the statement of the ABV who fired the fatal shot, they were told that the dead man had attacked the policeman after a warning shot had been fired and that the policeman had to act in self-defense.[19] They were pressured into agreeing to a cremation of the body and to having the clothes of the dead man destroyed.[20]

Hans-Jürgen Starrost's urn was buried in the cemetery in Rahnsdorf on June 3, 1981 in the presence of his immediate family.[21]

Martin Ahrends / Udo Baron / Hans-Hermann Hertle

1   See "Erstinformation des MfS/HA IX/4, 14.4.1981," in: BStU, MfS, HA IX Nr. 1430, Bl. 17–18.
2   Ibid., Bl. 18.
3   Ibid.
4   See ibid.
5   On this and the following, see "MfS-Bericht zur Befragung des Starrost, Hans-Jürgen, Potsdam, 15.4.1981," in: BStU, Ast. Potsdam, AP 728/83, Bl. 35; on the course of events see also Hannelore Strehlow, Der gefährliche Weg in die Freiheit, Potsdam, 2004, pp. 60–66.
6   "MfS-Bericht zur Befragung des Starrost, Hans-Jürgen, Potsdam, 15.4.1981," in: BStU, Ast. Potsdam, AP 728/83, Bl. 36.
7   "Bericht des Gefreiten [Name geschwärzt] zur Festnahme am 14.4.1981, 14.4.1981," in: BStU, Ast. Potsdam, AP 728/83, Bl. 50–52, here Bl. 51.
8   "Vernehmungsprotokoll des Zeugen [Name geschwärzt], Teltow, 14.4.1981," in: BStU, Ast. Potsdam, AP 728/83, Bl. 55.
9   "Untersuchungsbericht des MfS/Technische Untersuchungsstelle, 27.5.1981," in: BStU, Ast. Potsdam, AP 728/83, Bl. 27–29, here Bl. 28.
10 See "Erstinformation des MfS/HA IX/4, 14.4.1981," in: BStU, MfS, HA IX Nr. 1430, Bl. 16–17.

11 "Bericht von Major [Name geschwärzt] zur Festnahme einer männlichen Person in Teltow-Seehof am 14.4. 1981, 14.4.1981," in: BStU, Ast. Potsdam, AP 728/83, Bl. 41–42, here Bl. 42.

12 Hannelore Strehlow, *Der gefährliche Weg in die Freiheit,* Potsdam, 2004, p. 61.

13 "MfS-Bericht zur Befragung des Starrost, Hans-Jürgen, Potsdam, 15.4.1981," in: BStU, Ast. Potsdam, AP 728/83, Bl. 37.

14 Ibid.

15 See "Diagnose des Bezirkskrankenhauses Potsdam zu Hans-Jürgen Starrost, 20.5.1981," in: BStU, Ast. Potsdam, AP 728/83, Bl. 64.

16 See Hannelore Strehlow, *Der gefährliche Weg in die Freiheit,* Potsdam, 2004, p. 62.

17 See "Verfügung der Staatsanwaltschaft II bei dem Landgericht Berlin, 29.6.1995," in: StA Berlin, Az. 27/2 Js 1040/92, Bd. 2, Bl. 86–87, here Bl. 86.

18 "Erstinformation des MfS/HA IX/4, 14.4.1981," in: BStU, MfS, HA IX Nr. 1430, Bl. 18.

19 See "Aktenvermerk [der BVfS Potsdam/]Untersuchungsabteilung, 21.4.1981," in: BStU, Ast. Potsdam, AP 728/83, Bl. 80.

20 See Hannelore Strehlow, *Der gefährliche Weg in die Freiheit,* Potsdam, 2004, p. 62.

21 See "Aktenvermerk [der BVfS Potsdam/]Untersuchungsabteilung, 22.5.1981," in: BStU, Ast. Potsdam, AP 728/83, Bl. 82.

Thomas Taubmann

born on July 22, 1955

fatally injured on December 12, 1981
beneath the Böse Bridge
on the sector border between
Berlin-Prenzlauer Berg and Berlin-Wedding

During those memorable days in the winter of 1981, when the leaders of both German states were engaged in talks from December 11–13, a young man died in the middle of Berlin while trying to flee to the West. His death went unnoticed by the public. Not far from Berlin, in Hubertusschloss, a hunting lodge near the Werbellinsee lake, West German Chancellor Helmut Schmidt was engaged in negotiations with Erich Honecker, the Communist Party's general secretary and East Germany's state council chairman, over how to ease travel for passengers at the inner-German border. At the same time, Thomas Taubmann, driven to despair, went to the Wall in the belief that if he could get beyond it, his problems would be solved.

Thomas Taubmann was born in Berlin on July 22, 1955.[1] He grew up as an only child in Weissensee in the eastern part of the city. His mother came from West Berlin and the family had many relatives in the West with whom they kept in touch even after they had been separated by the Wall. The parents distanced themselves from the political regime and raised their children in the same spirit.

Thomas Taubmann went to school in Weissensee. He was a good swimmer and, for a time, he attended a sports school until the pressure became too much for him. After finishing tenth grade he completed an apprenticeship as a machine fitter in a house building combine. After this he trained to become a specialist for crane repairs. Because of his special technical skills, his company assigned him to the engineering school for mechanical engineering and electrical technology in Lichtenberg where he began his studies in 1977. He was already married and in 1976 the young couple gave birth to a son. It looked like a promising future awaited the young family.

But in 1979 the 24-year-old man's life changed abruptly. His marriage became troubled and ended in divorce. Shortly before completing his degree, Thomas Taubmann quit his studies. He waited on tables in various restaurants until he was assigned to work as an emergency fitter in "7. Oktober," a machine tool combine. After his divorce, he moved back to his parents' home for a while. Then he moved into a separate flat in the house, which was in such abysmal condition that he often fled to his grandmother's. Something threw him off track, he developed an alcohol problem and was unable to get back on course. One day in the fall of 1981 he went shopping but did not have any money on him to pay for his goods. When he tried to leave the shopping center with the unpaid items, he was caught. His parents' offered to pay for the damages, but the offer was rejected for "educational reasons." He was supposed to appear in court on December 14, 1981 and answer for his conduct – of all places in Weissensee, where his mother worked as a lay assessor. His father thought that his son probably found the situation humiliating and embarrassing for himself, but even more so for his mother. This may have been the final straw for him and, after long deliberation, or perhaps even after making a spontaneous decision, Thomas Taubmann decided to flee.

Saturday, December 12, 1981 was a day with light frost and clear skies. A thin sheet of snow covered the divided city.[2] Thomas Taubmann had a few drinks to bolster his courage. When a freight train heading for the city center made a short stop at the Berlin-Pankow station that evening, he used the opportunity to climb onto the train unnoticed. The 26-year-old man jumped down beneath the Böse Bridge, right at the Bornholmer Strasse border crossing. It can only be presumed what happened next. The Wall here was higher than it was elsewhere in the city, almost five meters tall, and he probably crashed against it. The Stasi deduced from the evidence that after Thomas Taubmann jumped, he fell under the freight train and was run over. Soon afterwards the driver of an oncoming train noticed a dark object on the tracks. He reported it to the transport police who later recovered the dead man.[3]

That same night the investigators of the transport police searched Thomas Taubmann's apartment and found a sealed envelope addressed to his parents. It contained a farewell letter that was dated December 11, the day before he tried to escape. In it Thomas Taubmann told his parents that he had to get as far away as possible from all the worries that were weighing him down and that he was going to Czechoslovakia to try and flee across the border between Czechoslovakia and Austria.[4] Evidently the young man changed his plans or, perhaps anticipating that his escape at the Berlin Wall might fail, he intentionally laid a false trail to protect his parents from being subjected to reprisals for knowing about his plan.

On the morning of Sunday, December 13, 1981, the investigators of the transport police questioned the parents about their son without saying why. Only after the father demanded an explanation did they answer vaguely that their son had died in an accident while under the influence of alcohol, but that the details had not yet been fully clarified. They brought the parents to the forensic institute of Charité Hospital to identify the body.

In consultation with the transport police, the Stasi decided that same day that the man's failed escape attempt should be "presented as a fatal accident in which the man was run over by a train and the case closed."[5] Thus the parents were not to be informed about the content of the farewell letter or even made aware of its existence.[6] A thorough investigation was conducted to determine whether anyone might have seen the incident from East or West Berlin or from a passing train.[7] Apparently, because the German-German summit talks were taking place, the East

German secret police was eager to keep knowledge of Thomas Taubmann's fatal escape attempt from the public.

Three days after his death, his parents were summoned to the transport police in Karlshorst and interrogated separately for over three hours. They initially tried to convince the father that his son had committed suicide, but the father found this difficult to believe. He insisted on knowing more details and learned about the farewell letter his son had written, although it was not given to him and he was not allowed to see it. Finally, his interrogators read him a few sentences out loud, but all he learned was that the "accident" had occurred in the border territory near Bornholmer Strasse.

Thomas Taubmann was buried in late January 1982 in the municipal cemetery in Weissensee in the presence of his relatives from the West and under the distrustful surveillance of the Security Service. Since the family had no knowledge of an escape attempt, they did not publicize the incident in the West.

Consequently, Thomas Taubmann's failed escape attempt did not become known until after 1990. Twenty-seven years after he died – a death his mother, who died in 1999, had never been able to get over – the father learned from Stasi files the exact circumstances of his son's death. Only then did he hold the farewell letter in his hands, not the original, but a copy, which ended with the words: "I know that in making this move I am shutting many doors behind me, but I am completely aware of the consequences. I will contact you on Monday at the latest."[8]

Hans-Hermann Hertle

1 Unless otherwise noted, the following presentation is based on a conversation conducted by Hans-Hermann Hertle and Lydia Dollmann with Thomas Taubmann's father, 8.12.2008, as well as on notes from the father on how the East German authorities treated the parents.
2 See "[Trapo], Ereignisortbefundsbericht, 12.12.1981," in: BStU, MfS, AP 7643/82, Bl. 9.
3 See "[BVfS Berlin/Abt. IX] Information, Berlin, den 13.12.1981," in: BStU, MfS, AP 7643/82, Bl. 4 – 6; "[Trapo], Ereignisortbefundsbericht, 12.12.1981," in: Ibid., Bl. 8 – 9; "Bericht der [MfS-]Hauptabteilung I/Grenzkommando Mitte/Abwehr/Unterabteilung GR-33 über das Auffinden einer tödlich verletzten Person, 13.12.1981," in: Ibid., Bl. 10 – 11.
4 See Thomas Taubmann's farewell letter to his parents, 11.12.1981, in: BStU, MfS, AP 7643/82, Bl. 59. Quoted with the permission of his father.
5 "[BVfS Berlin/]Abt. IX/SK, Aktenvermerk, Berlin, den 14.12.1981," in: BStU, MfS, AP 7643/82, Bl. 61.
6 Ibid.
7 "BVfS Berlin/Untersuchungsabteilung, Vernehmungsprotokoll des Zeugen K., Klaus-Peter, Berufsoffizier, Grenzregiment 33, Berlin, 13.12.1981," in: BStU, MfS, AP 7643/82, Bl. 33 – 34.
8 Thomas Taubmann's farewell letter to his parents, 11.12.1981, in: BStU, MfS, AP 7643/82, Bl. 59. Quoted with the permission of his father.

Lothar Fritz Freie

born on February 8, 1955

shot on June 4, 1982
near the Helmut-Just Bridge
on the sector border between
Berlin-Wedding and Berlin-Prenzlauer Berg
died from his bullet wounds on June 6, 1982

Lothar Fritz Freie, born on February 8, 1955 in Grossburgwedel in Lower Saxony, West Germany, wanted to study law and, after graduating from high school in 1977, moved with a schoolmate to West Berlin. But for unknown reasons, he quit his studies after four semesters. He showed up sporadically at his friend's apartment, his official residence. Unemployed and penniless, he struggled in the divided city for the next few years. Although he was "deteriorating" and having major financial difficulties, he did not take the advice of his friend, who had suggested that he stop by for a meal at least once a week.[1] During one of his visits he complained that he did not know how he could go on living this way.[2] The failed student no longer had an ID. Once he said that he had sold it, but later claimed he had left it at the "facility." His friend no longer understood him. Freie then asked his friend if he could somehow get him home, back to West Germany, but this was impossible from West Berlin without an identity card, and so he refused his friend's request. Indeed, it would have been a very risky act of friendship.

The night of June 4 was warm and cloudless. The moon was almost full and it was the only source of light on the grounds near the closed-down S-Bahn station at Bornholmer Strasse between the Böse Bridge in the north and Helmut-Just Bridge in the south, and an old railroad wall in the west and the five-meter-high border wall in the east. This was a typical "no man's land" area with waist-high weeds that had not been touched in years. The ground, strewn with old discarded tracks, brick debris from torn down railroad buildings and many rabbit holes, was hard to walk on, at least in the dark. There was only one track still in use in this area, which the border troops referred to as "front border territory:" the so-called Allied track. Only a few trains ran along here each week for the French garrison in the north of the city, but the tracks remained an unhindered connection between East and West Berlin.

On June 4, 1982 at about 11 p.m., the 27-year-old Lothar Fritz Freie entered the East Berlin "front border territory" from West Berlin and crossed the "Allied track" under the Helmut-Just Bridge heading north.[3] His upper body was bare and he was carrying his pullover in his hand. To this day it remains unclear what he was trying to do, but even later investigations found nothing to suggest a possible suicide attempt. Two border soldiers in a watchtower on the Helmut-Just Bridge noticed the intruder and reported it, but they soon lost track of him in the dark. A few hundred meters farther on, near the Böse Bridge, Freie came into view of the guards in the next observation tower. The two guards there were given the order to expel the "border violator" from the territory of East Germany. Both guards left their tower and, when they approached Lothar Fritz Freie from a distance of about 30 meters, they called out to him according to regulation: "Citizen of West Berlin! You have entered the territory of East Germany. Please leave our territory!"[4] According to the statements made by the border guards, Freie mumbled something incomprehensible in return, turned around and quickly walked along the tracks back the way he had come. He only had to go a few meters to the left to cross the S-Bahn tracks to reach West Berlin territory, but he probably did not realize this. He seemed to want to leave the forbidden area by way of the "Allied track" and take the same route that he had taken to get to where he was. He could have easily done this if the two guards on the watchtower at the Helmut-Just Bridge, which he had to pass by on his way back, had not received the order to arrest the "border violator."

The impassable railroad grounds stood between Lothar Fritz Freie and the two guards, who were unable to get through the deserted grounds quickly enough to cut him off. Unaware that Freie had just been ordered to leave the territory of East Germany, they called out to him to stop, after which Freie began to run. One of the guards fired a warning shot. Freie continued to run. The guard did not see where he was going and fell on his knees. At this point it seemed impossible for him to catch up with Freie. He aimed two shots at him. Lothar Fritz Freie collapsed and remained motionless on the "Allied track." When the guards reached him, he told them in a weak voice that they should just leave him there or shoot him.[5] The guards first dragged him to a railway signal box to get him out of view of the West. Then they took him to the watchtower and provided first aid. When they asked him what he was doing on East German territory, the man, seriously wounded and in a state of shock, said he wanted to "put up a tent."[6]

In the early morning hours of June 6, following two emergency operations, Lothar Fritz Freie died in the People's Police Hospital in Berlin-Mitte from the consequences of a bullet wound through the side of his pelvis. He was not inebriated. He was not checked for other intoxicants.[7]

Even according to East German law, shooting at a West Berliner who was clearly following the order to leave East German territory was illegal. But charges were not filed against the two border soldiers. On the contrary, both were commended and awarded honors. In order to facilitate a cover-up of the incident, they were both immediately transferred to another unit and never learned how severe Freie's injuries had been or that he had died.[8]

In late 1993 the Berlin district court tried the gunman, who was twenty years old at the time of the crime, as a youth for manslaughter and sentenced him to two years in prison. The sentence was commuted to probation.[9] His guard leader, who had been raised by his parents to be critical of the regime, admitted that while they were pursuing Freie he considered escaping himself, but decided against it because he feared his own comrade would shoot him. The court convicted him in 1995 of complicity in the crime and sentenced him to a year and eight months probation.[10]

On the West Berlin side, police and customs staff heard the shots and watched as the badly injured Lothar Fritz Freie was transported away. The incident received strong media attention. The West German federal government and West Berlin Senate immediately condemned the incident, stating that it stood in glaring contradiction to the aims of the Basic Treaty and the CSCE final act of Helsinki.[11] Hans-Otto Bräutigam, head of the Permanent Mission of the Federal Republic in East Germany, spoke with the East German foreign minister representative and referred to the incident as a "major encroachment on a human right recognized worldwide, namely the right to live," demanding that "the people responsible be held accountable."[12] The French city commander protested on behalf of the British and U.S. counterparts against the "most recent disregard for human life" and demanded once again "that a stop be put to these inhuman practices."[13]

A short time later the deputy official of East Germany responsible for visits informed the West Berlin Senate that a West Berliner had crossed the border to East Berlin on the night of June 4. The diplomat claimed that the man had insulted the border soldiers and assaulted them and could only be arrested "through extreme means." At the same time, he handed Gerhard Kunze, the Senate official for East Germany, a note of protest, demanding that the West Berlin Senate take "effective measures to prevent these kinds of serious attacks."[14] The East Berlin minister failed to mention that the "arrested man" had died.[15]

The East German secret police held on to the body for many weeks. It probably feared the public denunciations against East Germany that would follow after it was returned and the clearly evident bullet wounds were seen. Moreover, on June 11, 1982, the American president, Ronald Reagan, was paying a visit to West Berlin.

Finally, in August, the Stasi ordered the body to be quickly cremated and this was done on August 24, 1982 in the Baumschulenweg Crematorium. Five weeks later Lothar Fritz Freie was secretly buried in the common urn burial grounds of the cemetery there.[16] After this was done the Permanent Mission of the Federal Republic in East Berlin was notified and thus presented with a fait accompli.

Martin Ahrends / Udo Baron / Hans-Hermann Hertle

---

1 See "Vernehmung eines Freundes von Lothar Fritz Freie durch die West-Berliner Polizei vom 1.7.1982," in: StA Berlin, Az. 27 Js 22/91, Bd. 1, Bl. 25–26.

2 See "Anklageschrift der Staatsanwaltschaft Berlin gegen Andreas M. vom 16.2.1993," in: StA Berlin, Az. 27 Js 22/91, Bd. 2, Bl. 6–23.

3 On the course of events see "Urteil des Landgerichts Berlin in der Strafsache gegen Andreas M. vom 26.11. 1993, 2 Js 22/91," in: StA Berlin, Az. 27 Js 22/91, Bd. 3, n. pag. (pp. 1–31).

4 Ibid., p. 12.

5 See ibid., p. 16.

6 "Anhang zum zusammenfassenden Bericht des MfS/EG IX, 4.6.1982," in: BStU, MfS, GH 61/83, Bd. 1, Bl. 154.

7 See "Urteil des Landgerichts Berlin in der Strafsache gegen Andreas M. vom 26.11.1993, Az. 2 Js 22/91," in: StA Berlin, Az. 27 Js 22/91, Bd. 3, p. 11.

8 See ibid., p. 18.

9   See ibid.

10 See "Urteil des Landgerichts Berlin in der Strafsache gegen Wolfgang W. vom 9.5.1995, Az. 27 Js 1136/93," in: StA Berlin, Az. 27 Js 22/91, Bd. 4, Bl. 134 a ff.

11 *Der Tagesspiegel*, 6.6.1982.

12 "Vermerk des MfAA über ein Gespräch zwischen dem Leiter der Abteilung BRD im MfAA, Genossen Karl Seidel, mit dem Leiter der BRD-Vertretung, Dr. Hans-Otto Bräutigam, am 10.6.1982," in: BStU, MfS, GH 61/83, Bd. 1, Bl. 143–144.

13 *Der Tagesspiegel*, 6.6.1982.

14 "Massnahmeplan des MfS/HA IX, 7.6.1982, Anlage 2: Text des Protestes des MfAA der DDR gegenüber dem Westberliner Senat," in: BStU, MfS, GH 61/83, Bd. 1, Bl. 106–108.

15 *Frankfurter Allgemeine Zeitung*, 11.6.1982.

16 See "Schreiben des Städtischen Bestattungswesens, 30.9.1982," in: BStU, MfS, GH 61/83, Bl. 76.

Silvio Proksch

born on March 3, 1962

shot dead on December 25, 1983
at the Pankow municipal cemetery
on the sector border between
Berlin-Pankow and Berlin-Reinickendorf

S ilvio Proksch was born on March 3, 1962 in East Berlin. After finishing school he completed a bricklayer apprenticeship and then worked for a carpentry and joiner company. He lived with his brother and parents in the East Berlin district of Pankow. Nine of his siblings had already moved out of their parents' house. Silvio Proksch had been feeling constrained for a long time by the conditions in East Germany, but he had never spoken to anyone about concrete plans to escape before he tried to flee.[1]

Silvio Proksch left his parents' house with his brother on December 25, 1983 at about 7 p.m. They were both highly inebriated. Without having made any preparations, Silvio Proksch decided that he wanted to flee to West Berlin. "He said he wanted freedom and everything here made him sick," his brother later reported.[2] He only took the most important personal documents with him: his identity card, his training certification card and his social security identification. The weather seemed good for his undertaking. It was raining and misty. It is possible that family differences during the Christmas holidays had provided the final impetus for his decision to flee.[3] While they were walking towards the border, his brother tried to talk him out of his plan.

When the two brothers reached the Pankow Burger Park at the old Niederschönhausen pumping station near the Panke River, Silvio Proksch's brother stayed back in front of the cemetery, which was located directly on the border. Silvio Proksch climbed the cemetery fence that bordered the interior wall. He set off an alarm when he passed the signal fence at about 7:30 p.m. A border guard in a watchtower noticed him, called out to him and fired two warning shots. But Silvio Proksch continued undeterred towards the concrete wall. At the same time the border soldier began to fire shots aimed at the fleeing man. A bullet hit Silvio Proksch in his hip, shattering the right hip artery and femoral vein. He ran a few more meters before collapsing in front of the concrete wall.[4]

It took a long time before the twenty-one-year-old received any medical care and Silvio Proksch bled to death on the death strip.[5] He was declared dead upon arrival at the People's Police Hospital in Berlin-Mitte at 9:15 p.m.[6] A medical report from the Franziskus Hospital from 1992 stated: "All that can be said with certainty is that, had the young man, who had been shot, immediately been brought to a regular hospital with a properly trained anesthesia and surgery unit, the ligature of artery and vein combined with a professional blood transfusion would very likely have saved his life."[7] A short time later the guard was awarded the NVA border troop bronze medal of merit for his "brave and determined action."[8] In early November 1994 the Berlin district court convicted him of manslaughter and sentenced him to a year and nine months on probation.[9]

Silvio Proksch's brother heard the gunshots. After his brother was transported away, he sought out his older siblings and told them what had happened. His family waited worriedly for the official news to come but no one came to inform them of his death.[10] Meanwhile, a special commission of the East German secret police had taken over the case and decided that since the incident had not been noticed in West Berlin, the deadly shots should be covered up.

On December 28, 1983 one of Silvio Proksch's sisters reported her brother missing to the criminal investigation department of Berlin-Pankow, but did not receive a response until January 20, 1984. Another sister and her husband were sought out by the East German secret police and interrogated for ten hours in the East Berlin police headquarters. Even their 14-year-old son was subjected to an interrogation at his school. Each member of the family was also subsequently interrogated. Although the family knew from the brother what had happened, the Stasi agents denied that an escape attempt had taken place on December 25, 1983 and claimed that there had been neither a death nor a person arrested under the name Silvio Proksch. The Stasi also threatened to take legal steps if the family looked into the matter any further. They would be guilty of "slandering the state."[11]

A short time later Silvio Proksch's brother was arrested by the East German secret police for trifling offenses and imprisoned for more than two years. He was forced to agree in writing to keep quiet about his brother's escape attempt. After he was released from prison he was subjected to a "Berlin ban" and had to move to Eisenhüttenstadt an der Oder.[12]

After submitting many letters and complaints, in August 1990 the East German military state prosecutor finally told the family what had actually happened on December 25, 1983. The day after Christmas the East German secret police had taken Silvio Proksch's body to the military forensic institute in Bad Saarow. He was not listed in any death register of East Germany and his body has remained missing without a trace since December 30, 1983.[13]

Udo Baron

1 On the following, see Irene Agotz, Die Lügen der Stasi, in: Werner Filmer/Heribert Schwan, *Opfer der Mauer. Die geheimen Protokolle des Todes,* München, 1991, p. 22. On the course of events see: "Urteil des Landgerichts Berlin vom 9.11.1994," in: StA Berlin, Az. 2 Js 98/90, Bd. 5, Bl. 14 ff. See also "Protokoll der Zeugenvernehmung des Bruders von Silvio Proksch durch die Berliner Polizei, 12.9.1991," in: StA Berlin, Az. 2 Js 98/90, Bd. 2, Bl. 171/1–172/2.

2 Ibid., Bl. 172/2.

3 See "Urteil des Landgerichts Berlin vom 9.11.1994," in: StA Berlin, Az. 2 Js 98/90, Bd. 5, Bl. 14–15; Irene Agotz, *Die Lügen der Stasi,* p. 22.

4   See "Urteil des Landgerichts Berlin vom 9.11.1994," in: StA Berlin, Az. 2 Js 98/90, Bd. 5, Bl. 15–21.

5   See ibid., Bl. 21–22.

6   See Irene Agotz, *Die Lügen der Stasi,* p. 25.

7   "Gutachten des Franziskus-Krankenhauses zum Tötungsdelikt zum Nachteil Silvio Proksch, 18.2.1992," in: StA Berlin, Az. 2 Js 98/90, Bd. 4, Bl. 7.

8   See "Urteil des Landgerichts Berlin vom 9.11.1994," in: StA Berlin, Az. 2 Js 98/90, Bd. 5, Bl. 22.

9   See ibid., Bl. 1–2; on the trials, see Roman Grafe, *Deutsche Gerechtigkeit. Prozesse gegen DDR-Grenzschützen und ihre Befehlsgeber,* Berlin, 2004, here pp. 197–200.

10 See Irene Agotz, *Die Lügen der Stasi,* p. 22.

11 See ibid., pp. 22–24.

12 See "Protokoll der Zeugenvernehmung des Bruders von Silvio Proksch durch die Berliner Polizei, 12.9.1991," in: StA Berlin, Az. 2 Js 98/90, Bd. 2, Bl. 175–175/2.

13 See Irene Agotz, *Die Lügen der Stasi,* p. 25.

Michael Schmidt

born on October 20, 1964

shot dead on December 1, 1984
on Schulzestrasse,
near the Wollankstrasse S-Bahn station
on the sector border between
Berlin-Pankow and Berlin-Reinickendorf

Michael Schmidt was born on October 20, 1964 in Bernau near Berlin and grew up with a brother and sister in Schwanebeck near Berlin. After finishing school he completed training as a carpenter in a building repair company in Pankow. According to his father, he was not one to keep his opinions to himself.[1] When the Bernau military district unit pressured him to enlist for three years with the National People's Army, he refused. He also categorically refused to serve at the border and was said to have replied to his solicitors that he would not consider "shooting defenseless people in the back."[2]

He occasionally expressed an interest in fleeing to the West to his colleagues at work. As the first major wave of people leaving East Germany began in 1984, he made concrete plans to apply for an exit visa. But after speaking to his parents and in light of the common practice in East Germany of holding family members accountable for the actions of their children, he decided against it, mainly out of consideration for his brother, who was studying at the university.[3]

In November 1984 Michael Schmidt was assigned by his building repair company to a job very close to the border. Residential buildings on Wollank and Schulzestrasse were being rebuilt. From the buildings' top stories he was able to study the border facilities in detail. On November 30 he and his friends went to the disco of a youth club in Pankow. His friends recalled that he seemed like he was bidding farewell to them that evening as if he would not see them again for a long time.[4] He left the disco before midnight. In the early morning hours of December 1 he managed to gain access to one of the buildings on the border where he had been working. He was accompanied by another person who has remained unidentified to this day. Two wooden ladders were waiting for him at the construction site and he took them with him.

He first climbed over the wall to a back courtyard and then the first border barrier. His companion was no longer with him at this point. When he used the ladder to climb over the signal fence he triggered an optical and acoustic alarm. At this point the two guards in a tower 100 meters away were well aware of his presence. One guard fired from the tower; the other guard climbed down and began firing from the ground. Michael Schmidt had already reached the last obstacle. He leaned the ladder against the wall and climbed up it. He had already grasped the top of the wall with one of his arms when bullets hit him in the back and knee. He slipped, got caught with his foot on one of the rungs and fell to the ground.[5] "What the hell are you doing?" one of the guards asked Michael Schmidt excitedly, upon which he answered: "So you guys got me after all."[6]

The East German secret police made the East Berlin witnesses swear themselves to secrecy, but after the Wall fell they reported that, in addition to the first two guards, another three guards had also arrived, one of whom nudged the injured man on the ground with his foot.[7] They then dragged him by his legs to the patrol path, loaded him onto a military vehicle and carried him to the watchtower where he was out of view. Although Michael Schmidt begged for help, all they did was cover him with a blanket. Almost an hour passed before he was given medical care. At 4:25 a.m. an ambulance took him to the People's Police Hospital in Berlin-Mitte where he died from his wounds at 6:20 a.m.[8] To maintain secrecy Michael Schmidt was registered in the hospital files as "XY" and listed on the death certificate as "unidentified."[9]

According to a 1991 expert opinion of the university clinic in Berlin-Steglitz, Michael Schmidt's life could have been saved "with a probability bordering on certainty," had he been "brought quickly to a clinic and had immediate surgical measures been taken."[10] Charges filed by the Berlin prosecuting attorney for death by negligence were dismissed in March 1992 because it could not be accurately determined who was responsible for the late arrival of the ambulance and for the decision not to take him to a hospital closer by.[11]

Residents of the West Berlin district of Wedding were awoken at 3:15 in the morning by the shots fired at Michael Schmidt. West Berliner police officers and the French gendarmerie watched from a raised platform as the border guards searched the site and carried away the wounded man.[12] While the West German federal government, the West Berlin Senate and the western Allies reacted to the shots at the Wall "with outrage and strong protest,"[13] East Germany celebrated the 38th anniversary of the border troops on December 1, 1984.

That morning Michael Schmidt's parents noticed that his room was empty. When it was reported on western news later that day that an escape attempt, presumably fatal, had taken place near the Wollankstrasse S-Bahn station, they feared the worst. Very concerned, they went to the East German police in Bernau and to the nearby hospitals but were unable to find out anything about their son's whereabouts. The East German secret police gave them the runaround for four days and the East German police took three days to accept their missing persons' report. The authorities pretended to embark on a search campaign.[14] The parents were picked up by the East German secret police on December 4, 1984 and brought to the military state prosecutor's office in Berlin where they were informed of their son's death. They were lied to about the actual details surrounding his escape attempt and were told that their son had attacked a border soldier, so that he was "practically forced to engage in self-defense" by using his weapon. They were told that, "Despite all the medical efforts made," it was not possible to save the life of their son.[15]

The East German secret police pressured the parents to ensure that details about their son's death would not spread in East Germany or reach the western media. It threatened to put an end to their other son's studies and forbade them from having any contact with their relatives in the West.[16]

By mid-December 1989 Michael Schmidt's father had already requested information from the East German state prosecutor concerning the circumstances of his son's death, but the Berlin public prosecutor's office did not open an intensive investigation until after the two German states had been unified. The two guards, who had been honored with the "Medal for Exemplary Service at the Border" and awarded bonuses on the same day that Michael Schmidt died,[17] were convicted of joint manslaughter by the Berlin district court on February 5, 1992 and handed down a suspended sentence of a year and six months and a year and nine months.[18] The court stated that "they hadn't wanted to kill him, but they recognized the possibility that a shot might be fatal. Furthermore, they had been willing to take this risk in order to prevent the escape from being successful in accordance with their orders that they believed were binding."[19] Michael Schmidt's death later served as one of the main counts of an indictment in a trial held against members of the Communist Party Politburo and the National Defense Council of East Germany. The trial resulted in a number of year-long prison sentences. Preliminary proceedings against the responsible East German state prosecutors and Stasi agents for aiding and abetting a crime and obstructing justice had to be dismissed for lack of sufficient evidence in 1998.[20]

Michael Schmidt was buried in the cemetery in Schwanebeck on December 10, 1984 under East German secret police surveillance. In addition to his relatives and close friends, almost all of his work colleagues attended the funeral. The Stasi regarded this as a provocation and had them reprimanded.[21]

Udo Baron

1 See Horst Schmidt, Kaltblütiger Mord, in: Werner Filmer/Heribert Schwan, *Opfer der Mauer. Die geheimen Protokolle des Todes,* München, 1991, p. 35.
2 See ibid.
3 See "Protokoll der Zeugenvernehmung eines Freundes und Arbeitskollegen von Michael Schmidt durch die Berliner Polizei, 19.6.1991," in: StA Berlin, Az. 2 Js 63/90, Bd. 2, Bl. 113 b; "Protokoll der Zeugenvernehmung eines Arbeitskollegen von Michael Schmidt durch die Berliner Polizei, 1.8.1991," in: StA Berlin, Az. 2 Js 63/90, Bd. 3, Bl. 96-97.
4 See "Protokoll der Zeugenvernehmung eines Freundes und Arbeitskollegen von Michael Schmidt durch die Berliner Polizei, 19.6.1991," in: StA Berlin, Az. 2 Js 63/90, Bd. 2, Bl. 113-113 b.
5 See "Urteil des Landgerichts Berlin in der Strafsache gegen Udo W. und Uwe H., Az. 2 Js63/90 KLs (57/91), vom 5.2.1992," in: StA Berlin, Az. 2 Js 63/90, Bd. 4, Bl. 234-236.
6 Quoted from: Ibid., Bl. 237.
7 See "Protokoll der Zeugenvernehmung einer ehem. Anwohnerin des Grenzgebietes durch die Berliner Polizei, 16.4.1991," in: StA Berlin, Az. 2 Js 63/90, Bd. 2, Bl. 61-62; "Protokoll der Zeugenvernehmung eines ehem. Anwohners des Grenzgebietes durch die Berliner Polizei, 25.4.1991," in: StA Berlin, Az. 2 Js 63/90, Bd. 2, Bl. 81-82.
8 See "Urteil des Landgerichts Berlin in der Strafsache gegen Udo W. und Uwe H., Az. 2 Js63/90 KLs (57/91), vom 5.2.1992," in: StA Berlin, Az. 2 Js 63/90, Bd. 4, Bl. 237-239.
9 See ibid., Bl. 239.

10 "Gutachten des Universitätsklinikums Steglitz betr. Ermittlungsverfahren gegen ehemalige Grenzsoldaten wegen Verdachts des Mordes, hier: Begutachtung von Schussverletzungen beim Opfer Michael Schmidt, 26.6.1991," in: StA Berlin, Az. 2 Js 63/90, Bd. 2, Bl. 34.

11 See "Verfügung der Staatsanwaltschaft bei dem Kammergericht Berlin, Az. 2 Js 222/91, 26.3.1992," in: StA Berlin, Az. 2 Js 222/91, Bd. 3, Bl. 171–185.

12 See "Bericht der West-Berliner Polizei zum Ermittlungsverfahren wegen Totschlags durch unbekannte Angehörige der NVA, hier: Zwischenfall an der DL gegenüber der Einmündung Berlin 65, Nordbahnstrasse/Wilhelm-Kuhr-Strasse am 1.12.1984, 1.12.1984," in: StA Berlin, Az. 2 Js 63/90, Bd. 1, Bl. 8–10.

13 *Welt am Sonntag,* 2.12.1984; *Berliner Morgenpost,* 2.12.1984.

14 See Horst Schmidt, *Kaltblütiger Mord,* pp. 36–38.

15 Ibid., p. 38.

16 See ibid., p. 39.

17 See "Urteil des Landgerichts Berlin in der Strafsache gegen Udo W. und Uwe H., Az. 2 Js63/90 KLs (57/91), vom 5.2.1992," in: StA Berlin, Az. 2 Js 63/90, Bd. 4, Bl. 239–240. The defendants' appeal against the verdict was rejected by the Federal Court of Justice in November 1992 (Az. 5 StR 370/92 vom 3.11.1992). Both verdicts are documented in: Klaus Marxen/Gerhard Werle (eds.), *Gewalttaten an der deutsch-deutschen Grenze,* Bd. 2, 1. Teilband, Berlin, 2002, pp. 103–155. On the various trials concerning the case of Michael Schmidt see Roman Grafe, *Deutsche Gerechtigkeit. Prozesse gegen DDR-Grenzschützen und ihre Befehlsgeber,* Berlin, 2004, pp. 85–88, 220–221, 300–302, 331–337.

18 See "Urteil des Landgerichts Berlin in der Strafsache gegen Udo W. und Uwe H., Az. 2 Js63/90 KLs (57/91), vom 5.2.1992," in: StA Berlin, Az. 2 Js 63/90, Bd. 4, Bl. 220–221.

19 See ibid., Bl. 236.

20 "Verfügung der Staatsanwaltschaft Berlin, Az. 28 Js 23/96, 25.6.1998," in: StA Berlin, Az. 28 Js 23/96, Bd. 2, Bl. 20–31.

21 See Horst Schmidt, *Kaltblütiger Mord,* p. 40.

Rainer Liebeke

born on September 11, 1951

drowned on September 3, 1986
in Sacrower Lake
on the outer ring between
Gross Glienicke (Potsdam county)
and Berlin-Spandau

R ainer Liebeke drowned in Sacrower Lake north of Potsdam while trying to flee to the West just before his 35th birthday on September 3, 1986. He had been living with his wife and child in his hometown of Gotha. He was a trained motor mechanic, but worked as a taxi driver for the state-owned company "Kraftverkehr Erfurt." Rainer Liebeke was a passionate motorcyclist. As a member of the Gotha Motor Club he participated in all the important races that took place in East Germany for the 50-ccm bike category. In 1985 he advanced to a licensed racer in the East German General German Motor Sport Association (ADMV).[1]

He shared his enthusiasm for motorcycling with Dirk K. from Eisenach, who was nine years his junior. They had met in his sports club in 1980. In 1982 Dirk K. introduced Rainer Liebeke to a West German racer and his family and they were able to provide him with hard-to-find replacement parts for his bike. Over the following years their western colleague made a few visits to Gotha to see his motorcyclist friends in the East. They vacationed together at Lake Balaton in Hungary in 1986.

As soon as they returned from this vacation, things started to go downhill for Rainer Liebeke. First he learned that the ADMV planned to discontinue the race category he was in. Then he crashed during the Schleizer Triangle Race and broke his collar bone. His family advised him to give up racing, but as soon as he had recovered, he began changing his motorcycle to meet the standards for the larger engine capacity class. Dirk K., who, like Rainer Liebeke, was also affected by the changes in the motorcycling sport, helped him to convert his bike.[2]

On September 1 and 2, 1986, Dirk K. paid a visit to Rainer Liebeke, who was still on sick leave. Dirk K.'s mother thinks this must have been when the two men decided to flee to West Berlin together.[3] Rainer Liebeke's frustration with life in East Germany had begun in the early 1970s when he took a drive with a BMW that belonged to his cousin who was visiting Gotha from the West. The next day he was picked up at work by the secret police and interrogated for hours. According to his sister, this experience changed him. After that he felt constricted and patronized in East Germany.[4]

On September 2, 1986, the day of his escape, Rainer Liebeke told his wife that he was going with Dirk K. to see a mechanic in Karl-Marx-Stadt (now Chemnitz) about getting replacement parts for his motorcycle.[5] But instead of traveling to Karl-Marx-Stadt, the two men took a train to Potsdam. They headed from there to Sacrower Lake, the east side of which belonged to border territory. Dirk K. knew this area of the border well because he had served his military duty there from 1983 to 1985.[6]

The two men had to trudge through marshy grounds and thick reeds before they reached the Sacrower Lake by dark. It was 500 meters to the other side and they had to be very careful because spotlights lit up the area at irregular intervals. The younger man swam off quickly, but Rainer Liebeke was increasingly hindered by his collarbone injury. When they were still in Potsdam he had asked Dirk K. to tighten his shoulder bandage.[7] The men called out quietly to each other in order not to lose contact, but when Dirk K. reached the bank he realized that his friend was no longer behind him. He looked for him for a while but then decided not to further endanger himself and continued his flight through the woods to the Havel bank. Using a tree stake, Dirk K. was able to make it through the border grounds at a point almost exactly equidistant from two watchtowers. When he reached the Havel he triggered an alarm. But by the time the border guards began looking for him he had already swum across the border that ran through the middle of the river. The border troop commander noted in a report: "We lost his trace beyond the forward blocking element towards the Havel in the direction of the enemy."[8] Dirk K. reached the riverbank of West Berlin intact.[9]

Rainer Liebeke, however, did not survive the escape. A week later his body was discovered in the Sacrower Lake by two schoolchildren who notified the East German police. A short time later the crew of an East German border troop boat retrieved his body from the water and identified him from the personal documents they found on him.[10]

Rainer Liebeke's wife waited in vain for a message from her husband. She told the East German secret police that she had not known about any escape plans. An acquaintance from West Germany told her on the phone that her husband tried to escape on September 5, 1986 with a friend but never arrived in the West. She issued a missing persons' report four days later because she presumed that her husband was still alive and probably in prison. She and the other family members did not learn of his death from the East German secret police until September 19.[11] The widow was questioned by the East German secret police many times in the days that followed. She also started to feel ostracized and pushed around at work.[12] Her son was even picked up at school and questioned about his parents.[13]

The widow was denied both accident death benefits and life insurance benefits because the East German authorities were of the view that "the death [of Rainer Liebeke] involved criminal behavior caused by the deceased."[14]

The urn containing Rainer Liebeke's ashes was buried in the cemetery in Gotha on October 3, 1986.[15] His widow applied for an exit visa and was granted the right to resettle with her son in West Germany in 1988.

Udo Baron

1   See "Telegramm der BVfS Erfurt/Abt. IX an das MfS/HA IX und das MfS/ZKG über Fluchtversuch und Fahndung nach dem Mitflüchtling von Rainer Liebeke, 24.9.1986," in: BStU, Ast. Erfurt, AU 2100/87, Bd. 1, Bl. 87.

2   See "Untersuchungsbericht der BVfS Erfurt/Untersuchungsabteilung, 26.11.1986," in: BStU, Ast. Erfurt, AU 2100/87, Bd. 1, Bl. 194–195; "Vermisstenanzeige für Rainer Liebeke bei dem VPKA Gotha durch die Ehefrau von Rainer Liebeke, 12.9.1986," in: BStU, Ast. Erfurt, AU 2100/87, Bd. 2, Bl. 86–87.

3   See "Niederschrift des MfS/KD Eisenach über eine Aussprache mit den Eltern von Dirk K., 22.11.1986," in: BStU, Ast. Erfurt, AU 2100/87, Bd. 1, Bl. 156–157.

4   See conversation conducted by Udo Baron with Rainer Liebeke's sister, 29.10.2007.

5   On this and the following, see "Untersuchungsbericht der BVfS Erfurt/Untersuchungsabteilung, 26.11.1986," in: BStU, Ast. Erfurt, AU 2100/87, Bd. 1, Bl. 198.

6   Ibid., Bl. 198.

7   See "Niederschrift des MfS/KD Eisenach über eine Aussprache mit den Eltern von Dirk K., 22.11.1986," in: BStU, Ast. Erfurt, AU 2100/87, Bd. 1, Bl. 156.

8   "Untersuchungsbericht des Kommandeurs des Grenzkommandos Mitte zum Grenzdurchbruch DDR/Berlin (West) am 3.9.1986, 5.9.1986," in: BArch, GT 14514, Bl. 134.

9   See "Tagesmeldung Nr. 3/9/86 des MfS, 3.9.1986," in: BStU, MfS, HA I Nr. 10341, Bl. 400.

10 See "Anzeige durch das VPKA Potsdam über die Auffindung der Leiche von Rainer Liebeke, 12.9.1986," in: BStU, Ast. Erfurt, AU 2103/87, Bd. 3, Bl. 4–5; "Tagesmeldung Nr. 12/9/86 des MfS, 13.9.1986," in: BStU, MfS, HA I Nr. 10341, Bl. 377–379.

11 See conversation conducted by Udo Baron with Rainer Liebeke's widow, 18.2.2008; letter from Rainer Liebeke's sister Beate B. to Udo Baron, 1.11.2007; "Telegramm der BVfS Erfurt/Abt. IX an das MfS/HA IX und das MfS/ZKG über Fluchtversuch und Fahndung nach dem Mitflüchtling von Rainer Liebeke, 24.9.1986," in: BStU, Ast. Erfurt, AU 2100/87, Bd. 1, Bl. 87–88.

12 "Aktenvermerk des MfS/KD Gotha zum durchgeführten Gespräch mit der Person [Name geschwärzt; der Witwe von Rainer Liebeke, d. Verf.] am 27.10.1986, 28.10.1986," in: BStU, Ast. Erfurt, AU 2100/87, Bd. 1, Bl. 222.

13 See conversation conducted by Udo Baron with Rainer Liebeke's widow, 18.2.2008.

14 "Schreiben des MfS an die Staatliche Versicherung der DDR/Kreisdirektion Gotha, 11.12.1986," in: BStU, Ast. Erfurt, AU 2100/87, Bd. 4, Bl. 24.

15 Conversation conducted by Udo Baron with Rainer Liebeke's sister, 29.10.2007; conversation conducted by Udo Baron with Rainer Liebeke's widow, 18.2.2008.

René Gross

born on May 1, 1964

shot dead on November 21, 1986
near Karpfenteichstrasse
on the sector border between
Berlin-Treptow and Berlin-Neukölln

René Gross, born on May 1, 1964 in East Berlin, was a professional driver and worked for the state-owned company "Kühlautomat Berlin." He made no secret of his "hostile attitude towards East Germany."[1] He married in 1985 and that same year applied for the right to resettle in West Germany. Applications for permission to leave the country were submitted to the internal division of the district council office but rarely did anyone know if his request would be granted until a final decision had been made. Those who were granted permission to leave were usually informed of the decision only shortly before the designated date of their departure. After people submitted their request, they lived between hope and resignation and with a total uncertainty about where and how they would live through the next few years. René Gross was unable to endure being at the mercy of the authorities. He wanted to determine his own future.

Although his wife also wanted this, she preferred to stay in East Germany with their six-year-old son.[2]

When René Gross met 38-year-old Manfred Mäder, who had also submitted a request to leave, the two men soon agreed to flee to West Berlin in advance of their families.[3] They may have been encouraged by the fact that other people they knew had succeeded in fleeing to the West.[4]

On November 20, 1986 René Gross said goodbye to his wife in the afternoon, saying that "he just wanted to run an errand and would be right back."[5] He and Manfred Mäder stole a truck that night, a "W 50" with a tail-lift that could reach to the top of the Berlin Wall.[6] Early in the morning, at about 5:00 a.m., the two men drove at high speed towards the border that divided the Treptow and Neukölln districts of Berlin. They broke through a border gate in the interior security wall and through the signal fence. After turning sharply to the right the vehicle came to a halt parallel to the base of the concrete wall facing West Berlin.[7]

Guards on two watchtowers and guards on the ground rushed to the site and aimed automatic fire at the men until they both fell to the ground, either dead or severely injured. René Gross gave up his flight and crawled under the truck to seek protection from the flow of bullets but he was shot in the head. Manfred Mäder, who had jumped from the truck's tail-lift onto the top of the Wall, was hit by a bullet in his left thigh. He fell back onto the east side of the Wall and bled to death.[8]

The border soldiers involved in the incident were relieved of their duty and decorated the same day with the "Medal of Merit of the Border Troops of East Germany" in bronze – and invited to attend a banquet dinner.[9] An investigation of the incident opened by the East German military state prosecutor was suspended two months later with the explanation that the case involved fatal wounds "caused by self-inflicted actions."

The crime against René Gross remained unpunished, even in reunified Germany. Almost 18 years after the escape attempt the Berlin district court convicted the two men who shot Manfred Mäder of manslaughter and sentenced them to ten months probation.[10] But it could not be determined who had shot and killed René Gross.

Residents of the West Berlin district of Neukölln were awakened at about five o'clock in the morning by "explosion-like noises" accompanied by shots from a machine gun.[11] The West Berlin police and customs office tried to gather information about what had happened but they were not able to see the site of the incident. Given the dense population on the West Berlin side, the border troops and East German secret police decided against investigating the crime site and removed all the existing evidence for "political-operative reasons."[12] In order to prevent an "information flow," the Stasi blocked access to the public telephone of the border regiment that was involved in the incident.[13] The border soldiers involved had to swear to secrecy in writing and thereafter their mail was examined. The wives of the two dead men were kept under surveillance with the aim of "exerting influence on the prevention of conduct damaging to East Germany."[14]

On the morning of November 21, 1986 René Gross' wife heard on western radio about a failed escape attempt in the border area between Treptow and Neukölln. She had a feeling that it might have involved her husband. That same evening in the East German police headquarters in Berlin-Mitte she learned about her husband's death. She was interrogated and kept under surveillance by the East German secret police for a time in the hope that information could be gained about his escape preparations. The East German secret police forbade her from contacting the widow of Manfred Mäder.[15]

René Gross was buried a short time later in the cemetery in Berlin-Mahlsdorf.[16]

Udo Baron

1 "Information der BVfS Berlin/Abt. IX, 23.11.1986," in: BStU, MfS, HA I Nr. 5795, Bl. 60.
2 See "Protokoll der Zeugenvernehmung der Witwe von René Gross durch die Berliner Polizei, 29.1.1991," in: StA Berlin, Az. 27 Js/56 Js 275/03, Bd. 1, Bl. 90.
3 Ibid., Bl. 89
4 See "Protokoll der Zeugenvernehmung der Witwe von Manfred Mäder durch die Reutlinger Polizei, 14.4.1992," in: StA Berlin, Az. 27 Js/56 Js 275/03, Bd. 2, Bl. 58.
5 Ibid., Bl. 89.
6 See establishment of facts concerning circumstances of escape in: "Urteil des Landgerichts Berlin vom 10.5. 2004," in: StA Berlin, Az. 27 Js/56 Js 275/03, Bd. 7, Bl. 206–209.

7   See "Information der BVfS Berlin/Abt. IX, 23.11.1986," in: BStU, MfS, HA I Nr. 5795, Bl. 58.

8   See ibid.

9   See "Urteil des Landgerichts Berlin vom 10.5.2004," in: StA Berlin, Az. 27 Js/56 Js 275/03, Bd. 7, Bl. 210.

10 See ibid., Bl. 190–191.

11 *Süddeutsche Zeitung,* 22.11.1986.

12 "Information der BVfS Berlin/Abt. IX, 23.11.1986," in: BStU, MfS, HA I Nr. 5795, Bl. 60.

13 See "Bericht des MfS/HA I/Grenzkommando Mitte/Abteilung Abwehr über die Verhinderung eines Grenzdurch-
    bruches DDR-Berlin (West) am 21.11.1986, 21.11.1986," in: BStU, MfS, HA I Nr. 5795, Bl. 55.

14 "Information der BVfS Berlin/Abt. IX, 23.11.1986," in: BStU, MfS, HA I Nr. 5795, Bl. 63.

15 See "Protokoll der Zeugenvernehmung der Witwe von René Gross durch die Berliner Polizei, 29.1.1991," in:
    StA Berlin, Az. 27 Js/56 Js 275/03, Bd. 1, Bl. 90.

16 Ibid.

Manfred Mäder

born on August 23, 1948

shot dead on November 21, 1986
near Karpfenteichstrasse
on the sector border between
Berlin-Treptow and Berlin-Neukölln

Manfred Mäder, born on August 23, 1948 in Prenzlau, was a professional driver. At the end of the seventies he tried unsuccessfully to flee to the West through Czechoslovakia. He was sentenced to four and a half years in prison and served the term in the Bautzen II Penal Institution.

There were hardly any work opportunities available to Manfred Mäder after he was released from prison. His wife, who had married him in 1985, reported that "he had to do the lowest farm jobs that no one else wanted to do" and had to report to the East German police once a week. Manfred Mäder had moved in with her and her young daughter in an apartment located close to the Wall in Berlin-Treptow.[1] The following year the family applied for permission to leave East Germany.[2] Applications for permission to leave the country were submitted to the internal division of the district council office, but rarely did anyone know if his request would be granted until a final decision had been made. Those who were granted permission to leave were usually informed of the decision only shortly before the designated date of their departure. After people submitted their request, they lived between hope and resignation and with a total uncertainty about where and how they would live through the next few years. Manfred Mäder was unable to endure being at the mercy of the authorities. He wanted to determine his own future. When Manfred Mäder met René Gross, who had also submitted a request to leave, the two men soon agreed to flee to West Berlin in advance of their families.[3] They may have been encouraged by the fact that other people they knew had succeeded in fleeing to the West.[4]

On the evening of November 20, 1986 Manfred Mäder told his wife that "the escape was going to fly that night."[5] He would not be talked out of it and the couple said their goodbyes. He and René Gross stole a truck during the night, a "W 50" with a tail-lift that could reach to the top of the Berlin Wall.[6] Early in the morning, at about 5:00 a.m., the two men drove at high speed towards the border that divided the Treptow and Neukölln districts of Berlin. They broke through a border gate in the interior security wall and through the signal fence. After turning sharply to the right the vehicle came to a halt parallel to the base of the concrete wall facing

West Berlin.[7] Guards on two watchtowers and guards on the ground rushed to the site and aimed automatic fire at the men until they both fell to the ground, either dead or severely injured. Manfred Mäder, who had jumped from the truck's tail-lift onto the top of the Wall, was hit by a bullet in his left thigh. He fell back onto the east side of the Wall and bled to death. René Gross had given up his flight and crawled under the truck to seek protection from the bullets when he was shot in the head.[8]

The border soldiers involved in the incident were relieved of their duty and decorated the same day with the "Medal of Merit of the Border Troops of East Germany" in bronze – and invited to attend a banquet dinner.[9] An investigation opened by the East German military state prosecutor was suspended two months later with the explanation that the case involved fatal wounds "caused by self-inflicted actions."

Almost 18 years later the Berlin district court sentenced the men who had shot Manfred Mäder to a ten-month prison sentence commuted to probation for a "less serious case" of manslaughter.[10] It was not possible to determine who was responsible for shooting René Gross.

Residents of the West Berlin district of Neukölln were awoken at about five o'clock in the morning by "explosion-like noises" accompanied by shots from a machine gun.[11] The West Berlin police and customs office tried to gather information about what had happened but they were not able to see the site of the incident. Given the strong presence on the West Berlin side, the border troops and East German secret police decided against investigating the crime site and removed all the existing evidence for "political-operative reasons."[12] In order to prevent an "information flow," the Stasi blocked access to the public telephone booth in the border regiment involved in the incident.[13] The border soldiers involved had to swear to secrecy in writing and thereafter their mail was examined. The wives of the two dead men were kept under surveillance with the aim of "bearing influence on the prevention of conduct damaging to East Germany."[14]

By the morning of November 21, 1986 western radio stations had already reported on a failed escape attempt to West Berlin. Manfred Mäder's wife knew immediately that the fugitives might be her husband and his friend. That very evening the East German secret police paid her a visit and took her to the East German police headquarters in Berlin-Mitte for questioning. There she learned that her husband had been shot while trying to escape. She was forced to sign a document swearing to secrecy about the circumstances of his death and agreeing to invite only the closest family members to the funeral.

Manfred Mäder was buried in his parents' gravesite.

His wife was put off by the authorities for many months until finally, in December 1987, she was permitted to leave East Germany.[15]

Udo Baron

1   See "Protokoll der Zeugenvernehmung der Witwe von Manfred Mäder durch die Reutlinger Polizei, 14. 4. 1992," in: StA Berlin, Az. 27 Js/56 Js 275/03, Bd. 2, Bl. 58–59.

2   See "Information der BVfS Berlin/Abt. IX, 23. 11. 1986," in: BStU, MfS, HA I Nr. 5795, Bl. 58–63.

3   See "Protokoll der Zeugenvernehmung der Witwe von René Gross durch die Berliner Polizei, 29. 1. 1991," in: StA Berlin, Az. 27 Js/56 Js 275/03, Bd. 1, Bl. 89.

4   See "Protokoll der Zeugenvernehmung der Witwe von Manfred Mäder durch die Reutlinger Polizei, 14. 4. 1992," in: StA Berlin, Az. 27 Js/56 Js 275/03, Bd. 2, Bl. 58.

5   Ibid., Bl. 58.

6   See establishment of facts concerning circumstances of escape in: "Urteil des Landgerichts Berlin vom 10. 5. 2004," in: StA Berlin, Az. 27 Js/56 Js 275/03, Bd. 7, Bl. 206–209.

7   See "Information der BVfS Berlin/Abt. IX, 23. 11. 1986," in: BStU, MfS, HA I Nr. 5795, Bl. 58.

8   See ibid.

9   See "Urteil des Landgerichts Berlin vom 10. 5. 2004," in: StA Berlin, Az. 27 Js/56 Js 275/03, Bd. 7, Bl. 210.

10 See ibid., Bl. 190–191, 224 ff.

11 *Süddeutsche Zeitung*, 22. 11. 1986.

12 "Information der BVfS Berlin/Abt. IX, 23. 11. 1986," in: BStU, MfS, HA I Nr. 5795, Bl. 60.

13 See "Bericht des MfS/HA I/Grenzkommando Mitte/Abteilung Abwehr über die Verhinderung eines Grenzdurchbruches DDR-Berlin (West) am 21. 11. 1986, 21. 11. 1986," in: BStU, MfS, HA I Nr. 5795, Bl. 55.

14 "Information der BVfS Berlin/Abt. IX, 23. 11. 1986," in: BStU, MfS, HA I Nr. 5795, Bl. 63.

15 See "Protokoll der Zeugenvernehmung der Witwe von Manfred Mäder durch die Reutlinger Polizei, 14. 4. 1992," in: StA Berlin, Az. 27 Js/56 Js 275/03, Bd. 2, Bl. 60–61.

Michael Bittner

born on August 31, 1961

shot dead on November 24, 1986
near Nohlstrasse
on the outer ring between
Glienicke / Nordbahn (Oranienburg district)
and Berlin-Reinickendorf

Michael Bittner was born on August 31, 1961 in East Berlin. His father died early and he grew up with his mother and two siblings in Berlin-Pankow. After finishing school he completed a mason apprenticeship in a state-owned building repair company in Pankow. He spent much of his free time tending to masonry work on his mother's house.[1]

In May 1980 Michael Bittner was called up to serve his military duty with the National People's Army.[2] His mother recalled that he was often harassed there: "Michael landed in the bunker for the most minor offenses."[3] When Michael Bittner was released from the army in October 1981, he was a changed person. Looking back his mother described him as "quiet and introverted, sort of fearful and always ready to take off in case of a reserve enlistment."[4]

By April 1984 he had submitted an application to leave East Germany, which he hoped would be approved.[5] The state described his motives in a protocol, noting that he wanted "to be free and not have the state tell him what to do."[6] His request to leave was expressed very cautiously. The young man did not want to hurt the careers of his mother and siblings, nor did he want to be locked out of East Germany for an indefinite period after he emigrated. Hence, the East German secret police put him in the category of people wanting to leave that could be won back. He decided to flee after his petition to leave was repeatedly rejected.[7]

On November 23, 1986 Michael Bittner said goodbye to his brother, stating that his exit application had been approved but that he did not yet know when he could leave. He did not tell his brother or his mother about his plans to flee.[8] That night the 25-year-old man went through with his escape plan. It was 1:20 in the morning on November 24, 1986 when he approached the border grounds in Glienicke/Nordbahn. He had brought his personal documents that he would need in his new life in the West with him.[9] Using a wooden ladder he climbed over the interior wall and triggered an alarm. As he ran across the patrol path and security strip, the border guards, who were approximately 200 meters away, noticed him. Because the security strip in this area was rather narrow, Michael Bittner was able to quickly reach the last border wall. He leaned his ladder up against it and climbed up. The border guards fired directly at him just as he reached the top of the wall with his hands. Michael Bittner was hit in the back and fell backwards onto the ground.[10] "The bastard is hit" was the comment of one of the border guards, cited in eye-witness reports from the West.[11] At 1:50 a.m. the regiment doctor declared him dead. His body was soon taken to the military medical academy of the National People's Army in Bad Saarow for an autopsy and then picked up on November 28, 1986 by a Stasi vehicle. There has been no trace of it since then.[12]

Alarmed by the bullet shots, residents of the West Berlin side went to the border and were able to look through holes in the Wall and see Michael Bittner being carried away. A short time later, members of the West Berlin police, customs officials and the French gendarmerie had also arrived and tried to photograph and film the crime site.[13] By early morning news of the failed escape attempt was reported on West Berlin radio.[14] Over the next few days, western media continued to report in detail on the events that had occurred in northern Berlin.[15] Both the Berlin Senate and the West German federal government condemned the use of guns at the Wall.[16] The head of the Bonn chancellery, Wolfgang Schäuble, spoke of a "burden on relations between the Federal Republic and East Germany" and demanded that the East German government do everything possible "to put a stop to every form of violence at the German borders."[17] The three western Allies also reacted with outrage at this "most recent use of brutal violence that demonstrates a total lack of respect for human life."[18]

Just three days after the deadly shots were fired at René Gross and Manfred Mäder, the Communist Party leadership feared that the incident of November 24 could further damage its reputation. "The political sensibility of the state border to Berlin (West) makes it necessary to cover up the occurrence. Rumors about the incident must be prevented from spreading and information about it should not be permitted to reach West Berlin or [the] FRG," the Stasi wrote in a report on July 1988.[19] Hence the East German secret police did everything in its power to conceal the death of Michael Bittner and to create a legend about his disappearance. The border guards and the medical staff involved had to swear in writing that they would not speak about it. The public telephone in the barracks was blocked.[20] In order to explain his disappearance to his family and also to intimidate them, the East German secret police concocted a connection between Michael Bittner and a "criminal human trade gang" that supposedly "used unknown channels to smuggle him out of East Germany" on November 26, 1986.[21] It even opened a fake investigation against the dead man and issued a warrant for his arrest on December 4, 1986 for "engaging in treasonous agent activities against his country" and for "crossing the border illegally."[22] The death certificate and autopsy report were destroyed, as was the proof of his cremation and burial. The East German secret police entered into the registration files of Berlin-Pankow that Michael Bittner had immigrated to West Germany on December 9, 1986.[23]

Every since his disappearance his mother had lived in fear that he might have been the man that western media reported had died on November 24, 1986. The East German authorities denied that there had been a deadly incident at the Wall and insisted that he must have fled successfully to the West.

The uncertainty about the fate of her son continued to disturb his mother. In mid-January 1990, during the East German Peaceful Revolution, she requested information from the East German justice minister, Kurt Wünsche, about the disappearance of her son.[24] But a systematic investigation did not begin until after Germany had officially been reunified. At the end of 1997 the Berlin district youth court convicted both men responsible for shooting Michael Bittner to a youth sentence of one year and three months for manslaughter. The sentence was commuted to probation. The court was unable to determine whose bullets had hit and killed Michael Bittner, but was of the view that since both men had acted "consciously and jointly," they had to "assume responsibility for the bullets of the other."[25] Six months later the Berlin district court held another trial against the gunmen's supervisors. One was sentenced to two years in prison; the other to ten months. Both sentences were commuted to probation.[26]

But even after the criminal proceedings were settled, Michael Bittner's mother was unable to find peace. The body of her son was never located.

Udo Baron

1 See "Handschriftlicher Lebenslauf von Michael Bittner im Antrag auf Ausbürgerung zum Zweck der Übersiedlung in die BRD, 2.4.1984," in: BStU, Ast. Berlin, AOPK 5895/88, Bl. 27; "Abschlussbericht des MfS/KD Pankow zur OPK "Morgentau", 25.7.1988," in: BStU, Ast. Berlin, AOPK Nr. 5895/88, Bl. 119.

2 See "Handschriftlicher Lebenslauf von Michael Bittner, 2.4.1984," in: BStU, Ast. Berlin, AOPK Nr. 5895/88, Bl. 27.

3 Irmgard Bittner, Eine unglaubliche Geschichte, in: Werner Filmer/Heribert Schwan, *Opfer der Mauer. Die geheimen Protokolle des Todes,* München, 1991, p. 50.

4 Ibid.

5 See "Handschriftlicher Antrag auf Ausbürgerung zum Zweck der Übersiedlung in die BRD von Michael Bittner, 9.6.1986," in: BStU, Ast. Berlin, AOPK Nr. 5895/88, Bl. 51.

6 "Handschriftliches Protokoll des Rats des Stadtbezirks Berlin-Pankow über ein Gespräch mit dem Übersiedlungsersuchenden Michael Bittner, 5.9.1985," in: BStU, Ast. Berlin, AOPK Nr. 5895/88, Bl. 42.

7 See Irmgard Bittner, *Eine unglaubliche Geschichte,* pp. 51–52.

8 See ibid., p. 52; "Erstmeldung des MfS/HA IX/9, 27.11.1986," in: BStU, MfS, AU 3381/88, Bd. 1, Bl. 7.

9 See "Protokoll der Zeugenvernehmung der Mutter von Michael Bittner durch die West-Berliner Polizei, 16.1.1990," in: StA Berlin, Az. 2 Js 52/90, Bd. 5, Bl. 149.

10 See "Urteil des Landgerichts Berlin in der Strafsache gegen Hartmut B. und Olaf N., Az. 27/2 Js 52/90 Kls (8/92), vom 27.11.1997," in: StA Berlin, Az. 2 Js 52/90, Bd. 7a, Bl. 114f–114g.

11 Ibid., Bl. 114h.

12 See ibid., Bl. 114g.

13 See ibid., Bl. 114h; "Operative Meldung des MfS/HA I/GK Mitte/Unterabteilung GR 38, Hennigsdorf, 24.11.1986," in: BStU, MfS, HA I Nr. 5795, Bl. 92.

14 See report from *SFB 2,* 24.11.1986, 6:30 a.m.

15 See *Der Tagesspiegel,* 25.11.1986; *BZ,* 25.11.1986; *Berliner Morgenpost,* 25.11.1986; *Neue Osnabrücker Zeitung,* 25.11.1986.

16 See "39. Sitzung des Abgeordnetenhauses von Berlin, 27.11.1986," in: Plenarprotokolle des Abgeordnetenhauses von Berlin, 10. Wahlperiode, Bd. 3, Berlin 1986/87, pp. 2291–2294.

17 *Der Tagesspiegel,* 26.11.1986.

18 *Spandauer Volksblatt,* 25.11.1986.

19 "Abschlussbericht des MfS/KD Pankow zur OPK "Morgentau", 25.7.1988," in: BStU, Ast. Berlin, AOPK Nr. 5895/88, Bl. 118.

20 See "Urteil des Landgerichts Berlin in der Strafsache gegen Hartmut B. und Olaf N., Az. 27/2 Js 52/90 Kls

(8/92), vom 27.11.1997," in: StA Berlin, Az. 2 Js 52/90, Bd. 7a, Bl. 114g – 114h, 114j – 114k; "Bericht des MfS/HA I/Grenzkommando/Abteilung Abwehr Mitte über die Verhinderung eines Grenzdurchbruches DDR-Berlin (West) am 24.11.1986," in: BStU, MfS, HA I Nr. 5795, Bl. 105–106.

21 "Erstmeldung des MfS/HA IX/9, 27.11.1986," in: BStU, MfS, AU 3381/88, Bl. 7; see Irmgard Bittner, *Eine unglaubliche Geschichte,* pp. 53 – 55.

22 See "Verfügung des MfS/HA Untersuchung über die Einleitung eines Ermittlungsverfahrens gegen Michael Bittner, 27.11.1986," in: BStU, MfS, AU 3381/88, Bd. 1, Bl. 8; see "Haftbefehl des Stadtbezirksgerichts Berlin-Mitte gegen Michael Bittner, 4.12.1986," in: BStU, MfS, AU 3381/88, Bl. 11.

23 See "Protokoll des Militärstaatsanwalts der DDR-Grenztruppen zu den durchgeführten Überprüfungen im Zusammenhang mit der Eingabe [der Mutter von Michael Bittner, d.Verf.] vom 15.1.1990, 9.4.1990," in: StA Berlin, Az. 2 Js 52/90, Bd. 1, Bl. 43; Irmgard Bittner, *Eine unglaubliche Geschichte,* p. 56 – 57.

24 See Irmgard Bittner, *Eine unglaubliche Geschichte,* p. 56.

25 See "Urteil des Landgerichts Berlin in der Strafsache gegen Hartmut B. und Olaf N., Az. 27/2 Js 52/90 Kls (8/92), vom 27.11.1997," in: StA Berlin, Az. 2 Js 52/90, Bd. 7a, Bl. 114a, here Bl. 114m.

26 See "Urteil des Landgerichts Berlin in der Strafsache gegen Volker P., Udo R. und Dieter K., Az. 27 Js 71/97 Ks (1/98), vom 15.4.1998," in: StA Berlin, Az. 27 Js 71/97, Bd. 2, n. pag.

Lutz Schmidt

born on July 8, 1962

shot dead on February 12, 1987
near Rheingoldstrasse, near the
Waltersdorfer Chaussee border crossing
on the sector border between
Berlin-Treptow and Berlin-Neukölln

Lutz Schmidt, born on July 8, 1962 in Zittau, was an enthusiastic bike racer and considered to be very talented by his sport club.[1] At the age of 14 he was sent to East Berlin to attend the youth sports school SC Dynamo Berlin. He graduated from high school there and hoped to achieve a professional career as a sprinter. But as Lutz Schmidt got older, he was less and less willing to follow the political demands made by his trainer. His refusal to join the Communist Party led to a falling out with his sports club. As a consequence, his sports career ended abruptly and with it his dream of becoming a professional bicycle racer. Lutz Schmidt had to find a new field of work.

When he was 18 he met Karin and they soon decided to get married. Lutz Schmidt raised Karin's young daughter, Viktoria, as his own child. Soon a son, Karsten, was also born.[2] Now that his family's well-being was his most important priority, Lutz Schmidt trained to become an assembly metal worker. He served in the National People's Army as a motor mechanic and driver until April 1984. After that he planned to qualify as a master auto mechanic and hoped to open his own garage repair shop. But he ended up taking a job as a driver for the state-owned company "Autotrans" instead because the family wanted to build a house in Mahlow on the southeast edge of Berlin. He hoped that the job would make it easier for him to obtain materials he needed to build the house and that were hard to come by in East Germany.[3]

Still, life in East Germany did not really offer a promising future to Karin and Lutz Schmidt. Their contact with relatives in West Germany and the United States made them realize how different their life was to life in the West. They began to imagine a life for themselves in West Germany and wanted to offer their children a better chance in life. Nonetheless, they did not apply for an exit permit because they feared it might be disadvantageous to them both at work and privately. Instead, Lutz Schmidt hoped to use a visit to his relatives in Bremen to stay there permanently after which he would bring his family over. When his applications to visit his relatives in the West were repeatedly rejected, the couple decided that Lutz Schmidt should try to flee by himself and then bring the family over as part of the

East German policy of uniting families. He first began thinking about daring escape plans. He considered crossing the Baltic Sea to the West in a home-made submarine, but he soon gave the idea up. He then got to know Peter Sch. a little better, a fellow colleague at "VEB Autotrans," where he worked. They became friends and soon realized that they were both on the same wave length since Peter Sch. also wanted to leave East Germany.

Although Karin Schmidt had been informed of her husband's plans from the very beginning, she did not want to meet his partner or know the exact date of their planned escape. She feared she would not be able to bear the psychological strain and also worried that she might get into trouble with the authorities after the men had safely reached the West. The couple agreed on a signal to mark the day of the escape: If Lutz Schmidt's car was parked in the garage in the morning, then his wife would know that he had attempted his escape.[4]

Thursday, February 12, 1987, was a damp, cold, misty winter day. Visibility was less than 40 meters. Lutz Schmidt and Peter Sch. were both working the night shift. Over the past weeks they had used business trips to the border territory to find a good spot for their escape. This was the day they wanted to risk escape. They hoped that the weather conditions were to their advantage and that the soldiers would refrain from shooting at the border since East Berlin was expecting important guests from the West: Bernhard Vogel and Klaus von Dohnany, the minister presidents of the West German states Rheinland-Pfalz and Hamburg, were visiting Erich Honecker the next day. The men loaded two ladders onto to their truck that they had hidden in preparation for their escape and drove to the southeast edge of Berlin, to the sector border between Altglienicke and Rudow. Rheingoldstrasse, which was near Schönefeld airport, ran right into the death strip which was not more than 50 meters wide in this spot. The two men were driving at high speed and caught the attention of a police patrol car at about 9:20 p.m. East German policemen had been put on duty as reinforcement at the border because of the poor weather conditions. The police first mistook the escape car as a truck belonging to the border troops. Due to the poor visibility, the truck and patrol car almost collided head-on. Lutz Schmidt and Peter Sch. swerved the truck out of the way and drove off the road. Accelerating, they tried to get their vehicle back onto the road but the wheels kept spinning deeper into the soil. The two men jumped out of the truck and disappeared with their ladders into the fog. The policemen became suspicious and informed the nearby border guards. During later questioning, one of the two policemen stated that after about a minute "I heard shots from a machine pistol at the border."[5] Soon the notice came over the radio that "border troops had triggered 'option cemetery.'"[6]

That evening the difference between life and death occurred within less than 60 seconds.[7] When Lutz Schmidt and Peter Sch. climbed over the signal fence they triggered an alarm. One of the ladders got caught in the barbed wire. The two men ran with the remaining ladder to the front concrete wall and set it up against it. But the ladder slipped on the slanted concrete base and sank into the soft clay ground. Consequently, the ladder ended two meters below the top of the wall and neither man was able to climb to the top without the help of the other. With both men standing on the ladder, Lutz Schmidt, the stronger of the two, was able to give his partner a leg up onto the top of the 3.6-meter-high wall so that he could straddle himself on it. Then Peter Sch. leaned over and tried to pull Lutz Schmidt up but was unable to.

Meanwhile the two border guards were running toward the beacon light where the signal had been set off. When they recognized the fugitives in the fog, they opened automatic fire at short range. Squatting on the top of the wall, Peter Sch. was able to grasp Lutz Schmidt's hands, but when he tried to pull his friend up he lost his balance and fell onto the west side of the Berlin Wall. Lutz Schmidt fell back onto East German territory. As he fell he called to his friend: "Peter, take off!"[8] When he stood up a bullet fired by a border guard hit him in his breast cage and went into his heart. Peter Sch. succeeded in reaching West Berlin; Lutz Schmidt died in the death strip.

When Karin Schmidt woke up the next morning, she saw her husband's car parked in the garage. She became fearful when she heard the news on western television that only one of the two drivers who fled the night before had made it to West Berlin. No one at her husband's work place knew anything about it. She issued a missing persons' report. The next day she was summoned with her father-in-law to the office of the military state prosecutor in East Berlin. They were separated and informed by a staff officer of the military state prosecutor and Stasi that Lutz Schmidt had been shot and killed "when he had violently infiltrated a military protective area near the state border."[9] The East German secret police demanded that both of them maintain secrecy about the circumstances of his death. They were instructed to tell their own families, relatives and acquaintances that Lutz Schmidt had died in an automobile accident. The Stasi threatened that if they did not cooperate, the children would be taken away and handed over for adoption and that the wife would be committed to a psychiatric institute.[10] Stasi informants were assigned to watch Karin Schmidt and her family in Mahlow. Thereafter her mail was examined and her telephone tapped.[11] The principle aim of the Stasi "operative plan" against the dead man's wife was the "prophylactic prevention of information/news about the incident that could be used to cause political damage to interests of East Germany from leaking over the state border."[12]

Karin Schmidt was traumatized by the news of her husband's death and the threats of the Stasi. Her father-in-law, who rejected the Stasi's suggestion that he distance himself from his son's "crime," took over responsibility for the things that had to be negotiated with the Stasi.[13] Against the wishes of the widow, Lutz Schmidt was not buried in Mahlow, a village quite close to the border. He was buried on February 25, 1987 in his parents' family grave in Zittau, quite a distance away. The family told the mourners that Lutz Schmidt had died in a car accident. The Stasi was particularly concerned that western journalists might attend the burial and assigned a large number of Stasi agents to control and monitor the funeral.

Peter Sch.'s successful escape received a lot of attention in the West at first.[14] But on the political level little was done to get information from the East German authorities about the shots that had been fired on February 12, or to find out what happened to the second fugitive. The reason was a state visit from the East German leader, Erich Honecker, to Bonn that was planned for September 1987. The mayor of West Berlin, Eberhard Diepgen, had also invited the Communist Party general secretary to attend the city's 750th anniversary celebration. The politicians did not want the deaths at the Wall to disrupt the planned German-German diplomatic visits. As in the fall of 1986, it was striking how reservedly the Senate responded to inquiries and protests. During talks in preparation for President Ronald Reagan's visit to Berlin, Washington warned the West Berlin mayor not to be to "too soft" towards East Germany.[15] It was ultimately American authorities that announced in mid-March 1987 that Lutz Schmidt had been shot and killed in February. An article in the "Bild-Zeitung" about this alarmed the East German secret police.[16] It pressured the widow to "break off contact with people in Mahlow as soon as possible and more specifically to sell the house" so that things could "settle down" once and for all. "She and the children have to get out of Mahlow," the Stasi demanded of her father-in-law, who then organized the move.[17] The family hastily moved to Zittau in March. Lutz Schmidt's father demanded that the Stasi arrange to have a tenant move out so that Karin Schmidt could move into an apartment in her parent-in-law's semi-detached house a few months later.

In the 1990s Viktoria and Karsten Schmidt finally learned the truth about their father's death. When the archives were opened to the public, Karin Schmidt discovered that her father-in-law had been an informant for the East German secret police since 1975 and had been assigned to help cover up the circumstances of his son's death. Lutz Schmidt's father thought that given the Stasi's threats, his cooperation with the authorities would help the situation and protect his son's family.[18] But Karin Schmidt felt manipulated and betrayed by the conspiratorial activities that he had engaged in behind her back.[19]

By February 1990 Karin Schmidt was already ready to press charges in Zittau for the murder of her husband but the state prosecutor in charge there told her that that was pointless. In response she went to the East German general state prosecutor and demanded not only that her husband's murderer be punished, but also that her family be rehabilitated and granted financial compensation.[20] But a systematic investigation did not begin until after German reunification. On June 22, 1993 the Berlin public prosecutor's office brought charges against the border guards involved in the death of Lutz Schmidt who had received the "Medal for Exemplary Service at the Border" and three days of special leave for preventing an escape. Karin Schmidt served as joint plaintiff in the case and again later in the trials against the members of the Communist Party Politburo and the East German National Council of Defense. On March 21, 1995 the men who had shot and killed Lutz Schmidt were found guilty of joint manslaughter by the Berlin district court and sentenced as youths to a prison sentence of two years each. The sentences were commuted to probation. Moreover, "as a gesture of reconciliation," the two men had to pay Karin Schmidt a symbolic fine. The court explained that the "harsh sentence" was a consequence of the fact that given the command status at the time, there had been no compelling reason to use a weapon.[21] But the court also considered to the defendants' advantage that they had acted only with limited intent, had confessed at least in part and had expressed regret over the consequences of their actions.

Udo Baron / Hans-Hermann Hertle

1 On this and the following, see conversation conducted by Udo Baron with Karin Schmidt, 14.2.2007; conversation conducted by Udo Baron and Hans-Hermann Hertle with Lutz Schmidt's parents, 18.6.2007.
2 Conversation conducted by Udo Baron with Karin Schmidt, 14.2.2007.
3 Ibid.
4 Conversation conducted by Udo Baron with Karin Schmidt, 14.2.2007.
5 "Protokoll der Befragung des VP-Angehörigen [Name geschwärzt] durch die BVfS Berlin/Untersuchungsabteilung, 13.2.1987," in: BStU, Ast. Berlin, Abt. IX Nr. 12, Bl. 30–33, here Bl. 33.
6 "Bericht eines VP-Hauptwachtmeisters der VP-Inspektion Treptow, 13.2.1987," in: BStU, Ast. Berlin, Abt. IX Nr. 12, Bl. 34.
7 See establishment of facts concerning circumstances of escape in: "Urteil des Landgerichts Berlin in der Strafsache gegen Michael J. und Ekkehard T., Az. (513) 2 Js 101/90 KLs (59/93), vom 21. März 1995," in: StA Berlin, Az. 2 Js 101/90, Bd. 5, pp. 15–22; "Bericht des MfS/HA I/GKM/Abt. Abwehr über einen erfolgten und einen mit Anwendung der Schusswaffe verhinderten Grenzdurchbruch, 13.2.1987," in: BStU, MfS, HA I Nr. 14441, Bl. 547–553; "Information der BVfS Berlin/Abt. IX, 13.2.1987," in: BStU, MfS, HA I Nr. 14441, Bl. 557–562. Also see the presentation in Hannelore Strehlow, *Der gefährliche Weg in die Freiheit. Fluchtversuche aus dem ehemaligen Bezirk Potsdam,* Potsdam, 2004, pp. 52–55.
8 See "Urteil des Landgerichts Berlin in der Strafsache gegen Michael J. und Ekkehard T., Az. (513) 2 Js 101/90 KLs (59/93), vom 21. März 1995," in: StA Berlin, Az. 2 Js 101/90, Bd. 5, p. 19.
9 "Vermerk der BVfS Berlin/Abt. IX, 18.2.1987," in: BStU, Ast. Berlin, Abt. IX Nr. 12, Bl. 5.
10 Conversation conducted by Udo Baron with Karin Schmidt, 14.2.2007; conversation conducted by Udo Baron and Hans-Hermann Hertle with Lutz Schmidt's parents, 18.6.2007.
11 See "Eröffnungsbericht des MfS/KD Zossen zum OV "Jacob", 26.2.1987," in: BStU, Ast. Potsdam, AKG Nr. ZMA B 1241, Bl. 3–6; "Operativplan des MfS/KD Zossen zum OV "Jacob", 26.2.1987," in: Ibid., Bl. 7–9.
12 "Operativplan des MfS/KD Zossen zum OV "Jacob", 26.2.1987," in: BStU, Ast. Potsdam, AKG Nr. ZMA B 1241, Bl. 7.
13 See conversation conducted by Udo Baron with Karin Schmidt, 14.2.2007; conversation conducted by Udo Baron and Hans-Hermann Hertle with Lutz Schmidt's parents, 18.6.2007.
14 *Der Tagesspiegel,* 14.2.1987; *Bild-Zeitung,* 14.2.1987; *Berliner Morgenpost,* 14. und 15.2.1987; *Frankfurter Allgemeine Zeitung,* 17. und 19.2.1987; *Bild-Zeitung,* 25.2.1987.
15 See Hans-Hermann Hertle, *Die Berliner Mauer – Monument des Kalten Krieges,* Berlin, 2007, pp. 132–133.
16 "Junger Kipperfahrer von Mauer geschossen – Flüchtling heimlich beerdigt", in: *Bild-Zeitung,* 18.3.1987; "Schmidt wurde in Dresden beerdigt", in: *Berliner Morgenpost,* 19.3.1987.
17 See conversation conducted by Udo Baron and Hans-Hermann Hertle with Lutz Schmidt's parents, 18.6.2007; see also "Vermerk der BVfS Berlin/Abt. IX, 19.3.1987," in: BStU, Ast. Dresden, AIM 3170/90, Bd. 2, Bl. 50–52, here Bl. 51, 52.
18 See conversation conducted by Udo Baron and Hans-Hermann Hertle with Lutz Schmidt's parents, 18.6.2007.
19 See the interviews with Karin, Karsten and Viktoria Schmidt in the documentary "Wenn Tote stören – Vom Sterben an der Mauer", author: Florian Huber, NDR/ARD 2007; see also Sven-Felix Kellerhoff, "Gescheiterte Flucht löst Familientragödie aus", in: *Berliner Morgenpost,* 11.2.2007.
20 See "Schreiben von Karin Schmidt an den DDR-Generalstaatsanwalt, Juli 1990," in: StA Berlin, Az. 2 Js 101/90, Bd 1, Bl. 174.
21 See "Urteil des Landgerichts Berlin in der Strafsache gegen Michael J. und Ekkehard T., Az. (513) 2 Js 101/90 KLs (59/93), vom 21. März 1995," in: StA Berlin, Az. 2 Js 101/90, Bd. 5, esp. pp. 47–50.

Ingolf Diederichs

born on April 13, 1964

fatally injured in an accident on January 13, 1989
in the area of Böse Bridge / Bornholmer Strasse border crossing
on the sector border between
Berlin-Prenzlauer Berg and Berlin-Wedding

Ingolf Diederichs was born on April 13, 1964 in Wismar. After finishing school, he first trained to become a repair mechanic before studying trade school pedagogy at the Technical University of Dresden.[1]

Early in the evening of January 13, 1989, Ingolf Diederichs used a wooden folding ladder that he had made from the slats of a crib to climb from an S-Bahn train traveling from Pankow towards Schönhauser Allee. This was a unique S-Bahn line that allowed East German citizens to come very close to the West. As the train approached Bornholmer Strasse, passengers were a mere twenty meters from West Berlin, making the West seem very much "within reach." To counter this feeling, the Berlin Wall there was 5.4 meters high – higher than elsewhere. Trains sped through this part of their journey.

At about 6:30 p.m. Ingolf Diederichs jumped from a moving train at a point very close to the Bornholmer Strasse border crossing.[2] When he fell, he got caught on the train and was dragged with it. His head was seriously injured and caused his immediate death. An S-Bahn driver noticed the mangled body hanging between the long-distance tracks and the S-Bahn tracks as he passed over Böse Bridge. The East German secret police and border troops blocked off the route between Pankow and Schönhauser Allee in order to remove the body and secure evidence.[3]

It is not known what led the 24-year-old to risk such a dangerous undertaking. The East German secret police created what they called a "legend" to make the escape attempt appear to have been a mere accident. Ingolf Diederichs' relatives were only told that he died after falling out of a moving train.[4]

To determine whether someone else was responsible for the fugitive's death, the Berlin public prosecutor's office opened a preliminary investigation in late August 1994. The case was closed again the following month for lack of evidence indicating any external influence.[5]

Martin Ahrends / Udo Baron

1   See "Information der BVfS Berlin/Abt. IX, 14.1.1989," in: BStU, MfS, Sekr. Neiber Nr. 576, Bl. 130–132.

2   See "Lagebericht des Diensthabenden des MfS/HA I/Grenzkommando Mitte/Abt. Abwehr-Aufklärung, 13.1. 1989," in: BStU, MfS, HA I Nr. 6061, Bl. 20.

3   See "Rapport Nr. 13/89 des MfS/Zentraler Operativstab vom 13./14.1.1989," in: BStU, MfS, HA VII Nr. 5162, Bl. 69.

4   "Information der BVfS Berlin/Abt. IX, 14.1.1989," in: BStU, MfS, Sekr. Neiber Nr. 576, Bl. 131.

5   See "Verfügung der Staatsanwaltschaft II bei dem Landgericht Berlin, 5.10.1994," in: StA Berlin, Az. 27 AR 759/94, Bl. 11–12.

Chris Gueffroy

born on June 21, 1968

shot dead on February 5, 1989
on the Britzer Zweigkanal,
near the garden settlements "Harmonie" and "Sorgenfrei"
on the sector border between
Berlin-Treptow and Berlin-Neukölln

Chris Gueffroy, born on June 21, 1968 in Pasewalk, moved with his mother to Berlin when he was five years old.[1] When he was in the third grade, athletic scouts noticed his gymnastic talent and sent him to the youth sports school SC Dynamo Berlin. Chris Gueffroy was very hopeful that he would have a successful career as a gymnast. But he also felt increasingly constricted by the state-regimented daily routine. After he finished school he refused to pursue an officer's career track in the National People's Army and was consequently denied the right to study at the university. This destroyed his dream of becoming either an actor or a pilot. In September 1985 he began an apprenticeship in the Schönefeld airport restaurant near Berlin after which he worked in a number of different restaurants.

Chris Gueffroy had a better than average income as a waiter and enjoyed a strong degree of freedom, but he encountered the downside of his profession as well. He repeatedly told his mother how disgusted he was by the widespread corruption in the restaurant business. His friend Christian G., whom he had met at gastronomy school, shared his feelings. Chris Gueffroy, age twenty, began to find it increasingly unbearable to think that he would remain locked up with the knowledge that it would always be this way and that he would never have the freedom to decide for himself where he wanted to live.[2] In mid-January 1989, when Chris Gueffroy learned that he was to be conscripted into the National People's Army in May, he and Christian G. decided to leave East Germany.

The two young men chose not to submit an application for an exit visa to leave East Germany. They feared the harassment at work and in their personal lives that usually accompanied such a move. When they heard from friends that the order to shoot fugitives at the border had been lifted, they became convinced that they should try to flee over the Wall to West Berlin.[3]

Chris Gueffroy and Christian G. learned that the Swedish prime minister was going to pay a state visit to East Berlin in early February 1989 and they decided to plan their escape for February 5. They could not imagine that fugitives would be shot at during the official visit and they thought that, were they to be arrested, they would soon be deported to the West. But they had erred tragically on two counts:

The order to shoot was still in effect – and the Swedish prime minister had already left East Berlin.[4]

On February 5, 1989 both young men left the apartment they shared at 9 p.m. and approached the border area. They had told their family and friends that they were taking a trip to Prague.[5]

At around 10:30 p.m. they reached the small garden colony named "Harmonie" in the East Berlin district of Treptow. They waited for more than an hour in a tool shed and observed the border territory, waiting for an advantageous moment to flee. At around 11:30 p.m. they approached the border fortifications in front of the Britzer Zweigkanal, a canal that forms the border to the West Berlin district of Neukölln.[6] They had brought two self-made kedge anchors with them to help them get across the security grounds. The two athletic men were able to help each other climb over the three-meter-high interior wall without being noticed. Christian G. climbed up onto the top of the Wall first and helped pull Chris Gueffroy up from there.[7] They left one of the kedge anchors behind. When they crawled through the signal fence they set off an optical and acoustic alarm.

As both men ran towards the final obstacle, a three-meter-high stretch metal fence, they came under fire from two border guards. To escape the bullets they ran in the opposite direction along the fence and got caught in the fire of two other guards who were also shooting at them. They tried unsuccessfully to use the second kedge anchor to climb over the last fence, after which the two men tried again to help each other up with their hands. A border soldier about 40 meters away from Chris Gueffroy crouched down and fired single shots at the young man's feet. He hit them, but the injured man, in a state of shock, showed no reaction, so the gunman aimed higher. Chris Gueffroy was standing with his back to the fence when he was hit in the heart. He collapsed and died within minutes from his injuries.[8]

Christian G., injured, was arrested and sentenced in May 1989 to three years in prison for "a severe case of illegally attempting to cross the border." The West German government paid ransom to the Eastern authorities to have him released to the West in mid-October 1989.[9]

Many residents in the East and West heard the shots fired that night in the border territory. A West Berlin witness reported to the police that he heard at least ten shots and saw two men being carried away, one completely motionless.[10] West Berlin newspapers reported the next day on the failed escape attempt.[11]

Chris Gueffroy's mother had also heard the shots. Two days later she paid a visit to one of his friends and learned that her son had been planning to escape and that the shots fired the night before may have been directed at him. That very evening she was picked up by the East German secret police to "clarify circumstances." During the hours of interrogation she learned that her son was dead. The Stasi agents told her that Chris Gueffroy had been seriously injured during an attack on an East German "military security zone" and had died "despite the immediate medical care" that he had been given.[12]

Although the East German authorities did everything in their power to keep the death of Chris Gueffroy a secret, his brother managed to send the eastern paper "Berliner Zeitung" an obituary that was printed on February 21, 1989, making reference to a "tragic accident" that had occurred on February 6. The western media made the connection between the deceased and the shots fired at the border.[13]

Chris Gueffroy was buried on February 23, 1989 at the Baumschulenweg Cemetery in Berlin-Treptow amidst tremendous public sympathy. Well over 100 people paid him the last honors under the watchful eye of the East German secret police. Although the East German secret police imposed massive control measures,[14] a few western correspondents managed to enter East Germany in order to attend the funeral and report on it.[15] That same day a memorial cross in honor of Chris Gueffroy was erected on the West Berlin side of the Teltow Canal in Neukölln.[16] Opposition groups in East Germany publicized the murder of Chris Gueffroy in an "open letter to the population of East Germany." That fact that his murder was still referred to as a "tragic accident" during the funeral sermon was described as a shameful demonstration of just how steeped in lies East Germany was.[17]

After the Berlin Wall fell on November 9, 1989, Karin Gueffroy left no stone unturned in her search for information about the death of her son. On January 12, 1990 she pressed charges against "persons unknown" with the East German general state prosecutor.[18] After German re-unification the Central Investigating Agency for Governmental and Party Crimes took over the investigation. The Berlin public prosecutor opened the case amidst great public interest on May 27, 1991. Four former East German border guards stood trial for the shooting of Chris Gueffroy. It was the first of many trials against guards who had shot at fugitives at the Berlin Wall and their commanders. The Berlin district court came to its verdict on January 20, 1992: The gunman was found guilty of manslaughter and sentenced to three and a half years in prison.[19] The other defendants were either given suspended sentences or were acquitted. The court justified the long sentence for the one gunman, Ingo H., with the explanation that he had "revealed a very high degree of callousness and abjection."[20]

The Federal Court of Justice overturned the verdict on March 14, 1994 and referred the case to another chamber of the Berlin district court to be retried.[21] It criticized the Berlin district court for not paying enough consideration to the fact that the gunman stood at the very bottom of the military hierarchy and, unlike the people in positions of responsibility who had yet to be held accountable for their actions, the guards "were to a certain degree also victims of the border regime."[22] The outcome of this case created a precedent for later verdicts. Almost all the subsequent trials followed the court decision to exonerate the gunmen. Ingo H. was the only defendant in this case to be sentenced to a two year prison term by the Berlin district court in a subsequent trial, a sentence that was commuted to probation. His guard leader was acquitted due to "insufficient evidence of intention to kill."

The shooting of Chris Gueffroy threatened to politically isolate the Communist Party leadership in the spring of 1989. There was no end to the protests and diplomatic measures directed against the order to shoot fugitives at the Wall. On April 3, 1989 the Communist Party general secretary Erich Honecker revoked the order to shoot fugitives at the Wall – the existence of which had always been denied.[23] The shots fired at Chris Gueffroy and Christian G. were the last fatal bullets fired at the Berlin Wall.

A memorial column commemorating Chris Gueffroy was erected at Britzer Zweigkanal in Berlin-Treptow in 2003 in honor of his 35th birthday.

Udo Baron / Hans-Hermann Hertle

1 On this and the following, see conversations conducted by Udo Baron with Karin Gueffroy, 16.6.2006 und 22.1.2007; see also Roman Grafe, *Deutsche Gerechtigkeit. Prozesse gegen DDR-Grenzschützen und ihre Befehlsgeber,* Berlin, 2004, pp. 12–14.

2 Letter from Karin Gueffroy to Hans-Hermann Hertle, 18.1.2009.

3 Conversations conducted by Udo Baron with Karin Gueffroy, 16.6.2006 und 22.1.2007.

4 See "Urteil des Landgerichts Berlin in der Strafsache gegen Andreas K., Peter Sch., Mike Sch. und Ingo H., Az. (523) 2 Js 48/90 (9/91), vom 20.1.1992," in: StA Berlin, Az. 2 Js 48/90, Bd. 16, p. 44.

5 On the course of events see ibid., pp. 42 ff.; Karin Gueffroy, Eine Mutter klagt an, in: Werner Filmer/Heribert Schwan, *Opfer der Mauer. Die geheimen Protokolle des Todes,* München, 1991, pp. 62–65; "Protokoll der Zeugenvernehmung von Christian G. durch die West-Berliner Polizei, 4.12.1989," in: StA Berlin, Az. 2 Js 48/90, Bd. 1, Bl. 84–87; "Vernehmungsprotokoll von Christian G. durch die BVfS Berlin/Untersuchungsabteilung, 6.2.1989," in: BStU, Ast. Berlin, AU 3979/89, Strafakte Bd. 1, Bl. 23–32.

6 See "Urteil des Landgerichts Berlin in der Strafsache gegen Andreas K., Peter Sch., Mike Sch. und Ingo H., Az. (523) 2 Js 48/90 (9/91), vom 20.1.1992," in: StA Berlin, Az. 2 Js 48/90, Bd. 16, Bl. 45.

7 See "Protokoll der Zeugenvernehmung von Christian G. durch die West-Berliner Polizei, 4.12.1989," in: StA Berlin, Az. 2 Js 48/90, Bd. 1, Bl. 84.

8 See "Urteil des Landgerichts Berlin in der Strafsache gegen Andreas K., Peter Sch., Mike Sch. und Ingo H., Az. (523) 2 Js 48/90 (9/91), vom 20.1.1992," in: StA Berlin, Az. 2 Js 48/90, Bd. 16, Bl. 48–57.

9 See "Protokoll der Zeugenvernehmung von Christian G. durch die West-Berliner Polizei, 4.12.1989," in: StA Berlin, Az. 2 Js 48/90, Bd. 1, Bl. 86.

10 See "Strafanzeige des Polizeipräsidenten in Berlin, 6.2.1989," in: StA Berlin, Az. 2 Js 48/90, Bd. 1, Bl. 7–8; "Protokoll der Vernehmung eines Augenzeugen durch die West-Berliner Polizei, 16.1.1990," in: Ibid., Bl. 13–14.

11 See *Der Tagesspiegel,* 7.2.1989; *Bild-Zeitung,* 7.2.1989; *Berliner Morgenpost,* 7.2.1989.

12 "Protokoll des Militär-Oberstaatsanwalts/Abt. IA über ein Gespräch mit Karin Gueffroy am 7.2.1989, 8.2.1989," in: StA Berlin, Az. 2 Js 48/90, Bd. 3, Bl. 140–141; see also "Schreiben des Ministers für Staatssicherheit, Erich Mielke, an den Generalsekretär des ZK der SED, Erich Honecker, 25.2.1989," in: BStU, MfS, ZAIG Nr. 15217, Bl. 14–15; "Sachstandsbericht der BVfS Berlin/Abt. IX zur Durchführung schadensbegrenzender Massnahmen im Zusammenhang mit dem Vorkommnis an der Staatsgrenze der DDR zu Berlin (West) am 5.2.1989, 20.2.1989," in: BStU, MfS, ZAIG Nr. 15217, Bl. 78.

13 See *Der Tagesspiegel,* 23.2.1989; *Frankfurter Rundschau,* 23.2.1989.

14 See "Massnahmeplan des Leiters des MfS/KD Treptow zur Sicherung der Trauerfeier, 22.2.1989," in: BStU, MfS, ZAIG Nr. 15217, Bl. 64–65; "Bericht des Leiters des MfS/KD Treptow über den politisch-operativen Einsatz zur Sicherung der Trauerfeier und Urnenbeisetzung, 23.2.1989," in: Ibid., Bl. 61–62.

15 See Karl-Heinz Baum, "Von der stillen Grenze in ein stilles Grab," in: *Frankfurter Rundschau,* 24.2.1989; Monika Zimmermann, "Bewegter Abschied von dem jüngsten Opfer des Schiessbefehls," in: *Frankfurter Allgemeine Zeitung,* 24.2.1989, sowie *Süddeutsche Zeitung,* 24.2.1989; *Der Tagesspiegel,* 24.2.1989; *Die Tageszeitung,* 24.2.1989; *Die Welt,* 24.2.1989.

16 See "Lagefilm Nr. 54/89 des MfS/ZOS, 23.–24.2.1989," in: BStU, MfS, ZOS Nr. 31, Bd.1, Bl. 6.

17 "Offener Brief von Mitgliedern des Arbeitskreises Gerechtigkeit, der Initiativgruppe Leben, der Arbeitsgruppe Menschenrechte, des Jugendkonventes und der Arbeitsgruppe Friedensdienst an die Bevölkerung der DDR, Leipzig, 15.3.1989," in: Matthias-Domaschk-Archive, Berlin.

18 See "Strafanzeige des Anwalts von Karin Gueffroy wegen des Verdachtes der Tötung von Chris Gueffroy am 5.2.1989, 12.1.1990," in: StA Berlin, Az. 2 Js 48/90, Bd. 1, Bl. 92.

19 See "Urteil des Landgerichts Berlin in der Strafsache gegen Andreas K., Peter Sch., Mike Sch. und Ingo H., Az. (523) 2 Js 48/90 (9/91), 20.1.1992," in: StA Berlin, Az. 2 Js 48/90, Bd. 16, pp. 1–4; on this and the following see Roman Grafe, Die Prozesse wegen der Tötung des Mauerflüchtlings Chris Gueffroy, in: *Deutschland Archiv* 37 (2004), pp. 977–982.

20 "Urteil des Landgerichts Berlin in der Strafsache gegen Andreas K., Peter Sch., Mike Sch. und Ingo H., Az. (523) 2 Js 48/90 (9/91), vom 20.1.1992," in: StA Berlin, Az. 2 Js 48/90, Bd. 16, p. 185.

21 See "Urteil des Bundesgerichtshof in der Strafsache gegen Andreas K., Peter Sch., Mike Sch. und Ingo H., Az. 5 StR 418/92, vom 25.3.1993," in: StA Berlin, Az. 2 Js 48/90, Bd. 18, Bl. 102 ff.; "Urteil des Landgerichts Berlin in der Strafsache gegen Mike Sch. und Ingo H., Az. (527) 2 Js 48/90 Ks (3/93), vom 14.3.1994," in: StA Berlin, Az. 2 Js 48/90, Bd. 19, Bl. 59 ff. The verdicts in the Gueffroy case are documented in: Klaus Marxen/Gerhard Werle (eds.), *Gewalttaten an der deutsch-deutschen Grenze,* Bd. 2, 1. Teilband, Berlin, 2002, pp. 5–101.

22 See "Urteil des Bundesgerichtshof in der Strafsache gegen Andreas K., Peter Sch., Mike Sch. und Ingo H., Az. 5 StR 418/92, vom 25.3.1993," in: StA Berlin, Az. 2 Js 48/90, Bd. 18, Bl. 140.

23 "Niederschrift des Stellvertreters des Chefs und Chefs des Stabes der DDR-Grenztruppen, Generalmajor Teichmann, über die Rücksprache beim Minister für Nationale Verteidigung, i. V. Generaloberst Streletz, am 3.4.1989, 4.4.1989," in: BStU, MfS, HA I Nr. 5753, Bl. 2–5.

Winfried Freudenberg

born on August 29, 1956

fatally injured on March 8, 1989
in a hot-air balloon crash in Berlin-Zehlendorf
after flying over the sector border between
Berlin-Pankow and Berlin-Reinickendorf

Winfried Freudenberg was born on August 29, 1956 in Osterwieck in the Harz mountains and grew up in the Saxony-Anhalt community of Lüttgenrode, which was located close to the inner-German border. After completing an electrician apprenticeship, he took evening classes at the Halberstadt adult education center to acquire his high school degree. He then studied information technology in Ilmenau and graduated with an electrical engineering degree.[1]

He met the chemistry student Sabine W. in a student club. The young couple married in the fall of 1988 but soon recognized that few career prospects awaited them in East Germany. The two young adults were no longer willing to accept that the state denied them the opportunity to "travel, attend conferences, conduct research and have contact with people in the western countries," Sabine Freudenberg explained later.

The fact that he had lived within the border area, right by the barbed wire, "just a few hundred meters from another country that he could never enter," had strongly influenced her husband's desire for freedom.[2]

During a visit to relatives in West Germany two weeks before his wedding, Winfried Freudenberg expressed a determination to leave East Germany, but not without his wife.[3] Right after the wedding the couple began planning their escape with a gas balloon. To obtain the necessary natural gas needed for the balloon, Winfried Freudenberg took a job at an energy combine in the gas supply department and moved with his wife to an apartment in the East Berlin district of Prenzlauer Berg. The couple bought small, inconspicuous amounts of polyethylene sheets, a material commonly used for cold-frame windows and for tents. By taping 13-meter-long and two-and-a-half-meter-wide strips of the material with a special adhesive foil, the Freudenbergs began assembling a balloon, 13 meters high and 11 meters in diameter, in their apartment in January 1989. They wrapped the balloon in a net made of packaging string.[4]

Winfried Freudenberg chose not to have any contact with his relatives while they were constructing the balloon – behavior which puzzled them at the time. In retrospect they understand that he had wanted to protect them from having any knowledge about the escape plan since this might have gotten them into trouble with the authorities. By February the couple had completed all the preparations and began waiting for favorable wind conditions.

A moderate northeast wind was blowing on the evening of March 7.[5] The Freudenbergs packed the balloon, ballast and everything else that they wanted to take with them into a Trabant and drove to a Berlin gas supply control station near the Blankenburg S-Bahn station in the north of Berlin. Winfried Freudenberg had a key to the facility that he needed for his job. Just before midnight he began tapping gas from the station and filling the balloon with natural gas. The balloon slowly began to fill up, and a good hour later was clearly visible in the dark.

The flight with the balloon probably would have succeeded if it had not been for a young worker who was working as a part-time waiter. He had just gotten off work at 1:30 in the morning and was on his way home when he saw the balloon from a distance of about 500 to 600 meters. He knew that "East German citizens had managed to get away using a balloon" in the past and he later testified that this is what led him to notify the East German police.[6]

It was just past 2 a.m. when a police car slowed down in front of the grounds of the control station. Fearing that the balloon did not yet have enough gas to carry two people, they decided that Winfried Freudenberg should take off by himself. He cut the tether cables and rose up into the night sky. Shortly after launching, the ballast bags rubbed against a high-voltage cable striking sparks and causing a blackout in the neighboring garden settlement. Because gas was leaking, the East German policemen decided against shooting at the fugitive. They feared that the gas might cause an explosion.[7]

The hasty take-off had unexpected consequences. Without the weight of his wife, Winfried Freudenberg rose much faster and higher than he had intended. A reconstruction of his flight route concluded that he flew over the border to West Berlin unnoticed at 20 kilometers an hour and arrived at the Tegel air field where he probably tried to land. But the release cord that was supposed to allow the balloon to open and sink appeared initially not to have functioned. He either lost ballast or he threw it down to the airport to draw attention to his emergency situation. But this loss of weight caused him to rise even higher. Over Tegel he got caught in a northern current, and evidence suggests that he had reached an altitude of at least 2000 meters since that was the height at which this other wind direction was noticeable. Winfried Freudenberg had calculated that the flight would take a good half hour – instead he was aloft for many hours. Floating at great heights and in freezing temperatures, he cowered over a wooden post above Berlin, first traveling westward, then southward. At daybreak a pedestrian saw him floating over the Teufelsberg hill and thought it was a weather balloon.

At approximately 7:30 in the morning, Winfried Freudenberg flew over the West Berlin district of Zehlendorf. Just another few hundred meters and he would have reached Kleinmachnow and been back in East German territory. The exact cause of the crash is not known, but the West Berlin police surmised that he had in the end managed to let out enough gas to cause the balloon to descend rapidly. Wind currents gave him another boost upward making the balloon brake suddenly. This, in turn, spun Winfried Freudenberg out of his position and caused him to fall to the ground.[8] The empty balloon landed in the branches of a tree on Potsdamer Chaussee at the corner of Spanische Allee. Winfried Freudenberg crashed down into the garden of a villa just a few hundred meters away. Almost every bone in his body was broken and no internal organ was left uninjured. He died immediately.

Two men from the East German secret police were waiting for Sabine Freudenberg when she arrived at their apartment in Prenzlauer Berg in the early morning. Personal documents had flown out of the balloon at take-off revealing the couple's identity and address. Sabine Freudenberg was arrested and interrogated. She was charged with "attempting to breach the border."

At the same time the East German secret police opened a comprehensive control and surveillance operation against everyone acquainted with the Freudenbergs, including against relatives in the East and in the West, against friends, acquaintances and colleagues from their neighborhood and workplace. They also attempted to investigate western journalists and prevent them from reporting from East Germany.[9] But the effectiveness of all these measures was minimized by the immense shock that this daring escape attempt and its fatal end caused in both the West and the East. Just a few weeks earlier, the East German leaders had signed the Vienna CSCE document which obliged them to respect the right of every individual to leave any country, including his own, and allow for the right of that individual to return to his own country unhindered. The document obliged the country to not only legally guarantee this right, but also to have its implementation monitored.[10] Despite all the counter-measure plans developed by the Stasi, the East German leadership was still having to defend itself to the international world just as it had after Chris Gueffroy was murdered. It was also impossible for the Stasi to keep its dealings with Winfried Freudenberg's wife a secret.

The attorney's office Vogel, which represented Sabine Freudenberg, suggested that the West German federal government might be willing to pay ransom for her release to the West, but she rejected this option. In the end she was sentenced to "only" three years probation. She received amnesty on October 27, 1989.[11]

Winfried Freudenberg's body was delivered from West Berlin to East Berlin on April 7, 1989. An autopsy was conducted in the Institute of Forensic Medicine of Humboldt University after which the body was cremated. Winfried Freudenberg was buried on April 24, 1989 in Lüttgenrode amidst immense public sympathy and under the conspiratorial surveillance of the East German secret police. "Measures to prevent hostile negative activities in connection with the funeral were introduced. Their effectiveness benefited from the favorable burial location within the border security area."[12]

This kind of burial and advantageous situation would not present itself again. Winfried Freudenberg was the last person to die in Berlin as a consequence of the Berlin Wall, which fell exactly eight months and one day after his tragic accident.

Martin Ahrends / Udo Baron / Hans-Hermann Hertle

1   See "Handgeschriebener Lebenslauf von Winfried Freudenberg vom 20.6.1983," in: BStU, Ast. Berlin, AU 5302/89, Bd. 1, Bl. 169.

2   Zit. nach: Ursula von Bentheim, "Mit dem Wind in den Tod," in: *Berliner Morgenpost,* 14.4. (part 1), 15.4. (part 2) and 18.4.1990 (part 3), here part 2.

3   See "Bericht der West-Berliner Polizei, 14.3.1989," in: StA Berlin, Az. 6 AR 162/91, Bd. 2, Bl. 90–91.

4   See "Erklärung zur Herstellung eines Ballons, 9.3.1989," in: BStU, Ast. Berlin, AU 3901/89, Bl. 221; see also "Information Nr. 111/89 des MfS-ZAIG an Erich Honecker u.a. über das ungesetzliche Verlassen der DDR durch eine männliche Person mittels Gasballon nach Westberlin am 8. März 1989, 9.3.1989 [signed by Erich Honecker]," in: BStU, MfS, ZAIG Nr. 3745, Bl. 1–5.

5   On the following see the three-part series from Ursula von Bentheim, "Mit dem Wind in den Tod," in: *Berliner Morgenpost,* 14.4., 15.4. and 18.4.1990, and Hans Michael Kloth, "Sterben bis zum Schluss," in: *Der Spiegel* Nr. 32, 6.8.2001, pp. 74–75.

6   See "Zeugenvernehmungsprotokoll des Passanten durch die BVfS Berlin, 13.3.1989," in: BStU, Ast. Berlin, AOP 5119/89, Bd. 1, Bl. 81–83, here Bl. 82; see also "Zeugenvernehmungsprotokoll des Passanten durch die Ost-Berliner Volkspolizei, 8.3.1989," in: BStU, Ast. Berlin, AU 3901/89, Bd. 2, Bl. 3–5.

7   "Zeugenvernehmungsprotokoll eines beteiligten Volkspolizisten der VPI Pankow durch die Ost-Berliner Volkspolizei, 8.3.1989," in: BStU, Ast. Berlin, AU 3901/89, Bd. 2, Bl. 10–12, here Bl. 12; see also "Eröffnungsbericht der BVfS Berlin/Abteilung VII zum Operativen Vorgang "Regler", 10.3.1989," in: BStU, Ast. Berlin, AOP 5119/89, Bd. 1, Bl. 7.

8   See "Bericht der West-Berliner Polizei, 14.3.1989," in: StA Berlin, Az. 6 AR 162/91, Bd. 2, Bl. 95–103; *Berliner Morgenpost,* 10.3.1989.

9   "Operativplan der BVfS Berlin/Abteilung VII zum Operativen Vorgang "Regler", 14.3.1989," in: BStU, Ast. Berlin, AOP 5119/89, Bd. 1, Bl. 9–13.

10 See "Konferenz über Sicherheit und Zusammenarbeit in Europa, Abschließendes Dokument des Wiener KSZE-Folgetreffens, Wien, 15. Januar 1989," dok. in: *Deutschland Archiv* 4/1989, pp. 467 ff.

11 See *Berliner Morgenpost,* 18.4.1990.

12 See "MfS-Vermerk [vermutlich MfS/HA IX], 11.4.1989," in: BStU, MfS, Sekr. Neiber Nr. 498, Bl. 40.

**East German border soldiers who were killed by military deserters,
fellow soldiers, fugitives, an escape helper or a West Berlin policeman
while on duty**

Jörgen Schmidtchen

born on June 28, 1941

shot dead on April 18, 1962
at Gleisdreieck Griebnitzsee
on the outer ring between
Potsdam-Babelsberg and Berlin-Zehlendorf

The military border regime established by the East German leadership at the Berlin Wall did not only frighten people off: It bred counterviolence. In individual cases, fugitives, military deserters and escape helpers assisting others to flee used weapons against border guards in securing passage to West Berlin. There were also incidents in which members of the armed units guarding the border fortifications in and around Berlin were killed or injured. Jörgen Schmidtchen was the first border policeman to die while on duty at the border with West Berlin after the Wall was built.

He was shot by the cadet Peter Böhme who, with his comrade Wolfgang G., had tried to flee from Potsdam to West Berlin on the night leading into April 18, 1962.[1] The official version of what happened, a "legend" publicized with great fanfare in East Germany, claimed that Jörgen Schmidtchen was "murdered by an agent while trying to prevent an armed border breach."[2] During the East German era, he was celebrated as a martyr who had sacrificed his life for peace and fatherland. The following words were spoken at his military memorial service: "Our fallen comrade knew how important his duty was to preserving freedom. And he fulfilled this task conscientiously up to the last beat of his heart, thereby adding a glorious chapter to Socialist heroism. All your comrades will emulate you. Many border soldiers will be trained to follow your example of boldness, courage and heroism. [...] You will live on through our deeds."[3]

The real Jörgen Schmidtchen got lost amid this kind of exploitative propaganda. Born and raised in Leipzig, according to official records, he began an apprenticeship as a galvanizer after finishing school. He then worked as a skilled laborer for the state-owned industrial plant in Ludwigsfelde, where he was distinguished as a young activist.[4] At the age of 19 he signed up to serve with the German Border Police. He was assigned to the "Grenzbereitschaft Blankenfelde," a police unit stationed in the south of Berlin that was responsible for guarding the border region between West Berlin and the East German district of Potsdam.

On the night leading into April 18, 1962, Jörgen Schmidtchen, who had achieved the rank of private, had been assigned to guard duty with the soldier R. in Potsdam-

Babelsberg at a post called "Gleisdreieck." They began their shift at one o'clock in the morning on the inoperative S-Bahn grounds at the border to the West Berlin housing settlement "Kohlhasenbrück." Before starting duty they were informed that there was a search being conducted in Potsdam and its environs for two armed members of the NVA [National People's Army] who had disappeared from an officers' school. Evidently, when the guard leader Schmidtchen and his junior guard R. heard a noise at around 2:30 a.m., they did not make any connection to this warning. They left the former railway gatehouse they had been in to check out the situation and came upon two men in uniform. Later the soldier R. reported that Schmidtchen had assumed the two men were on duty patrol. He approached them unsuspectingly and spoke to them. Suddenly shots were fired.[5] Later it was determined that the bullets had come from the weapon of the 19-year-old cadet Peter Böhme, who had wanted to flee to West Berlin with his comrade, Wolfgang G.[6] Jörgen Schmidtchen fell to the ground and presumably died immediately. After the soldier R. returned fire, a shoot-out ensued during which Peter Böhme was also fatally wounded. Wolfgang G. however, remained uninjured and was able to make it safely to West Berlin. The next day he was quoted in the press as saying: "It was horrible. But we had no other choice. It was us or them."[7]

The commander of the 2nd Border Brigade to which Schmidtchen belonged concluded in his investigation report that Schmidtchen had acted imprudently. "The guard leader's conduct was not in accordance with the circumstances at hand given the fact that the border guards had received detailed information about the situation, in particular about the search measures, and that the deserters were armed. His unguarded approach to the alleged duty guards demonstrates this."[8]

Not a single critical word was spoken externally by the military leadership about Jörgen Schmidtchen. A day after he died he was promoted to sergeant "for fulfilling his duty to secure the state border in an exemplary fashion." His parents received a one-time payment of 500 marks for financial support.[9] The funeral at the Leipzig-Schönefeld Cemetery was carried out with all the military honors. Over the following years streets and schools were named after Jörgen Schmidtchen, including the 33rd Polytechnic secondary school in Potsdam. As part of the border troops' effort to foster tradition, commemorating a border soldier who was killed on duty was considered a high priority. In the "Walter Junker" troop formation, a memorial room and commemorative grove were established to remind future generations of border soldiers guarding the Wall between Potsdam and West Berlin that Jörgen Schmidtchen was one of the "unforgotten heroes of the East German troops."[10]

Christine Brecht

1 See the biography of Peter Böhme in this book.
2 "Aufstellung der NVA/Stadtkommandantur Berlin/Abt. Operativ über von Westberliner Banditen ermordete bzw. verletzte Grenzsoldaten, 9.9.1966," in: BArch, VA-07/6008, Bl. 358.
3 "Er lebt in unseren Taten weiter," in: Volksarmee, Wochenblatt der NVA, Nr. 28, Juli 1963.
4 See "Er fiel beim Schutz des Friedens. Vor 25 Jahren wurde Jörgen Schmidtchen an der Staatsgrenze ermordet," in: Märkische Volksstimme, 18.4.1987.

5 See "Bericht der NVA/Bepo/2.GB (B)/Der Kommandeur betr. schwerer Grenzdurchbruch unter Anwendung der Schusswaffe und mit tödlichem Ausgang, 18.4.1962," in: BArch, VA-07/8370, Bl. 129–135.

6 See "Verfügung der Staatsanwaltschaft bei dem Kammergericht [2 Js 150/90], 18.8.1992," in: StA Berlin, Az. 2 Js 150/90, Bd. 2, Bl. 202–207.

7 "Sterbender gab Feuerschutz," in: *BZ,* 19.4.1962.

8 "Bericht der NVA/Bepo/2.GB (B)/Der Kommandeur betr. schwerer Grenzdurchbruch unter Anwendung der Schusswaffe und mit tödlichem Ausgang, 18.4.1962," in: BArch, VA-07/8370, Bl. 135.

9 "Befehl Nr. 43/62 des MdI/Kommando/Bepo zur Beförderung und Prämierung bei der Bereitschaftspolizei, 19.4.1962," in: StA Berlin, Az. 2 Js 150/90, Bd. 3, Bl. 111.

10 "Plötzlich hallten Schüsse an der Grenze. 25. Jahrestag der Ermordung des Unteroffiziers Schmidtchen", in: *Brandenburgische Neueste Nachrichten,* 18./19.4.1987.

Peter Göring

born on December 28, 1940

killed accidentally by a ricochet bullet on May 23, 1962
at the Spandauer Schifffahrts Canal
near the Sandkrug Bridge
on the sector border between
Berlin-Mitte and Berlin-Tiergarten

The news that there had been an armed conflict between East Berlin border guards and West Berlin policemen at the Spandauer Schifffahrts Canal spread like wildfire across both sides of the city. Members of the 1st Border Brigade opened fire on the 14-year-old Wilfried Tews from Erfurt to stop him from escaping. He was seriously injured before he could be pulled onto the western bank.[1] When the border guards' bullets struck West Berlin, the police officers there provided the fugitive with covering fire. The 21-year-old border guard Peter Göring was fatally injured by a ricochet bullet.

Given the ongoing East-West confrontation, Peter Göring's death was politically explosive. The East German leadership reacted aggressively, placing the blame on the West Berlin Senate. It publicized a photo of the dead man lying on the ground and announced that he had been a murder victim of the "Frontstadt-OAS," a reference to the terror attacks of nationalist French Algerians.[2] One propaganda poster proclaimed that, with this "assassination," the "reactionary forces and their henchmen in the form of the front city police" once again demonstrated that they were "the enemy of our people."[3] Hand in hand with the damning of the enemy came the glorification of the dead man from their own ranks. It was propagated that "Peter Göring was young and had loved life, which is why he stood guard at the East German state border in Berlin."[4]

In a radio speech, Willy Brandt, the mayor of Berlin, expressed his support for the police officer who had assisted the defenseless fugitive. He also expressed his regret over the death of the border policeman. Peter Göring, he said, was a new victim of the Wall. "We don't know what kind of man he was since the clichés and slogans of the other side do not tell us anything. But responsibility for his fate lies with those who built the Wall."[5]

The official version of Peter Göring's life that was publicized throughout East Germany was, in fact, both vague and portentous.[6] Born in December 1940 to a working-class family in Dresden, Peter Göring was young when he experienced the hardships of a war that cost his father his life. He grew up in Dresden in a children's home named "Weisser Hirsch." After finishing school he completed an apprenticeship as a cast fettler. He then began agriculture work in response to the party's appeal to young workers to work the land. In April 1960, he apparently enlisted voluntarily to serve "honorary duty" with the "armed organs" of East Germany. He was transferred in June of the following year to the "anti-fascist protective wall" and, because of his readiness to serve, remained a role model for all comrades.[7] As a token of appreciation, he was posthumously promoted from private to sergeant. The inscription on the gravestone that Peter Göring was given after his state funeral in Luchau, Saxony advanced this view further: "He was shot perfidiously by West Berlin police while faithfully fulfilling his duty to protect the state border in Berlin."[8] Peter Göring's mother was also integrated into the official commemoration of her son and continued to participate actively in it her entire life.[9]

Official documents from the East and West, however, show that the murder claim was a fabrication. Military and judiciary files, which were under lock and key in East Germany, prove without a doubt that Peter Göring was actively involved in the exchange of fire and was fatally hit while firing directly at the fugitive Wilfried Tews. In doing so, Göring violated the regulations that forbade arms from being used against children or directed at the West. Moreover, in opposition to the clear orders of his post leader, he left his watchtower in order to get into a better shooting position.[10] West Berlin investigation files reveal that on the other side of the canal, a police officer noticed the border guard who was shooting at that moment. The protocol stated that because the West Berlin officer felt threatened, he returned the fire, "upon which the Vopo [East German policeman] suddenly disappeared and presumably was fatally hit."[11]

The exchange of fire was in full swing when he was shot. After the sound of the last shot trailed off, the lifeless body of the border guard was found between two walls that blocked access to the river bank.[12] The forensic investigation in East Berlin determined that the bullets that hit and killed Peter Göring had not been fired directly. The injuries were caused by a ricochet bullet that had bounced off one of the walls.[13]

The investigation was re-opened in the 1990s. Whatever charges had been made against the West Berlin policeman who was believed to have fatally injured Peter Göring were dropped in July 1991 with the explanation that since he had fired his gun to protect himself and the fugitive, his conduct was justified as an act of self-defense and emergency assistance.[14] Three former East German guards were accused of attempted manslaughter of the fugitive Wilfried Tews, which led to a trial in June 1996.[15] But during the main proceedings the court was unable to determine which guard had fired the shots and the defendants were acquitted.[16]

The court concluded in its decision that the shots that injured Wilfried Tews, causing him to suffer from their consequences for the rest of his life, may even have been fired by Peter Göring. But this could not be proven with any certainty.

Christine Brecht

1 See "Schwerer Grenzzwischenfall am Humboldt-Hafen," in: *Die Welt,* 24.5.1962; "Vopo-Opfer kämpft mit dem Tode," in: *BZ,* 25.5.1962.

2 See "Blutige Provokation an der Staatsgrenze," in: *Neues Deutschland,* 24.5.1962, and "Mordüberfall der Frontstadt-OAS. Zorn erfüllt unser Land," in: *Neues Deutschland,* 25.5.1962. The abbreviation OAS stands for "Organisation de l' Armée Secrète." Founded in April 1961 under the leadership of generals of the French Algerian Army, the OAS used terror attacks in France to fight against the de-colonization of Algeria.

3 "Peter Göring durch Frontstadt-OAS ermordet," Plakat der Politabteilung der 1. Grenzbrigade, o.D. [Mai 1962], in: BArch, DY 30/IV 2/12/75, Bl. 248.

4 "Gefallen im Ersten Weltkrieg? Gefallen im Zweiten Weltkrieg?," Plakat, o.D. [Mai 1962], Archive of the Berlin Wall Foundation.

5 "Abschrift eines Schreibens von Heinrich Albertz/Innensenator West-Berlin (darin Abschrift von einem Redebeitrag von Willy Brandt am 27.5.1962 in der RIAS-Sendung "Wo uns der Schuh drückt"), o.D. [Mai 1962]," in: BStU, MfS, ZAIG Nr. 101713, Bl. 102–104, here Bl. 103.

6 The authors Thomas Brasch and Lothar Trolle used this material in 1971 in their bitingly ironic play titled "The Exemplary Life and Death of Peter Göring. Biography of a Happy Citizen." The play was promptly banned after its premier.

7 See BArch, GTÜ/AZN 663, n. pag., and "Ein blühendes Menschenleben ist nicht mehr," in: *Neues Deutschland,* 25.5.1962.

8 See "Bericht des MdI/Bepo/1.GB (B)/Kommandeur betr. Errichtung eines Grabsteines für den durch Westberliner Polizeiangehörige ermordeten Genossen Unteroffizier Peter Göring, 4.6.1962," in: BArch, DY 30/IV 2/12/75, Bl. 285–287, here Bl. 287.

9 See "Mutter Peter Görings zu Gast im VPKA," in: *Neuer Tag,* 1.4.1981.

10 See "Spitzenmeldung des MdI/Bepo/1.GB (B)/O.p.D. betr. verbrecherische Provokation Westberliner Polizeikräfte mit Anwendung der Schusswaffe gegen eigene Grenzsicherungskräfte, 23.5.1962," in: BArch, VA-07/8400, Bl. 2, and "Bericht des MdI/Bepo/1.GB (B) zum Vorkommnis in der 2. Kompanie der III. GA am 25.5.1962 um 17.35 Uhr," in: Ibid., Bl. 6–8.

11 "Abschrift aus dem Tagebuch des am Schusswechsel beteiligten West-Berliner Polizisten des RKB 27, 23.5.1962," in: StA Berlin, Az. 2 Js 102/91, Bd. 2, Bl. 9. See also "Niederschrift der Vernehmung des am Schusswechsel beteiligten West-Berliner Polizisten durch die West-Berliner Polizei, 24.5.1962," in: Ibid., Bl. 17–20.

12 "Bericht des MdI/Bepo/1.GB (B) zum Vorkommnis in der 2. Kompanie der III. GA am 25.5.1962 um 17.35 Uhr," in: BArch, VA-07/8400, Bl. 8.

13 See "Schlussbericht [des MfS]/Abt. K/Dez.U/Mordkommission, 23.6.1962," in: BStU, Ast. Potsdam AKK Nr. 1672/82, Bl. 23–31, here Bl. 28–29.

14 See "Ermittlungen gegen westliche Todesschützen," in: *Süddeutsche Zeitung,* 8.7.1991; "West-Berliner Polizist schoss in Notwehr," in: *Berliner Morgenpost,* 13.7.1991.

15 See "Anklageschrift der Staatsanwaltschaft II bei dem Landgericht Berlin (27/2 Js 102/91), 24.6.1996," in: StA Berlin, Az. 2772 Js 102/91, Bd. 5, Bl. 130–173.

16 See "Urteil des Landgerichts Berlin vom 14.6.2002," in: Ibid., Bd. 7, Bl. 103–147.

Reinhold Huhn

born on March 8, 1942

shot dead on June 18, 1962
on the corner of Jerusalemer Strasse / Zimmerstrasse
on the sector border between
Berlin-Mitte and Berlin-Kreuzberg

Reinhold Huhn was the youngest child of a farmer family living in Braunsberg, East Prussia. His mother died in an accident when he was three years old. At the end of 1946 the family was forced to leave East Prussia, which then belonged to Poland, and find a new home in Adorf, in Vogtland. After completing his schooling, Reinhold Huhn trained to become a cattle breeder and later worked on a state-owned farm in the Plauen district. When he was 18 he enlisted with the police force and began his service in Karl-Marx-Stadt – now Chemnitz – in September 1960. In June 1961 his unit was transferred to East Berlin and involved in constructing the Wall. Afterwards he belonged to the East Berlin border brigade.[1]

On the afternoon of June 18, 1962, Reinhold Huhn, as a guard of the 4th Border Division, was stationed in the middle of the city at the corner of Jerusalemer Strasse and Zimmerstrasse. The border fortifications here ran right through Berlin's former newspaper district. Not far away on the West Berlin side, the Springer Verlag was building its new publishing house. Reinhold Huhn had been standing guard at the border strip with his guard leader, Private H., since 3 p.m. that day.[2] At about 5:20 p.m. they saw a man approaching from the East Berlin border house at Zimmerstrasse 56.[3] The building, blocked off with barbed wire fencing, was still inhabited on the upper levels, but the ground floor had already been evacuated and the front door was sealed shut. The building could only be entered from the back courtyard on Jerusalemer Strasse. Since the man was heading towards the East Berlin city center, the two border guards were not suspicious at first. But when he returned an hour later with two women and two children, the guard leader ordered Reinhold Huhn to conduct an identity check. He approached the people in the border strip and demanded through the security fence that they show their papers.

The man who had been observed by the border guards was named Rudolf Müller. He was a former border-crosser (someone who commuted across the border daily to work) and had lived apart from his family in West Berlin ever since the Wall had been built. He was planning to bring his wife, their two children and his sister-in-law through a tunnel to the west side of the city that afternoon. After other escape plans had failed, he dug underground for many weeks with his brothers and other helpers until the tunnel, which ran from the grounds of the Springer Verlag to the basement of the building at Zimmerstrasse 56, was finished.[4] Rudolf Müller later described what happened: When Reinhold Huhn approached the small group, Rudolf Müller had his family continue on. To dissuade the young border guard from carrying out his security check, he told him that they were on their way to a birthday party.[5] But when the guard went to carry out his orders anyway, Rudolf Müller reached into the inner pocket of his jacket, pulled out his pistol and pulled the trigger. Hit in the chest at close range, Reinhold Huhn fell down and bled to death.[6] The guard leader H. immediately opened fire on the fugitives, who still were able to get through the tunnel and reach West Berlin safely.

Two days later the East Berlin authorities demanded Rudolf Müller's extradition.[7] They had no doubt that he was responsible for the death of Reinhold Huhn. The West Berlin Senate aligned itself with Rudolf Müller, who was immediately flown to West Germany with his family.[8]

Rudolf Müller told the West Berlin police that he had only hit the border guard, causing him to fall down, and that the fatal shot had come from the other border soldier who had shot at the fugitives. Believing Rudolf Müller's version of the events, the western media accused the second guard of having killed his comrade, depicting him as a "trigger-happy Vopo" [East German policeman].[9] The investigation opened in West Berlin against Rudolf Müller was closed in November 1962.[10]

East Germany chose to see a malicious act of murder and declared Reinhold Huhn a victim of western warmongers.[11] The Communist Party had all the East Berlin border units conduct roll calls and assemblies during which it was claimed that "the cowardly and malicious murder attack" had been ordered directly by Adenauer and Brandt and was the "fault of the blood-stained German military."[12]

The border troop leaders were instructed to organize a politically demonstrative funeral ceremony.[13] Reinhold Huhn's body was laid out in the barracks of his unit in Berlin-Rummelsburg. Soldiers, officers and delegates from factories and schools were called on to bid farewell at the open coffin. Reinhold Huhn was buried in his hometown of Adorf in Saxony with military honors.[14]

A year later the East Berlin city commander Poppe dedicated a memorial plaque at the site where Reinhold Huhn had been shot.[15] In the 1970s this site on Jerusalemer Strasse was expanded into a central memorial for border soldiers who died while serving at the Berlin Wall. Schützenstrasse, a nearby street, was renamed Reinhold-Huhn-Strasse in 1966. After East Germany ceased to exist, the memorial was removed and Reinhold-Huhn-Strasse again became Schützenstrasse.

At the end of the nineties, the death of Reinhold Huhn once again made the headlines. Following a long and drawn out trial, Rudolf Müller was charged by the Berlin district court in April 1999 with manslaughter and sentenced to a year in prison commuted to probation.[16] In the main court proceedings, he admitted to having shot Reinhold Huhn, but claimed it was in self-defense. The court, however, came to the conclusion that the act was not justified by either self-defense or emergency assistance to others. According to the verdict, Reinhard Huhn at no time threatened the life and health of Rudolf Müller and his family.

Both the convicted man and the relatives of Reinhold Huhn appealed the decision. Rudolf Müller hoped to be acquitted; Reinhold Huhn's relatives said they wanted a just evaluation of the crime. In 2000 the Federal Court of Justice revised the verdict, finding Rudolf Müller guilty of murder, but it did not change the original sentence. The court found that "in the concrete crime situation in which the border guard wanted only to perform a security check, it recognized malice, an objective prerequisite characteristic of murder" and pointed out the "outstanding significance of the legally protected right to life."[17]

The court's decision remains controversial today. Rudolf Müller felt that the conviction equated him with a cold-blooded murderer. Reinhold Huhn's relatives could not understand the mild sentence, given the legal assessment of the crime.[18] The chief judge's hope that she had found a "penalty that would satisfy" all was not fulfilled.[19]

Christine Brecht / Maria Nooke

1 See "Chronik der IV. Grenzabteilung/1.GB, 24.6.1961 bis 31.12.1962," in: BArch, VA-07/16661, Bl. 105.

2 See "Niederschrift der Zeugenvernehmung des Postenführers von Reinhold Huhn durch die Mordkommission der Volkspolizei (Abt. K/Dez.U), 19.6.1962," in: BStU, MfS, AU 23/85, Nr. XV/2807/62 (Untersuchungsvorgang Rudolf Müller), Bl. 131-137.

3 See "Bericht des MdI/Bepo/1.GB (B)/Kommandeur über den Mordanschlag auf einen Grenzposten der IV. Grenzabteilung am 18.6.1962 in der Jerusalemer Strasse, 19.6.1962," in: BArch, VA-07/16925, Bl. 10-17, here Bl. 12, and the extensive collection of reports, plans and photos, in: BArch, VA-07/8400, Bl. 50-112.

4 See Rudolf Müller, *Tunnelflucht in Berlin,* Norderstedt, 2007.

5 "Bericht der West-Berliner Polizei, 4.7.1962, Ermittlungsverfahren gegen Rudolf Müller," in: StA Berlin, StA 27/2 Js 281/93, Bd. 1, Bl. 38-39. On the course of events see also Dietmar Arnold/Sven Felix Kellerhoff, *Die Fluchttunnel von Berlin,* Berlin, 2008, p. 99.

6 See "Urteil des Landgerichts Berlin vom 22.4.1999 (Az. 1 Kap Js 1422/90 KS)," in: StA Berlin, StA 27/2 Js 281/93, Bd. 3, n. pag.

7 See "Senat stellt sich vor Fluchthelfer," in: *Der Tagesspiegel,* 21.6.1962.

8 See "Fluchthelfer auf Bewährung verurteilt," in: *Frankfurter Rundschau,* 23.4.1999.

9 See press reports, such as "Vopos erschossen den eigenen Kameraden," in: *Berliner Morgenpost,* 19.6.1962; "Schiesswütige Vopos töten eigenen Posten," in: *Der Tagesspiegel,* 19.6.1962.

10 See "Beglaubigte Abschrift der Verfügung vom 28. November 1962 aus 2P Js 841/62 der Staatsanwaltschaft bei dem Landgericht Berlin, Ermittlungssache gegen Müller, Rudolf wegen Mord, Bl. 44-46," in: StA Berlin, StA 27/2 Js 281/93, Bd. 1, Bl. 52-56.

11 See, for example, "Mitteilung der Pressestelle des MdI (ADN), o.D. [19.6.1962]," in: BArch, VA-07/8400, Bl. 77, and *Neues Deutschland,* 20.6.1962.

12 "Bericht des MdI/Bepo/1.GB (B)/Politabteilung über die bisherige Auswertung der Ermordung unseres Genossen Unteroffizier Huhn, 22.6.1962," in: BArch, DY 30/IV 2/12/76, Bd. 3, Bl. 215-219, here Bl. 215.

13 See "Plan zur Aufbahrung und Überführung" (Abschrift), 20.6.1962," in: BArch, VA-07/8400, Bl. 100-105.

14 See "Abschied von einem treuen Sohn der DDR," in: *Neues Deutschland,* 23.6.1962.

15 See "Gedenktafel für Reinhold Huhn," in: *Neues Deutschland,* 13.1.1963; "Sie gaben ihr Leben für unseren Frieden," in: *Neues Deutschland,* 14.8.1966.

16 See "Urteil des Landgerichts Berlin gegen Rudolf Müller vom 22.4.1999 (Az. 1 Kap Js 1422/90 KS)," in: StA Berlin, StA 27/2 Js 281/93, Bd. 3, n. pag.; "Todesschütze in Fall Huhn verurteilt," in: *Berliner Zeitung,* 23.4.1999; "Fluchthelfer auf Bewährung verurteilt," in: *Berliner Morgenpost,* 23.4.1999.

17 See excerpts from the verdicts of the Federal Court of Justice from 5.7.2000, published in: *Neue Juristische Wochenschrift* 2000, Heft 41, p. 3079.

18 Conversation conducted by Maria Nooke with a brother of Reinhold Huhn, 26.1.2009.

19 See "Schüsse auf DDR-Grenzer waren Mord," in: *Süddeutsche Zeitung,* 6.7.2000.

Günter Seling

born on April 28, 1940

shot on September 29, 1962
in Teltow-Seehof at the southwest outer ring
died from his bullet wounds
on September 30, 1962

"It has now been announced that a member of the Soviet zone border troops was buried with military honors last Friday at the Stahnsdorf Cemetery near Berlin. The soldier was shot by a comrade who, due to the thick fog, mistook him for a fugitive."[1] That was how the West German newspaper "Die Welt" reported the death of an East German border soldier in October 1962. In the "Tagesspiegel," a West Berlin paper, it was noted: "The West Information Office has reported that last Friday a member of the Soviet zone border troops was buried with 'military honors' at the cemetery in Stahnsdorf near Berlin. He was shot early Tuesday morning by a comrade on duty who, because of the thick fog, assumed that he was a fugitive and shot him."[2]

The victim, 22-year-old Sergeant Günter Seling, was born on April 28, 1940 in Stahnsdorf near Berlin, where he lived until his death. Günter Seling had been serving in the National People's Army since April 1959, having joined the military before the general draft was introduced in East Germany. At the time of his death he belonged to the Heinersdorf border military unit that was stationed on the southern edge of the city, on the border between West Berlin and Teltow.

On September 29, 1962 he had been assigned patrol duty as guard leader. The border troop reports show that at about 5 o'clock in the morning he approached the guard area of soldier W.[3] Visibility was poor; a thick fog had set in. Günter Seling's job was to conduct what was called a "post control," to check on the border guards on duty without warning to see if they were conducting themselves according to regulation. Apparently when he approached the soldier W., he made a noise to draw attention to himself. In response W., the 19-year-old soldier, loaded his machine pistol, because he thought it might be someone trying to flee.

What happened next is described differently in various documents. The report that the commander of the 2nd Border Brigade prepared for Erich Honecker, the Communist Party Politburo member responsible for security issues, stated that, as the gun was being loaded, a sheaf of fire, four bullets in total, was released from the MPi, critically injuring Sergeant Seling in his head."[4] According to this version, the shots were fired by accident.

The report of the city commander of Berlin of the previous day suggested that W. had aimed and fired the shots intentionally. The report stated that the moment Seling approached, "without calling out or firing a warning shot, W. responded to a noise with four shots of continuous fire from the MPi, thereby severely injuring Sergeant S. in the head."[5] Günter Seling was quickly taken to the nearest hospital in Kleinmachnow and operated on immediately. He died from his injuries at three in the morning.

The victim was granted a funeral "with all the military honors" while the soldier W. was taken into custody and subjected to an interrogation by the military state prosecutor for negligent use of a weapon.[6] The documents do not reveal the outcome of the proceedings. After the state of East Germany ceased to exist it was not deemed necessary to try the gunmen. The Berlin public prosecutor in charge of the preliminary investigation in 1994 saw "no indication of a deliberate killing or violent offense" and concluded that "with regard to the law," the act presents an example "merely of involuntary homicide."[7]

With hindsight and independently of the question of the soldier W.'s personal guilt, it was possible to determine that it was the special conditions at the border and in the East German border troops that had been responsible for Günter Seling's death. He was shot because he was mistaken for a fugitive when he approached the border guard. Günter Seling's death shows that the pressure on guards to prevent so-called "border breaches" and, if necessary, to use their weapons to do so, was so immense that in cases of doubt border guards even shot at their own comrades.

Border guards who succeeded in fleeing to the West in the 1960s reported on the fatal incident but did not reveal the identity of the victim. They attested that at that time the accident had been reported on at duty assemblies in the neighboring border companies. According to these reports, a soldier had accidentally shot a sergeant who he thought was a fugitive.[8] In September 1968, on the basis of witness testimonies, this death was added to the list of "victims of the Wall" maintained by the West Berlin police headquarters.[9] In contrast to the other border soldiers who were killed, Günter Seling was not publicly mourned in East Germany. Evidently, this did not appear opportune to the political and military leaders, given the circumstances of his death.

Christine Brecht

1 *Die Welt,* 11.10.1962.

2 *Der Tagesspiegel,* 11.10.1962.

3 See "Bericht der NVA/2. GB/Kommandeur an Erich Honecker betr. Sicherheitsfragen, 1.10.1962," in: BArch, DY 30/IV 2/12/77, Bd. 4, Bl. 117–118, and "Operative Tagesmeldung Nr. 34/62 der NVA/Stadtkommandantur Berlin/Operative Abt., 30.9.1962," in: BArch, VA-07/4726, Bd. 1, Bl. 1061.

4 "Bericht der NVA/2.GB/Kommandeur an Erich Honecker betr. Sicherheitsfragen, 1.10.1962," in: BArch, DY 30/IV 2/12/77, Bd. 4, Bl. 117.

5 "Operative Tagesmeldung Nr. 34/62 der NVA/Stadtkommandantur Berlin/Operative Abt., 30.9.1962," in: BArch, VA-07/4726, Bd. 1, Bl. 1061.

6 "Bericht der NVA/2.GB/Kommandeur an Erich Honecker betr. Sicherheitsfragen, 1.10.1962," in: BArch, DY 30/IV 2/12/77, Bd. 4, Bl. 118.

7 "Verfügung der Staatsanwaltschaft II bei dem Kammergericht Berlin (27 AR 45/94), 19.4.1994," in: StA Berlin, Az. 27 AR 45/94, Bl. 9.

8 See "Schreiben des GStA Braunschweig an den Generalbundesanwalt beim Bundesgerichtshof in Karlsruhe betr. Erfassung von SBS- und SBZ-Rechtsbrüchen, in: Zentrale Beweismittel- und Dokumentationsstelle der Landesjustizverwaltungen in Salzgitter, Az. I AR-ZE 949/64, Bl. 1–3," in: BArch, B 197/3180, Bl. 1–3.

9 "Vermerk der West-Berliner Polizei, 23.9.1968," in: Ibid., Bl. 9.

Siegfried Widera

born on February 12, 1941

knocked out by fugitives on August 23,
1963 near the Massante Bridge
on the sector border between
Berlin-Treptow and Berlin-Neukölln
died from his injuries on September 8, 1963

Siegfried Widera belonged to the 5th company of Border Regiment 42, which was responsible for guarding the border in the southeast of the city between the districts of Treptow and Neukölln. On the evening of August 23, 1963, the 22-year-old corporal was posted with Sergeant T. on the Massante Bridge that was blocked off by the Wall and barbed wire. At the time, canal excavation work was being carried out on the East Berlin side and construction workers were often seen working there during the day. Although the construction work had stopped in the early evening, Siegfried Widera and his junior guard did not suspect anything at 7 p.m., when three men began tampering with an excavator. They were wearing workers' suits and Sergeant T. later reported that it looked as though they were repairing the excavator.[1] In truth they were employed by a state-run company that was conducting the excavation work and had access to the border territory for a number of weeks. The workers were hoping to take advantage of this situation and flee to West Berlin. They engaged the two border guards in a conversation and soon realized that the two men were completely unsuspecting. Nonetheless, the fugitives felt they had no choice but to knock the two guards out so that they could get by them, cross the bridge and reach the other side of the city.[2]

Before they realized what was happening, Siegfried Widera and his assisting guard were knocked down with fists and an iron rod. Then the fugitives ran past the barriers on the Massante Bridge and, although the guard T. began shooting at them, they reached the West Berlin bank on the other side uninjured. The next day West Berlin press reported how they had cleverly outmaneuvered the border guards.[3] The West did not yet know that Siegfried Widera had been badly injured and was in critical condition. He had suffered a fracture to the base of the skull and died two weeks later on September 8 in the Köpenick Municipal Hospital, probably having never regained consciousness.[4]

Citing the press office of the East German Ministry of National Defense, the Communist Party newspaper, "Neues Deutschland," stated that the fatal injuries were inflicted on him by "Girrmann bandits." This baseless accusation was a reference to one of the most successful West Berlin groups involved in helping people escape to the West. But East Germany used the propaganda as a way to conceal the truth and the fact that violence had been employed against border guards. Instead, they fabricated their own version of what happened, creating a "legend" that was upheld at all the memorial events in honor of Siegfried Widera. The story stated that "wirepullers," those behind the crime, also had "Jörgen Schmidtchen, Peter Göring and Reinhold Huhn on their consciences."[5] But the concluding report of the border troop leadership clearly shows that internally the events were evaluated quite differently. It stated that Widera and the other guard had acted in violation of their orders, had been overly trustful and that this had contributed to their being besieged and to the escape operation's success.[6] This view of the situation was conveyed to the border soldiers of the unit in the obligatory "evaluation" and was incorporated into police classes to encourage discipline and alertness among the border soldiers.

Siegfried Widera, who was born in 1941 in Silesia and grew up after the war in Mansfelder Land on the edge of the Harz Mountains, was nonetheless glorified in East Germany as a hero of the "socialist fatherland." He had worked as a lathe operator, and official reports claimed that he joined the border service voluntarily in October 1960. In the annals of the East German border troops it was written that "on the historical day of August 13, 1961" he was "assigned to the anti-fascist protective barrier in Berlin" and that he always fulfilled his duty with courage and determination.[7] He was still a corporal when he died but was posthumously promoted to sergeant.[8] Siegfried Widera had been married just weeks before he died. His widow was expecting a child. During the public mourning ceremony on the market square of the mining town of Hettstedt, she was handed a letter of condolence from state and party chairman Walter Ulbricht.[9] Siegfried Widera was buried with military honors in nearby Gorenzen, his wife's hometown.

After the East German media reported in detail on the funeral ceremonies for the border soldier, the West German authorities opened an investigation against the fugitives. The men asserted that it had not been their intention to harm Widera. One of them testified that in no way had they planned to use violence. "Violence was supposed to be completely avoided. Our motto had been to get over the fence unnoticed."[10] Another stressed that "I was very unhappy to learn that a young man had to die because of my actions. [...] I am distraught by the whole thing and can't cope with it, although I know I acted in an emergency situation."[11] The charges were dropped in April 1969 because it had not been possible to prove that the fugitives' actions were premeditated or that they had committed joint homicide.[12]

After the East German state ceased to exist, the Berlin public prosecutor's office reopened the case. This time the investigation was focused on the former guard, T., who had opened fire at the fugitives although he had suffered a concussion. But based on Stasi files, it had to be assumed that he was only half conscious when he fired his weapon and thus no charges were brought against him either.[13]

Christine Brecht

447

1 See "Abschlussbericht der NVA/4.GB/Stellvertreter Rückwärtige Dienste des Kommandeurs der 4.GB zum gewaltsamen schweren Grenzdurchbruch im Grenzabschnitt 1 des GR-42, WG Massantebrücke, 24.8.1963," in: BArch, VA-07/6002, Bl. 14–19.

2 See "Niederschrift der Zeugenvernehmungen der Flüchtlinge durch die West-Berliner Polizei, 30.8.1963," in: StA Berlin, Az. 27/2 Js 666/92, Bd. 1, Bl. 11–13.

3 See "Flucht im Kugelhagel," in: *BZ,* 24.8.1963; "Grenzposten überwältigt und geflohen," in: *Spandauer Volksblatt,* 25.8.1963; "Ostberliner Grenzposten niedergeschlagen," in: *Die Welt,* 26.8.1963.

4 See "Todesanzeige für Siegfried Widera, ausgestellt vom Städtischen Krankenhaus Köpenick, 9.9.1963," in: StA Berlin, Az. 27/2 Js 666/92, Bd. 2, Bl. 8.

5 "Unteroffizier Widera von Frontstadtbanditen ermordet," in: *Neues Deutschland,* 10.9.1963. See also later commemorative articles, for example on the 15th anniversary of his death, in: *Junge Welt,* 8.9.1978, and on his 40th birthday, in: *Neues Deutschland,* 13.2.1981.

6 See "Abschlussbericht der NVA/4.GB/Stellvertreter Rückwärtige Dienste des Kommandeurs der 4. GB zum gewaltsamen schweren Grenzdurchbruch im Grenzabschnitt 1 des GR-42, WG Massantebrücke, 24.8.1963," in: BArch, VA-07/6002, Bl. 18.

7 "'Unvergessen sind, die ermordet wurden an dieser Grenze' (Unteroffizier Siegfried Widera), Festansprache des Mitgliedes des Politbüros des ZK der SED und Minister für Nationale Verteidigung, Heinz Hoffmann, zum 30. Jahrestag der GT der DDR," in: BArch, GTÜ/AZN 6653, n. pag.

8 See "Chronik der Stadtkommandantur Berlin, 23.8.1962 bis 30.11.1963," in: BArch, VA-07/3133, Bl. 96–97.

9 See media reporting on the funeral ceremonies in Hettstedt and Gorenzen, in: *Neues Deutschland,* 12.9.1963, and in: *Die Volksarmee,* Wochenzeitung der Nationalen Volksarmee, Nr. 38/1963.

10 "Niederschrift der Beschuldigten-Vernehmung von einem der Flüchtlinge durch die westdeutsche Polizei in Ludwigshafen, 11.12.1963," in: StA Berlin, Az. 27/2 Js 666/92, Bd. 1, Bl. 42–55, here Bl. 47. See also "Niederschrift der Beschuldigtenvernehmung von einem der Flüchtlinge durch die westdeutsche Polizei in Hannover, 14.2.1964," in: Ibid., Bl. 62–70.

11 "Niederschrift der Beschuldigtenvernehmung von einem der Flüchtlinge durch die westdeutsche Polizei in Ludwigshafen, 5.5.1963," in: Ibid., Bl. 72–82, here Bl. 81–82.

12 See "Verfügung des Oberstaatsanwalts von Frankenthal (9 Js 438/63), 3.4.1969," in: Ibid. Bl. 142–149.

13 See "Verfügung der Staatsanwaltschaft II bei dem Landgericht Berlin (27/2 Js 666/92), 21.10.1994," in: Ibid., Bd. 2, Bl. 157–159.

Egon Schultz

born on January 4, 1943

shot dead on October 5, 1964
in the courtyard of Strelitzer Strasse 55
on the sector border between
Berlin-Mitte and Berlin-Wedding

I n December 1964, balloons floated over the Wall onto the east side of the city near the "Checkpoint Charlie" border crossing. Fliers were attached to them with a letter to the mother of Egon Schultz, a border guard who had recently been killed. The text of the flier had been written by the escape helpers, whom the East German press a few weeks earlier had accused of murder.[1] "We speak on behalf of our group, which over the last half year built a tunnel through which 57 fugitives fled and at the entrance to which your son was shot." The composers of the letter conveyed to the mother their sympathy and described their view of what happened during the escape operation that ended with the border soldier's death. "The causative murderer is the East German secret police. These men, with great acting skill, first pretended to be fugitives. Reluctant to intervene themselves, they instead fetched the soldier and had him clarify the situation. But the real murderer is the system that addressed the massive flight of its citizens not by removing the cause of the problem, but by building a WALL and giving the order for Germans to shoot Germans."[2]

Egon Schultz was born in 1943 in Pomerania. He was seven years old when his parents moved with their two sons from Poland to East Germany. The family re-settled in Gross Stove near Rostock and moved into Rostock in 1957. Egon Schultz attended the Borwin School in Rostock through the 10th grade. During this time he developed an interest in becoming a teacher. He liked working with children and, after he joined the FDJ, the Communist Party youth organization, he watched over the younger schoolchildren as a pioneer group leader.[3] In July 1960 he was admitted to the Institute for Teacher Training in Putbus on the island of Rügen and began training as an elementary school teacher.[4] He came from a working-class family – his father was a driver, his mother worked as a waitress and his brother, four years older, had trained to become a house painter. The parents hoped that their youngest son would get a higher degree.[5] Just what the state expected of Egon Schultz during his studies was conveyed to him after his "enlistment" in the teacher training institute: "We hope that you will apply all your energies, both professionally and socially, towards achieving successful studies."[6]

After studying for two years, Egon Schultz began a practical teaching year at a school in Rostock-Dierkow. Egon Schultz met Michael Baade, a colleague, at the weekly study meetings and they became friends. On September 1, 1963 he began teaching a first grade class. But soon after the school year began, Egon Schultz was conscripted into the East German military (NVA).[7] He signed on as an enlisted soldier to serve in the military for three years and was assigned to the border troops on November 2. A short time later he wrote to his friend about his first impressions: "All we do here is answer to someone else's bidding. […] You don't have to think at all, as long as you run when the whistle is blown. I think I will gradually become stupid here."[8] Egon Schultz wrote a number of letters to his friend in which he described his daily life as a soldier. He told him how exhausting his duty was but also wrote about his attempts to meet a girl despite the fact that he was in uniform. The budding young sergeant also wrote about his success in shooting training. He became a candidate for the Communist Party in August 1964.[9] He proved himself to be a "class-conscious guard of the state border," not just within the border troops, but also towards his former students, who often sent him letters. "It is a good job to protect our fatherland from its enemy," he wrote to his friend's class, which had become his sponsor.[10] After completing his officer training, he began his duty as group leader in Border Regiment 34 in Berlin-Mitte in the spring of 1964. According to official biographies, on October 7, 1964, the anniversary of East Germany's founding, he was going to be honored with a medal for best soldier.[11]

On October 4, 1964 Sergeant Egon Schultz was assigned as a reserve to the command post at Arkonaplatz in Berlin-Mitte.[12] It was almost midnight when a Stasi officer demanded backup support from the border guards. They were ordered to investigate and arrest suspicious individuals at Strelitzer Strasse 55.[13] The property was situated very close to the border barriers that extended along Bernauer Strasse. But Egon Schultz and his comrades were not informed of the real purpose of the operation: The Stasi had learned from informants about an escape operation.[14] While checking out the area near the border, the two Stasi agents had come upon two men who were assisting an escape operation in the foyer of the building at Strelitzer Strasse 55. The escape helpers mistook the Stasi men for fugitives. Claiming that they had to fetch a friend who had just been released from custody, the Stasi men, pretending to be fugitives, were able to leave the building.[15] While they organized back-up support from the border troops, the escape helpers waited for them to return.

Over many months, the West Berlin students had managed to secretly build a 145-meter-long tunnel to East Berlin. The tunnel began at a closed down bakery on Bernauer Strasse and continued eleven meters underground to an outhouse located in the courtyard of the building at Strelitzer Strasse 55. It later became famous as "Tunnel 57," referring to the number of people who had succeeded in escaping through it. One of the escape helpers was Reinhard Furrer, the future astronaut. He waited with three other escape helpers on the East Berlin side, ready to direct fugitives to the tunnel's opening. At about half past midnight, the unidentified men returned with the border soldiers. It was dark and Reinhard Furrer recognized much too late that a gun was pointed in his direction. Familiar with the surroundings, he quickly receded into the courtyard and before disappearing into the tunnel, warned his friends of the danger. The sound of shots cracked through the darkness. The escape helpers were able to rescue themselves at the last minute and enter the safety of the West, but Egon Schultz, hit by ten bullets, fell to the ground in the courtyard. There was no way to help him. He died on the way to the People's Police Hospital.[16]

Within a few hours the East German news reported the death of the border troop sergeant, who had been "treacherously murdered by shots fired by West Berlin agents."[17] The media reports on the east and west sides rapidly poured in.[18] The East German propaganda declared Egon Schultz a heroic martyr and attacked the murderers and the supposed wire-pullers working behind the scenes. Although the escape helpers' action was criticized in the West, it was acknowledged that they had acted in self-defense.[19]

In both the East and the West, investigations were opened against the escape helpers, most of whom had themselves fled from East Germany at one time.[20] They admitted to the West Berlin investigators that one of them had fired a gun, but there was no proof that the bullet that caused Egon Schultz's death was from that gun. The East Berlin state prosecutor's office had refused to comply with official requests from West Berlin for assistance in clarifying the case. Instead East Germany demanded that the supposed murderer be extradited.[21] In November 1965 the West Berlin public prosecutor closed the case against the escape helpers. They were only charged a fine for illegal possession of a weapon.[22] At this point there were already indications that Egon Schultz may have been shot by one of his own comrades. After fleeing to the West, another border soldier, K., reported in June 1965 that during a border troop duty evaluation his guard leader had stated that "an accident had occurred last night in another regiment. [...] A guard leader, he reported, was shot and killed by his junior guard." A short time later, in politics class, this presentation of the incident was retracted as false.[23]

The results of the East Berlin investigation conducted by the city commander and the Stasi were classified as top secret. They realized that Egon Schultz had been shot by an escape helper but that the fatal shot that killed the soldier had come from the Kalashnikov of one of his comrades.[24] To conceal the truth, the Stasi had the autopsy files disappear from Charité Hospital.[25] In the Communist Party Central Committee's division for security issues, an evaluation of the incident determined that both Stasi agents "when they first encountered the terrorists [...] had demonstrated political inconsistency and acted tactically irresolutely. [...] Even their fabrication of a legend was a mistake in the concrete situation. [...] More practical decision-making and better instructions to the border security forces, as well as a more advantageous deployment of the available forces and means, would most likely have prevented the tragic consequences."[26]

Just two days before the East German state's 15th anniversary and right before a new border pass agreement was to be signed with the West Berlin Senate allowing West Berliners to visit the East, the events that played out in the courtyard of Strelitzer Strasse 55 provided the Communist Party leadership with advantageous conditions for a political campaign.[27] For propaganda reasons, the accidental death of Egon Schultz by East German border soldiers was attributed to the West Berlin escape helpers and presented as an act of murder. The gunmen actually responsible for the death were not legally prosecuted.[28] The escape helpers, however, were investigated, although an indictment was ultimately never issued.[29]

The East German state leadership turned the funeral ceremony for Egon Schultz in the Friedrich-Engels barracks in Berlin, as well as the state funeral with military honors that took place in his hometown, Rostock, into political demonstrations. As a member of the Communist Party Politburo, Erich Honecker made a speech in the presence of members of the Communist Party Central Committee and the border troop leadership in which he attributed responsibility for the death of Egon Schultz to the West, making reference to the current policies of mutual understanding. "Hence the deadly shots were also against the new border pass agreement; they were directed against the anti-fascist protective barrier that has been preserving our and your peace since August 13."[30]

When the coffin was transferred from Berlin to Rostock, tens of thousands of workers followed government orders to line the streets and pay their last respects to Egon Schultz. He was buried in the New Cemetery in Rostock, accompanied by the tune of "Undying Victim," thereby establishing his death in the tradition of the international workers' movement. As part of the commemorative pioneer assembly, on the day of his funeral, the school in Rostock where he had been a teacher was given the honorary name "Egon Schultz Secondary School." In the end, more than a hundred collectives, schools and institutions were named after Egon Schultz.[31] The former teacher was glorified into a socialist fighter.[32] On January 4, 1965, a memorial plaque. which commemorated his death while also denouncing the West Berlin agents involved in the "assassination," was erected at house no. 55 on Strelitzer Strasse, which was renamed Egon-Schultz-Strasse on August 13, 1966.[33] The dead man was commemorated at this site, and at many others, often in the presence of his parents.

In 1992, as the violent acts at the border were being legally prosecuted, a case was opened with regard to Egon Schultz for suspicion of negligent homicide. It entailed the investigation of all the people involved in the incident, including the Stasi agents and the border troops.[34] The socialist paper "Neues Deutschland" embarked on a major campaign asking for donations to help cover the costs of legal counsel and court fees for the border soldiers who, from the viewpoint of the fundraising initiators, were being unlawfully prosecuted. Almost 200,000 German marks were donated, managed by the Society for Legal and Humanitarian Aid, an association of former Stasi, border troop and Communist Party members.[35] The investigation determined without a doubt that Christian Zobel, the escape helper from the West, had fired the first shot in order to prevent Reinhard Furrer and himself from being arrested. The bullet was lodged in Egon Schultz's lung but did not kill him. The fatal shot had come from the Kalashnikov of a border soldier who, on instructions from a Stasi officer, had fired shots in the dark courtyard and unintentionally hit Egon Schultz, who then died from internal bleeding.[36] It was accepted by the court that the border soldier who had fired the deadly shot had acted in self-defense. The case was dismissed since he had been ordered to fire.[37]

In response to the investigation against the border guards and Stasi agents, in May 1994, private individuals pressed charges against Reinhard Furrer for supposedly murdering Egon Schultz. Egon Schultz's mother, who had supported the accusation, was represented by a renowned West Berlin law firm. Additional charges were also filed with the Berlin public prosecutor's office.[38] When Reinhard Furrer died in an airplane accident in September 1995 and it became known that Christian Zobel had already passed away, the lawyers representing Egon Schultz's mother filed charges against the other escape helpers as murder accomplices. The case was dropped in the summer of 1999 "because the shots fired by Zobel [involved] an excess crime that cannot be attributed to the other persons charged."[39]

The circumstances that led to Egon Schultz's death continue to polarize views today.[40] What remains indisputable, however, is that Egon Schultz was a victim of the Wall. A few escape helpers and a friend erected a new memorial plaque on the building at Strelitzer Strasse 55 honoring Egon Schultz as a Wall victim and finally putting an end to the propaganda and lies concerning his death.

Maria Nooke

1 Flier with an open letter to Egon Schultz' mother, December 1964, in: Archive of the Berlin Wall Foundation; see "Information über das Verbreiten von Hetzflugblättern an der Staatsgrenze der DDR, 31.12.1964," in: BStU, MfS, HA I Nr. 3805, Bl. 71–73.

2 Ibid.

3 "Beurteilung von Egon Schultz durch den Klassenlehrer/Stellvertretenden Direktor, 24.8.1960," in: Michael Baade Archive, Rostock.

4 "Schreiben zur Einberufung an Egon Schultz, Diesterweg-Institut für Lehrerbildung Putbus, 16.7.1960," in: Michael Baade Archive, Rostock.

5 Conversation conducted by Maria Nooke with Michael Baade, 2.10.2006, Archive of the Berlin Wall Foundation.

6 "Schreiben zur Einberufung an Egon Schultz, Diesterweg-Institut für Lehrerbildung Putbus, 16.7.1960," in: Michael Baade Archive, Rostock.

7 "Aufforderung zur Musterung, Wehrkreiskommando Rostock, 8.9.1963," in: Michael Baade Archive, Rostock.

8 Letter from Egon Schultz to Michael Baade, 10.11.1963, in: Michael Baade Archive, Rostock.

9 "Bericht der NVA, Kommandeur der 1. Grenzbrigade, über den hinterhältigen Mord an Uffz. Schultz, 5.10.1964," in: BArch, VA-07/16925, Bl. 27–42, here Bl. 27.

10 See letter from Egon Schultz to Michael Baade, 21.12.1963, in: Michael Baade Archive, Rostock, and letter from Egon Schultz to Michael Baade's school class, 29.12.1963," in: Michael Baade Archive, Rostock.

11 See "Kurzbiographien ermordeter Grenzsoldaten, Zusammenstellung des Kommandos der Grenztruppen," in: StA Berlin, Az 2 Js 772/92, Bl. 140.

12 "Bericht der NVA, Kommandeur der 1. Grenzbrigade, über den hinterhältigen Mord an Uffz. Schultz 5.10.1964," in: BArch VA-07/16925, Bl. 27–42.

13 "MfS/[HA XX/5], Bericht über die Befragung der am Einsatz beteiligten Grenzsoldaten," in: BStU, MfS AU 8795, Bd. 1, Bl. 106–107.

14 See "MfS/HA XX/5, Bericht über einen Einsatz zur Aufklärung der Tunnelflucht nach zwei inoffiziellen Hinweisen, 6.10.1964," in: BStU, MfS, AU 8795, Bd. 2, Bl. 81–84; "Protokoll der Zeugenvernehmung der Kontaktperson Horst Lange durch die HA XX/5, 5.10.1964," in: Ibid., Bl. 101–109; "Treffbericht des MfS über Informationen zur Tunnelflucht durch GM "Drescher", 5.10.1964," in: BStU Ast. Berlin, AIM 5890/91, Teil A, Bd. 1, Bl. 101–103.

15 On the circumstances of events from the viewpoint of the Stasi, see "Bericht über die Ermordung des Genossen Uffz. Schultz durch die HA IX/7, 13.10.1964," in: BStU, MfS, AU 8795/65, Bd. 1, Bl. 29–55.

16 "Bericht des Untersuchungsorgans des MfS zum gegenwärtigen Stand in der Mordsache Uffz. Schultz, 8.10.1964," in: BStU, MfS, AU 8795/65, Bd. 1, Bl. 15–17, here Bl. 16.

17 *ADN*, 5.10.1964; "Unteroffizier Egon Schultz von Westberliner Agenten ermordet," in: *Neues Deutschland*, 6.10.1964; "Hinterhältiger Mord an Grenzsoldaten," in: *Berliner Zeitung*, 6.10.1964.

18 Collection of press articles and agency notices, investigation of unknown individuals, in: BStU, MfS, AU 8795/65, Bd. VI, Bl. 1–135, and in: BStU, MfS, AS Nr. 418/84, Bd. 1, Bl. 1–109.

19 See z.B. "Fluchthelfer erschossen den Grenzposten Schultz," in: *Der Tagesspiegel*, 7.10.1964; "Fluchthelfer schoss in Notwehr," in: *BZ*, 7.10.1964; "Der dritte Mann war ein Grepo," in: *Berliner Morgenpost*, 7.10.1964.

20 See the trial before the Berlin district court, Az. 2 P Js 924/64, in: StA Berlin, Az 27/2/Js 772/92, and BStU, MfS, AU 8795, Gerichtsakte, Bd. 1 und 2.

21 See the exchange of letters between the East German general state prosecutor and the West Berlin investigative authority, 1964–1965, in: BStU, MfS, AU 8795, Bd. 1, Bl. 22–27, as well as the media reporting on 7.10.1964 in West Berlin.

22 See "Urteil des Landgerichts von Berlin-Tiergarten gegen die Fluchthelfer vom 26.5.1966," in: StA Berlin, Az 1 Kap. Js 1001/94, Bd. 1, Bl. 28–31.

23 "Protokoll der Befragung des geflüchteten Grenzsoldaten Wolf-Dieter K., 4.6.1965," in: Az 2 P Js 924/64, Bl. 201–202. See also "Vopo Schultz von seinen Kameraden erschossen," in: *Berliner Morgenpost*, 9.11.1965.

24 In addition to a retained pistol bullet, the autopsy report documents nine other bullet wounds, although most of these shots came from a Kalashnikov, and were fired at Egon Schultz after he was already lying on the ground. See "Obduktionsprotokoll des GMI der HU," in: BStU, MfS, AU 8795, Gerichtsakte Bd. 1, Bl. 69–86, here Bl. 84–85, and "MfS, Technische Untersuchungsstelle, Ballistische Gutachten zum Untersuchungsauftrag vom 8.10.1964," in: BStU, MfS, AU 8795, Bd. 1, Bl. 134–150.

25 See entries in the autopsy book and in the registry book of bodies of the Humboldt University Institute for Forensic Medicine, as well as the pertaining investigation by the ZERV, in: StA Berlin, Az. 27/2 Js 772/92, Bd. 2, Bl. 134–149.

26 "Information der Abteilung Sicherheitsfragen beim ZK der SED zur Überprüfung der Abläufe im Zusammenhang mit dem Tod von Egon Schultz," in: BArch DY/30/IV, AZ 12/82, Bl. 9–15, here Bl. 13.

27 On this see the reporting in *"Neues Deutschland"* and in *"Armeefilmschau"* Nr. 11/1964 (4), Bundeswehr Information and Media Headquarters, St. Augustin.

28 See "Einschätzung der Staatsanwaltschaft bei dem Kammergericht Berlin, 25.7.1994," in: StA Berlin, Az 1 Kap Js 1001/94, Bd. 1, Bl. 8–23, here Bl. 10.

29 The case against an unidentified escape helper declared murderer was suspended on June 12, 1964. See BStU, MfS, AU 8795/65, Bd. 1, Bl. 19–20.

30 "Rede von Erich Honecker auf der Trauerfeier für Egon Schultz am 9. Oktober 1964 in der Friedrich-Engels-Kaserne in Berlin," in: *Neues Deutschland*, 10.10.1964.

31 "Aufstellung von Kollektiven und Institutionen mit dem Namen Egon Schultz, o.D.," in: Michael Baade Archive, Rostock. See also the information from a member of the Permanent Commission of the Name-Bearing Collective of the Border Troops in: "Kommen nun auch westdeutsche ‚Mauerschützen' vor Gericht?", in: *Neues Deutschland*, 6.1.1993.

32 See the description of his life in the children's book by Herbert Mühlstädt, 172 *Tage. Aus dem Leben des Lehrers Egon Schultz,* Kinderbuchverlag Berlin, 1974.

33 See *Neues Deutschland,* 13.8.1966

34 "Ermittlungsverfahren gegen Unbekannt, später gegen Nagel, Manfred K. und Volker M.," in: StA Berlin, Az 27/2 Js 772/92.

35 "Spenden sind weiterhin Quelle für Beistand mit verfolgten DDR-Bürgern," in: *Neues Deutschland*, 2.6.1998.

36 See "Sektionsergebnis des GMI der HU, 5.10.1964," in: BStU, MfS, AU 8795, Gerichtsakte, Bd. 1, Bl. 68–85, and "Aussage von Prof. Prokop zur Wirkung der Pistolenschussverletzung, 9.10.1964," in: Ibid., Bl. 86.

37 "Staatsanwaltschaft bei dem Kammergericht Berlin, Einstellungsverfügung im Verfahren gegen Nagel, M. und K. zum Nachteil von Zobel, Furrer und Egon Schultz, 25. Juli 1994," in: StA Berlin, Az 27/2 Js 772/92, Bl. 76–95. See also "Pressemitteilung der Senatsverwaltung für Justiz, Arbeitsgruppe Regierungskriminalität, 26.8.1994," in: StA Berlin, 1 Kap Js 1001/94, Bl. 120.

38 "Schreiben von Karl-Heinz K. an die Staatsanwaltschaft bei dem Landgericht Berlin, 11.5.1994," in: StA Berlin, Az 1 Kap Js 1001/94, Bd. 1, Bl. 1; "Schreiben von Rechtsanwalt Vendey an den Generalstaatsanwalt bei dem Landgericht Berlin, 21.7.1994," in: Ibid., Bl. 5, and "Entwurf eines Antwortschreibens auf die Sammelanzeige von H.N., o.D.," in: Ibid., Bd. V, Bl. 12–13.

39 "Verfügung der Staatsanwaltschaft I bei dem Landgericht Berlin im Verfahren gegen die wegen angeblicher Beihilfe zum Mord beschuldigten Fluchthelfer, 15. Juni 1999," in: Ibid., Bl. 1–14.

40 See, for example, the biography of Egon Schultz in: Kurt Frotscher/Horst Liebig, *Opfer der deutschen Teilung. Beim Grenzschutz getötet,* Schkeuditz, 2005, pp. 129–137, or the presentation on the website http://home.snafu.de/veith/ehrenhain.htm.

Rolf Henniger

born on November 30, 1941

shot dead on November 15, 1968
in the Babelsberg Palace Park
on the outer ring between
Klein Glienicke (Potsdam city district)
and Berlin-Zehlendorf

Rolf Henniger was born on November 30, 1941 in Saalfeld in East Thuringia.
After finishing school he trained with the German railway company to become
a train driver. He had just gotten married when he received his draft notice to serve
in the border troops in November 1967. After completing his training he was assigned as military driver and border guard to a border regiment in Potsdam-Babelsberg. In October 1968, on the 19th anniversary of the East German state, Rolf
Henniger was promoted ahead of schedule to the rank of private for "exemplary
achievement," something that was not uncommon on such occasions.[1]

Two weeks before his 27th birthday, on the evening of November 15, 1968,
Rolf Henniger was driving his guard leader in a Trabant "Kübel" along the security strip through the border territory of Babelsberg Palace Park. His superior would
be the only witness to survive what happened next. Shortly before reaching the
command post situated on the bridge that crossed the Teltow Canal into the Klein
Glienicke enclave, the guard leader noticed a man in uniform standing behind a
tree. He first assumed that he was a local member of the Klein Glienicke East German police force. Since the entire area was border territory, Rolf Henniger received
the order to put the vehicle into reverse and to drive back 15 meters. As they were
driving backwards, the guard leader called out to the unidentified soldier and
asked him who he was.[2]

The man hiding behind the tree was Horst Körner, a 21-year-old constable of
the East German police force who was fleeing to West Berlin with a loaded machine pistol. When he saw that he had been seen, Horst Körner opened fire on the
army vehicle.[3] He shot automatic fire at the driver through the front windshield at
close range. Hit by a number of bullets in the head and chest, Rolf Henniger collapsed behind the steering wheel. The soldier in the passenger seat was able to
drop out of the vehicle. He put his machine pistol into firing position and brought
Horst Körner down with numerous bursts of fire.

That, at least, is how the investigation report of the East German secret police
documented the incident. Years later, the Berlin public prosecutor did not question
its accuracy,[4] but at the time, the details were not made public. The East Berlin

press agency, ADN, merely reported the following day that "an armed agitator" had tried to violently break through the East German state border and that a border soldier was fatally injured. The agitator was also shot and killed.[5]

Rolf Henniger was buried in his hometown of Saalfeld amidst an elaborate display of propaganda on November 21, 1968. The family was not allowed to participate in any of the funeral arrangements.[6] His coffin was wrapped in the East German flag, placed on an open truck and paraded through the city, accompanied by the NVA guard of honor, local brigade groups and members of the Soviet Army.[7] The Berlin city commander, Helmut Poppe, stated that the heroism displayed by Rolf Henniger served to foil a criminal attack on socialism and peace. He added that "this cowardly act of murder" fills "the hearts and heads of the army members and workers of East Germany with an overwhelming hatred toward the imperialist henchmen and wirepullers." The East German television program "Aktuelle Kamera" and other East German media reported on this.[8] Rolf Henniger was posthumously promoted and awarded the National People's Army medal of achievement in gold. Later, the BSG locomotive stadium in Saalfeld and a number of youth collectives in factories and schools were named after him.[9]

The Berlin city commander instructed the guard leader who had witnessed Rolf Henniger's death and shot Horst Körner to pay a visit to Henniger's bereaved family on his birthday. Staff sergeant Wolfgang B. was not only a soldier in the border troops. He was also an informant of the Stasi who operated under the code name "Helmut Anton." The Stasi arranged with him a "line of conduct," which called on him to investigate the mood of the family and conceal from them the fact that the deceased had been shot by an East German police constable.[10] Although the perpetrator had not been officially identified and it was not known where the weapon had come from, the truth was not easy to conceal. Countless rumors and speculations spread about Rolf Henniger's death. The East German secret police collected and documented all the various views on the case that were circulating in the different Saalfeld factories and determined that, in general, the people in Saalfeld felt they had been fed half-truths and given abstruse official information; some even wondered whether one of Henniger's comrades or perhaps Henniger himself had tried to flee to the West.[11]

The family also had their doubts about the official version of his death. The Stasi learned that Rolf Henniger's stepfather believed his son had "wanted to flee the republic, which led to his being shot down by a member of the NVA border guards."[12] Apparently, Rolf Henniger had confided to close family members that he intended to flee. Even his relatives in southern Germany, who had requested information from the West Berlin police about what had really happened on the night of November 15, had been aware of Henniger's plans to flee.[13] But the West Berlin police could not provide any information. They had heard shots being fired that night, but did not know what had transpired.

Year after year Sergeant Rolf Henniger was officially commemorated in East Germany. His gravesite was decorated and the myth of a hero was kept alive by the military, party and state. But for years the question of how Rolf Henniger had really died continued to pre-occupy his closest relatives.

When the East German archives were opened and the police and public prosecutor opened an investigation in the 1990s, the background of the incident finally came to light. The truth – that a desperate East German policeman had killed a border soldier while fleeing – was not suitable "as a warning or as a reminder to more vigilantly protect the border and prevent further attacks by the imperialist class enemy of East Germany."[14] It was also not a good tale of heroism, which is why it was concealed from the family as a state secret.

But the heroic border soldier Rolf Henniger only existed in the propaganda. His closest relatives kept the family secret from the state that the young man whose life was taken on November 15, 1968 had probably been waiting for his own opportunity to flee.

Martin Ahrends / Udo Baron / Hans-Hermann Hertle

1   See "Kurzbiografien ermordeter Grenzsoldaten, o.D.," in: StA Berlin, Az. 27 Js 131/91, Bd. 3, Bl. 192; "Unvergessen sind, die ermordet wurden an dieser Grenze," in: StA Berlin, Az. 27 Js 131/91, Bd. 3, Bl. 193–196.

2   "Information des MfS/HA IX/9, 17.11.1968," in: BStU, MfS, AS 34/70, Bl. 30–31.

3   On this and the following see ibid., and "MfS/KD Potsdam/Abt. VII, Versuchter Grenzdurchbruch unter Anwendung der Schusswaffe mit Todesfolge," in: BStU, MfS, AS 34/70, Bl. 34–38.

4   See "Vermerk der Staatsanwaltschaft Berlin, 25.1.1994," in: StA Berlin, Az. 27/2 Js 131/91, Bd. 3, Bl. 114–117, here Bl. 114.

5   "NVA-Grenzsoldat von Provokateur ermordet," in: Neues Deutschland, 17.11.1968.

6   See the files on Rolf Henniger's burial, in: BArch, VA-07/18353, Bl. 453 ff.

7   See "Bericht des MfS/HA I/Abwehr B über die Beisetzung des ermordeten Unteroffiziers Rolf Henniger, 22.11. 1968," in: BStU, MfS, ZAIG Nr. 10713, Bl. 186–187.

8   See Neues Deutschland, 22.11.1968; Berliner Zeitung, 22.11.1968; Volksarmee Nr. 48/1968. The speeches held at the funeral are presented in: BArch, VA-07/18353, Bl. 490 ff.

9   See Neues Deutschland, 16.11.1978.

10 See "Bericht des MfS/HA I/Abwehr B über die Beisetzung des ermordeten Unteroffiziers Rolf Henniger, 22.11. 1968," in: BStU, MfS, ZAIG Nr. 10713, Bl. 187; see also "Abschrift eines Berichtes über den Besuch der nächsten Angehörigen des Uffz. Rolf Henniger, 2.12.1968," in: BStU, MfS, ZAIG Nr. 10713, Bl. 160–161.

11 "Informationsbericht des MfS/KD Saalfeld, 21.11.1968," in: BStU, MfS, ZAIG Nr. 10713, Bl. 180–182.

12 Ibid., Bl. 181.

13 See the letter and questioning of Rolf Henniger's family, 20.12.1968, 16.1.1969 and 28.8.1969, in: StA Berlin, Az. 27/2 Js 131/91, Bd. 1, Bl. 23/24, 26 und 44.

14 See Märkische Volksstimme, 21.11.1968.

Ulrich Steinhauer

born on March 13, 1956

shot dead on November 4, 1980
near Schönwalde, across from Eiskeller
on the outer ring between
Schönwalde (Nauen district) and Berlin-Spandau

Ulrich Steinhauer, born on March 13, 1956 in Behrenshagen in the Ribnitz-Damgarten district at the Baltic Sea, grew up as the third of five children. His father was a warehouse clerk in the state-owned fiber board factory in Ribnitz-Damgarten. His mother, a housewife, raised the children. From 1962 to 1970 Ulrich Steinhauer attended elementary school in Behrenshagen and the Rudolf-Harbig Secondary School in Damgarten. After completing his carpenter apprenticeship in the farming intercompany in Damgarten in 1973, the company hired him as a skilled worker. His youngest sister Ilona described her brother as a frugal youth who saved his money to go on vacation. Every summer he took a trip through East Germany with a tent.[1]

In November 1979 Ulrich Steinhauer was called up for military service with Border Regiment 40 in Oranienburg. Although the family maintained casual contact with people in the West – the mother's brother had lived in West Germany since 1961 – and the parents were not members of the Communist Party, the border troops were apparently convinced that his background – coming from a large working-class family from the coast – was assurance enough that he could be trusted to serve reliably at the border. "Now almost a year has passed," Ulrich Steinhauer wrote in a letter to his parents in April 1980. "Time seems to fly by. My time in the army can't be over soon enough. Next year at this time the world will look quite different."[2]

After completing basic training he was assigned in May 1980 to Border Regiment 34 in Gross Glienicke in the north of Berlin.[3] Like most of his comrades, he was not an enthusiastic border soldier and counted the days until his release. "Only in a very extreme situation" would he use his weapon, Ulrich Steinhauer told his superiors in the border regiment, who criticized him for being "too quiet" and for not doing more "than what he thought was right."[4] He had told his sister Ilona that he wanted to put his 18 months of military service behind him without ever having to shoot at anyone and he hoped he would never find himself in that kind of situation. One thing her brother said remained particularly vivid in her memory: "You never know who you are standing there with. Is he my friend or my enemy?"[5] On November 2, 1980 he wrote his parents and sister that he had become a private and guard leader. He ended the letter with: "172 more days. Waiting for an answer."[6] By the time his letter was delivered to the family on November 7, Ulrich Steinhauer had already been dead for three days.

November 4, 1980 was a cold autumn day. Ulrich Steinhauer was assigned to serve duty from 1 p.m. to 9 p.m. as guard leader at the Staaken-Schönwalde border section, across from Eiskeller in the West Berlin district of Spandau.[7] He was scheduled together with Egon B. who had just recently been assigned to the unit in Gross Glienicke. Ulrich Steinhauer had no idea that his junior guard was planning to flee to the West and that he had singled out this particular border section to carry out his plan. At their first meeting Ulrich Steinhauer made a friendly impression on Egon B. – not like the other "harsh" guard leaders. He later explained that this had led him to hope that his guard leader would not get in the way of his escape.[8]

They were both controlled during a routine check early that afternoon.[9] Egon B. thought he was safe from any further checks after that. It was just past 4 p.m. when he embarked on his plan. According to regulation, Ulich Steinhauer, as guard leader, should have been patrolling a few meters to the right or left behind his junior guard. If the facts presented by Egon B. are to be believed, Ulrich Steinhauer must have been walking a few meters in front of him when B., unnoticed by his guard leader, pulled a plug to deactivate the border communication system.[10] Then he unlocked his gun and loaded it. Startled by the noise, Ulrich Steinhauer supposedly turned towards him. "Don't fool around," he said to his junior guard and removed his own machine gun from his shoulder.[11] "I am taking off now, throw down your weapon!" Egon B. later reported having called out to him while shooting two shots over his head as a warning.[12] But instead of throwing off his weapon, Egon B. claimed that Ulrich Steinhauer pointed his gun at him and that Egon B. responded by firing five shots. But the bullet that badly injured Ulrich Steinhauer, causing him to collapse, was not fired from the front. The bullet that pierced his heart had entered from his back. He died before a doctor arrived.[13] Border soldiers soon dragged the dead man and his weapon out of the death strip, but a short time later their superiors ordered them to return the body to the area where it had been found.[14] These circumstances, and the fact that the border guards could not recall where they had found which weapon, made it highly unlikely that the results provided to West Berlin by the East German general state prosecutor had been attained through a reliable forensic investigation.[15] The dead man was kept on the ground in the border strip on view to western media for an entire day – allegedly this was necessary in order to reconstruct the case.

Egon B. rode his military bike through the border strip to an area where the Berlin Wall was lower than usual. He leaned his bike against it, stood on top of the bike saddle and climbed over the final barrier to West Berlin.[16] He went right to the West Berlin police and reported what he had done and was taken into police custody. The West Berlin public prosecutor rejected the East German state prosecutor's request to have him extradited to East Germany, explaining that in East Germany, young adult perpetrators between the ages of 18 and 21, regardless of their development, are tried not as youths but as adults. Experience had shown that East German law did not take into account the German criminal law relating to youthful offenders, in particular "that a young person between the age of 18 and 21 cannot be held responsible for his actions in the same way as an adult can."[17] In response to a formal request, the East German attorney general provided the West Berlin authorities with large amounts of evidence, but it was limited in its usefulness given the failure to effectively secure the crime site.[18]

The West Berlin public prosecutor's office was certain that Egon B. had not acted impulsively, that his crime had been well-prepared and that he had fired his gun intentionally. The five shots were fired in quick succession – not leaving any time for the dialog that Egon B. claimed took place with his victim.[19] Because the shot into his back demonstrated malice, he was charged with murder.

But the Berlin district youth court found that it had not been sufficiently proven without a doubt that the deadly shots in the back were fired first. For this reason for the main court proceedings the charge was reduced from murder to manslaughter.[20] In the fall of 1981 the youth court found Egon B. guilty of manslaughter and sentenced him as a youth to six years in prison.[21] The court rejected the defense's claim of a "justifiable emergency," explaining that B.'s interest in fleeing without conflict did not outweigh Ulrich Steinhauer's interest in staying alive. In a conflict between freedom and life, life takes priority,[22] the court stated, adding that his self-serving conduct shifted the crime "very close" to murder.[23]

The defendant appealed the verdict, leading the Federal Court of Justice to lift the sentence and refer the case to another youth court, which ultimately confirmed the six-year prison sentence in June 1982.[24] In early February 1983 the sentence was once again appealed successfully to the Federal Court of Justice and retried a second time by the Berlin district court, which commuted the sentence to four years and nine months probation. Its decision was based on the fact that the defendant's conduct demonstrated that he deeply regretted his actions and was completely aware of the breadth of his guilt.[25] The Berlin Superior Court of Justice had already granted his early release from prison in June 1982.[26]

The East German secret police continued to treat the "murder" case of Egon B. as an operative procedure. With the help of informants from the West, the Stasi was kept up to date on all the details of his new life in West Germany.[27] A plan was made to have him "transferred" back to East Germany after which threatening letters were to be employed to try to manipulate him into committing suicide.[28]

Ulrich Steinhauer was posthumously promoted to sergeant. He was awarded a combat medal "for service to the people and fatherland" by the East German defense minister, Heinz Hoffmann, in "honor of his exemplary and selfless fulfillment of his duty." The FDJ youth association awarded the deceased the "Arthur-Becker-Medal" in gold. He was buried with military honors on November 12, 1980 at the Old Cemetery in Ribnitz-Damgarten.[29] The funeral service was organized by the authorities; the family had no say in the matter.

A border company, a school, a memorial boxing tournament, streets and work collectives were named after Ulrich Steinhauer. On his birthday and on the anniversary of his death, and on the "day of the border troops," a wreath was placed on his grave. His death was politically exploited and his relatives were unable to stop this. "That was a huge burden to us, especially for mother," Ulrich Steinhauer's sister Ilona recalled. "My brother was only doing his service. They took him from us a second time when they turned him into a hero."[30]

Martin Ahrends / Udo Baron / Hans-Hermann Hertle

1 Conversation conducted by Hans-Hermann Hertle with Ilona Jahnke, 1.11.2008.
2 Letter from Ulrich Steinhauer to his parents and his sister, Oranienburg, 13.4.1980" (privately owned by Ilona Jahnke).
3 See "Erstinformation des MfS/HA IX/6, 5.11.1980," in: BStU, MfS, HA IX Nr. 5529, Bl. 5–6.
4 "Ausspracheprotokoll, o.D.," in: BStU, MfS, AOP 3507/91, Bd. 3, Bl. 212–213.
5 Statement by Ilona Jahnke, Ulrich Steinhauer's sister, in: "Der Fall B. und die Rachepläne der Stasi," film documentary, director: Dirk Simon, 45 min., MDR 2004. The German film is a short version of the English original: "Between the Lines," director: Dirk Simon, 81 min., ©Titelbild Berlin 2004.
6 Letter from Ulrich Steinhauer to his parents and his sister, 2.11.1980 (privately owned by Ilona Jahnke).
7 On the following presentation of the establishment of facts regarding the circumstances of the crime see: "Urteil der 9. grossen Strafkammer – Jugendkammer – des Landgerichts Berlin in der Strafsache gegen Egon B., Az. (509) 1 P KLs 5/81 (39/81), vom 15.10.1981," in: BStU, MfS, Sekr. Neiber Nr. 425, esp. Bl. 110–115; see also "Erstinformation des MfS/HA IX/6, 5.11.1980," in: BStU, MfS, HA IX Nr. 5529, Bl. 5–9, and "Protokoll der Zeugenvernehmung des Kontrollstreifenführers durch das MfS, Gross Glienicke, 6.11.1980," in: BStU, MfS, HA IX Nr. 967, Bl. 211.
8 See "Urteil der 9. grossen Strafkammer – Jugendkammer – des Landgerichts Berlin in der Strafsache gegen Egon B., Az. (509) 1 P KLs 5/81 (39/81), vom 15.10.1981," in: BStU, MfS, Sekr. Neiber Nr. 425, Bl. 111–112.
9 See "Protokoll der Zeugenvernehmung des Kontrollstreifenführers durch das MfS, Gross-Glienicke, 6.11.1980," in: BStU, MfS, HA IX Nr. 967, Bl. 211.
10 See Urteil der 9. grossen Strafkammer – Jugendkammer – des Landgerichts Berlin in der Strafsache gegen Egon B., Az. (509) 1 P KLs 5/81 (39/81), vom 15.10.1981," in: BStU, MfS, Sekr. Neiber Nr. 425, Bl. 112–113.
11 Ibid., Bl. 113.
12 Ibid.
13 See "Bericht des um 17.30 Uhr am Tatort eintreffenden Arztes, 4.11.1980, 21.15 Uhr," in: BArch, GTÜ 10676, Bl. 128, and "Erstinformation des MfS/HA IX/6, 5.11.1980," in: BStU, MfS, HA IX Nr. 5529, Bl. 7–8.
14 See *Berliner Morgenpost,* 2.10.1981; "Tatortuntersuchungsprotokoll des Ministeriums des Innern HA/Kriminalpolizei zum Verdacht des Mordes an Steinhauer, Ulrich, 6.11.1980," in: BStU, MfS, HA IX Nr. 967, Bl. 2.
15 See "Information der BVfS Berlin/Abt. IX über die Fahnenflucht von Egon B., 5.11.1980," in: BStU, MfS, AU 5577/84, Bd. 1, Bl. 115–119.
16 See "Urteil der 9. grossen Strafkammer – Jugendkammer – des Landgerichts Berlin in der Strafsache gegen Egon B., Az. (509) 1 P KLs 5/81 (39/81), vom 15.10.1981," in: BStU, MfS, Sekr. Neiber Nr. 425, Bl. 114–115.
17 "Schreiben des Generalstaatsanwalts bei dem Kammergericht an den DDR-Generalstaatsanwalt, 7.11.1980," in: BStU, MfS, AU 5577/84, Bd. 7, Bl. 51–52.
18 See "Schreiben der Staatsanwaltschaft bei dem Landgericht Berlin an den Generalstaatsanwalt der DDR, 7.11.1980," in: BStU, MfS, AU 5577/84, Bd. 7, Bl. 53.
19 See the pertaining statements from the prosecuting attorney, Lucas Wedhorn, in: "Der Fall B. und die Rachepläne der Stasi," film documentary, director: Dirk Simon, MDR 2004.
20 See "B.: Ich habe ungezielt geschossen," in: *Berliner Morgenpost,* 29.9.1981.
21 See "Urteil der 9. grossen Strafkammer – Jugendkammer – des Landgerichts Berlin in der Strafsache gegen Egon B., Az. (509) 1 P KLs 5/81 (39/81), vom 15.10.1981," in: BStU, MfS, Sekr. Neiber Nr. 425, Bl. 104.
22 Ibid., p. 23.
23 See reporting on the trial: "Sechs Jahre Haft für geflüchteten 'DDR'-Soldaten," in: *Die Welt,* 16.10.1981; "Geflüchteter DDR-Grenzsoldat wegen Totschlags verurteilt," in: *Der Tagesspiegel,* 16.10.1981.
24 See "Urteil des Bundesgerichtshofs, Az. 5 StR 96/82, vom 23.3.1982"; "Urteil der 18. grossen Strafkammer – Jugendkammer – des Landgerichts Berlin in der Strafsache gegen Egon B., Az. (518) 1 PKLs 5/81 (26/82), vom 2.6.1982".

25   See "DDR-Grenzer erschoss auf der Flucht Streifenführer – Gericht mildert Strafmass", in: *Berliner Morgenpost,*
     2.2.1983; "Strafmass gegen früheren DDR-Grenzer herabgesetzt," in: *Der Tagesspiegel,* 2.2.1983.

26   See "Haftverschonung für früheren DDR-Grenzsoldaten," in: *Frankfurter Allgemeine Zeitung,* 29.6.1982.

27   See "OV 'Mörder'", in: BStU, MfS, AOP 3507/91, Bd. 1–10; see also "Information des MfS/HVA Nr. A/032722/
     05/09/89/03, 5.9.1989," in: BStU, MfS, ZKG Nr. 1477, Bl. 13–14.

28   See the objectives, operative plans and plan of action of the OV "Murderer," in: BStU, MfS, AOP 3507/91,
     Bd. 1–10; "Der Fall B. und die Rachepläne der Stasi", film documentary, director: Dirk Simon, MDR 2004.

29   *Neues Deutschland,* 13.11.1980.

30   Statement by Ilona Jahnke, Ulrich Steinhauer's sister, in: "Der Fall B. und die Rachepläne der Stasi," film docu-
     mentary, director: Dirk Simon, MDR 2004.

Other Cases of Death and Alleged Cases[1]

Other Cases of Death

Deaths on the Border Crossings

Hundreds of mostly elderly people traveling from the East and West died between 1961 and 1989 during or after passing through a checkpoint at a Berlin border crossing, usually as a result of heart attacks. In our research of various archival holdings, we found that the cases of death at border crossings were intermittently and unsystematically documented. We were able to verify at least 251 cases. Achieving a more exact count of all the deaths that occurred at a Berlin border crossing would have required evaluating all the daily reports transmitted by the border troops over the 28 years – a time consuming task that could not be undertaken within the framework of this project. Alternatively, our team chose to examine the East Berlin transport police reports concerning the Friedrichstrasse station border crossing, although these files are incomplete, as the surveillance films and reports for the years 1971 to 1978, and 1989, are missing. Hence one third of the entire time period is not documented.[2] Where both collections are intact, discrepancies exist regarding death cases. Nevertheless, according to these files, at least 227 deaths occurred at the Friedrichstrasse station border crossing, involving 164 East Germans, 40 West Berliners, 20 West Germans, one Czech and two East Germans who, after receiving permission to immigrate to West Germany, wanted to pass through the border crossing.

The sources often do not identify the exact location or circumstances of a given death, leaving it ambiguous as to whether the person died during or after going through the checkpoint, or perhaps during an interrogation. Thus not every case of death documented by the transport police is necessarily related to the border regime. To validate the claim that the particular control situation at the Friedrichstrasse station border crossing led to a significantly higher number of deaths compared to other stations, a control sample was conducted on the deaths that occurred in all the East Berlin stations in 1984. That year 23 deaths were registered at the Friedrichstrasse station border crossing compared to 29 deaths for all the other East Berlin stations combined.

On August 23, 1961, just a few days after the Wall was erected, Frieda K., a 58-year-old woman from West Berlin, died at the Friedrichstrasse station border crossing. It was the next to last day that West Berliners were still permitted to travel to East Berlin. A report of the East Berlin transport police states without further explanation that Frieda K. was handed over to the criminal investigation department at around 11:45 a.m. for the purpose of "examining a travel permit." What then happened is described as follows: "When asked by Div. K. [criminal division] whether she feared going through the checkpoint, she said yes. After responding, she fainted and died of a heart attack in the interrogation room of Div. K."[3]

The East German border checkpoints, jointly operated by the border troops, secret police and customs agency, were secured by menacing barriers. The border troops were in charge of military security, in particular the prevention of escapes. Their observation towers and command posts were highly visible and they patrolled the Friedrichstrasse station with machine pistols and German shepherds. The security, control and surveillance of all passenger traffic, including searches and arrests, were the responsibility of the passport control unit of the secret police, which disguised itself by wearing the uniform of the border troops.[4] The actual examination of travelers and goods was carried out by the customs agency. Checks conducted on suspicious people took place in special rooms outside of customs clearance or in garages of the border customs officials, who had their own interrogation, search and detention rooms.

During the entire era of East Germany, travelers experienced the passport controls at the East German border crossings – on the transit routes, at the entrances and exits to East Germany or when traveling between East and West Berlin – as extremely stressful situations because of the psychological pressure. It was not uncommon for travelers to be harassed. Sometimes they were forced to wait an inordinately long time without explanation. On other occasions they were taken away for questioning for the most minor of offences. Some were threatened with an entry or exit ban, which, if enforced, could put an end to contact between relatives and friends. Many people feared this ban and were intimidated by the unfriendly passport control and customs officers against whom they were defenseless at these sites.

The deaths that occurred at the border crossings were not usually made public. The deaths of Kurt Krüger in 1965 and Rudolf Burkert in 1983 are exceptions. Both men suffered fatal heart attacks while being subjected to interrogations by East German border authorities at border crossings in Berlin.

The Case of Kurt Krüger

On April 25, 1965, Kurt Krüger, a 59-year-old businessman from West Berlin, went to visit relatives in the eastern part of the city. When he was traveling back to West Berlin, customs officials at the Invalidenstrasse border crossing discovered twenty eggs in his car that he allegedly had not properly declared. Kurt Krüger had to pull over to a special parking area where he was interrogated. He apparently suffered a heart attack during questioning. When his daughter, who had waited in the car, entered the security barrack to check on her father, she found him lying on the floor gasping for air. She demanded medical assistance, but according to the daughter, it took forty-five minutes for a doctor to arrive. All efforts to resuscitate him came too late. Kurt Krüger, who had previously suffered two heart attacks, died on the way to East Berlin's Charité Hospital.[5]

The Case of Rudolf Burkert

On April 10, 1983, Rudolf Burkert, a 45-year-old innkeeper, was traveling with an acquaintance in transit through East Germany on his way from Asendorf near Bremen to West Berlin. The two men were planning to attend a boxing event in the Deutschlandhalle, an arena in West Berlin. They also planned to briefly visit relatives in the East. Rudolf Burkert met his cousin and his daughter for lunch at "Magdeburger Börde," the motorway service area located just beyond the border in East Germany.[6] The motorway service areas along the transit route were kept under scrupulous surveillance by the secret police. Meetings between East and West citizens were always regarded with suspicion, especially when there was a transfer of goods involved. For this reason Rudolf Burkert drove with his eastern relatives to the nearest parking lot to quickly transfer the gifts from one trunk to the other. He had brought candy and catalogs with him, as well as a pair of used safety belts and loudspeakers.[7] Later the cousin stated in an interrogation by the Stasi that these kinds of goods were practically worthless in the West, but in East Germany they served as a valuable form of currency.[8] Rudolf Burkert and his cousin did not seem aware of the fact that the transit parking lots were under hidden surveillance at this time. The cousin was intercepted right after the meeting and interrogated. At about 1:30 p.m., when Rudolf Burkert and the man with him reached the Drewitz border crossing, they were pulled out of the vehicle line and directed to a garage. When the garage doors closed, the feeling that one was completely at the mercy of the armed men in uniform was reinforced. The car was inspected and the passenger traveling with Rudolf Burkert was interrogated first. At about 2 p.m. it was Rudolf Burkert's turn for questioning. The intimidating preliminaries to these kinds of interrogations were not documented in any reports, but they were nonetheless well known: Without making any concrete accusations, the interrogators made it clear that they "knew everything" and that not telling the whole truth would only make things worse. Rudolf Burkert was seated in front of the uniformed officers, isolated from the other transit travelers as if he were a potentially dangerous criminal. He did not know of what he was being accused or when he would be allowed to leave the room. The East German border authorities clearly intended to make these situations as stressful as possible for the people they were interrogating.

According to the protocol, in answer to the first three questions regarding his transit trip, Rudolf Burkert provided information on everything of which he thought he might be accused: He spoke of the meeting with his cousin at the motorway service area and about giving him the "western goods" in the parking lot. At 2:30 p.m., when he was asked: "What was the reason for your handing over the objects on the transit route?" he suddenly collapsed and fell to the ground where he remained motionless. Measures to resuscitate him failed. The doctor who was summoned arrived a half hour later and was only able to pronounce him dead. The interrogation protocol noted succinctly: "Because the traveler died, the customs check and foreign currency exchange could not be completed."[9]

Three days later, on April 13, the deceased was handed over to a West German undertaker at the Helmstedt border crossing. His wife left the coffin open and noticed external injuries which led her to request a forensic examination. On April 14, Rudolf Burkert's dead body was examined in Bassum by two forensic doctors from the University of Hamburg. The autopsy report specified a heart attack as the cause of death, but also noted external injuries that suggested violence inflicted while he was still alive. In response, the public prosecutor of Verden opened an investigation. Under the headline "Transit Traveler Struck Dead by East German Officials," the "Berliner Morgenpost," a West Berlin newspaper, proclaimed that Burkert's external injuries "were without a doubt caused by punches," citing the coroners, whose statements did not rule out this possibility.[10] A few days later, Helmut Kohl, chancellor of West Germany at the time, contacted the East German Communist Party leader Erich Honecker in regard to the Burkert issue and demanded a thorough investigation.[11] The Bavarian premier Franz Josef Strauss went so far as to refer to a "case of murder."[12] Three weeks after Burkert's funeral, and in connection with both the Burkert case and a West German loan of more than a million marks to East Germany, it was agreed upon in a confidential exchange between Strauss and the East German mediator, Alexander Schalck-Golodkowski, that customs inspections at all the East German border control points were to be conducted humanely.[13] The case flared up in the western media until Burkert's "agonal fall" following sudden cardiac death was reconstructed in the Drewitz interrogation barrack in the presence of one of the Hamburg coroners who had conducted the autopsy. Apparently, there was sufficient evidence to prove that Burkert's external injuries had been caused by his fall and not by physical violence. Photographs were taken of the reconstructed fall: Rudolf Burkert hit his head on the desk in front of him, slid down sideways, hit his head on the heater and fell to the ground. A new autopsy was conducted in East Berlin. The forensic doctors there confirmed the results of the Hamburg autopsy report and agreed that Rudolf Burkert's death was caused by "an acute failure of the heart as a consequence of his preexisting heart condition." According to this report, Burkert suffered from coronary artery calcinations that were so severe "that a sudden cardiac death could occur at any time induced by the most minimal amount of stress or even without any stress [...]."[14]

The investigation results of the Burkert case were passed from the East to the West through the highest political channels (from Ewald Moldt, then the permanent representative of East Germany to the Federal Republic of Germany, to Philipp Jenninger, minister of state in the Federal Chancellery). In response, the public prosecutor of Verden announced that the forensic medical report showed that Burkert had died a natural death. It remained unproven "whether the acute heart failure was related to the questioning of Burkert by the East German authorities."[15] The investigation was closed and Rudolf Burkert was buried. The case appeared to be over.

In August 1990, the public prosecutors in Verden and Celle refused to reopen the investigation of the death since no new factors had surfaced after the Wall fell. In April 1995, the German magazine "Stern" published a story that raised new questions about the case, claiming that the furniture in the room had been arranged incorrectly when the reconstruction was conducted in 1983: The article stated that the table Rudolf Burkert had slipped off of had not been positioned next to the heater, as claimed, but in the middle of the room.[16] In response, the Neuruppin public prosecutor reopened the case in the fall of 1997, only to file it away again a short time later after the witness statements quoted in the "Stern" were checked. "The information from 'Stern' does not correspond with the investigation results," wrote the Neuruppin public prosecutor in the closing deposition.[17]

By the end of April 1983, "Der Spiegel" news magazine had already noted with prescience that "it appears unlikely that what took place in the Drewitz barrack on that Sunday will ever be clarified with certainty."[18]

Reactions in the East and West

Shortly after Rudolf Burkert's death, two more people died at East German border control posts along the inner German border. Heinz Moldenhauer, aged 68, suffered a fatal heart attack on April 26, 1983 while being "lectured" at the Wartha border crossing. Günter Zöllner died four days later during an interrogation at the Marienborn border crossing. These fatalities at East German border crossings caused a major stir in the West and were widely discussed in the media. People demonstrated against the East German border regime and held silent protests in honor of the victims.[19] The public debate focused on the physical and mental tension suffered by westerners at the border crossing when they traveled into or through East Germany. "Even the 'normal' procedures put a strain on the circulatory system and caused a feeling of pressure around the stomach area," wrote the West German newspaper "Frankfurter Allgemeine Zeitung." "If you are pulled out of line and forced to endure an interrogation or a 'lecture' in a certain tone and with uncertain consequences, it is inevitable that this menacing situation will evoke nervousness and fear."[20] For travelers with a heart condition, this extremely stressful situation could lead to a sudden cardiac arrest. A heart specialist described the possible effects of experiencing fear while crossing the East German border: "Within seconds there is a flicker in the heart chamber and the heart stops beating. Not enough blood reaches the brain and coronary vessels. The person loses consciousness and dies."[21]

The situation became less tense in early May 1983 when East Germany relaxed its control measures at the East German border crossings. Luggage inspections became rare and the information on customs forms identifying goods being carried into the country was rarely verified. Transit passengers began describing the customs processing "as extremely polite and courteous."[22] The West German government lessened its criticism. In response to a parliamentary inquiry by Eduard Lintner, CDU/CSU parliamentary party speaker for German political issues, the Federal Ministry of Intra-German Relations declared on May 11, 1983 that it had no information "from East Germany, from relatives of the deceased, or other sources" pertaining to any "deaths occurring during controls or interrogations." There was also no indication of any deaths occurring as a consequence of harassment or threats of violence. However, it could not be ruled out that mental stress caused by the controls may have "endangered health in individual cases." The ministry also noted that, for this reason, the West German federal government repeatedly pointed out the difficulties related to border customs processing for travelers and "demanded of East Germany that these inconveniences at the inner German border and in transit traffic to and from Berlin (West) be eliminated."[23]

The fact that the chancellor referred to the deaths at the East German border control posts in his state of the union address on June 26, 1983 underscored how important this issue was to the West German government: "Grave incidents occurred in Berlin transit traffic and travel in East Germany this year. We were all deeply pained by the death of two people. It has raised public awareness of the problem of harsh border controls."[24] But this was only partially true. The public had been moved by the issue of westerners being harassed when traveling to East Germany. But during the short period between the death of Rudolf Burkert and the chancellor's state of the union address, six East German citizens also died at the Friedrichstrasse station border crossing. However, no one but their relatives took notice of their deaths because they were kept secret in East Germany. The reports of the East Berlin transport police reveal the exact circumstances under which these deaths occurred:

- on the morning of April 19, 1983, Albert W., aged 75, died of heart failure;
- on the evening of May 6, 1983, Walter K., aged 70, died of a heart attack during his re-entry into East Berlin, and in the presence of his wife;
- in the early morning of May 10, 1983, Ingeborg St., aged 53, fainted while exiting to West Berlin, and died;
- on the morning of June 8, 1983, Margarete G., aged 89, died of "natural heart failure" while re-entering East Berlin;
- on the evening of June 14, 1983, Herbert W., aged 72, died of heart failure while re-entering East Berlin;
- on the afternoon of June 22, 1983, Lieselotte K., aged 70, from Hennigsdorf, whose visa had expired, died of acute heart failure.[25]

At least 19 people in 1983 and at least as many in the following years did not survive crossing the border at the Friedrichstrasse station. As in previous decades, the deaths in the "Tränenpalast" ("palace of tears," the building where border control and customs processing took place) were kept secret from the public in both parts of Germany well into the eighties. The families were left to grieve alone. Many of them remain traumatized today because of the circumstances under which they lost their husbands and wives, mothers and fathers, sons and daughters.

The Case of Luise B.

Joachim B.'s family was divided by the Berlin Wall. His mother and sister lived in West Berlin. He lived with his family in East Germany, in a northern suburb of Berlin.[26] In the 1980s, his mother required special care. His wife Luise, who became an invalid at an early age due to a heart defect, looked after her mother-in-law. As a pensioner she was allowed to travel to West Berlin regularly, but Joachim B. was only permitted to visit his mother on special occasions. On one of the few occasions that they were allowed to travel to West Berlin together, the couple stood in the passport control line to exit the Friedrichstrasse station and Luise B.

confided to her husband how much she feared the men in uniform. A nightmarish feeling overcame her each time. "When I die, it will be here," she sighed.

On September 17, 1985, Luise B. set off, as she had done many times before, to visit her mother-in-law in West Berlin. They had agreed that her husband would pick her up at the Friedrichstrasse station when she returned at 5 p.m. In the early evening Joachim B. joined the crowd of East Berliners waiting for visitors to arrive. Every now and then a small door opened and released people who were either arriving in or returning to East Berlin. But Joachim B. waited in vain for his wife. He tried to get information on her whereabouts. Finally, he was able to call his mother in the West from a payphone in the station, but all he learned was that Luise had left on time. Had he perhaps missed his wife? Could she have taken another exit? Joachim B. drove home, but his wife was not there. He drove back to East Berlin with his son and inquired of the customs agency in the basement of the Friedrichstrasse station whether a Frau B. had been detained. She had not. Eventually, the son found out from the transport police that his mother was in the Friedrichshain Hospital. Only then did the husband learn that his wife had died while re-entering East Berlin at the Friedrichstrasse station. He was not permitted to see her that evening, nor was he given an explanation as to why this was the case. Only after her body was transferred to their hometown was Joachim B. able to bid farewell to his wife.

The husband's efforts to find out more about the circumstances of his wife's death both before and after the Wall fell led to nothing. The only related document ever found was an East Berlin transport police "surveillance film" classified under "Number 1913, 6 p.m." It notes: "Death of a traveler: On 17.09.1985 at 3:29 p.m. in the St. Frie [Friedrichstrasse Station] after re-entry, the East German citizen, Luise, born 1926 [...], died of heart failure. SHW 3170 with Dr. B. and death certificate issued at the site, natural death. Body was transferred to Berlin-Friedrichshain Hospital – VPKA Oranienburg per FS 115 dead, to inform [the] family."[27] The death is registered in the report, but it is not revealed under what circumstances Luise died, whether it was before or after she passed through the passport control, or perhaps even during an interrogation.

The high number of travelers who died at East German border crossings was an inseparable part of the Berlin Wall and the East German border regime. If the Wall had not existed, these deaths would not have occurred and the controls would not have been necessary. Hence, these stressful situations, particularly dangerous for the elderly and people with weak hearts, would not have taken place. The incidents of death at border crossings generally did not appear to involve direct external violence or a failure on the part of East German agencies to render assistance. Although the exact number of people who died is not known and only a few typical fates can be presented here, they are nevertheless in their own way also victims at the Berlin Wall.

Suicides and Fatal Accidents

An additional 101 deaths were documented during the research conducted by our project. These were deaths identified as accidents or suicides "at the Wall" or "because of the Wall," as well as deaths that occurred at or near the Wall in which the victim did not qualify as a direct victim of the East German border regime according to the project's definition of a victim. Twenty-four of these cases involved suicides. Twenty-three of the victims came from West Berlin. Twenty-seven of the people were members of the East German border troops. Fifty-three bodies were found in border waterways or in the stretch of land known as "sub-base territory" or "no-man's land," which was located directly in front of the Wall on the west side but which belonged officially to East Germany. Another 14 accident victims, who died outside of the border area, are also accounted for here. In some cases it was not possible to identify the victim or to determine the person's origins or the circumstances and background of his or her death. The results of the final research on fatal accidents and suicides are presented below. For reasons of privacy, complete names are not provided, but dates and locations are listed so that the information can be verified.

Suicides as a Consequence of the Wall and Division

One death that occurred "because" of the Wall involved the physician Dr. Wilhelm P. from the East Berlin district of Mitte. According to information provided by his wife, he suffered from depression and committed suicide at the end of August 1961 as a consequence of the Wall's being built and his fear that it would cause him to lose his livelihood.[28] The East German police evaluation of the "deceased" stated that he was "strongly oriented towards the West, his son attended school in West Berlin, and P. was convinced that his practice would be taken away from him in the near future."[29]

A new study conducted by Udo Grashoff on suicides in East Germany was unable to confirm the widespread assumption held in the West at the time[30] that the construction of the Berlin Wall caused a wave of suicides among East Berliners.[31] Wilhelm P.'s suicide was not, however, unusual. Many suicides occurred during the 28 years of division. In a close examination of the circumstances, these acts could be perceived as having been related to the existence of the Wall and the country's division, but knowing the specific causes of a suicide is generally difficult. An additional complexity arises from the fact that, for ideological reasons, suicides in East Germany were largely taboo.[32] According to Grashoff, the state was able to almost completely conceal the causes and motivations of a suicide by stating that the person who committed suicide was mentally unstable. This, in turn, caused suspicions among the population, leading people to mistrust official information. Peter B., for example, hanged himself in the Plänterwald in the East Berlin district of Treptow on November 1, 1984 for unknown reasons. His relatives, friends and acquaintances, however, were convinced that he had died while trying to escape. When this news reached the West, a cross was erected to Peter B. at the Reichstag. After the East German state collapsed, the official information that he had hanged himself was verified.[33]

In cases that involved an actual suicide, the assumption that it was undertaken out of distress over the existence of the Wall or because of the consequences the division brought with it can rarely be proven. It is highly likely that Ida Z., an unmarried woman from East Berlin, Karl-Heinz I., a soldier in the National People's Army, and the East German police officers Adolf L. and Wilhelm P. killed themselves in August and September 1961 for reasons related to the construction of the Wall. At the time it was believed in the West that Ida Z. had committed suicide on September 29, 1961 "due to the cavalier manner in which her request for permission to move to West Berlin was rejected."[34] Karl-Heinz I., a captain in the East German National People's Army, shot himself with his service weapon on August 13, 1961 near Hennigsdorf. As a member of the 1st Armored Rifle Division, he was involved in "securing" the closure of the border on the very first day. The deceased left behind the following note: "I am no long able to fulfill my duty. I am too weak to do it. I ask my wife to forgive me. It is better this way."[35] Alfred L. was a lieutenant in the East German police and belonged to the operative staff of the East German police headquarters of Prenzlauer Berg. He was found shot dead at the Prenzlauer Berg water tower on August 14, 1961. His service pistol was said to be lying next to him.[36]

In addition to despair and loneliness caused by the Berlin Wall, Grashoff, who examined a number of individual cases, attributes other motives, which were caused by the effects of being "walled in," for committing suicide. These include the difficulties and conflicts involved in flight and emigration, failure to adjust to life in the West and the ban on contacting people in the West. One example of this is the case of Wolfgang B. It is said that he hanged himself soon after he arrived in the Marienfelde refugee center in West Berlin because he was distressed by the fact that his daughter did not want to join him.[37] In another example, Grashoff describes the deadly trip taken by a young man who rammed his car into the Wall on the west side of Berlin in the spring of 1987 after he was refused permission to visit his parents in East Germany.[38] As in this case, the ban on travel established by East Germany often caused loneliness and despair, particularly among people who had difficulties adjusting to life in the West. In addition to suicides committed by desperate refugees and individuals requesting permission to immigrate to the West, Grashoff also documents a wide range of suicidal behavior caused by conflicts related to loved-ones who had engaged in successful or failed escape attempts, or who had applied for exit permits or immigrated to the West. One officer cadet shot himself in the fall of 1987 while on guard duty because his parents' application to leave the East had caused him to be expelled from officer's college, to be demoted to basic military training and to lose his permission to study at the university.[39] Given the polymorphic nature of human fates and the insufficient documentation of motives, it is not possible to identify all the deaths that were caused by the existence of the Wall.

Border Soldier Suicides and Fatal Accidents

Documented deaths involving border guards account for at least 15 cases of suicide, four accidents and eight incidents with firearms, but this figure does not claim to represent all deaths. In most cases the death could be proven, but additional background information was entirely lacking. As was the case with all members of the "armed organs" in the East, suicides and fatal accidents involving border soldiers were "incidents subject to registration." They usually led to an investigation by the military state prosecutor[40] and an autopsy of the body.[41] When there was reason to suspect that political motives or Stasi interests were involved, the Stasi Central Department I, which was responsible for military intelligence, was also notified. Nonetheless, in many cases the background information, circumstances and motives remain undocumented or are not revealed in the existing files. In some cases it was not even possible to clarify what had actually happened.

The fundamental question arises as to what degree deaths involving border soldiers – be it by suicide, accident or firearms – were actually the result of conflicts caused by border duty or the difficult conditions within the border troops. The following investigated cases involving accidents shed light on this issue. Gerhard L., a petty officer second class from Rostock, was a member of the boat crew of Border Regiment 38. During a rotation maneuver on May 12, 1974, he fell into the Oder-Havel Canal near Hennigsdorf and drowned.[42] Private Klaus B. from Walthersdorf in the Annaberg district was stationed at the border troop post in Wassmannsdorf, south of Berlin. On July 28, 1977 he was scheduled to serve guard duty together with Private L. Apparently the two men were careless in handling their weapons. Private L. pulled the release on his gun so far back that a cartridge from the magazine was pushed into the barrel. Since he had his finger on the trigger, a shot was fired, hitting Klaus B. in his chest and killing him.[43] The 21-year-old soldier Fritz F. was also fatally shot on December 29, 1964 by a comrade with whom he was on duty in a boat on the border waters, "when the hunting gun was discharged during a hunt for wild ducks on the Gross-Glienicker Lake."[44] Lothar J. was also the victim of a firearms incident in August 1961. He was a driver in the Dreilinden Company at the time and also serving as an informer for the Stasi under the code name "Rotkirch." On August 14 he was supposed to transport arrested individuals from the Drewitz station to the People's Police Hospital in Potsdam. Soldier F. was also part of the transfer operation. When he climbed into the vehicle, a bullet was released from his weapon. It penetrated the back wall of the driver's cab and fatally injured Lothar J.[45] In December 1962, Norbert A. was serving on the boat crew of the checkpoint control division of the 1st Berlin Border Brigade. He was accidentally shot by his comrade Wolfgang M. on December 27 when Wolfgang M. was cleaning his weapon. He had jokingly pointed his gun at him and a bullet was fired. Wolfgang M. was held in confinement for ten days as punishment. The incident was investigated thoroughly and the case was taken over by the military state prosecutor.[46]

In evaluating suicides committed by border soldiers, both personal problems and the special conditions within the border troops have to be considered. In most cases, however, it was not possible to clarify the background circumstances either because a thorough investigation was never conducted or was not documented in its entirety.[47] It should also be noted that from the viewpoint of the East German investigating agencies, the reasons and circumstances for the act were, for ideological and military reasons, usually found or claimed to be of a private nature. Andreas J., a sergeant in the East German border troops, was part of Border Training Regiment 39 stationed in Berlin-Wilhelmshagen. He died on September 11,

1984 in an East Berlin hospital where he had been taken after swallowing an over-dose of pills.[48] In a brief farewell letter he assured his parents and siblings: "It has only to do with military problems," and added: "There is no point in going into the details now."[49] A few days earlier Andreas J. had been arrested for violating duty and battle readiness when he left the troop post to visit his girlfriend without permission.[50] On November 10, 1965, Private Friedo-Erich S., a member of Border Regiment 37, injured his head severely by a shot fired from his own machine pistol. He died the next day in an East Berlin hospital. It remains unclear whether it was an accident or an act of suicide.[51] The suicide on September 22, 1963 of Peter H. from the 5th Company of Border Regiment 35 is explained tersely in the border troop chronicle: The guard shot himself while on duty on Liesenstrasse after having "quarreled with his wife."[52] Sergeant Rüdiger K. was a member of Border Regiment 42. He took his own life on July 18, 1965 in his parents' apartment in Oranienburg by inhaling coal gas.[53] Mario D. from Border Regiment 34 killed himself while on guard duty on April 10, 1980 by shooting himself in his abdomen with his service gun.[54] According to the military state prosecutor files, Mario D. had serious conflicts with his supervisors.[55] It is quite possible that, like Andreas J., the cause of Mario D.'s conflicts and problems within his border troop service had to do with his refusal to use his weapon. Achieving a more precise understanding of why these men killed themselves is difficult since the reasons for suicide were censored before they were entered into official documents. Both the military state prosecutor and the Stasi were inclined to find the causes of suicide and attempted suicide by NVA members in the soldier's personality. The causes were usually interpreted as being rooted in a specific disposition or caused by "heart sickness," a "weariness of life," "loneliness" or simply a "weakness of character." Work conflicts or grievances within the East German army – such as harassment by senior soldiers, drastic punishments for minor offences, the unfulfilled desire to be released from duty early, pressure on border troop soldiers, surveillance by fellow soldiers serving as informants, the fear of having to shoot someone or conflicts of conscience after having shot someone – were generally trivialized or ignored.

At the same time it should be acknowledged that the reasons for suicide vary greatly and often do go back to childhood experiences. It would be too simple to generally blame the border regime for the suicides of border guards. Nonetheless, on the basis of the military files on suicide and attempted suicides from 1983 to 1988, Dietmar Schultke concludes that every fourth suicide attempt was directly or indirectly related to the unyielding border regime. According to his data, the most common motives were refusal to serve in the military, fear, being overworked while on border duty and harassment.[56] The soldiers serving in the border troops were, in fact, under constant surveillance by a dense network of informers. Many of them felt the strain of their service at the border.[57] Contrary to Schultke's theory that many of the border guards broke down under the psychological terror of the Stasi, Grashoff's data show that the suicide rate within the border troops did not differ from the rate within the units of the National People's Army.[58] "There is no indication that the suicide rate of border soldiers in the 1980s was higher than that of the other troop divisions of the NVA. The suicide rate of the border troops was also not higher than that among civilians of the same age group."[59] This assertion, however, does not rule out that the causes of individual cases of suicide, as well as accidents, among border soldiers were rooted in the East German border regime.

Bodies Found in the Border Waters and in "No Man's Land"

Daily reports from the East German border troops, the East Berlin and Potsdam police departments and the West Berlin police document that a number of bodies were found in the border waterways and on the East German territory known as "no man's land," which was situated on the west side of the Berlin Wall. The bodies retrieved from the water were not always found at the place of death, especially when a long period had passed between the time of death and the time of discovery. Nevertheless, there are generally good reasons to suspect that these cases involved victims of the East German border regime because of their proximity to the border and border fortifications. For this reason all cases that were registered in archives or published on victim lists involving bodies found in border waters and in the border territory were researched by our team. In some cases it was possible to confirm that the dead person was, in fact, a fugitive attempting to flee to the West.[60] In other cases it was determined that a causal relationship between the death and the East German border regime did not exist. It was established that both East Berliners and West Berliners committed suicide or suffered accidents in the waterways in the center and on the edge of the city for reasons that had nothing to do with the border fortifications or the Berlin Wall. There were, however, a number of bodies found in the waters for which the background circumstances could not be sufficiently established. There were also a number of West Berliners found dead within "no man's land." This strip of land on the West Berlin side of the Wall in front of the actual border fortifications could usually be reached without difficulty from the west side. No less than 53 people were documented as being found dead in this "no man's land" and in the border waters. Some of these people were included on the victim lists of the "Working Group 13th of August" and on other lists;[61] others are presented here for the first time. In many cases investigation files from the time when the bodies were discovered, as well as pre-investigation and investigative files from the 1990s, were available for research purposes. Although these files show that these were not cases of violence leading to criminal proceedings, the staff of the Investigating Agency for Governmental and Party Crimes (ZERV) was nonetheless able to unearth revealing information. Inquiries into the federal archive of Stasi files (BStU), however, tended to be less fruitful.[62]

Bodies Found in the Berlin Border Waters

The monthly report of the East Berlin Water Protection Agency indicates that an East Berliner named Günter H. was retrieved from the Spree River on January 30, 1979. The man had been reported missing since the night before. Evidence suggests that he had fallen off an ice breaker anchored on the Stralau Peninsula.[63] In another case, Johannes T., a 74-year-old East Berliner who lived in the Treptow district in the border territory, was found dead in a water ditch on January 18, 1975, not far from Kiefholzstrasse.[64] It is highly unlikely that he had been trying to escape since, as a pensioner, he was allowed to travel to West Berlin.

Kurt H. was pulled out of the Teltow Canal on the west side of the city on November 4, 1967. The West Berliner, it turned out, had swallowed prussic acid before going into the water.[65] On August 7, 1969, Bernhard J., another native of West Berlin, who lived in the Kreuzberg district, was pulled out of the Spree by the East Berlin Water Protection Agency near the Gröbenufer riverbank in Kreuzberg. According to the East Berlin autopsy report, the 34-year-old man had drowned the previous day while drunk.[66] Louise M., who was found dead on April 16, 1963 by East German border soldiers conducting clean-up work on an underwater barrier in the Teltow Canal, was first registered as an unidentified water corpse and later identified as a resident of West Berlin. The 68-year-old woman had lived in the West Berlin district of Lichterfelde, not far from the site where her body was discovered. The West Berlin police investigation conducted at the time showed that she had committed suicide.[67]

When he entered the waters in May 1963, Ismet C., a Turkish citizen living in West Berlin, had apparently decided to take his life because he was suffering from a serious illness. Members of the East German border troops found his body on May 31, 1963 in the Gross-Glienicker Lake through the middle of which ran the border.[68] In another case, an East German, initially unidentified, was retrieved from the Niederneuendorfer Lake on the West Berlin side. A letter found on the body when it was discovered on March 20, 1966 identified the woman as Gertrud W., born on July 27, 1899 in Königsberg, last residence in Birkenwerder, and reported missing since January 9, 1966. She had apparently confided to her son her intention to commit suicide after her husband left her in November 1965.[69] An escape attempt can be ruled out in this case, as in many others, since Gertrud W. was already retired and allowed to travel to the West. In fact, shortly before she disappeared she had spent the Christmas holidays with her daughter in West Berlin. The Polish boatman Franciszek M. did not need to escape through the border fortifications in order to reach the West either. But he did not return after taking leave from his ship to go to West Berlin on December 5, 1980. Two months later a Hamburg skipper found his body in the Spree near the Oberbaum Bridge. East German border soldiers retrieved the body from the water after the West Berlin police activated a water rescue alarm that had been installed on the bank of the Spree in Kreuzberg in October 1975. According to the autopsy report, he had been intoxicated when he drowned.[70]

Evidence verifies that these and many other cases did not involve victims of the East German border regime, but in other cases it was not possible to eliminate the possibility or to prove that a connection existed. Sometimes the victim's identity could not be established; sometimes neither the original documents nor reports from historical witnesses were able to shed light on how the person found in the water had died. Bodies found in waterways often remain a mystery to the authorities. Even when the autopsies found no indication of third-party fault, it was not always possible after the fact to determine how the body came to be in the water in the first place and whether it entailed a suicide, an accident or a crime.

A body retrieved from the Spree just before the Schilling Bridge on July 8, 1965 was registered at the time in West Berlin.[71] Because the body had decomposed by then, the West Berlin authorities assumed it was linked to the death of an unknown fugitive who had drowned at the same site on January 19 of that year.[72] This suspicion has yet to be confirmed or dismissed.[73] Daily reports from the East German border troops found in the 1990s suggested that the remains of a human body had been discovered that day during cleaning operations at an underwater border barrier at the Schilling Bridge and that it was handed over to Humboldt University's Forensic Medicine Institute. But these documents do not provide insight into the results of the East Berlin investigation and no other relevant East German police and Stasi files on the case were found.[74]

There are also information gaps in documents drawn up by West Berlin authorities concerning bodies found in waterways. For example, one unsolved case involves an unidentified body retrieved from the Landwehr Canal on the west side of the sector border on September 15, 1963.[75] In this case the retrieval efforts on the western bank were also observed and registered by East Berlin. An East German report states that at approximately 11:30 a.m. "a male body wearing boots and a strapped-on pistol was retrieved from the Landwehr Canal by the crew of two West Berlin fire trucks. A crowd of approximately 100 people had gathered. The situation returned to normal at about 12:50 p.m."[76] The West Berlin press did not report on the incident, nor was an incident report issued by the West Berlin police. In the 1990s, ZERV investigators found that there was little documentation showing what knowledge the West Berlin authorities had on the case at the time – not from the fire department, the state bureau of criminal investigation nor the state security police.[77] If there had been reason to suspect that the dead man had been a victim of the East German border regime, there would have been more documentation; thus it can be assumed that this case did not involve a victim of the Wall, although this remains to be proven.

Even when the identity of a body was established, questions often remained unanswered. Once the suspicion was raised that it may have been a fugitive trying to escape, it was very difficult to eliminate the rumor later. When young people inexplicably disappeared and were later found dead in border waterways, both the authorities and family members were inclined to believe that they may have died while trying to escape. The parents of Klaus S. suspected and presumably still suspect this to this day. Their son's dead body was retrieved from the Spree on July 18, 1970 in the Berlin district of Mitte. He had turned 19 just one month earlier. His parents remained suspicious of the information they had received from the East German authorities claiming that their son had died in an ordinary accident. They assumed that their son had been shot while trying to escape and that this information was being concealed from them. When the East German state collapsed, they hoped to learn the truth about his death and sought information from criminal investigation agencies in the early 1990s. An investigation was opened[78] that revealed that an autopsy had been conducted on Klaus S.'s body in East Berlin. According to the autopsy report, there was no indication of a bullet wound and the cause of death was documented as drowning. The investigators from the

ZERV, however, found it unlikely that Klaus S. had drowned while trying to escape because his body was found quite a distance from the sector border. Documents from the border troops or the Stasi that might have corroborated the parents' suspicions, shed light on the circumstances of his death or documented the retrieval of the body evidently do not exist.

In the case involving the death of Wilfried M, a 20-year-old border troop sergeant, a clear suspicion exists that he may have lost his life while trying to escape. A search was already underway when his body was retrieved from the Spree River at the Elsen Bridge some distance from the sector border on May 30, 1972. He had belonged to Border Regiment 33, which was stationed in the East Berlin district of Treptow, and it was believed that he had deserted his unit.[79] He had left his unit without permission the previous day, but it is still unclear where he went or how he died. ZERV investigators ruled out third-party involvement on the basis of the autopsy findings of the East Berlin Institute of Forensic Medicine.[80] The report stated that M. was intoxicated when he drowned.

According to a report from the East Berlin Water Protection Agency, the body of Thomas B. was also retrieved from the Spree at the Elsen Bridge in the East Berlin district of Treptow on March 17, 1978.[81] The 20-year-old East Berliner had been missing for weeks. His parents stated that he had left their apartment in a drunken state after a fight on the evening of January 27, saying that he was going into the water.[82] When he did not return the next day, his mother reported him missing to police. A short time later she had to stand by and watch as their apartment was searched because the authorities suspected that their son had fled to the West. After his body was found, the police informed his parents and they were presented with objects and clothing, which they recognized as their son's and which had been found on the dead body. Here, too, the autopsy found no signs of external violence; the coroners noted the cause of death as "probably drowning." Whether Thomas B. departed this life voluntarily or whether he had tried to flee to West Berlin remains unclear.

The fate of 18-year-old Barbara B. from the Mitte district of East Berlin is also ambiguous. When the talented gymnast did not return home after training on the evening of January 12, 1962, her parents became worried and reported her missing to the police. But the East German police suspected that Barbara B. had "illegally left" East Germany, as so many other young East Berliners had done after the Wall was built.[83] Many weeks passed during which Barbara B.'s parents and siblings waited in vain for a sign of life from her. Finally, on April 5, 1962, her body was retrieved from the Spree, not far from the sector border. The East Berlin police report states that on that morning "the dead body of an approximately 20-year-old female was pulled out of the Spree beneath the underpass at the Friedrichstrasse S-Bahn station. Based on its condition, it must have been in the water for many weeks. The body was brought to the Institute of Forensic Medicine and an autopsy was ordered by the general state prosecutor."[84] The dead person was soon identified as Barbara B. Drowning was found to be the cause of death.[85] Within her family, however, the rumor spread that Barbara B. may have been shot while trying to escape.[86] Investigations conducted after the East German state came to an end were unable to confirm this suspicion. But without clarifying the background and circumstances of her death, the investigators of the ZERV could not definitively rule out the possibility that Barbara B. may have drowned while trying to escape.

Bodies Found in "No Man's Land"

On March 16, 1982, Christian T., a West Berliner who evidently suffered from depression, went into an area of "no man's land" in front of the Wall on the western edge of the city, poured ethyl alcohol over his body and set himself on fire.[87] His suicide recalls acts of protest against the communist system, but whether or to what degree his death was politically motivated is not revealed by the available reports. At least eight West Berliners were found dead in "no man's land."[88] Bodies found in this area of land, which belonged to East Germany, were retrieved by members of the border troops. Only in the case of Rudolf W., a patient at the Spandau Psychiatric Clinic who was found dead on August 12, 1989 on the border to the East German district of Nauen, did East Germany oblige the request to have the body retrieved by the West Berlin fire department.[89] In all the other cases, responsibility for the investigation fell to the Stasi. If the discovery and retrieval of the body went unnoticed in the West, the Stasi kept the incident secret. Hence, four deaths were not discovered until after the East German state collapsed.[90] The remaining cases, however, made the headlines.[91] To provide just one example: The body of 78-year-old Anna Kirste was found on the bank of the Landwehr Canal on November 8, 1974 by two West Berlin children, who immediately reported their macabre discovery to the police. But before a retrieval team could be formed on the west side of the city, the Stasi ordered the body to be transported to the East Berlin Institute of Forensic Medicine.[92] According to the autopsy report, Anna Kirste had died weeks earlier without external interference. The deceased was diagnosed with a weak heart that had caused a physical breakdown, possibly causing her to freeze to death. It remained unclear how the elderly lady got from Kreuzberg to the stretch of "no man's land" in Treptow. The West Berlin investigation did find out "that there was a sad story behind the spectacular incident." The retired unmarried woman had recently cleared out her apartment on Falkensteinstrasse in Kreuzberg and tried to move in with her daughter, who lived in East Berlin, but the East German authorities had sent her back to West Berlin. After that the woman's son, who lived in West Germany, had his mother housed in a residence of the German Red Cross. She disappeared without a trace a short time later. The report ended with the comment: "Whether the lonely woman took her own life out of despair or had wanted to cross through the border fortifications to get to her daughter remains, for the time being, unclear."[93]

The death of Peter U. also remains a mystery. According to Stasi files, his body was found on November 18, 1987 by a patrol of Border Regiment 44 in a wooded area near Potsdam-Babelsberg, 150 meters from the closed-off train tracks that ran between Berlin-Wannsee and Potsdam.[94] The Stasi district administration in Potsdam that was in charge of the case estimated that the body had been lying at the site for five weeks. Signs of violence or "traces of corpse transport to the territory" were not found. Peter U. had his driver's license and identification card on him, which stated that his last residence was located in Berlin-Wedding. Born on August 17, 1958 in Adelaide, Australia, he was 29 years old at the time of his death.

No doubt unreported cases of dead bodies found in "no man's land" also exist. It cannot be completely ruled out that new findings may emerge in the future to help clarify unsolved cases or other suspected cases. There is, however, no reason to assume that the East German Ministry of State Security aimed to create "legends" or engage in "cover-up measures" in regard to the cases of death presented here. That was apparently only done for cases involving West Berliners who were found dead in "no man's land." In none of these cases is there any indication that the dead were shot by border guards or that they may have died as a consequence of border guards' actions or inaction.

Fatal Accidents and Deaths Outside the Border Territory

Our research found that in 14 cases people did not die in the border territory, or at least not at the Berlin Wall. Contrary to our initial suspicion, in each of these cases there was neither a spatial nor a causal connection between the death and the Berlin Wall. This includes four cases of death caused by firearms that did not, however, occur at the Wall. The four cases, registered as suspected cases, were found on the list compiled by the "Working Group 13th of August." One of the men had been a member of the East German police and was shot on September 15, 1964 on the Czechoslovakian border by Czech soldiers who were fleeing to West Berlin or West Germany.[95] According to information provided by the agency responsible for the Stasi archive (BStU), the border soldiers Günter M. and A. were shot and killed on the inner German border on December 24, 1971 by an NVA soldier who had deserted his unit. Contrary to other claims, Horst H. was not a border guard, and he was shot and killed by a Soviet guard in Stendal on August 3, 1989 when he entered a building belonging to the Soviet armed forces in a drunken state.[96]

Most of the remaining cases involved fatal accidents. Two accidents occurred on subway or S-Bahn tracks on East Berlin territory. Paul G. was evidently drunk on August 25, 1972 when he was fatally injured after jumping off a moving subway train between the Rosenthaler Platz and Bernauer Strasse stations.[97] The 23-year-old Rolf Peter B. was also intoxicated on April 16, 1988 when he fell out of the S-Bahn train between the Friedrichstrasse and Humboldthain stations.[98]

Two other accidents involved NVA soldiers who were long believed to have died while trying to escape. A West German brochure from 1962, for example, states that "Axel B., around 27 years old from Güterglück, Zerbst distr. (Soviet zone), according to his relatives, was shot and killed in the Soviet zone at the end of September 1961 while attempting to flee to Berlin (West). Axel B.'s mother received the news from the East German police that her son had died in an accident at the border."[99] This data was based on information that western authorities received from a West Berlin woman, but which turned out to be unfounded. Axel B., who at the time belonged to a NVA signal corps, died in a serious car accident near Strausberg on September 27, 1961. The car, traveling at high speed, rammed into a tree at a curve in the road. The driver of the car and two other passengers also died.[100] Sergeant Hans-Joachim R. was fatally injured on September 2, 1961, "presumably while carelessly handling a small caliber pistol."[101] The man, who was serving in a NVA flak unit stationed in the city of Brandenburg, died from his injuries. The relatives, however, were suspicious of the official information. Until her death, his mother continued to believe that he was the fugitive, unidentified at the time, who had been shot and killed in the Teltow Canal on August 29, 1961.[102]

Alleged Cases of Death

Several of the 575 cases researched during the project were found not to involve a death. The suspicion that an incident had ended in death could not be confirmed in 76 cases. Thirty of these alleged cases involved incidents in which fugitives or other Wall victims survived a shooting or accident.[103] In 46 cases, the suspicion of death was unfounded because the events in question never took place.[104] Furthermore, the "Working Group 13th of August" counted three deaths on its list twice.[105] A few of these cases will be described below. Since survivors were sometimes falsely counted as fatal victims of the East German border regime, their fates are also addressed here.

For example, according to the "Working Group 13th of August," two people came under fire at the Berlin Wall on December 10, 1961 and drowned.[106] East Berlin police reports seem to corroborate these facts, stating that that evening two fugitives swimming towards the West Berlin bank in the Spandau Schifffahrts Canal were detected and shot at. It stated further that the whereabouts of the two people could not be determined. The report nevertheless concludes that "It is highly unlikely that the border violators reached the other side of the canal."[107] West Berlin police and press reports, however, show that this assumption was wrong. Both fugitives, two young men aged 21 and 23, reached the other side, cold, but otherwise unscathed.[108]

It is hardly surprising that in cases of doubt, the border guards and their supervisors were inclined to declare the attempted escape a failure rather than to admit that a fugitive had gotten away from them. For this reason daily reports from the East German police and border troops that were based primarily on information from the guards on duty are an important source for suspected cases, but only with the knowledge that they do not always provide reliable information on an incident's outcome. False information from border guards, for example, led to the belief that a fugitive was shot and killed at the Osthafen on the night leading into September 4, 1962.[109] Both East and West reports document that a shooting took place at Osthafen that night and that the Spree River was searched the following morning. The West side assumed that they were searching for a fugitive who had been shot and had sunk into the water.[110] Border troop reports confirm this assumption, claiming that a head had been seen in the water between Osthafensteg and the Oberbaum Bridge and had sunk beneath the water's surface after shots were fired.[111] But the search for the "border violator who was presumably killed" was unsuccessful.[112] In truth, the fugitive who was supposedly shot never existed. Thirty years later the two guards involved in the shooting convincingly admitted to the public prosecutor that they had fired their guns "out of frustration" and then, fearing a reprimand, had claimed to have shot at a fugitive.[113]

Sometimes real events – be these either a successful or failed escape attempt, or another incident that occurred at the Berlin Wall – were behind cases which were originally thought to have ended in death but, in fact, did not. Not all fugitives were as fortunate as the two young men who managed to escape uninjured on December 10, 1961 although they had come under fire. It was usually East German fugitives who survived this kind of violence. Of the 30 people involved in known cases, 26 had tried to get across the border fortifications. Ten people managed to reach the West under a hail of bullets; three of these fugitives suffered bullet wounds. In sixteen cases the escape attempt failed and the fugitives were arrested. Nine people were injured by bullets fired by the border guards; four of them, the East Berlin woman Elke M., the Soviet military deserter Mindijan A., the East German citizen Wilfried S. and the border guard Hans H., were not East Germans trying to flee to the West.

In other cases the initial suspicion was found to be baseless because no one had died or been hurt, such as the shooting at the Osthafen on September 4, 1962 that is mentioned above. These cases were usually registered and prosecuted by the judicial authorities without the names ever being published on a victim list. Altogether 46 of the alleged cases could be eliminated after examination.[114]

False suspicions were usually based on witness statements made to western law enforcement authorities about events that had supposedly taken place. Someone, for example, had claimed that Bernd Lünser, who fell to his death on October 4, 1961 while trying to flee to West Berlin from the rooftop of a building on the Bernauer Strasse sector border, had been accompanied by another person who had been beaten to death in the attic of the border house. This claim, based on eyewitness reports, was spread by the western press and initiated a police investigation. An anonymous letter from East Berlin that reached the West Berlin judicial authority appeared to confirm the suspicion. "Imagine," it read, "the friend of the student with a grave on Bernauer Str. – those pigs beat him to death up in the attic."[115] East German files, however, leave no doubt that Bernd Lünser attempted to flee alone.[116] Udo Düllick was also alone on October 5, 1961 when he drowned in the Spree just before reaching the West Berlin riverbank following a dramatic chase.[117] West Berlin eye-witnesses claimed that they had seen one or two other people fleeing with him who were also killed that night. Although the claim has now been proven wrong, the rumor continues to spread.[118]

As these examples show, the western authorities looked into every suspicious incident. At the end of 1962, for example, a West Berlin woman told the police that a Swiss student she knew had observed a young man being shot at the Friedrichstrasse border crossing on December 6, 1962.[119] After fleeing from East Germany in 1963, another witness claimed that a friend of his brother's had been shot and killed in late 1962 or early 1963 while trying to escape. His mother had written to him about it.[120] In February 1963 a border guard who managed to escape declared that a sergeant had boasted of having shot two fugitives in Gross Glienicke.[121] But in each of these cases, the investigations conducted at the time and the research conducted by the ZERV in the 1990s were unable to confirm the suspicions.

In other cases charges were not filed until the 1990s. A former border guard, for example, filed charges in 1990 against a former fellow soldier. He stated that back when East Germany existed, the other soldier claimed to have shot and killed a fugitive on Bernauer Strasse in the fall of 1962. No information in the files of the border troops or the Stasi was found to corroborate this claim. The Berlin public prosecutor's office ultimately came to the conclusion that the man who had pressed charges had merely wanted to take revenge, hence the investigation was closed.[122]

These alleged cases turned out not to be based on real incidents, at least not on ones in which anyone was harmed. But there were other cases in which people who were "believed dead" had actually survived. Gerhard K., for example, had wanted to flee from the East to the West in the north of the city on October 27, 1961. West Berliners at the time had seen the fugitive shot and carried away without showing any sign of life. "Unidentified man shot dead in Reinickendorf, Wilhelmsruh S-Bahn Station," read a victim list compiled by the West Berlin senator of the interior in 1962.[123] A brochure published by the Federal Ministry for All-German Affairs that same year stated: "The critically injured individual was brutally dragged back through the barbed wire for 30 meters and left on the ground for an hour before he was carried away. He died the following morning in a hospital in the Soviet sector."[124] The death notice traveled over circuitous routes from the East to the West. At the time it was not possible to check its accuracy, but there was also no reason to question it. Gerhard K., in fact, survived, and later he reported that he had been imprisoned for his attempted escape.[125]

Some of the survivors are still registered as fatalities today. The "Working Group 13th of August," for example, claims that Elke Märtens died on June 10, 1966.[126] The woman from West Berlin, 21 years old at the time, did, in fact, come under fire on June 15, 1965 when she and Hermann Döbler accidentally crossed the border to the outskirts of East Germany in a motorboat.[127] Her companion was fatally wounded, but Elke Märtens survived her critical injuries. She did, however, suffer permanent damage from the bullet that grazed her head. In the 1990s, when an investigation was opened against the former border guard who fired the shots, she was questioned as a witness.[128] She had married by then, and still lived in Berlin, although under a different name. Because of her health, she preferred not to appear before the court. Her fate had made major headlines in the 1960s, but now she shied away from public attention. Nevertheless, journalists tracked down the woman, who was 50 years old by then, and reported on her story.[129]

The fates of survivors like Gerhard K. and Elke Märtens suggest that people who suffered violence at the Wall – if they did not die from it – were affected by it their entire lives. Günter K. evidently struggled his whole life with the effects of a failed escape that had left him with a walking disability. He had come under heavy fire at the border between the Berlin districts of Treptow and Neukölln on October 5, 1969 and was arrested with critical injuries.[130] Twenty years later, when the Wall fell in November 1989, he moved to Upper Bavaria, where he received temporary accommodation in a housing complex for repatriates, but because of his physical impairment he was unable to find work. In December 1990 he inquired of the Berlin justice senator as to whether he qualified for compensation for the injuries he had sustained during his escape attempt. His inquiry led to an investigation of the guards who had shot him. Günter K. did not live to see the outcome of the trial. He died sick and lonely in 1995.[131]

Inconclusive Cases

Archival documents could not be found for all the registered suspected cases. Eight cases remain unresolved. These cases, most of them from the recent lists of the "Working Group 13th of August," supposedly involved a death. Since the Working Group does not publish its sources, our team conducted its own research in all the relevant archives and information offices in search of records pertaining to these cases – not an easy task since the minimal details provided offered few starting points for research into the cases and the incidents were difficult to verify.

In one example, it lists the death of an unknown border troop soldier, but does not provide either an exact date or location. The man was supposedly shot and killed before July 29, 1970. This may refer to the NVA soldier Willi Born, who took his own life a short time earlier after his escape attempt failed, or to the border soldier Friedhelm Ehrlich, who – presumably without the intent to flee – was shot and killed in the border territory. The vague data available made it impossible to clarify this case. Another case involved a child who allegedly died in an accident, but neither the name nor the sex of the child, who supposedly died in 1968 between the two bridges in Klein Glienicke, is known. The information came from an informer's report which merely stated that due to the death, access to the embankment had been blocked off. Research at the resident and death registries provided no clues. The search for related reports in the Federal Archive was also without success.

Based on earlier information from the "Working Group 13th of August," Günther Gums was supposedly shot and killed during an attempted escape on March 26, 1963. Neither the files of the border troops nor the public prosecutor's investigation files mention an incident of this kind on that date or around that time. The Working Group took his name off its list of Berlin Wall victims that was published on August 13, 2008. The information on Günther Heim, who supposedly was shot and killed on February 27, 1963 while trying to escape, and on Joachim Stephan, whose death near the Marschall Bridge was dated November 22, 1966, have also been removed from the list, although no explanation was given for the deletions. Without a valid way to check these cases they remain inconclusive, even though they are no longer on the Working Group's list.

The "Working Group 13th of August" list still includes the Soviet military deserter Michail Pustowoit, who supposedly committed suicide on July 29, 1980 after he was discovered in Berlin. The name of the escape victim Lutz Schmidt was also added to the list in 2007. According to the information provided, Lutz Schmidt was born on September 14, 1952 and was supposedly shot dead on February 21,

1981 during an escape attempt. Hence he cannot be the fugitive of the same name who died at the Wall in 1987.[132] According to the BStU, there is, in fact, a man with this name and birth date, but the Stasi never recorded his involvement in an escape attempt. The public prosecutor's office never opened an investigation in connection with this name or an incident with this date.

The eighth case is based on falsely cited sources from the West Berlin police list.[133] It claims that the lifeless body of an unknown transport police officer was carried away on a truck from the closed-down subway station at Bernauer Strasse on October 16, 1972. The entry was supposedly based on a newspaper report in the "Berliner Morgenpost" from October 26, 1972. This edition of the paper, however, does not contain this information. Research of all the relevant holdings of the police, the BStU and the Federal Archive found nothing about this incident. The above text makes clear why the eight alleged cases could not be clarified.

Unsolvable Cases

In 16 alleged cases, it could not be determined whether victims at the Berlin Wall were involved or not. All of these cases involved bodies found in the border waterways. In each case the ZERV or the public prosecutor's office found nothing in its investigations of violent acts at the Wall and border to suggest that a violent crime or a connection to the border regime existed and, consequently, the investigations were closed. Our interest, however, was in examining whether there had been an escape attempt or an accident in the border territory in which assistance was denied. If this had been the case, then such victims would qualify as victims at the Berlin Wall. The names of seven of these people are known; the others could not be identified.[134] Often the bodies or body parts were not found until many weeks after the person had died. In a few cases the body had been in the water for so long that it had decomposed or had been mangled beyond recognition by boat propellers and it was impossible to determine if the body was that of a man or a woman. Sometimes it could not be determined whether the person came from East or West Berlin. On a few occasions it was suspected that the body parts discovered may have belonged to two different people.[135] In some cases identities may have been confused or incidents mixed up. The "Working Group 13th of August," for example, lists the death of an unidentified 18-year-old citizen of East Germany who supposedly drowned in the Teltow Canal on April 16, 1989. According to the findings of the Stasi, however, the dead man retrieved from the Teltow Canal on April 17, 1989 was from West Berlin and he was estimated to be about 40 years old.[136] Another case of a probable mix-up concerns two youths who tried to escape across the Spree near the Reichstag on the same day. Andreas K. managed to reach West Berlin unscathed; Heiko F.'s escape was unsuccessful, but he did not die.[137] Nevertheless, it cannot be ruled out that the death in the Teltow Canal was perhaps related to the border regime.

On June 19, 1964, border troops reported the discovery of a female body in Griebnitzsee, a lake on the outer ring of Berlin close to the border grounds. The retrieval was carried out by the Potsdam police department.[138] In this case, too, it was not clear whether an escape attempt had been involved. To clarify these kinds of cases, research was carried out on the findings and observations from West Berlin concerning bodies found in waterways during the time period in question. Another body was, in fact, found in the Havel River near the Grunewald Tower at the same time as the death in Griebnitzsee, but it had belonged to an Israeli who died in a swimming accident and was not related to the dead body retrieved from the border waters. No new insights were gained from the documents researched.[139] In another case, a female body was found on March 31, 1968 in the Britzer Zweig Canal.[140] Reports on drowned bodies in West Berlin for this time period included the suicide of a woman from Wedding in the Plötzensee lake, and a resident of Schöneberg who was found in the Landwehr Canal.[141] Here, too, there appears to be no link between the cases that could help clarify the circumstances of the cases in question.

Occasionally, previously existing files were destroyed or could not be found again, as in the case of the male body that the West Berlin fire department pulled out of the Landwehr Canal at Schlesischer Busch on September 16, 1963. Although the East German police report indicates that a large crowd had gathered, no files on the incident could be found from holdings of the West Berlin police, the state bureau of criminal investigation, the state security police, the fire department or the Institute of Forensic Medicine. According to information provided by the municipal fire department to the investigating public prosecutor in 1995, files on operations are only kept for five years.[142] The West Berlin press did not report on this incident either. Thus, in this case, it remains unclear whether a Wall death was involved or not. In all the unclear cases, additional sources were sought to determine whether or not they involved a Wall death, but for Otto M., Barbara B., Klaus Sch., Wilfried M., Thomas B., Christian G., Carsten D.G. and the nine unidentified dead people pulled out of the border waters, no additional documents could be found.

Concluding Remarks

For at least 136 people who died at the Berlin Wall between 1961 and 1989, it could be proven that a causal or spatial connection existed between their deaths and either an attempted escape or actions taken by the East German armed forces in the border territory. Beyond these well-defined criteria, the examples described above show that the delineation between victims *at the* Wall and the more broadly defined victims *of the* Wall tends to be less clear. For most of the people who died at the Berlin border crossings – the total number is much higher than the 251 cases of death that we have documented here – information on the exact place and circumstances of the deaths was not available. The cases of suicide, fatal accidents involving civilians and border soldiers and bodies found in the border waters and in "no man's land" are even more difficult to judge.

Regardless of the very different ways there are of calculating how many people died, all the people who died at the Berlin Wall – and at the inner and outer German border– are evidence and consequences of the violence used by the Communist Party leadership to maintain its power and preserve the existence of the East German state. In addition to the fatal victims, a vast number of people were injured during escape attempts. Furthermore, forced evacuations of the border territories caused thousands of East German citizens to lose their homes.

The other side of the story is presented by the 40,000 East Germans who, between the construction of the Wall and the fall of the Wall, succeeded in fleeing through the border fortifications, often under daring circumstances and with the knowledge that they were risking their lives. It remains unclear exactly how many escapes failed either because the people were discovered or betrayed. Tens of thousands of people who had wanted to escape were arrested between 1961 and 1989, either while they were still planning their escapes or when they had set off for the border. Statistics of the East German general state prosecutor's office show that close to 110,000 proceedings were conducted between 1961 and 1988 against people charged with "flight from the Republic" or an "unauthorized border crossing."[143] According to a study on political prisoners based on a control sample of East German criminal statistics, between 1960 and 1988 prison sentences for "flight from the Republic" were imposed throughout East Germany in more than 71,000 cases.[144] Moreover, especially in the seventies and eighties, East German citizens who applied for an exit permit to leave East Germany for the West were ostracized, discriminated against and criminalized. Tens of thousands of people who tried to claim their right to freedom of movement were imprisoned for "interfering with national or societal activities" (§ 214 DDR-StGB), for "establishing illegal contact" (§ 219 DDR-StGB), for "treasonous communication of information or agent activities" (§§ 99, 100 DDR-StGB) and for "public vilification" (§ 220 DDR-StGB).

People who wanted no more than to leave their country were ostracized, imprisoned, injured and killed. This violation of human rights was part of a political system that could not exist without a wall – it collapsed when the Wall fell.

1 Text: Martin Ahrends, Udo Baron and Hans-Hermann Hertle ("Death at the Border Crossings") and Christine Brecht (the other sections); editing: Maria Nooke.
2 See "Lagefilme und Rapporte der Transportpolizei / Abschnitt Berlin / Operativstab," in: PHS, Bestand Trapo.
3 "Rapport Nr. 235/61 der Transportpolizei / Abschnitt Berlin / Operativstab, Berlin, 24.8.1961, p. 3," in: PHS, Bestand Trapo.
4 See "Ministerrat der DDR / MfS / HA VI, Ordnung über die Durchführung der Paßkontrolle an den Grenzübergangsstellen der DDR – Paßkontrollordnung," in: BStU, MfS, VI/Ltr./RuG/534/78. In response to inquiries from travelers, the staff of the Passport Control Unit (PKE) was said to be part of the "East German Border Troop Command." (See ibid., Punkt I/1, p. 9). See Monika Tantzscher, *Hauptabteilung VI: Grenzkontrollen, Reise- und Touristenverkehr, MfS-Handbuch, Teil III/14*, published by the Bundesbeauftragte für die Unterlagen des Staatssicherheitsdienstes der ehemaligen DDR, Berlin, 2005.
5 See *Der Tagesspiegel*, 27.4.1965; *Berliner Morgenpost*, 27.4.1965
6 See "Ergebnis der Überprüfung zum natürlichen Tod des Bürgers der Bundesrepublik Deutschland, Rudolf Burkert, am 10. April 1983," in: BArch, DY 30/2393, Bl. 36–44.
7 See ibid.
8 "Protokoll der Vernehmung des angeheirateten Cousins von Rudolf Burkert durch die BVfS Magdeburg/ Abteilung Transitüberwachung Autobahn, 10.4.1983, 13.00 Uhr," in: BStU, MfS, HA IX Nr. 3552, Bl. 49.
9 "Vernehmung [des Grenzzollamts Drewitz] zur Person Burkert, Rudolf, [10.4.1983], 14.00 Uhr," in: BStU, MfS, HA IX Nr. 3965, Bl. 9.

10 *Berliner Morgenpost,* 16.4.1983.

11 See "Abschrift des Telefonats Kohl – Honecker vom 18.4.1983," in: Heinrich Potthoff, *Die »Koalition der Vernunft«. Deutschlandpolitik in den 80er Jahren,* Munich, 1995, pp. 112–118.

12 *Der Spiegel,* 25.4.1983

13 *Der Tagesspiegel,* 13.11.1994; see also Franz Josef Strauß, *Die Erinnerungen,* Berlin, 1989, pp. 470ff.

14 "Gerichtsmedizinische Stellungnahme des Instituts für Gerichtliche Medizin der Charité der Humboldt-Universität in der Leichensache Rudolf Burkert, 22.4.1983," in: BStU, MfS, HA IX Nr. 3965, Bl. 91.

15 *Frankfurter Allgemeine Zeitung,* 27.4.1983.

16 See *Stern,* 12.4.1995.

17 "Vermerk der Staatsanwaltschaft Neuruppin vom 8. August 1997," in: StA Neuruppin, Az. 61 AR-16/97, Bl. 77.

18 *Der Spiegel,* 25.4.1983.

19 See "Hinweis [des MfS] zur Durchführung einer »Protestaktion« am 23.4.1983 in Westberlin im Zusammenhang mit der Hetzkampagne um den Tod des DDR-Bürgers Burkert an der Grenzübergangsstelle Drewitz," in: BStU, MfS, HA IX Nr. 3552, Bl. 35–36.

20 *Frankfurter Allgemeine Zeitung,* 29.4.1983.

21 *BZ,* 28.4.1983.

22 *Die Welt,* 7.5.1983.

23 "Antwort des Parlamentarischen Staatssekretärs des Bundesministeriums für innerdeutsche Beziehungen, Dr. Hennig, Deutscher Bundestag," Drucksache 10/64.

24 "Bericht zur Lage der Nation," Deutscher Bundestag, Plenarprotokoll 10/16 vom 23.6.1983, p. 991.

25 See "Lagefilme der Transportpolizei/Abschnitt Berlin/Operativstab" of those days, in: PHS, Bestand Trapo.

26 On this and the following, see the conversation Hans-Hermann Hertle conducted with Joachim B., 2.6.2009.

27 See "Lagefilm der Transportpolizei/ODH, 17.9.1985–18.9.1985," in: PHS, Bestand Trapo.

28 See "Meldung der Volkspolizei, 31.8.1961," in: LAB, C Rep. 303-26-01, Nr. 239, Bl. 135; "Informationsberichte der PdVP für die Zeit vom 26.8.–2.9.1961," in: LAB, Bestand PdVP-Rapporte, Nr. 237, Bl. 182.

29 Ibid.

30 See, for example, "Zeichen kommunistischer Unmenschlichkeit: Erschütterndes Ansteigen der Selbstmordziffern und anderer Verzweiflungstaten in Ost-Berlin," in: *Bulletin des Presse- und Informationsamtes der Bundesregierung,* 24.1.1962.

31 See Udo Grashoff, *"In einem Anfall von Depression ...." Selbsttötungen in der DDR,* Berlin, 2006, pp. 218–227.

32 On the suicide taboo and its development, see ibid., pp. 470–474.

33 See contemporary documents in: StA Berlin 2 Js 130/91, and data from the victim lists of the "Working Group 13th of August."

34 See "Liste 'Opfer der Mauer' des Polizeipräsidenten in Berlin 15.6.1962," and "'Aufstellung über die bei Fluchtversuchen an der DL getöteten Personen' des Senators für Inneres von Berlin, 21.2.1963," in: BArch, B 137, Nr. 15650, no pag. See also Bundesministerium für gesamtdeutsche Fragen (ed.), *Ulbrichts Mauer. Zahlen, Fakten, Daten,* Bonn/Berlin, 1962, and Bundesministerium für gesamtdeutsche Fragen (ed.), *Verletzungen der Menschenrechte. Unrechtshandlungen und Zwischenfälle an der Berliner Sektorengrenze seit Errichtung der Mauer,* 2nd edition, Bonn/Berlin, n.d. (1962).

35 "Untersuchungsbericht der HA I/MB V/Unterabteilung 1. MSD,15.8.1961," in: BStU, MfS, ZAIG Nr. 459, here Bl. 6.

36 See "Tagesrapport der HV der DVP/Operativstab, 15.8.1961," in: BArch, DO 1/11.0/1350, Bl. 244.

37 See contemporary documents in: StA Berlin, Az. 2 Js 1103/92, and data from the victim lists of the "Working Group 13th of August."

38 See Grashoff, *"In einem Anfall von Depression,"* p. 148.

39 See ibid., p. 133.

40 See Heinz Josef Wagner, *Die Militärjustiz der DDR. Unter besonderer Berücksichtigung der Rechtsprechung der Militärgerichte,* 2 vol., Berlin, 2006.

41 It can be assumed that the border troop files do not register all these cases since suicides committed in hometowns were usually only registered by the local investigation police.

42 See "Tagesmeldung 132/74 der NVA/Kommando der Grenztruppen, 13.5.1974" in: BArch, GT 6395, Bl. 131–133; see also contemporary documents in: StA, Az. 27 AR 100/95, and data from the victim lists of the "Working Group 13th of August."

43 See "Rapport Nr. 209/77 der BDVP," in: BLHA, MdI, PA, Rep. 471/15.2. Nr. 543, and data from the victim lists of the "Working Group 13th of August."

44 "Operative Tagesmeldung 364/64 der NVA/Stadtkommandantur Berlin/Operative Abteilung, 30.12.1964," in: BArch, VA-07/6030, Bl. 261–264, here Bl. 264.

45 See BStU, MfS, AIM 287/62, Personalakte, Bl. 20, 23–25, 27–30; BArch, Pt 7799, Bl. 5–96, and data from the victim lists of the "Working Group 13th of August."

46 See "Bericht von Oltn. B., 1. Grenzbrigade, an Stadtkommandant Poppe, 27.12.1962," in: BArch, VA-07/8455, Bd. 2, Bl. 431–435.

47 Inquiries made to the Federal Archive/Military Archive were only successful on three cases addressed here: Andreas J., Mario D. and Henry F., although the latter belonged to the border training unit in Rudolstein. Inquiries to the BStU only led to information regarding Mario D.

48 See "Tagesmeldung, Kommando der Grenztruppen, 12.9.1984," in: BArch, GTÜ 12454-Rot, Bl. 36–39, here Bl. 39, and BArch, DVW 13/92816 and BArch, GTÜ 12454 Rot, Bl. 36–39.

49 "Abschiedsbrief von Andreas J. an seine Eltern und Geschwister, 11.9.1984," in: BArch, DVW 13/92816, n. pag.

50 "Abschlußbericht, 6.9.1984," in: BArch, DVW 13/92816, n. pag.

51 See contemporary documents in the investigative files on the death of Heinz Cyrus in: StA Berlin, Az. 2 Js 85/90.

52 "Chronik der 1. Grenzbrigade 1962/63," in: BArch, VA-07/16642, Bl. 51.

53 See "Kurzinformation über Ergebnisse der Grenzsicherung, NVA/Stadtkommandantur Berlin/Oberoffizier für Auswertung, 25.7.1965," in: BArch, VA-07/6004, Bl. 121–123; "Kurzinformation der NVA/Stadtkommandantur Berlin/Operative Abteilung, 5.8.1965," in: Ibid., Bl. 124–129, and data from the victim lists of the "Working Group 13th of August."

54 "Abschlußbericht über die Selbsttötung des Soldaten des Kompanie- und Batteriechefs/GR 34, 14.4.1980," in: BStU, ASt. Potsdam, ZMA Wit Nr. 748, Bl. 72–76; also in: BArch, DVW 13/66894, Bl. 20–24.

55 Ibid.

56 See Dietmar Schultke, *"Keiner kommt durch." Die Geschichte der innerdeutschen Grenze* 1945–1990, 3rd ed., Berlin, 2004, pp. 124–127; Ibid., "Das Grenzregime der DDR. Innenansichten der siebziger und achtziger Jahre," in: APuZ, B 50/97, pp. 43–52.

57 See Jochen Maurer, "Die Bewachung der Bewacher. Die Arbeit der Staatssicherheit in den Grenztruppen der DDR," in: *Militärgeschichte. Zeitschrift für historische Bildung*, Vol. 1/2008, pp. 10–13.

58 Grashoff, "*In einem Anfall von Depression*," p. 95.

59 Ibid., p. 99.

60 See the biographical essays in this book on Philipp Held, Erna Kelm, Günter Wiedenhöft, Horst Plischke, Wolf-Olaf Muszynski, Norbert Wolscht, Rainer Gneiser, Bernd Lehmann, Henri Weise and Rainer Liebeke.

61 See, for example, Werner Filmer/Heribert Schwan, *Opfer der Mauer. Die geheimen Protokolle des Todes*, Munich, 1991.

62 According to the BStU, MfS daily reports for Berlin and Potsdam do not exist for all time periods of interest here.

63 See "WSI, Insp. Bln., ODH-Bereich, Monatsberichte, Januar–Dezember 1979," in: LAB, C Rep. 303-26-02, Karton-Nr. 989.

64 See contemporary documents in: StA Berlin, Az. 27 AR 718/94.

65 See contemporary documents in: StA Berlin, Az. 27 AR 53/95, and data from the victim lists of the "Working Group 13th of August."

66 See contemporary documents in: StA Berlin, Az. 27 AR 645/94, and data from the victim lists of the "Working Group 13th of August."

67 See "Sofortmeldung [des GR 38] über den Fund einer Leiche, 16.4.1963," in: BArch, VA-07/8462, Bl. 174; "Ereignismeldung, 17.4.1963," in: PHS, Bestand Ereignismeldungen der West-Berliner Schutzpolizei; *Berliner Morgenpost*, 18.4.1963; see also contemporary documents in: StA Berlin, Az. 27 AR 67/92, and data from the victim lists of the "Working Group 13th of August."

68 "See "Sofortmeldung [des GR 38] über den Fund einer Leiche, 21.5.1963," in: BArch, VA-07/8462, Bl. 210; *Der Tagesspiegel*, 22.5.1963 and 31.5.1963; see also contemporary documents in: StA Berlin, Az. 7 AR 31/92, and data from the victim lists of the "Working Group 13th of August."

69 See "Operative Tagesmeldung, NVA/Stadtkommandantur Berlin/Operative Abteilung, 22.3.1966," in: BArch, VA-07/6035, Bl. 136–137; "Ereignismeldung, 22.3.1966," in: PHS, "Bestand Ereignismeldungen der West-

Berliner Schutzpolizei"; *BZ*, 21.3.1966; *Der Tagesspiegel,* 22.3.1966; See also contemporary documents in: StA Berlin, Az. 27 AR 55/95, and data from the victim lists of the "Working Group 13th of August."

70 See "Lagefilm, 4./5.2.1981," in: PHS, Bestand PdVP-Rapporte; *Berliner Morgenpost*, 5.2.1981; *Der Tagesspiegel*, 5.2.1981; see also contemporary documents in: StA Berlin, Az. 27 AR 79/95, and data from the victim lists of the "Working Group 13th of August."

71 See "Ereignismeldung, 9.7.1965," in: PHS, Bestand Ereignismeldungen der West-Berliner Schutzpolizei.

72 On the death of the unknown fugitive, see the biographical essay in this book.

73 See contemporary documents in: StA Berlin, Az. 27 AR 89/97 and Az. 7 AR 390/92.

74 Other authors, however, count the person in this unsolved case as a Wall victim. See the data from the victim lists of the "Working Group 13th of August" and Filmer/Schwan, *Opfer der Mauer*.

75 See data from the victim lists of the "Working Group 13th of August" which also counts this unidentified person as a Wall victim, although the identity and circumstances of death are not clarified.

76 "PdVP-Rapport Nr. 258, 16.9.1963," in: PHS, Bestand PdVP-Rapporte.

77 See contemporary documents in: StA Berlin, Az. 27 AR 187/95. ZERV investigations found that the fire department operation files are generally not kept for more than 15 years, but that the state bureau of criminal investigation has to maintain its files on unidentified dead and missing people for 25 years.

78 See documents in: StA Berlin, Az. 2 Js 388/92.

79 See "Tagesmeldung 151/72, NVA/Kommando der Grenztruppen/Operativer Diensthabender, 31.5.1972," in: BArch, GT 6382, Bl. 79–82, here Bl. 81, and data from the victim lists of the "Working Group 13th of August."

80 See contemporary documents in: StA Berlin, Az. 27 AR 1/95. According to the BStU, Stasi files were not preserved. An inquiry to the Federal Archive/Military Archive found that military state prosecutor files do not exist either.

81 "Monatsbericht der Wasserschutzinspektion Berlin," in: LAB, C Rep. 303-26-02, Karton-No. 989, n. pag. These are documents from the East Berlin police that had not been viewed or evaluated until now. Thomas B. is not registered on the victim lists of the "Working Group 13th of August."

82 See contemporary documents in: StA Berlin, Az. 27 AR 13/95.

83 See "PdVP-Rapport, 20.1.1962," in: PHS, Bestand PdVP-Rapporte. The name Barbara B. is listed under the heading, "Suspicion of exiting East Germany illegally."

84 "PdVP-Rapport, 6.4.1962," in: PHS, Bestand PdVP-Rapporte. See also "Grenzrapport, MdI/Bereitschaftspolizei/1. Grenzbrigade (B), 6.4.1962," in: BArch, VA-07/4752, Bd. 1, Bl. 42–46, here Bl. 46.

85 See contemporary documents in: StA Berlin, Az. 27 Js 317/92.

86 See "Ermittlungsbericht der MfS-HA Kader und Schulung/Abt. Kader/Referat 6, 13.10.1965," in: BStU, MfS, KS III, 66/77, Bl. 2, 21–23.

87 See contemporary documents in: StA Berlin, Az. 27 Js 173/96, and the news reporting in *BZ*, *Berliner Morgenpost* and *Tagesspiegel* on March 18 and 19, 1982.

88 The "Working Group 13th of August" lists all eight cases as victims at the wall.

89 See contemporary documents in: StA Berlin, Az. 27 AR 71/93.

90 These four cases involved Raimund M., Helmut B., Hans-Joachim M. and Peter U.

91 The deceased were Anna Kirste, Christian T., Willi B. and Rudolf W.

92 See "Information zum Leichenfund des MfS/HA IX/7, 9.1.1974," in: BStU, MfS, AS 109/77, Bl. 4–7; "Abschlußbericht der PdVP, Abt. Morduntersuchungskommission, 18.1.1974," in: Ibid., Bl. 10–12, and contemporary documents in: StA Berlin, Az. 27 AR 2/95.

93 *Berliner Morgenpost*, 11.1.1974.

94 See the reports in: BStU, MfS, HA I Nr. 10442, Bl. 67, 69, 74, 76–77, and BStU, MfS, HA I Nr. 14780.

95 See BArch, VA-01/5089, Bl. 270–276.

96 On this case, see files in: StA Berlin, Az. 27 Js/56 Js 277/03.

97 See contemporary files in: StA Berlin, Az. 27 AR 9/95, and data from the victim lists of the "Working Group 13th of August."

98 See "PdVP-Rapport Nr. 76/88," in: PHS, Bestand PdVP-Rapporte; *Berliner Morgenpost,* 17.4.1988.

99 See Bundesministerium für gesamtdeutsche Fragen (ed.), *Verletzungen der Menschenrechte. Unrechtshandlungen und Zwischenfälle an der Berliner Sektorengrenze seit Errichtung der Mauer*, 2nd printing, Bonn/Berlin, n.d. (1962), and data from the victim lists of the "Working Group 13th of August."

100 See the description of the case in: StA Berlin: 2 Js 112/90.

101 See "Bericht der DVP über besondere Vorkommnisse, 3.9.1961," in: BLHA, Rep. 471/15.1, Bd. 223, Bl. 56.

102 See contemporary documents in: StA Neuruppin, Az. 61 Js 23/95 (betr. Tod von Roland Hoff).

103 Of these 30 alleged cases, 17 were investigated on the basis of data from the "Working Group 13th of August," although by 2008, this association only had seven of these cases on its list. Five of these cases were registered in one of the following publications: Werner Filmer/Heribert Schwan, *Opfer der Mauer. Die geheimen Protokolle des Todes*, Munich, 1991; Heiner Sauer/Hans-Otto Plumeyer, *Der Salzgitter-Report. Die Zentrale Erfassungsstelle berichtet über Verbrechen im SED-Staat*, Munich, 1991. Five others were examined because they had been kept on the list of the public prosecutor's office. One case was discovered by chance during an examination of state prosecutor files. Another case was added on the basis of eye-witness statements. And finally, the last of these alleged cases was based on an initial suspicion derived from our own archival research.

104 These were usually cases from the unpublished list of the Berlin public prosecutor's office. Seven were taken from the list of the "Working Group 13th of August." By 2008, however, only four of these cases were still on its list.

105 In 2008 two cases, Henri Weise and Barbara B., were still counted twice on the list of the "Working Group 13th of August.

106 See the list of the "Working Group 13th of August" from 2008, p. 8.

107 "Rapport Nr. 342 der HV DVP, 11.12.1961," in: BArch, DO 1/11.0/1358, Bl. 176–193, here Bl. 179. See also "Spitzenmeldung, Kommando Bereitschaftspolizei, 10.12.1961," in: BArch, VA-07/4724, Bd. 1, Bl. 94.

108 See "Ereignismeldung, 11.12.1961," in: PHS, Bestand Ereignismeldungen der West-Berliner Schutzpolizei; *Der Tag*, 12.12.1961.

109 See Filmer/Schwan, *Opfer der Mauer*, p. 107. The authors believe the victim in question was probably Ernst Mundt, who was shot the same day but many hours later at a different site at the Wall. See also Volker Koop, *"Den Gegner vernichten." Die Grenzsicherung der DDR,* Bonn, 1996, p. 368.

110 See "Ereignismeldung, 5.9.1962," in: PHS, Bestand Ereignismeldungen der West-Berliner Schutzpolizei; *Der Tagesspiegel*, 5.9.1962.

111 See BArch, VA-07/4753, Bd. 3, Bl. 31, and VA-07/4726, Bd. 1, Bl. 59–61, here Bl. 61.

112 Ibid.

113 See StA Berlin, Az. 27 Js 1087/93. See also Koop, *"Den Gegner vernichten"*; Filmer/Schwan, *Opfer der Mauer.*

114 Of these 46 cases, the "Work Group 13th of August" names seven from 2005 to 2007 and only four in 2008, two of which were allegedly Düllick's companions. Most of the cases (27 altogether) were examined because they were also on the Berlin public prosecutor's list. Another five were added on the basis of our own research (three from contemporary press reports, one from LAB research, one during the evaluation of court case files pertaining to a different case) and six named in the Salzgitter Report (and in part in Filmer/Schwan), plus one case named by Filmer/Schwan and by Koop.

115 See "Abschrift eines anonymen Briefes aus Ost-Berlin, WB Polizei, 10.4.1962," in: StA Berlin, Az. 27 Js 140/90, Bd. 1, Bl. 43.

116 See "Verfügung der Staatsanwaltschaft, 14.7.1995", ibid., Bd. 3, Bl. 4–8, and the biographical essay on Bernd Lünser in this book.

117 See StA Berlin, Az. 27 Js 143/90, and the biographical essay on Udo Düllick in this book.

118 See Alexandra Hildebrandt, *Neue Zahl der ermittelten Todesopfer*, Berlin, 2008, p. 8.

119 See StA Berlin, Az. 27 Js 241/93.

120 See StA Berlin, Az. 27 Js 456/92.

121 See StA Berlin, Az. 27 Js 278/93.

122 See StA Berlin, Az. 27 Js 254/90.

123 See "Der Polizeipräsident in Berlin, Liste »Opfer der Mauer«, 15.6.1962," in: BArch, B 137, No. 15650, n. pag.

124 Bundesministerium für gesamtdeutsche Fragen (ed.), *Verletzungen der Menschenrechte. Unrechtshandlungen und Zwischenfälle an der Berliner Sektorengrenze seit Errichtung der Mauer,* 2nd edition, Bonn/Berlin, n.d. (1962), here p. 20. In the first edition of the "Salzgitter-Report" report, published in 1991, and in the documentation, *Opfer der Mauer*, by Werner Filmer and Heribert Schwan, published the same year, Gerhard K. is referred to as the unknown victim. He also appears on the lists of the "Working Group 13th of August" from 2005 to 2007; but not in that from 2008.

125 See contemporary documents in: StA Berlin, Az. 27/2 Js 142/90.

126 See Alexandra Hildebrandt, *Neue Zahl der ermittelten Todesopfer*, Berlin, 2008, p. 9.

127 See the biographical essay on Hermann Döbler in this book.

128 See the files in: StA Berlin, Az. 2 Js 161/90, Bd. 2, Bl. 49–51.

129 See *BZ*, 23.9.1993; *Die Welt,* 21.10.1993 and 26.10.1993; *Berliner Kurier,* 18.11.1993.

130 Günter K. is registered on the victim lists of the "Working Group 13th of August" from 2005 to 2007. His name no longer appears on the list from 2008.

131 See files in: StA Berlin, Az. 2 Js 2/91.

132 See the biographical essay on Lutz Schmidt in this book.

133 "Opfer der Mauer." Polizeiliche Liste des Polizeipräsidenten in Berlin/Abt. I, o.O. (Berlin), n.d. (1990), Part 3.

134 Otto M. (found dead in the Spree River on 14.3.1962), Barbara B. (found dead in the Spree River on 5.4.1962), Klaus Sch. (found dead in the Spree River on 18.7.1970), Wilfried M. (found dead in the Spree River on 30.5.1972), Thomas B. (found dead in the Spree River on 17.3.1978), Christian G. (found dead in the Spree River on 17.2.1987), Carsten DG. (drowned on 6.7.1988) and nine other unidentified bodies retrieved from the water on the following days: 15.9.1963, 19.6.1964, 7.10.1964, 8.7.1965, 21.11.1966, 31.3.1968, 16.4.1976, 26.3.1979,17.4.1989.

135 "PdVP-Rapporte Nr. 8458 und 8459 mit Informationen über die Bergung von Leichenteilen am Osthafen am 2.3.1976, 17.3.1976, 16.4.1976," in: PHS, Bestand PdVP-Rapporte.

136 "Erstmeldung/Vorkommnisuntersuchung der BVfS Potsdam, 19.4.1989," in: BStU, Ast. Potsdam, AKG Nr. 2478, Bl. 111; see also handwritten note [MfS HA IX], 17.4.1989, in: MfS HA IX Nr. 1304, Bd. 1, Bl. 123.

137 On the two young men's escape, see *Berliner Morgenpost,* 18.4.1989; *Der Tagesspiegel,* 18.4.1989; BZ, 18.4.1989.

138 "Tagesmeldung Nr. 16/VI/64 des Operativen Diensthabenden der NVA, 20.6.1964," in: BArch VA-01/5088, Bl. 71–72.

139 "Eilmeldung der West-Berliner Polizei, 20.6.1964," in: PHS, Bestand Grenzvorkommnisse.

140 "Eilmeldung der West-Berliner Polizei, 1.4.1968," in: PHS, Bestand Grenzvorkommnisse.

141 "Zwei Wasserleichen von der Polizei identifiziert," in: *Berliner Morgenpost,* 3.4.1968; "Berliner Notizen," in: *Der Tagesspiegel,* 2.4.1968.

142 See contemporary documents in: StA Berlin, Az. 27 AR 187/95; see also "PdVP-Rapport Nr. 258, 16.9.1963," in: PHS, Bestand PdVP-Rapporte.

143 See "Statistisches Material des GStA" in: Johannes Raschka, *Justizpolitik im SED-Staat. Anpassung und Wandel des Strafrechts während der Amtszeit Honeckers,* Cologne, Weimar, Vienna, 2000, p. 314 ff.; see also: Stiftung Gedenkstätte Berlin-Hohenschönhausen (ed.), *Die vergessenen Opfer der Mauer. Flucht und Inhaftierung in Deutschland 1961–1989,* Berlin, n.d. (2004), p. 33.

144 See Jürgen Wilke/Wilhelm Heinz Schröder, *Politische Gefangene in der DDR – eine quantitative Analyse,* Cologne, 1997, p. 92.

Appendix

Chronological Overview of 136 Victims at the Wall

Fugitives who were either shot, suffered a fatal accident or took their own lives at the Berlin Wall between 1961 and 1989; individuals from the East and the West who did not intend to flee but were killed or suffered a fatal accident in the border territory

Year	Name	Born	Died	Circumstances of death	p.
1961	Ida Siekmann	08-23-1902	08-22-1961	Fatally injured while trying to escape	36
	Günter Litfin	01-19-1937	08-24-1961	Shot while trying to escape	39
	Roland Hoff	03-19-1934	08-29-1961	Shot while trying to escape	42
	Rudolf Urban	06-06-1914	09-17-1961	Died from injuries incurred while trying to escape	45
	Olga Segler	07-31-1881	09-26-1961	Died from injuries incurred while trying to escape	48
	Bernd Lünser	03-11-1939	10-04-1961	Fatally injured under fire while trying to escape	50
	Udo Düllick	08-03-1936	10-05-1961	Drowned under fire while trying to escape	53
	Werner Probst	06-18-1936	10-14-1961	Shot while trying to escape	56
	Lothar Lehmann	01-28-1942	11-26-1961	Drowned while trying to escape	59
	Dieter Wohlfahrt	05-27-1941	12-09-1961	Shot while helping others to escape	62
	Ingo Krüger	01-31-1940	12-11-1961	Drowned while trying to escape	65
	Georg Feldhahn	08-12-1941	12-19-1961	Drowned while trying to escape	68
1962	Dorit Schmiel	04-25-1941	02-19-1962	Shot while trying to escape	71
	Heinz Jercha	07-01-1934	03-27-1962	Shot while helping others to escape	74
	Philipp Held	05-02-1942	April 1962	Drowned while trying to escape	77
	Klaus Brueske	09-14-1938	04-18-1962	Shot while trying to escape	80

Year	Name	Born	Died	Circumstances of death	p.
	Peter Böhme	08-17-1942	04-18-1962	Shot while trying to escape	83
	Horst Frank	05-07-1942	04-29-1962	Shot while trying to escape	86
	Lutz Haberlandt	04-29-1938	05-27-1962	Shot while trying to escape	89
	Axel Hannemann	04-27-1945	06-05-1962	Shot while trying to escape	91
	Erna Kelm	07-21-1908	06-11-1962	Drowned while trying to escape	94
	Wolfgang Glöde	02-01-1949	06-11-1962	Accidentally shot while playing in the border area	96
	Siegfried Noffke	12-09-1939	06-28-1962	Shot while helping others to escape	99
	Peter Fechter	01-14-1944	08-17-1962	Shot while trying to escape	102
	Hans-Dieter Wesa	01-10-1943	08-23-1962	Shot while trying to escape	106
	Ernst Mundt	12-02-1921	09-04-1962	Shot while trying to escape	109
	Anton Walzer	04-27-1902	10-08-1962	Shot while trying to escape	112
	Horst Plischke	07-12-1939	11-19-1962	Drowned while trying to escape	115
	Ottfried Reck	12-14-1944	11-27-1962	Shot while trying to escape	117
	Günter Wiedenhöft	02-14-1942	12-06-1962	Drowned while trying to escape	120
1963	Hans Räwel	12-11-1941	01-01-1963	Shot while trying to escape	123
	Horst Kutscher	07-05-1931	01-15-1963	Shot while trying to escape	126
	Peter Kreitlow	01-15-1943	01-24-1963	Shot while trying to escape	129
	Wolf-Olaf Muszynski	02-01-1947	Feb. 1963	Drowned while trying to escape	133
	Peter Mädler	07-10-1943	04-26-1963	Shot while trying to escape	135
	Klaus Schröter	02-21-1940	11-04-1963	Shot at while trying to escape and drowned due to injuries	138
	Dietmar Schulz	10-21-1939	11-25-1963	Fatally injured while trying to escape	141
	Dieter Berger	10-27-1939	12-13-1963	Shot while trying to escape	143
	Paul Schultz	10-02-1945	12-25-1963	Shot while trying to escape	146

Year	Name	Born	Died	Circumstances of death	p.
1964	Walter Hayn	01-31-1939	02-27-1964	Shot while trying to escape	149
	Adolf Philipp	08-17-1943	05-05-1964	West Berliner shot in the border area	152
	Walter Heike	09-20-1934	06-22-1964	Shot while trying to escape	155
	Norbert Wolscht	10-27-1943	07-28-1964	Drowned while trying to escape	158
	Rainer Gneiser	01-10-1944	07-28-1964	Drowned while trying to escape	161
	Hildegard Trabant	06-12-1927	08-18-1964	Shot dead while trying to escape	163
	Wernhard Mispelhorn	11-10-1945	08-20-1964	Shot at while trying to escape and died of his injuries	166
	Hans-Joachim Wolf	08-08-1947	11-26-1964	Shot while trying to escape	169
	Joachim Mehr	04-03-1945	12-03-1964	Shot while trying to escape	172
1965	Unidentified fugitive		01-19-1965	Drowned while trying to escape	175
	Christian Buttkus	02-21-1944	03-04-1965	Shot while trying to escape	177
	Ulrich Krzemien	09-13-1940	03-25-1965	Drowned as a West Berliner in border waters	181
	Peter Hauptmann	03-20-1939	05-03-1965	Shot in the border area with no intent to escape	185
	Hermann Döbler	10-28-1922	06-15-1965	West Berliner shot in the border area	188
	Klaus Kratzel	03-03-1940	08-08-1965	Fatally injured while trying to escape	191
	Klaus Garten	07-19-1941	08-18-1965	Shot while trying to escape	194
	Walter Kittel	11-21-1942	10-18-1965	Shot while trying to escape	197
	Heinz Cyrus	06-05-1936	11-11-1965	Fatally injured under fire while trying to escape	201
	Heinz Sokolowski	12-17-1917	11-25-1965	Shot while trying to escape	204
	Erich Kühn	02-27-1903	12-03-1965	Shot while trying to escape	207
	Heinz Schöneberger	06-07-1938	12-26-1965	Shot while helping others to escape	210
1966	Dieter Brandes	10-23-1946	01-11-1966	Shot at while trying to escape and died of his injuries	213
	Willi Block	06-05-1934	02-07-1966	Shot while trying to escape	216

Year	Name	Born	Died	Circumstances of death	p.
	Jörg Hartmann	10-27-1955	03-14-1966	Shot while trying to escape	220
	Lothar Schleusener	01-14-1953	03-14-1966	Shot while trying to escape	223
	Willi Marzahn	06-03-1944	03-19-1966	Shot while trying to escape or committed suicide	226
	Eberhard Schulz	03-11-1946	03-30-1966	Shot while trying to escape	229
	Michael Kollender	02-19-1945	04-25-1966	Shot while trying to escape	232
	Paul Stretz	02-28-1935	04-29-1966	West Berliner shot in the border area	235
	Eduard Wroblewski	03-03-1933	07-26-1966	Shot while trying to escape	238
	Heinz Schmidt	10-26-1919	08-29-1966	West Berliner shot in the border area	241
	Andreas Senk	1960	09-13-1966	Drowned in border waters	244
	Karl-Heinz Kube	04-10-1949	12-16-1966	Shot while trying to escape	246
1967	Max Sahmland	03-28-1929	01-27-1967	Shot at while trying to escape and drowned because of his injuries	250
	Franciszek Piesik	11-23-1942	10-17-1967	Drowned while trying to escape	253
1968	Elke Weckeiser	10-31-1945	02-18-1968	Shot while trying to escape	255
	Dieter Weckeiser	02-15-1943	02-19-1968	Shot while trying to escape	255
	Herbert Mende	02-09-1939	03-10-1968	Shot while trying to escape	258
	Bernd Lehmann	07-31-1949	05-28-1968	Drowned while trying to escape	262
	Siegfried Krug	07-22-1939	07-06-1968	Shot as a West Berliner in the border area	265
	Horst Körner	07-12-1947	11-15-1968	Shot while trying to escape	269
1969	Johannes Lange	12-17-1940	04-09-1969	Shot while trying to escape	272
	Klaus-Jürgen Kluge	07-25-1948	09-13-1969	Shot while trying to escape	275
	Leo Lis	05-10-1924	09-20-1969	Shot while trying to escape	277
1970	Christel Wehage	12-15-1946	03-10-1970	Committed suicide after a failed escape with a hijacked airplane	280

Year	Name	Born	Died	Circumstances of death	p.
	Eckhard Wehage	07-08-1948	03-10-1970	Committed suicide after a failed escape with a hijacked airplane	280
	Heinz Müller	05-16-1943	06-19-1970	Shot as a West Berliner in the border area	283
	Willi Born	07-19-1950	07-07-1970	Committed suicide after a failed escape attempt	285
	Friedhelm Ehrlich	07-11-1950	08-02-1970	Shot with no intent to escape	287
	Gerald Thiem	09-06-1928	08-07-1970	West Berliner shot in the border area	290
	Helmut Kliem	06-02-1939	11-13-1970	Shot in the border area with no intent to escape	293
	Christian Peter Friese	01-05-1948	12-25-1970	Shot while trying to escape	296
1971	Rolf-Dieter Kabelitz	06-23-1951	01-30-1971	Shot at during an escape attempt and died of his injuries	299
	Wolfgang Hoffmann	09-01-1942	07-15-1971	West Berliner fatally injured after being arrested in East Berlin	302
	Werner Kühl	02-10-1949	07-24-1971	West Berliner shot in the border area	307
	Dieter Beilig	09-05-1941	10-02-1971	West Berliner shot in the border area	312
1972	Horst Kullack	11-20-1948	01-21-1972	Shot at while trying to escape and died of his injuries	316
	Manfred Weylandt	07-12-1942	02-14-1972	Shot while trying to escape	319
	Klaus Schulze	10-13-1953	03-07-1972	Shot while trying to escape	322
	Cengaver Katranci	1964	10-30-1972	Drowned in border waters	325
1973	Holger H.	1971	01-22-1973	Suffocated during his parents' successful escape attempt	327
	Volker Frommann	04-23-1944	03-05-1973	Fatally injured while trying to escape	329
	Horst Einsiedel	02-08-1940	03-15-1973	Shot while trying to escape	333
	Manfred Gertzki	05-17-1942	04-27-1973	Shot while trying to escape	337
	Siegfried Kroboth	04-23-1968	05-14-1973	Drowned in border waters	341
1974	Burkhard Niering	09-01-1950	01-05-1974	Shot while trying to escape	344
	Johannes Sprenger	12-03-1905	05-10-1974	Shot while trying to escape	347
	Giuseppe Savoca	04-22-1968	06-15-1974	Drowned in border waters	351

Year	Name	Born	Died	Circumstances of death	p.
1975	Herbert Halli	11-24-1953	04-03-1975	Shot while trying to escape	354
	Cetin Mert	05-11-1970	05-11-1975	Drowned in border waters	358
	Herbert Kiebler	03-24-1952	06-27-1975	Shot while trying to escape	361
	Lothar Hennig	06-30-1954	11-05-1975	Shot during a search operation in the border area with no intent to escape	364
1977	Dietmar Schwietzer	02-21-1958	02-16-1977	Shot while trying to escape	369
	Henri Weise	07-13-1954	May 1977	Retrieved dead from the Spree River near the Marschall Bridge	372
1980	Marienetta Jirkowsky	08-25-1962	11-22-1980	Shot while trying to escape	376
1981	Dr. Johannes Muschol	05-31-1949	03-16-1981	West German shot in the border area	380
	Hans-Jürgen Starrost	06-24-1955	05-16-1981	Shot at while trying to escape and died of his injuries	385
	Thomas Taubmann	07-22-1955	12-12-1981	Fatally injured while trying to escape	389
1982	Lothar Fritz Freie	02-08-1955	06-06-1982	West Berliner shot in the border area	392
1983	Silvio Proksch	03-03-1962	12-25-1983	Shot while trying to escape	396
1984	Michael Schmidt	10-20-1964	12-01-1984	Shot while trying to escape	399
1986	Rainer Liebeke	09-11-1951	09-03-1986	Drowned while trying to escape	403
	René Gross	05-01-1964	11-21-1986	Shot while trying to escape	406
	Manfred Mäder	08-23-1948	11-21-1986	Shot while trying to escape	409
	Michael Bittner	08-31-1961	11-24-1986	Shot while trying to escape	412
1987	Lutz Schmidt	07-08-1962	02-12-1987	Shot while trying to escape	416
1989	Ingolf Diederichs	04-13-1964	01-13-1989	Fatally injured while trying to escape	421
	Chris Gueffroy	06-21-1968	02-05-1989	Shot while trying to escape	423
	Winfried Freudenberg	08-29-1956	03-08-1989	Fatally injured while trying to escape in a balloon	428

East German border soldiers who were killed by military deserters, fellow soldiers, fugitives, an escape helper or a West Berlin policeman while on duty:

Year	Name	Born	Died	Circumstances of Death	p.
1962	Jörgen Schmidtchen	06-28-1941	04-18-1962	Shot by an NVA officer cadet who was also killed	434
	Peter Göring	12-28-1940	05-23-1962	Fatally injured by a ricochet bullet fired by a West Berlin policeman	437
	Reinhold Huhn	03-08-1942	06-18-1962	Shot by a West Berlin escape helper	440
	Günter Seling	04-28-1940	09-30-1962	Accidentally shot by an East German border soldier	443
1963	Siegfried Widera	02-12-1941	09-08-1963	Died of injuries after being knocked out by fugitives	446
1964	Egon Schultz	01-04-1943	10-05-1964	Accidentally shot by an East German border soldier	449
1968	Rolf Henniger	11-30-1941	11-15-1968	Shot by an East German policeman who had deserted and was also killed	456
1980	Ulrich Steinhauer	03-13-1956	11-04-1980	Shot by a border soldier who had deserted	459

Bibliography

Aanderud, Kai-Axel/Knopp Guido (eds.): *Die eingemauerte Stadt. Die Geschichte der Berliner Mauer*, Recklinghausen, 1991.

Ackermann, Volker: *Der "echte" Flüchtling. Deutsche Vertriebene und Flüchtlinge aus der DDR 1945–1961*, Osnabrück, 1995.

Agotz, Irene: "Die Lügen der Stasi," in: Filmer, Werner / Schwan, Heribert (eds.): *Opfer der Mauer. Die geheimen Protokolle des Todes*, Munich, 1991, p. 22.

Arnold, Dietmar/Kellerhoff, Sven Felix: *Die Fluchttunnel von Berlin*, Berlin, 2008.

Atzl, Isabel/Hess,Volker/Schnalke, Thomas (eds.): *Zeitzeugen Charité. Arbeitswelten der Psychiatrischen und Nervenklinik 1940–1999*, Münster, 2005.

Bahr, Christian: *Mauerstadt Berlin. Brennpunkt Bernauer Straße*, Berlin, 2009.

Bittner, Irmgard: "Eine unglaubliche Geschichte," in: Filmer, Werner/Schwan, Heribert (eds.): *Opfer der Mauer. Die geheimen Protokolle des Todes*, Munich, 1991, p. 50.

Brautigam, Hans-Otto: *Ständige Vertretung. Meine Jahre in Ost-Berlin*, Hamburg, 2009.

Bundesministerium für Gesamtdeutsche Fragen (ed.): *Ulbrichts Mauer. Zahlen, Fakten, Daten*, Bonn/Berlin, 1962.

Bundesministerium für Gesamtdeutsche Fragen (ed.): *Verletzungen der Menschenrechte. Unrechtshandlungen und Zwischenfälle an der Berliner Sektorengrenze seit Errichtung der Mauer*, Bonn/Berlin, 1962.

Bundesministerium für innerdeutsche Beziehungen (ed.): *Der Bau der Mauer durch Berlin. Faksimilierter Nachdruck der Denkschrift von 1961*, Bonn, 1986.

Bundesministerium für innerdeutsche Beziehungen (ed.): *Zehn Jahre Deutschlandpolitik. Die Entwicklung der Beziehungen zwischen der Bundesrepublik Deutschland und der Deutschen Demokratischen Republik 1969–1979. Bericht und Dokumentation*, Bonn, 1980.

Camphausen, Gabriele/Nooke, Maria (eds.): *Die Berliner Mauer/The Berlin Wall. Ausstellungskatalog, Dokumentationszentrum Berliner Mauer*, Dresden, 2002.

Cramer, Michael: *Berliner Mauer-Radweg*, Rodingersdorf, 2004.

Dalos, György: *Der Vorhang geht auf. Das Ende der Diktaturen in Osteuropa*, Munich, 2009.

Deutsches Nationalkomitee für Denkmalschutz (ed.): *Die Berliner Mauer. Vom Sperrwall zum Denkmal*, vol. 76/1, Bonn, 2009.

Detjen, Marion: *Ein Loch in der Mauer. Die Geschichte der Fluchthilfe im geteilten Deutschland 1961–1989*, Munich, 2005.

Diedrich, Torsten/Ehlert, Hans/Wenzke, Rüdiger (eds.): *Im Dienste der Partei. Handbuch der bewaffneten Organe der DDR*, Berlin, 1998.

Diedrich, Torsten/Wenzke, Rüdiger: *Die getarnte Armee. Geschichte der Kasernierten Volkspolizei der DDR 1952 bis 1956*, Berlin, 2002.

Dunkhorst, Giordana: *Hoher Preis für coole Klamotten. Jugendliche "Aussteiger" in der DDR um 1980. Eine Schülerarbeit im Rahmen des Geschichtswettbewerbs des Bundespräsidenten*, Berlin, 2007.

Effner, Bettina / Heidemeyer, Helge (eds.): *Flucht im geteilten Deutschland. Erinnerungsstätte Notaufnahmelager Marienfelde*, Berlin, 2005.

Eisenfeld, Bernd / Engelmann, Roger: *13. 8. 1961. Mauerbau. Fluchtbewegung und Machtsicherung*, Bremen, 2001.

Eisenfeld, Bernd: *Die Zentrale Koordinierungsgruppe. Bekämpfung von Flucht und Ausreise*, Berlin, 1995.

Feversham, Polly / Schmidt, Leo: *Die Berliner Mauer heute. Denkmalwert und Umgang*, Berlin, 1999.

Filmer, Werner / Schwan, Heribert (eds.): *Opfer der Mauer. Die geheimen Protokolle des Todes*, Munich, 1991.

Flemming, Thomas / Koch, Hagen: *Die Berliner Mauer. Geschichte eines politischen Bauwerks*, Berlin, 1999.

Frotscher, Kurt / Liebig, Horst: *Opfer der deutschen Teilung. Beim Grenzschutz getötet*, Schkeuditz, 2005.

Gieseke, Jens: *Mielke-Konzern. Die Geschichte der Stasi 1945–1990*, Stuttgart / Munich, 2001.

Grafe, Roman: *Deutsche Gerechtigkeit. Prozesse gegen DDR-Grenzschützen und ihre Befehlsgeber*, Munich, 2004.

Grafe, Roman: *Die Grenze durch Deutschland. Eine Chronik von 1945 bis 1990*, Berlin, 2002.

Grashoff, Udo: *In einem Anfall von Depression. Selbsttötungen in der DDR*, Berlin, 2006.

Gueffroy, Karin: "Eine Mutter klagt an," in: Filmer, Werner / Schwan, Heribert (eds.): *Opfer der Mauer. Die geheimen Protokolle des Todes*, Munich, 1991, pp. 62–65.

Hannemann, Charlotte: "In schwerer Zeit," in: Filmer, Werner / Schwan, Heribert (eds.): *Opfer der Mauer. Die geheimen Protokolle des Todes*, Munich, 1991, pp. 102–103.

Harrison, Hope M.: *Driving the Soviets up the Wall. Soviet-East German Relations, 1953–1961*, Princeton, N. J., 2003.

Hauswald, Harald / Rathenow, Lutz: *Ost-Berlin. Leben vor dem Mauerfall*, Berlin, 2005.

Heidemeyer, Helge: *Flucht und Zuwanderung aus der SBZ / DDR 1945 / 1949–1961*, Düsseldorf, 1994.

Hertle, Hans-Hermann / Jarausch, Konrad H. / Kleßmann, Christoph (eds.): *Vom Mauerbau zum Mauerfall. Ursachen – Verlauf – Auswirkungen*, Berlin, 2002.

Hertle, Hans-Hermann: *Chronik des Mauerfalls. Die dramatischen Ereignisse um den 9. November 1989*, 11th ed., Berlin, 2009.

Hertle, Hans-Hermann: *Der Fall der Mauer. Die unbeabsichtigte Selbstauflösung des SED-Staates*, 2nd ed., Opladen / Wiesbaden, 1999.

Hertle, Hans-Hermann: *Die Berliner Mauer – Monument des Kalten Krieges*, Berlin, 2007.

Hildebrandt, Alexandra: *Die Mauer. Zahlen, Daten*, Berlin, 2001.

Hildebrandt, Rainer: *Es geschah an der Mauer / It happened at the Wall / Cela s'est passé au mur*, 21st ed., Berlin, 2004.

Jeschonnek, Friedrich / Riedel, Dieter / Durie, William: *Alliierte in Berlin: 1945 – 1994. Ein Handbuch zur Geschichte der militärischen Präsenz der Westmächte*, Berlin, 2002.

Kaminsky, Anna (ed.): *Orte des Erinnerns. Gedenkzeichen, Gedenkstätten und Museen zur Diktatur in SBZ und DDR*, Berlin, 2007.

Klausmeier, Axel / Schmidt, Leo: *Mauerreste – Mauerspuren. Der umfassende Führer zur Berliner Mauer*, Berlin, 2004.

Koop, Volker: *"Den Gegner vernichten." Die Grenzsicherung der DDR*, Bonn, 1996.

Kowalczuk, Ilko-Sascha: *Endspiel. Die Revolution von 1989 in der DDR*, Munich, 2009.

Kunze, Gerhard: *Grenzerfahrungen. Kontakte und Verhandlungen zwischen dem Land Berlin und der DDR 1949 – 1989*, Berlin, 1999.

Laabs, Rainer / Sikorski, Werner: *Checkpoint Charlie und die Mauer. Ein geteiltes Volk wehrt sich*, Berlin, 1997.

Lapp, Peter Joachim / Ritter, Jürgen: *Die Grenze. Ein deutsches Bauwerk*, 5th ed., Berlin, 2006.

Lapp, Peter Joachim: *Gefechtsdienst im Frieden. Das Grenzregime der DDR 1945 – 1990*, Bonn, 1999.

Lemke, Michael: *Die Berlinkrise 1958 – 1963*, Berlin, 1995.

Lienicke, Lothar / Bludem, Franz: *Todesautomatik. Die Stasi und der Tod des Michael Gartenschläger*, Frankfurt a. M., 2003.

Lindenberger, Thomas: *Volkspolizei. Herrschaftspraxis und öffentliche Ordnung im SED-Staat 1952 – 1968*, Cologne, 2003.

Litfin, Jürgen: *Tod durch fremde Hand. Das erste Maueropfer in Berlin und die Geschichte einer Familie*, Husum, 2006.

LStU Sachsen-Anhalt (ed.): *Tod in der Spree. Zur Erinnerung an Klaus Schröter, erschossen auf der Flucht am 4. 11. 1963*, Magdeburg, 2001.

Mann, Ulf: *Tunnelfluchten. Grenzgänger, Wühlmäuse, Verräter*, Berlin, 2005.

Marxen, Klaus / Werle, Gerhard (eds.): *Strafjustiz und DDR-Unrecht. Dokumentation, 2. Teilband: Gewalttaten an der deutsch-deutschen Grenze*, Berlin, 2002.

Marxen, Klaus / Werle, Gerhard / Schäfter, Petra: *Die Strafverfolgung von DDR Unrecht. Fakten und Zahlen*, Berlin, 2007.

McAdams, James A.: *Germany Divided: From the Wall to Reunification*, Princeton, 1993.

Melis, Damian von / Bispinck, Henrik: *"Republikflucht." Flucht und Abwanderung aus der SBZ / DDR 1945 – 1961*, Munich, 2006.

Mitdank, Joachim: *Die Berlin-Politik zwischen 17. Juni 1953, dem Viermächteabkommen und der Grenzöffnung 1989. Erinnerungen eines Diplomaten*, Berlin, 2003.

Mühlstädt, Herbert: *172 Tage. Aus dem Leben des Lehrers Egon Schultz*, Berlin, 1974.

Müller, Bodo: *Faszination Freiheit. Die spektakulärsten Fluchtgeschichten*, 4th ed., Berlin, 2001.

Müller, Rudolf: *Tunnelflucht in Berlin*, Norderstedt, 2007.

Müller-Hegemann, Dieter: *Die Berliner Mauer-Krankheit. Zur Soziogenese psychischer Störungen,* Herford, 1973.

Neubert, Ehrhart: *Geschichte der Opposition in der DDR 1949–1989,* 2nd ed., Berlin, 2000.

Neubert, Ehrhart: *Unsere Revolution. Die Geschichte der Jahre 1989/90,* Munich, 2008.

Nooke, Maria: *Der verratene Tunnel. Geschichte einer verhinderten Flucht im geteilten Berlin,* Bremen, 2002.

Nooke, Maria: "Erfahrungen und Herausforderungen im gesellschaftlichen Aufarbeitungsprozess in Gedenkstätten zur zweiten deutschen Diktatur," in: Stiftung Haus der Geschichte (ed.): *Gedenkstätten und Besucherforschung,* Bonn, 2004.

Oplatka, Andreas: *Der erste Riss in der Mauer. September 1989 – Ungarn öffnet die Grenze,* Vienna, 2009.

Petschull, Jürgen: *Die Mauer. August 1961. Zwölf Tage zwischen Krieg und Frieden,* 3rd ed., Hamburg, 1990.

Pond, Elizabeth: *Beyond the Wall. Germany's Road to Unification,* Washington D.C., 1993.

Potthoff, Heinrich: *Im Schatten der Mauer. Deutschlandpolitik 1961 bis 1990,* Berlin, 1999.

Pragal, Peter/Stratenschulte, Eckart D.: *Der Monolog der Lautsprecher und andere Geschichten aus dem geteilten Berlin,* Munich, 1999.

Preuschen, Henriette von/Schmidt, Leo: *On Both Sides of the Wall. Preserving Monuments and Sites of the Cold Wall Era/Auf beiden Seiten der Mauer. Denkmalpflege an Objekten aus der Zeit des Kalten Krieges,* Bad Münstereifel, 2005.

Rathje, Wolfgang: *"Mauer-Marketing" unter Erich Honecker,* Kiel, 2001.

Rehlinger, Ludwig A.: *Freikauf. Die Geschäfte der DDR mit politisch Verfolgten 1963–1989,* Berlin/Frankfurt a. M., 1991.

Rühle, Jürgen/Holzweißig Gunter (eds.): *13. August 1961. Die Mauer von Berlin,* 3rd ed., Cologne, 1988.

Rummler, Thoralf: *Die Gewalttaten an der deutsch-deutschen Grenze vor Gericht,* Baden-Baden, 2000.

Sälter, Gerhard: *Der Abbau der Berliner Mauer und noch sichtbare Reste in der Berliner Innenstadt,* Berlin, 2004.

Sälter, Gerhard: *Grenzpolizisten. Konformität, Verweigerung und Repression in der Grenzpolizei und den Grenztruppen der DDR 1952–65,* Berlin, 2009.

Sauer, Heiner/Plumeyer, Hans-Otto: *Der Salzgitter-Report. Die Zentrale Erfassungsstelle berichtet über Verbrechen im SED-Staat,* Munich, 1991.

Schaad, Martin: *"Dann geh doch rüber." Über die Mauer in den Osten,* Berlin, 2009.

Schmelz, Andrea: *Migration und Politik im geteilten Deutschland während des Kalten Krieges. Die Ost-West-Migration in die DDR in den 1950er und 1960er Jahren,* Opladen, 2002.

Schmidt, Horst: "Kaltblütiger Mord," in: Filmer, Werner/Schwan, Heribert (eds.): *Opfer der Mauer. Die geheimen Protokolle des Todes,* Munich, 1991, p. 35.

Schnurre, Wolfdietrich: *Die Mauer des 13. August*, Berlin, 1962.

Scholze, Thomas / Blask, Falk: *Halt! Grenzgebiet! Leben im Schatten der Mauer*, Berlin, 1992.

Schöne, Jens: *Die Friedliche Revolution*, Berlin, 2009.

Schultke, Dietmar: *"Keiner kommt durch." Die Geschichte der innerdeutschen Grenze 1945–1990*, 2nd ed., Berlin, 2000.

Schumann, Karl F. et al.: *Private Wege der Wiedervereinigung. Die deutsche Ost-West-Migration vor der Wende*, Weinheim, 1996.

Shell, Kurt L.: *Bedrohung und Bewährung. Führung und Bevölkerung in der Berlin-Krise*, Cologne / Opladen, 1965.

Steininger, Rolf: *Berlinkrise und Mauerbau 1958–1963*, 4th ed., Munich, 2009.

Stiftung Gedenkstätte Berlin-Hohenschönhausen (ed.): *Die vergessenen Opfer der Mauer. Flucht und Inhaftierung in Deutschland 1961–1989*, Berlin, 2003.

Strehlow, Hannelore: *Der gefährliche Weg in die Freiheit. Fluchtversuche aus dem ehemaligen Bezirk Potsdam*, Potsdam, 2004.

Taylor Frederick: *Die Mauer: 13. August 1961 bis 9. November 1989*, Munich, 2009.

Tantzscher, Monika: *Hauptabteilung VI: Grenzkontrollen, Reise- und Touristenverkehr, MfS-Handbuch*, Part III / 14, ed. by Bundesbeauftragte für die Unterlagen des Staatssicherheitsdienstes der ehemaligen DDR, Berlin, 2005.

Trzeciok, Peter: *Die Mauer um West-Berlin. Grenzerkundungen 1986–2003*, Berlin, 2004.

Tusa, Ann: *The Last Division. Berlin and the Wall*, London, 1996.

Uhl, Matthias / Wagner, Armin (eds.): *Ulbricht, Chruschtschow und die Mauer. Eine Dokumentation*, Munich, 2003.

Ulrich, Maren: *Geteilte Ansichten. Erinnerungslandschaft deutsch-deutsche Grenze*, Berlin, 2006.

Wagner, Armin: *Walter Ulbricht und die geheime Sicherheitspolitik der SED*, Berlin, 2002.

Wenzel, Otto: *Kriegsbereit. Der Nationale Verteidigungsrat der DDR 1960–1989*, Cologne, 1995.

Wenzke, Rüdiger (ed.): *Staatsfeinde in Uniform. Widerständiges Verhalten und politische Verfolgung in der NVA*, Berlin, 2005.

Wettig, Gerhard: *Chruschtschows Berlin-Krise, 1958–1963*, Munich, 2006.

Wetzlaugk, Udo: *Die Alliierten in Berlin*, Berlin, 1988.

Whitney, Craig R.: *Advocatus Diaboli: Wolfgang Vogel – Anwalt zwischen Ost und West*, Berlin, 1993.

Wolf, Stephan: *Hauptabteilung I: NVA und Grenztruppen, MfS-Handbuch*, Part III / 13, ed. by Bundesbeauftragte für die Unterlagen des Staatssicherheitsdienstes der ehemaligen DDR, 2nd ed., Berlin, 2005.

Wolfrum, Edgar: *Die Mauer. Geschichte einer Teilung*, München, 2009.

Wolle, Stefan: *Die heile Welt der Diktatur. Alltag und Herrschaft in der DDR 1971–1989*, Berlin, 1998.

Wyden, Peter: *Wall. The Inside Story of Divided Berlin*, New York, 1989.

Abbreviations

ADMV	Allgemeiner Deutscher Motorsportverband / General (East-)German Motor Sport Association
ADN	Allgemeiner Deutscher Nachrichtendienst (DDR) / East German press agency
AIM	Archivierter IM-Vorgang / archived informer file
AKG	Auswertungs- und Kontrollgruppe / evaluation and control group
AOP	Archivierte Operative Personenkontrolle / archived operative personal data check
Az.	Aktenzeichen / file reference
BArch	Bundesarchiv / Federal Archive
BdVP	Bezirksdirektion der Deutschen Volkspolizei / East German police district authority
Bepo	Bereitschaftspolizei / riot police
BG	Bezirksgericht / district court
BGH	Bundesgerichtshof / Federal Court of Justice
BLHA	Brandenburgisches Landeshauptarchiv / Brandenburg Central State Archive
BMG(F)	Bundesministerium für gesamtdeutsche Fragen / Federal Ministry of All-German Affairs
BRD	Bundesrepublik Deutschschland / FRG Federal Republic of Germany
BStU	Die Bundesbeauftragte für die Unterlagen des Staatssicherheitsdienstes der ehemaligen DDR / Federal Commissioner for the Records of the State Security Service of the former German Democratic Republic
BVfS	Bezirksverwaltung für Staatssicherheit / District Administration for State Security
BZ	Berliner Zeitung (West Berlin newspaper)
CSCE	Conference on Security and Cooperation in Europe
ČSSR	Tschechoslowakische Sozialistische Republik / Czechoslovakian Socialist Republic
DDR	Deutsche Demokratische Republik / GDR German Democratic Republic (East Germany)
DGP	Deutsche Grenzpolizei / German border police
FAZ	Frankfurter Allgemeine Zeitung (West German newspaper)
FDJ	Freie Deutsche Jugend / Free German Youth
GA	Grenzabteilung / Border Department
GB	Grenzbrigade / Border Brigade
GI	Geheimer Informant (des MfS) / Stasi secret informer
GMS	Gesellschaftlicher Mitarbeiter für Sicherheit (des MfS) / Stasi secret informer

GR	Grenzregiment/Border Regiment
GStA	Generalstaatsanwalt/Generalstaatsanwaltschaft/ General state prosecutor
HA	Hauptabteilung/Central Department
HV	Hauptverwaltung/Central Administration
HVA	Hauptverwaltung Aufklärung/ Central Administration for Intelligence
IGM	Institut für Gerichtliche Medizin der Humboldt Universität/Charité/ Forensic Institute of Humboldt University/Charité
IM	Inoffizieller Mitarbeiter (des MfS)/ Stasi unofficial informer
KD	Kreisdienststelle/district office
KPP	Kontrollpassierpunkt/checkpoint
KSZE	Konferenz für Sicherheit und Zusammenarbeit in Europa/ CSCE Conference on Security and Cooperation in Europe
LAB	Landesarchiv Berlin/State Archive of Berlin
LPG	Landwirtschaftliche Produktionsgenossenschaft/ Agricultural Production Cooperative
MdI	Ministerium des Innern der DDR/ East German Ministry of Interior
MfNV	Ministerium für Nationale Verteidigung der DDR/ East German Ministry of National Defense
MfS	Ministerium für Staatssicherheit/ Ministry of State Security
MZA	Militärisches Zwischenarchiv Potsdam/ Potsdam Military Interim Archive
ND	Neues Deutschland (Communist Party newspaper in East Germany)
NVA	Nationale Volksarmee/National People's Army
NVR	Nationaler Verteidigungsrat/National Defense Council
OPK	Operative Personenkontrolle (des MfS)/ operative personal data check
OStA	Oberstaatsanwalt/senior public prosecutor
OT	Operative Tagesmeldung/operative daily report
OV	Operativer Vorgang (des MfS)/ Stasi operative transaction
PdVP	Präsidium der Volkspolizei/ East Berlin police presidium
PHS	Polizeihistorische Sammlung des Polizeipräsidenten in Berlin/ Police Historical Collection of the Berlin Police President
PKE	Passkontrolleinheit/passport control unit
RIAS	Rundfunk im amerikanischen Sektor/ Radio in the American sector

SAPMO	Stiftung Archiv der Parteien und Massenorganisationen der DDR / Foundation Archive of Parties and Mass Organizations of East Germany
SED	Sozialistische Einheitspartei Deutschlands / Socialist Unity Party (Communist Party in East Germany)
SK	Stadtkommandant / city commander
SKB	Stadtkommandantur Berlin / Berlin command headquarters
StA	Staatsanwaltschaft / public prosecutor
Trapo	Transportpolizei / transport police
VEB	Volkseigener Betrieb / state-owned enterprise
VP	Volkspolizei / East German police
VPI	Volkspolizei-Inspektion / East German police inspection
VPKA	Volkspolizeikreisamt / East German police local office
ZAIG	Zentrale Auswertungs- und Informationsgruppe / Central evaluation and information group
ZERV	Zentrale Ermittlungsstelle für Regierungs- und Vereinigungskriminalität / Investigating Agency for Governmental and Party Crimes
ZK	Zentralkomitee / Central Committee
ZKG	Zentrale Koordinierungsgruppe / Central Coordination Group
ZMA	Zentrale Materialablage / Central Document Storage

List of Illustrations

Acknowledgments

Our special thanks go foremost to all the families and friends of the deceased who have supported us and helped us with their critical comments and suggestions. Their encouragement inspired us to carry on and their sustained sorrow over the loss of loved ones made us understand the importance of our task. We continue to encourage corrections, criticism and suggestions, especially from families and friends to whom we have not yet spoken.

We are grateful to the Berlin Wall Association, represented by Dr. Gabriele Camphausen and Minister Manfred Fischer, for supporting our research project, and to the many people who closely followed its development and progress, in particular: Dr. Pertti Ahonen, Lars Amelung (Bundesarchiv Koblenz), Sabine Berthold (Bundeszentrale für politische Bildung), Dr. Michael Brettin, Peter Brinkmann, Helga-Christine Broneske, Hermann Bubke, Hans Dankwardt, StA Klaus Deutschländer, Giordana Dunkhorst, Bettina Effner, Mrs Engler (GStA Braunschweig, Abteilung ZBDoSt), Gisela Erler (Landesarchiv Berlin), Dr. Bärbel Fest (Polizeihistorische Sammlung des Polizeipräsidenten in Berlin), Harald Fiss, Günter Ganßauge, Sylvia Gräfe (Bundesarchiv Berlin), OStA Dr. Hans-Jürgen Grasemann, Dr. Britta Grell, OStA Herwig Großmann, Georg Hardenberg, Dr. Helge Heidemeyer (BStU), Prof. Dr. Klaus-Dietmar Henke, Florian Huber, Cornelia Jabs (BStU), OStA Bernhard Jahntz (StA Berlin), Dr. Dieter Kabisch, Bernd Keichel, Hagen Koch, Astrid Kowalik-Bonkat, Hilde Kroll, Senatsdirigent a.D. Gerhard Kunze, Christian Ladwig (†), Erika Laurent, Birte Lock (Deutschlandradio), Dr. Ulrich Mählert, Dr. Egbert Meyer (Deutschlandradio), Marianne Naujoks (Bundesarchiv, Militärarchiv Freiburg), Dr. Knut Nevermann, Pfarrer Christian Ohm, Dr. Susanne Olbertz, Brigitta Osterland, Gerald Praschl, Ute Räuber (Bundesarchiv Berlin), GStA Dr. Erardo Rautenberg, Mr Rehmann (Verwaltung der StA Berlin), Dr. Michael Roik, Annelie Rosenmüller (BStU), Gisela Rüdiger (BStU), Pfarrer i. R. Ekkehard Runge, Dr. Gerhard Sälter, GStA a.D. Christoph Schaefgen, Thorsten Schilling (BpB), Dr. Detlef Schmiechen-Ackermann, Gabriele Schnell, Ltd. OStA Gerd Schnittcher, Michael Schultheiß, Manfred Staude (Archiv der StA Berlin), Prof. Dr. Peter Steinbach, Hannelore Strehlow (BStU), Maximilian Tauscher, Dr. Werner Vennewald, Berit Walter (Bundesarchiv Koblenz), Hans-Werner Weber, Frau Wildner (Standesamt Potsdam), Prof. Dr. Manfred Wilke, OStA Burkhard Zuppke.

We also are indebted to the student assistants who helped us far beyond our expectations: Benedikt Glatz, Lucia Halder, Georg Heilmann, René Schlott, Clemens Villinger, Wiebke Volkmann and Mareen Walus.

Alphabetical Register of the 136 Victims

About the Authors

Martin Ahrends was born in 1951. He completed his Abitur secondary school degree in Potsdam in 1970 and studied music, philosophy and theater in Berlin. Later he worked as editor of a journal of serious music and joined the scholarly staff of the Comic Opera. In 1982, after he was banned for political reasons from working in his profession, he applied for an exit permit to leave East Germany that was approved in 1984. He worked in Hamburg from 1986 to 1996 as an editor and freelancer for the weekly newspaper *Die Zeit* and later became a freelance writer. His publications, including literary narratives, essays and novels, have been published by Kiepenheuer & Witsch in Cologne and the Aufbau Verlag in Berlin. He is a member of PEN.

Dr. Udo Baron, born in 1963, is a political scientist, contemporary historian and journalist. After working for the "Enquete-Kommissionen des Deutschen Bundestages zur Aufarbeitung der SED-Diktatur" and the "Forschungsverbund SED-Staat" of the Free University of Berlin, he joined the staff of the research project "Victims at the Berlin Wall." In 2008 he was put in charge of overseeing leftist extremism for the Lower Saxony Ministry of Internal Affairs, Athletics and Integration. His areas of expertise include East German Communist Party activities in the West, political party history and political extremism.

Christine Brecht was born in 1966 and studied history, philosophy and political science in Berlin. As a historian and exhibition curator, her areas of expertise include the cultural history of knowledge in the modern world, Berlin contemporary history and the history and theory of exhibitions, remembrance and commemoration. From 2005 to 2007 she was part of the staff of scholars for the project "Victims of the Berlin Wall," conducted by the Center for Contemporary History Potsdam and the Berlin Wall Association. She has published works on the history of the Berlin Wall and escape and emigration from East Germany, as well as a monograph in 2009 about an East German business situated at the border.

Lydia Dollmann was born in 1967 and studied political science at the Free University of Berlin. She has contributed to contemporary history projects on National Socialism and East German history. Her most recent publication is "Chwalek, Martha (1899–1986). Widerstand im Schatten des Ehemannes," in: Siegfried Mielke (ed.): *Gewerkschafterinnen im NS-Staat: Verfolgung, Widerstand, Emigration*, Essen, 2008.

Dr. Hans-Hermann Hertle was born in 1955 and studied history and political science in Marburg and Berlin. From 1985 to 1999 the academic publicist and social researcher was part of the staff of scholars at the "Zentralinstitut für sozialwissenschaftliche Forschung" and worked on various German Research Foundation (DFG) projects at the Free University of Berlin. He joined the staff of scholars at the Center for Contemporary History Potsdam in December 1999. He has published several works on social and contemporary history and has produced documentary films and radio feature presentations. His work has been honored with numerous awards, including the Friedrich-Wilhelm-Murnau-Kurzfilmpreis (1999), Bayerischer Fernsehpreis (2000) and the Grimme-Preis (2005).

Books of his published by the Ch. Links Verlag: *Chronik des Mauerfalls*, 1996; *Das Ende der SED* (co-edited with Gerd-Rüdiger Stephan), 1997; *Mauerbau und Mauerfall* (co-edited with Konrad H. Jarausch and Christoph Kleßmann), 2002; *Risse im Bruderbund. Die Krim-Gespräche Honecker – Breshnew* (co-edited with Konrad H. Jarausch), 2006; *Die Berliner Mauer – Monument des Kalten Krieges. The Berlin Wall – Monument of the Cold War*, 2007.

Dr. Maria Nooke was born in 1958. She studied religious education and worked on projects with children in the church and youth groups. After 1989 she studied sociology, psychology and pedagogy and has been involved in contemporary history projects on National Socialism and East German history. She has held academic and directorial responsibilities at the Berlin Wall Memorial since 1999. In 2009 she was appointed deputy director of the Berlin Wall Foundation. She received her PhD degree in 2007 and has published contemporary history and biographical publications on National Socialism, East German opposition and the history of German division, including *Der verratene Tunnel. Geschichte einer verhinderten Flucht im geteilten Berlin*, Bremen, 2002. Books of hers published by Ch. Links Verlag: *Für Umweltverantwortung und Demokratisierung. Die Forster Oppositionsgruppe in der Auseinandersetzung mit Staat und Kirche*, 2008.